한국의 토익 수험자 여러분께,

토익 시험은 세계적인 직무 영어능력 평가 시험으로, 지난 40여 년간 비즈니스 현장에서 필요한 영어능력 평가의 기준을 제시해 왔습니다. 토익 시험 및 토익스피킹, 토익라이팅 시험은 세계에서 가장 널리 통용되는 영어능력 검증 시험으로, 160여 개국 14,000여 기관이 토익 성적을 의사결정에 활용하고 있습니다.

YBM은 한국의 토익 시험을 주관하는 ETS 독점 계약사입니다.

ETS는 한국 수험자들의 효과적인 토익 학습을 돕고자 YBM을 통하여 'ETS 토익 공식 교재'를 독점 출간하고 있습니다. 또한 'ETS 토익 공식 교재' 시리즈에 기출문항을 제공해 한국의 다른 교재들에 수록된 기출을 복제하거나 변형한 문항으로 인하여 발생할 수 있는 수험자들의 혼동을 방지하고 있습니다.

복제 및 변형 문항들은 토익 시험의 출제의도를 벗어날 수 있기 때문에 기출문항을 수록한 'ETS 토익 공식 교재'만큼 시험에 잘 대비할 수 없습니다.

'ETS 토익 공식 교재'를 통하여 수험자 여러분의 영어 소통을 위한 노력에 큰 성취가 있기를 바랍니다.

감사합니다.

Dear TOEIC Test Takers in Korea,

The TOEIC program is the global leader in English-language assessment for the workplace. It has set the standard for assessing English-language skills needed in the workplace for more than 40 years. The TOEIC tests are the most widely used English language assessments around the world, with 14,000+ organizations across more than 160 countries trusting TOEIC scores to make decisions.

YBM is the ETS Country Master Distributor for the TOEIC program in Korea and so is the exclusive distributor for TOEIC Korea.

To support effective learning for TOEIC test-takers in Korea, ETS has authorized YBM to publish the only Official TOEIC prep books in Korea. These books contain actual TOEIC items to help prevent confusion among Korean test-takers that might be caused by other prep book publishers' use of reproduced or paraphrased items.

Reproduced or paraphrased items may fail to reflect the intent of actual TOEIC items and so will not prepare test-takers as well as the actual items contained in the ETS TOEIC Official prep books published by YBM.

We hope that these ETS TOEIC Official prep books enable you, as test-takers, to achieve great success in your efforts to communicate effectively in English.

Thank you.

입문부터 실전까지 수준별 학습을 통해 최단기 목표점수 달성!

ETS TOEIC® 공식수험서 스마트 학습 지원

www.ybmbooks.com에서도 무료 MP3를 다운로드 받을 수 있습니다.

ETS 토익 모바일 학습 플랫폼!
ETS 토익기출 수험서 앱

구글플레이   앱스토어

- **교재 학습 지원**
  - LC 음원 MP3
  - 교재 해설 동영상 강의
  - 교재/부록 모의고사 채점 분석
  - 단어 암기장

- **부가 서비스**
  - 데일리 학습(토익 기출문제 풀이)
  - 토익 최신 경향 무료 특강
  - 토익 타이머

- **모의고사 결과 분석**
  - 파트별/문항별 정답률
  - 파트별/유형별 취약점 리포트
  - 전체 응시자 점수 분포도

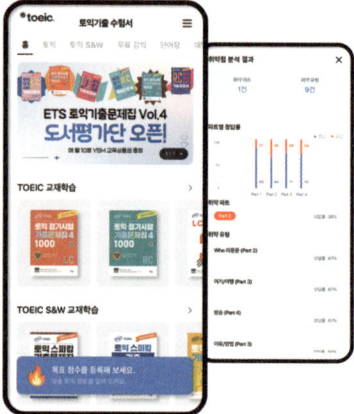

ETS 토익 학습 전용 온라인 커뮤니티!
ETS TOEIC® Book 공식카페

etstoeicbook.co.kr

- **강사진의 학습 지원**   토익 대표강사들의 학습 지원과 멘토링
- **교재 학습관 운영**   교재별 학습게시판을 통해 무료 동영상 강의 등 학습 지원
- **학습 콘텐츠 제공**   토익 학습 콘텐츠와 정기시험 예비특강 업데이트

ETS 토익 단기공략 650+

최신 개정판

무료 동영상 강의

LC
RC

ETS 토익 단기공략
650⁺

발행인	허문호
발행처	YBM
편집	이태경, 이진열, 이혜원, 김현식
디자인	김현경, 정규리
마케팅	고영노, 장은선, 김동진, 박찬경, 하재희, 임재민, 류혜윤, 문근호, 고은
초판인쇄	2025년 6월 20일
3쇄발행	2025년 11월 1일
신고일자	1964년 3월 28일
신고번호	제1964-000003호
주소	서울시 종로구 종로 104
전화	(02) 2000-0515 [구입문의] / (02) 2000-0305 [내용문의]
팩스	(02) 2285-1523
홈페이지	www.ybmbooks.com
ISBN	978-89-17-24377-2

ETS, the ETS logo, TOEIC and 토익 are registered trademarks of Educational Testing Service, Princeton, New Jersey, U.S.A., used in the Republic of Korea under license. Copyright © 2025 by Educational Testing Service, Princeton, New Jersey, U.S.A. All rights reserved. Reproduced under license for limited use by YBM. These materials are protected by United States Laws, International Copyright Laws and International Treaties. In the event of any discrepancy between this translation and official ETS materials, the terms of the official ETS materials will prevail. All items were created or reviewed by ETS. All item annotations and test-taking tips were reviewed by ETS.

서면에 의한 저자와 출판사의 허락 없이 내용의 일부 혹은 전부를 인용 및 복제하거나 발췌하는 것을 금합니다.
낙장 및 파본은 교환해 드립니다.
구입 철회는 구매처 규정에 따라 교환 및 환불 처리됩니다.

ETS 토익
단기공략
650+

최신개정판

무료
동영상 강의

LC

RC

PREFACE

Dear test taker,

The purpose of this book is to help you prepare for success on the TOEIC® Listening and Reading Test. A good TOEIC score is a valuable asset for demonstrating your English communication proficiency to colleagues and clients in Korea and globally.

This book provides practical steps that you can follow during a two-week or four-week program of study to help you in your preparation for the TOEIC test. Use your TOEIC test score as a respected professional credential and a sign that you are ready to take your career to the next level. Your TOEIC score is recognized globally as evidence of your English-language proficiency.

With **〈ETS 토익 단기공략 650+〉**, you will have the tools you need to ensure you are thoroughly prepared for the TOEIC test. This book contains key study points that will familiarize you with the test format and content, and you will be able to practice at your own pace. The test questions are created by the same test specialists who develop the TOEIC test itself, and the book contains questions taken from actual TOEIC tests.

Here are some features of **〈ETS 토익 단기공략 650+〉**.

- This book features carefully selected questions from actual TOEIC tests, chosen specifically for their advanced level of difficulty, and contains three full-length actual TOEIC tests.

- All TOEIC Listening and Reading test content is included in one book that is suitable for two-week or four-week short-term study plans.

- You will hear the same voice actors that are used for the actual TOEIC Test.

- Key study points are provided to help you achieve your target score with the least amount of time and effort.

In preparing for the test with **〈ETS 토익 단기공략 650+〉**, you can be confident that you are taking the best approach to maximizing your TOEIC test score. Use **〈ETS 토익 단기공략 650+〉** to become familiar with the test, including actual test tasks, content, and format. You will be well prepared to demonstrate to the world your proficiency in English communication by taking the TOEIC test and receiving your score report.

We hope that you will find this high-quality resource to be of the utmost use, and we wish you all the very best success.

출제기관이 만든 점수대별
단기 완성 전략서!

⊙ 최신 기출 문항으로 보강된 단기 완성 시리즈
풍부한 최신 기출 문항과 최신 출제 경향을 반영한 ETS의 체계적인 공략법으로 구성된 고품질의 단기 완성 전략서이다.

⊙ 단기 목표 달성에 최적화된 구성
LC와 RC를 한 권으로 구성하여 학습 부담은 줄이고, 목표 점수 달성에 필요한 핵심 내용만을 수록하여 학습 효율은 높였다.

⊙ 정기시험과 동일한 성우 음원
토익 정기시험 성우가 실제 시험과 동일한 속도와 발음으로 녹음한 음원으로 실전에 완벽하게 대비할 수 있다.

⊙ 토익 최신 경향을 반영한 명쾌한 분석과 해설
최신 출제 경향을 완벽하게 분석하고 반영하여 목표 점수를 달성하게 해줄 해법을 낱낱이 제시하고 있다.

⊙ 점수 상승을 돕는 다양한 부가 학습자료 제공
실전에 보다 완벽하게 대비할 수 있도록 실전 모의고사 1회분을 추가로 제공하며, 이해를 돕는 동영상 강의와 기출어휘 PDF, APP을 무료로 제공한다.

CONTENTS

LC

PART 1
INTRO		018
UNIT 01	인물 중심 사진	020
UNIT 02	사물/배경 중심 사진	026
PART 1 빈출 표현		030

PART 2
INTRO		036
UNIT 03	Who/What/Which 의문문	038
UNIT 04	When/Where 의문문	042
UNIT 05	Why/How 의문문	046
UNIT 06	일반/선택 의문문	050
UNIT 07	부정/부가 의문문	054
UNIT 08	요청·제안 의문문/평서문	058
PART 2 빈출 표현		062

PART 3
INTRO		068
UNIT 09	주제·목적 문제/화자·장소 문제	070
UNIT 10	세부 사항 문제/문제점·걱정거리 문제	076
UNIT 11	요청·제안 문제/다음에 할 일 문제	082
UNIT 12	의도 파악 문제	088
UNIT 13	시각 정보 문제	094
PART 3 빈출 표현		100

PART 4
INTRO		106
UNIT 14	전화 메시지	108
UNIT 15	공지/안내/회의	112
UNIT 16	광고/방송/보도	116
UNIT 17	인물/강연/설명	120
UNIT 18	여행/견학/관람	124
PART 4 빈출 표현		128

RC

PART 5&6

INTRO		134
UNIT 01	문장의 구성 요소	136
UNIT 02	명사	144
UNIT 03	대명사	152
UNIT 04	형용사	160
UNIT 05	부사	166
UNIT 06	동사의 형태와 종류	172
UNIT 07	수 일치	178
UNIT 08	시제	184
UNIT 09	능동태와 수동태	192
UNIT 10	to부정사와 동명사	198
UNIT 11	분사	206
UNIT 12	전치사와 접속사	214
UNIT 13	부사절 접속사	222
UNIT 14	관계대명사	228
UNIT 15	명사절 접속사	234
UNIT 16	비교구문	240
UNIT 17	어휘 1: 명사/형용사	246
UNIT 18	어휘 2: 동사/부사	258

PART 7

INTRO		272
UNIT 19	편지/이메일	274
UNIT 20	회람/공지/광고/기사	282
UNIT 21	기타 양식	290
UNIT 22	복수 지문	298
PART 7 빈출 표현		308

정답과 해설 (책 속의 책)
실전 모의고사 (별책)

무료 동영상 강의
기출 포인트를 짚는 핵심 강의로 토익 단기완성!

TOEIC 소개

» TOEIC

Test of English for International Communication(국제적 의사소통을 위한 영어 시험)의 약자로서, 영어가 모국어가 아닌 사람들을 대상으로 일상생활 또는 비즈니스 상황에서 필요한 실용영어 능력을 갖추었는지 평가하는 시험이다.

» 시험 구성

구성	PART	유형		문항 수	시간	배점
Listening	Part 1	사진 묘사		6	45분	495점
	Part 2	질의 응답		25		
	Part 3	짧은 대화		39		
	Part 4	짧은 담화		30		
Reading	Part 5	단문 빈칸 채우기		30	75분	495점
	Part 6	장문 빈칸 채우기		16		
	Part 7	독해	단일 지문	29		
			이중 지문	10		
			삼중 지문	15		
Total		7 Parts		200문항	120분	990점

» 평가 항목

LC	RC
사진 묘사 문장을 듣고 이해하는 능력	문장 구조를 파악해 문장에서 필요한 품사, 어휘 등을 찾는 능력
질의/응답하는 문장을 듣고 이해하는 능력	글의 목적, 주제, 의도 등을 파악하는 능력
짧은 대화에서 주고받은 내용을 파악할 수 있는 능력	장문에서 특정한 정보를 찾을 수 있는 능력
담화에서 핵심이 되는 정보를 파악할 수 있는 능력	글의 내용에서 추론할 수 있는 능력
화자의 의도나 함축된 의미를 이해하는 능력	뜻이 유사한 단어의 정확한 용례를 파악하는 능력

※ 성적표에는 전체 수험자의 평균과 해당 수험자가 받은 성적이 백분율로 표기되어 있다.

수험 정보

» 시험 접수

시험 약 2개월 전부터 아래와 같은 방법으로 접수할 수 있다.
인터넷 접수: TOEIC위원회 공식 홈페이지(https://exam.toeic.co.kr/)를 통해 접수
모바일 접수: TOEIC위원회 공식 어플리케이션 또는 모바일 웹사이트
 (https://m.exam.toeic.co.kr)를 통해 접수

» 시험장 준비물

신분증	규정 신분증만 가능 (주민등록증, 운전면허증, 기간 만료 전의 여권, 공무원증 등)
필기구	연필, 지우개 (볼펜이나 사인펜은 사용 금지)

» 시험 진행 시간

09:20	입실 (9:50 이후 입실 불가)
09:30 ~ 09:45	답안지 작성에 관한 오리엔테이션
09:45 ~ 09:50	휴식
09:50 ~ 10:05	신분증 확인
10:05 ~ 10:10	문제지 배부 및 파본 확인
10:10 ~ 10:55	듣기 평가 (LISTENING TEST)
10:55 ~ 12:10	독해 평가 (READING TEST)

» 성적 확인

성적은 TOEIC 홈페이지에 안내된 성적 발표일에 인터넷 홈페이지, 어플리케이션을 통해 확인 가능하다. 최초 성적표 발급은 우편 또는 온라인을 통해 수령 가능하며, 재발급은 성적 유효기간(시험 시행일로부터 2년) 내에만 가능하다. 단, 유효기간은 공공기관에 한하여 2023년 4월부터 5년으로 연장되었다.

» 토익 점수

TOEIC 점수는 듣기 영역(LC) 점수와 읽기 영역(RC) 점수, 그리고 두 영역을 합계한 전체 점수로 구성된다. 각 영역의 점수는 5점 단위로 5점에서 495점까지 주어지고, 두 영역을 합계한 전체 점수는 10점에서 990점까지 주어진다. TOEIC 성적은 각 문제 유형의 난이도에 따른 점수 환산표에 의해 결정된다.

LC 출제 유형 및 경향 분석

PART 1

문제 유형 및 출제 비율

사람을 주어로 행동이나 상태를 묘사하는 문제의 비중이 가장 높다. 최근 주어가 다양하고 보기가 긴 문제들이 출제되고 있다.

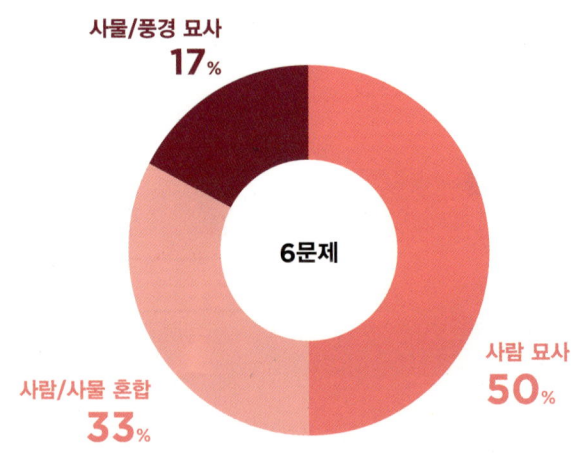

PART 2

문제 유형 및 출제 비율

의문사 의문문이 거의 절반을 차지하며 일반 의문문과 평서문도 비중 있게 출제된다. 질문에 대해 우회적으로 응답하는 문제 비중이 높아지고 있다.

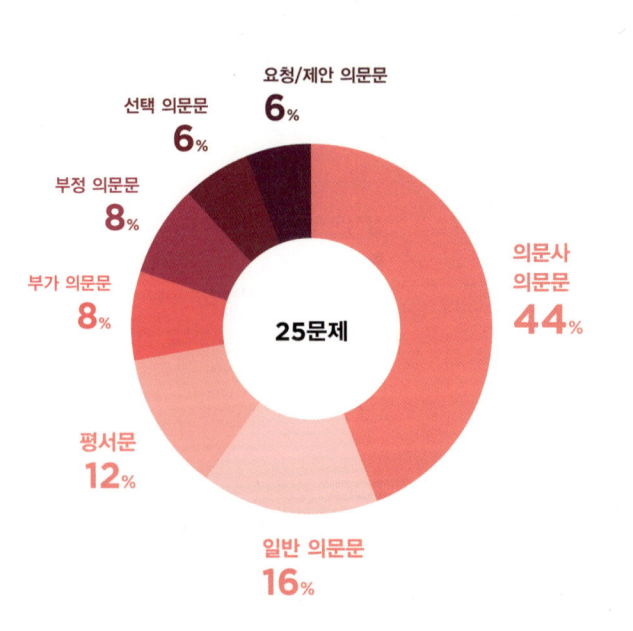

PART 3

문제 유형 및 출제 비율

세부 사항을 물어보는 문제가 가장 많이 출제되며, 의도 파악 문제와 시각 정보 문제가 각각 2문항과 3문항씩 고정적으로 출제된다. 대화에서 사용된 표현을 다른 말로 paraphrasing한 보기가 정답으로 자주 출제된다.

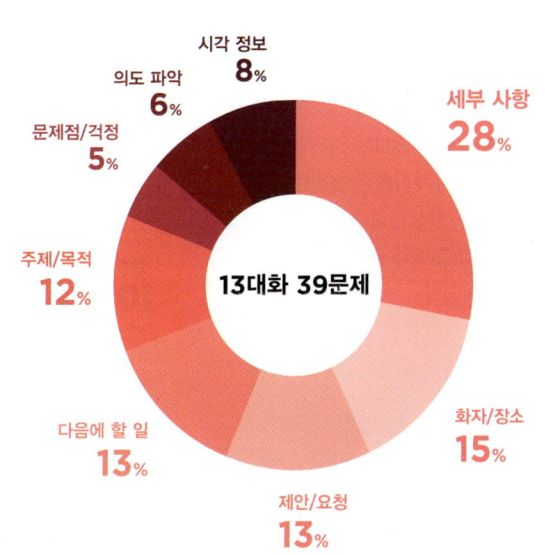

PART 4

담화 유형 및 출제 비율

전화 메시지와 공지/안내/회의 발췌록 등의 출제 빈도가 가장 높다. 담화 곳곳에 흩어져 있는 단서들로 정답을 유추해야 하는 문제가 고난도로 출제된다.

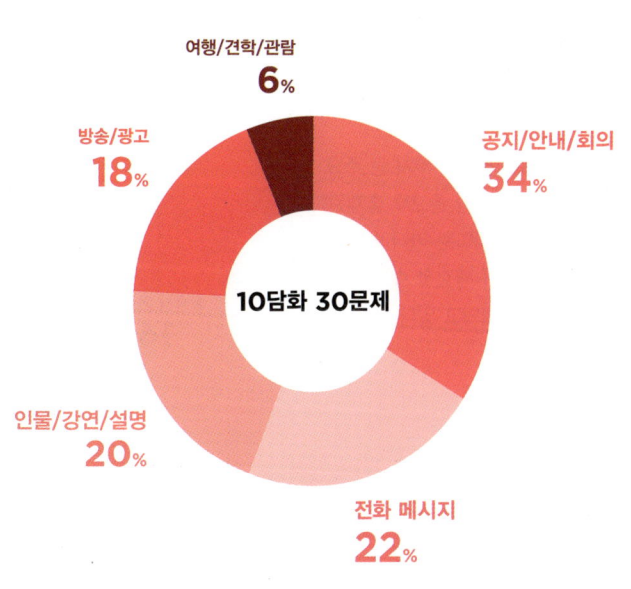

RC 출제 유형 및 경향 분석

PART 5
문법 문제 유형 및 출제 비율

주요 품사 자리를 판단하는 문제와 전치사와 접속사/부사를 구별하는 문제가 주로 출제된다. 그 외 준동사, 관계사, 명사절 접속사 관련 문제가 고난도로 출제된다.

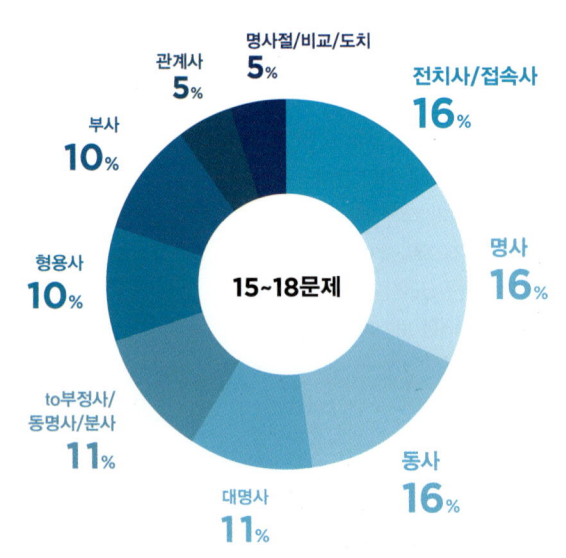

PART 5
어휘 문제 유형 및 출제 비율

명사, 동사, 형용사, 부사 등 주요 품사 어휘 문제가 골고루 출제된다. 최근 어휘의 의미뿐 아니라 문법적인 구조를 알아야 해결할 수 있는 문제들도 출제되고 있다.

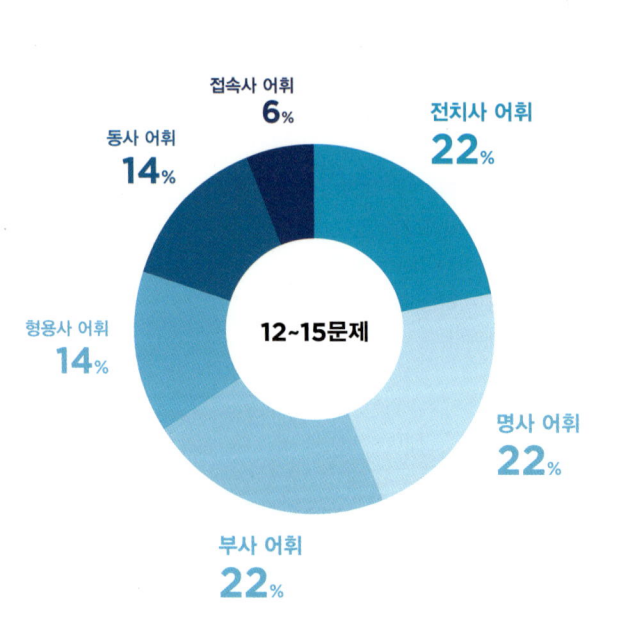

PART 6

문제 유형 및 출제 비율

문법과 어휘 문제가 비슷한 비중으로 골고루 나오며, 빈칸에 알맞은 문장을 고르는 문제가 매 지문마다 1문항 출제된다. PART 5와 달리 문맥과 전체 흐름을 파악해야 풀 수 있는 문제들이 출제된다.

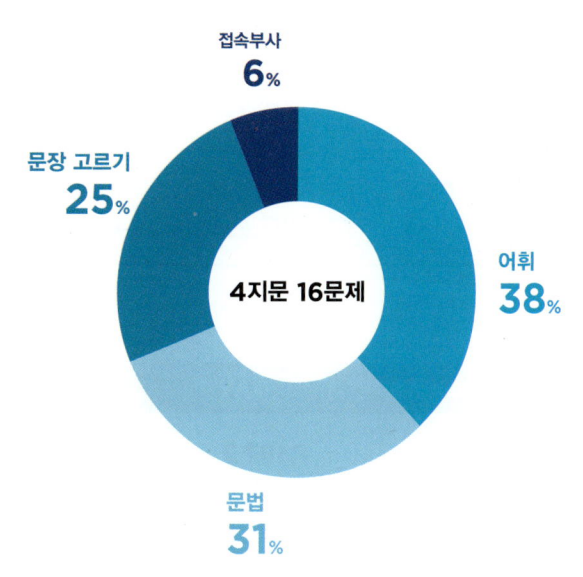

PART 7

지문 유형 및 출제 비율

이메일/편지, 기사, 공지/안내문, 광고, 메시지 대화 지문은 거의 항상 나오는 유형이다. 문제 유형으로는 세부 사항, 주제/목적, 추론 등이 있으며 문장 삽입, 의도 파악 문제가 각 2문항씩 고정적으로 출제된다. 복수 지문에서는 연계 문제가 항상 출제된다.

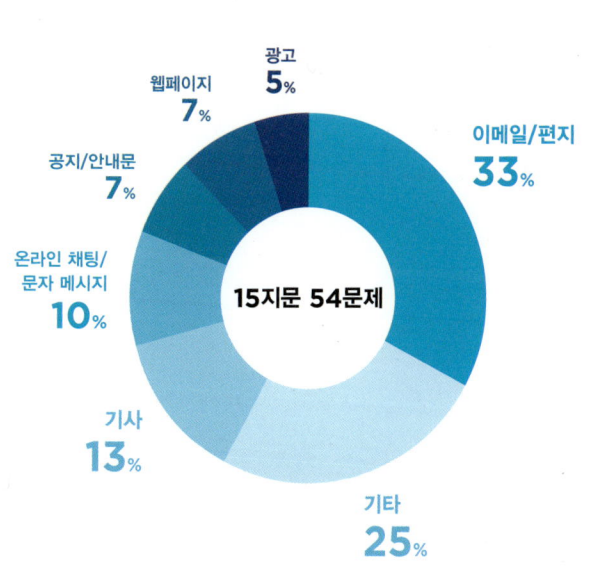

2주 완성 플랜

초단기에 토익 650점 이상을 달성하고자 하는 중급 수험생을 위한 2주 완성 플랜

	DAY 1	DAY 2	DAY 3	DAY 4	DAY 5
LC	PART 1 UNIT 1~2	PART 2 UNIT 3~4	PART 2 UNIT 5~6	PART 2 UNIT 7~8	PART 3 UNIT 9~10
RC	PART 5&6 UNIT 1~3	PART 5&6 UNIT 4~6	PART 5&6 UNIT 7~9	PART 5&6 UNIT 10~12	PART 5&6 UNIT 13~15

	DAY 6	DAY 7	DAY 8	DAY 9	DAY 10
LC	PART 3 UNIT 11	PART 3 UNIT 12~13	PART 4 UNIT 14	PART 4 UNIT 15~16	PART 4 UNIT 17~18
RC	PART 5&6 UNIT 16~18	PART 7 UNIT 19	PART 7 UNIT 20	PART 7 UNIT 21	PART 7 UNIT 22

4주 완성 플랜

단기에 차근차근 토익 650점 이상을 달성하고자 하는 중급 수험생을 위한 4주 완성 플랜

	DAY 1	DAY 2	DAY 3	DAY 4	DAY 5
LC	PART 1 UNIT 1	PART 1 UNIT 2	PART 2 UNIT 3	PART 2 UNIT 4	PART 2 UNIT 5
RC	PART 5&6 UNIT 1	PART 5&6 UNIT 2	PART 5&6 UNIT 3	PART 5&6 UNIT 4	PART 5&6 UNIT 5

	DAY 6	DAY 7	DAY 8	DAY 9	DAY 10
LC	PART 2 UNIT 6	PART 2 UNIT 7	PART 2 UNIT 8	PART 1, 2 UNIT 1~8 복습	PART 3 UNIT 9
RC	PART 5&6 UNIT 1~5 복습	PART 5&6 UNIT 6	PART 5&6 UNIT 7	PART 5&6 UNIT 8	PART 5&6 UNIT 9

	DAY 11	DAY 12	DAY 13	DAY 14	DAY 15
LC	PART 3 UNIT 10	PART 3 UNIT 11	PART 3 UNIT 12~13	PART 3 UNIT 9~13 복습	PART 4 UNIT 14
RC	PART 5&6 UNIT 10	PART 5&6 UNIT 6~10 복습	PART 5&6 UNIT 11	PART 5&6 UNIT 12	PART 5&6 UNIT 13

	DAY 16	DAY 17	DAY 18	DAY 19	DAY 20
LC	PART 4 UNIT 15	PART 4 UNIT 16	PART 4 UNIT 17	PART 4 UNIT 18	PART 4 UNIT 14~18 복습
RC	PART 5&6 UNIT 14	PART 5&6 UNIT 15~16	PART 5&6 UNIT 17~18	PART 7 UNIT 19~20	PART 7 UNIT 21~22

LISTENING
COMPREHENSION

PART
1

사진 묘사

INTRO
UNIT 01 인물 중심 사진
UNIT 02 사물/배경 중심 사진
PART 1 빈출 표현

 무료 강의

INTRO PART 1 사진 묘사

총 6문항

Part 1은 사진을 보면서 4개의 보기를 듣고, 그중에서 사진을 가장 잘 묘사한 보기를 고르는 유형입니다.

▶ PART 1 이렇게 풀자

STEP 1
음원을 듣기 전 사진 파악

STEP 2
음원을 들으면서 오답 보기 소거

(A) A man is watering a plant.
(B) A man is ~~sliding a chair~~ under a desk.
(C) A man is ~~using a computer~~.
(D) A man is ~~drawing curtains~~ across a window.

STEP 3
정답 선택

(A)

▶ 오답을 소거하자

음원을 듣기 전에 사람의 동작이나 상태, 사물의 이름과 위치 등을 파악한 다음, 음원을 들으면서 오답을 소거하다 보면 쉽게 정답을 찾을 수 있습니다. 오답 유형은 크게 두 가지로 나뉩니다.

❶ 사진과 다른 동작이나 상태 표현이 들리면 오답입니다.

A woman is ~~carrying~~ a pile of books. 여자가 책 더미를 나르고 있다.
→ **A woman is stacking some books on a shelf.**
   여자가 선반에 책을 쌓고 있다.

She's ~~putting on~~ glasses. 여자가 안경을 쓰고 있는 중이다.
→ **She's wearing glasses.** 여자가 안경을 쓰고 있다.

⚠ 착용하고 있는 동작을 나타내는 put on과 착용한 상태를 나타내는 wear를 혼동하지 않도록 주의합니다.

❷ 사진에 없는 단어가 들리면 오답입니다.

Some ~~boats~~ are docked along the beach.
배들이 해변을 따라 정박해 있다.

Some ~~children~~ are climbing on a ~~rock~~. 어린이들이 바위를 오르고 있다.

→ **A path extends along the shore.**
   길이 해안을 따라 나 있다.

▶ 동작이나 상태를 묘사하는 동사의 형태에 주목하자

Part 1에서는 주어 뒤에 나오는 동사를 듣는 것이 중요합니다. 동작이나 상태를 묘사하는 동사의 시제는 다음과 같습니다.

❶ 현재진행 시제 주로 사람의 동작을 묘사할 때 사용합니다.

| 주어+is/are+-ing | 주어가 ~하고 있다 |

She's pressing a button on a telephone. 여자가 전화기의 버튼을 누르고 있다.
A woman is facing a computer screen.
여자가 컴퓨터 화면을 마주보고 있다.

❷ 현재 시제 현재의 상태를 나타낼 때 사용합니다.

| 주어+is/are+형용사 | 주어가 ~한 상태이다 |
| 주어+is/are+전치사구 | 주어가 ~에 있다 |

Some baskets are full of fruit. 바구니에 과일이 가득하다.
Some merchandise is on display. 상품들이 진열되어 있다.

❸ 현재완료 시제 행동이나 움직임이 완료되었을 때 사용합니다.

| 주어+has/have p.p. | 주어가 ~했다 |

A tourist has stopped to look at a document.
한 관광객이 문서를 보기 위해 멈춰 섰다.

❹ 현재 수동태/현재완료 수동태 주로 사물의 위치나 상태를 묘사할 때 사용합니다.

| 주어+is/are p.p. | 주어가 ~되어 있다 |
| 주어+has/have been p.p. | |

Tables are covered with tablecloths. 탁자들이 식탁보로 덮여 있다.
An umbrella has been closed on a terrace. 테라스에 파라솔 하나가 접혀 있다.

UNIT 01 인물 중심 사진

무료 강의

1 1인 사진

사람이 한 명만 등장하는 사진으로, 주로 사람의 동작이나 상태를 묘사하는 문장이 출제됩니다.

> **핵심 포인트 1** 4개의 보기가 모두 동일한 주어로 시작하면서 현재진행(is/are + -ing) 시제로 사진을 묘사하는 문제가 주로 출제됩니다. 이런 경우 주어보다는 -ing 부분을 집중해서 들어야 합니다.
> **핵심 포인트 2** 사람의 손이 닿아 있거나 사진에서 두드러지는 사물에 유의해야 합니다.

▶ 기출 사진으로 분석하는 정답 vs. 오답   🔊 650_P1_01

동작 묘사

- 정답 She's **preparing** some food. 여자가 음식을 준비하고 있다.
- 오답 She's ~~setting~~ the table. 여자가 식탁을 차리고 있다.
- 정답 She's **holding** kitchen utensils. 여자가 조리도구를 들고 있다.
- 오답 She's ~~washing~~ some mixing bowls. 여자가 믹싱볼들을 닦고 있다.

  ⚠ mixing bowls처럼 구체적인 사물명 대신에 kitchen utensils처럼 포괄적인 단어로 묘사하는 경우도 많습니다.

사진 속 명사와 사진에 없는 명사

- 정답 She's examining **a vase**. 여자가 꽃병을 보고 있다.
- 오답 She's cutting ~~some flowers~~. 여자가 꽃을 자르고 있다.
- 정답 She is holding **a pottery item**. 여자가 도자기 제품을 들고 있다.
- 오답 She is serving ~~some customers~~. 여자가 고객을 응대하고 있다.

상태 묘사와 동작 묘사

- 정답 A man is **crouching down** near some plants.
  남자가 식물 근처에 쭈그리고 앉아 있다.
- 오답 A man is ~~digging~~ in a garden. 남자가 정원에서 땅을 파고 있다.
- 정답 A man is **wearing** a hat. 남자가 모자를 쓰고 있다.
- 오답 A man is ~~putting on~~ a hat. 남자가 모자를 쓰고 있는 중이다.

  ⚠ put on, try on은 입거나 착용하고 있는 동작을 묘사하는 표현입니다.

ETS 유형 연습

음원을 듣고 사진을 가장 잘 묘사한 문장을 고르세요.
다시 듣고 빈칸을 채우세요.

🔊 650_P1_02

정답과 해설 p.002

1.

   (A) He's _____ lamps on a wall.
   (B) He's _____ to set up work supplies.
   (C) He's _____ a paintbrush in a sink.
   (D) He's _____ some windows with paper.

2.

   (A) A woman is _____ a restaurant.
   (B) A woman is _____ some trash into a bin.
   (C) A woman is _____ a meal to some customers.
   (D) A woman is _____ containers from a dining area.

3.

   (A) She's _____ money into a cashbox.
   (B) She's _____ a serving utensil.
   (C) She's _____ food on paper plates.
   (D) She's _____ supplies from a vehicle.

4.

   (A) The woman's _____ a display case in a hallway.
   (B) The woman's _____ a display of books.
   (C) The woman's _____ books on a counter.
   (D) The woman's _____ merchandise on a rack.

② 2인 이상 사진

사람이 2명 이상 등장하는 사진으로, 사람들의 공통된 동작/상태 또는 개별적인 동작/상태를 묘사하는 문장이 출제됩니다.

> **핵심 포인트 1** 2인 사진: 두 사람의 공통된 동작이나 상태를 먼저 파악합니다. 공통점이 없는 경우, 각각의 인물이 개별적으로 하는 동작이나 상태에 주목합니다.
>
> **핵심 포인트 2** 3인 이상 사진: 다수의 사람들이 하는 동작 → 개별 행동을 하는 사람 → 눈에 띄는 배경이나 사물 순서로 잘 출제됩니다.

▶ **기출 사진으로 분석하는 정답 vs. 오답**   🔊 650_P1_03

2인 사진 – 공통 동작

정답 Some people are **standing near a notice board**.
사람들이 게시판 근처에 서 있다.

오답 Some people are ~~hanging a map~~ on a sign.
사람들이 표지판에 지도를 걸고 있다.

2인 사진 – 개별 동작

정답 One of the men is **holding a cane**.
남자들 중 한 명이 지팡이를 들고 있다.

오답 One of the men is ~~closing his bag~~.
남자들 중 한 명이 가방을 닫고 있다.

3인 이상 사진 – 공통 동작

정답 Some people are **meeting in a conference room**.
사람들이 회의실에서 회의를 하고 있다.

오답 ~~The women are sitting~~ at a table. 여자들이 테이블에 앉아 있다.

⚠️ 일부 사람들만 하고 있는 개별 동작을 공통 동작처럼 묘사하는 오답 문장에 주의해야 합니다.

3인 이상 사진 – 개별 동작

정답 A waiter is **taking an order**.
웨이터가 주문을 받고 있다.

오답 The man is ~~giving his menu~~ to a waiter.
남자가 웨이터에게 메뉴를 건네주고 있다.

ETS 유형 연습

음원을 듣고 사진을 가장 잘 묘사한 문장을 고르세요.
다시 듣고 빈칸을 채우세요.

🔊 650_P1_04

정답과 해설 p.003

1.

   (A) Two men are _____ a wall.

   (B) A man is _____ a cord.

   (C) A man is _____ to his coworker.

   (D) _____ are using tools.

2.

   (A) The woman is _____ a newspaper in half.

   (B) The woman is _____ a sign on the wall.

   (C) The man is _____ a cup to his mouth.

   (D) The man is _____ a counter.

3.

   (A) The people are _____ outdoors.

   (B) The people are _____ under a tent.

   (C) Some of the people are _____ bushes.

   (D) Some of the people are _____ a snack.

4.

   (A) Some people are _____ in a lobby.

   (B) Some people are _____ an escalator.

   (C) Some people are _____ on a balcony.

   (D) Some people are _____ a staircase.

ETS 실전 문제

1.
   (A)   (B)   (C)   (D)

2.
   (A)   (B)   (C)   (D)

3.
   (A)   (B)   (C)   (D)

4.
   (A)   (B)   (C)   (D)

5.
   (A)   (B)   (C)   (D)

6.
   (A)   (B)   (C)   (D)

7.
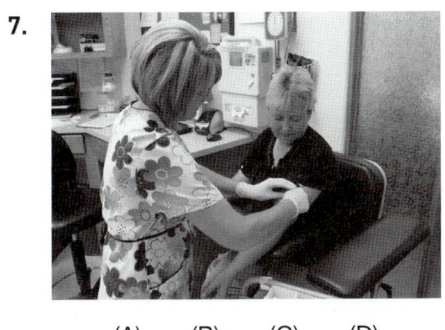
(A)　　(B)　　(C)　　(D)

8.
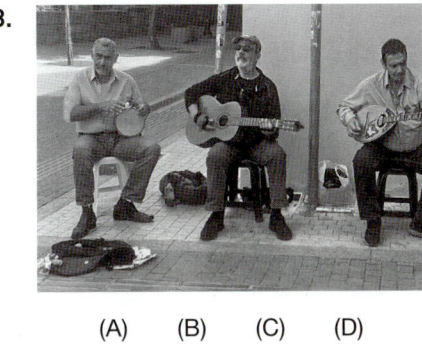
(A)　　(B)　　(C)　　(D)

9.
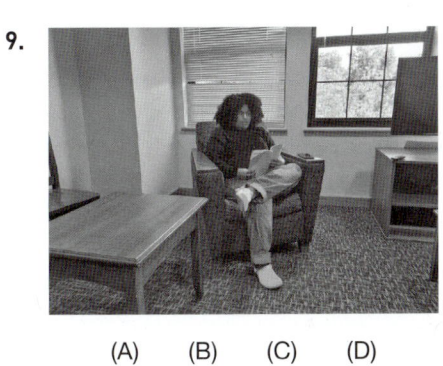
(A)　　(B)　　(C)　　(D)

10.
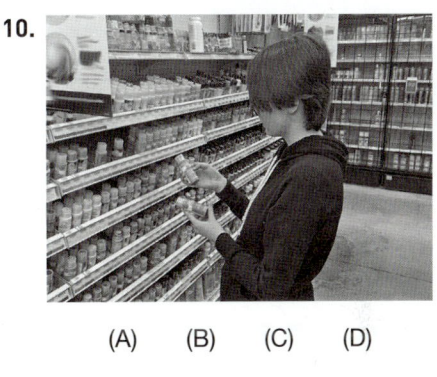
(A)　　(B)　　(C)　　(D)

11.

(A)　　(B)　　(C)　　(D)

12.
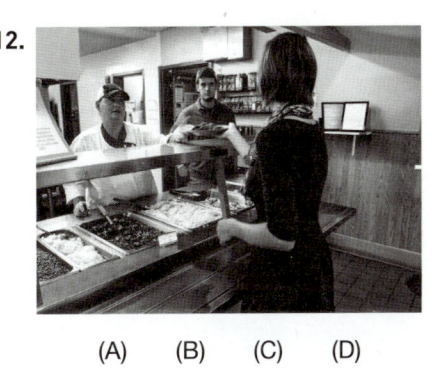
(A)　　(B)　　(C)　　(D)

UNIT 02 사물/배경 중심 사진

무료 강의

❶ 사물/배경 사진

사물이나 공원, 거리, 호수 등과 같은 배경이 중심이 되는 사진으로, 사물의 위치나 상태를 묘사하는 문제가 주로 출제됩니다.

> **핵심 포인트 1** 사진에 보이는 사물의 위치와 상태를 정확히 묘사하는지 확인해야 합니다.
> **핵심 포인트 2** 동사 be being p.p.에 유의해야 합니다. 이는 '~되고 있다'라는 의미로 그 행위를 하는 사람이 있어야 합니다. 사람이 없는 사진에 be being p.p.가 들리면 오답일 확률이 높습니다.

▶ 기출 사진으로 분석하는 정답 vs. 오답   🔊 650_P1_06

사물 주어

- **정답** Some **chairs** are arranged **around a table**.
  몇몇 의자들이 테이블 주위에 배치되어 있다.
- **오답** Some **food** is ~~being served~~. 음식이 제공되고 있다.
  ⚠ 사진에 food와 serve 하는 사람이 보이지 않습니다.

TIP be being displayed(전시되고 있다), be being cast(드리워지고 있다)는 사람이 없는 사진에서도 정답이 될 수 있습니다.

- Shadows **are being cast** on a patio.
  그림자가 테라스에 드리워지고 있다.

❷ 인물/사물 혼합 사진

특별히 부각되는 부분이 없는 사진에서는 인물과 사물, 배경에 대한 묘사를 모두 다루는 문제가 출제됩니다.

> **핵심 포인트** 사진의 중심이 되는 부분뿐 아니라 주변 배경까지 놓치지 않고 파악해야 합니다. 주어를 잘 듣고 인물, 사물, 배경 중 어떤 부분을 언급하는지 파악한 뒤, 제대로 묘사하는지 확인합니다.

▶ 기출 사진으로 분석하는 정답 vs. 오답   🔊 650_P1_07

인물 주어

- **정답** Workers are **carrying cargo**. 근로자들이 화물을 나르고 있다.
- **오답** Some people are ~~walking down~~ a ramp.
  몇몇 사람들이 경사로를 내려가고 있다.

사물 주어

- **정답** **Cargo is being carried up a ramp.** 화물이 경사로 위로 운반되고 있다.
- **오답** A ~~ladder has been left on the ground~~. 사다리가 땅에 놓여 있다.

ETS 유형 연습

음원을 듣고 사진을 가장 잘 묘사한 문장을 고르세요.
다시 듣고 빈칸을 채우세요.

🔊 650_P1_08
정답과 해설 p.007

1.

   (A) _____ has been left outside.
   (B) _____ has been removed from a wheelbarrow.
   (C) There's a _____ leaning against a wall.
   (D) There's a _____ under an archway.

2.

   (A) _____ are crossing at an intersection.
   (B) Trees are _____ on both sides of a street.
   (C) People are _____ to board a bus.
   (D) Lines are _____ on a road.

3.

   (A) Some pictures are _____ on the ground.
   (B) Some artwork is _____ on a wall.
   (C) A man is _____ a picture.
   (D) A man is _____ a jacket.

4.

   (A) _____ are viewing a city from a distance.
   (B) _____ is obscured by clouds.
   (C) Several people are _____ a low wall.
   (D) A woman is _____ her helmet on a ledge.

UNIT 02 | 사물/배경 중심 사진 **027**

ETS 실전 문제

1.
   (A) (B) (C) (D)

2.
   (A) (B) (C) (D)

3.
   (A) (B) (C) (D)

4.
   (A) (B) (C) (D)

5.
   (A) (B) (C) (D)

6.
   (A) (B) (C) (D)

7.

(A)　　(B)　　(C)　　(D)

8.

(A)　　(B)　　(C)　　(D)

9.

(A)　　(B)　　(C)　　(D)

10.

(A)　　(B)　　(C)　　(D)

11.

(A)　　(B)　　(C)　　(D)

12.

(A)　　(B)　　(C)　　(D)

PART 1 | 빈출 표현

🔊 650_P1_10

동작/자세 묘사

hanging up ~을 걸고 있다
holding 들고 있다
picking up ~을 집고 있다
pointing at ~을 가리키고 있다
extending (팔·다리를) 뻗고 있다
reaching for ~로 손을 뻗고 있다
handing 건네고 있다
pulling 끌고 있다
drawing 끌어당기고 있다
pressing 누르고 있다
tying (끈을) 묶고 있다
waving 손을 흔들고 있다
lying on ~에 누워 있다
leaning against[on] ~에 기대어 있다
relaxing 쉬고 있다
sitting 앉아 있다 (= be seated)
standing in line 줄을 서 있다
kneeling 무릎을 꿇고 있다
bending over 몸을 구부리고 있다
crouching down 쭈그리고 앉아 있다
walking along ~을 따라 걷고 있다
entering 들어가고 있다
exiting 나가고 있다
crossing 건너고 있다
passing through ~을 지나가고 있다
climbing 올라가고 있다
hiking 하이킹하고 있다

plugging in ~의 플러그를 꽂고 있다
typing 타자를 치고 있다
preparing 준비하고 있다
paying for ~의 값을 지불하고 있다
posting 게시하고 있다
placing 놓고 있다
removing 치우고[옮기고] 있다
watering 물을 주고 있다
facing 향하고[마주보고] 있다

동작 vs. 상태

putting[trying] on 입고[입어보고] 있다 (동작)
taking off 벗고 있다 (동작)
wearing 입고 있다 (상태)
getting on/off 올라타고/내리고 있다 (동작)
boarding 탑승하고 있다 (동작)
riding 타고 있다 (상태)

시선

looking at ~을 보고 있다
peering into ~을 들여다보고 있다
examining 살펴보고 있다
studying 살펴보고 있다
inspecting 살피고[검사하고] 있다
reviewing 검토하고 있다
overseeing 감독하고 있다
staring at ~을 뚫어지게 보고 있다

작업

- operating 작동시키고 있다
- adjusting 조절하고 있다
- arranging 배열[정리]하고 있다
- organizing 정리하고 있다
- lifting 들어 올리고 있다
- loading (짐을) 싣고 있다
- unloading (짐을) 내리고 있다
- carrying 나르고 있다
- stacking 쌓고 있다
- piling up 쌓아 올리고 있다
- wiping 닦고 있다
- mopping (대걸레로) 닦고 있다
- polishing 닦고 있다, 광을 내고 있다
- sweeping 쓸고 있다
- filling 채우고 있다
- stocking (물건을) 채우고 있다
- pouring 붓고 있다
- digging 파고 있다
- planting 심고 있다
- mowing (잔디를) 깎고 있다
- hammering 망치로 치고 있다
- installing 설치하고 있다
- fixing 고치고 있다
- repairing 수리하고 있다
- serving (음식을) 제공하고 있다, (손님을) 응대하고 있다
- taking measurements 치수를 재고 있다
- replacing 교체하고 있다

사물 설명 동사

- be arranged 정리되어 있다
- be attached 부착되어 있다
- be hung 걸려 있다
- be mounted (벽에) 걸려 있다, (받침대에) 얹혀 있다
- be suspended 매달려 있다
- be displayed 진열되어 있다(= be on display)
- be packed 포장되어 있다
- be positioned 자리잡고 있다
- be propped against[on] ~에 기대어져 있다
- be scattered 흩어져 있다
- be secured 묶여[고정되어] 있다
- be stacked[piled] 쌓여 있다
- be filled with ~로 채워져 있다
- be stocked 채워져 있다
- be separated by ~로 분리되어 있다
- be decorated with ~로 장식되어 있다
- be exhibited 전시되어 있다
- be occupied 사용되고 있다
- be unoccupied 사용되지 않고 있다(= be empty)
- be left 놓여 있다
- be placed 놓여 있다
- be spread out 펼쳐져 있다
- be set 준비되어 있다
- be open/closed 열려/닫혀 있다
- be turned on/off 켜져/꺼져 있다
- be propped up 받쳐져 있다
- be fallen 쓰러져 있다

PART 1 | 빈출 표현

배경 설명 동사

overlook 내려다보고 있다
lead to ~로 이어져 있다
run (길이) 나 있다
pass through ~을 지나고 있다
extend 뻗어 있다
line 늘어서 있다
cross over ~을 가로지르고 있다
span 가로질러 있다
border ~와 경계를 이루고 있다
surround ~을 둘러싸고 있다
stretch 뻗어 있다
flow 흐르고 있다
stand 서 있다
be reflected 비치고 있다
be crowded with ~로 붐비고 있다
be parked 주차되어 있다
be docked 정박되어 있다
be situated 놓여 있다
be set up 설치되어 있다
be planted 심어져 있다
be covered with ~로 덮여 있다
be under construction 공사 중이다
be tiled 타일이 깔려 있다
be laid out 가지런히 펼쳐져 있다
be lined up 줄지어 있다
be obscured by ~에 가려져 있다
be rolled up 말려 있다

실내 사물

display case 진열장
shelf 선반
rack 걸이, 선반
crate 나무 상자
cargo 화물
equipment 장비
workstation 작업대
work supplies 작업 용품
toolbox 도구상자
ladder 사다리
laptop 노트북 컴퓨터
bulletin board 게시판
trash bin 쓰레기통
light bulb 전구
light fixture 조명 (기구)
rug 깔개, 카펫
blanket 담요
sink 싱크대
counter 조리대; 계산대
cupboard 찬장
container 용기, 그릇
tray 쟁반
kitchen utensil 조리 도구
cash register 금전 등록기
flower pot 화분
wheelbarrow 손수레
artwork 예술 작품

실외 사물

patio 야외 테라스
patio umbrella 파라솔
awning 차양, 비[해] 가리개
handrail (계단) 난간
staircase 계단
lamppost 가로등
doorway 출입구
pavement 인도, 포장 도로
walkway 산책로, 보도
curb 도로 경계석
ramp 경사로
driveway 진입로
bush 덤불
fence 울타리, 담
pond 연못
fountain 분수대
archway 아치 통로
pillar 기둥
garage 차고, 주차 건물
pantry 식품 저장실

장소

shore 물가, 해변
harbor 항구
dock 부두
outdoor market 노천 시장
intersection 교차로
platform 승강장, 플랫폼
lobby 로비
construction site 공사장

위치

in the middle of ~ 중간에
on the top of ~ 맨 위에, 꼭대기에
on the floor 바닥에
in front of ~ 앞에
at the back of ~ 뒤에
in the corner of ~ 구석에
across from ~ 맞은편에
alongside ~ 옆에, ~ 나란히
on both sides of ~ 양쪽에
next to ~ 옆에
side by side 나란히
in a shaded area 그늘진 곳에
across the water 물 건너에
along the beach 해변을 따라
toward the stream 개울 쪽으로
against the wall 벽에 기대어
from the ceiling 천장에서
through an intersection 교차로를 지나서
down a road 도로를 따라
from a distance 멀리서
in a row 일렬로

LISTENING
COMPREHENSION

PART
2

질의 응답

INTRO
UNIT 03 Who/What/Which 의문문
UNIT 04 When/Where 의문문
UNIT 05 Why/How 의문문
UNIT 06 일반/선택 의문문
UNIT 07 부정/부가 의문문
UNIT 08 요청·제안 의문문/평서문
PART 2 빈출 표현

 무료 강의

INTRO
PART 2 질의 응답

📄 총 25문항

Part 2는 한 개의 질문과 세 개의 대답을 듣고 질문에 가장 적절한 대답을 고르는 유형입니다.

▶ PART 2 이렇게 풀자

STEP 1
첫 4단어를 듣고 핵심 의도 파악
Where do we keep our office supplies?

> **STEP 2**
오답 보기 소거하며 듣기
(A) ~~That's a nice tie.~~
(B) In the storage cabinet.
(C) ~~Two o'clock on Thursdays.~~

> **STEP 3**
정답 선택
(B)

▶ 빈출 오답 유형을 알아두자

❶ 질문과 상관없는 대답 – 다른 주어, 다른 시제, 다른 개념

Q **Who** came up with our new slogan?
누가 새 슬로건을 생각해 냈죠?

A ~~This escalator~~ goes down. (**X**)
이 에스컬레이터는 내려갑니다.

→ **Someone on the marketing team.** (**O**)
마케팅 팀의 누군가요.

❷ 의문사 의문문에 Yes/No로 대답

Q **When** will the road works begin?
언제 도로 공사가 시작될까요?

A Yes, it will. (**X**) 네, 그럴 겁니다.

→ **In late April.** (**O**) 4월 말에요.

❸ 발음이 같거나 비슷한 단어로 대답

Q Which **supplier** do you use for fruits?
과일에는 어떤 공급업체를 쓰세요?

A In the ~~supply~~ closet. (**X**) 물품 창고예요.

→ **The one on Edgewood Street.** (**O**)
에지우드 가에 있는 곳이요.

❹ 연상 어휘로 대답

Q This is the best **Italian restaurant** in town.
이 곳이 마을 최고의 이탈리안 식당이에요.

A ~~Pasta and a salad.~~ (**X**) 파스타와 샐러드요.

→ **It's where I take all of my clients.** (**O**)
제가 고객들을 접대하는 곳이에요.

▶ 만능 답변을 잡자

의문문에 '모른다'라고 대답하면 정답이 됩니다. 비슷한 맥락의 표현들을 기억해 두세요.

❶ 모르겠어요.

I don't know. 모르겠어요.
I'm not sure. 모르겠어요.
I have no idea. 전혀 몰라요.

Nobody knows. 아무도 몰라요.
It's not certain yet. 아직 확실하지 않아요.
I wish I knew. 저도 알았으면 좋겠네요.

❷ 알아볼게요.

I'll check. 확인해 볼게요.
I'll find out. 알아볼게요.
Let me check. 확인해 볼게요.
Let me figure it out. 알아볼게요.

I'll ask the supervisor. 상사에게 물어 볼게요.
I'll call ~ and find out. ~에 전화해서 알아볼게요.
Let me talk to my manager. 매니저에게 얘기해 볼게요.

❸ 나중에 알려줄게요.

I'll let you know later. 나중에 알려 줄게요.
It'll be announced this afternoon. 오늘 오후에 공지될 거예요.
I'll tell you all about it when I get back. 돌아와서 전부 다 말해 줄게요.

❹ ~에게 물어보세요. / ~가 알아요. / ~가 도와줄 거예요.

Ask the receptionist. 안내데스크 직원에게 물어보세요.
Oscar might know. 오스카가 알고 있을 거예요.
Check with Mr. Carter. 카터 씨에게 확인해 보세요.
Didn't your supervisor tell you? 상사가 말해주지 않았나요?

❺ 아직 결정되지 않았어요.

They are still deciding. 아직 결정하지 못했어요.
It hasn't been decided yet. 아직 결정되지 않았어요.
The board is reviewing it. 이사회에서 검토 중이에요.
It hasn't been announced. 공지되지 않았어요.

❻ 상황에 따라 달라요.

It depends. 상황에 따라 달라요.
It's up to the board. 이사회에 달려 있어요.

UNIT 03 Who/What/Which 의문문

무료 강의

1 Who 의문문

Who로 시작하면서 특정 행위의 주체나 대상을 묻는 질문으로, 매회 1~3문제 출제됩니다.

> **핵심 포인트** 사람 이름 또는 직책이 답변으로 제시되거나, 해당 사람에게 닿을 수 있는 방법을 말할 수도 있습니다.

▶ 빈출 질문 & 응답 패턴

🔊 650_P2_01

사람 이름 Mr./Ms./Dr. 등의 호칭이나 낯선 단어가 들리면 사람 이름일 확률이 높습니다.

Q **Who approved** the budget estimate?   누가 예산안을 승인했나요?
A **Mr. Allawi** did.   알라위 씨가 했어요.

직업/직책/부서명/회사명 이름 대신 그 사람이 소속된 곳으로 답할 수 있습니다.

Q **Who's in charge** of scheduling employees' work shifts?   직원 업무 교대 일정은 누가 짜요?
A **The factory supervisor.**   공장 감독관이요.

부정 대명사 특정 인물을 구체적으로 언급하지 않고 someone, no one 등으로 답할 수 있습니다.

Q **Who authorized** that purchase?   그 구매건은 누가 승인했나요?
A **Someone** in the accounting department.   회계부 사람이요.

1인칭 대명사 I/We 해당하는 사람이 누구인지 묻는 질문에 본인이라고 또는 본인이 아니라고 말하는 것은 자연스러운 응답입니다.

Q **Whose turn** is it to buy lunch?   누가 점심을 살 차례인가요?
A **I** already bought it.   제가 이미 샀어요.

우회적 응답 장소나 정보의 출처를 알려 주는 식의 답변도 정답이 될 수 있습니다.

Q **Who should I call** to set up my printer?   프린터 설치는 누구한테 전화해야 해요?
A **The phone number's on your desk.**   당신 책상 위에 번호가 있어요.

 ETS Check Up   🔊 650_P2_02   정답과 해설 p.011

다음 질문을 먼저 읽고 음원을 들은 후 적절한 응답을 고르세요.

1. Who can bring the clients upstairs?   (A) (B) (C)
2. Who's getting the lunch order today?   (A) (B) (C)
3. Who came up with our new slogan?   (A) (B) (C)
4. Who do you think we should offer the position to?   (A) (B) (C)
5. Who's managing the bookstore tomorrow?   (A) (B) (C)

❷ What/Which 의문문

What/Which(+명사)로 시작하는 의문문으로 매회 2~3문제 정도 출제됩니다.

핵심 포인트   의문사 뒤에 오는 명사를 들어야 정답을 선택할 수 있습니다.

▶ 빈출 질문 & 응답 패턴   🔊 650_P2_03

명사구 답변   대상을 묻는 What 의문문은 명사구를 이용한 단답형 정답이 자주 나옵니다.

Q	**What's the price** of this item? (가격)	이 물건은 얼마인가요?
A	**Five euros.**	5유로요.
Q	**What time are we meeting** with the architect? (시간)	건축가와 몇 시에 만나나요?
A	**Right after lunch.**	점심 직후요.
Q	**What floor** is the workshop on? (층수)	워크숍은 몇 층에서 하나요?
A	**The sixth.**	6층요.

대명사 one   어떤 '것/사람'을 묻는 Which 의문문은 대명사 one을 이용한 정답이 가장 흔합니다.

Q	**Which shoes** are on sale this weekend?	이번 주말에는 어떤 신발들이 할인되나요?
A	The **ones** on this table.	이 탁자 위에 있는 것들이요.
Q	**Which event space** would you like to use?	어떤 행사 장소를 이용하고 싶으세요?
A	I like the **one** we used last year.	작년에 우리가 썼던 곳이 좋아요.

의견   'What do you think of/about ~?'은 의견을 묻는 질문이므로 호불호를 표현하는 응답이 가장 자연스럽습니다.

Q	**What do you think of** the new floor plan?	새 평면도 어떻게 생각하세요?
A	It's **a good design**.	디자인이 괜찮네요.
Q	**What did you think of** the training video?	교육 영상 어땠어요?
A	I thought it was **very helpful**.	매우 유익했던 것 같아요.

✅ ETS Check Up   🔊 650_P2_04 정답과 해설 p.012

다음 질문을 먼저 읽고 음원을 들은 후 적절한 응답을 고르세요.

1. What happens at the weekly meetings?   (A) (B) (C)
2. Which of these companies is accepting résumés?   (A) (B) (C)
3. What time does the train arrive?   (A) (B) (C)
4. Which company developed this software?   (A) (B) (C)
5. What do you think of this month's budget?   (A) (B) (C)

ETS 유형 연습

다음 말을 듣고 적절한 응답을 고르세요.
다시 듣고 빈칸을 채우세요.

🔊 650_P2_05
정답과 해설 p.013

1. Mark your answer.
   (A)   (B)   (C)

   _____ the floor plan?
   (A) They're _____.
   (B) Only _____.
   (C) Mr. Bryson _____.

2. Mark your answer.
   (A)   (B)   (C)

   What's _____?
   (A) _____ and water.
   (B) On Atlantic _____.
   (C) She _____ her bicycle.

3. Mark your answer.
   (A)   (B)   (C)

   Which carpet was _____?
   (A) _____ the hallway.
   (B) Yes, _____.
   (C) _____ the counter.

4. Mark your answer.
   (A)   (B)   (C)

   What's the topic of _____?
   (A) _____.
   (B) I'm _____.
   (C) No, _____.

5. Mark your answer.
   (A)   (B)   (C)

   Who's _____ to help me contact _____?
   (A) A _____ for five percent off.
   (B) I know Bianca is _____.
   (C) _____ of dollars.

ETS 실전 문제

🔊 650_P2_06

1. Mark your answer on your answer sheet.
2. Mark your answer on your answer sheet.
3. Mark your answer on your answer sheet.
4. Mark your answer on your answer sheet.
5. Mark your answer on your answer sheet.
6. Mark your answer on your answer sheet.
7. Mark your answer on your answer sheet.
8. Mark your answer on your answer sheet.
9. Mark your answer on your answer sheet.
10. Mark your answer on your answer sheet.
11. Mark your answer on your answer sheet.
12. Mark your answer on your answer sheet.
13. Mark your answer on your answer sheet.
14. Mark your answer on your answer sheet.
15. Mark your answer on your answer sheet.
16. Mark your answer on your answer sheet.
17. Mark your answer on your answer sheet.
18. Mark your answer on your answer sheet.
19. Mark your answer on your answer sheet.
20. Mark your answer on your answer sheet.
21. Mark your answer on your answer sheet.
22. Mark your answer on your answer sheet.
23. Mark your answer on your answer sheet.
24. Mark your answer on your answer sheet.
25. Mark your answer on your answer sheet.

UNIT 04 When/Where 의문문

무료 강의

1 When 의문문

When으로 시작하면서 어떤 일이 발생하는 시점을 묻는 질문으로, 매회 2~3문제 출제됩니다.

핵심 포인트 시간을 직접적으로 나타내거나, 어느 행위 전후로 답변할 수 있습니다.

▶ 빈출 질문 & 응답 패턴
650_P2_07

특정 시점 - 전치사구 전치사(at, in, by, until 등)가 들어간 구체적 시간 표현 정답이 자주 나옵니다.

Q **When will Mr. Ota finish** his conference call? 오타 씨는 언제 전화회의가 끝나시나요?
A **In about five minutes.** 5분 정도 후예요.

특정 시점 - 부사구 부사(ago, sometime, soon, earlier 등)가 들어간 구체적 시간 표현 정답도 많습니다.

Q **When did you join** the company? 언제 입사했나요?
A **Three years ago.** 3년 전예요.

부사절 표현 before, after, as soon as 등의 부사절 접속사로 시작하는 표현도 있습니다.

Q **When will the renovation start?** 보수공사가 언제 시작되나요?
A **After** the budget is approved. 예산안이 승인되고 나서요.

모른다 응답 '들은 바 없다, 확인해 보겠다, (담당자에게) 물어보라, (자료를) 참고하라' 등 여러 표현으로 등장합니다.

Q **When will the conveyor belt be fixed?** 컨베이어 벨트가 언제 수리될까요?
A **Let's ask Mr. Miller.** 밀러 씨에게 물어봅시다.

우회적 응답 구체적인 시점으로 답하는 대신 시점과 관련된 단서를 우회적으로 제시하기도 합니다.

Q **When will the sales report be ready?** 판매 보고서는 언제 준비되나요?
A **I just have to add** a few more tables. 표 몇 개만 더 삽입하면 돼요.

✓ ETS Check Up
650_P2_08 정답과 해설 p.018

다음 질문을 먼저 읽고 음원을 들은 후 적절한 응답을 고르세요.

1. When does the grocery store close? (A) (B) (C)
2. When's your next dental checkup? (A) (B) (C)
3. When will the construction begin? (A) (B) (C)
4. When do we need to register for the sales seminar? (A) (B) (C)
5. When will you have the results of the customer survey? (A) (B) (C)

❷ Where 의문문

Where로 시작하는 의문문으로 매회 2문제 정도 출제됩니다.

> **핵심 포인트** 주로 장소나 위치에 대해서 묻지만, 물건이나 정보의 출처를 묻기도 합니다. When 의문문에 어울리는 답변을 선택하지 않도록 주의합니다.

▶ 빈출 질문 & 응답 패턴
🔊 650_P2_09

장소·위치 전치사(at, in, on, near, across 등)가 들어간 장소·위치 표현 정답이 가장 많습니다.

Q **Where did you meet** with Ms. Jenkins? 젠킨스 씨와 어디에서 만났나요?
A **In the cafeteria.** 구내식당에서요.

사람 물건을 갖고 있거나 사용 중인 사람이 답이 되기도 합니다.

Q **Where can I get** an ink cartridge for the printer? 이 프린터용 잉크 카트리지는 어디에 있죠?
A **Jacob** has the key to the supply room. 제이콥한테 비품실 열쇠가 있어요.

출처 물건의 출처로는 물건을 준 사람이나 구입처, 정보의 출처로는 웹사이트, 신문, 설명서 등이 답이 될 수 있습니다.

Q **Where did you get** that beautiful scarf? 그 멋진 스카프는 어디에서 샀나요?
A It was a **gift from my colleague**. 제 동료가 준 선물이에요.

모른다 응답 '들은 바 없다, 확인해 보겠다, (담당자에게) 물어보라, (자료를) 참고하라' 등 여러 표현으로 등장합니다.

Q **Where do I board** the plane to London? 런던행 비행기는 어디서 탑승하나요?
A **Check your boarding pass.** 탑승권을 확인해 보세요.

✅ ETS Check Up
🔊 650_P2_10 정답과 해설 p.019

다음 질문을 먼저 읽고 음원을 들은 후 적절한 응답을 고르세요.

1. Where did you store the extra name tags?   (A) (B) (C)
2. Where will the conference be held next month?   (A) (B) (C)
3. Where was Mr. Wagner yesterday?   (A) (B) (C)
4. Where can I attend an evening course?   (A) (B) (C)
5. Where's the library branch going to be built?   (A) (B) (C)

ETS 유형 연습

다음 말을 듣고 적절한 응답을 고르세요.
다시 듣고 빈칸을 채우세요.

🔊 650_P2_11

정답과 해설 p.020

1. Mark your answer.
   (A)   (B)   (C)

   When will the _____?
   (A) They haven't given us _____.
   (B) A new _____.
   (C) Through the _____.

2. Mark your answer.
   (A)   (B)   (C)

   Where can I find _____?
   (A) No, it's not _____.
   (B) By _____.
   (C) _____ at Greenville Office Supplies.

3. Mark your answer.
   (A)   (B)   (C)

   When will the _____?
   (A) I _____ that store.
   (B) _____ sometime.
   (C) No, _____.

4. Mark your answer.
   (A)   (B)   (C)

   When will the manager's _____?
   (A) During the _____.
   (B) The _____, downstairs.
   (C) Yes, it's _____ now.

5. Mark your answer.
   (A)   (B)   (C)

   _____ this article?
   (A) In yesterday's _____.
   (B) It's about _____.
   (C) Yes, I have a _____.

ETS 실전 문제

🔊 650_P2_12
정답과 해설 p.021

1. Mark your answer on your answer sheet.
2. Mark your answer on your answer sheet.
3. Mark your answer on your answer sheet.
4. Mark your answer on your answer sheet.
5. Mark your answer on your answer sheet.
6. Mark your answer on your answer sheet.
7. Mark your answer on your answer sheet.
8. Mark your answer on your answer sheet.
9. Mark your answer on your answer sheet.
10. Mark your answer on your answer sheet.
11. Mark your answer on your answer sheet.
12. Mark your answer on your answer sheet.
13. Mark your answer on your answer sheet.
14. Mark your answer on your answer sheet.
15. Mark your answer on your answer sheet.
16. Mark your answer on your answer sheet.
17. Mark your answer on your answer sheet.
18. Mark your answer on your answer sheet.
19. Mark your answer on your answer sheet.
20. Mark your answer on your answer sheet.
21. Mark your answer on your answer sheet.
22. Mark your answer on your answer sheet.
23. Mark your answer on your answer sheet.
24. Mark your answer on your answer sheet.
25. Mark your answer on your answer sheet.

UNIT 05 Why/How 의문문

1 Why 의문문

Why로 시작하면서 어떤 일의 원인이나 이유, 목적을 묻는 질문으로, 매회 1~2문제씩 출제됩니다.

핵심 포인트 답변으로 제시하는 이유가 질문의 내용과 잘 맞는지 끝까지 들어야 합니다.

▶ 빈출 질문 & 응답 패턴   🔊 650_P2_13

Because가 있는 문장 Because로 시작하면서 이유를 설명하는 문장은 정답일 수 있습니다.

- Q **Why has there been a delay** in shipping these orders? 왜 이 주문품의 배송이 지연됐나요?
- A **Because** we ran out of packing materials. 포장재가 떨어졌거든요.
  - 오답 함정 Because the order has arrived. 주문품이 도착했거든요.
  → Because는 함정으로 사용되기도 하므로 이유를 말하는 문장이 맞는지 끝까지 들어야 합니다.

Because가 없는 문장 Because를 생략하고 이유를 설명하는 문장이 정답인 경우가 가장 많습니다.

- Q **Why do you want to exchange** this coat? 왜 이 코트를 교환하시려는 거죠?
- A It's the wrong size. 사이즈가 맞지 않아요.

to부정사구 '~하기 위해'라는 뜻의 목적을 설명하는 to부정사구 표현도 있습니다.

- Q **Why is the legal department having a party?** 법무팀에서 왜 파티를 여는 거죠?
- A **To welcome** some new employees. 신입 직원 몇 명을 환영하기 위해서요.

모른다 응답 '들은 바 없다, 확인해 보겠다, (담당자에게) 물어보라, (자료를) 참고하라' 등 여러 표현으로 등장합니다.

- Q **Why did Juan decline** the job offer? 후안은 왜 그 일자리 제안을 거절했죠?
- A I have no idea. 모르겠어요.

부정 의문문 〈Why+동사+not〉의 부정 의문문도 출제되는데, Because 없이 이유를 설명하는 문장이 가장 흔한 정답 유형입니다.

- Q **Why isn't the printer working?** 왜 프린터가 작동하지 않죠?
- A It's out of ink. 잉크가 떨어졌어요.

✅ ETS Check Up   🔊 650_P2_14   정답과 해설 p.026

다음 질문을 먼저 읽고 음원을 들은 후 적절한 응답을 고르세요.

1. Why isn't Matt's contact information in the company directory?   (A) (B) (C)
2. Why do we need three copies of the contract?   (A) (B) (C)
3. Why are the technicians here?   (A) (B) (C)
4. Why were our expenses over budget last month?   (A) (B) (C)
5. Why aren't these scarves included in the clearance sale?   (A) (B) (C)

 How 의문문

How로 시작하는 의문문으로 매회 2문제 정도 나옵니다.

> **핵심 포인트** 방법이나 의견을 묻는 문제가 주로 출제되지만, 〈How+형용사/부사〉의 형태로 수량, 가격, 기간 등을 묻는 문제도 출제됩니다.

▶ 빈출 질문 & 응답 패턴   🔊 650_P2_15

방법 '어떻게'라고 묻고 그에 대한 방법 및 수단을 알려 주는 답변이 정답인 경우가 가장 많습니다.

Q **How will you notify** the applicants? 　　지원자들에게 어떻게 통지할 건가요?
A I'll **call them**. 　　전화하려고요.

의견·상태 형용사나 부사로 의견이나 상태를 표현하는 답변이 많습니다.

Q **How is Ivan's new job** at the law firm **going**? 　　법률회사에서 이반의 새 일은 좀 어떤가요?
A He seems to be **doing quite well**. 　　꽤 잘하고 있는 것 같아요.

수량 How many 질문에는 수량, How much 질문에는 가격을 나타내는 수 표현이 정답인 경우가 많습니다.

Q **How many** people are there in the art department? 　　예술부서에는 사람이 몇 명 있나요?
A Around **twenty**. 　　대략 20명이요.

빈도 How often 질문에는 빈도를 나타내는 수 관련 표현(once, twice, every 등)이 정답입니다.

Q **How often** is the hotel swimming pool cleaned? 　　호텔 수영장은 얼마나 자주 청소하나요?
A **Every morning**. 　　매일 아침마다요.

시간·기간 How long 질문에는 기간, How soon/late 질문에는 시간 관련 수 표현이 정답입니다.

Q **How late** does the store stay open? 　　그 가게는 얼마나 늦게까지 문을 여나요?
A It closes **at nine**. 　　9시에 문을 닫아요.

✅ ETS Check Up   🔊 650_P2_16 정답과 해설 p.027

다음 질문을 먼저 읽고 음원을 들은 후 적절한 응답을 고르세요.

1. How do I get to the doctor's office?　　(A) (B) (C)
2. How was your stay at the hotel?　　(A) (B) (C)
3. How long have you been gardening?　　(A) (B) (C)
4. How much is this umbrella?　　(A) (B) (C)
5. How often do you charge your phone?　　(A) (B) (C)

ETS 유형 연습

다음 말을 듣고 적절한 응답을 고르세요.
다시 듣고 빈칸을 채우세요.

🔊 **650_P2_17**
정답과 해설 p.028

1. Mark your answer.
   (A)   (B)   (C)

   Why should we _____ of the city?
   (A) _____ of Maple and Third Street.
   (B) Yes, the _____.
   (C) _____ haven't been here before.

2. Mark your answer.
   (A)   (B)   (C)

   _____ for the conference?
   (A) _____ our new model.
   (B) Just _____.
   (C) I'd _____.

3. Mark your answer.
   (A)   (B)   (C)

   _____ is the company offering this summer?
   (A) I brought my _____.
   (B) _____ yet.
   (C) OK, I'll _____ now.

4. Mark your answer.
   (A)   (B)   (C)

   Why is the store _____ today?
   (A) No, it isn't _____.
   (B) Yes, I _____ today.
   (C) It's a _____.

5. Mark your answer.
   (A)   (B)   (C)

   _____ does this tea kettle _____?
   (A) With _____, please.
   (B) Oh, you should _____.
   (C) I _____.

ETS 실전 문제

🔊 650_P2_18

1. Mark your answer on your answer sheet.
2. Mark your answer on your answer sheet.
3. Mark your answer on your answer sheet.
4. Mark your answer on your answer sheet.
5. Mark your answer on your answer sheet.
6. Mark your answer on your answer sheet.
7. Mark your answer on your answer sheet.
8. Mark your answer on your answer sheet.
9. Mark your answer on your answer sheet.
10. Mark your answer on your answer sheet.
11. Mark your answer on your answer sheet.
12. Mark your answer on your answer sheet.
13. Mark your answer on your answer sheet.
14. Mark your answer on your answer sheet.
15. Mark your answer on your answer sheet.
16. Mark your answer on your answer sheet.
17. Mark your answer on your answer sheet.
18. Mark your answer on your answer sheet.
19. Mark your answer on your answer sheet.
20. Mark your answer on your answer sheet.
21. Mark your answer on your answer sheet.
22. Mark your answer on your answer sheet.
23. Mark your answer on your answer sheet.
24. Mark your answer on your answer sheet.
25. Mark your answer on your answer sheet.

UNIT 06 일반/선택 의문문

1 일반 의문문

의문사 없이 Be동사/Do동사/조동사/Have동사로 시작하는 의문문으로 매회 4문제 정도 나옵니다.

핵심 포인트 의문사 의문문과는 달리 Yes/No로 응답할 수 있으며 다양한 내용이 출제됩니다.

▶ 빈출 질문 & 응답 패턴　　　　　　　　　　　　　　　　650_P2_19

Yes/No 응답　〈Yes+긍정 내용〉과 〈No+부정 내용〉으로 구성된 응답이 출제됩니다.

Q **Was that the last bus** to the airport?　　　저 버스가 공항행 마지막 버스였나요?
A **No, there's another one soon.**　　　아니요, 곧 또 한 대가 올 거예요.

Yes/No 대체 표현　Yes는 Sure, Okay, No는 Unfortunately, Not yet, I don't think so 등으로 대체되기도 합니다.

Q **Are you going to join** that new fitness center?　　　새로 생긴 헬스클럽에 등록할 건가요?
A **I don't think so.**　　　아니요.

Yes/No가 빠진 응답　Yes/No를 생략한 채 Yes/No의 의미를 나타내는 응답이 가장 흔합니다.

Q **Does your store carry** any tomato sauce?　　　이 가게에 토마토 소스가 있나요?
A **It's in aisle sixteen**.　　　16번 통로에 있어요.

되묻는 응답　질문에 답하는 데 필요한 추가 정보 등을 되묻는 답변도 정답이 될 수 있습니다.

Q **Do I have to replace my car's tires?**　　　제 차의 타이어를 교체해야 할까요?
A **When did you buy the car?**　　　언제 차를 사셨는데요?

간접 의문문 응답　간접 의문문에는 Yes/No 답변이 가능하고, 의문사에 해당하는 내용을 답하면 됩니다.

Q **Do you know where** the library is?　　　도서관이 어디에 있는지 아시나요?
A **Yes**, it's **around the corner**.　　　네, 모퉁이를 돌면 있어요.

✅ ETS Check Up　　　　　　　　　　　　　　650_P2_20　정답과 해설 p.034

다음 질문을 먼저 읽고 음원을 들은 후 적절한 응답을 고르세요.

1. Do you want to see a play tomorrow night?　　　(A) (B) (C)
2. Was the advertising team informed about the leadership change?　　　(A) (B) (C)
3. Has the gallery received our shipment of artwork?　　　(A) (B) (C)
4. Does the chef use local ingredients?　　　(A) (B) (C)
5. Do you know what kind of car you'd like to lease?　　　(A) (B) (C)

❷ 선택 의문문

〈A or B〉 형태로 or가 들어가 A와 B 중 어떤 것을 선택할지 묻는 의문문으로, 매회 2문제 정도 출제됩니다.

핵심 포인트 빈출 정답 패턴이 골고루 답으로 나오는데, 우회적 응답이 정답인 경우가 많습니다.

▶ 빈출 질문 & 응답 패턴   🔊 650_P2_21

둘 중 하나 선택 질문에서 제시된 두 가지 중 하나를 선택하는 답변이 정답으로 나옵니다.

Q Are you going to buy **the small suitcase or the backpack**?   작은 여행가방과 배낭 중 뭘 사실 건가요?
A I decided to get **the backpack**.   배낭을 사기로 했어요.

둘 다 선택 혹은 거부 '둘 다 좋다' 혹은 '둘 다 안 하겠다'라고 답할 수 있습니다.

Q Are you going to watch **the movie or the game**?   영화와 경기 중 어떤 걸 볼 거예요?
A **Neither**, I'm too tired.   둘 다 안 봐요, 너무 피곤하거든요.

상관없음 '둘 중 어느 쪽이든 상관없다'는 답변이 들리면 정답일 확률이 매우 높습니다.

Q Can I pay **by credit card or** do I have to pay **cash**?   신용카드와 현금 중 어떤 걸로 계산해야 하나요?
A **Either is fine**.   어느 쪽이든 상관없습니다.

제3의 선택 질문에서 주어진 두 가지가 아닌 제3의 것을 선택하는 응답도 있습니다.

Q Should I turn **at this traffic light or the next one**?   이번 신호등에서 방향을 바꿔야 하나요, 아니면 다음 번 신호등에서인가요?
A **Wait until the one at Maple Street**.   메이플 로 신호등이 나올 때까지 기다리세요.

우회적 응답 둘 중 하나를 선택할 경우, 질문에서 주어진 선택 사항을 반복하지 않고 우회적으로 돌려 답변하는 경우가 많습니다.

Q Do you want to hire **one or two interns** for the summer?   올 여름에 인턴을 한 명 채용하실 건가요, 아니면 두 명 채용하실 건가요?
A **The budget's quite small** this year.   올해 예산이 꽤 빠듯해요.

✅ ETS Check Up   🔊 650_P2_22 정답과 해설 p.035

다음 질문을 먼저 읽고 음원을 들은 후 적절한 응답을 고르세요.

1. Does Henry speak Spanish or Italian?   (A) (B) (C)
2. Are you presenting your research today or tomorrow?   (A) (B) (C)
3. Would you like this shirt or a smaller one?   (A) (B) (C)
4. Do you want my home or work phone number?   (A) (B) (C)
5. Should we reserve the conference room for one hour or two?   (A) (B) (C)

ETS 유형 연습

다음 말을 듣고 적절한 응답을 고르세요.
다시 듣고 빈칸을 채우세요.

🔊 650_P2_23
정답과 해설 p.036

1. Mark your answer.
   (A)   (B)   (C)

   Are these _____?
   (A) No, could you _____?
   (B) It's _____.
   (C) He's a _____.

2. Mark your answer.
   (A)   (B)   (C)

   Will the next shipment be _____?
   (A) A free _____.
   (B) I _____ a truck.
   (C) Our _____ that.

3. Mark your answer.
   (A)   (B)   (C)

   Are you _____ in the small conference room?
   (A) No, _____ the board.
   (B) In the _____.
   (C) _____ with a projector.

4. Mark your answer.
   (A)   (B)   (C)

   Should we _____ today, or _____ OK?
   (A) They got _____.
   (B) Yes, I _____.
   (C) It _____ to me.

5. Mark your answer.
   (A)   (B)   (C)

   Do your employees _____?
   (A) The _____ today.
   (B) Yes, _____.
   (C) That job is _____.

ETS 실전 문제

🔊 **650_P2_24**
정답과 해설 p.037

1. Mark your answer on your answer sheet.
2. Mark your answer on your answer sheet.
3. Mark your answer on your answer sheet.
4. Mark your answer on your answer sheet.
5. Mark your answer on your answer sheet.
6. Mark your answer on your answer sheet.
7. Mark your answer on your answer sheet.
8. Mark your answer on your answer sheet.
9. Mark your answer on your answer sheet.
10. Mark your answer on your answer sheet.
11. Mark your answer on your answer sheet.
12. Mark your answer on your answer sheet.
13. Mark your answer on your answer sheet.
14. Mark your answer on your answer sheet.
15. Mark your answer on your answer sheet.
16. Mark your answer on your answer sheet.
17. Mark your answer on your answer sheet.
18. Mark your answer on your answer sheet.
19. Mark your answer on your answer sheet.
20. Mark your answer on your answer sheet.
21. Mark your answer on your answer sheet.
22. Mark your answer on your answer sheet.
23. Mark your answer on your answer sheet.
24. Mark your answer on your answer sheet.
25. Mark your answer on your answer sheet.

UNIT 07 부정/부가 의문문

무료 강의

1 부정 의문문

부정 의문문은 대부분 사실을 확인하는 내용이지만 제안을 하거나 동의를 구하는 경우도 있으며, 매회 2문제 정도 나옵니다.

핵심 포인트 not을 제외한 내용에 대해 일반 의문문과 같은 방식으로 답을 찾으면 됩니다.

▶ 빈출 질문 & 응답 패턴   650_P2_25

Yes/No 응답   〈Yes+긍정 내용〉과 〈No+부정 내용〉으로 구성된 응답이 출제됩니다.

Q Aren't you working next week? 다음 주에 근무하시지 않나요?
A No, I'll be on vacation. 아니요, 저는 휴가예요.

Yes/No가 빠진 응답   Yes/No를 생략한 채 Yes/No의 의미를 나타내는 응답도 있습니다.

Q Isn't the store closed? 그 상점은 문을 닫지 않았나요?
A It's open 24 hours a day. 거기는 하루 종일 영업해요.

모른다 응답   '들은 바 없다, 확인해 보겠다, (담당자에게) 물어보라, (자료를) 참고하라' 등 여러 표현으로 등장합니다.

Q Isn't Mr. Tao opening a new office in town? 타오 씨가 시내에 새 사무실을 열지 않나요?
A I haven't talked to him lately. 최근에 그와 얘기를 나눈 적이 없어요.

우회적 응답   Yes/No를 직접적으로 답하는 대신 참고할 수 있는 상황이나 관련 사항을 우회적으로 제시하는 답변도 자주 나옵니다.

Q Don't I need to make another doctor's appointment? 진료 예약을 또 해야 하지 않나요?
A Most patients only come in once a year. 환자분들 대부분이 일 년에 한 번만 오세요.

되묻는 응답   제안하거나 동의를 구하는 질문에는 직접 해달라고 요청하거나 추가 관련 정보를 되묻는 응답이 정답이 될 수 있습니다.

Q Shouldn't we update the price? 가격표를 수정해야 하지 않을까요?
A Could you do it? 직접 해 주시겠어요?

✓ ETS Check Up   650_P2_26   정답과 해설 p.042

다음 질문을 먼저 읽고 음원을 들은 후 적절한 응답을 고르세요.

1. Shouldn't the drywall have been delivered by now? (A) (B) (C)
2. Shouldn't we have dinner soon? (A) (B) (C)
3. Aren't we offering a free-ticket promotion next week? (A) (B) (C)
4. Shouldn't the roof be inspected for potential leaks? (A) (B) (C)
5. Isn't Alonso moving into an apartment in the city? (A) (B) (C)

❷ 부가 의문문

부가 의문문은 평서문 끝에 문장의 내용을 확인하는 의문문이 붙은 형태로, 매회 2문제 정도 나옵니다.

핵심 포인트 평서문의 내용에 대해 일반 의문문과 같은 방식으로 답을 찾으면 됩니다.

▶ 빈출 질문 & 응답 패턴
🔊 650_P2_27

Yes/No 응답 〈Yes+긍정 내용〉과 〈No+부정 내용〉으로 구성된 응답이 출제됩니다.

Q **You have a receipt** for the purchase, don't you?   구매 영수증이 있으신 거죠?
A **No, I left it at home.**   아니요, 집에 두고 왔어요.

Yes/No 대체 표현 Yes는 Sure, Okay, Absolutely, No는 Unfortunately, Not yet 등으로 대체되기도 합니다.

Q **The gymnastics class was really fun**, wasn't it?   체조 수업이 정말 재미있었죠?
A **Absolutely** — I really enjoyed myself.   그럼요, 정말 즐거웠어요.

Yes/No가 빠진 응답 Yes/No를 생략한 채 Yes/No의 의미를 나타내는 응답도 있습니다.

Q **You rescheduled my Tuesday appointments**, didn't you?   제 화요일 일정은 조정하신 거죠?
A **All of them except for Mr. Park's.**   박 씨와의 일정만 빼고 전부요.

모른다 응답 '들은 바 없다, 확인해 보겠다, (담당자에게) 물어보라, (자료를) 참고하라' 등 여러 표현으로 등장합니다.

Q **Ron's last day at work is Friday**, isn't it?   론의 마지막 근무일이 금요일이죠?
A **I don't really know.**   잘 모르겠어요.

우회적 응답 Yes/No를 직접적으로 답하는 대신 참고할 수 있는 상황이나 관련 사항을 우회적으로 제시하는 답변도 자주 나옵니다.

Q **I e-mailed you the presentation**, didn't I?   제가 발표자료를 이메일로 보내드렸죠?
A **My computer is broken.**   제 컴퓨터가 고장났어요.

✅ ETS Check Up
🔊 650_P2_28   정답과 해설 p.043

다음 질문을 먼저 읽고 음원을 들은 후 적절한 응답을 고르세요.

1. That meeting was called by Ms. Romero, wasn't it?   (A) (B) (C)
2. That photocopy machine is broken, isn't it?   (A) (B) (C)
3. You drive to work every day, don't you?   (A) (B) (C)
4. You used to own that furniture store, didn't you?   (A) (B) (C)
5. You're meeting Monica tomorrow, aren't you?   (A) (B) (C)

ETS 유형 연습

다음 말을 듣고 적절한 응답을 고르세요.
다시 듣고 빈칸을 채우세요.

🔊 650_P2_29
정답과 해설 p.044

1. Mark your answer.
   (A)   (B)   (C)

   My car will _____, won't it?
   (A) I _____.
   (B) All _____.
   (C) It _____ how busy we are.

2. Mark your answer.
   (A)   (B)   (C)

   Isn't the _____ tomorrow?
   (A) A _____.
   (B) Sure, I can _____ those.
   (C) No, he _____.

3. Mark your answer.
   (A)   (B)   (C)

   You don't _____ now, do you?
   (A) Yes, this is _____.
   (B) I _____, thanks.
   (C) No, I just _____.

4. Mark your answer.
   (A)   (B)   (C)

   Hasn't the _____ been repaired?
   (A) Thanks for the _____.
   (B) The funding was _____.
   (C) I have _____.

5. Mark your answer.
   (A)   (B)   (C)

   That building's still _____, isn't it?
   (A) Maybe the _____.
   (B) Yes, it's _____ in October.
   (C) Yes, it's _____ six.

ETS 실전 문제

1. Mark your answer on your answer sheet.
2. Mark your answer on your answer sheet.
3. Mark your answer on your answer sheet.
4. Mark your answer on your answer sheet.
5. Mark your answer on your answer sheet.
6. Mark your answer on your answer sheet.
7. Mark your answer on your answer sheet.
8. Mark your answer on your answer sheet.
9. Mark your answer on your answer sheet.
10. Mark your answer on your answer sheet.
11. Mark your answer on your answer sheet.
12. Mark your answer on your answer sheet.
13. Mark your answer on your answer sheet.
14. Mark your answer on your answer sheet.
15. Mark your answer on your answer sheet.
16. Mark your answer on your answer sheet.
17. Mark your answer on your answer sheet.
18. Mark your answer on your answer sheet.
19. Mark your answer on your answer sheet.
20. Mark your answer on your answer sheet.
21. Mark your answer on your answer sheet.
22. Mark your answer on your answer sheet.
23. Mark your answer on your answer sheet.
24. Mark your answer on your answer sheet.
25. Mark your answer on your answer sheet.

UNIT 08 요청·제안 의문문 / 평서문

무료 강의

❶ 요청·제안 의문문

상대에게 요청하거나 제안하는 방법으로 다양한 형태의 질문이 매회 2~3문제 정도 출제됩니다.

> **핵심 포인트** 요청 사항에 대한 질문 또는 수락/거절하는 이유만 제시하는 답변도 답이 될 수 있습니다.

▶ 빈출 질문 & 응답 패턴   🔊 650_P2_31

수락하는 응답 Sure, Absolutely, Of course 등의 표현이 정답으로 제시됩니다.

Q **Can you help** me plant these flowers? 이 꽃을 심는 걸 좀 도와 주시겠어요?
A **Sure**, let me get some gardening gloves. 물론이죠, 원예용 장갑을 가져올게요.

거절하는 응답 거절할 때는 Sorry, I'm not sure ~, I don't think ~, Thanks, but ~ 등의 표현이 정답입니다.

Q **Would you like help** revising the contracts? 계약서를 수정하는 걸 도와드릴까요?
A **Thanks, but** I'm almost done. 고맙습니다만, 거의 다 했어요.

Yes/No 응답 Why don't you/we ~?, What/How about ~?은 Yes/No 표현으로 응답이 가능합니다.

Q **Why don't you come** to the beach with us? 우리와 함께 해변에 가는 게 어때요?
A **Sure**. When are you leaving? 좋아요. 언제 떠날 거예요?

 * Why don't you/we ~?는 간혹 이유(왜 ~하지 않나요?)를 묻는 문제로도 출제되어 Because 응답이 정답이 될 수도 있습니다.

되묻는 응답 제안 및 요청 사항에 대해 추가 정보를 되묻는 응답이 정답이 될 수 있습니다.

Q **Would you like to go see** the opera tonight? 오늘 밤에 오페라 공연 보러 가실래요?
A **When does it start**? 언제 시작하는데요?

우회적 응답 Yes/No에 해당하는 내용을 직접적으로 말하는 대신 참고할 수 있는 상황 등을 우회적으로 제시하는 답변도 나옵니다.

Q **Could I borrow** your book on finance? 당신의 금융 관련 책을 빌릴 수 있을까요?
A **I gave it to Amanda.** 아만다에게 줬어요.

✅ ETS Check Up   🔊 650_P2_32 정답과 해설 p.050

다음 질문을 먼저 읽고 음원을 들은 후 적절한 응답을 고르세요.

1. Can I help you carry those books? (A) (B) (C)
2. Would you mind taking notes for me at the seminar? (A) (B) (C)
3. Can I borrow a hammer? (A) (B) (C)
4. Wouldn't you like to join the team for dinner? (A) (B) (C)
5. Why don't we ride together to the conference? (A) (B) (C)

❷ 평서문

평서문은 정보 전달, 의견이나 감정의 제시, 문제점 제기, 제안 및 요청 사항 등을 언급하는 문장으로 매회 2~3문제가 출제됩니다.

> **핵심 포인트** 다양한 답변이 나올 수 있어 난이도가 가장 높은 문제 유형으로, 오답을 걸러내면서 들으면 정답을 고르는 데 도움이 됩니다.

▶ 빈출 질문 & 응답 패턴 🔊 650_P2_33

정보 전달 응답 제시된 정보에 따른 후속 조치를 제안하거나 정보에 대해 호응하는 내용 등이 정답으로 자주 나옵니다.

- Q I need to look over the report before two. — 2시 전에 보고서를 검토해야 해요.
- A I'll get it to you right away. — 지금 바로 가져다 드릴게요.

의견 및 감정 제시 제시된 문장 내용에 대해 맞장구를 치는 등 호응하거나 반대 의사를 밝히는 응답이 나옵니다.

- Q The security system **needs to be repaired**. — 보안 시스템을 수리해야 해요.
- A Yes, it's urgent. — 맞아요, 시급합니다.

문제점 제기 문제점에 대한 해결책을 제시하는 답변이 가장 흔한 정답입니다.

- Q Mr. Miller hasn't arrived yet. — 밀러 씨가 아직 안 왔어요.
- A Let's start without him. — 우리끼리 시작합시다.

수락/거절 응답 제안 혹은 요청하는 내용에는 수락하거나 거절하는 응답이 정답입니다.

- Q **Let's take a break** for fifteen minutes. — 15분 동안 쉬도록 하죠.
- A That sounds like a good idea. — 좋은 생각이에요.

되묻는 응답 제시된 정보에 관련된 추가 정보나 상대의 의견을 되묻는 응답이 정답이 될 수 있습니다.

- Q My doctor just opened a new office in town. — 제 주치의가 얼마 전 시내에 개원했어요.
- A Where's it located exactly? — 위치가 정확히 어디죠?

✅ ETS Check Up 🔊 650_P2_34 정답과 해설 p.051

다음 질문을 먼저 읽고 음원을 들은 후 적절한 응답을 고르세요.

1. I just bought a new telephone. (A) (B) (C)
2. I can't find the paper you asked me to sign. (A) (B) (C)
3. Let's take a break for a few minutes. (A) (B) (C)
4. Let's find out if Mr. Gao wants to manage this account. (A) (B) (C)
5. I'd like to see your speech for the awards ceremony. (A) (B) (C)

ETS 유형 연습

다음 말을 듣고 적절한 응답을 고르세요.
다시 듣고 빈칸을 채우세요.

🔊 650_P2_35
정답과 해설 p.052

1. Mark your answer.
   (A)   (B)   (C)

   My computer _____.
   (A) We began at _____.
   (B) Yes, I _____ early.
   (C) Maybe it's not _____.

2. Mark your answer.
   (A)   (B)   (C)

   Let's have Dr. Lu _____.
   (A) Yes, I do.
   (B) That's _____.
   (C) No, there's _____.

3. Mark your answer.
   (A)   (B)   (C)

   Everyone in the department is going to _____.
   (A) What was the _____?
   (B) I didn't _____.
   (C) _____ in the basket.

4. Mark your answer.
   (A)   (B)   (C)

   Can you _____ for me on Friday?
   (A) I'm _____ Hiroki.
   (B) The _____ is locked.
   (C) Yes, some _____ covers.

5. Mark your answer.
   (A)   (B)   (C)

   Could you _____ to the airport?
   (A) No, I _____ any.
   (B) Sure, _____ your flight?
   (C) About _____.

ETS 실전 문제

🔊 650_P2_36
정답과 해설 p.053

1. Mark your answer on your answer sheet.
2. Mark your answer on your answer sheet.
3. Mark your answer on your answer sheet.
4. Mark your answer on your answer sheet.
5. Mark your answer on your answer sheet.
6. Mark your answer on your answer sheet.
7. Mark your answer on your answer sheet.
8. Mark your answer on your answer sheet.
9. Mark your answer on your answer sheet.
10. Mark your answer on your answer sheet.
11. Mark your answer on your answer sheet.
12. Mark your answer on your answer sheet.
13. Mark your answer on your answer sheet.
14. Mark your answer on your answer sheet.
15. Mark your answer on your answer sheet.
16. Mark your answer on your answer sheet.
17. Mark your answer on your answer sheet.
18. Mark your answer on your answer sheet.
19. Mark your answer on your answer sheet.
20. Mark your answer on your answer sheet.
21. Mark your answer on your answer sheet.
22. Mark your answer on your answer sheet.
23. Mark your answer on your answer sheet.
24. Mark your answer on your answer sheet.
25. Mark your answer on your answer sheet.

PART 2 | 빈출 표현

650_P2_37

직업/직책

receptionist 접수직원
plumber 배관공
accountant 회계사
consultant 컨설턴트
mechanic 정비사
technician 기술자
architect 건축가
assistant 비서, 부하 직원
supervisor 관리자, 감독관
project manager 프로젝트 매니저(= PM)
department manager 부서장
director 이사
board of directors 이사진
(vice) president (부)회장
CEO 최고경영자(= Chief Executive Officer)

부서명

human resources (department) 인사부
accounting department 회계부
sales department 영업부
marketing department 마케팅부
customer service department 고객서비스부
shipping department 배송부
maintenance department 관리부
finance department 재무부
payroll department 경리부
quality control department 품질 관리부
public relations department 홍보부

과거 표현

yesterday 어제
last year 작년에
three weeks ago 3주 전에
a couple of days ago 이틀쯤 전에
since last spring 지난 봄 이후로
in the past 과거에
the day before yesterday 그저께

현재 표현

these days 요즘
right now 당장
currently 현재
almost every day 거의 매일
on a weekly basis 매주
sometimes 때때로(= occasionally)
quite recently 꽤 최근에

미래 표현

this afternoon 오늘 오후에
in ten minutes 10분 후에
not until next Monday 다음 주 월요일이 되어야
by the end of the week 금요일까지
later today 오늘 늦게
within a week 한 주 내로
sometime next month 다음 달쯤에
soon 곧
at the latest 늦어도

장소/행사 명사

warehouse 창고
auditorium 강당
headquarters 본사
main office 본사, 본점
branch (office) 지사, 지점
art exhibition 미술 전시회
conference 회의, 학회
press conference 기자 회견

위치/방향 표현

in the conference room 회의실에서
on the third floor 3층에
in the auditorium 강당에서
down the street 길 따라 아래로
at the west terminal 서쪽 터미널에
on the next corner 다음 모퉁이에
downstairs 아래층에
upstairs 위층에
right across the hall 복도 바로 맞은편에
behind the building 건물 뒤에
in front of the store 상점 앞에
right over there 바로 저쪽에
to the right[left] 오른쪽[왼쪽]으로
in the filing cabinet 파일 캐비닛 안에
somewhere in the north 북부쪽 어딘가에
in the mailbox 우편함 안에
in the front[back] row 앞[뒷]줄에
on the bottom[top] shelf 맨 아래[위] 선반에

이유

due to heavy traffic 교통 체증 때문에
due to severe weather 악천후 때문에
due to road construction 도로 공사 때문에
due to circumstances 상황 때문에
because of a schedule change 일정 변경 때문에
because it's the wrong size 사이즈가 맞지 않아
because of the power failure 정전 때문에
because it's too narrow 너무 좁기 때문에
because there wasn't enough space
충분한 공간이 없었기 때문에
because they postponed the launch
그들이 출시를 연기했기 때문에
because I'll be out of town
출장을 갈 예정이기 때문에
because he retired 그가 퇴직했기 때문에

목적

to meet with a customer 고객을 만나기 위해
to thank us for our hard work
우리의 노고에 감사하기 위해
in order to get a refund 환불을 받기 위해
in order to finish early 빨리 끝내기 위해서
for a business trip 출장을 위해
for a dentist appointment 치과 예약 때문에
to welcome 환영하기 위해
to reserve 예약하기 위해
to discuss 논의하기 위해
to advertise 광고하기 위해
to increase efficiency 효율성을 높이기 위해

PART 2 | 빈출 표현

방법/수단

in writing 서면으로
in person 직접, 손수 (= personally)
by bus[plane] 버스[비행기]로
by cash 현금으로
by credit card 신용카드로
by overnight delivery 익일 배송으로
by accident 우연히, 실수로
through an Internet search 인터넷 검색으로
through fund-raising events 모금 행사를 통해서

기간/빈도

biweekly 격주로 (= every two weeks)
for two days 이틀간
once in a while 가끔
once/twice 한 번/두 번
three times a week 일주일에 세 번
for years 수년간
during lunch 점심시간 동안에
during a break 쉬는 시간에
more than 10 years 10년 이상
at least once a month 최소 한 달에 한 번
within the next month 다음 달 내로
usually just on Saturdays 보통 토요일에만
until noon 정오까지
throughout the next three weeks
앞으로 3주 동안
as soon as we arrive 우리가 도착하자마자
no later than Friday 늦어도 금요일까지

모른다

Nobody knows. 아무도 모르죠.
I don't really know. 잘 모르겠어요.
I have no idea. 몰라요.
I'm not sure. 잘 모르겠어요.
We're not sure yet. 아직 잘 모르겠어요.
Not that I know of. 제가 알기로는 아니에요.
I don't know anything about it.
그것에 대해선 전혀 몰라요.
I wish I knew. 저도 알았으면 좋겠네요.
She didn't mention it. 그녀가 말하지 않았어요.
I'll find out for you. 제가 알아볼게요.
Let's ask ~. ~에게 물어보죠.

정해지지 않았다

I'm still considering it. 아직 고려 중이에요.
I'm still waiting. 여전히 기다리고 있어요.
I'm still thinking about it.
아직 생각 중이에요.
The manager is reviewing it.
매니저가 검토 중입니다.
I haven't decided yet.
아직 결정하지 않았어요.
It hasn't been decided yet.
아직 결정되지 않았어요.
It depends on the design.
디자인에 따라 달라요.
It's not certain yet.
아직 확실하지 않아요.
It hasn't been announced.
발표가 안 났어요.

둘 중 한 가지 선택

I prefer a window seat. 창가 쪽 좌석이 더 좋아요.

I feel like eating out. 외식을 하고 싶어요.

I'll take a bigger one. 큰 걸로 할게요.

It's nicer outside. 바깥이 좋겠네요.

Let's stay indoors. 실내에 있죠.

I'd better go soon. 바로 가는 게 좋겠어요.

Yes, I'll be with you shortly. 네, 곧 갈게요.

Sorry, I can't right now. 미안하지만 지금은 안 돼요.

I chose July this year. 올해는 7월로 결정했어요.

Whichever costs less. 어느 것이든 더 저렴한 거요.

둘 다 선택 / 상관없음

Both would be good. 둘 다 좋겠어요.

I like both of them. 둘 다 좋아요.

It doesn't matter. 상관없어요.

It's up to you. 당신에게 달렸습니다.

Whichever you like. 원하시는 대로요.

Either is fine with me. 둘 중 어느 것이든 좋아요.

둘 다 선택 안 함

I don't like either of them. 둘 다 별로예요.

I prefer neither.
둘 다 좋아하지 않습니다.

Neither, thanks.
고맙지만, 둘 다 됐습니다.

None of us can stay late.
우리 중 누구도 늦게까지 있을 수 없어요.

Yes 대체 표현(수락/동의)

Certainly. / Absolutely. / Definitely. / Why not? 물론이죠.

No problem. 문제없어요.

Not at all. 전혀요.

I'd love to. / I'd be happy[glad] to. / I'm glad to. / I'd be delighted to. 기꺼이 그러죠.

That's what we expected.
그게 우리가 기대했던 바예요.

I think so too. 나도 그렇게 생각해요.

Go ahead. / Be my guest. 그렇게 하세요.

I'd appreciate it. 그렇게 해주시면 고맙겠습니다.

That sounds good to me. 좋은 거 같네요.

Yes, I think we'd better. 네, 그게 낫겠어요.

OK, I'll do it right away. 네, 바로 할게요.

No 대체 표현(거절/부정)

I'm sorry, (but) ~ 미안하지만 ~

Unfortunately, ~ 유감스럽게도[아쉽게도] ~

Sorry, I have an appointment then.
미안하지만 그때 약속이 있어요.

Actually, I already have. 실은 벌써 했습니다.

I'm almost done, thanks. 고맙지만, 거의 다 했어요.

I have other plans. 다른 약속이 있어요.

I'm afraid I can't. 그럴 수 없어요.

I wish I could. 그럴 수 있다면 좋겠네요.

I'll consider it. 고려해 볼게요.

Just wait a minute, please. 잠시만 기다려 주세요.

I'll let you know later. 나중에 알려드릴게요.

LISTENING
COMPREHENSION

PART
3

LISTENING
COMPREHENSION

PART
4

패러프레이징 빈출 표현
(단어 → 단어)

rule 규칙	→ regulation 규정
deliver 배달하다	→ ship 배송하다
attach 첨부하다	→ include 포함하다
journal 학술지	→ publication 출판물
display 진열하다	→ exhibit 전시하다
event 행사	→ occasion 행사
holiday 휴가	→ vacation 휴가
footwear 신발(류)	→ shoes 신발
switch 전환하다	→ transfer 옮기다
upcoming 다가오는	→ future 미래의
relocate 이전하다	→ move 이사하다
aircraft 항공기	→ flight 항공편
produce 생산하다	→ develop 개발하다
show 보여 주다	→ present 제시하다
profitable 수익성 있는	→ lucrative 수익이 되는
donate 기부하다	→ contribute 기부하다
paperwork 서류	→ document 문서
feedback 피드백	→ comment 의견
sufficient 충분한	→ adequate 충분한
abroad 해외로	→ overseas 해외로
thoroughly 철저히	→ carefully 신중하게
inside 내부에	→ indoors 실내에
free 무료의	→ complimentary 무료의
walk 걷다	→ stroll 거닐다
reasonable 가격이 적정한	→ affordable 가격이 합당한

패러프레이징 빈출 표현
(단어 → 구)

submit 제출하다	→ turn in 제출하다
postpone 연기하다	→ put off 연기하다
cancel 취소하다	→ call off 취소하다
land 착륙하다	→ touch down 착륙하다
attend 참석하다	→ participate in 참석하다
review 검토하다	→ go over 검토하다
visit 방문하다	→ drop by 들르다
contact 연락하다	→ get in touch with 연락하다
collaborate 협력하다	→ work together 협력하다
exercise 운동하다	→ work out 운동하다
revise 수정하다	→ make a correction 수정하다
distribute 배부하다	→ hand out 나눠 주다
install 설치하다	→ set up 세우다
mayor 시장	→ government official 공무원
ship 배송하다	→ send out 발송하다
consult 참고하다	→ refer to 참고하다
register 등록하다	→ sign up 등록하다
detour 우회로	→ alternate route 우회로
assistant 조수, 보좌	→ staff member 직원
quarterly 분기별의	→ every three months 3개월마다
telecommuting 재택근무	→ working from home 재택근무
unavailable 이용할 수 없는	→ out of stock 재고가 없는
join 가입하다	→ become a member 회원이 되다

PART 3 | 빈출 표현

쇼핑

brand-new 새로 출시된
inventory 재고
damaged item 손상된 물품
refund 환불
shipment 배송
flyer 전단, 광고지
deliver 배송하다(= ship)
receipt 영수증

식당

cuisine 요리법, 요리
beverage 음료
chef 주방장
food stand 매점
assorted 여러 가지의, 갖은
vegetarian 채식주의자(의)
spicy 양념 맛이 강한, 매운

병원

checkup (건강) 검진
examine 검진하다(= see a doctor)
symptom 증상
treatment 치료, 처치
prescription 처방전
medication 약
pharmacy 약국
act up (병이) 재발하다

은행

deposit 예금하다
withdraw 인출하다
transfer 송금하다(= remit)
balance 잔고, 잔액
due (돈을) 지불해야 하는
exchange rate 환율
savings account 보통 예금
interest rates 금리, 이자율

부동산

rent 임대료
lease 임대[임차]하다
deposit 보증금
landscaping 조경
tenant 세입자
property 부동산, 건물
renovation 개보수(= improvement)

교통

departure 출발
timetable 시간표
flight 비행; 비행편
express train 급행 기차
one-way[round] trip 편도[왕복] 여행
aisle[window] seat 통로[창가] 쪽 좌석
tow 견인하다
be stuck in traffic 교통 체증으로 꼼짝달싹 못하다

인사 업무

coworker 동료
colleague 동료
employee 직원, 종업원
staff (전체) 직원
predecessor 전임자
replacement 후임자(= successor)
performance 업무 실적
raise 급여 인상
benefit (급여 외) 혜택, 수당
cover 맡다, 담당하다
time sheet 근무 시간 기록표
take over the position 직책을 맡다

구인 & 구직

position 일자리, 직위
résumé 이력서
qualifications 자격요건
candidate 지원자, 후보자
complete (양식을) 작성하다
submit 제출하다
hire 고용하다
recruit 모집하다
portfolio 포트폴리오, (사진·그림 등의) 작품집
employment agency 직업 소개소
recommendation letter 추천서
job opening 일자리 공석(= job vacancy)

사무기기

office supplies 사무용품
copier 복사기(= photocopier)
computer components 컴퓨터 부품
installation 설치
stockroom 비품 저장실
malfunction (기계가) 제대로 작동하지 않다
run out of ~이 떨어지다
place an order 주문하다
out of order 고장 난
find a new supplier[vendor]
새로운 납품업체를 구하다

여가

leave 휴가; 떠나다
vacation 휴가; 휴가를 보내다
sightseeing 관광
destination 목적지
accommodations 숙박시설
single room 1인실
itinerary 여행 일정표
landmark 랜드마크, 주요 지형지물
jet lag 시차증(시차로 인한 피로)
go on a trip 여행 가다
make a reservation 예약하다(= book)
travel agency 여행사
take a guided tour 가이드가 딸린 여행을 하다

PART 3 | 빈출 표현

🔊 650_P3_26

업무 전반

- **headquarters** 본사(= head office)
- **branch office** 지점
- **paperwork** 서류 업무
- **deadline** 마감시한
- **paycheck** 급여
- **extension** 내선, 구내전화
- **return one's call** 답신 전화하다
- **security badge** 사원증(= ID badge)
- **bulletin board** 게시판
- **transfer** 인사이동 시키다
- **identification card** 신분증
- **promote sales** 판촉하다
- **sign a contract** 계약서에 서명하다
- **submit a proposal** 제안서를 제출하다
- **work overtime** 초과 근무하다, 잔업하다
- **work late** 야근하다

출퇴근 / 휴가

- **medical leave** 병가(= sick leave)
- **maternity leave** 출산 휴가
- **access card** 출입증
- **flexible working hours** 탄력근무제
- **take a day off** 하루 휴가를 내다
- **get out of work** 퇴근하다
- **call in sick** 아파서 결근하겠다고 전화하다
- **cover one's shift** ~의 근무를 대신하다

회의 / 일정

- **presentation** 프레젠테이션, 발표
- **meeting room** 회의실
- **conference call** 전화회의
- **videoconferencing** 화상회의
- **agenda** 의제, 안건
- **handout** 유인물, 인쇄물
- **chart** 차트, 도표
- **(annual) budget report** (연간) 예산 보고서
- **market survey** 시장 조사
- **available** (사람을 만날) 시간이 있는
- **scheduling conflict** 일정 겹침
- **attend the meeting** 회의에 참석하다

사내 행사

- **banquet** 연회
- **invitation** 초대장
- **attendee** 참석자
- **retirement** 퇴직, 은퇴
- **venue** 개최지, 행사장
- **register** 등록하다
- **corporate event** 기업 행사
- **company retreat** 회사 야유회
- **trade show** 무역 박람회
- **foundation ceremony** 창립식
- **attend a training session** 교육 과정에 참석하다
- **call off** 취소하다(= cancel)

	4/13	4/14	4/15
9:00 A.M.	Time 1	Time 2	Lorenzo Ross
10:00 A.M.	Ife Cho	Kavi Gu	Ilya Aslan
2:00 P.M.	Vivek Raj	Time 3	Time 4

7. Which position is the man applying for?

   (A) Head chef
   (B) Data analyst
   (C) Human resources manager
   (D) Web site designer

8. Why does the man need to reschedule an interview?

   (A) He has a dentist appointment.
   (B) His car needs repairs.
   (C) He has a project deadline.
   (D) He will be on vacation.

9. Look at the graphic. Which time slot will the man most likely choose?

   (A) Time 1
   (B) Time 2
   (C) Time 3
   (D) Time 4

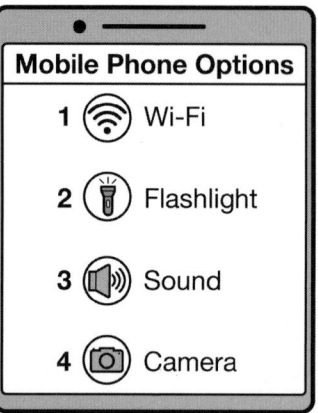

10. Who most likely are the speakers?

    (A) Plumbers
    (B) Electricians
    (C) Weather forecasters
    (D) Computer technicians

11. Look at the graphic. What mobile phone option did the woman use?

    (A) Option 1
    (B) Option 2
    (C) Option 3
    (D) Option 4

12. What does the man suggest doing?

    (A) Taking a picture
    (B) Checking a schedule
    (C) Going to a store
    (D) Updating some software

ETS 실전 문제

Interview Schedule

Candidate	Interview Time
Ms. Ogawa	Monday, 10:00 A.M.
Ms. Lee	Tuesday, 2:00 P.M.
Mr. Jebreen	Thursday, 11:00 A.M.
Mr. Alvarez	Friday, 3:00 P.M.

1. Why has the speakers' business been busy lately?
   (A) A new branch location was opened.
   (B) A new product was launched.
   (C) Some prices have been reduced.
   (D) An advertising campaign has been successful.

2. Where do the speakers work?
   (A) At a bank
   (B) At an airport
   (C) At a car dealership
   (D) At a software company

3. Look at the graphic. Which candidate will the man interview by himself?
   (A) Ms. Ogawa
   (B) Ms. Lee
   (C) Mr. Jebreen
   (D) Mr. Alvarez

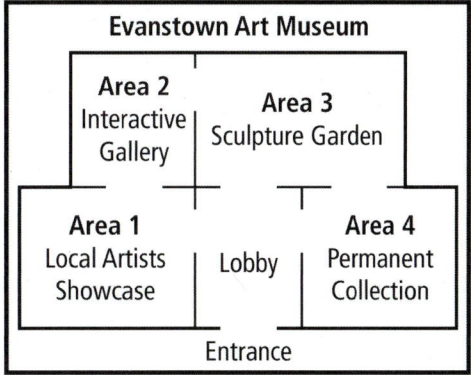

4. Why is the woman in town?
   (A) To visit a friend
   (B) To attend a conference
   (C) To interview for a job
   (D) To conduct an inspection

5. Look at the graphic. Which area of the museum is closed?
   (A) Area 1
   (B) Area 2
   (C) Area 3
   (D) Area 4

6. What does the man say is being offered?
   (A) Hourly tours
   (B) Free parking
   (C) A catalog
   (D) A discount

ETS 유형 연습

문제를 먼저 읽은 후 대화를 들으면서 답을 고르세요.
다시 듣고 빈칸을 채우세요.

🔊 650_P3_24
정답과 해설 p.092

1.
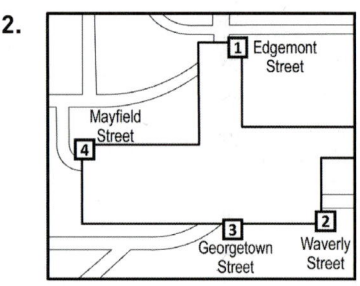

Look at the graphic. How much will the man pay per month?

(A) $200   (B) $300
(C) $500   (D) $900

W *Latest Fashion Magazine*, sales department. How may I help you?

M Hi. I've been a fan of your fashion magazine for some time, and now I'd like to _____ _____ for my business in it.

W Thank you! _____ are you looking for?

M I'd like to go with the _____ and make it a recurring ad each month.

2.
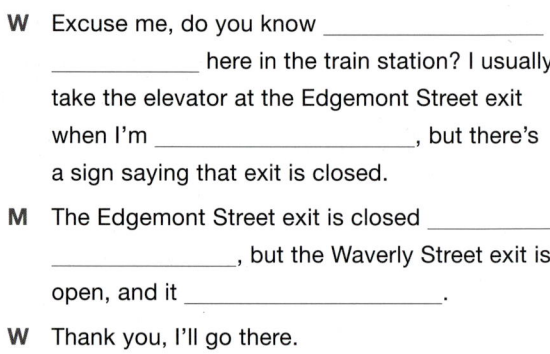

Look at the graphic. Which exit will the woman go to?

(A) Exit 1   (B) Exit 2
(C) Exit 3   (D) Exit 4

W Excuse me, do you know _____ _____ here in the train station? I usually take the elevator at the Edgemont Street exit when I'm _____, but there's a sign saying that exit is closed.

M The Edgemont Street exit is closed _____ _____, but the Waverly Street exit is open, and it _____.

W Thank you, I'll go there.

3.
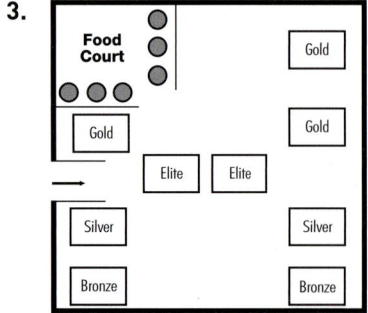

Look at the graphic. What type of booth does the man reserve?

(A) Elite   (B) Gold
(C) Bronze (D) Silver

M Hello, I'd _____ for this year's garden show.

W We have _____. I suggest one of the "Elite" locations.

M I will take one of the spots _____ _____. I'm guessing there'll be _____ there. Do I need to pay now?

W Just a deposit.

2 시각 정보 문제 – 지도·기타

건물의 평면도, 마을 약도, 좌석 배치도와 같은 지도가 시각 정보로 자주 출제되고, 안내 표지판, 순서도, 할인 쿠폰과 같은 기타 시각 정보도 종종 출제됩니다.

> **핵심 포인트** 대화를 듣기 전에 시각 정보의 종류와 내용을 미리 확인하고, 무엇에 유의해서 들을지 유추하면 정답을 찾는 데 도움이 됩니다.

빈출 질문 Look at the graphic. Where will the man sell his product?
시각 정보에 따르면, 남자는 어디에서 제품을 판매하겠는가?

Look at the graphic. Which road will the speakers take next?
시각 정보에 따르면, 화자들은 다음에 어떤 길로 갈 것인가?

▶ ETS 기출 예제

🔊 650_P3_23

W Hello, Mr. Clement? This is Asako Kimura calling. I manage the Brookstone Farmers Market. We're pleased to let you know that a spot has opened up.

M That's great! Where should I set up my stand?

W Are you familiar with the layout? **Your stand will be located between the flower and the vegetable stands.**
→ 지도 상의 위치를 나타내기 위한 표현이 나왔습니다.

여 안녕하세요, 클레멘트 씨? 아사코 키무라입니다. 저는 브룩스톤 파머스 마켓을 관리하고 있어요. 자리가 생겼다는 소식을 알려드리게 되어 기쁩니다.

남 잘됐네요! 가판대는 어디에 설치하면 되나요?

여 배치를 잘 알고 계시나요? 가판대는 꽃 판매대와 채소 판매대 사이에 위치하게 될 거예요.

Farmers Market Map		
②	Flowers	③
Bakery		Vegetables
①		④
Cheese	Entrance	Fruits

파머스 마켓 지도		
②	꽃	③
빵		채소
①		④
치즈	출입구	과일

Look at the graphic. Where will the man sell his product?

(A) Location 1 (B) Location 2
(C) Location 3 (D) Location 4

시각 정보에 따르면, 남자는 어디에서 제품을 판매하겠는가?

(A) 위치 1 (B) 위치 2
(C) 위치 3 (D) 위치 4

> **정답이 들리는 단서 표현** 시각 정보로 지도가 나오는 문제에서는 위치나 방향을 나타내는 표현들이 자주 등장합니다.

next to ~ 옆에	**in the rear of** the building 건물 뒤편에
directly across from ~ 바로 맞은편에	**closest to** the snack counter 스낵 코너에서 가장 가까운
at the corner of A **and** B A와 B가 만나는 모퉁이에	The new terminal is being built **next to** the parking area. 새 터미널은 주차 구역 옆에 건설될 거예요.

ETS 유형 연습

문제를 먼저 읽은 후 대화를 들으면서 답을 고르세요.
다시 듣고 빈칸을 채우세요.

🔊 650_P3_22
정답과 해설 p.091

1.

Guest Name:	Eric Peterson
Nightly Rate:	$95.00
Airport Transfer:	$15.00
Restaurant Charges:	$45.00 (two meals)
Miscellaneous:	$20.00

Look at the graphic. Which amount on the bill will be changed?

(A) $95   (B) $15
(C) $45   (D) $20

W   May I have the key card to your room so I can begin _____?

M   I _____. Sorry about that. My name's Eric Peterson. I was in room 615.

W   So... I will have to add an _____ _____ of seven dollars to your bill for the key card.

2.

Training Schedule

8:00 A.M.	Tour facility
9:30 A.M.	Collect samples
10:30 A.M.	Record test results
Noon	Staff lunch
1:30 P.M.	Learn safety protocols

Look at the graphic. What time does the conversation most likely take place?

(A) At 8:00 A.M.   (B) At 9:30 A.M.
(C) At 10:30 A.M.   (D) At 1:30 P.M.

W   And now, for _____, I'm going to teach you how to record the _____.

M   OK—and the water that flows through this facility is _____, right?

W   Right. That way, we can ensure that it meets our water-treatment plant's _____.

M   That makes sense.

3.

Nutrition Information
Serving Size: 200 grams
Calories: 150

Amount Per Serving	
Fat	5 grams
Protein	11 grams
Sugar	32 grams
Sodium	40 milligrams

Look at the graphic. Which of the ingredients does the man express concern about?

(A) Fat   (B) Protein
(C) Sugar   (D) Sodium

M   Is there a yogurt that's _____ but also has a lot of protein?

W   Here's one of _____ of blueberry yogurt. See, there's a lot of protein...

M   Mmm—nice! But my doctor told me I shouldn't _____—and it would put me over the daily amount he recommended. That's more than 30 grams!

W   In that case, I'd suggest _____ of this yogurt.

UNIT 13 시각 정보 문제

무료 강의

1 시각 정보 문제 – 표·그래프

'Look at the graphic.'으로 시작하여 대화 내용을 시각 정보와 연계시켜야만 정답을 고를 수 있는 문제가 매회 3문제씩 출제됩니다. 일정표, 주문서, 송장 같은 표가 가장 많이 출제되고, 수익이나 매출 변화 그래프도 출제됩니다.

> **핵심 포인트** 시각 정보에 제시된 키워드가 대화에 그대로 등장하는 경우가 많으므로, 시각 정보 내 키워드를 먼저 파악하면 정답을 찾는 데 도움이 됩니다.

빈출 질문
Look at the graphic. Which product did the woman buy? 시각 정보에 따르면, 여자는 어떤 제품을 샀는가?
Look at the graphic. When will the man work at the event?
시각 정보에 따르면, 남자는 언제 행사에서 일할 것인가?

▶ ETS 기출 예제

🔊 650_P3_21

W How can I help you?
M Hi, my mobile phone isn't working correctly.
W OK. **First, can you tell me the phone's serial number?**
→ 시각 정보의 키워드인 serial number가 그대로 등장했습니다.
M Sorry, I'm not exactly sure where to find that.
W The serial number is under the settings menu.
M OK, give me a second to find that.

여 무엇을 도와드릴까요?
남 안녕하세요, 제 휴대폰이 제대로 작동하지 않아요.
여 그렇군요. 먼저, 휴대폰 일련 번호를 알려 주시겠어요?
남 죄송해요, 어디에 있는지 잘 모르겠어요.
여 일련 번호는 설정 메뉴 밑에 있어요.
남 알겠어요, 잠깐만 기다려 주시면 찾을게요.

Software version	8.2	>
Model	250–73	>
Capacity in GB	124	>
Serial Number	36998	>

소프트웨어 버전	8.2
모델	250-73
용량(GB)	124
일련 번호	**36998**

Look at the graphic. Which number will the man give the woman?

(A) 8.2
(B) 250-73
(C) 124
(D) **36998**

시각 정보에 따르면, 남자는 어떤 번호를 여자에게 주겠는가?
(A) 8.2 (B) 250-73
(C) 124 (D) 36998

정답이 들리는 단서 표현 막대 그래프와 선 그래프에서는 최고점이나 최저점을 나타내는 최상급 표현이 정답으로 자주 등장합니다.

the largest number 가장 큰 수치

what they like **the best** 가장 좋아하는 것

the second most popular 두 번째로 인기 있는

the lowest rate 최저 요금

the least amount 가장 적은 양

It's clear which one our customers like **the best**.
우리 고객들이 어떤 것을 가장 좋아하는지가 분명하네요.

13. What good news does the woman share?
    (A) A product launch has been scheduled.
    (B) A contract has been signed.
    (C) Some expenses have been reduced.
    (D) Some customer reviews have been positive.

14. What type of business do the speakers most likely work for?
    (A) A marketing firm
    (B) A department store
    (C) A clothing manufacturer
    (D) A software developer

15. Why does the man say, "she's learned more than five already"?
    (A) To offer reassurance
    (B) To recommend a pay raise
    (C) To show surprise
    (D) To reject a request for training

16. In which industry do the speakers most likely work?
    (A) Landscaping
    (B) Tourism
    (C) Architecture
    (D) Television

17. What does the woman say she will send the man?
    (A) Updated drawings
    (B) Meeting notes
    (C) A cost estimate
    (D) A video recording

18. What does the man imply when he says, "I'm going to a professional-development seminar next week"?
    (A) He will receive a certificate soon.
    (B) He needs additional time to finish a task.
    (C) He would like the woman to attend.
    (D) He hopes to earn a promotion.

19. What did the man do this morning?
    (A) He organized a workspace.
    (B) He gave a presentation.
    (C) He printed event invitations.
    (D) He e-mailed some guidelines.

20. What does the woman ask the man to do?
    (A) Train a new employee
    (B) Destroy some documents
    (C) Make a restaurant reservation
    (D) Sign a vendor contract

21. Why does the man say, "I have a client meeting in Midtown this afternoon"?
    (A) To request assistance
    (B) To explain a delay
    (C) To offer to perform a task
    (D) To complain about a schedule

22. Why does the man congratulate the woman?
    (A) She was recently promoted.
    (B) She published an article.
    (C) She finished a degree program.
    (D) She developed a new product.

23. What is the man concerned about?
    (A) Meeting a deadline
    (B) Staying within a budget
    (C) Running out of supplies
    (D) Providing good customer service

24. Why does the woman say, "they like to be informed regularly about our products"?
    (A) To make a complaint
    (B) To offer advice
    (C) To describe a company policy
    (D) To suggest getting help with a task

ETS 실전 문제

1. What does the company sell?
   (A) Calculators
   (B) Cameras
   (C) Laptop computers
   (D) Kitchen appliances

2. Why does the woman say, "our customers want a compact design"?
   (A) To reject a suggestion
   (B) To express surprise
   (C) To offer reassurance
   (D) To ask for help

3. What will the woman do tomorrow?
   (A) Meet some clients
   (B) Select some images
   (C) E-mail a report
   (D) Make a presentation

4. What does the woman imply when she says, "Two hours wasn't enough"?
   (A) A deadline has been extended.
   (B) A project took longer than expected.
   (C) She was late arriving to an event.
   (D) She enjoyed a performance.

5. Why has the man been busy?
   (A) He was preparing for a presentation.
   (B) He was designing a brochure.
   (C) He was reporting on customer comments.
   (D) He was reviewing a performance.

6. What does the woman suggest the man do?
   (A) Arrive early
   (B) Invite a coworker
   (C) Test a new product
   (D) Recommend some medicine

7. What problem does the woman have?
   (A) She lost her ticket.
   (B) She cannot access her bonus points.
   (C) Her flight has been delayed.
   (D) Her luggage is too heavy.

8. Why does the man say, "your seat is in the main cabin"?
   (A) To correct an assumption
   (B) To give directions
   (C) To expedite a request
   (D) To express approval

9. What will the woman most likely do next?
   (A) Pay a fee
   (B) Request a new seat
   (C) Walk to a gate
   (D) Speak with a manager

10. Where do the speakers need to be at 2:00 P.M.?
    (A) At an office
    (B) At an airport
    (C) At a train station
    (D) At a convention center

11. What will the speakers do in Janville?
    (A) Conduct some research
    (B) Present at a seminar
    (C) Inspect a facility
    (D) Meet with investors

12. What does the man mean when he says, "we'll have Internet access at all times"?
    (A) He has changed an Internet provider.
    (B) He does not need to make any copies.
    (C) The woman should not complain about poor service.
    (D) The woman can complete an assignment online.

ETS 유형 연습

문제를 먼저 읽은 후 대화를 들으면서 답을 고르세요.
다시 듣고 빈칸을 채우세요.

🔊 650_P3_19
정답과 해설 p.083

1. What does the man mean when he says, "It was time for something like that"?
   (A) He is concerned about a work deadline.
   (B) He wants to hold meetings more often.
   (C) He thinks a project is a good idea.
   (D) He hopes to hold a special event.

   M I just noticed _____ in the lobby.
   W It's just regular _____—to improve the lobby's overall appearance.
   M Oh, OK.... It was time for something like that.
   W I heard the crews will even put up antique photos showing the _____—more than a century ago.

2. What does the man mean when he says, "I was just about to drop off these parts"?
   (A) He does not have time to help.
   (B) He was unaware of an order cancellation.
   (C) He needs a printed invoice.
   (D) He is close to finishing his work for the day.

   W Ryan, I need your _____. I know you have some deliveries to make, but _____ it?
   M Asher's Automotive Repair Shop is starting a big job today. I was just about to drop off these parts.
   W It won't _____ to unload the shipment.

3. What does the man imply when he says, "I have so many responsibilities right now"?
   (A) He would like some assistance.
   (B) He should be considered for a promotion.
   (C) He does not have time for a task.
   (D) He wants to extend a deadline.

   W Adem, _____ on the *Marketing Milestones* radio show!
   M That's great. I hope _____ the blog now.
   W Do you think now would be a _____ _____? There's a lot of interest these days in _____ using AI technology. I bet it would be popular.
   M I have so many responsibilities right now.

4. What does the man mean when he says, "That's not a bad idea"?
   (A) He would like to hear more suggestions.
   (B) He prefers the original plan.
   (C) He agrees with the proposed solution.
   (D) He has a better idea.

   W We'll have to _____ we've asked you to do.
   M Do you know _____ you'd like to put off?
   W Well, I know we talked about _____ wing—but that's very expensive. So, if we don't make that addition, that's all we may need to cut.
   M You know, that's not a bad idea. Let's see _____ if I take the library out of the renovation proposal.

② 의도 파악 문제 – 문맥상 의미

대화 속 말의 숨은 의도를 파악하는 문제 중, 해당 대화 상황에만 적용되는 문맥상 의미를 묻는 문제도 매회 출제됩니다.

> **핵심 포인트** 다양한 상황에서 쓸 수 있는 말이 제시문으로 등장하므로, 반드시 제시된 문장과 앞뒤 대화의 흐름을 파악해 해당 문장이 구체적으로 암시하는 바를 이해해야 문제를 풀 수 있습니다.

빈출 질문 What does the man mean when he says, "~"? 남자가 "~"라고 말할 때 무엇을 의미하는가?
What does the woman imply when she says, "~"? 여자가 "~"라고 말할 때 무엇을 암시하는가?

▶ ETS 기출 예제　🔊 650_P3_18

M Thanks again, Xinyu, for helping me find this space. This is the perfect spot for the teahouse.

W I'm happy to help! **But remember, you still need to submit an offer.** This is a really popular location.
→ 여자가 공간을 마음에 들어 하는 남자에게 제안서를 제출할 것을 재촉하고 있습니다.

M I understand. But I need to confirm all this with my business partner.

W Absolutely. Call me when the two of you have agreed on the offer.

(What) does the (woman mean) when she says, "This is a really popular location"?

(A) Parking will be difficult.
(B) The man can earn high profits.
(C) A dining area will need to be expanded.
(D) The man needs to act quickly.

남 신유, 이 공간을 찾는 데 도움을 주셔서 다시 한번 감사드려요. 찻집에 딱 맞는 장소네요.

여 도와드릴 수 있어서 기뻐요! 하지만 아직 제안서를 제출해야 한다는 것을 잊지 마세요. 이곳은 정말 인기 있는 장소예요.

남 알겠어요. 하지만 제 동업자와 이 모든 걸 확정해야 해요.

여 물론이죠. 두 분께서 제안에 동의하시면 전화 주세요.

여자가 "이곳은 정말 인기 있는 장소예요"라고 말할 때 **무엇을 의미**하는가?
(A) 주차가 어려울 것이다.
(B) 남자는 높은 수익을 낼 수 있다.
(C) 식사 공간이 확장되어야 할 것이다.
(D) 남자는 신속하게 행동해야 한다.

정답이 들리는 단서 표현　문맥상 의미를 파악하는 문제는 다음과 같은 표현이 들릴 때 정답을 포착해야 합니다.

거절
W Can you lead a tour of our factory tomorrow morning?
M **I'm supposed to train some new employees all morning.**
　[문맥상 의미] He cannot take on the job.

내일 오전에 공장 견학을 진행할 수 있어요?
오전 내내 신입 사원들을 교육해야 해요.
남자는 일을 맡을 수 없다.

승낙
M I'd like to talk to you about the spring jacket designs. Maybe after your meeting?
W **My meeting was canceled.**
　[문맥상 의미] She is available to discuss an issue.

당신과 봄 재킷 디자인에 대해 논의하고 싶어요. 아마 당신 회의 끝난 후에요?
제 회의가 취소되었어요.
여자는 문제에 대해 논의할 수 있다.

ETS 유형 연습

문제를 먼저 읽은 후 대화를 들으면서 답을 고르세요.
다시 듣고 빈칸을 채우세요.

🔊 650_P3_17

정답과 해설 p. 082

1. Why does the woman say, "I really like to cook in my free time"?
   (A) To describe her professional background
   (B) To express her concern about nutrition
   (C) To decline an invitation
   (D) To indicate a preference

2. Why does the man say, "The train leaves in one minute"?
   (A) To urge a quick decision
   (B) To announce an early departure
   (C) To deny a ticket purchase
   (D) To assure the woman that she has arrived in time

3. Why does the woman say, "If you wouldn't mind"?
   (A) To suggest a solution
   (B) To ask for permission
   (C) To make a complaint
   (D) To accept an offer

4. Why does the man say, "That meeting is at two o'clock"?
   (A) To remind the woman of a meeting's start time
   (B) To invite the woman to attend a meeting
   (C) To express disappointment about a meeting time
   (D) To request help with meeting preparations

M Hello. Domani Real Estate. Alberto speaking. _____ you?

W Hi. I'm _____ in Brazelton next month, and I'd like to rent an apartment downtown.

M OK. _____ apartment are you looking for?

W One with _____. Oh, and I really like to cook in my free time.

W Hello. Can I still _____ for the 9:05 train to Amsterdam? It's not too late, is it?

M I'm sorry. The train leaves in one minute. However, there are trains at 10:50 A.M. and 12:30 P.M. There are _____.

W I'll _____.

M This is Jacob from the landscaping company. I'm afraid we won't be able to _____ _____ tomorrow.

W I'm going to _____ for two weeks starting this Thursday. I wanted to give you a key to the gate, so you'd be able to _____.

M OK. Then what if I come by tomorrow anyway, just to _____?

W If you wouldn't mind. I'll be at home _____ _____.

W Hi, Ilya. I have been _____ to the company server for the past five minutes, but it hasn't been working at all.

M Did you try _____?

W Oh yeah, I always forget to do that. So, are you planning to _____ about management training opportunities at two?

M That meeting is at two o'clock. Maybe I can _____.

UNIT 12 | 의도 파악 문제 **089**

UNIT 12 의도 파악 문제

1 의도 파악 문제 – 목적

대화 중에 나올 짧은 문장 하나를 질문에서 미리 보여 주고, 그 말의 숨은 의도를 묻는 문제가 매회 2문제씩 출제됩니다. 그중 화자가 그 말을 하는 구체적인 '목적'을 묻는 문제가 매회 출제됩니다.

> **핵심 포인트** 대화를 듣기 전 문제에 제시된 문장을 반드시 먼저 읽고, 대화를 들을 때 해당 제시문을 놓치지 않고 들어야 정답을 고를 수 있습니다.

빈출 질문
Why does the man say, "~"? 남자는 왜 "~"라고 말하는가?
Why does the woman say, "~"? 여자는 왜 "~"라고 말하는가?

▶ ETS 기출 예제   🔊 650_P3_16

W Hey, Samir. How's it going?

M **I'm so tired of this financial report! I've been working on it for the last five hours.**
→ 남자가 재무 보고서를 5시간째 작성 중이라고 푸념하고 있습니다.

W Well, the work day's almost over.

M That's true—I'm off in half an hour.

(Why) does the (woman) say, "the work day's almost over"?
(A) To end a meeting.   → 제시문을 먼저 확인합니다.
(B) To express surprise
(C) **To comfort the man**
(D) To correct the man

여 안녕, 사미르. 잘 지내요?
남 이 재무 보고서 정말 지긋지긋해요! 5시간째 작성하고 있어요.
여 음, 근무시간이 거의 끝나가요.
남 그렇긴 하죠. 30분 후면 퇴근이네요.

여자는 왜 "근무시간이 거의 끝나가요"라고 말하는가?
(A) 회의를 끝내려고
(B) 놀라움을 표현하려고
(C) **남자를 위로하려고**
(D) 남자의 실수를 바로잡으려고

정답이 들리는 단서 표현 목적을 파악하는 문제는 다음과 같은 표현이 들릴 때 정답을 포착해야 합니다.

지연
M Why is the elevator still out of order?
W **They are waiting for some new parts to arrive.**
[목적] To explain a delay

왜 엘리베이터가 여전히 고장이죠?
새 부품이 도착하길 기다리고 있어요.
지연 이유를 설명하려고

우려
W I'm still on my way to the office, so I'm afraid I won't be able to go over our presentation materials with you.
M Oh. **The meeting starts soon.**
[목적] To express a concern

아직 사무실로 가는 중이라, 발표 자료를 함께 검토하지 못할 것 같아요.
아. 회의가 곧 시작하는데요.
우려를 표현하려고

13. What does the man say he has tickets for?
    (A) A city tour
    (B) An art show
    (C) A baseball game
    (D) A music concert

14. Why does the woman say she does not want the tickets?
    (A) She plans to work late that night.
    (B) She will be at a different event.
    (C) She will be away on vacation.
    (D) She prefers other types of events.

15. What will the man most likely do next?
    (A) Place information on a bulletin board
    (B) Attend a lunch meeting with clients
    (C) Prepare for a sports game
    (D) Call to ask for a refund

16. What type of business does the man own?
    (A) A film production studio
    (B) An electronics store
    (C) An event-planning service
    (D) An advertising firm

17. What does the man ask the woman about?
    (A) Recycling some items
    (B) Making some repairs
    (C) Hiring a consultant
    (D) Changing a meeting location

18. What does the woman offer to send the man?
    (A) A refund
    (B) A timetable
    (C) A map
    (D) A contract

19. What are the speakers expecting to be delivered?
    (A) Mobile phone parts
    (B) Office furniture
    (C) Construction materials
    (D) Some vehicles

20. How did the man already know about a problem?
    (A) He attended a meeting.
    (B) He read an article.
    (C) He listened to a radio broadcast.
    (D) He watched a television program.

21. What does Sabine suggest a driver do?
    (A) Use a navigation system
    (B) Contact an information center
    (C) Take an alternate route
    (D) Stop for fuel

22. Where does the woman most likely work?
    (A) At a hotel
    (B) At an architectural firm
    (C) At a movie theater
    (D) At a restaurant

23. What is causing a problem?
    (A) A delayed opening
    (B) An incorrect bill
    (C) Noise from construction work
    (D) A shortage of trained staff

24. What will the woman probably do next?
    (A) Speak to her manager
    (B) Send a confirmation e-mail
    (C) Offer a reduced rate
    (D) Check for an available room

ETS 실전 문제

1. What does the man say is needed for a team's improvement?
   (A) A larger field
   (B) High-quality coaching
   (C) Additional athletes
   (D) New equipment

2. What does the woman suggest?
   (A) Contacting a city official
   (B) Changing a schedule
   (C) Traveling to different cities
   (D) Attracting more sponsors

3. What does the man say he will do?
   (A) Write a job listing
   (B) Speak to the players
   (C) Search for local businesses
   (D) Organize a workshop

4. Where do the speakers work?
   (A) At a national park
   (B) At a travel agency
   (C) On a farm
   (D) In a market

5. What does the woman ask the man to do?
   (A) Arrange a display
   (B) Unload some boxes
   (C) Update a contact list
   (D) Order supplies

6. Why does the man say he cannot complete the task today?
   (A) He has to make a delivery.
   (B) He needs additional information.
   (C) No one is available to help.
   (D) The weather is bad.

7. What has the man been hired to do?
   (A) Handle customer complaints
   (B) Develop new products
   (C) Repair electrical equipment
   (D) Drive a truck

8. According to the woman, what is important to the company?
   (A) Teamwork
   (B) Employee satisfaction
   (C) Environmental sustainability
   (D) Innovation

9. What will the man most likely do next?
   (A) Complete some paperwork
   (B) Get an identification badge
   (C) Tour a facility
   (D) Prepare a presentation

10. What is the report about?
    (A) Loan applications
    (B) Software updates
    (C) Revised hiring plans
    (D) Possible business locations

11. What does the woman say she is pleased about?
    (A) The changes in market prices
    (B) The availability of skilled workers
    (C) The presentation of some information
    (D) The reduction of some expenses

12. What does the man suggest?
    (A) Hiring a consultant
    (B) Including more photographs
    (C) Rescheduling a presentation
    (D) Requesting a product demonstration

ETS 유형 연습

문제를 먼저 읽은 후 대화를 들으면서 답을 고르세요.
다시 듣고 빈칸을 채우세요.

🔊 650_P3_14
정답과 해설 p. 075

---

1. What will the man most likely do next?
(A) Make an appointment
(B) Provide a reference
(C) Purchase some merchandise
(D) Leave a message

M I'm _____ and your company for the great job you did catering for our business luncheon last week.

W Oh, don't thank me. Your event was _____ _____, Nadia.

M If Nadia's in the office, I'd like to _____.

W Actually, she's out today. But I can _____ _____ so that you can leave her a message.

---

2. What will the speakers do next?
(A) Look at fuel prices
(B) Review customer complaints
(C) Update staffing schedules
(D) Organize training programs

W I hear that we've had _____ recently.

M In fact, I've just been _____. Our driver _____, but there was heavy traffic on the way to the airport, and she nearly missed her flight.

W We should probably _____ scheduled in the area.

M And we have some other issues to consider as well. _____—we'll need to decide what to do.

---

3. What does the woman say she will do next?
(A) Update a file
(B) Sign a contract
(C) Discuss a price
(D) Transfer a call

W I have a _____ on the phone. Since I'm really busy today, I was going to ask Steven to show the apartment, but he isn't _____.

M I noticed he forgot his mobile phone on his desk there. I might have _____ to show the client the third-floor apartment.

W That would be great. OK, I'll _____ _____ now.

---

4. What does the woman say she will do this afternoon?
(A) File a maintenance request
(B) Contact a decorator
(C) Arrange some furniture
(D) Create some flyers

W Thanks for agreeing to photograph the house my agency is putting on the market! Your photos should _____ of a fast sale.

M I hope so. _____ with the decorator that _____ that day?

W No, but I'll do that this afternoon.

UNIT 11 | 요청·제안 문제 / 다음에 할 일 문제 **085**

❷ 다음에 할 일 문제

화자가 다음에 할 일을 묻는 문제로 매회 5문제 정도 출제되고, 특히 세 번째 문제로 주로 출제됩니다.

> **핵심 포인트** 한 대화에서 마지막 문제로 출제되기 때문에 단서는 주로 대화 후반부에 언급됩니다. 미래 시점의 말이나 제안을 나타내는 표현에서 정답의 단서를 찾을 수 있습니다.

다음에 할 일
What will the man do next? 남자는 다음에 무엇을 할 것인가?
What is the man going to do next? 남자는 다음에 무엇을 할 것인가?
What does the woman say she will do? 여자는 무엇을 하겠다고 말하는가?
What will the speakers most likely do next? 화자들은 다음에 무엇을 할 것 같은가?

▶ ETS 기출 예제

🔊 650_P3_13

M I'd like to discuss a marketing strategy with you.
W OK, what did you have in mind?
M I was thinking of using social media to connect with customers directly.
W That's a wonderful plan! **Why don't I set up a meeting with the rest of the marketing team?**
→ 제안의 표현이 곧 정답으로 연결됩니다.

남 당신과 마케팅 전략을 논의하고 싶어요.
여 좋아요, 생각해 둔 게 있나요?
남 소셜 미디어를 이용해서 고객과 직접 소통할까 생각하고 있었어요.
여 멋진 계획이에요! 제가 나머지 마케팅 팀원들과 회의를 잡아 볼까요?

(What) does the (woman) say she (will do)?
(A) Revise a project timeline
(B) Obtain a construction estimate
(C) Provide a sales forecast
(D) Arrange a team meeting

여자는 **무엇을** 하겠다고 말하는가?
(A) 프로젝트 일정표 수정
(B) 공사 견적서 입수
(C) 예상 매출 제공
(D) 팀 회의 주선

정답이 들리는 단서 표현 다음에 할 일을 묻는 문제는 다음과 같은 표현이 들릴 때 정답을 포착해야 합니다.

미래 시점
I'll have a technician **look** at the equipment.
I'll call Khan **and ask** him if he'd be able to switch shifts with me.
I'll stop by your office right now.

기술자를 불러 장비를 점검하도록 할게요.
칸에게 전화해서 저와 근무시간을 바꿀 수 있는지 물어볼게요.
지금 바로 당신 사무실에 들를게요.

제안
I can call some landscaping firms to get some prices.
I can e-mail you our latest brochure for your reference.
Let me ask my manager if I can leave early tomorrow.

조경 회사 몇 군데에 전화해서 가격을 알아볼게요.
참고해 보실 수 있게 이메일로 당사의 최신 안내책자를 보내드리겠습니다.
내일 일찍 퇴근할 수 있는지 제 상사에게 물어볼게요.

ETS 유형 연습

문제를 먼저 읽은 후 대화를 들으면서 답을 고르세요.
다시 듣고 빈칸을 채우세요.

🔊 650_P3_12
정답과 해설 p.074

1. What does the woman ask for?
   (A) An address
   (B) A password
   (C) A phone number
   (D) An account number

   M Hello, my name is Fred Kane, and I'm calling from the Clearsea Electronics Company. I'd like to _____ dollars from our short-term savings account to our long-term account.
   W No problem, sir. What's the _____ that you're _____?
   M The account number is 67843.

2. Where does the woman suggest going?
   (A) To a restaurant
   (B) To a coffee shop
   (C) To an ice cream shop
   (D) To a company cafeteria

   W Do you want to _____ near the ice cream shop?
   M Oh, I went there last week and I _____ _____. There were too many people and there wasn't _____ between the tables.
   W Really? That's too bad.

3. What does the man ask the woman to do?
   (A) Wait in the lobby
   (B) Update an application
   (C) Wear a badge
   (D) Provide photo identification

   W Hi, I'm Petra Barlow. I have an _____ a position in the accounting department here at Houseman Incorporated.
   M Hello, Ms. Barlow. Let me _____. While I do that, would you _____ _____ so it's easy to see?
   W Yes, of course.

4. What suggestion does the man make about the logo?
   (A) Fixing the position
   (B) Adding a picture
   (C) Changing the color
   (D) Increasing the size

   W Did you have a chance to _____ of the new book cover?
   M Yes, I _____, and I think it's really good. I do have one suggestion though. I think our publishing company's logo is _____ compared to the other information. How about _____ so people can see it better?
   W That's a good idea.

UNIT 11 | 요청·제안 문제 / 다음에 할 일 문제   083

UNIT 11 요청·제안 문제 / 다음에 할 일 문제

무료 강의

① 요청·제안 문제

요청이나 제안 사항에 대해 묻는 문제는 매회 5문제 정도 출제되고, 특히 세 번째 문제로 주로 출제됩니다.

> **핵심 포인트** 한 대화에서 마지막 문제로 출제되기 때문에 단서는 주로 대화 후반부에 언급됩니다. 요청이나 제안을 할 때 사용하는 빈출 표현을 알아두면 정답을 고르는데 도움이 됩니다.

요청	What does the man ask the woman to do? 남자는 여자에게 무엇을 해 달라고 요청하는가?
	What is the woman asked to do? 여자는 무엇을 하라고 요청 받는가?
제안	What does the woman offer to do? 여자는 무엇을 하겠다고 제안하는가?
	What does the man suggest/recommend? 남자는 무엇을 제안/추천하는가?

▶ ETS 기출 예제

🔊 650_P3_11

W I was looking for the cookware that was used in your cooking demonstration last week, but I don't see any on the shelf. Do you have any more in stock?

M No, sorry. We sold out of those quickly.

W Do you know if one of your other stores might have them in stock?

M Let me check. Here, it looks like we have them at our Silver Creek store. **I'll call and ask them to hold a set for you.**
→ 제안의 표현인 I'll이 등장했습니다.

여 지난주 요리 시연에 사용된 조리 기구를 찾고 있었는데, 진열대에 안 보이네요. 재고가 더 있나요?

남 없어요, 죄송합니다. 빨리 매진되었어요.

여 다른 매장들 중 한 곳에 재고가 없을까요?

남 확인해 볼게요. 여기 있네요. 실버 크릭 매장에 있는 것 같아요. **제가 전화해서 고객님을 위해 한 세트 챙겨 놓으라고 요청할게요.**

(What) does the (man) (offer) to do?
(A) Check a catalog
(B) Wrap a gift
(C) Issue a refund
(D) Call another store

남자는 무엇을 하겠다고 제안하는가?
(A) 카탈로그 확인
(B) 선물 포장
(C) 환불
(D) 다른 매장에 전화하기

> **정답이 들리는 단서 표현** 요청·제안 문제는 다음과 같은 표현이 들릴 때 정답을 포착해야 합니다.

요청	**I'll need** your photo ID.	사진이 있는 신분증을 주세요.
	Could you place an order for some more bottles today?	오늘 병 몇 개를 추가로 주문해 주시겠어요?
	(Please) switch off the power of the machine.	기계의 전원을 꺼 주세요.
제안	**(I think) you should** consider leading a discussion.	토론을 진행하는 걸 고려해 보셨으면 해요.
	I'll check with him and see if he can start to work earlier.	그가 일을 더 일찍 시작할 수 있는지 확인해 볼게요.
제공	**(If you'd like,) I could[can]** mail you some samples.	(원하시면) 제가 샘플을 몇 개 보내드릴게요.
	I can take care of that. I'll send an e-mail to them.	제가 처리할게요. 그들에게 이메일을 보낼게요.

13. Where do the speakers most likely work?
    (A) At a television studio
    (B) At an electronics shop
    (C) At a bookstore
    (D) At a printshop

14. What task is the woman assigned?
    (A) Finalizing a budget
    (B) Interviewing a job candidate
    (C) Ordering refreshments
    (D) Creating a display

15. What does the man expect to do by the end of the day?
    (A) Make an announcement
    (B) Apply for a permit
    (C) Schedule a delivery
    (D) Review a list

16. Where does the woman work?
    (A) At a post office
    (B) At a restaurant
    (C) At a computer repair shop
    (D) At a pharmacy

17. What is the man concerned about?
    (A) Hours of operation
    (B) Fees for a service
    (C) A lost item
    (D) A mistake on an invoice

18. What will the woman most likely do next?
    (A) Check on an order
    (B) Speak to a colleague
    (C) Verify an address
    (D) Take a break

19. Where do the men most likely work?
    (A) At department store
    (B) At a hotel
    (C) At a tourism agency
    (D) At a gym

20. What problem do the speakers mainly discuss?
    (A) A canceled tour
    (B) A delayed flight
    (C) Some missing luggage
    (D) Some damaged parcels

21. What service does the woman ask about?
    (A) Food
    (B) Laundry
    (C) Internet
    (D) Transportation

22. What does the engineering team need the man to do?
    (A) Order some raw materials
    (B) Hire a researcher
    (C) Write a press release
    (D) Register a patent

23. What is significant about some new batteries?
    (A) They are inexpensive to produce.
    (B) They are simple to replace.
    (C) They use environmentally friendly materials.
    (D) They take up less space.

24. Why should Asako and Tariq attend a meeting?
    (A) To receive a new assignment
    (B) To offer expertise
    (C) To practice a presentation
    (D) To discuss a new policy

ETS 실전 문제

1. How is the man's new film different from his previous ones?
   (A) It uses special effects.
   (B) It is a documentary.
   (C) It has a different screenwriter.
   (D) It has a smaller cast.

2. What does the man say was challenging?
   (A) Conducting auditions
   (B) Staying within budget
   (C) Filming in poor weather
   (D) Meeting a release date

3. What does the woman say she read about a filming location?
   (A) It was discovered by accident.
   (B) It had a lot of background noise.
   (C) It has become a tourist destination.
   (D) It was expensive to reserve.

4. What event are the speakers discussing?
   (A) A film festival
   (B) A groundbreaking ceremony
   (C) A lecture series
   (D) A picnic

5. What problem does the man mention?
   (A) A weather forecast is bad.
   (B) A building permit has not been issued.
   (C) A structure is being repaired.
   (D) A guest speaker is unavailable.

6. What does the woman decide to do?
   (A) Request a refund
   (B) Reschedule an event
   (C) Reserve a different venue
   (D) Speak with a supervisor

7. Where does the conversation most likely take place?
   (A) At a flower shop
   (B) At a clothing store
   (C) At a laundromat
   (D) At a restaurant

8. What good news does the man share?
   (A) Business hours have been extended.
   (B) A second location has opened.
   (C) Some items have been discounted.
   (D) A new shipment recently arrived.

9. What does the man tell the woman she can do?
   (A) Pay with a credit card
   (B) Join a loyalty program
   (C) Arrange for delivery
   (D) Return an item

10. What did the man recently do?
    (A) He took some cooking classes.
    (B) He earned a promotion at work.
    (C) He completed a renovation project.
    (D) He moved to a new apartment.

11. Why is the man disappointed?
    (A) Some prices have increased.
    (B) Certain brands of items are not offered.
    (C) A store's business hours have changed.
    (D) A location is inconvenient.

12. What does the woman offer to do?
    (A) Provide a brochure
    (B) Report some feedback
    (C) Apply a discount
    (D) Place a special order

ETS 유형 연습

문제를 먼저 읽은 후 대화를 들으면서 답을 고르세요.
다시 듣고 빈칸을 채우세요.

🔊 650_P3_09
정답과 해설 p.067

1. What problem are the men discussing?
   (A) A piece of furniture is too big.
   (B) A project has been delayed.
   (C) Some equipment has been damaged.
   (D) Some upgrades have not been approved.

M1 We've moved all the _____ in. Now let's work on the living room stuff.
M2 That sounds good, but I think this couch is going to be _____ the door. Maybe we can _____ on it?
M1 Hm. That should work.
W Sorry to bother you, but will you _____ _____ in the house by this evening?

2. What problem does the woman mention?
   (A) She cannot locate a store.
   (B) She cannot install a program.
   (C) She cannot print some documents.
   (D) She cannot replace an ink cartridge.

W Hi, I'm _____. The problem is, um, every time I try to _____ on both sides of the paper, the _____ in the machine.
M I'm sorry to hear that. Unfortunately, we can't _____ over the phone.
W I guess I'll _____ to the store this afternoon.

3. What is the woman concerned about?
   (A) The rate of production
   (B) The availability of staff
   (C) The temperature of a room
   (D) The cost of shipping

W I'm _____ on assembly line number three. The machine that seals the mobile phone boxes isn't _____ it should.
M1 Oh, we've had trouble with that machine in the past. _____ again, I think we'd better just replace it.
M2 I agree. But we should try to get a new one put in as soon as possible, or we might have to _____.

4. What problem does Ms. Reed mention?
   (A) An invoice is incomplete.
   (B) An office has closed.
   (C) A document is missing.
   (D) A measurement is incorrect.

M Hello? Ms. Reed?
W Hello, Mr. Park. Could you possibly _____ _____? I _____ for the front entrance.
M Certainly. It'll _____ to print the plan, though. If you come by my office around three o'clock, I'll _____ for you by then.

UNIT 10 | 세부 사항 문제 / 문제점·걱정거리 문제 079

2 문제점·걱정거리 문제

기기 고장, 교통편 및 일정 지연, 예약, 업무 등과 관련된 문제점이나 걱정거리를 묻는 문제로, 매회 2문제 정도 출제됩니다.

핵심 포인트 반전이나 역접의 표현 뒤에서 문제점이나 걱정거리가 언급되는 경우가 많으므로, 이 부분에 유의하며 대화를 들으면 정답을 찾는 데 도움이 됩니다.

문제점	What problem does the woman mention?	여자는 어떤 문제를 언급하는가?
걱정거리	What is the man concerned about?	남자는 무엇을 걱정하는가?
	Why are the speakers concerned?	화자들은 왜 걱정하는가?

▶ ETS 기출 예제

🔊 650_P3_08

M We really enjoyed meeting you at the interview, and I'd like to offer you the position of Assistant Director.

W Thanks so much for the offer. I'm very interested in the job, **but my only concern is how I would get to work. I don't own a car, and I know there aren't any public transportation options in the area**.
→ 반전·역접의 표현인 but 뒤로 문제점이 이어지고 있습니다.

M Actually, I have some good news for you. Our company has just launched an employee shuttle service from the nearby train station.

남 면접에서 만나 봬서 정말 즐거웠어요. 조감독 자리를 제안하고 싶어요.

여 제안해 주셔서 정말 감사합니다. 그 일에 관심이 많지만, 단 하나 걱정스러운 건 어떻게 출근할까 하는 거예요. 전 차가 없는데 제가 알기로 이 지역에는 대중교통 수단이 없거든요.

남 실은 좋은 소식이 있어요. 우리 회사는 가까운 기차역에서 오는 직원 셔틀 서비스를 막 시작했어요.

(What) is the (woman) (concerned about)?
(A) The availability of staff
(B) The cost of a move
(C) A delay in production
(D) A lack of transportation options

여자는 무엇을 걱정하는가?
(A) 직원 활용 가능성
(B) 이사 비용
(C) 생산 지연
(D) 교통편 부족

정답이 들리는 단서 표현
문제점·걱정거리 문제는 다음과 같은 표현이 들릴 때 정답을 포착해야 합니다.

반전·역접	But / However Unfortunately Actually	그러나 유감스럽게도 실은
고장이 난	out of order / down / broken down / not working / not functioning / malfunctioning	고장이 난
부족한·떨어진	out of power out of fuel out of stock	전원이 나간 연료가 떨어진 품절된
일정 지연	delayed behind schedule	지연된 일정보다 늦게

ETS 유형 연습

문제를 먼저 읽은 후 대화를 들으면서 답을 고르세요.
다시 듣고 빈칸을 채우세요.

🔊 650_P3_07

정답과 해설 p.065

1. When will the man probably start seeing clients tomorrow?
   (A) At 9 A.M.
   (B) At 10 A.M.
   (C) At 11 A.M.
   (D) At 1 P.M.

M Susan, could you _____ client tomorrow?
W Sure, Mr. Miller. When is the _____ see him?
M The mechanic told me that my car should be ready by ten. So, _____.
W OK, I'll _____ in at eleven.

2. What is the man pleased to learn about?
   (A) A new transportation option will be available.
   (B) A work schedule has been changed.
   (C) Employees will receive a salary increase.
   (D) Extra vacation days will be awarded.

W Luis, I didn't see you at the supervisors' meeting, but there's _____ for factory employees.
M What's the news?
W The company's going to start _____ service to and from the Metrorail station.
M _____.

3. Why is the woman unable to answer the man's question?
   (A) She has not heard back from a hotel.
   (B) She does not have Internet access.
   (C) An event budget has not been provided.
   (D) A director has been out of town.

M Divya, I have a question about the _____ _____ banquet. Do you know _____ _____ this year?
W I'm still waiting to _____ from the South York Hotel that we can use their ballroom. _____, we can host as many clients as we like.
M Oh, OK. Please let me know _____.

4. What does the man say about the Claremont property?
   (A) It is close to his business.
   (B) It has a historical building.
   (C) He hopes to redevelop it.
   (D) He has decided to sell it.

W Hello, Mr. Wilson? This is Susan Chung—a reporter for the local newspaper. I'm following up on a report that you _____ the vacant Claremont property site.
M I lead a community group that _____ the Claremont property into the biggest park in the city. _____ are really excited about this possibility.
W I imagine you'll need to _____ to the city.
M That's right.

UNIT 10 | 세부 사항 문제 / 문제점·걱정거리 문제   077

UNIT 10 세부 사항 문제 / 문제점·걱정거리 문제

무료 강의

1 세부 사항 문제

'누가/언제/어디서/무엇을/어떻게/왜'의 의문사로 다양한 세부 사항을 묻는 문제로, 매회 12문제 정도 출제됩니다.

> **핵심 포인트** 질문에 등장한 키워드가 대화에 그대로 나오는 경우가 많으므로, 문제의 키워드를 미리 파악하고 대화를 들으면 정답을 쉽게 고를 수 있습니다.

언급 내용	What does the woman say about an item?	여자는 제품에 대해 무엇을 언급하는가?
세부 정보	What is the man unable to do?	남자는 무엇을 할 수 없는가?
	Why is Mr. Dubois unavailable?	두보아 씨는 왜 시간이 안 되는가?

▶ ETS 기출 예제

🔊 650_P3_06

M You know, there's a new Indian restaurant that opened on Samson Street yesterday. It's just five minutes away. Why don't you try it?

W Oh, that sounds good. It's so nice to be able just to walk to a restaurant from home and not have to worry about parking my car.

M If you go there <u>this week</u>, you'll get a ten percent discount because it's their opening week.
→ 질문의 키워드인 this week가 그대로 등장했습니다.

남 어제 샘슨 가에 인도 식당이 새로 개업했어요. 5분 거리밖에 안 돼요. 한번 가 보는 게 어때요?

여 오, 좋아요. 집에서 식당까지 그냥 걸어서 갈 수 있고 주차 걱정도 안 해도 되니까 너무 좋아요.

남 이번 주에 거기 가면 개업 첫 주라서 10퍼센트 할인 받을 거예요.

What does the man say is available (this week)?

(A) Reserved parking
(B) Product samples
(C) Cooking classes
(D) Discounted prices

남자는 **이번 주**에 무엇이 가능하다고 말하는가?
(A) 예약 주차
(B) 제품 샘플
(C) 요리 교실
(D) 할인가

> **정답이 들리는 단서 표현** 세부 사항 문제는 다음과 같은 표현이 들릴 때 정답을 포착해야 해야 합니다.

질문	지문 속 단서
What **recently happened** in the company? 최근에 회사에 무슨 일이 있었는가?	We **recently just** hired several new people. 우리는 최근에 신입사원을 몇 명 고용했어요.
What does the man say he will do **in March**? 남자는 3월에 무엇을 하겠다고 말하는가?	I'll be on vacation **in March**. 저는 3월에 휴가를 갈 거예요.
Why does the man **apologize**? 남자는 왜 사과하는가?	(I'm) **sorry, but** I'm running late. 죄송하지만, 늦을 것 같아요.
What does the woman **want** to buy? 여자는 무엇을 사길 원하는가?	**I'd like to** purchase some furniture for my restaurant. 제 식당에 들어갈 가구를 구입하고 싶어요.

076

13. What is the conversation mainly about?
    (A) Making travel arrangements
    (B) Submitting receipts for expenses
    (C) Applying for a business loan
    (D) Having a computer repaired

14. According to the man, why is the new system better?
    (A) Payments are processed faster.
    (B) It is less expensive to operate.
    (C) Scheduling is done online.
    (D) A warranty is included.

15. What will the woman most likely do next?
    (A) Change an appointment time
    (B) Consult with another colleague
    (C) Create electronic documents
    (D) Correct a bank statement

16. Where is the conversation taking place?
    (A) At a hair salon
    (B) At a doctor's office
    (C) At a clothing store
    (D) At a photography studio

17. Why is Marcus unable to keep an appointment?
    (A) His certification has expired.
    (B) He was unable to find the necessary supplies.
    (C) His car is not working.
    (D) He is home sick.

18. When will the woman most likely return?
    (A) Later this afternoon
    (B) Tomorrow
    (C) On Wednesday
    (D) On Saturday

19. Why is the man calling?
    (A) To apply for a job
    (B) To arrange a tour
    (C) To request an identification card
    (D) To join a sports club

20. What does the woman tell the man to bring?
    (A) A discount coupon
    (B) A completed form
    (C) An admission ticket
    (D) A list of references

21. What does the woman say can be found on a Web site?
    (A) Directions
    (B) Photographs
    (C) Office hours
    (D) Open positions

22. What are the speakers discussing?
    (A) An annual inspection
    (B) A new software program
    (C) Malfunctioning equipment
    (D) Employee work schedules

23. What is the woman concerned about?
    (A) Exceeding a budget
    (B) Satisfying some customers
    (C) A staff shortage
    (D) A production delay

24. What does the woman request?
    (A) A floor plan
    (B) A list of names
    (C) An e-mail update
    (D) A company policy

ETS 실전 문제

1. What are the speakers discussing?
   (A) Recruiting new employees
   (B) Reducing travel expenses
   (C) Developing a new product
   (D) Updating a company logo

2. According to the man, what is important to the company?
   (A) Environmental sustainability
   (B) Customer loyalty
   (C) Workplace safety
   (D) Professional development

3. What will the woman most likely do next?
   (A) Research competitors' prices
   (B) Launch a package design contest
   (C) Consult industry experts
   (D) Create a survey for customers

4. Why is the woman calling?
   (A) To ask about a music festival
   (B) To apply for a job
   (C) To enter a contest
   (D) To find out a song title

5. Where does the man work?
   (A) At a music store
   (B) At a recording studio
   (C) At a radio station
   (D) At a talent agency

6. Who most likely is Yuliya Maksim?
   (A) An event coordinator
   (B) A sound engineer
   (C) An announcer
   (D) A musician

7. What type of event is the man attending?
   (A) A new-hire orientation
   (B) A job fair
   (C) A safety training
   (D) An awards ceremony

8. What is the man's occupation?
   (A) Architect
   (B) Train operator
   (C) Auto mechanic
   (D) Electrician

9. What does the woman give the man?
   (A) A parking pass
   (B) A meal voucher
   (C) A floor map
   (D) A program schedule

10. What are the speakers discussing?
    (A) An interview schedule
    (B) A client complaint
    (C) A performance review
    (D) A conference presentation

11. Where do the speakers most likely work?
    (A) At a hospital
    (B) At a hotel
    (C) At a law firm
    (D) At a career center

12. What does the woman ask the man to do?
    (A) Review a policy
    (B) Respond to an e-mail
    (C) Set up some equipment
    (D) Provide some documents

ETS 유형 연습

문제를 먼저 읽은 후 대화를 들으면서 답을 고르세요.
다시 듣고 빈칸을 채우세요.

🔊 650_P3_04
정답과 해설 p.059

1. Where most likely are the speakers?
(A) At a restaurant
(B) At a theater
(C) At a sports stadium
(D) At a shopping center

M I was here for _____, and I think I left my jacket on the back of my seat. I was sitting in the _____.
W I'll have to check. Can you _____ _____ like?
M It's dark blue and _____ on the left side.

2. Who most likely is the woman?
(A) A supermarket owner
(B) A food critic
(C) A chef
(D) A photographer

M Thanks for meeting with me, Ms. Breton. I'm a big fan of your _____ and really like _____.
W That's great. And how would I fit in?
M I want to _____ on our Web site. Here are some _____ we've planned in the past for you to look at.

3. Where does the man work?
(A) At a car rental agency
(B) At an automotive repair shop
(C) At an express delivery service
(D) At a driver's license office

M Hi, this is Larry from Millwood Automotive Repairs. I'm _____ on a truck. I'm calling to see whether your _____. The model number on the tires is RCL forty-four.
W I'm afraid we don't have it _____ right now. I could order it for you, and it would be _____ in three working days. _____?
M Not really.

4. Where is the conversation taking place?
(A) At a train station
(B) At an airport
(C) At a bus terminal
(D) At a car rental agency

M Hello, I'd like to _____ for the 3 o'clock train to Chicago.
W Unfortunately, sir, that train's _____. Here's a copy of the _____.
M Hmmm... if I wait for the 3:40 train, I'll have time to _____ before leaving.

2 화자·장소 문제

대화의 화자가 누구인지, 대화가 이루어지는 장소가 어디인지를 묻는 문제는 매회 6문제 정도 출제됩니다.

> **핵심 포인트** 단서가 대화 초반에 대부분 제시되지만 그렇지 않은 경우에는 다른 문제들을 먼저 풀고 나서 마지막에 정답을 선택해도 좋습니다.

직업·신분	Who is the woman?	여자는 누구인가?
	What is the man's job?	남자의 직업은 무엇인가?
근무처	Where do the speakers most likely work?	화자들은 어디에서 일할 것 같은가?
대화 장소	Where most likely are the speakers?	화자들은 어디에 있는 것 같은가?

▶ ETS 기출 예제

🔊 650_P3_03

W Excuse me, do you work here? **I'm interested in one of the cameras on display behind the counter.**
→ 카메라 가게에서 일어난 대화임을 알 수 있습니다.

M Oh, **you mean this one—the Balani X13**?
→ 남자의 직업은 카메라 가게 점원입니다.

W Yes, that's it.

M Just so you know, the battery that's included doesn't last very long—you might want to buy an extra one if you're planning to use the camera a lot.

여 실례합니다만 여기 직원이세요? 제가 카운터 뒤에 진열된 카메라들 중 하나에 관심이 있어서요.

남 아, 이거 말씀하시는 거죠, 발라니 X13?

여 네, 맞아요.

남 참고로 말씀드리면, 카메라에 들어 있는 배터리는 오래 가지 않아요. 카메라를 자주 사용하실 거라면 여분으로 하나 더 사시는 게 좋을 겁니다.

(Who) most likely is the (man)?
(A) A store clerk
(B) A magazine journalist
(C) A museum director
(D) A professional photographer

남자는 누구인 것 같은가?
(A) 가게 점원
(B) 잡지사 기자
(C) 박물관 관장
(D) 전문 사진작가

정답이 들리는 단서 표현 화자·장소 문제는 다음과 같은 표현이 들릴 때 정답을 포착해야 합니다.

자기 소개	Mr. Colson, **I'm a journalist** for *Health and Wellness Magazine*. 직업 A journalist	콜슨 씨, 저는 〈헬스 앤 웰니스 매거진〉의 기자입니다. 기자
업무 관련 단어	Take a look at the layout for the **next issue** of our **cooking magazine**. 근무처 At a magazine publisher	우리 요리 잡지 다음 호 레이아웃을 좀 보세요. 잡지 출판사
제품	A customer is looking for **this winter boot** in a size ten. 대화 장소 At a shoe store	손님이 이 겨울 부츠를 10사이즈로 찾고 있어요. 신발 매장

ETS 유형 연습

문제를 먼저 읽은 후 대화를 들으면서 답을 고르세요.
다시 듣고 빈칸을 채우세요.

🔊 650_P3_02
정답과 해설 p.058

1. Why is the man calling?
   (A) To open an account
   (B) To report an error
   (C) To place an order
   (D) To return an item

   M   Hello, I'm _____ for a set of headphones I saw in your catalog.
   W   All right, I can _____. Can you give me the _____ for those?
   M   I have the catalog right here—if you can give me a moment, I'll check it and see.

2. What are the speakers discussing?
   (A) A telephone bill
   (B) An electricity bill
   (C) A weather report
   (D) A broken air conditioner

   M   I got a _____ in the mail today. It's so expensive!
   W   Mine is too. I guess that's because I've been _____ so much in this hot weather.
   M   So have I, but I still don't think I should have been billed this much. Maybe I should _____ and find out if the rates have gone up.

3. Why is the man calling?
   (A) To update his contact information
   (B) To open a new account
   (C) To apply for a loan
   (D) To report a lost card

   M   I'm calling to speak with someone about _____. Is this something I can do over the phone?
   W   Unfortunately, to open an account, you'll have to come to the bank with _____. Would you like to _____ an account manager?
   M   No, I'll just stop by when I can.

4. What are the speakers mainly discussing?
   (A) Holding a workshop
   (B) Creating a menu
   (C) Organizing a trip
   (D) Reviewing some applications

   M   Ms. Johnson, I'm planning the company's cafeteria menu for next month, and I'd like to add _____ to what I'll be cooking. Would that be OK with you?
   W   That'd be fine. I'm sure _____ for vegetarian dishes.
   M   I have _____ for vegetarian meals. I can make a few for _____.

UNIT 09 주제·목적 문제 / 화자·장소 문제

무료 강의

1 주제·목적 문제

대화 전체의 주제 또는 목적을 묻는 문제는 매회 4문제 정도 출제됩니다.

> **핵심 포인트** 첫 화자가 화두를 꺼내면서 그와 관련된 내용의 대화가 이어지므로 인사말 이후 처음 2~3문장에서 대부분 답이 나옵니다. 대화 초반을 놓치지 않고 듣는 것이 중요합니다.

주제	What are the speakers discussing?	화자들은 무엇에 관해 이야기하고 있는가?
	What are the speakers talking about?	화자들은 무엇에 관해 이야기하고 있는가?
	What is the topic of the conversation?	대화의 주제는 무엇인가?
목적	Why is the man/woman calling?	남자/여자는 왜 전화하고 있는가?

▶ ETS 기출 예제

🔊 650_P3_01

M Is that today's newspaper, Isabella? **There's an advertisement in there about a photography contest.**
→ 화두를 꺼낸 후 대화 주제가 바로 등장합니다.

W I haven't seen it yet. What page is it on?

M I don't know, but it's in the Features section. I was thinking you should enter that great picture you took of the buildings in New York last summer.

남 이자벨라, 그거 오늘 신문인가요? 거기에 사진 공모전 광고가 실려 있던데요.

여 아직 못 봤는데요. 몇 면에 있나요?

남 모르겠어요, 특집 기사면인데요. 당신이 지난 여름 뉴욕에서 찍었던 멋진 건물 사진을 출품하면 어떨까 생각했어요.

(What) are the (speakers) (discussing)?
(A) A book review
(B) A magazine article
(C) A newspaper advertisement
(D) A travel brochure

화자들은 무엇에 대해 이야기하고 있는가?
(A) 서평
(B) 잡지 기사
(C) 신문 광고
(D) 여행 책자

정답이 들리는 단서 표현	주제·목적 문제는 다음과 같은 표현이 들릴 때 정답을 포착해야 합니다.	
전화를 건 용건	**I'm calling to** get some assistance with my laptop.	노트북 컴퓨터에 대해 도움을 받고자 전화했어요.
상황/사실 언급	**I have an appointment** with Dr. Ramirez tomorrow, but I'm afraid I have to reschedule.	내일 라미레즈 박사님과 진료 예약이 잡혀 있는데 일정을 변경해야 할 것 같아요.
소식 전달	**Did you hear the news** about our company merger with Geller Solutions?	우리 회사가 겔러 솔루션즈와 합병할 거라는 소식 들으셨어요?
요청/제안	**We need to plan** our strategy for next month's business exposition.	다음 달 비즈니스 박람회를 위한 전략을 세워야겠어요.

▶ PART 3 이렇게 풀자

STEP 1
음원을 듣기 전

❶ 문제 파악

문제를 미리 읽으면서 대화문을 듣는 동안 어떤 부분에 초점을 두어야 할지 파악합니다. 성우가 Part 3의 Directions를 읽어주는 동안 첫 세트인 32번~34번 문제를 읽어 둡니다.

❷ 키워드 표시

문제의 핵심이 되는 키워드를 표시해 두면, 정답 단서가 들렸을 때 더 쉽게 포착할 수 있습니다. 키워드에는 의문사, 명사, 동사, 시간 표현 등이 해당됩니다.

32. (Why) is the (woman) (calling)? → 여자는 왜 전화를 하고 있는가?
33. (What) does the (man) say about the (service)? → 남자는 서비스에 대해 무엇을 말하는가?
34. (What) does the (woman) (ask) (permission) to do? → 여자는 무슨 허락을 구하는가?

❸ 문제에 나온 화자 파악

문제에 나온 화자가 주로 정답의 단서를 말합니다.

Why is the **woman** calling? → 여자가 말하는 부분에서 정답이 나옵니다.
What does the **man** say about the service? → 남자가 말하는 부분에서 정답이 나옵니다.
⚠ What is **the man asked** to do? → 여자가 말하는 부분에서 정답이 나옵니다.

STEP 2
음원을 들으면서

❹ 정답 선택하기

정답의 단서는 대부분 문제 순서대로 나옵니다. 따라서 대화 전반부가 나올 때 첫 번째 문제를 보고 있다가 단서가 들리면 바로 정답을 고르고 다음 문제로 넘어가서 다음 단서를 기다리면 됩니다.

STEP 3
음원을 들은 후

❺ 문제를 읽어주는 동안 다음 세트 문제 파악

대화문이 끝나면 성우가 문제를 읽어줍니다. 각 문제를 읽을 때마다 8초간의 문제 풀이 시간이 함께 주어지는데, 이 시간 동안 다음 세트의 문제들을 미리 파악해 둡니다.

INTRO
PART 3   짧은 대화

총 13지문, 39문항

Part 3는 남녀가 번갈아 가며 이야기하는 대화문을 듣고 그에 따른 문제를 푸는 유형입니다. 문제 수가 39개나 되므로 LC에서 가장 비중이 큰 파트입니다.

▶ **PART 1, 2와 이런 점이 다르다**

1. 대화문 하나를 듣고 문제를 세 개씩 풀어야 합니다. 1세트가 [대화문 1개 + 문제 3개]로 총 13세트(39문제)입니다.
2. 시험지에 문제와 보기가 제시되어 있어, 대화문을 듣는 동시에 읽으면서 문제를 풀어야 합니다.

Questions 32 through 34 refer to the following conversation.

🔊 음원

W   Hello, I'm calling from the customer service department of Le Star Shoes. You recently purchased a pair of boots from us, and I wanted to know if you're satisfied with your purchase.

↓

M   Oh. Yes, I'm very pleased with your service. I was especially impressed that I could order a pair of shoes and receive them the very next day!

↓

W   That's great. We appreciate the positive feedback. Would you mind if we shared your comments on our Web site?

↓

32. Why is the woman calling? 8초
33. What does the man say about the service? 8초
34. What does the woman ask permission to do? 8초

📄 문제지

32. Why is the woman calling?
    (A) To offer a refund
    (B) To promote a new product
    (C) To extend an invitation
    (D) To collect feedback

↓

33. What does the man say about the service?
    (A) Delivery is fast.
    (B) Returning merchandise is easy.
    (C) Representatives are helpful.
    (D) Fees are reasonable.

↓

34. What does the woman ask permission to do?
    (A) Postpone a shipping date
    (B) Substitute an item
    (C) Post some comments
    (D) Charge an account

↓

다음 세트 준비!

[35~37]

짧은 대화

INTRO
UNIT 09 주제·목적 문제/화자·장소 문제
UNIT 10 세부 사항 문제/
문제점·걱정거리 문제
UNIT 11 요청·제안 문제/다음에 할 일 문제
UNIT 12 의도 파악 문제
UNIT 13 시각 정보 문제
PART 3 빈출 표현

 무료 강의

짧은 담화

INTRO
UNIT 14 전화 메시지
UNIT 15 공지/안내/회의
UNIT 16 광고/방송/보도
UNIT 17 인물/강연/설명
UNIT 18 여행/견학/관람
PART 4 빈출 표현

 무료 강의

INTRO PART 4 — 짧은 담화

총 10지문, 30문항

Part 4는 한 사람이 말하는 담화문을 듣고 그에 따른 세 문제를 푸는 유형으로, 총 10세트[담화문10개＋문제30개]가 출제됩니다.

▶ **PART 3와 똑같다**

2인 이상이 말하는 대화문이 아닌 혼자서 말하는 담화문인 점만 제외하면, 문제 유형이나 문제 풀이 방식은 **Part 3**와 같습니다.

Questions 71 through 73 refer to the following announcement.

🔊 음원

M Hi everyone. I hope you're enjoying the conference. Uhm... before we get started with the next presentation, I have a quick announcement.

↓

You should have received a prepaid ticket for the welcome dinner tonight, in your registration packet. But it looks like some of the packets were missing them.

↓

So... if you didn't get one, I'll be in the lobby distributing tickets during the break at three o'clock. You just need to present your conference badge in order to receive your ticket. So don't forget it, OK?

↓

71. Who most likely are the listeners? 8초
72. What problem does the speaker mention? 8초
73. According to the speaker, what will some listeners need to do? 8초

📋 문제지

71. Who most likely are the listeners?
    (A) Concert performers
    (B) Technical support staff
    (C) Conference attendees
    (D) Restaurant servers

↓

72. What problem does the speaker mention?
    (A) A room has not been reserved.
    (B) Some tickets were not distributed.
    (C) A speaker is unavailable.
    (D) A microphone is not working.

↓

73. According to the speaker, what will some listeners need to do?
    (A) Keep their receipts
    (B) Follow some signs
    (C) Wait in line
    (D) Show some identification

↓

다음 세트 준비!

[74~76]

▶ PART 4 이렇게 풀자

STEP 1
음원을 듣기 전

❶ 문제 파악

문제를 미리 읽으면서 담화문을 듣는 동안 어떤 부분에 초점을 두어야 할지 파악합니다. 성우가 Part 4의 Directions를 읽어주는 동안 첫 세트인 71번~73번 문제를 읽어 둡니다.

❷ 키워드 표시

문제의 핵심이 되는 키워드를 표시해 두면, 정답 단서가 들렸을 때 더 쉽게 포착할 수 있습니다. 키워드에는 의문사, 명사, 동사, 시간 표현 등이 해당됩니다.

71. (Who) most likely are the (listeners)? → 청자들은 **누구**일 것 같은가?
72. (What problem) does the (speaker) (mention)? → 화자는 **무슨 문제**를 언급하는가?
73. According to the speaker, (what) will some (listeners) (need to do)? → 화자에 따르면, 일부 **청자들**은 **무엇**을 해야 하는가?

❸ 화자와 청자 구분

문제에서 화자(speaker)에 대해 묻는지 청자(listener)에 대해 묻는지를 구분해야 합니다.

Where does the **speaker** most likely work? → 화자가 일하는 곳
Who most likely are the **listeners**? → 청자의 직업

STEP 2
음원을 들으면서

❹ 정답 선택하기

정답의 단서는 대부분 문제 순서대로 나옵니다. 담화 전반부가 나올 때 첫 번째 문제를 보고 있다가 단서가 들리면 바로 정답을 고르고 다음 문제로 넘어가서 다음 단서를 기다리면 됩니다.

STEP 3
음원을 들은 후

❺ 문제를 읽어주는 동안 다음 세트 문제 파악

담화문이 끝나면 성우가 문제를 읽어줍니다. 각 문제를 읽을 때마다 8초간의 문제 풀이 시간이 함께 주어지는데, 이 시간 동안 다음 세트의 문제들을 미리 파악해 둡니다.

UNIT 14 전화 메시지

예약 확인, 업무 요청 등 발신자가 남기는 전화 메시지와 공공기관 등의 자동 안내 녹음 메시지가 거의 매회 출제됩니다.

> **핵심 포인트** 메시지 초반에 화자의 신분/근무지, 메시지의 주제에 대한 단서가 나오므로 첫 2~3문장을 놓치지 않고 듣는 것이 중요합니다. 메시지를 듣는 청자가 누구인지 묻는 경우 전체 지문의 흐름을 통해 추론해야 할 때도 있습니다.

빈출 질문
Who most likely is the speaker/listener? 화자/청자는 누구인 것 같은가?
Where does the speaker work? 화자는 어디에서 근무하는가?
What does the speaker ask about? 화자는 무엇에 대해 묻고 있는가?

▶ ETS 기출 예제

🔊 650_P4_01

인사/소개
Hello, Mr. Clark. ❶ **This is Roger calling from the Lost Property office at the Wharton train station.**

용건
❷ **A passenger found your wallet this morning and turned it in to us.**

요청/당부
When you come to retrieve your wallet, ❸ **you will need to give the attendant your item reference number.** It's 5492. Please remember to have this number when you come to the station. We cannot return your wallet unless you present this information.

❶ 저는 워튼 기차역 분실물 관리소의 로저입니다.
❷ 승객 한 분이 오늘 아침 귀하의 지갑을 습득해서 저희에게 주셨습니다.
❸ 안내원에게 조회 번호를 제시하셔야 합니다.

정답과 해설 p.096

1. Where does the speaker work?
   화자는 어디에서 근무하는가?
   장소 문제 → 인사 직후 자기소개에 주목

   정답 At a train station
   기차역

2. What is the speaker calling about?
   화자는 무엇에 대해 전화하는가?
   주제 문제 → 초반부 듣고 주제 파악하기

   정답 A lost item
   분실물

3. What does the speaker ask the listener to do?
   화자는 청자에게 무엇을 해달라고 요청하는가?
   요청 사항 문제 → 요청문에 주목

   정답 Present a reference number
   조회 번호 제시하기

질문의 단서가 되는 주요 표현

Thank you for calling Chester City Theater's business office. 화자는 어디에서 일하는가?
I'm calling to confirm your reservation for a one-way shuttle bus. 전화의 목적은 무엇인가?
Please call us again during regular office hours. 화자는 무엇을 요청하는가?
This is Jim from Thompsonville Garage with a message for Gloria Blanton. 화자는 누구인 것 같은가?

ETS 유형 연습

문제를 먼저 읽은 후 담화를 들으면서 답을 고르세요.
다시 듣고 빈칸을 채우세요.

🔊 650_P4_02

정답과 해설 p.096

[1-2]

1. What type of work will take place at the Medford office?
   (A) An air-conditioning system will be installed.
   (B) A roof will be repaired.

2. Why does the speaker prefer to hire the Classion Company?
   (A) It charges reasonable prices.
   (B) It has a lot of experience.

I'm calling with an update on our regional office in Medford. As you know, we need to have a _____ installed for the building. I received bids from three companies, and luckily, they're all within our budget. But I think we should give the contract to the Classion Company. They've been _____ for over twenty years and have done several installations in _____ like ours.

[3-4]

Floor Plan: Third Floor

Supply Closet	Stairwell	
		3-B
3-A		
3-C	Elevator	3-D

3. Who most likely is the message for?
   (A) A repair person
   (B) A real estate agent

4. Look at the graphic. Which apartment does the Garcia family live in?
   (A) 3-A   (B) 3-B

I'm calling because one of the apartment units has _____. Could you _____ later this afternoon or tomorrow morning? It's the one the Garcia family lives in... you know... the corner apartment on the third floor, _____ _____? Their phone number is 555-0148. Please _____ to arrange a time to make the repair.

[5-6]

5. Why is the speaker calling?
   (A) To finalize a menu
   (B) To announce a venue change

6. What does the speaker say about Millson Conference Center?
   (A) It has received an award.
   (B) It is undergoing some repairs.

Hi, Ivan. I have some bad news. We had to _____ of the awards dinner next Friday night. Unfortunately, some water pipes burst in the kitchen at the Millson Conference Center, and the _____ will take over a week to complete. I was able to book a new venue across town at Tulip Hall. It's farther away, but it's our _____.

ETS 실전 문제

1. Where does the speaker most likely work?
   (A) At an Internet service provider
   (B) At an electricity company
   (C) At a newspaper
   (D) At a bank

2. What will the listener do on October 15 ?
   (A) Start a new job
   (B) Leave for vacation
   (C) Cancel a subscription
   (D) Move to a new location

3. Why would the listener call a phone number?
   (A) To request a printed schedule
   (B) To provide feedback on a service
   (C) To make changes to an account
   (D) To request additional information

4. Why is the woman calling?
   (A) To reschedule a flight reservation
   (B) To notify a customer of a delay
   (C) To confirm transportation details
   (D) To provide driving directions

5. What time will the shuttle bus arrive at Jackson Telecommunications?
   (A) 3:15 P.M.
   (B) 4:15 P.M.
   (C) 5:15 P.M.
   (D) 6:15 P.M.

6. What is the listener asked to do?
   (A) Give payment to the driver
   (B) Be prepared to provide identification
   (C) Allow extra time for check-in
   (D) Confirm the number of passengers

7. What does the speaker's company sell?
   (A) Cookware
   (B) Clothing
   (C) Jewelry
   (D) Luggage

8. What does the speaker mean when he says, "your videos are very popular"?
   (A) The listener will need to continue traveling.
   (B) The listener can reach a lot of people.
   (C) The listener should upgrade some equipment.
   (D) The listener should speak to a talent agent.

9. What does the speaker recommend doing?
   (A) Giving out a prize
   (B) Touring a facility
   (C) Meeting with a consultant
   (D) Watching a demonstration

10. Who most likely is the speaker?
    (A) An electrician
    (B) A car mechanic
    (C) A carpenter
    (D) A telephone repair person

11. What does the speaker say he will have to do?
    (A) Contact another store
    (B) Collect a deposit
    (C) Replace a broken part
    (D) Consult a colleague

12. Why should the listener call back?
    (A) To set up an appointment
    (B) To confirm a delivery time
    (C) To speak to a department manager
    (D) To authorize a charge

13. Why is the speaker calling?
    (A) To respond to a complaint
    (B) To decline a job offer
    (C) To confirm service availability
    (D) To reschedule a reservation

14. What problem does the speaker mention?
    (A) A driver went to the wrong address.
    (B) A driver was delayed by roadwork.
    (C) A form was not filled out accurately.
    (D) A form was not submitted on time.

15. What will the listener receive?
    (A) A revised contract
    (B) A company policy
    (C) A discounted ticket
    (D) A free ride

16. Who is the speaker most likely calling?
    (A) A family member
    (B) A friend
    (C) A client
    (D) A coworker

17. What does the speaker imply when he says, "It's rush hour"?
    (A) A business' schedule has changed.
    (B) A project was poorly timed.
    (C) A suggestion will not work.
    (D) A bus is crowded.

18. What does the speaker ask the listener to do?
    (A) Give a presentation
    (B) Make an appointment
    (C) Mail some packages
    (D) Purchase a gift

Locations
- Sports stadium, 300 kilometers away
- Indoor mall, 15 kilometers away
- City center, 120 kilometers away
- Residential home, 50 kilometers away

19. What industry does the speaker most likely work in?
    (A) Architecture
    (B) Film
    (C) Shipping
    (D) Real estate

20. What will the speaker send to the listener?
    (A) A floor plan
    (B) An itinerary
    (C) Some receipts
    (D) Some photos

21. Look at the graphic. Which location does the speaker refer to?
    (A) Sports stadium
    (B) Indoor mall
    (C) City center
    (D) Residential home

UNIT 15 공지 / 안내 / 회의

다수의 고객을 대상으로 한 안내, 회사 직원들을 대상으로 한 공지, 업무 관련 회의 내용 등이 출제됩니다.

> **핵심 포인트** 청자가 보통 여러 사람인 경우가 많기 때문에, 'listeners(청자들)'에 대해 묻는 문제가 자주 나옵니다. 특히 지문에서 언급되는 문제점이나 화자가 청자들에게 요청/제안하는 내용을 놓치지 않고 듣는 것이 중요합니다.

빈출 질문
What problem does the speaker mention? 화자는 어떤 문제점을 언급하는가?
What does the speaker ask the listeners to do? 화자는 청자들에게 무엇을 해달라고 요청하는가?
What does the speaker offer to do? 화자는 무엇을 해주겠다고 제안하는가?

▶ ETS 기출 예제

🔊 650_P4_04

안내 주제/대상
❶ Congratulations on completing your flight attendant training! You're now ready for your first work assignments.
세부 사항
❷ You have all submitted your lists of airports that you would like to be assigned to. I'm reviewing your preferences and will give you your location assignments by the end of the week.
요청/당부
But before you leave, ❸ we're going to take a group photo, so please come to the front of the room. We'll post the photo on our internal company Web site.

❶ 비행기 승무원 교육 수료를 축하드립니다.
❷ 여러분 모두 배정받고 싶은 공항 목록을 제출하셨습니다.
❸ 단체 사진을 찍을 테니, 방 앞쪽으로 나와 주세요.

정답과 해설 p.102

1. Who most likely are the listeners? 청자들은 누구일 것 같은가?
   대상 문제 → 도입부에 청자의 직업 정보에 주목
   정답 Flight attendants
   비행기 승무원

2. According to the speaker, what did the listeners submit?
   화자에 따르면, 청자들은 무엇을 제출했는가?
   세부 사항 문제 → 초반부 키워드 'submitted'에 주목
   정답 Work location preferences
   선호하는 근무 장소

3. What are the listeners asked to do next?
   청자들은 다음에 무엇을 하라고 요청받는가?
   요청 사항 문제 → 후반부의 요청문에 주목
   정답 Assemble for a photo
   사진을 찍기 위해 모이기

> **질문의 단서가 되는 주요 표현**
>
> **Welcome you all on your first day of work.** 청자는 누구일 것 같은가?
> **Sign up[Register] for** the program today. 화자가 청자들에게 무엇을 하라고 요청하는가?
> **I'd like to show** a video of our president's speech. 청자들은 다음에 무엇을 할 것 같은가?
> **Come up with** some ideas by the end of the week. 청자들은 다음에 무엇을 하라고 요청받는가?

ETS 유형 연습

문제를 먼저 읽은 후 담화를 들으면서 답을 고르세요.
다시 듣고 빈칸을 채우세요.

🔊 650_P4_05
정답과 해설 p.102

[1-2]

1. What problem does the speaker mention?
   (A) A building will be without power.
   (B) Some computers must be replaced.

2. What does the speaker say he will do?
   (A) Send colleagues a message
   (B) Meet with team leaders

Our office building will be _____ Saturday morning and, uh, the _____ for about three hours. For any of you planning to come in on Saturday, _____ by one o'clock. I'll _____ once the work's done.

[3-4]

3. What is the speaker mainly discussing?
   (A) Changing a menu
   (B) Opening a new location

4. According to the speaker, what are available in the stockroom?
   (A) Utensils
   (B) Aprons

I want to talk about a big change coming to our restaurant soon. We're going to start a _____ _____. Basically, our diners will have a special four-course meal that we select, instead of the diners choosing _____ from a full menu. OK, now one last thing. _____ have arrived. Please _____ from the stockroom before the dinner shift starts.

[5-6]

5. What is the purpose of the announcement?
   (A) To report a schedule change
   (B) To give directions to an event

6. When will the event begin?
   (A) At 1:00 P.M.
   (B) At 6:00 P.M.

Ladies and gentlemen, I'm sorry to announce that tonight's football game _____ _____, due to heavy rain conditions. We _____ six P.M. In the meantime, we encourage you to _____, which are now open. Please note there are no refunds, but you can exchange your ticket for a future game by _____ next to the main gate.

ETS 실전 문제

1. Where most likely is the announcement being made?
   (A) At a paint store
   (B) At a post office
   (C) At a manufacturing plant
   (D) At a construction site

2. What has caused a problem?
   (A) Some paint has spilled.
   (B) Some machinery is jammed.
   (C) Some packages have not been delivered.
   (D) Some products have been damaged.

3. What are the listeners instructed to do?
   (A) Turn off their machines
   (B) Meet with a supervisor
   (C) Clean up the area
   (D) Go to the staff room

4. Where does the meeting most likely take place?
   (A) At a food processing facility
   (B) At a coffee shop
   (C) At a conference center
   (D) At a supermarket

5. What does the speaker say he is excited about?
   (A) Moving to a new location
   (B) Expanding a selection
   (C) Replacing some equipment
   (D) Adding a parking area

6. What would the speaker like the listeners to do?
   (A) Check a shift schedule
   (B) Set up a display
   (C) Provide some feedback
   (D) Clean a work area

7. What is the main topic of the announcement?
   (A) A recycling policy
   (B) An inventory procedure
   (C) Employee payroll
   (D) Computer maintenance

8. Why is the company making a change?
   (A) To increase revenue
   (B) To attract new employees
   (C) To comply with the local laws
   (D) To take advantage of a new technology

9. According to the speaker, what will happen on Thursdays?
   (A) Discarded materials will be picked up.
   (B) Machinery will be serviced.
   (C) Employees will be paid.
   (D) Supply orders will be processed.

10. Where most likely are the listeners?
    (A) At a ferry terminal
    (B) At a sports stadium
    (C) At a train station
    (D) At an airport

11. What does the speaker announce?
    (A) A loyalty discount
    (B) An unexpected delay
    (C) A building policy
    (D) A café opening

12. What should the listeners be prepared to show?
    (A) Their tickets
    (B) Their bags
    (C) A coupon
    (D) Some identification

13. What is the purpose of the meeting?
    (A) To welcome new employees
    (B) To review some procedures
    (C) To schedule some equipment upgrades
    (D) To announce a new product line

14. What does the speaker say about Friday?
    (A) A supervisor is retiring.
    (B) A client will be visiting.
    (C) Cold weather is predicted.
    (D) Survey results will be published.

15. Where do the listeners most likely work?
    (A) At a television station
    (B) At a home-improvement store
    (C) At a real estate agency
    (D) At a water company

16. Who most likely is the audience for this talk?
    (A) Catering staff
    (B) A maintenance crew
    (C) A group of musicians
    (D) Concert attendees

17. Why are listeners invited to visit the green tents?
    (A) To get water
    (B) To purchase food
    (C) To check a schedule
    (D) To pick up a T-shirt

18. According to the woman, what will happen at 6:00 P.M.?
    (A) A contest winner will be announced.
    (B) Performers will sign autographs.
    (C) Equipment will be checked.
    (D) Cleanup will begin.

Grocery Store Directory

Aisle	Products
1	Frozen Food
2	Beverages, Tea, Coffee
3	Cereal, Granola Bars
4	Snacks, Condiments

19. What item has a customer found?
    (A) A car key
    (B) A mobile phone
    (C) A wallet
    (D) An identification card

20. Look at the graphic. Which aisle is under renovation?
    (A) Aisle 1
    (B) Aisle 2
    (C) Aisle 3
    (D) Aisle 4

21. Why will the store close early?
    (A) There is a holiday.
    (B) Inventory will be taken.
    (C) A private event will be held there.
    (D) There is a temporary staffing shortage.

UNIT 16 광고 / 방송 / 보도

무료 강의

제품/행사/업체 등을 알리는 광고나 교통 방송, 일기 예보, 또는 다양한 주제를 다루는 라디오 방송이 출제됩니다.

핵심 포인트 광고되는 대상, 방송/뉴스의 주제를 묻는 문제가 자주 나오므로, 첫 2~3문장을 놓치지 않고 들어야 정답의 단서를 쉽게 찾을 수 있습니다.

빈출 질문
What is the speaker advertising? 화자는 무엇을 광고하는가?
What is the speaker mainly discussing? 화자는 주로 무엇을 이야기하는가?

▶ ETS 기출 예제

🔊 650_P4_07

광고 대상 소개
❶ At Oak Tree Apparel, we've built a reputation for making men look their very best in the latest formal wear fashions.

세부 사항
❷ It's the individualized attention from our helpful staff that keeps our customers coming back. And now, to serve you better, ❸ we're keeping our doors open longer. Beginning next week, we'll be open for business from nine A.M. until nine P.M. every day. Come in and see why we're ranked number one in the city for customer satisfaction.

다음에 일어날 일

❶ 오크 트리 어패럴은 최신 정장 패션으로 남성분들을 최고의 모습으로 꾸며드린다는 명성을 쌓아 왔습니다.

❷ 고객분들이 계속 재방문하시는 것은 저희 직원들의 개인 맞춤 서비스 때문입니다.

❸ 다음 주부터, 매일 아침 9시부터 저녁 9시까지 문을 엽니다.

정답과 해설 p.108

---

1. **What** is the **speaker** **advertising**? 화자는 무엇을 광고하는가?
   광고 대상 문제 → 광고 도입부의 업체 소개에 주목

   정답 A clothing store
   옷 가게

---

2. According to the speaker, **what** do **customers** **like** about the business?
   화자에 따르면, 고객들이 업체에 대해 무엇을 좋아하는가?
   세부 사항 문제 → 키워드 'customers like'에 주목 → keeps our customers coming back

   정답 Its personalized service
   맞춤형 서비스

---

3. **What** will **happen** at the business **next week**?
   다음 주에 업체에서 무슨 일이 일어날 것인가?
   다음에 일어날 일 문제 → 'next week'에 주목

   정답 Operating hours will be extended.
   영업 시간이 연장될 것이다.

질문의 단서가 되는 주요 표현

Are you looking for healthy lunch options? Come to VG Bistro.
Visit our Web site to watch our video tutorials.
Our new shoes will last much longer **than ordinary shoes**.
I'll be right back after a commercial break.

어떤 업체가 광고되고 있는가?
청자들은 왜 웹사이트를 방문해야 하는가?
신제품은 어떤 점이 특별한가?
청자들은 다음에 무엇을 듣게 될 것인가?

ETS 유형 연습

문제를 먼저 읽은 후 담화를 들으면서 답을 고르세요.
다시 듣고 빈칸을 채우세요.

🔊 650_P4_08

정답과 해설 p.108

[1-2]

1. What is happening this weekend?
   (A) An art gallery opening
   (B) A music festival

2. Why does the speaker recommend checking social media?
   (A) To view a schedule
   (B) To volunteer for an event

This weekend's weather will be _____ —perfect for attending the annual Summerton Jazz Extravaganza. You won't want to miss it. There'll be lots of _____ performing on three stages. To see the list of _____, visit the Summerton social media page.

[3-4]

Mishu E-readers	
Model	Display Size
PT-250	15 centimeters
DX-16	16 centimeters
DX-32	17 centimeters
DX-64	18 centimeters

3. Look at the graphic. Which e-reader has an app for video chatting?
   (A) PT-250
   (B) DX-64

4. What does the speaker say visitors to the Mishu Web site can do?
   (A) Read customer reviews
   (B) Purchase a product

Buy a Mishu E-reader today and _____ _____. Mishu customers can carry _____ on one device! The model with _____ size even has an application installed for video chatting. Visit the Mishu Web site "Customer Feedback" section to read for yourself what _____ _____ about their devices.

[5-6]

5. What benefit of the project did the governor mention?
   (A) Shorter commutes
   (B) More local jobs

6. Who will be interviewed after the break?
   (A) The governor
   (B) Community residents

At a press conference today, the governor announced that _____ in Starks County. The governor emphasized that the hospital will _____ —helping to boost the local employment rate. After the break, I'll talk with _____ of Starks County. They've raised concerns that the _____ will have a negative impact on wildlife in the area.

ETS 실전 문제

1. What is being advertised?
   (A) A fitness center
   (B) An apartment complex
   (C) A hotel
   (D) An amusement park

2. According to the speaker, what will the listeners appreciate most about Ocean Springs?
   (A) An outdoor pool
   (B) A self-serve coffee bar
   (C) Affordable pricing
   (D) Convenient parking

3. What does the speaker suggest the listeners do online?
   (A) Download a brochure
   (B) Take a virtual tour
   (C) Schedule a visit
   (D) Read some reviews

4. What is currently under construction?
   (A) A tunnel
   (B) A bridge
   (C) A wind farm
   (D) A solar farm

5. How will local residents benefit from a project?
   (A) City streets will be cleaner.
   (B) A service will be less expensive.
   (C) More jobs will be added.
   (D) Commuting time will be shorter.

6. How can the listeners find out more?
   (A) By visiting a Web site
   (B) By signing up for a newsletter
   (C) By watching an interview
   (D) By attending a community meeting

7. Who most likely is the speaker?
   (A) A marine biologist
   (B) A news reporter
   (C) A local official
   (D) A boat captain

8. According to the speaker, what can business owners expect?
   (A) An increase in customers
   (B) A reduction in energy costs
   (C) Higher tax rates
   (D) Fewer parking restrictions

9. What will Marjorie Kelley most likely discuss?
   (A) Road conditions
   (B) Business opportunities
   (C) Wildlife conservation
   (D) Boating safety

10. What kind of business is being advertised?
    (A) A flower shop
    (B) A hair salon
    (C) An event-planning company
    (D) A clothing store

11. What can the business provide free of charge?
    (A) A product sample
    (B) A customer loyalty card
    (C) Personal consultations
    (D) Expedited shipping

12. How can the listeners obtain a discount?
    (A) By using a special code
    (B) By mentioning an ad at checkout
    (C) By spending a certain amount
    (D) By making a customer referral

13. What is the topic of the podcast?

    (A) Interior decorating
    (B) Architecture
    (C) Travel photography
    (D) Money management

14. Why does the speaker say, "returning items is an inconvenience"?

    (A) To explain a delay
    (B) To advise caution
    (C) To justify a complaint
    (D) To recommend a policy change

15. What does the speaker say he will do next?

    (A) Interview a guest
    (B) Announce future topics
    (C) Thank a sponsor
    (D) Answer some questions

16. Where is the speaker?

    (A) At a television studio
    (B) At a car dealership
    (C) At a parking garage
    (D) At city hall

17. According to the speaker, what happened yesterday?

    (A) A contract was signed.
    (B) A new product went on sale.
    (C) An article was published.
    (D) A construction project began.

18. What will the speaker do next?

    (A) Demonstrate a process
    (B) Review a product
    (C) Take a tour
    (D) Conduct an interview

ENTRANCE CLOSINGS	
Entrance	Month
Metro Station	May
Bridge Street	June
Orchard Street	July
Stadium Avenue	August

19. What event is the speaker discussing?

    (A) A music festival
    (B) A holiday celebration
    (C) An opening ceremony
    (D) A sporting event

20. Look at the graphic. When is the event being held?

    (A) In May
    (B) In June
    (C) In July
    (D) In August

21. How can the listeners find more information?

    (A) By visiting a Web site
    (B) By listening to a podcast
    (C) By speaking to an agent
    (D) By downloading a mobile application

UNIT 17 인물/강연/설명

새로운 직원, 행사의 연설자 등을 소개하는 내용이나 학회, 박람회 등의 행사에서 강연하거나 설명하는 내용이 출제됩니다.

핵심 포인트 소개 대상의 세부 사항에 대해 묻거나, 특히 다음에 할 일이나 미래에 일어날 일을 묻는 문제가 자주 출제되므로, 지문의 후반부를 놓치지 않고 듣는 것이 중요합니다.

빈출 질문 What will the speaker (most likely) do next? 화자는 다음에 무엇을 할 것인가?

▶ ETS 기출 예제

🔊 650_P4_10

인사	❶ Hi everyone, I hope that you've been enjoying this year's architecture conference.	❶ 안녕하세요, 여러분. 올해의 건축 학회를 즐기고 계시길 바랍니다.
담화의 목적	I'm here to introduce a new product from my company, New Wave Printers.	
세부 사항	Now, you've all used a software program to create models to present a building idea to clients. Well, ❷ with our new 3D printer, the Replicon 3000, you'll experience the most accurate tool on the market for making professional-quality presentation models.	❷ 3D 프린터 레플리콘 3000으로, 시중에서 가장 정확한 도구를 경험하게 되실 겁니다.
다음에 일어날 일	❸ I'd like to show you models that I've made with the Replicon 3000 so you can see just how precise the outcome is.	❸ 제가 레플리콘 3000으로 만든 모형을 몇 개 보여드리고 싶습니다.

정답과 해설 p.114

1. Where is the talk most likely being given?
   담화는 어디에서 이루어지고 있는 것 같은가?
   장소 문제 → 인사 중 언급되는 장소에 주목
   정답 At a professional conference
   전문 학회

2. What does the speaker emphasize about the Replicon 3000? 화자는 레플리콘 3000에 대해 무엇을 강조하는가?
   세부 사항 문제 → 키워드 'Replicon 3000'에 주목
   정답 Its accuracy
   정확성

3. What will the speaker do next?
   화자가 다음에 할 일은 무엇인가?
   다음에 할 일 문제 → 앞으로 할 행동을 표현하는 'I'd like to'에 주목
   정답 Display some models
   몇몇 모형 보여주기

질문의 단서가 되는 주요 표현

I'm honored by this award for Employee of the Year. 연설의 목적은 무엇인가?
Thank you for attending tonight's Business Seminar. 청자들은 어떤 종류의 행사에 참여했는가?
Dr. Smith **is known for his work** as the director of the research lab. 스미스 박사는 무엇으로 유명한가?

ETS 유형 연습

문제를 먼저 읽은 후 담화를 들으면서 답을 고르세요.
다시 듣고 빈칸을 채우세요.

🔊 650_P4_11

정답과 해설 p.114

[1-2]

1. What type of photography is the talk about?
   (A) Fashion
   (B) Travel

2. According to the speaker, what helps a photographer take a good picture?
   (A) Automated focus
   (B) A light source

If you're new to _____, don't worry. As an award-winning photojournalist who has worked _____, I'm here to share with you some easy ways to take an awesome photo. Even _____, the basic principles still apply. Above all, I recommend that you _____. It makes a significant difference in the quality of the image you're capturing.

[3-4]

3. What is the purpose of the speech?
   (A) To inaugurate a company
   (B) To accept an award

4. Why does the speaker say, "I couldn't have done it without my team"?
   (A) She does not have the skills for a task.
   (B) She wants to thank her colleagues.

I feel truly honored by _____ here at Flint and Gray Banking. At the beginning of the year, I was asked to _____ for our account holders. After ten months of _____, we are now able to release a fully functioning application to our users. But I couldn't have done it without my team of programming specialists. They all did a fabulous job. So for that, please join me in giving them a _____.

[5-6]

5. Where is the speech being given?
   (A) At a press conference
   (B) At a trade show

6. How is a business different from its competitors?
   (A) It allows for flexible work schedules.
   (B) It processes international paychecks.

Thanks for stopping by our booth. This is my company's first time at _____. Momentum Online helps businesses like yours _____ new staff. Our Web site allows employers to browse résumés from talented professionals in a variety of specialties. But unlike other Internet-based employment services, our company provides a platform that even makes it possible to pay employees _____. Successful companies and skilled freelancers are already _____.

UNIT 17 | 인물/강연/설명

ETS 실전 문제

1. Where most likely is the interview being held?
   (A) At a health clinic
   (B) At a radio station
   (C) At a publishing company
   (D) At a television studio

2. What is Dr. Meyer's specialty?
   (A) Allergy treatments
   (B) The science of exercise
   (C) Nutritional supplements
   (D) The study of sleep

3. What will Dr. Meyer talk about today?
   (A) A trip she has taken
   (B) An award she has received
   (C) A book she has written
   (D) A foundation she has started

4. Who most likely is the speaker?
   (A) An accountant
   (B) A lawyer
   (C) An engineer
   (D) An architect

5. What problem with a building project does the speaker mention?
   (A) It may require many permits.
   (B) It may violate a local regulation.
   (C) A neighbor has complained about it.
   (D) Costs have exceeded the original budget.

6. What will the speaker most likely do next?
   (A) Respond to questions
   (B) Contact some clients
   (C) Share new cost projections
   (D) Show an image

7. Who is the speaker most likely addressing?
   (A) Equipment suppliers
   (B) Factory employees
   (C) A board of directors
   (D) Potential customers

8. According to the speaker, what will listeners do first?
   (A) Have their pictures taken
   (B) Fill out a survey
   (C) Meet with a nurse
   (D) Watch a video

9. What will the supervisors do?
   (A) Demonstrate machinery operation
   (B) Review an annual budget
   (C) Submit performance records
   (D) Distribute special clothing

10. What field does Dr. Hoffman work in?
    (A) Business
    (B) Education
    (C) Medicine
    (D) Engineering

11. What is said about young people aged thirteen to eighteen?
    (A) They buy more electronics than adults do.
    (B) They frequently participate in after-school programs.
    (C) They prefer online reading sources.
    (D) They are healthier than young people of previous generations.

12. What will Dr. Hoffman do at the end of the week?
    (A) Release a report
    (B) Host a conference
    (C) Accept an award
    (D) Start a new job

13. What is the class mainly about?
    (A) Nature photography
    (B) Native plants
    (C) Weather patterns
    (D) Camping skills

14. What is different about today's class?
    (A) It will end an hour early.
    (B) It will be filmed.
    (C) It will be led by a substitute teacher.
    (D) It will be held indoors.

15. What will the speaker do next?
    (A) Set up some equipment
    (B) Divide the group into pairs
    (C) Take attendance
    (D) Distribute some booklets

16. What will the demonstration video show the listeners how to do?
    (A) Install a ceiling fan
    (B) Assemble a sofa
    (C) Build a computer
    (D) Tile a shower

17. What does the speaker say the listeners can find in a box?
    (A) A manual
    (B) An invoice
    (C) Some coupons
    (D) Some tools

18. What does the speaker suggest having a friend help with?
    (A) Lifting a part
    (B) Conducting a test
    (C) Measuring an area
    (D) Reading instructions

Project	Cost
Bike Lanes	$1 million
Library Expansion	$2 million
Parking Garage	$2.5 million
Community Center	$3 million

19. Who most likely is the speaker?
    (A) An accountant
    (B) A business owner
    (C) A city official
    (D) An architect

20. Look at the graphic. How much will the selected project cost?
    (A) $1 million
    (B) $2 million
    (C) $2.5 million
    (D) $3 million

21. What will the speaker do next?
    (A) Show a video
    (B) Provide additional information
    (C) Visit a library
    (D) Present an award

UNIT 18 여행 / 견학 / 관람

무료 강의

관광지를 소개하거나 공장, 시설 등을 견학하며 해당 장소나 관람 순서 등을 설명하는 내용이 출제됩니다.

핵심 포인트 여행/견학/관람 장소의 세부 사항을 묻거나 문제에서 제시된 문장의 의도를 파악하는 문제도 출제됩니다.
문제에서 제시된 키워드가 지문에서 직접 언급되거나 간접적으로 나타나므로, 그 주변을 놓치지 않고 듣는 것이 중요합니다.

빈출 질문 What is included in the brochure? 안내 책자에 무엇이 포함되어 있는가?
Why does the speaker say, "~"? 화자는 왜 "~"라고 말하는가?

▶ ETS 기출 예제

🔊 650_P4_13

인사/소개	❶ **Welcome to the Museum of Ancient History.** I'm your guide.	❶ 고대사 박물관에 오신 것을 환영합니다.
안내 및 세부 사항 설명	Right now we're in the Egyptian Gallery. We have a lot of unusual artifacts on display. ❷ **Some of you have already asked if you'll get to see some of the famous painted masks you've heard about in books and movies.** As our art conservation experts have told us, those objects are easily damaged by light.	❷ 몇 분께서 책과 영화에서 들은 몇몇 유명한 채색 가면을 볼 수 있는지 벌써 물어보셨는데요.
관련 정보	However, ❸ **if you'd like to learn more about the masks, we have a fantastic book available in the gift shop.**	❸ 가면에 대해 더 알고 싶으시면, 기념품점에서 멋진 책을 구입하실 수 있습니다.

정답과 해설 p.120

1. (Where) is the tour (taking place)? 관람은 어디에서 이루어지고 있는가?
   장소 문제 → 인사 중 언급되는 장소에 주목

   정답 At a history museum
   역사 박물관

2. (Why) does the speaker say, "those objects are easily damaged by light"?
   화자는 왜 "그 물건들은 빛에 의해 쉽게 손상됩니다"라고 말하는가?
   의도 파악 문제 → 제시문 주변에 언급되는 내용에 주목

   정답 To explain why some items are not on display
   일부 품목이 전시되지 않은 이유를 설명하려고

3. (How) can the (listeners) (find) more (information)?
   청자들은 어떻게 추가 정보를 찾을 수 있는가?
   세부 사항 문제 → 키워드 'find more information'에 주목 → learn more

   정답 By purchasing a book
   책을 구입함으로써

질문의 단서가 되는 주요 표현

On this tour, **we'll** visit some buildings with different architectural styles. 관광의 주된 초점은 무엇인가?
Let me show you how those machines work. **Follow me.** 사람들이 다음에 갈 장소는 어디인가?
We apologize for the delay due to poor weather conditions. 지연의 원인은 무엇인가?

ETS 유형 연습

문제를 먼저 읽은 후 담화를 들으면서 답을 고르세요.
다시 듣고 빈칸을 채우세요.

🔊 650_P4_14
정답과 해설 p.120

[1-2]

1. Where does the speaker most likely work?
   (A) At a photography studio
   (B) At an art museum

2. What is *Blanchard's Gaze*?
   (A) A book
   (B) A painting

We will now be _____ named Gold Hall. For this next part of our tour, I ask that you please refrain from taking pictures. The first painting, here on our right, is *The Look*, arguably _____ by Esmeralda Blanchard. What exactly is the woman in the painting looking at? Well, if you guessed the gardener by the pond, you are correct. Historians have recently confirmed this through a letter Blanchard wrote to her sister. You can read more about the correspondence in *Blanchard's Gaze*, _____ which is available in the gift shop.

[3-4]

3. What most likely will listeners do first?
   (A) Watch how tea is produced
   (B) Touch the texture of tea leaves

4. What does the speaker imply when he says, "you won't be able to go through all of them"?
   (A) A product comes in many varieties.
   (B) Some items are very expensive.

Welcome to Danmere Tea Company's factory tour. The first thing we'll do on our tour is visit interactive Introduction Hall, where you'll have the chance to _____ of various textures. Then we'll see the _____ on the factory floor, and finally—in our new Danmere Tasting Room—you'll get to _____ tea drinks. Trust me… you won't be able to go through all of them. I encourage you to walk around and see all the offerings before making your choices. Now, if everyone is ready, let's begin the tour.

[5-6]

5. Where is the talk most likely taking place?
   (A) On an airplane
   (B) On a boat

6. According to the speaker, what will the listeners have an opportunity to do?
   (A) Shop for food and gifts
   (B) Listen to live music

Welcome to beautiful Thompson Lake. Please be advised that _____ approximately two hours. We'll make one stop to give everyone a chance to walk around and _____. There's a _____ near the dock where we're stopping. We'll stay for 30 minutes and then _____ promptly. Please be sure to remain close to _____, so you can hear me announce when we're ready to go.

UNIT 18 | 여행/견학/관람 **125**

ETS 실전 문제

1. According to the speaker, what will be the main focus of the tour?
   (A) Architectural styles
   (B) Local cuisine
   (C) Literary figures
   (D) Traditional farming

2. What does the speaker say about Morales Avenue?
   (A) A famous author used to live there.
   (B) It is the location of a yearly festival.
   (C) It is closed to vehicles.
   (D) A city wall used to stand there.

3. According to the speaker, what can listeners do at the museum?
   (A) View a short film
   (B) Purchase some souvenirs
   (C) See a reproduction of the city
   (D) Attend a lecture

4. According to the speaker, what is unique about a tour?
   (A) It takes place at night.
   (B) It includes gardening tips.
   (C) It ends with a magic show.
   (D) It occurs only once a year.

5. What does the speaker say to avoid?
   (A) Touching the displays
   (B) Recording videos
   (C) Taking photos with a flash
   (D) Speaking loudly

6. Where does the speaker say the listeners can find refreshments?
   (A) In a garden
   (B) In a reception area
   (C) In a cafeteria
   (D) In a gift shop

7. Where is the announcement most likely being heard?
   (A) At a banquet hall
   (B) At a shopping center
   (C) At an aquarium
   (D) At an art museum

8. According to the speaker, what can visitors do at the customer service desk?
   (A) Enter a raffle
   (B) Get a map of the building
   (C) Sign up for a membership
   (D) Rent a locker

9. What does the speaker say will happen in fifteen minutes?
   (A) A show will start.
   (B) The café will begin serving lunch.
   (C) Advance tickets will go on sale.
   (D) A tour group will meet.

10. What is the subject of the talk?
    (A) The score from a sporting event
    (B) The contents of an art exhibit
    (C) The route for a boat ride
    (D) The view from a tower

11. According to the speaker, what is unusual about today?
    (A) Tickets are half price.
    (B) The sky is clear.
    (C) A bridge is closed.
    (D) An island is crowded.

12. What will listeners do in 30 minutes?
    (A) Get on a bus
    (B) Exit a room
    (C) Meet at a bench
    (D) Return a headset

13. What did the listeners receive in the reception lobby?

(A) A printed recipe
(B) A product sample
(C) A discount coupon
(D) An entry ticket

14. What does the speaker say the listeners will learn about?

(A) A company's history
(B) An upcoming marketing campaign
(C) A production process
(D) A safety procedure

15. According to the speaker, what recently took place?

(A) A negotiation
(B) A renovation
(C) A relocation
(D) A merger

16. What type of volunteer work are the listeners going to do?

(A) Arts education
(B) Health services
(C) Community development
(D) Environmental conservation

17. Why does the speaker say, "each of you will be assigned a mentor"?

(A) To reject a proposal
(B) To request feedback
(C) To correct some information
(D) To encourage participation

18. What does the speaker remind the listeners about?

(A) Taking some notes
(B) Wearing safety glasses
(C) Signing a waiver
(D) Reading a manual

Exhibit	On loan from ...
Painting Achievements	The Portuguese Fund
Modern Printing	The Acker Family
Swiss Photography	Bern University
Dutch Sculpture	The Amsterdam Collection

19. What did the Megahurst Art Gallery recently do?

(A) It opened a new location.
(B) It began offering art classes.
(C) It joined an art organization.
(D) It stopped permitting photography.

20. What is included with the brochure?

(A) A discount coupon
(B) A restaurant menu
(C) A schedule of events
(D) A membership application

21. Look at the graphic. What exhibit will the tour group visit first?

(A) Painting Achievements
(B) Modern Printing
(C) Swiss Photography
(D) Dutch Sculpture

PART 4 | 빈출 표현

제품/서비스 문의 메시지

contact 연락하다
extension (number) 내선번호
respond to ~에 대해 회신하다
inquiry about ~에 대한 문의
receipt 영수증
policy 정책, 방침
manufacturer 제조업체, 생산자
discount 할인(하다)
bill 청구서, 계산서
statement 내역서
purchase 구매(하다)
shipment 운송품, 선적
merchandise 상품, 물품(= goods)
retailer 소매업자
place an order 주문하다
customer service representative 고객 서비스 담당자

고장/수리 메시지

recall 회수하다
replace 교체하다
fix 수리하다, 고치다(= repair)
manufacturing flaw 제조 결함
inconvenience 불편
compensate 보상하다
purchase price 구매가
mailing address (우편물을 받는) 주소

일정 문의

appointment 약속, 예약
reschedule 예정을 다시 세우다, 일정을 변경하다
be delayed 지연되다
shop hours (가게의) 영업 시간
office[business] hours 업무 시간
hours of operation 운영 시간
confirm a reservation 예약을 확정하다
make a reservation 예약하다

메시지

reach 연락이 닿다
beep 삐 하는 소리
hotline 핫라인, 직통 전화 (번호)
tone 발신음, 신호음
connect 연결하다
star key (전화기) 별표(*)
pound key (전화기) 우물 정자(#)
voice mail 음성 사서함
automated message 자동 응답 메시지
leave a message 메시지를 남기다
take a message 메시지를 받아 적다
return one's call ~에게 회신 전화를 하다
get back to ~에게 나중에 회신 전화를 하다
stay on the line 전화를 끊지 않고 기다리다
after the tone 신호음이 나온 후에

사내 공지

bulletin board 게시판
board of directors 이사회
on short notice 충분한 예고 없이, 갑자기
security policy 보안 정책
ID badge 신분증, 사원증
go into effect 실시되다
check in 출입 절차를 밟다
work assignment 작업 할당
modify 변경하다, 바꾸다
maintenance 관리, 정비
installation 설치
expand 확장하다
service person 수리공, 정비공
energy-efficient 에너지 효율성이 좋은
safety measures 안전 조치

교통 안내 방송

flight 항공편
destination 목적지
arrivals board 도착 안내 게시판
due to ~ 때문에
engine trouble 엔진 고장
proceed to ~로 가다
shut down (기계가) 멈추다, 정지하다, 정지시키다

쇼핑 센터

patron 고객; 후원자
register 금전등록기, 계산대
sales representative 영업사원
grocery 식료품, 잡화
retail outlet 소매점
raffle 추첨 행사, 경품 행사
shopping complex 쇼핑 단지
coatroom 휴대품 보관소
checkout (counter) 계산대
customer service counter 고객 서비스 창구

행사장

performance 공연
exhibition 전시회
ticket counter 매표소
complimentary 무료의
audience 청중, 관람객
demonstration 시범 설명
sound equipment 음향 장비
auditorium 강당
hold 열다, 개최하다
arrange 미리 정하다, 준비하다
opening ceremony 개막식, 개회식
establishment 시설, 업체
prepare for ~을 준비하다
can't wait to 빨리 ~하고 싶어 하다

PART 4 | 빈출 표현

인물 소개

commitment 헌신, 전념
congratulate 축하하다
guest speaker 초청 연사
keynote speaker 기조 연설자
inspire 격려하다, 영감을 주다
positive attitude 긍정적인 태도
contribute 공헌하다, 기여하다

시상식

honored 영예로운
fabulous 멋진
present an award to ~에게 시상하다
best known for ~로 가장 유명한[잘 알려진]
do an outstanding job 뛰어난 업적을 이루다
prestigious award 권위 있는 상
awards ceremony 시상식
recognize (공로를) 인정하다, 표창하다
devoted 헌신적인
thanks to ~ 덕분에
on behalf of ~을 대표해서, ~을 대신해서
be pleased to ~하게 되어 기쁘다
announce that ~을 알리다
make a speech 연설하다 (= give a speech)
win an award 상을 받다
meet[achieve] a goal 목표를 달성하다
give a round of applause for
~에게 큰 박수를 보내다

관광/견학

event hall 이벤트 홀
cafeteria 구내 식당
snack bar 매점
kiosk 매점
refreshments 다과, 음식물
landmark 주요 지형지물, 역사적 건조물
state-of-the-art 최첨단의, 최고급의
turn off mobile phones 휴대폰을 끄다
take pictures of ~ 사진을 찍다
souvenir 기념품
itinerary 여행 일정
historical site 유적지
brochure 안내 책자
tourist attraction 관광 명소
scenic spot 경치 좋은 장소

광고

a new line (상품의) 새로운 종류, 신제품 라인
beverage 음료
machine 기계
appliance (가전)제품
office furniture 사무용 가구
art supplies 미술용품
catering order 출장 음식 주문
product 상품, 물품

패러프레이징 빈출 표현 (단어 → 단어)

see 보다	→ view 보다
staff 직원	→ employee 직원
e-mail 이메일을 보내다	→ send 보내다
submit 제출하다	→ send 보내다
gather 모이다	→ meet 만나다
type 타자를 치다	→ enter 입력하다
release 공개하다	→ introduce 소개하다
encourage 권장하다	→ advise 조언하다
supermarket 슈퍼마켓	→ store 상점
outing 야유회	→ trip (짧은) 여행
productivity 생산성	→ efficiency 효율성
movie 영화	→ film 영화
footwear 신발(류)	→ shoes 신발
policy 정책	→ procedure 절차
head 책임자, 장	→ supervisor 관리자
competition 경연대회	→ contest 시합
thoroughly 철저히	→ carefully 신중하게
recently 최근에	→ lately 최근에
space 공간	→ room 자리, 공간
author 저자	→ writer 작가
electronically 온라인으로	→ online 온라인으로
revitalize 부흥시키다	→ improve 향상시키다
singer 가수	→ performer 공연자
dessert 디저트	→ refreshments 다과
appointment 진료 예약	→ consultation (의사와의) 상담

패러프레이징 빈출 표현 (단어 → 구 / 구 → 단어)

film 촬영하다	→ direct a film 영화를 감독하다
expo 박람회	→ trade show 무역 박람회
collaborate 협력하다	→ work together 함께 일하다
in-flight 기내의	→ on an airplane 기내에서
order 주문하다	→ place an order 주문하다
mayor 시장	→ city official 시 공무원
distribute 배부하다	→ hand out 나누어 주다
establish 설립하다	→ set up 세우다
economist 경제학자	→ economic expert 경제 전문가
guitar 기타	→ musical instrument 악기
detour 우회로	→ alternate route 대체 도로
sign up 신청하다	→ register 등록하다
come up with ~을 생각해 내다	→ brainstorm 아이디어를 모으다
take a look at ~을 살펴보다	→ inspect 점검하다
schedule an appointment 약속을 잡다	→ contact 연락하다
receive your money back 돈을 돌려 받다	→ refund 환불
a lot less noisy 훨씬 덜 시끄러운	→ quiet 조용한
songwriter and singer 작곡가 겸 가수	→ musician 음악가

READING COMPREHENSION

PART 5 & 6

단문, 장문 빈칸 채우기

INTRO
UNIT 01 문장의 구성 요소
UNIT 02 명사
UNIT 03 대명사
UNIT 04 형용사
UNIT 05 부사
UNIT 06 동사의 형태와 종류
UNIT 07 수 일치
UNIT 08 시제
UNIT 09 능동태와 수동태
UNIT 10 to부정사와 동명사
UNIT 11 분사
UNIT 12 전치사와 접속사
UNIT 13 부사절 접속사
UNIT 14 관계대명사
UNIT 15 명사절 접속사
UNIT 16 비교구문
UNIT 17 어휘 1: 명사/형용사
UNIT 18 어휘 2: 동사/부사

 무료 강의

INTRO
PART 5 & 6 — 단문, 장문 빈칸 채우기

📄 PART 5 30문항,
PART 6 16문항

Part 5는 완전한 한 문장을 만들기 위해 빈칸에 들어갈 단어나 어구를 선택지에서 고르는 유형으로, 총 30문제가 출제됩니다. Part 6는 완전한 지문을 만들기 위해 4개의 빈칸에 들어갈 단어나 어구, 문장을 선택지에서 고르는 유형으로, 총 4개의 지문(16문제)이 출제됩니다.

▶ PART 5와 PART 6는 이런 점이 다르다

1. Part 5는 완전한 한 문장을 완성하고, Part 6는 완전한 한 지문을 완성합니다.
2. Part 6는 Part 5와는 달리 한 문장 안에서 정답의 근거를 찾지 못하는 경우가 많습니다.

▶ PART 5는 이렇게 풀자

101. All tags should be ------- attached to luggage.

(A) secure
(B) security
(C) securely
(D) securing

102. Prices on select sofas will be ------- by up to 50 percent this weekend only.

(A) softened
(B) arranged
(C) reduced
(D) made

101 〔문법 문제〕

빈칸과 주변 요소 간의 관계를 살펴봅니다. 문장의 주어와 동사, 빈칸에 필요한 품사 등을 파악할 수 있으면 비교적 쉽게 해결할 수 있는 문제 유형입니다.

→ 빈칸은 수동태 동사 be attached를 수식하는 부사 자리이다. 따라서 (C) securely가 정답이다.

102 〔어휘 문제〕

문장의 주어, 동사, 목적어 중심으로 해석한 후, 빈칸 주변 단어를 확인합니다. 문장의 상황이나 뉘앙스에 맞는 어휘를 선택해야 하므로 빠르게 읽고 해석하는 것이 중요합니다.

→ 빈칸 뒤의 by up to 50 percent this weekend only와 함께 '(가격이) 50퍼센트까지 할인되다'라는 의미를 완성하는 (C) reduced가 정답이다.

▶ PART 6는 이렇게 풀자

Santina Botanical Garden boasts an impressively wide-ranging collection of rosebushes. Indeed, the ------- features hundreds of rose varieties. ------- are rare and ancient specimens. Among
     131.   **132.**
these are double-blooming roses, climbing roses, heirloom roses, and even the rare blue rose, which actually appears lilac in color. Santina's rose garden is spread out ------- approximately
                                                                                133.
2,200 square meters of land. Seventeen full-time gardening and landscaping experts dedicate themselves to tending these treasured roses. ------- .
                                                                        134.

131. (A) booklet   (B) posting
       (C) property   (D) method

132. (A) Others   **(B) Some**
       (C) None   (D) Both

133. (A) by   (B) from
       (C) after   (D) across

134. (A) This floral marvel is not to be missed, so plan your visit accordingly.
       (B) Rose arrangements make spectacular anniversary gifts.
       (C) On the other hand, Santina Botanical Garden is privately owned.
       (D) That year, we showcased vibrant water plants in our large pond.

131   어휘 문제

Part 6의 어휘 문제는 Part 5와 달리 한 문장 안에서 정답을 찾을 수 없는 경우도 있습니다. 따라서 전체 글의 흐름을 파악해야 하거나, 문장 앞뒤의 유기적 관계를 파악해야 한다는 점에 유의해야 합니다.

→ 빈칸 앞 문장에서 산티나 식물원(Santina Botanical Garden)에 대해 언급하고 있으므로 식물원을 대신할 수 있는 (C) property가 정답이다.

132 / 133   문법 문제

Part 6의 문법 문제는 대게 한 문장 안에서 정답을 찾을 수 있지만, 시제나 대명사 문제는 앞뒤 문맥, 글의 종류 및 주제 등을 통해 정답을 찾아야 합니다.

→ **132** 빈칸 앞에서 수백 종의 장미를 언급했고, 빈칸 뒤 rare and ancient specimens는 수백 종의 장미 중 일부이므로 '일부'를 나타내는 대명사 (B) Some이 정답이다.

→ **133** 빈칸 뒤 approximately 2,200 square meters of land와 함께 '약 2,200평방미터의 땅에 걸쳐 있다'는 의미가 되어야 자연스러우므로 전치사 (A) by가 정답이다.

134   문장 고르기 문제

① 전반적인 지문 흐름과 빈칸 앞뒤 문장을 확인합니다.
② 선택지를 빈칸에 넣어 글의 흐름이 자연스러운지 확인합니다.
③ 지문에서 언급하지 않은 아이디어를 사용한 오답을 소거합니다.

→ 빈칸 앞 글 전반에 걸쳐 산티나 식물원의 훌륭한 장미 나무 컬렉션에 대해 홍보하고 있으므로 글을 마무리하는 마지막에는 꽃 구경을 놓치지 않도록 방문 계획을 잘 세우라는 당부가 나오는 것이 글의 흐름상 자연스럽다. 따라서 (A)가 정답이다.

UNIT 01 문장의 구성 요소

무료 강의

1 주어와 동사

문장에는 반드시 동사가 있으며 be동사, 일반동사, <조동사 + 동사>의 형태로 존재합니다.

We **are** friends.
We always **go** together.

▶ **주어** | 동작을 행하는 주체

주어는 우리말로 '~은[는], ~이[가]'에 해당하는 말로, 주로 사람이나 사물, 개념을 나타내는 (대)명사가 주어 역할을 담당합니다. 물론 주어인 명사를 꾸미는 말이 함께 와서 길어질 수도 있습니다.

All employees must wear a uniform. 모든 직원은 유니폼을 입어야 한다.
　　주어

The flight to Tokyo was delayed. 도쿄행 항공편이 지연되었다.
　주어　　주어를 꾸미는 말 (UNIT 12 전치사와 접속사 참고)

The computers repaired by the technician are now ready for use.
　주어　　　주어를 꾸미는 말 (UNIT 11 분사 참고)
그 기술자에 의해 수리된 컴퓨터들은 이제 사용할 수 있다.

> **LEVEL UP** 주어 없이 동사원형으로 시작하는 명령문
>
> 명령문은 주어인 you가 생략된 형태, 즉 주어 없이 동사로 시작하는데, 이때 동사는 동사원형으로만 등장합니다.
>
> Please **send** me your final draft. 당신의 최종 원고를 제게 보내주세요.
> 　　　~~sends, sending~~

▶ **동사** | 사람이나 사물의 움직임이나 상태를 나타내는 말

동사는 주어 뒤에서 주어의 동작이나 상태를 나타내는 말입니다. be동사는 물론이고 <조동사(will, can 등)+동사원형>도 이에 해당합니다. 한 개의 절에는 한 개의 동사만 존재하고, 동사 앞에 to가 붙거나 뒤에 -ing가 붙은 형태는 동사가 아닙니다.

Mobile phones **are** very useful. 휴대전화들은 매우 유용하다.
　　　　　　동사

We **replaced** the fax machine. 우리는 팩스기를 교체했다.
　　동사

Employees working late **should lock** the door. 늦게까지 일하는 직원들은 문을 잠가야 한다.
　　　　　　　　　　　동사

ETS 유형 연습

다음 문장의 빈칸에 들어갈 알맞은 말을 고르세요.

정답과 해설 p.126

STEP 1

1. The main ------- of the new electronic notepad is Internet use.
   (A) function
   (B) functional

2. Mr. Lee recently ------- a tour of the company's main production facility.
   (A) to conduct
   (B) conducted

3. ------- of the shipment should be expected within ten days.
   (A) Receive
   (B) Receipt

4. Please ------- the enclosed survey and return it to our office.
   (A) complete
   (B) completed

STEP 2

5. During the contract talks, Ms. Imura proved that she is an excellent -------.
   (A) negotiate
   (B) negotiated
   (C) negotiating
   (D) negotiator

6. The ------- of the carpet can be completed as soon as the office furniture is moved.
   (A) installed
   (B) installation
   (C) installers
   (D) install

7. Online shoppers should note that products may ------- in appearance from the images shown on a Web site.
   (A) different
   (B) differed
   (C) to differ
   (D) differ

8. Mr. Caine requested that the board ------- be rescheduled.
   (A) met
   (B) meets
   (C) to meet
   (D) meeting

| 어휘 | 1 main 주요한　function 기능; 기능을 하다　2 production facility 생산 시설　3 shipment 선적(물)　receipt 수령, 받기; 영수증　4 enclosed 동봉된　complete 작성하다　5 contract 계약　talks 협상, 회담　prove 입증하다　negotiator 협상가　6 complete 완료하다　install 설치하다　installation 설치　7 note 유의하다　appearance 외관　differ 다르다　8 board 이사회　reschedule 일정을 변경하다

② 목적어

타동사 뒤에는 목적어가 오는데
명사(구), 대명사, to부정사, 동명사, 명사절이
대표적인 목적어 형태입니다.

The peacock has beautiful **feathers**.
It likes **to sing**.

▶ **목적어** | 주어+동사+목적어

대부분의 동사 뒤에는 우리말의 '~을[를]'에 해당하는 목적어가 등장합니다. 이렇게 뒤에 목적어가 필요한 동사를 '타동사'라고 부르며 (대)명사나 to부정사구, 동명사구, 명사절이 타동사 뒤에서 목적어 역할을 하게 됩니다.

명사	We **had** <u>a discussion</u> with the sales staff. 우리는 영업사원들과 논의했다. 　　　동사　목적어(명사)	
	Mr. Baek **gives** <u>new employees</u> <u>an orientation</u>. 백 씨는 신입사원들에게 예비 교육을 해준다. 　　　　　　동사　　목적어 1(~에게)　　목적어 2(~을)	
	→ 동사에 따라 목적어 두 개가 나오는 경우도 있습니다. give(주다), offer(제공하다) 등의 동사가 이에 해당됩니다.	
대명사	Corv Graphics **will help** <u>us</u> to create a new logo. 코브 그래픽 사는 우리가 새 로고를 만드는 데 도움을 줄 것이다. 　　　　　　　동사　　목적어(대명사)	
to부정사구	They **agreed** <u>to revise</u> the plan. 그들은 계획을 수정하는 것에 동의했다. 　　　동사　　목적어(to부정사)	
동명사구	Ms. Eaves **suggested** <u>changing</u> the current supplier. 이브 씨는 현 납품 업체를 바꿀 것을 제안했다. 　　　　　　동사　　목적어(동명사)	
명사절	Apollo, Inc. **announced** <u>that it is acquiring Luzon Manufacturing</u>. 　　　　　　　동사　　　　목적어(주어+동사로 이루어진 명사절) 아폴로 사는 루존 제조사를 인수할 것이라고 발표했다.	

> **LEVEL UP**　목적어가 필요 없는 자동사
>
> 동사 뒤에 목적어가 없는 경우도 있습니다. 예를 들어 '오르다, 상승하다'라는 뜻의 rise 같은 동사가 '~을 상승하다'라고 해석되면 어색하죠? 이렇게 목적어가 필요 없는 동사들을 '자동사'라고 부르는데 이런 자동사 뒤에는 주로 부사나 전치사구가 등장한다는 점을 기억해 두면 좋습니다.
>
> Prices **are rising** <u>sharply</u>. 물가가 급격히 오르고 있다.
> 　　　　　　　　　부사
> The CEO **spoke** <u>to the shareholders</u>. CEO는 주주들에게 호소했다.
> 　　　　　　전치사(to)+명사(the shareholders)로 이루어진 전치사구

ETS 유형 연습

다음 문장의 빈칸에 들어갈 알맞은 말을 고르세요.

정답과 해설 p.126

STEP 1

1. The city's library will accept ------- of used books until June 30.
   (A) donates
   (B) donations

2. Local artists sell their handmade ------- every Saturday morning.
   (A) creative
   (B) creations

3. Mr. Martin has decided ------- the planning meeting because of a scheduling conflict.
   (A) postpones
   (B) to postpone

4. After remaining high for several days, temperatures finally fell ------- yesterday.
   (A) slight
   (B) slightly

STEP 2

5. CEO Donald Farajo issued a brief ------- on the merger proposal to the international financial press.
   (A) stated
   (B) stating
   (C) statement
   (D) state

6. Electric vehicles are expected to gain wider ------- once their battery life is improved.
   (A) acceptance
   (B) acceptable
   (C) acceptingly
   (D) accepted

7. Remember to obtain written ------- from a supervisor before placing an order for office supplies.
   (A) authorize
   (B) authorized
   (C) authorizes
   (D) authorization

8. Mr. Oliver gave the customers some samples to show ------- what the fabric looked like.
   (A) they
   (B) them
   (C) their
   (D) themselves

| 어휘 | 1 accept 받다 used 사용된, 중고의 2 handmade 수제의, 수공의 creative 창조의, 창의적인 creation 창작(품)
3 decide 결정하다 planning 기획 scheduling conflict 일정상의 충돌 4 slightly 조금 5 issue 발표하다
brief 간략한 merger proposal 합병 제안 financial 금융의 press 언론 6 vehicle 차량 gain 얻다
acceptance 수용, 받아들임 7 obtain 얻다 office supplies 사무용품 authorization 승인 8 fabric 옷감

UNIT 01 | 문장의 구성 요소

3 보어

동사 뒤에는 주어나 목적어를 보충하는 보어가 오는데 명사나 형용사가 그 역할을 합니다.

He is **a superhero**. 명사 보어
He is **fantastic** and **powerful**. 형용사 보어

▶ **주격 보어** | 주어+동사+주격 보어

보어는 주어나 목적어의 성질, 상태, 신분 등을 보충 설명하는 말로, 명사나 형용사가 보어 역할을 합니다. 주격 보어란 주어의 의미를 보충하는 말입니다.

주어 + be동사 ~이다   become ~이 되다   remain ~인 채로 남다
         appear ~인 듯하다 seem ~처럼 보이다   stay ~인 채로 머무르다   + 주격 보어

Mr. Kraus **was** a major **asset** to the sales team. 크라우스 씨는 판매팀의 핵심 인재였다.
→ 보어가 주어와 동격(크라우스 씨 = 핵심 인재)일 때, 즉 '~이다'라고 해석이 되는 주격 보어 자리에는 명사가 옵니다.

The number of technicians available **is insufficient**. 작업 가능한 기술자 인원이 불충분하다.
→ 보어가 주어의 상태를 표현할 때, 즉 '~(하)다'라고 해석이 되는 주격 보어 자리에는 형용사가 옵니다.

▶ **목적격 보어** | 주어+동사+목적어+목적격 보어

목적격 보어란 목적어를 보충 설명하는 말로, 명사나 형용사가 사용되며 부사는 보어가 될 수 없습니다. '목적어와 목적격 보어'의 관계는 '주어와 주격 보어'의 관계처럼 이해하면 됩니다.

주어 + make ~이 …하게 만들다   keep ~을 …로 유지하다
       find ~이 …임을 알다/깨닫다 consider ~을 …라고 여기다   + 목적어 + 목적격 보어

The music **made** the performance (**impressive** / impression / impressively). 음악은 공연을 감명 깊게 만들었다.
→ 목적격 보어가 목적어인 the performance의 상태를 설명하므로 형용사 impressive가 옵니다.

I **found** the book **easy**. 나는 그 책이 쉽다고 생각했다.
I **found** the book **easily**. 나는 그 책을 쉽게 찾아냈다.
→ easy는 목적어인 the book의 상태를 설명하는 목적격 보어로 쓰였습니다. 하지만 easily는 목적격 보어가 아니라 동사 found를 수식하는 부사라서 보어와는 달리 생략할 수도 있습니다.

ETS 유형 연습

다음 문장의 빈칸에 들어갈 알맞은 말을 고르세요.

정답과 해설 p.127

STEP 1

1. Sun Foods, Inc., has become a ------- in selling processed foods in China.
   (A) leader
   (B) leading

2. Ms. Chu was extremely ------- to receive the award for outstanding sales performance.
   (A) happy
   (B) happily

3. With its light weight, the latest Apurage vacuum cleaner is ------- to carry.
   (A) ease
   (B) easy

4. Experts remain ------- about the stability of Eastside Technology's stock.
   (A) optimistically
   (B) optimistic

STEP 2

5. Ms. Inoue is ------- that she can finalize the budget proposal next week.
   (A) positivity
   (B) positives
   (C) positively
   (D) positive

6. Due to her strong background, Ms. Sakai was a natural ------- to lead Celina Legal Associates.
   (A) choose
   (B) chosen
   (C) to choose
   (D) choice

7. The competition for qualified medical personnel has become ------- in recent years.
   (A) intense
   (B) intensity
   (C) intensively
   (D) intensifying

8. Many of our employees have reported that they have found the new computer program quite -------.
   (A) benefit
   (B) benefits
   (C) benefitting
   (D) beneficial

| 어휘 | 1 processed food 가공식품 2 extremely 매우, 극도로 outstanding 뛰어난 performance 실적 3 weight 무게 vacuum cleaner 진공 청소기 4 expert 전문가 stability 안정성 stock 주식 5 finalize 마무리 짓다 budget 예산 proposal 제안 6 due to ~ 때문에 choice 선택된 사람[것] 7 qualified 자격을 갖춘 personnel 직원 intense 치열한 8 benefit 혜택; 이익을 얻다, ~에게 이롭다 beneficial 유익한, 이로운

UNIT 01 | 문장의 구성 요소

ETS 실전 문제

1. Business travelers should purchase a suitcase that meets all the ------- for an airplane carry-on.
   (A) requires
   (B) requiring
   (C) requirements
   (D) required

2. Amplono Industries' latest product is a ------- of a mobile phone and a lightweight tablet computer.
   (A) combine
   (B) combination
   (C) combines
   (D) combined

3. The main ------- of the Pine Ridge Hotel is its stunning views of the countryside.
   (A) appeal
   (B) appeals
   (C) appealed
   (D) appealing

4. The Felton Engineering Conference ------- are pleased to have Dr. Gerard Wylie as this year's keynote speaker.
   (A) organizers
   (B) organizing
   (C) organizational
   (D) organizationally

5. The consensus among the members of the focus group is that the salad dressing is ------- enough.
   (A) sweeten
   (B) sweet
   (C) sweetly
   (D) sweetest

6. Please ------- the owner's manual before using your Kivi Craft oven for the first time.
   (A) consulting
   (B) consulted
   (C) consults
   (D) consult

7. It is Namgung Consulting's policy to make a job ------- without delay when the right applicant is found.
   (A) offerings
   (B) is offered
   (C) offer
   (D) offers

8. The finance department has submitted an initial budget ------- for upgrading our billing system.
   (A) estimate
   (B) estimates
   (C) estimating
   (D) estimations

9. McDuffy Cleaners and Tailors is known for its expert ------- of formal wear.
   (A) alters
   (B) altered
   (C) alterations
   (D) alterable

10. Sometimes employees need ------- to take risks and try new ways to solve problems.
    (A) encouraged
    (B) to encourage
    (C) encouragement
    (D) encouragingly

Questions 11-14 refer to the following e-mail.

To: Employees <employees@braffordtech.com>
From: Joanna Spatz <joanna.spatz@braffordtech.com>
Date: September 5
Subject: Party for Camella Bard

Hello everyone,

As you know, one of our sales representatives, Camella Bard, was ------- a few months ago. As part of her new role, she was given ------- sales responsibilities. These new duties have required her to spend the last four weeks on the road. Although we have not seen Camella for some time, she is still very much a part of the Brafford Tech family here at the office. I am ------- organizing a party to celebrate her new role and welcome her back to the office when she returns in two weeks. ------- . I would appreciate the help, and I hope that all of you can be there.

Sincerely,

Joanna Spatz

11. (A) honored
    (B) featured
    (C) promoted
    (D) discovered

12. (A) to increase
    (B) increases
    (C) increase
    (D) increased

13. (A) also
    (B) then
    (C) therefore
    (D) nevertheless

14. (A) Please let me know if you are able to contribute anything.
    (B) The company has a lot to celebrate this year.
    (C) Camella has worked for Brafford Tech for more than six years.
    (D) We hope that Camella returns to the office within the year.

UNIT 02 명사

무료 강의

❶ 명사의 역할과 자리

명사는 문장에서 주어, 목적어, 보어 역할을 합니다.

Cake is delicious. 주어
We can't resist **cake**. 목적어
That is Dad's birthday **cake**! 보어

▶ **명사의 형태** | -tion/-sion/-ance/-ment/-ty 등으로 끝나는 단어

| participation 참가 | discussion 토론 | assistance 도움 | movement 이동 | ability 능력 |

▶ **명사의 역할**

❶ 주어	동사 앞	The **seminar was canceled** because of rain. 비 때문에 세미나가 취소되었다.
❷ 목적어	타동사 뒤	The inspectors **checked** the **equipment** yesterday. 조사관들이 어제 장비를 점검했다.
	전치사 뒤	Dr. Aoki is an expert **in education**. 아오키 박사는 교육 분야의 전문가이다. → 전치사 뒤에는 항상 명사가 따라오는데 그 명사를 전치사의 목적어라고 합니다.
❸ 보어		Mr. Bacon **was** a **consultant** at a hospital. 베이컨 씨는 병원의 상담가였다.

→ 동사나 전치사 바로 뒤에 항상 명사부터 나오는 것은 아닙니다. 명사를 수식하는 형용사가 먼저 오는 경우도 많습니다.

The company provides **educational programs**. 그 회사는 교육 프로그램을 제공한다.
　　　　　동사　　　　　형용사　　　명사

▶ **명사의 자리**

❶ a(n) / the 뒤

　The receptionist called **an ambulance**. 접수원이 구급차를 불렀다.

❷ 소유격 뒤

　The price of **Ashland Food's stock** increased. 애쉴랜드 푸드 사의 주가가 올랐다.

❸ 형용사 뒤

　We hired **additional employees**. 우리는 추가 인력들을 고용했다.

ETS 유형 연습

다음 문장의 빈칸에 들어갈 알맞은 말을 고르세요.

정답과 해설 p.129

STEP 1

1. A ------- of souvenirs can be found in the gift shop.
   (A) various
   (B) variety

2. Please remember to include your -------- at the bottom of the order form.
   (A) signed
   (B) signature

3. The ------- of cameras is prohibited during the performance.
   (A) operate
   (B) operation

4. For reasons of -------, anyone entering the construction area must wear a hard hat.
   (A) safety
   (B) safely

STEP 2

5. According to last month's -------, retail sales are expected to double this quarter.
   (A) report
   (B) to report
   (C) reported
   (D) reportedly

6. A thorough ------- of paragraph 6 should be made before the letter is signed.
   (A) revision
   (B) revised
   (C) revising
   (D) revise

7. Richbrock Art Museum has one extremely valuable ------- in its collection.
   (A) drawing
   (B) drawn
   (C) draw
   (D) drew

8. Kumiko Sekine will give a ------- on watercolor techniques on May 3.
   (A) demonstration
   (B) demonstrating
   (C) demonstrated
   (D) demonstrators

| 어휘 | 1 souvenir 기념품 2 at the bottom of ~의 하단에, 밑바닥에 3 be prohibited 금지되다 performance 공연
4 construction area 건설 현장 hard hat 안전모 5 retail 소매 double 두 배가 되다 quarter 사분기
6 thorough 철저한 revision 검토, 수정 7 extremely 극히 valuable 귀중한 drawing 그림
8 give a demonstration 시연해 보이다 watercolor 수채화 technique 기법 demonstrator 시연하는 사람

2 셀 수 있는 명사와 셀 수 없는 명사

셀 수 없는 명사는 앞에 a(n)을 쓰지 않고, 뒤에 -(e)s를 붙일 수 없습니다.

Access is strictly prohibited.
An access (**X**)　　**Access**es (**X**)

▶ **셀 수 있는 명사** | 가산명사

셀 수 있는 명사를 쓸 때는 하나(단수)인지, 여러 개(복수)인지를 반드시 표시해야 합니다. 단수명사 앞에는 하나를 의미하는 a(n)을 붙이고 복수명사는 마지막에 -(e)s를 붙입니다.

We plan to hire ＋ an assistant. / assistants. / ~~assistant.~~

우리는 보조 한 명을 고용할 계획이다.
보조들을

→ 가산명사는 관사나 -(e)s 없이 단독으로 쓸 수 없습니다.

빈출 가산명사

price 가격	estimate 견적(서)	opening 공석	product 제품
permit 허가증	refund 환불	location 위치	order 주문
discount 할인	result 결과	increase 증가	plan 계획

▶ **셀 수 없는 명사** | 불가산명사

셀 수 없는 명사는 단수, 복수의 개념이 없어서 앞에 a(n)이 올 수 없으며 뒤에 -(e)s도 붙지 않습니다. 하지만 형태는 단수와 동일하므로 뒤에 오는 동사도 단수 형태가 됩니다.

Access / ~~An access~~ / ~~Accesses~~ ＋ to this building **is** restricted. 이 건물에 대한 접근이 제한됩니다.

빈출 불가산명사

advice 조언	research 연구	information 정보	furniture 가구
access 접근	employment 고용	luggage/baggage 짐	machinery 기계류
consent 동의	stationery 문구류	equipment 장비	merchandise 상품

LEVEL UP　사람 명사는 대표적인 가산명사

동사 뒤에 -er[or], -ee, -ant, -ist 등이 붙으면 '~하는 사람'을 의미하는 명사가 됩니다. 사람 명사는 관사나 -(e)s 없이 단독으로 쓸 수 없는 데 유의합니다.

employer 고용주	employee 직원	consumer 소비자	supervisor 상사
applicant 지원자	accountant 회계사	assistant 조수	client 고객
candidate 후보자	representative 직원	receptionist 접수원	guide 안내인
architect 건축가	critic 비평가	professional 전문가	official 공무원

ETS 유형 연습

다음 문장의 빈칸에 들어갈 알맞은 말을 고르세요.

정답과 해설 p.130

STEP 1

1. The best salespeople first establish a ------- of trust with their potential buyers.
   (A) sense
   (B) senses

2. A processing fee of $3.00 will be added to ------- received by telephone.
   (A) order
   (B) orders

3. Mr. Rivera has just been appointed to a senior management -------.
   (A) position
   (B) positions

4. Star Transportation ordered new office ------- last month.
   (A) furniture
   (B) desk

STEP 2

5. The supervisors decided to delay ------- until they could fill the entire order.
   (A) ship
   (B) shipped
   (C) shipper
   (D) shipment

6. So far this quarter, regional sales of compact cars have surpassed industry analysts' -------.
   (A) predicts
   (B) predicted
   (C) predictions
   (D) predictable

7. D & Y Beauty Corporation plans to add at least one ------- overseas in the next year.
   (A) locations
   (B) location
   (C) locates
   (D) locating

8. On -------, our employees stay with the company for about six years.
   (A) average
   (B) averagely
   (C) averaging
   (D) averaged

| 어휘 | 1 establish 확립하다 trust 신뢰 potential 잠재적인 2 processing fee 수수료 order 주문(품); 주문하다
3 be appointed 임명되다 management 경영, 관리 4 transportation 운송 5 supervisor 관리자 entire 전체의 6 so far 지금까지 sales 매출 compact car 소형차 surpass 초과하다 analyst 분석가 predict 예상하다, 예측하다 prediction 예상, 예측 7 at least 적어도, 최소 overseas 해외에 8 average 평균; 평균 ~이 되다

③ 한정사의 개념과 종류

한정사는 명사의 의미를 한정하는 말로, 명사에 따라 어울리는 한정사가 각기 다릅니다.

The dog wants **a few** bones.
The cat wants **a little** meat.
The pig wants **all** the food.

▶ 한정사의 개념

명사의 의미를 한정시키는 말을 한정사라고 하는데 셀 수 있는 명사(가산명사)의 단수형 앞에는 반드시 한정사가 와야 합니다.

▶ 한정사의 종류

❶ 관사: a(n) 뒤에는 셀 수 있는 명사(가산명사)의 단수형을 쓰고, the 뒤에는 어떤 명사든지 쓸 수 있습니다.

관사	셀 수 있는 명사	셀 수 없는 명사
a(n)	a computer, ~~a computers~~	~~an equipment~~
the	the computer, the computers	the equipment

❷ 소유격: my(나의), Mr. Glenn's(글렌 씨의) 등의 소유격 뒤에는 모든 종류의 명사가 올 수 있습니다.

❸ 수량 표현: 수나 양을 나타내는 수량 표현의 경우 각각 어울리는 명사의 종류가 정해져 있습니다.

수량 표현	가산명사				불가산명사
	단수		복수		
each 각각의 every 모든	each every	computer			
both 둘 다 few 거의 없는 a few 몇몇의 several 몇몇의 many 많은 a number of 많은 a variety of 다양한			both few a few several many a number of a variety of	computers	
little 거의 없는 a little 조금 있는 much 많은					little a little much	equipment
some 약간의 most 대부분의 all 모든			some most all	computers	some most all	equipment

Please answer **each** question in the form. 양식에 있는 각각의 질문에 답하세요.
~~many~~

They reorder products **every two months**. 그들은 두 달마다 제품을 재주문한다.

→ every는 단수명사와 쓰이지만 〈every + 기수 + 복수명사〉 형태로 쓰여 '~마다'라는 의미를 나타낼 수도 있습니다.

ETS 유형 연습

다음 문장의 빈칸에 들어갈 알맞은 말을 고르세요.

정답과 해설 p.130

STEP 1

1. Mr. Montoya's biography of former president John Kendall is the subject of ------- debate.
   (A) much
   (B) many

2. The new Boulin sports car has several ------- that distinguish it from last year's model.
   (A) feature
   (B) features

3. Due to an unavoidable -------, Mr. Khan will postpone the teleconference until Thursday.
   (A) conflict
   (B) conflicts

4. Maucir Travel Agency offers ------- flights at reduced prices.
   (A) much
   (B) some

STEP 2

5. Productivity increased 23 percent in the first ------- months after the protocols were revised.
   (A) few
   (B) small
   (C) high
   (D) late

6. All ------- to the auto production plant must register at the security checkpoint.
   (A) visit
   (B) visitation
   (C) visitors
   (D) visiting

7. The president of Paterson Industrial Solutions has signed a number of important ------- this month.
   (A) contract
   (B) contracts
   (C) contracted
   (D) contracting

8. Most ------- have completed a paid internship at the company headquarters.
   (A) apply
   (B) applicants
   (C) applied
   (D) applicant

| 어휘 | 1 biography 전기 former 이전의 subject 주제, 대상 debate 논란, 논쟁 2 distinguish A from B A와 B를 구별하다 3 unavoidable 피할 수 없는 postpone 미루다, 연기하다 teleconference 화상회의 4 at reduced prices 할인된 가격에 5 productivity 생산성 protocol 프로토콜, 규약 revise 수정하다 6 security checkpoint 보안 검문소 visitation 방문, 시찰 7 contract 계약, 계약서 8 paid 유급의

UNIT 02 | 명사 149

ETS 실전 문제

1. After collecting more information about its customer base, Kolby Corp. will present a business plan to potential -------.
   (A) investing
   (B) investors
   (C) invests
   (D) invested

2. Amusement park ride operators must review the safety-protocol checklist at the start of ------- work period.
   (A) always
   (B) whose
   (C) every
   (D) all

3. Kasis Art Gallery encourages every ------- to read the guidelines carefully before submitting exhibition proposals.
   (A) apply
   (B) applied
   (C) applicant
   (D) application

4. Cool Reads' Web site specializes in the ------- of electronic books to public libraries.
   (A) distributed
   (B) distributor
   (C) distribution
   (D) distributes

5. Combining humor and musical talent, ------- by the Arieli Sisters have attracted large audiences to Café Baron.
   (A) performances
   (B) performed
   (C) performance
   (D) to perform

6. Participants in Rodel's culinary-internship program should report to Mr. Gerard in the dining area to receive their initial -------.
   (A) assignment
   (B) assigns
   (C) assigned
   (D) assigning

7. The entrance on Somers Street will be closed ------- day so that a new automatic door can be installed.
   (A) like
   (B) full
   (C) all
   (D) same

8. ------- order of Gladinoe's ice cream is specially packaged so that it stays frozen during shipment.
   (A) Each
   (B) Several
   (C) All
   (D) Either

9. Mr. Pennington gave clients a helpful ------- to increase their sales profits.
   (A) suggest
   (B) suggested
   (C) suggestion
   (D) suggestions

10. Employee performance evaluations are conducted ------- six months.
    (A) even
    (B) less
    (C) soon
    (D) every

Questions 11-14 refer to the following article.

Enjoy Stuffed Peppers with No Frying

My family loves chiles rellenos. Who can ------- those delicious deep-fried stuffed peppers
                                           11.
filled with yummy cheese? However, if you are like many people, you do not make them often

because they are high in calories. That is why I have developed a healthier version that has

become a family ------- . Start with whole green canned chiles and place them in a baking
                   12.

dish. ------- , layer the chiles with tomatoes and low-fat cheese. Then, top them with a couple
       13.

of eggs mixed with a little flour and milk. ------- . I cook the dish at 350 degrees for about a
                                               14.

half hour.

11. (A) discover
    (B) resist
    (C) import
    (D) locate

12. (A) favor
    (B) favoring
    (C) favored
    (D) favorite

13. (A) Next
    (B) If not
    (C) In any case
    (D) Otherwise

14. (A) Please let me know if you like them.
    (B) Some people prefer hot peppers.
    (C) Finally, bake them until they are puffy.
    (D) I borrowed the recipe from my mother.

UNIT 03 대명사

무료 강의

❶ 인칭대명사

인칭대명사는 문장에서의 역할[격]과 지칭 대상에 따라 형태가 달라집니다.

I love my baby.
My baby loves me too.

▶ 인칭대명사의 형태

명사를 대신해서 쓰는 말을 대명사라고 합니다. 그 중 인칭대명사는 '나', '너', '그것들'처럼 사람이나 사물을 가리키는 말로, 문장에서 담당하는 역할[격]과 지칭하는 대상이 무엇인지 등에 따라 형태가 달라집니다.

		주격 ~은[는], ~이[가]	소유격 ~의	목적격 ~을, ~에게	소유대명사 ~의 것	재귀대명사 ~ 자신
1인칭	나	I	my	me	mine	myself
	우리	we	our	us	ours	ourselves
2인칭	너	you	your	you	yours	yourself
	너희	you	your	you	yours	yourselves
3인칭	그	he	his	him	his	himself
	그녀	she	her	her	hers	herself
	그것	it	its	it	—	itself
	그들/그것들	they	their	them	theirs	themselves

▶ 주격, 소유격, 목적격

❶ **주격 인칭대명사:** 동사 앞 주어 자리에는 주격 인칭대명사를 씁니다.

　She will quit her job next month. 그녀는 다음 달에 일을 그만둘 것이다.
　<u>주격</u>

❷ **소유격 인칭대명사:** 명사 앞에서 명사를 수식하는 한정사로 쓰입니다.

　Mr. Watts talked about **his** report briefly. 왓츠 씨는 자신의 보고서에 대해 간단히 말했다.
　　　　　　　　　　　　　<u>소유격</u>

❸ **목적격 인칭대명사:** 동사나 전치사 뒤에는 목적격 인칭대명사를 씁니다.

　Ms. Diaz is busy, but I could ask **her** for **you**. 디아즈 씨는 바쁘지만 내가 너를 위해 그녀에게 물어볼게.
　　　　　　　　　　　　　　　　<u>목적격</u>　<u>목적격</u>

152

ETS 유형 연습

다음 문장의 빈칸에 들어갈 알맞은 말을 고르세요.

STEP 1

1. The mechanics became more efficient as ------- began using the new technology.
   (A) themselves
   (B) they

2. Mr. Kensington has already filed the expense report for ------- recent trip to Hong Kong.
   (A) his
   (B) him

3. Ms. Williams has given ------- a detailed schedule for constructing the new workstations.
   (A) we
   (B) us

4. Although the staff has grown, Mr. Lee continues to conduct all client meetings -------.
   (A) him
   (B) himself

STEP 2

5. If Mr. Motholo had stayed in Pretoria a day longer, ------- could have toured the factory.
   (A) him
   (B) he
   (C) his
   (D) himself

6. There will be a meeting tomorrow to answer ------- questions about the vacation policy.
   (A) you
   (B) your
   (C) yours
   (D) yourself

7. We were informed by the property owner that the rent should be paid directly to -------.
   (A) her
   (B) hers
   (C) she
   (D) herself

8. Applicants for the graphic designer position must submit ------- portfolios by May 30.
   (A) their
   (B) them
   (C) they
   (D) themselves

| 어휘 | 1 mechanic 정비공   efficient 효율적인   2 file 제출하다; 보관하다   expense report 지출 결의서   3 detailed 상세한   construct 짓다, 건설하다   workstation 근무하는 자리   4 conduct 진행하다, 수행하다   6 vacation 휴가   policy 정책   7 inform 알리다   property owner 건물주   rent 임대료   directly 직접   8 applicant 지원자   position 직책   submit 제출하다

❷ 소유대명사와 재귀대명사

소유대명사는 '소유격 + 명사'로 '~의 것'이라는 의미를 나타냅니다.

my + cheese = **mine**

▶ 소유대명사

〈소유격+명사〉의 역할을 하는 소유대명사는 '~의 것'이라고 해석하며, 명사처럼 주어, 목적어, 보어 자리에 모두 쓸 수 있습니다.

❶ 주어: 동사 앞에 옵니다.

My backpack is too heavy, but **yours** / ~~you~~ is lightweight. 내 배낭은 너무 무거운데, 네 것은 가볍다.
= your backpack (소유격 your + 명사 backpack)

❷ 목적어: 타동사나 전치사 뒤에 옵니다.

Of the three ideas, the judge chose **mine** / ~~me~~. 세 가지 아이디어 중에서 심사위원은 내 것을 선택했다.
= my idea

❸ 보어: 주어나 목적어의 보충어로 쓰입니다.

The mobile phone on Ms. Ryo's desk is **hers** / ~~her~~. 료 씨의 책상에 있는 휴대폰은 그녀의 것이다.
= her mobile phone

▶ 재귀대명사

myself(나 자신)처럼 인칭대명사의 소유격이나 목적격에 -self[selves]를 붙인 형태로 '~ 자신', '직접'이라고 해석합니다.

조건	위치	예문
주어와 목적어가 같을 때	목적어 자리	**Carlos** can introduce **himself** / ~~him~~ in English. 　주어　　　　　　　　　　목적어 = Carlos 카를로스는 영어로 자기 자신을 소개할 수 있다.
주어나 목적어를 강조할 때 (생략 가능)	문장 끝이나 명사 뒤	**The investors** visited the factory (**themselves**). 　주어　　　　　　　　　　　　　주어 강조 = **The investors** (themselves) visited the factory. 투자자들은 공장을 (직접) 방문했다.
관용적 표현	전치사 뒤	Jill has written the article **by herself**. 질은 혼자서 그 기사를 썼다. → by oneself(= on one's own) 혼자 힘으로, 혼자서

ETS 유형 연습

다음 문장의 빈칸에 들어갈 알맞은 말을 고르세요.

STEP 1

1. Drivers are asked to park ------- cars within the white lines.
   (A) their
   (B) theirs

2. To prepare ------- for a job interview, Mr. Paik read about the company's history.
   (A) yourselves
   (B) himself

3. Mr. Wong will travel to the management seminar in Singapore on -------.
   (A) his own
   (B) him

4. Barton Maintenance employees determined next month's work schedule -------.
   (A) them
   (B) themselves

STEP 2

5. We will position ------- as the premier refrigerator among quality kitchen appliances.
   (A) we
   (B) us
   (C) our
   (D) ours

6. Dr. Schmidt is not sure that her assistant can complete the investigation by -------.
   (A) his
   (B) him
   (C) his own
   (D) himself

7. Customer inquiries can be difficult to answer on -------.
   (A) yours
   (B) yourself
   (C) your own
   (D) you

8. Mr. Yu often mentions that green tea is a favorite refreshment of -------, so a tea assortment would be a thoughtful gift.
   (A) himself
   (B) him
   (C) his
   (D) he

| 어휘 | 1 be asked to ~하도록 요청 받다   2 prepare 준비하다   3 travel 여행하다   management 경영
4 maintenance 정비, 유지 (보수)   determine 결정하다   5 position 배치하다, 자리를 잡다   premier 최고의
quality 우수한, 양질의   appliance 가전제품   6 be sure that ~을 확신하다   assistant 조수, 보조   complete
완수하다, 완성하다   investigation 조사   7 inquiry 문의   8 assortment 모음, 종합   thoughtful 사려 깊은

3 지시대명사와 부정대명사

지시대명사 those 뒤에 수식어가 붙으면 '~하는 사람들' 이라는 의미입니다.

those interested in music 음악에 관심이 있는 사람들

▶ 지시대명사 this/these와 that/those

이전에 언급된 사물이나 사람을 가리키는 말로 거리나 시간상 가까운 것은 this(이것), 먼 것은 that(저것)으로 표현하며 복수형은 these(이것들), those(저것들)입니다. 각각 명사 앞에서 그 명사를 한정하는 지시형용사로 쓰일 수도 있습니다.

This is a quick update on the program. 이것은 프로그램에 관한 간단한 수정 사항입니다.
These/Those programs are no longer available. 이/저 프로그램들은 더 이상 운영되지 않습니다.

> **LEVEL UP** those who: ~하는 사람들
> 뒤에 수식어가 붙은 those는 '~하는 사람들'을 의미합니다.
> **Those who** use the parking area must obtain a permit. 주차장을 사용하는 사람들은 허가증을 받아야 한다.
> **Those** (who are) **interested** in the seminar should register in advance. 그 세미나에 관심 있는 사람들은 미리 등록해야 한다.

▶ 부정대명사

수량	부정대명사	of the+복수/불가산 명사: ~중에서	동사의 수
단수	one 하나 each 각각 either 둘 중 하나 neither 둘 중 어느 쪽도 아닌	of the restaurants (복수명사)	is great.
복수	few 거의 없는 both 둘 다 several 몇몇 many 많은 some 일부 any 누구든/무엇이든 most 대부분 all 전부	of the restaurants (복수명사)	are great.
단수	some 일부 any 누구든/무엇이든 most 대부분 all 전부 much 다량	of the information (불가산명사)	is great.

▶ one, another, the other, (the) others의 차이

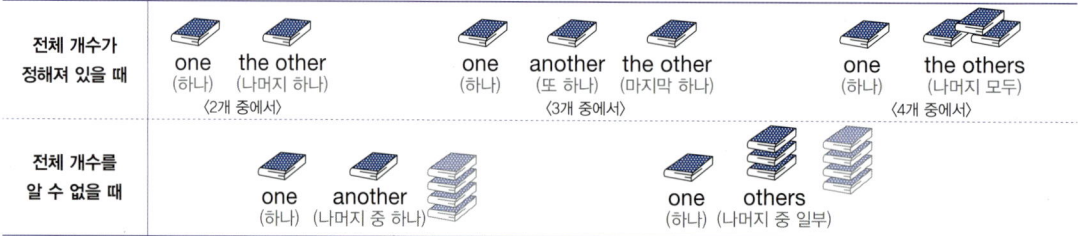

Among five balls, **one** is red, **another** is yellow, and **the others** are blue.
5개의 공 중 하나는 빨강, 다른 하나는 노랑, 나머지 전부(3개)는 파랑이다.

→ each other(2명), one another(3명 이상)는 '서로'라는 의미의 대명사로, 목적어로 쓰입니다.

ETS 유형 연습

다음 문장의 빈칸에 들어갈 알맞은 말을 고르세요.

STEP 1

1. ------- mechanic has worked at Mr. Kim's Auto Shop for years.
   (A) This
   (B) These

2. ------- of the employees are searching the archives for the missing folder.
   (A) Much
   (B) Many

3. Mr. Hahn and Ms. Smalls have similar job duties, and ------- hope for promotions.
   (A) one
   (B) both

4. Dr. Hemana and Dr. Wareham have known ------- since they were university students.
   (A) another one
   (B) each other

STEP 2

5. ------- who work in the shipping office must receive training in the new mailing procedures label.
   (A) One
   (B) Each
   (C) Those
   (D) Themselves

6. Of the two mobile phones, one has an 8 megapixel camera, and ------- features a 12 megapixel camera.
   (A) another
   (B) others
   (C) the other
   (D) the others

7. In order to finish the candidate interviews, ------- of the recruiters will need to stay another day.
   (A) all
   (B) much
   (C) other
   (D) others

8. ------- interested in the position should submit a completed form before February 21.
   (A) These
   (B) Those
   (C) Every
   (D) They

| 어휘 | 1 auto shop 자동차 정비소 2 search 찾다 archive 기록 보관소 missing 없어진 3 similar 비슷한 duty 의무 promotion 승진 4 since ~한 이래로 5 shipping office 배송 사무실 procedure 절차 6 megapixel 100만 화소 feature 특징을 이루다 7 candidate 지원자, 후보자 recruiter 채용 담당자 8 interested 관심이 있는 submit 제출하다 completed 작성된, 완성된

ETS 실전 문제

1. Both Dialah's Boutique and Galena Fashions have social media links on ------- Web sites.
   (A) they
   (B) their
   (C) them
   (D) theirs

2. Although Daminger Beauty Products and Sasso Cosmetics have not been profitable this year, ------- expect revenues to increase next quarter.
   (A) another
   (B) both
   (C) either
   (D) least

3. Please ensure that the service contract for ------- machinery includes inspections.
   (A) us
   (B) ourselves
   (C) ours
   (D) our

4. Ms. Newman said she will complete the quarterly report ------- since most of the accounting staff is on vacation.
   (A) she
   (B) her
   (C) hers
   (D) herself

5. Maybear Bakery promises that ------- bread products are dairy free.
   (A) themselves
   (B) its
   (C) itself
   (D) they

6. Only ------- scientists directly involved in the research project are allowed to enter the laboratory.
   (A) which
   (B) those
   (C) this
   (D) what

7. The president of Macropa, Inc., took it upon ------- to investigate the reasons for the company's narrowing profit margin.
   (A) his
   (B) him
   (C) himself
   (D) he

8. Recent customer feedback shows that ------- Galpran line of footwear is lightweight and affordable.
   (A) our
   (B) us
   (C) we
   (D) ourselves

9. Hikers can improve ------- level of fitness by choosing trails with several hills.
   (A) them
   (B) their
   (C) theirs
   (D) themselves

10. Putting ------- preference aside, Ms. Shang approved the design favored by the majority.
    (A) hers
    (B) her own
    (C) she
    (D) herself

Questions 11-14 refer to the following e-mail.

To: All Employees
From: Shinya Futagi
Date: 17 November
Subject: System test

Dear Staff:

Next week, we will be conducting a safety drill to test our new alarm system. There are two points of action for you to consider. First, familiarize yourself this week with the exit nearest to your workstation. Please remember that next week when the alarm sounds, you should exit the building in a calm, ------- manner. -------. Second, once you are out of the building, go
                                                       11.   12.
directly to the sidewalk on Cooper Street. ------- will be there to check attendance. Be sure
                                                    13.
to check in with me once you arrive. The entire drill ------- only a few minutes. If you have any
                                                              14.
questions or concerns, please reach out to me.

Sincerely,

Shinya Futagi
Safety Liaison

11. (A) suspicious
    (B) orderly
    (C) previous
    (D) inward

12. (A) Security will give you a badge when you enter.
    (B) Vermer Alarms provided our new alarm system.
    (C) Safety drills are conducted at random times.
    (D) Please leave immediately from wherever you are in the building.

13. (A) I
    (B) He
    (C) You
    (D) They

14. (A) took
    (B) is taking
    (C) should take
    (D) could have taken

UNIT 04 형용사

무료 강의

❶ 형용사의 개념과 역할

형용사는 명사를 수식하거나, 명사의 상태나 특성을 설명합니다.

There is a **huge** tree. 명사 수식
The tree is **huge**. 명사 설명

▶ 형용사의 개념과 형태

형용사는 good voice(좋은 목소리)의 good처럼 명사의 성질이나 상태를 나타내는 말로, 일반적으로 -able, -ive, -ful 등으로 끝나는 형태가 많습니다.

형용사 어미	형용사		형용사 어미	형용사	
-able[ible]	available 이용 가능한	possible 가능한	-al	personal 개인적인	additional 추가의
-ive	expensive 값비싼	creative 창조적인	-ous	famous 유명한	previous 이전의
-ful	careful 조심스러운	successful 성공적인	-ary	necessary 필요한	temporary 임시의
-ic	realistic 현실적인	specific 구체적인	-ate	private 사적인	fortunate 운 좋은

→ -able[ible]로 끝나면 '~할 수 있는, ~ 가능한'이라는 의미로 주로 해석됩니다.

▶ 형용사의 역할

❶ 명사 수식: 주로 명사 앞에서 명사를 꾸미는 수식어 역할을 합니다.

The staff is making **considerable** changes. 직원들은 상당한 변화를 이루어 내고 있다.
　　　　　　　　　　　　　　　　↑
　　　　　　　　　　　　　　　　명사

❷ 주어 보충: be동사, become, seem, remain 등의 동사 뒤에서 주어를 보충하는 주격 보어로 쓰일 수 있습니다.

The document was **informative**. 그 문서는 유익했다.
　　　주어　　　　　주격 보어

❸ 목적어 보충: make, keep, find, consider 등의 동사가 있을 때 그 동사의 목적어 뒤에서 목적격 보어로 쓰일 수 있습니다.

Most customers **found** the manual **helpful**. 대부분의 고객들은 설명서가 유용하다고 생각했다.
　　　　　　　　　　　목적어　　목적격 보어

ETS 유형 연습

다음 문장의 빈칸에 들어갈 알맞은 말을 고르세요.

STEP 1

1. If you have a ------- meal request, please tell the ticket agent when booking your flight.
   (A) special
   (B) specialize

2. The clothing shop is ------- because it sells quality uniforms at competitive prices.
   (A) success
   (B) successful

3. The coordinators are asking the focus groups to provide ------- criticism.
   (A) construction
   (B) constructive

4. The finance department will outline its ------- growth plans at the all-staff meeting.
   (A) strategic
   (B) strategically

STEP 2

5. Centerville Library will host a series of free classes about ------- subjects for the community next month.
   (A) vary
   (B) varies
   (C) various
   (D) variously

6. Pietro's Fine Ice Cream is available in a range of ------- flavors.
   (A) popular
   (B) popularly
   (C) popularity
   (D) popularizes

7. The sales goal set by the management team seems ------- to most of the staff.
   (A) realist
   (B) realism
   (C) realistic
   (D) realistically

8. Dr. Sugiyama's current academic work is focused on ------- research projects in behavioral psychology.
   (A) collaborate
   (B) collaboration
   (C) collaborates
   (D) collaborative

| 어휘 | **1** ticket agent 탑승권 판매원 **2** quality 품질이 좋은; 품질 competitive 경쟁력 있는 **3** coordinator 진행자 criticism 비평, 비판 constructive 건설적인 **4** finance department 재무부 strategic 전략적인 **5** vary 다르다 various 다양한 variously 다양하게 **6** a range of 다양한 **7** realistic 현실적인 **8** academic 학문의 behavioral psychology 행동 심리학 collaborate 협력하다 collaboration 협력 collaborative 협력적인, 공동의

2 주의해야 할 형용사

형태가 비슷하지만 뜻이 서로 다른 형용사에 주의해야 합니다.

The painting is **impressive**. 인상적인
The man is **impressed**. 감명 받은

▶ 분사 형용사 (UNIT 11 분사 참고)

-ing로 끝나는 형용사		-ed로 끝나는 형용사	
leading 선두의	following 다음의	detailed 상세한	established 자리를 잡은
lasting 지속적인	promising 유망한	motivated 의욕적인	experienced 노련한
challenging 힘든	encouraging 고무적인	required 필수의	attached 첨부된

Mr. Kwon is a (**promising** / ~~promised~~) candidate. 권 씨는 유망한 후보이다.
Advance registration is (**required** / ~~requiring~~) for the conference. 그 학회는 사전 등록이 필수적이다.

▶ 헷갈리는 형용사

reliable/dependable 믿을 만한	responsible 책임이 있는	considerable 상당한	favorable 우호적인
reliant/dependent 의존적인	responsive 민감한	considerate 사려 깊은	favorite 좋아하는
comprehensible 이해할 수 있는	informative 유익한	impressive 인상적인	confident 확신하는
comprehensive 포괄적인	informed 잘 아는	impressed 감명 받은	confidential 기밀의
respectable 존경할 만한	respected 존경 받는	successful 성공적인	industrial 산업의
respective 각각의	respectful 공손한	successive 연속적인	industrious 근면한

All personal information is (**confidential** / ~~confident~~). 모든 개인 정보는 기밀이다.

▶ be + 형용사 + 전치사

be responsible for	~에 대한 책임이 있다	be dedicated[committed] to	~에 헌신하다, 전념하다
be recognized for	~을 인정받다	be promoted to	~로 승진하다
be eligible for = be entitled to	~에 자격이 있다	be accessible by	~로 접근할[이용할] 수 있다
be dependent on	~에 의존하다	be aware of	~을 알다, 인지하다
be concerned[anxious] about	~에 대해 걱정하다	be capable of	~을 할 수 있다(= be able to do)
be familiar with	~에 익숙하다	be exempt from	~에서 면제되다

Team leaders **are responsible for** their teams. 팀장들은 팀을 책임진다.
Some Koreans **are capable of** speaking English. 일부 한국인은 영어로 말할 수 있다.
= are able to speak English

ETS 유형 연습

다음 문장의 빈칸에 들어갈 알맞은 말을 고르세요.

정답과 해설 p.137

STEP 1

1. ------- assembly-line workers tend to be more attentive.
   (A) Experienced
   (B) Experiencing

2. Mr. Moore's speech made a ------- impression on the audience.
   (A) lasted
   (B) lasting

3. Everyone at the concert was ------- by Ms. Vincenzi's outstanding performance.
   (A) impressive
   (B) impressed

4. Wellbeing Aid, Inc., is ------- to meeting the specific needs of its customers.
   (A) dedicated
   (B) dedication

STEP 2

5. Farmers are predicting good crop harvests as a result of recent ------- weather conditions.
   (A) favors
   (B) favorable
   (C) favor
   (D) favoring

6. Winthrop Strategies is seeking to employ a ------- individual who consistently meets deadlines.
   (A) motivate
   (B) motivated
   (C) motivation
   (D) motivations

7. The office building inspection revealed some minor flaws but no ------- damage.
   (A) structuring
   (B) structural
   (C) structurally
   (D) structures

8. The new printer is more ------- than the old one, which had to be repaired frequently.
   (A) reliable
   (B) faithful
   (C) prohibitive
   (D) methodical

| 어휘 | 1 assembly-line 조립 라인   tend to ~하는 경향이 있다   attentive 세심한, 주의 깊은   2 impression 인상   audience 청중   3 outstanding 뛰어난   5 predict 예상하다, 예견하다   good crop 풍작   harvest 수확, 추수   as a result of ~의 결과로   favor 호의, 친절   favoring 형편에 맞는, 선호하는   6 individual 개인   consistently 일관되게   meet a deadline 마감일을 맞추다   8 frequently 자주

ETS 실전 문제

1. The kiosk on Harvey Street offers a ------- selection of newspapers and magazines.
   (A) diverse
   (B) diversify
   (C) diversifies
   (D) diversely

2. The consultants recommended that a more ------- staffing plan be put in place within three months.
   (A) efficiency
   (B) efficiently
   (C) efficient
   (D) efficiencies

3. Thanks to a highly ------- management team, Wu Logistics has experienced unprecedented growth this year.
   (A) competency
   (B) competently
   (C) competence
   (D) competent

4. Ms. Patel was ------- about her first day on the job at Haighton Industries, but everything went extremely well.
   (A) anxious
   (B) anxiously
   (C) anxiety
   (D) anxiousness

5. Complimentary breakfast is served daily from 6:00 A.M. to 9:30 A.M. for ------- guests.
   (A) register
   (B) registers
   (C) registered
   (D) to register

6. Zach Hartvigsen's latest book explores ------- moments in the history of modern architecture.
   (A) significance
   (B) significant
   (C) significantly
   (D) signifies

7. The self-storage industry is currently testing ------- technologies for enhanced automation.
   (A) promise
   (B) to promise
   (C) promising
   (D) promises

8. After ------- effort, we have succeeded in redesigning the keyboard.
   (A) consider
   (B) considerable
   (C) considerate
   (D) considerably

9. Consumers have been very ------- of our efforts to reduce the amount of unsolicited mail that they receive.
   (A) appreciating
   (B) appreciate
   (C) appreciative
   (D) appreciation

10. There is no ------- evidence that the reformulated allergy medication is any more effective than the existing one.
    (A) persuaded
    (B) persuasion
    (C) persuasive
    (D) persuade

Questions 11-14 refer to the following advertisement.

Strawberry Moon celebrates springtime with May price breaks on all mattresses!

Relieve your aches and pains with a Strawberry Moon state-of-the-art mattress. Strawberry Moon's natural foam mattresses are engineered to promote a restful night's sleep, helping you wake up every day feeling ------- . Our mattresses offer support ------- your back as
11.   12.
well as durability and comfort. ------- , every mattress we manufacture is antibacterial and
13.
hypoallergenic.

------- To learn more about these savings and to browse our entire inventory, please visit
14.
www.strawberrymoon.ca.

11. (A) refreshed
    (B) refreshment
    (C) refreshes
    (D) refresh

12. (A) on
    (B) off
    (C) in
    (D) for

13. (A) Nevertheless
    (B) Consequently
    (C) In addition
    (D) To summarize

14. (A) Extra-firm mattresses are available by special order only.
    (B) Purchase a mattress before May 31 to obtain a special discount.
    (C) Please note that our Toronto showroom will be closed on Mondays in June.
    (D) Satisfied customers are encouraged to post positive reviews.

UNIT 05 부사

무료 강의

❶ 부사의 개념과 역할

부사는 동사, 형용사, 부사를 수식하거나 문장 전체를 수식합니다.

The man **desperately** wants some water. 동사 수식
The weather is **extremely** hot. 형용사 수식

▶ 부사의 개념과 형태

부사는 방법이나 정도 등을 설명하는 말로, (대)명사를 제외한 모든 품사뿐만 아니라 문장 전체도 수식할 수 있습니다. 대체로 '~하게'라고 해석되며 '형용사+-ly'의 형태가 많습니다.

형용사+-ly	strongly 강력하게 highly 매우	sharply 급격하게 closely 밀접하게	carefully 신중하게 lately 최근에	suddenly 갑자기 hardly 거의 ~ 않다
그 밖의 형태	well 잘, 훨씬 also 또한 already 이미, 벌써	very 매우 too 너무, 또한 still 여전히, 그런데도	then 그때 quite 꽤 yet 아직, 벌써	even 심지어 just 딱, 방금 ever 언제나

▶ 부사의 역할

❶ 동사 수식

주어+**부사**+동사   The president **personally** greets new employees. 회장은 직접 신입사원들을 환영한다.
동사(+목적어)+**부사**   Please **finish** the sales report **quickly**. 신속히 판매 보고서를 작성해 주세요.
조동사+**부사**+본동사   The client must **fully** understand all the paperwork. 고객은 모든 서류를 완전히 이해해야 한다.
be동사+**부사**+p.p.[-ing] The meeting was **originally** scheduled for May 13. 회의는 원래 5월 13일로 예정되어 있었다.
have+**부사**+p.p.   Our office has **recently** moved. 우리 사무실은 최근에 이사했다.

❷ 형용사, 부사, 구, 문장 전체 수식

부사는 동사 외에도 형용사나 부사, 구, 문장 전체를 수식할 수 있습니다.

The **extremely** hot weather lowered productivity. 극도로 더운 날씨가 생산성을 떨어뜨렸다.
　　　　　└─ 형용사 수식

We would **very** much like to hire you as an advisor. 우리는 당신을 고문으로 모시길 간절히 바랍니다.
　　　　　└─ 부사 수식

You should register for the seminar **well** in advance. 그 세미나는 한참 전에 등록해야 한다.
　　　　　　　　　　　　　　　　　└─ 전치사구 수식

Fortunately, no one was seriously injured. 다행히 아무도 심하게 다치지 않았다.
└─ 문장 전체 수식

ETS 유형 연습

다음 문장의 빈칸에 들어갈 알맞은 말을 고르세요.

STEP 1

1. You can have a ------- different opinion from your colleagues on the matter.
   (A) complete
   (B) completely

2. Apply the sunblock lotion to exposed skin and rub until it is ------- absorbed.
   (A) fully
   (B) full

3. Please adjust the volume knob ------- so the sound is not too loud.
   (A) slight
   (B) slightly

4. The municipal road repaving project is ------- on schedule.
   (A) current
   (B) currently

STEP 2

5. The legal department will ------- examine the contract and provide feedback by Friday.
   (A) close
   (B) closer
   (C) closeness
   (D) closely

6. Checks deposited after 5:00 P.M. are ------- posted within two business days.
   (A) type
   (B) typical
   (C) typically
   (D) types

7. Unfortunately, Sunbee Snacks' new protein-rich granola bars are not ------- available.
   (A) widening
   (B) widest
   (C) widely
   (D) wider

8. Mi-Sun Park's artwork ------- combines classical elements with modern materials.
   (A) skill
   (B) skilled
   (C) skillful
   (D) skillfully

| 어휘 | 1 opinion 의견 colleague 동료 completely 완전히 2 apply 바르다 exposed 노출된 rub 문지르다 absorb 흡수하다 fully 완전히 3 adjust 조절하다 knob 손잡이 4 municipal 시의 repave (도로를) 재포장하다 on schedule 예정대로인 5 legal 법적인 examine 검토하다 6 check 수표 deposit 입금하다 typically 보통, 일반적으로 7 protein-rich 단백질이 풍부한 8 combine 결합하다 element 요소 material 재료

② 빈출 부사 정리

특정 동사 또는 표현과 함께 잘 쓰이는 부사가 있습니다.

Her score has **sharply** increased.

▶ 빈출 부사

증가/감소 강조 부사	증가/감소/변화를 나타내는 동사(increase, decrease, rise, fall, replace, change 등)와 잘 어울립니다.
	sharply 급격하게 slightly 약간 gradually 점진적으로 steadily 꾸준히 considerably/substantially 상당히
	Customer satisfaction **increased steadily** after the store opened. 그 매장을 연 뒤로 고객 만족도가 꾸준히 높아졌다.
숫자 수식 부사	빈칸 뒤에 숫자 표현이 있으면 숫자 수식 부사와 어울립니다.
	nearly/almost/approximately/about 대략, 거의 at least 최소한 just/only 오직
	The factory produces **approximately** 300 vehicles per year. 그 공장은 1년에 대략 300대의 차량을 생산한다.
시간 강조 부사	before(~ 전에)나 after(~ 후에)의 앞에 위치하여 '직전에', '직후에'를 의미합니다.
	shortly/immediately/soon/right 곧, 즉시
	There will be a snack break **immediately after** the lecture. 강연 직후에 간식 시간이 있을 것이다.
접속부사	앞뒤 문장의 의미를 연결하는 부사로, 주로 콤마(,)와 함께 사용됩니다.
	however 하지만 nevertheless 그럼에도 불구하고 moreover 게다가 therefore 그러므로 otherwise 그렇지 않으면
	The new antivirus program is easy, cheap, and, **moreover**, it's effective. 새로운 바이러스 퇴치 프로그램은 쉽고 싸며, 게다가 효과적이다.
부정부사	부정(否定)의 의미를 나타냅니다.
	never 결코 ~ 않다 hardly/scarcely/seldom/rarely 거의 ~ 않다
	The tenants **hardly** use the back gate. 세입자들은 뒷문을 거의 이용하지 않는다.

▶ 자주 어울려 쓰이는 부사 표현

reasonably[affordably] priced	가격이 적당한	conveniently located	위치가 편리한
originally scheduled	원래 예정된	temporarily closed	일시적으로 폐쇄된
review thoroughly[carefully]	철저히[꼼꼼히] 검토하다	widely known	널리 알려진
regularly check[inspect]	정기적으로 점검하다	clearly indicate	명확하게 나타내다

The clinic is **conveniently located** near the campus.
그 병원은 캠퍼스 인근 편리한 곳에 위치하고 있다.

ETS 유형 연습

다음 문장의 빈칸에 들어갈 알맞은 말을 고르세요.

STEP 1

1. The contractors say they will begin the renovation work ------- before 8 A.M. tomorrow.
   (A) shortly
   (B) short

2. The elevators in the north wing will be ------- closed for maintenance next week.
   (A) temporarily
   (B) cautiously

3. Sales of new cars are down ------- five percent this quarter.
   (A) nearly
   (B) quite

4. ------- opened as a modest tourist hotel, Agafya Inn is now a full-service resort.
   (A) Originally
   (B) Original

STEP 2

5. The bookshelf from Malden Furniture arrived on time, but one of the parts was ------- damaged.
   (A) slight
   (B) slighted
   (C) slightly
   (D) slighting

6. Please leave ------- six chairs in the conference room and remove any extras.
   (A) more
   (B) rather
   (C) just
   (D) quite

7. Kristi Driver is a well-known therapist, and her services are very ------- priced.
   (A) strongly
   (B) internally
   (C) reasonably
   (D) repeatedly

8. The management plans to replace employee office chairs -------.
   (A) soon
   (B) therefore
   (C) both
   (D) easy

| 어휘 | 1 contractor 하청업체 renovation 보수 2 wing 부속 건물 3 quarter 분기 4 modest 크지 않은 originally 원래 5 bookshelf 책장 on time 제시간에 part 부품 damage 손상시키다 6 remove 치우다 7 well-known 잘 알려진 therapist 치료사 8 replace 교체하다

ETS 실전 문제

1. Despite heavy competition, Mr. Tashjian was able to expand his consulting business -------.
   (A) is profiting
   (B) profitable
   (C) profited
   (D) profitably

2. Pearl Fashion has opened its third shop in the ------- popular Reiser Mall in downtown Miami.
   (A) tightly
   (B) evenly
   (C) highly
   (D) solely

3. Rather than replace all machinery at once, engineers at the Hartford plant decided to replace it ------- over the next five years.
   (A) slightly
   (B) gradually
   (C) familiarly
   (D) previously

4. Although the job took ------- six hours to complete, the workers will be paid for a full eight-hour shift.
   (A) during
   (B) until
   (C) right
   (D) only

5. Monstad Construction, the company that will renovate our hotel lobby, comes ------- recommended.
   (A) high
   (B) higher
   (C) highest
   (D) highly

6. Serena Safety Alarms offers home security systems that are ------- priced.
   (A) reason
   (B) to reason
   (C) reasonable
   (D) reasonably

7. Applicants are advised to ------- proofread all application materials before submitting them.
   (A) careful
   (B) caring
   (C) carefully
   (D) cares

8. Before its expansion, Lomas Restaurant ------- served about 50 patrons per hour.
   (A) reported
   (B) reportable
   (C) reports
   (D) reportedly

9. Zoellner Company found building costs to be ------- high in the western part of the county.
   (A) surprise
   (B) surprised
   (C) surprising
   (D) surprisingly

10. Iron Ace's high-quality power tools are sold at over 10,000 retailers -------.
    (A) nation
    (B) national
    (C) nationality
    (D) nationwide

Questions 11-14 refer to the following e-mail.

To: a.crimmins@anyasgifts.com.au
From: payments@orangebellwireless.com.au
Date: 7 September
Subject: Payment processed

Dear Ms. Crimmins,

We have received your payment of $71.39. The amount has been credited to your account, and no ------- action is required on your part. ------- , if you wish to change your next payment
  11.   12.
due date, you may do so by logging in to your account at www.orangebellwireless.com.au/
portal. ------- . Customers tell us that they find this new version of our app much easier to use
      13.
than the previous version. We hope you will ------- .
                                         14.

Thank you for being a loyal customer. We appreciate your business.

Orange Bell Wireless

---

11. (A) further
(B) furthers
(C) furthered
(D) furthering

12. (A) Instead
(B) However
(C) In particular
(D) For example

13. (A) It is our privilege to be your wireless services provider.
(B) This information will provide you with additional examples.
(C) We have rescheduled the due date for your next payment.
(D) You can also access your account on our newly redesigned mobile app.

14. (A) continue
(B) respond
(C) agree
(D) join

UNIT 06 동사의 형태와 종류

무료 강의

1 동사의 형태

동사에는 기본형(~하다), 완료형(~했다), 수동형(~되다), 진행형(~ 중이다) 등 다양한 형태가 있습니다.

Something **has changed**. 완료형

▶ 동사의 형태 변화

종류	동사		동사 아님	
	현재형(~이다/~하다)	과거형(~했다)	과거분사형(~된)	현재분사형(~하는)
be동사	is, are	was, were	been	being
규칙 변화 동사	return	return**ed**	return**ed**	return**ing**
불규칙 변화 동사	begin	began	begun	beginning

→ 과거분사, 현재분사는 be동사나 have동사와 결합하면 동사로 쓰일 수 있습니다.

▶ 동사원형이 오는 경우

❶ 주어가 없는 명령문 **Please change** the layout of this chart. 이 도표의 구성을 바꾸세요.

❷ 조동사 뒤 The assistant **will change** the coffee filters. 비서가 커피 필터를 교체할 것이다.
(will = 미래를 나타내는 조동사)

❸ 3인칭 단수(he, she, it 등)가 아닌 주어의 현재 시제
The rules change frequently. 규정이 자주 바뀐다.
Mr. Roberts often **changes** his mind. 로버츠 씨는 자주 마음을 바꾼다. (Mr. Roberts = 3인칭 단수)
→ 주어가 3인칭 단수이면 동사원형에 -(e)s를 붙입니다.

▶ 과거분사형(p.p.)이 오는 경우

❶ 수동태 be + p.p.: ~되다
The plan **was changed** abruptly. 계획이 갑자기 바뀌었다. (UNIT 9 능동태와 수동태 참고)

❷ 완료 시제 have + p.p.: ~했다
The Internet **has changed** our lives. 인터넷은 우리의 삶을 바꾸었다. (UNIT 8 시제 참고)

▶ 현재분사형(-ing)이 오는 경우

진행 시제 be + -ing: ~하고 있다
The paintings **are changing** the atmosphere of the room. 그림들이 방의 분위기를 바꾸고 있다. (UNIT 8 시제 참고)

ETS 유형 연습

다음 문장의 빈칸에 들어갈 알맞은 말을 고르세요.

정답과 해설 p.142

STEP 1

1. Please ------- your hotel key at the front desk when you go out.
   (A) to leave
   (B) leave

2. The latest lecture by Jee-Soo Lee can ------- online.
   (A) view
   (B) be viewed

3. The Darlingstone Hotel ------- a complimentary breakfast to all of its guests.
   (A) offering
   (B) is offering

4. Mr. Hu's innovative ideas were ------- enthusiastically by the Bercier Group's marketing staff.
   (A) received
   (B) receive

STEP 2

5. The CEO has ------- an invitation to meet with the press.
   (A) decline
   (B) declined
   (C) declines
   (D) declining

6. To ensure prompt return of your laundry, ------- your hotel room number on the tag provided.
   (A) wrote
   (B) written
   (C) write
   (D) writing

7. Next week we will be ------- a new accounting software program.
   (A) introduce
   (B) introduction
   (C) introduced
   (D) introducing

8. All orders for office supplies must be ------- to Ms. Reaton by Thursday at noon.
   (A) submitting
   (B) submit
   (C) submitted
   (D) submission

| 어휘 | 1 front desk 프런트 데스크 2 latest 최근의 lecture 강의 3 complimentary 무료의 4 innovative 획기적인, 혁신적인 enthusiastically 열렬하게, 열광하여 5 press 언론, 기자들 decline 거절하다 6 ensure 보장하다 prompt 신속한, 즉각적인 laundry 세탁물 tag 꼬리표, 번호표 7 accounting 회계 8 order 주문(서), 주문품 office supplies 사무용품 submit (서류 등을) 제출하다 submission 제출

UNIT 06 | 동사의 형태와 종류

2 자동사와 타동사

자동사는 목적어가 필요 없지만, 타동사는 뒤에 목적어가 반드시 필요합니다.

Kites **fly**. 자동사
A girl **flies** a kite. 타동사+목적어

▶ 자동사의 개념

목적어가 필요 없는 동사로, 자동사 뒤에는 명사가 오지 않고 주로 전치사구나 부사가 옵니다.

Some of the passengers **talked** loudly. 몇몇 승객들은 큰 소리로 (부사) 이야기했다.
              자동사 in the station. 역에서 (전치사구)
                  ~~loudness~~. 큰 소리를

▶ 토익에 자주 출제되는 자동사 + 전치사

rely[depend] on ~에 의존하다	agree with[on] ~에 동의하다	collaborate with/on ~와/~에 협력하다
consist of ~로 구성되다	specialize in ~을 전문으로 하다	deal with ~을 다루다
comply with ~을 준수하다	adhere to ~에 들러붙다	refer to ~을 참고하다, 언급하다
participate in ~에 참가하다	respond[react] to ~에 응답[반응]하다	appeal to ~에 호소하다

The staff members usually **agree with** the manager's decisions. 직원들은 대체로 부장의 결정에 동의한다

▶ 타동사의 개념

타동사 뒤에는 목적어(명사)가 반드시 있어야 하고, 부사나 전치사구는 목적어 역할을 대신할 수 없습니다.

Mr. Crown finally **finished** **the budget report**. 크라운 씨는 마침내 예산 보고서를 완성했다.
                  타동사   목적어

▶ 자동사로 헷갈리기 쉬운 타동사

| discuss ~에 대해 논의하다 | attend ~에 참석하다 | accompany ~와 동반하다 | oppose ~에 반대하다 |
| explain ~에 대해 설명하다 | contact ~와 연락하다 | notify ~에게 통지하다 | await ~을 기다리다 |

We will soon **discuss** ~~about~~ **technical matters**. 우리는 곧 기술적인 문제에 대해 논의할 것이다.

> **LEVEL UP** 뒤에 전치사가 따라오는 자동사
>
> 동사 어휘를 선택할 때 자동사와 타동사 구별에 유의해야 합니다. 문장을 해석하면서 빈칸 뒤에 전치사가 있는지 살펴보고 전치사가 있다면 그 전치사와 어울리는 자동사를 선택합니다.
>
> Mr. Femi (**participated** / ~~attended~~) **in** the symposium. 페미 씨는 그 심포지엄에 참석했다.

ETS 유형 연습

다음 문장의 빈칸에 들어갈 알맞은 말을 고르세요.

STEP 1

1. Every member of the team should ------- with the new regulations.
   (A) comply
   (B) keep

2. The new line of products will surely ------- a lot of customers.
   (A) appeal
   (B) attract

3. All employees are required to ------- annual evaluations every December.
   (A) agree
   (B) complete

4. Ms. Ishimura generously offered to ------- the invitation in person.
   (A) respond
   (B) deliver

STEP 2

5. The planning team will ------- a survey to determine how much storage is needed.
   (A) remain
   (B) act
   (C) decide
   (D) conduct

6. Most residents of Vilica rely ------- agriculture for their livelihood.
   (A) on
   (B) from
   (C) into
   (D) of

7. Medateli Foods ------- in crafting products that are rich in health-giving vitamins and minerals.
   (A) authorizes
   (B) modernizes
   (C) realizes
   (D) specializes

8. The construction workers ------- with their colleagues to make sure that they meet the deadline.
   (A) collaborate
   (B) collaborating
   (C) collaborates
   (D) collaboration

| 어휘 | 1 regulation 규정 2 surely 분명히 4 generously 친절하게, 관대하게 in person 직접 5 determine 알아내다 storage 보관(소) 6 resident 주민, 거주자 livelihood 생계, 살림살이 7 craft 제조하다 authorize 재가하다 modernize 현대화하다 realize 깨닫다 8 collaboration 협력

ETS 실전 문제

1. The financial review board has stated that no budget proposal may ------- ten pages.
   (A) excessive
   (B) excess
   (C) exceeding
   (D) exceed

2. All new employees are required to ------- in the three-day orientation.
   (A) attend
   (B) take
   (C) inquire
   (D) participate

3. For the last fifteen years, Tatella, Inc. has ------- consistently among the nation's ten leading toy manufacturers.
   (A) rank
   (B) ranked
   (C) ranking
   (D) ranks

4. Kimura Consulting is offering a workshop to ------- its employees' writing skills.
   (A) improve
   (B) explore
   (C) market
   (D) select

5. Customers who ------- to our newsletter will save 15 percent on their first purchase.
   (A) alert
   (B) propose
   (C) receive
   (D) subscribe

6. Glideline Technologies ------- in archiving records and retrieving lost data.
   (A) consists
   (B) interests
   (C) inspects
   (D) specializes

7. The Tyneside Recreation Department ------- suggestions for new programs until the end of this month.
   (A) has accepted
   (B) will be accepting
   (C) accepting
   (D) to accept

8. Keyomon restaurants can be ------- in a wide variety of locations, from urban centers to coastal towns.
   (A) finding
   (B) found
   (C) having found
   (D) find

9. For the best results, allow the glue to dry for twenty minutes to ensure that it ------- to the surface of the wood.
   (A) utilizes
   (B) polishes
   (C) complies
   (D) adheres

10. The Director of Finance and the Director of Personnel responded quite ------- to the question about budget increases.
    (A) differently
    (B) difference
    (C) differed
    (D) differing

Questions 11-14 refer to the following article.

MELBOURNE (26 April)—Tinley Tint, one of Australia's oldest cosmetics companies, has named Stella Chou to replace CEO Clifford Bigsby, who is retiring this week. Over the past ten years, Ms. Chou has held various leadership positions within the company. Most recently, she served as its chief operating officer. In that ------- , she oversaw the rapid expansion of Tinley Tint's global presence. Tinley Tint ------- has distribution centers in more than twenty countries. "It is an honor to ------- as leader of this innovative company," Ms. Chou said in a press release. "The cosmetics industry is about more than just products. It's about empowering people to express their uniqueness. Our employees understand this. ------- ."

11. (A) capacity
    (B) development
    (C) group
    (D) location

12. (A) too
    (B) now
    (C) mostly
    (D) strictly

13. (A) picks
    (B) picking
    (C) have picked
    (D) be picked

14. (A) I am delighted that they have been nominated for this award.
    (B) They deserve most of the credit for Tinley Tint's success.
    (C) Our best-selling lipstick was the first product we developed.
    (D) Tinley Tint will be hiring about 50 more employees this year.

UNIT 07 수 일치

무료 강의

1 수 일치의 개념과 동사의 형태

단수명사 뒤에는 단수동사가 오고, 복수명사 뒤에는 복수동사가 옵니다.

A bean is red.
Three peas are green.

▶ 수 일치의 개념

주어와 동사의 수를 일치시키는 것을 수 일치라고 합니다.

▶ 단수동사와 복수동사의 형태

① 일반동사

명사는 복수일 때 -(e)s를 붙이는 데 반해 동사는 단수일 때 -(e)s를 붙여요. 즉 단수동사는 동사원형에 -(e)s가 붙은 형태를 의미하고 복수동사는 동사원형이 됩니다.

Mr. Watson attends the conference every year. 왓슨 씨는 매년 그 학회에 참석한다.
　단수주어　　단수동사

Our employees attend the conference every year. 우리 직원들은 매년 그 학회에 참석한다.
　복수주어　　복수동사

② be동사, do동사, have동사

	be동사	do동사	have동사
단수	is, am, was	does	has
복수	are, were	do	have

The festival is popular around the world.
그 축제는 전 세계적으로 인기가 있다.

Spanish festivals are popular around the world.
스페인의 축제들은 전 세계적으로 인기가 있다.

IGC Inc. does not produce heavy machinery.
IGC사는 중장비를 생산하지 않는다.

They have not produced heavy machinery.
그들은 중장비를 생산한 적이 없다.

ETS 유형 연습

다음 문장의 빈칸에 들어갈 알맞은 말을 고르세요.

STEP 1

1. The library's e-mail system ------- notified patrons of the new hours of operation.
   (A) has
   (B) have

2. Our research ------- were published in the July issue of *Breakthrough*.
   (A) result
   (B) results

3. The manufacturer ------- the warranty on its latest camera models by twelve months.
   (A) extend
   (B) has extended

4. Second-quarter ------- were significantly above our expectations.
   (A) earning
   (B) earnings

STEP 2

5. Event organizers ------- an increase in the number of vendors at this year's art festival.
   (A) anticipate
   (B) anticipates
   (C) anticipating
   (D) to anticipate

6. Ms. Seon ------- to highlight earnings for the month of August at the upcoming board meeting.
   (A) planning
   (B) were planned
   (C) plans
   (D) plan

7. Our most important goal this year ------- to cut our expenses and save money.
   (A) are
   (B) is
   (C) have
   (D) do

8. Factory ------- have helped Zubiri Footwear to improve the design of its running shoes.
   (A) test
   (B) tests
   (C) tested
   (D) testing

| 어휘 | 1 notify 공지하다　patron 고객, 이용자　operation 운영　2 publish 게재하다, 출판하다　issue (잡지의) 호　3 manufacturer 제조사, 제조업자　warranty 품질 보증　latest 최신의, 최근의　4 significantly 상당히　expectation 기대　earnings 수익　5 organizer 기획자, 주최자　vendor 판매 업체　anticipate 기대하다　6 highlight 부각시키다, 강조하다　upcoming 다가오는　board meeting 이사진 회의　7 expense 비용　8 footwear 신발(류)

❷ 주의해야 할 수 일치

주어를 수식하는 어구는 주어-동사 수 일치에 영향을 미치지 않습니다.

The man carrying many glasses **looks** busy.

▶ 수식어가 붙은 주어와 동사의 수 일치

주어와 동사 사이에 수식어가 있으면 주어와 동사의 사이가 멀어져 수 일치 여부를 판단하기가 쉽지 않습니다. 이런 경우에는 전체 문장 구조를 파악해서 주어와 동사를 찾은 후에 수 일치를 판단하면 됩니다.

Each security camera (in the laboratories) **operates** 24 hours a day. 실험실의 각 보안 카메라는 24시간 작동한다.
　　　　　　　　　　　전치사구　　　　　　　　 ~~operate~~

Each security camera (installed in the laboratories) **operates** 24 hours a day.
　　　　　　　　　　　　　분사구 (UNIT 11 분사 참고)

Each security camera (that was installed in the laboratories) **operates** 24 hours a day.
　　　　　　　　　　　　　관계대명사절 (UNIT 14 관계대명사 참고)

▶ 주의해야 할 주어

❶ 고유명사나 동명사(-ing)로 시작하는 주어는 단수 취급

Acer Solutions (**offers** / ~~offer~~) effective accounting programs. 에이서 솔루션즈는 효율적인 회계 프로그램을 제공한다.

Taking pictures (**is** / ~~are~~) not allowed in the museum. 박물관에서 사진 촬영은 허용되지 않는다.

❷ a number of / the number of

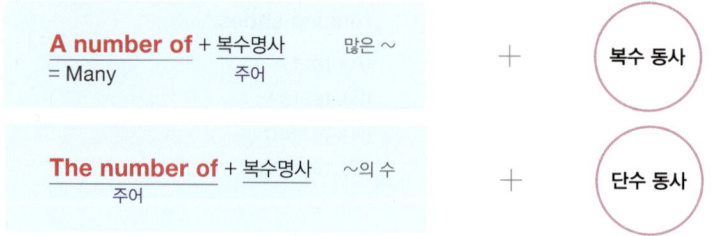

A number of **suitcases** (**were** / ~~was~~) missing. 많은 여행용 가방들이 없어졌다.

The number of tourists (**has** / ~~have~~) decreased. 여행객의 수가 감소했다.

❸ 부분을 나타내는 표현

most, some, half	of the + 단수 명사	+ 단수 동사
	of the + 복수 명사	+ 복수 동사

Most of the marketing staff members (**are** / ~~is~~) on vacation. 마케팅 팀원들은 대부분이 휴가 중이다.

ETS 유형 연습

다음 문장의 빈칸에 들어갈 알맞은 말을 고르세요.

STEP 1

1. Tedeschi Shoes ------- a discount to students of Brinkley University.
   (A) offer
   (B) offers

2. The number of smartphone users ------- expected to increase by 30% this year.
   (A) is
   (B) are

3. Sharing design ideas with co-workers ------- you to receive feedback from them.
   (A) enable
   (B) enables

4. Discount ------- for Thursday evening's jazz concert are available in Ms. Klein's office.
   (A) ticket
   (B) tickets

STEP 2

5. Everyone involved in the Greenfield project ------- in company housing.
   (A) reside
   (B) resides
   (C) residing
   (D) have resided

6. Most of the songs on Georgia Berne's latest CD ------- very popular with teenagers.
   (A) are
   (B) is
   (C) be
   (D) have

7. A number of vehicles ------- parked illegally every night despite the city's strict regulations.
   (A) being
   (B) been
   (C) is
   (D) are

8. The ------- provided by the consultant are supposed to improve staff productivity.
   (A) suggestion
   (B) suggest
   (C) suggestions
   (D) suggesting

| 어휘 | 1 discount 할인 offer 제공하다   2 be expected to ~할 것으로 예상되다   3 co-worker 동료   enable A to A가 ~하는 것을 가능하게 하다   4 available 이용[구입] 가능한   5 involved in ~에 연관된   reside 살다, 거주하다   6 latest 최신의   7 illegally 불법적으로   despite ~에도 불구하고   strict 엄격한   regulation 규정, 규제   8 be supposed to ~할 것으로 추정되다, ~하기로 되어 있다   improve 향상시키다   productivity 생산성

ETS 실전 문제

1. Trains for Gruyville ------- at 9:00 A.M. Monday through Friday.
   (A) depart
   (B) is departed
   (C) departs
   (D) is departing

2. Royce Glass Company's free installation offer ------- from May 1 until August 31.
   (A) extends
   (B) extending
   (C) extensive
   (D) extensively

3. The deadline to sign up for one of the job-related courses ------- February 10.
   (A) is
   (B) are
   (C) have been
   (D) are being

4. ------- for the reception were supplied by J. Lister Design.
   (A) Decorate
   (B) Decorations
   (C) Decoration
   (D) Decorating

5. The office complex ------- on the outskirts of the pedestrian shopping area.
   (A) will be built
   (B) built
   (C) are building
   (D) builder

6. The ------- for the MacNeill project is hanging on the wall in the first floor conference room.
   (A) schedule
   (B) scheduled
   (C) schedules
   (D) scheduler

7. This week only, spend over $200 and your order ------- for free overnight shipping.
   (A) qualification
   (B) qualifies
   (C) qualify
   (D) qualifying

8. The documents in the filing cabinet ------- to be organized alphabetically.
   (A) need
   (B) needs
   (C) needing
   (D) to need

9. Tax laws passed recently ------- the majority of family-owned businesses in the province.
   (A) has benefited
   (B) have benefited
   (C) having benefited
   (D) has been benefited

10. The ------- given by author Michiko Hirota was received well by the employees of Ergan, Inc.
    (A) addresses
    (B) addressable
    (C) addressed
    (D) address

Questions 11-14 refer to the following letter.

Council Member Deborah Hsu
451 Forest Place, Ground Floor
Huxton, RI 02310

Dear Council Member Hsu,

I am writing on behalf of my fellow community members to request more bicycle lanes in our town. The development of new business facilities near residential areas ------- the distance we need to commute. The opening of a bicycle shop on Holleyhill Avenue attests to the increase in bicycle usage. In fact, the *Huxton Daily* made note of ------- in an article earlier in the year.

I understand that the council approved plans on September 6 for bicycle lane development on Teasdale Street and Port Avenue. I fully support these -------, -------. Please improve the safety and efficiency of our roads by adding bicycle lanes.

Thank you.

Sincerely,

Gabriel Richards

11. (A) shorten
    (B) has shortened
    (C) shortening
    (D) to shorten

12. (A) this
    (B) which
    (C) few
    (D) them

13. (A) companies
    (B) groups
    (C) measures
    (D) factories

14. (A) In fact, more bicycle safety courses should be provided.
    (B) In addition, new bicycle shops have been opened.
    (C) In other words, riding a bicycle is good exercise.
    (D) Indeed, I feel that more bicycle lanes should follow.

UNIT 08 시제

무료 강의

1 현재/과거/미래 시제

현재에 일어난 일은 현재 시제로, 과거에 일어난 일은 과거 시제로 표현합니다.

I **finished** my homework **yesterday**.
I **will do** my homework **tomorrow**.

▶ **현재 시제** | 동사원형 또는 〈동사원형+-(e)s〉

현재의 상태, 반복되는 사건이나 습관, 일반적인 사실 등을 표현합니다.

― 현재 시제와 함께 쓰는 말 ―
| always 항상 | often/frequently 자주 | usually 보통 |
| sometimes 가끔 | every week[month] 매주[매달] | regularly/periodically 정기적으로 |

We **hire** additional staff **every year**. 우리는 매년 직원을 추가로 채용한다.

▶ **과거 시제** | 동사원형+-(e)d

특정한 과거 시점에 일어난 일이나 과거의 상태를 표현합니다.

― 과거 시제와 함께 쓰는 말 ―
| yesterday 어제 | last week[month] 지난주[달] | previously 이전에 |
| in+(과거) 연도 ~년에 | 시간 표현+ago ~ 전에 | recently 최근에 |

Ms. Spencer **worked** for a bank **in 2010**. 스펜서 씨는 2010년에 은행에서 일했다.
Our sales **increased** by 10 percent **last year**. 우리의 매출은 지난해 10퍼센트 증가했다.

▶ **미래 시제** | will/be going to+동사원형

미래의 일에 대한 추측이나 의지를 표현합니다.

― 미래 시제와 함께 쓰는 말 ―
| tomorrow 내일 | next week[month] 다음 주[달] | this coming Monday 다가오는 월요일에 |
| soon/shortly 곧 | in the near future 가까운 미래에 | as of/effective+미래 시점 ~부터 |

There **will be** a special event **tomorrow**. 내일 특별 행사가 있을 것이다.
Mr. Cohen **will resign** as president **next month**. 코헨 씨는 다음 달 사장직에서 물러날 것이다.

ETS 유형 연습

다음 문장의 빈칸에 들어갈 알맞은 말을 고르세요.

STEP 1

1. Mr. Kang ------- his printing business 25 years ago in Busan, South Korea.
   (A) will start
   (B) started

2. Zellacor Software, Inc., frequently ------- information technology specialists.
   (A) hires
   (B) hiring

3. The company dinner party ------- held this coming Saturday at Royal Hotel.
   (A) will be
   (B) has been

4. The award ------- to Hiroshi Suzuki at last night's dinner.
   (A) was presented
   (B) has presented

STEP 2

5. Businesses on Ellory Avenue ------- early yesterday to allow work crews to repave the street.
   (A) are closed
   (B) to close
   (C) closing
   (D) closed

6. The current system ------- users to access their online banking accounts by entering a password.
   (A) allowed
   (B) allow
   (C) allows
   (D) allowing

7. A new ordering process for all Engbert Appliance products ------- into effect as of next month.
   (A) will come
   (B) come
   (C) came
   (D) has come

8. Last year, the Hansford Automobile catalog ------- air-conditioning as a standard feature in all automobiles.
   (A) listed
   (B) list
   (C) listing
   (D) to list

| 어휘 | **2** technology 기술 specialist 전문가 hire 고용하다 **3** be held 열리다 **4** award 상 present 주다 **5** work crew 작업반 repave (도로를) 재포장하다 **6** access 접속하다 account 계좌 allow A to A가 ~하는 것을 허락하다 **7** process 절차, 과정 come into effect 시행되다 **8** automobile 자동차 air-conditioning 에어컨 장치 feature 기능, 특징 list 리스트[목록]에 포함시키다[언급하다]

② 진행 시제

어떤 시점에 진행 중인 동작이나 사건은 진행 시제로 표현합니다.

He **is dancing** now.

▶ **현재진행** | am/are/is + -ing

'~하는 중이다'라고 해석되며 현재 시점에 진행 중인 일을 나타냅니다. 또한 미래를 의미하는 부사와 함께 쓰여서 가까운 미래에 예정된 일을 표현할 수도 있습니다.

┌─ 현재진행 시제와 함께 쓰는 말 ─────────────────────────────┐
│ (right) now 지금   at the moment 지금   currently/presently 현재 │
└──┘

The store clerk **is talking** with a customer **now**. 가게 점원은 지금 고객과 이야기하고 있다.
The board meeting **is starting** **soon**. 이사회가 곧 시작된다. (가까운 미래)

▶ **과거진행** | was/were + -ing

과거 특정 시점에 진행 중이던 동작이나 사건을 나타냅니다.

They **were discussing** the matter **at 9 last night**. 그들은 어젯밤 9시에 그 문제를 논의하고 있었다.
When I went in his office, he **was writing** an e-mail.
내가 그의 사무실에 갔을 때 그는 이메일을 쓰고 있었다.

▶ **미래진행** | will be + -ing

미래 특정 시점에 진행되고 있을 사건이나 동작을 나타냅니다.

I **will be staying** in New York **next week**. 나는 다음 주에 뉴욕에 머무르고 있을 것이다.
The technician **will be fixing** the heaters **this afternoon**.
그 기술자는 오늘 오후에 난방기들을 수리하고 있을 것이다.

ETS 유형 연습

다음 문장의 빈칸에 들어갈 알맞은 말을 고르세요.

정답과 해설 p.149

STEP 1

1. Due to overbooking, some Telco Bus passengers ------- now waiting over five hours.
   (A) are
   (B) were

2. Pohang residents will ------- to elect their new mayor this time next week.
   (A) be voting
   (B) voted

3. Ms. Yoon ------- from jet lag when she returned on Thursday.
   (A) will suffer
   (B) was suffering

4. The visitors ------- touring our production facilities at 10 A.M. tomorrow morning.
   (A) were
   (B) will be

STEP 2

5. A service engineer from PX Copytime ------- the broken copy machine at the moment.
   (A) repair
   (B) repairs
   (C) will repair
   (D) is repairing

6. Flunge, Inc., ------- a new representative to the investors' meeting next February.
   (A) send
   (B) sending
   (C) will be sending
   (D) were sent

7. When Paxton Enterprises ------- its textile division, several middle managers were laid off.
   (A) were restructured
   (B) restructures
   (C) was restructuring
   (D) to restructure

8. Mornesse Hardware ------- free flashlights to the first 50 customers next Friday.
   (A) is offering
   (B) having offered
   (C) was offered
   (D) to offer

| 어휘 | 1 due to ~ 때문에   overbooking 초과 예약 2 elect 선출하다   mayor 시장   vote 투표하다 3 jet lag 시차증 return 되돌아오다   suffer (고통 등을) 겪다 4 visitor 방문객   production 생산   facility 시설 5 broken 고장 난 repair 수리하다 6 representative 대표; 대표하다   investor 투자자 7 textile 섬유 (산업), 직물   restructure 구조 조정하다, 개혁하다 8 free 무료의   flashlight 손전등

③ 완료 시제

과거의 어떤 시점보다 더 과거에 일어난 일은 과거완료로 표현합니다.

The ship **had left** before she **arrived**.

▶ **현재완료** | have/has + p.p.

과거에 발생한 일이나 상태가 현재까지 계속되거나 영향을 미치고 있음을 나타냅니다. '~했다, ~해오고 있다, ~해본 적 있다' 등으로 해석됩니다.

― 현재완료 시제와 함께 쓰는 말 ―

| recently/lately 최근에 | for + 기간 ~ 동안 |
| since + 과거 시점 ~ 이래로 | over[for/in] the last[past] + 기간 지난 ~에 걸쳐[동안] |

The business **has grown** significantly **since 2012**. 2012년 이후로 사업이 상당히 성장했다.

They **have worked** together **for the last two years**. 그들은 지난 2년 동안 함께 일했다.

> **LEVEL UP** 명확한 과거 시점과 함께 쓸 수 없는 현재완료 시제
> 현재완료 동사는 명확한 과거 시점을 나타내는 last + 시점, ago, yesterday 등과 함께 쓸 수 없습니다.
> The plant (**stopped** / ~~has stopped~~) operating **last week**. 공장은 지난주에 가동을 멈췄다.

▶ **과거완료** | had p.p.

과거의 어떤 시점을 기준으로 그보다 더 이전 과거에 일어난 일을 나타냅니다.

― 과거완료 시제와 함께 쓰는 말 ―

| before + 주어 + 과거 동사 ~하기 전에 | by the time + 주어 + 과거 동사 ~했을 때 즈음에 |

Many fans **had arrived** at the concert **before** the performance **started**.
공연이 시작하기 전에 많은 팬들이 콘서트장에 도착해 있었다.

▶ **미래완료** | will have p.p.

과거나 현재에 시작된 일이 미래까지 계속되거나 미래의 특정 시점에 완료될 것임을 나타냅니다.

― 미래완료 시제와 함께 쓰는 말 ―

| by the time + 주어 + 현재 동사 ~할 때 즈음에 | by + 시점 ~까지 |

I **will have left** the office **by the time** you **come**.
당신이 올 때 즈음에 나는 이미 퇴근하고 없을 것이다.

ETS 유형 연습

다음 문장의 빈칸에 들어갈 알맞은 말을 고르세요.

정답과 해설 p.149

STEP 1

1. Working conditions ------- greatly since the new CEO joined Loopa Investments.
   (A) improved
   (B) have improved

2. The two companies ------- an agreement on a merger plan one month ago.
   (A) reached
   (B) have reached

3. Mr. Imola's net profit rate ------- slightly risen for the last three quarters.
   (A) has
   (B) was

4. Several Tiger Gym health clubs ------- recently in the city center.
   (A) have opened
   (B) will have opened

STEP 2

5. More university students ------- in internships in the last five years than ever before.
   (A) were participated
   (B) have participated
   (C) participating
   (D) will participate

6. The 10:17 A.M. train ------- already left before Mr. Abaki's team arrived at the station.
   (A) has
   (B) had
   (C) is
   (D) will have

7. We ------- ten inquiries since the advertisement ran in last week's edition of the newspaper.
   (A) receive
   (B) have received
   (C) will receive
   (D) receiving

8. By the time Ms. Valspar retires, she ------- to increase the company's market share significantly.
   (A) manages
   (B) will have managed
   (C) managed
   (D) has been managing

| 어휘 | 1 working conditions 근무 환경   greatly 대단히   2 agreement 합의, 계약서   merger 합병   3 net profit rate 순수익률   slightly 약간   quarter 사분기   4 city center 도심부   5 internship 인턴 프로그램   than ever before 과거 어느 때보다   participate in ~에 참가하다, 참여하다(= take part in)   6 leave 떠나다   arrive 도착하다   station 역   7 inquiry 문의, 조회   advertisement 광고   8 retire 은퇴하다   market share 시장 점유율   significantly 상당히

ETS 실전 문제

1. Maggie Williams, the purchasing manager, currently ------- requested supplies at the end of each week.
   (A) ordered
   (B) orders
   (C) order
   (D) ordering

2. Next month, Berges Art Studio ------- 25 percent off all classes.
   (A) was offered
   (B) offered
   (C) will offer
   (D) has been offering

3. According to the Harton Fashion Chronicle, many designers ------- green and brown fabrics for their autumn collections this year.
   (A) to use
   (B) are using
   (C) had been used
   (D) were used

4. Polansky Data International ------- transportation for all employees attending the digital media conference in Liverpool next week.
   (A) has arranged
   (B) was arranged
   (C) arranging
   (D) arrangements

5. Dr. Suzuki arrived for the awards ceremony on time even though her train ------- twenty minutes late.
   (A) is leaving
   (B) will leave
   (C) to leave
   (D) had left

6. At Gaude University, the graduation rate has increased by 55 percent ------- the past decade.
   (A) over
   (B) behind
   (C) near
   (D) toward

7. Real estate agents in Stranton anticipate that property values ------- in the coming year.
   (A) increasingly
   (B) increasing
   (C) will increase
   (D) to increase

8. The Salisbury Nature Club's treasurer ------- and suggested revisions to the budget for the next financial quarter.
   (A) is examining
   (B) has examined
   (C) will examine
   (D) to examine

9. Monthly account statements are ------- available for review online.
   (A) now
   (B) well
   (C) gently
   (D) brightly

10. Because of a sudden decrease in sales, Mikkelsen Clothing suspended its current advertising campaign and ------- it substantially.
    (A) to modify
    (B) will be modifying
    (C) having modified
    (D) modifying

Questions 11-14 refer to the following notice.

To all staff:

You may be aware that a minor electrical fire was extinguished on the first floor of our building last night. -------11.------- , the fire was contained quickly, so the damage is minimal. However, the kitchenette and tables are -------12.------- today. Electricians arrived this morning to inspect and replace the wiring. -------13.------- . We are grateful to our overnight security crew for taking quick action.

Regardless of whether you use the kitchenette regularly, your manager -------14.------- to distribute vouchers for free refreshments at the company cafeteria.

—Judy Ng, Facilities Manager

11. (A) Repeatedly
    (B) Fortunately
    (C) Normally
    (D) Kindly

12. (A) arranged
    (B) incomplete
    (C) furnished
    (D) unavailable

13. (A) A new restaurant has just opened a mere block from our office.
    (B) There is not enough money in the budget for this.
    (C) When they are done, the space will be cleaned thoroughly.
    (D) Please let your manager know if you can attend the team luncheon.

14. (A) has been authorized
    (B) had been authorized
    (C) authorizes
    (D) authorized

UNIT 09 능동태와 수동태

무료 강의

1 수동태의 개념과 형태

주어가 다른 대상으로부터 어떤 행위를 당하는 경우 수동태로 표현합니다.

The thief **stole** a treasure. 능동태
A treasure **was stolen** by the thief. 수동태

▶ 능동태와 수동태의 개념

영어는 주어가 어떤 행위를 직접 행하는 능동태와, 주어가 다른 대상으로부터 어떤 행위를 당하는 수동태로 구분할 수 있습니다. 능동태는 '~하다'로, 수동태는 '~해지다, ~하게 되다'로 해석됩니다.

▶ 수동태의 형태

기본 형태는 〈be동사+p.p.(과거분사)〉입니다. 여기서 주어의 수와 시제에 따라 be동사의 형태가 달라집니다.

현재 과거 미래	be+p.p.	am/are/is+p.p. was/were+p.p. will be+p.p.	The letter **is sent** by mail. 편지는 우편으로 전달된다. The letter **was sent** by mail. 편지는 우편으로 전달되었다. The letter **will be sent** by mail. 편지는 우편으로 전달될 것이다.
현재진행 과거진행 미래진행	be being +p.p.	am/are/is+being+p.p. was/were+being+p.p. will be+being+p.p.	All computers **are being repaired**. 모든 컴퓨터가 수리되고 있다. All computers **were being repaired**. 모든 컴퓨터가 수리되고 있었다. All computers **will be being repaired**. 모든 컴퓨터가 수리되고 있을 것이다.
현재완료 과거완료 미래완료	have been +p.p.	have/has+been+p.p. had+been+p.p. will have+been+p.p.	The plan **has been changed**. 계획이 변경되었다. The plan **had been changed**. 계획이 변경되어 있었다. The plan **will have been changed**. 계획이 변경되어 있을 것이다.

▶ 수동태 문장의 형성

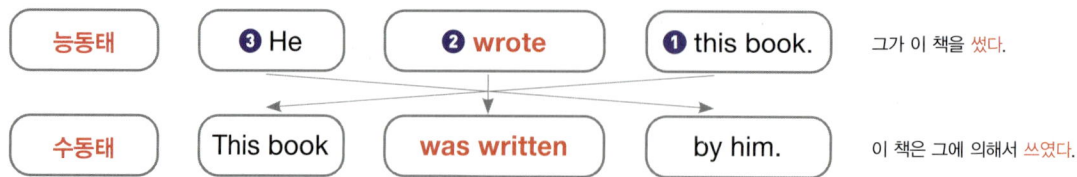

❶ 능동태의 목적어 this book이 주어 자리로 옵니다.

❷ 수동태 동사의 형태 〈be+p.p.〉가 되도록 동사 wrote를 주어의 수와 시제에 맞게 was written으로 바꿉니다.

❸ 능동태의 주어 He는 〈by+목적격〉인 by him으로 바꿉니다. 단, 이 부분은 생략 가능합니다.

→ 능동태 문장의 목적어를 주어로 해서 만든 문장이 수동태이므로 목적어를 갖는 타동사만이 수동태가 될 수 있습니다.
 즉, 뒤에 목적어가 오지 않는 자동사는 수동태로 쓰이지 않습니다.

ETS 유형 연습

다음 문장의 빈칸에 들어갈 알맞은 말을 고르세요.

정답과 해설 p.152

STEP 1

1. Candidates for the position must ------- their applications by the end of the month.
   (A) submit
   (B) be submitted

2. A list of engineers nominated for a design award is ------- to this e-mail.
   (A) attaching
   (B) attached

3. The requested information should be ------- carefully in the space provided.
   (A) writing
   (B) written

4. The seminar will be attended ------- professionals in the food service industry.
   (A) of
   (B) by

STEP 2

5. Due to the airline strike, Mr. Jarvela ------- his plans to travel to Rome.
   (A) postponing
   (B) to postpone
   (C) should be postponed
   (D) had to postpone

6. Our quality control department tests all products before they are ------- to retailers.
   (A) shipped
   (B) shipment
   (C) ships
   (D) shipping

7. The report on the city's train system ------- to the public last Tuesday.
   (A) to release
   (B) have released
   (C) is releasing
   (D) was released

8. An updated list of job opportunities ------- on Island Hopper's Web page.
   (A) is posted
   (B) posting
   (C) are posting
   (D) post

| 어휘 | 1 candidate 지원자, 후보자 application 지원서 2 nominate (후보로) 지명하다 award 상 attach 첨부하다 3 requested 요청된 carefully 신중하게 provided 제공된 4 professional 전문가 food service industry 외식산업 5 strike 파업 postpone 미루다 6 quality control 품질 관리 retailer 소매업자 ship 배송하다 7 public 일반인들, 대중 release 공개하다 8 opportunity 기회 post 게시하다

② 능동태와 수동태 구별하기

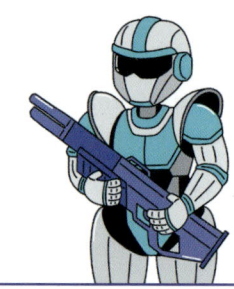

항상 전치사와 함께 쓰이는 수동태 구문이 있습니다.

The future warrior **is equipped with** weapons.

▶ 능동태와 수동태 구별하기

동사 자리가 능동태인지 수동태인지는 동사 뒤의 목적어 유무에 따라 결정됩니다. 동사 자리 뒤에 목적어가 있으면 능동태, 동사 자리 뒤에 목적어가 없으면 수동태가 됩니다.

❶ 능동태: 빈칸 뒤에 한정사(관사, 소유격, 수량 형용사 등)가 있다면 그 뒤에 명사인 목적어가 있음을 알 수 있습니다.

A famous architect (**built** / ~~was built~~) **the museum**.
유명한 건축가가 그 박물관을 건립했다.

Ablexar Co. (**is building** / ~~is being built~~) **its new plant**.
애블렉서 사는 새로운 공장을 짓고 있다.

❷ 수동태: 빈칸 뒤에 전치사나 부사가 왔거나 또는 문장이 빈칸으로 끝났다면 목적어가 없는 수동태 자리일 확률이 높습니다.

Conference room B (**is being prepared** / ~~is preparing~~) **by Ms. Yoon**.
B회의실이 윤 씨에 의해 준비되고 있다.

The sales presentation (**will be prepared** / ~~will prepare~~) **soon**.
곧 영업 발표가 준비될 것이다

▶ 수동태 + 전치사 구문

in	be engaged in ~에 종사하다	be interested in ~에 관심이 있다	be involved in ~에 관련되다
to	be committed to ~에 전념하다 = be dedicated[devoted] to	be accustomed to ~에 익숙하다 = be used to	be exposed to ~에 노출되다 be related to ~와 관계가 있다
with	be satisfied with ~에 만족하다 be pleased with ~에 기뻐하다	be concerned with ~에 관련되다 be associated with ~와 관련되다	be equipped with ~을 갖추고 있다 be crowded with ~로 붐비다

Many people **are interested in** the seminar. 많은 사람들이 세미나에 관심이 있다.

The DX printer **is equipped with** a scanner. DX 프린터는 스캐너를 갖추고 있다.

Professor Lee **is committed to** teaching students. 이 교수는 학생들을 가르치는 일에 전념한다.
= dedicated, devoted

ETS 유형 연습

다음 문장의 빈칸에 들어갈 알맞은 말을 고르세요.

정답과 해설 p.152

STEP 1

1. The company handbook ------- the topics of compensation, bonuses, and overtime.
   (A) is covered
   (B) covers

2. The best trailer for small boats ------- by Tow-Well Manufacturing.
   (A) is made
   (B) is making

3. Better marketing strategies can always -------.
   (A) are developing
   (B) be developed

4. Both the designers and photographers are satisfied ------- the fall catalog.
   (A) for
   (B) with

STEP 2

5. Mr. Ling is ------- a revised schedule to the show's host as well as to the guest speakers.
   (A) distribute
   (B) distributing
   (C) distributes
   (D) distributed

6. A large number of team members are interested ------- the upcoming workshop.
   (A) in
   (B) of
   (C) to
   (D) for

7. Both the model number and the serial number ------- on the back of every watch.
   (A) were engraving
   (B) are engraved
   (C) to be engraved
   (D) engrave

8. Many problems with locks ------- by a simple repair or adjustment.
   (A) solved
   (B) could solve
   (C) can solve
   (D) can be solved

| 어휘 | 1 compensation (노고의) 보상, 보수   cover 다루다   3 strategy 전략   develop 개발하다   5 revised 수정된   as well as ~뿐만 아니라   distribute 나눠 주다, 분배하다   6 a number of 많은   upcoming 다가오는   7 serial number 일련 번호   engrave 새기다   8 lock 자물쇠   repair 수리; 수리하다   adjustment 조절, 조정

UNIT 09 | 능동태와 수동태

ETS 실전 문제

1. Dave Minsent, a lawyer from Alsager, was ------- to serve on the town council.
   (A) election
   (B) electoral
   (C) elect
   (D) elected

2. The Silvau Division is now ------- a full line of steel products at a new modern facility just outside the city.
   (A) manufacturer
   (B) being manufactured
   (C) manufactured
   (D) manufacturing

3. All passengers ------- to stay seated while the bus is in motion.
   (A) can require
   (B) are required
   (C) are requiring
   (D) have required

4. Jae Kwon's collection of photographs ------- the subtle changes of light across the mountain landscape.
   (A) exposes
   (B) expose
   (C) is exposed
   (D) are exposing

5. The newly renovated laboratory is equipped ------- state-of-the-art research equipment and security cameras.
   (A) by
   (B) with
   (C) in
   (D) to

6. The technical manuals for the True Photo Printer ------- into Spanish by contractors from A-Language, Inc.
   (A) translation
   (B) were translated
   (C) translator
   (D) are translating

7. Anyone who ------- the missing warehouse key should return it to Mr. Shah.
   (A) find
   (B) was found
   (C) finds
   (D) is found

8. The various measures used to determine annual salary increases ------- to as the merit criteria.
   (A) are referred
   (B) referring
   (C) have referred
   (D) to refer

9. The winter agenda of the company's community service club ------- later this afternoon.
   (A) circulated
   (B) has circulated
   (C) has been circulating
   (D) will be circulated

10. The Web site of Miller Hardware Store is ------- for viewing on mobile phones.
    (A) simplification
    (B) simplified
    (C) simplifies
    (D) simplifying

Questions 11-14 refer to the following guidelines.

The *Opalwood Tribune* welcomes letters from readers. Because space is limited, we cannot print ------- submissions we receive. We give priority to letters that provide a new perspective on issues of local interest, particularly if the issue ------- in a recent article. We also prefer letters that do not exceed 200 words. ------- .

Please be sure to include your name and contact information so the editors can notify you if your letter is ------- for publication.

11. (A) any
    (B) total
    (C) all
    (D) original

12. (A) mentioned
    (B) has mentioned
    (C) being mentioned
    (D) was mentioned

13. (A) Therefore, we do not publish anonymous letters.
    (B) Submissions that are longer than that may be edited.
    (C) The use of such words is not allowed in our publication.
    (D) Please do not write us more frequently than this.

14. (A) selected
    (B) completed
    (C) opened
    (D) continued

UNIT 10 to부정사와 동명사

무료 강의

① to부정사의 형태와 역할

to부정사는 문장에서 명사, 형용사, 부사 역할을 합니다.

She exercises hard **to lose weight**.

▶ to부정사의 형태

to부정사는 〈to+동사원형〉의 형태로 대표적인 준동사 중 하나입니다. 준동사란 동사에서 비롯되었으나 동사가 아닌 다른 품사(명사, 형용사, 부사)로 쓰이는 것들을 말합니다. to부정사, 동명사, 분사가 이에 해당되는데 동사처럼 목적어를 취할 수 있고, 부사의 수식을 받을 수도 있습니다.

The producers will meet **to arrange** the schedule. 제작자들이 일정을 짜기 위해 모일 것이다.
<u>　　　　　　　　　　　　　　　　　目적어　　</u>

▶ to부정사의 역할

to부정사는 문장에서 명사, 형용사, 부사의 역할을 합니다.

❶ 명사 역할(~하는 것, ~하기): 명사처럼 문장의 주어, 목적어, 보어 자리에 올 수 있습니다.

주어　**To meet** the deadline is necessary. 반드시 마감일을 맞춰야 한다.
　　　= **It** is necessary **to meet** the deadline. → 주어가 너무 길면 뒤로 보내고 그 자리에 가주어 it을 씁니다.
　　　It is necessary **for him to meet** the deadline. 그는 반드시 마감일을 맞춰야 한다.
　　　→ to부정사의 의미상 주어는 〈for+목적격〉의 형태로 표시합니다.

목적어　The film producers **decided to delay** the release date. 영화 제작자들은 개봉일을 늦추기로 결정했다.

보어　　Our goal **is to develop** cutting-edge technology. 우리의 목표는 최신 기술을 개발하는 것입니다.

❷ 형용사 역할(~할, ~하는): 명사의 뒤에 위치해 앞에 나온 명사를 수식하는 형용사 역할을 할 수 있습니다.

The government announced **a plan to reduce** traffic congestion. 정부는 교통 혼잡을 줄이기 위한 계획을 발표했다.

❸ 부사 역할(~하기 위하여): 문장에서 목적을 나타냅니다.

The conference location was changed **to accommodate** 150 participants.
　　　　　　　　　　　　　　　　　= in order to accommodate
150명의 참가자들을 수용하기 위해 회의 장소가 변경되었다.

ETS 유형 연습

다음 문장의 빈칸에 들어갈 알맞은 말을 고르세요.

STEP 1

1. The management team decided ------- the project because of budget constraints.
   (A) cancel
   (B) to cancel

2. One of your tasks as a computer programmer is ------- our Web site.
   (A) update
   (B) to update

3. Ms. Dodson has so many assignments ------- complete that she cannot take a day off.
   (A) for
   (B) to

4. ------- fine furniture, Mr. Taylor uses special wood that is not available in stores.
   (A) To build
   (B) To building

STEP 2

5. Rings on display in the jewelry case can be sized ------- fit any finger.
   (A) to
   (B) will
   (C) so
   (D) upon

6. To ------- clinic volunteers, Laradore Hospital administrators will provide refreshments.
   (A) thankful
   (B) thanks
   (C) thanking
   (D) thank

7. In order to ------- properly, this machine must be serviced at regular intervals.
   (A) functions
   (B) functional
   (C) functioning
   (D) function

8. ------- is possible for a robot to carry out several tasks at the same time.
   (A) It
   (B) This
   (C) That
   (D) There

| 어휘 | 1 decide 결정하다 budget 예산 constraint 제약 2 task 업무 3 assignment 업무 complete 완료하다 take a day off 하루 쉬다 4 fine 훌륭한, 질 좋은 5 size 치수를 바꾸다 fit 맞다 6 volunteer 자원봉사자 administrator 관계자, 관리자 refreshments 다과 7 properly 제대로 service 정비하다 interval 간격 function 기능을 하다; 기능 8 possible 가능한 carry out 수행하다 at the same time 동시에

② 자주 출제되는 to부정사 표현

어떤 동사는 to부정사를 목적어로 취합니다.

I hope to be beautiful someday.
  expect

▶ 동사 + to부정사

want to ~하고 싶다	decide to ~하기로 결정하다	tend to ~하는 경향이 있다
would like to ~하고 싶다	need to ~해야 한다	hope to ~하기를 바라다
plan to ~할 계획이다	expect to ~하기를 기대하다	try to ~하려고 노력하다
agree to ~하는 데 동의하다	fail to ~하지 못하다	(= strive to)

The personnel department **plans to hold** a retirement party. 인사과는 퇴직 기념 파티를 열 계획이다.
The local government **agreed to protect** the forest. 지방 정부는 숲을 보호하는 데 동의했다.

▶ 명사 + to부정사

ability to ~할 능력	time to ~할 시간	effort to ~하려는 노력
right to ~할 권리	chance to ~할 기회	failure to ~하지 못함
way to ~할 방법	opportunity to ~할 기회	plan to ~할 계획

Moss & Co. is seeking a **way to maximize** profits. Moss & Co 사는 수익을 극대화할 방안을 모색하고 있다.

▶ be동사 + 형용사/분사 + to부정사

be ready to ~할 준비가 되다	be pleased to ~하게 되어 기쁘다
be allowed to ~하는 것이 허락되다	be advised to ~하도록 권고받다
be able to ~할 수 있다	be likely to ~할 것 같다
be expected to ~하리라 예상되다, ~할 것이다	be designed to ~하도록 고안되다
be willing to 기꺼이 ~하다	be scheduled to ~할 예정이다
be asked to ~하도록 요청받다	be required to ~하는 것이 필수적이다

We **were able to find** a replacement for Lydia Parry. 우리는 리디아 패리의 후임을 구할 수 있었다.
His flight **is expected to arrive** late. 그의 비행편이 늦게 도착할 것으로 예상된다.

ETS 유형 연습

다음 문장의 빈칸에 들어갈 알맞은 말을 고르세요.

STEP 1

1. Ms. Adrina hopes to ------- the deadline to finish her financial report.
   (A) extend
   (B) extending

2. Teachers are ------- to arrive early on Monday in order to meet the new students.
   (A) expectations
   (B) expected

3. Duncan Enterprise plans ------- its first store in Manila this year.
   (A) to open
   (B) opened

4. We are pleased ------- subscribers' letters on matters of interest to our readers.
   (A) to publish
   (B) publishing

STEP 2

5. We at TPG Financial Planning welcome the opportunity ------- you in your business.
   (A) assisting
   (B) to assist
   (C) assisted
   (D) assistant

6. National Bank officials have taken the necessary steps ------- another computer system failure.
   (A) prevented
   (B) to prevent
   (C) prevent
   (D) were prevented

7. The City Chorus is scheduled ------- at the dedication of the new library building.
   (A) is performing
   (B) will perform
   (C) to perform
   (D) performance

8. The board of Lee & Zhang, Inc. has concluded that it is time ------- the computer network.
   (A) upgrades
   (B) will upgrade
   (C) to upgrade
   (D) upgrading

| 어휘 | 1 deadline 마감일 financial 재정의 extend 연장하다 2 expectation 기대, 예상 4 subscriber 구독자 matter of interest 관심사 publish 발표하다, 출판하다 5 welcome 환영하다 opportunity 기회 assist 돕다 6 official 공무원, 임원 take steps 조치를 취하다 failure 고장, 장애 prevent 막다, 방지하다 7 dedication 개관식; 헌신 perform 공연하다 8 board 이사회 conclude 결론 내리다

③ 동명사의 개념과 명사와의 차이점

어떤 동사는 동명사를 목적어로 취합니다.

Everyone **enjoys**   **playing** the game.
             practices

▶ 동명사의 개념과 역할

〈동사원형+-ing〉의 형태로 동사의 성격이 있지만 동사가 아니라 명사로 쓰이는 단어를 동명사라고 합니다. 명사처럼 문장에서 주어, 보어, 목적어 역할을 합니다.

주어   **Boosting** sales volume **is** our goal for this quarter.   판매량을 올리는 것이 이번 분기 우리의 목표다.

보어   Our main concern **is promoting** our brand image.   우리의 주 관심사는 브랜드 이미지를 제고하는 것이다.

목적어   The renovation project **includes replacing** floor tiles.   수리 계획은 바닥 타일을 교체하는 것을 포함한다.

동명사를 목적어로 취하는 동사

enjoy 즐기다	finish 마치다	postpone[delay] 미루다	consider 고려하다	recommend 추천하다
suggest 제안하다	include 포함하다	keep 계속하다	avoid 피하다	give up 포기하다

▶ 동명사와 명사의 차이

동사에서 파생된 동명사는 명사와 달리 뒤에 목적어를 취할 수 있고, 부사의 수식을 받을 수도 있습니다. 전치사 뒤 목적어 자리 빈칸에는 명사 역할을 하는 단어(명사, 대명사, 동명사 등)가 들어가야 하는데, 빈칸 뒤에 명사가 있다면 그 빈칸은 동명사 자리가 될 수 있습니다.

Wilson Fashion is famous for (**skillfully** / ~~skillful~~) **making** leather belts.
윌슨 패션은 솜씨 있게 가죽 벨트를 제작하는 것으로 유명하다.
→ 동명사를 수식할 수 있는 것은 부사입니다.

This report is about (**improving** / ~~improvement~~) **productivity**.   이 보고서는 생산성을 높이는 것에 관한 것이다.
→ 전치사와 명사 사이 빈칸은 동명사 자리일 확률이 높습니다.

▶ 동명사 관용 표현

spend 시간[돈] (in) -ing ~하는 데 시간[돈]을 쓰다	be[get] used to -ing ~하는 데 익숙해지다
have trouble/difficulty -ing ~하는 데 어려움을 겪다	look forward to 명사/-ing ~을 기대하다
be busy -ing ~하느라 바쁘다	on/upon -ing ~하자마자
by -ing ~함으로써	play a role in -ing ~하는 데 역할을 하다

We are **looking forward to** (**meeting** / ~~meet~~) you soon.   곧 당신을 만나기를 기대합니다.

ETS 유형 연습

다음 문장의 빈칸에 들어갈 알맞은 말을 고르세요.

STEP 1

1. To avoid ------- a late fee, you have to return the books by the due date.
   (A) paying
   (B) pay

2. ------- yourself to the audience is the first step of your presentation.
   (A) Introduction
   (B) Introducing

3. ------- arriving at the airport, take the free shuttle bus to the Hotel Marois.
   (A) On
   (B) From

4. The dieticians recommend ------- a well-balanced and healthy breakfast daily.
   (A) eating
   (B) eat

STEP 2

5. Personnel must sign the register before ------- any confidential papers from vaults.
   (A) removed
   (B) remover
   (C) removal
   (D) removing

6. Maga Electronics, Inc., spent over a million dollars ------- new mobile phones last year.
   (A) develop
   (B) developing
   (C) is developed
   (D) developed

7. Senior management has considered ------- a ban on the personal use of work computers.
   (A) institute
   (B) instituted
   (C) institution
   (D) instituting

8. Playo Construction plays a critical role ------- helping our company achieve its goals on every project.
   (A) since
   (B) though
   (C) much
   (D) in

| 어휘 | 1 avoid 피하다   late fee 연체료   due date 기일, 마감일   2 audience 청중   4 dietician 영양사   well-balanced 균형 잡힌   daily 매일   5 personnel 직원   register 기록부   confidential 기밀의   vault 보관실, 금고   6 mobile phone 휴대전화   develop 개발하다   7 senior management 고위 경영진   ban 금지   personal 개인적인, 사적인   institute 시행하다, 실시하다; 협회   institution 제정, 설립, 기관   8 construction 건설, 공사   achieve 성취하다

ETS 실전 문제

1. The business consultant suggests ------- the merger plan carefully before negotiations begin.
   (A) review
   (B) reviews
   (C) reviewing
   (D) reviewed

2. ------- additional audio books is part of the head librarian's plan to modernize the library's collections.
   (A) Purchases
   (B) Purchasing
   (C) Has purchased
   (D) Will be purchasing

3. We at the Ribeiro Agency strive ------- all communication with our clients clear and to the point.
   (A) to make
   (B) making
   (C) to be made
   (D) having made

4. All employees of Future Styles Co. are looking forward to ------- their new designers.
   (A) meet
   (B) met
   (C) meeting
   (D) have met

5. Our goal is to establish supply-chain efficiencies ------- increase revenue growth.
   (A) while
   (B) in order to
   (C) also
   (D) by the time

6. The publisher's goal is ------- the daily circulation figure of 80,000 by next year.
   (A) to surpass
   (B) surpassed
   (C) surpass
   (D) surpassing

7. Mr. Jung will present the results of the marketing study to the president after he has had a chance ------- them.
   (A) to review
   (B) reviewer
   (C) reviewed
   (D) is reviewing

8. If you wish to pay for this computer workshop by ------- your credit card, please contact Linda Wagner at 555-4236.
   (A) used
   (B) using
   (C) usage
   (D) usable

9. It is important for companies ------- professional development opportunities in order to retain qualified staff.
   (A) offering
   (B) offer
   (C) to offer
   (D) offered

10. Mercox Cosmetics hopes ------- its number one ranking in consumer growth by expanding its market.
    (A) to defend
    (B) defense
    (C) defending
    (D) defended

Questions 11-14 refer to the following article.

Growing a Garden in Limited Space

Many vegetable lovers enjoy growing their own food at home. ------- . To save space, you
                                                                  11.
can grow different plants together. Bush beans, ------- , are fast growers and can be planted
                                                   12.
between tomatoes, a slower-growing plant. The ------- plants will help prevent the growth of
                                                 13.
weeds as the tomatoes mature. Once the beans are grown, the vegetables can be harvested
and the plants removed. This will create room for the tomatoes ------- growing and leave
                                                                  14.
valuable nutrients in the soil. Ultimately, your garden's yield will increase and the health of
your plants will be significantly improved.

11. (A) Tomato plants are commonly found in home gardens.
(B) Gardening can be very time-consuming.
(C) Yet, finding space for everything you want to grow can be a struggle.
(D) Deciding what to grow is an essential part of the process.

12. (A) however
(B) as a result
(C) for example
(D) on the other hand

13. (A) natural
(B) colorful
(C) rare
(D) extra

14. (A) continuing
(B) to continue
(C) could continue
(D) have continued

UNIT 11 분사

1 분사의 형태와 역할

분사에는 능동이나 진행을 의미하는 현재분사(-ing)와 수동이나 완료를 의미하는 과거분사(-ed)가 있습니다.

a **wandering** cat   **fallen** leaves

▶ 분사의 형태와 의미

	형태	의미	예문
현재분사	동사원형+-ing	~한, ~하고 있는 (능동, 진행)	falling leaves 떨어지는 잎사귀들
과거분사	동사원형+-ed	~된 (수동, 완료)	fallen leaves (이미) 떨어진 잎사귀들

▶ 분사의 역할

형용사처럼 명사를 수식하거나 보충하는 역할을 합니다. 그리고 to부정사나 동명사와 마찬가지로 동사는 아니지만 동사의 성질이 있어서 뒤에 목적어가 올 수 있고 부사의 수식을 받을 수 있습니다.

❶ 명사 앞에서 수식

All **damaged** merchandise should be returned within a week. 모든 손상된 제품은 일주일 이내에 반품되어야 한다.

❷ 명사 뒤에서 수식

Mr. Allen sent **an e-mail accepting** the job offer. 앨런 씨는 그 일자리 제안을 수락하는 이메일을 보냈다.

> **LEVEL UP** 분사가 명사를 뒤에서 수식하는 경우 분사 뒤 목적어 유무로 능동/수동을 판단
>
> 대체로 분사 뒤에 목적어(명사)가 있으면 -ing, 뒤에 목적어가 없고 전치사구나 부사가 있으면 -ed가 옵니다.
>
> Dylan watched **a documentary discussing** Jazz. 딜런은 재즈를 다룬 다큐멘터리를 보았다.
> 목적어
>
> **The records stored** on the first floor are available now. 1층에 보관된 기록물들은 현재 열람할 수 있다.
> 전치사구

❸ 보어

The topic of the seminar **was interesting**. 세미나의 주제는 흥미로웠다.

Assistants should **keep** the items **organized**. 조수들은 물품들을 정돈되게 유지해야 한다.

→ 보어를 필요로 하는 동사는 UNIT 1 문장의 구성 요소를 참고하세요.

ETS 유형 연습

다음 문장의 빈칸에 들어갈 알맞은 말을 고르세요.

정답과 해설 p.158

STEP 1

1. The country's ------- exports have caused great concern among economic experts.
   (A) decrease
   (B) decreasing

2. The city's building codes have become very ------- to accommodate.
   (A) complicated
   (B) complicate

3. Any person ------- in a legal case is advised to consult a lawyer.
   (A) involving
   (B) involved

4. The discount offer is not valid on tickets ------- before publication of this advertisement.
   (A) purchased
   (B) purchases

STEP 2

5. Because of minor bridge repairs, trains will run with ------- frequency from May 12 to May 25.
   (A) reduce
   (B) reduced
   (C) reduces
   (D) reduction

6. Your personal digital files will remain ------- safely on our online server.
   (A) store
   (B) storage
   (C) stores
   (D) stored

7. The brochure ------- all the vendors for the trade show will be sent out next week.
   (A) list
   (B) listing
   (C) lists
   (D) listed

8. Mr. Vargas makes a point of including ------- notes in the welcome cards for new employees.
   (A) handwrite
   (B) to handwrite
   (C) handwrites
   (D) handwritten

| 어휘 | 1 export 수출 cause 야기하다 concern 우려 expert 전문가 2 accommodate 수용하다 complicate 복잡하게 하다 3 legal case 소송 be advised to ~하도록 권고 받다 4 valid 유효한 publication 게재, 발표 5 minor 경미한, 작은 frequency 빈도 reduce 줄이다 reduction 감소 6 personal 개인적인, 사적인 remain ~한 상태로 있다 safely 안전하게, 무사히 store 저장하다 7 brochure 안내책자 vendor 공급업체 trade show 산업 박람회 list 나열하다 8 make a point of -ing ~하는 것을 잊지 않다 handwrite 손으로 쓰다

UNIT 11 | 분사 **207**

② 현재분사 vs. 과거분사

분사와 명사가 능동 관계이면 현재분사, 수동 관계이면 과거분사를 씁니다.

a **confusing** puzzle　　a **confused** child

▶ 현재분사
분사가 나타내는 행위를 명사가 직접 행하는 주체라면 '능동' 관계이므로 현재분사를 씁니다.

Online games enjoy **increasing** popularity.　온라인 게임은 늘어나는 인기를 누리고 있다.

The event **introducing** X-530 will be held next week.　X-530을 소개하는 행사가 다음 주에 열릴 것이다.

▶ 과거분사
분사가 나타내는 행위를 명사가 당하는 입장이면 '수동' 관계이므로 과거분사를 씁니다.

The **completed** form should be submitted by this Friday.　작성된 양식은 이번 주 금요일까지 제출되어야 한다.

The discount offer is not valid on tickets **purchased** online.　온라인에서 판매된 티켓은 할인 혜택이 적용되지 않는다.

▶ 토익에 자주 출제되는 분사 표현

┌─ 현재분사 + 명사 ───┐
demanding task 힘든 일	missing luggage 분실 수하물	rewarding job 보람 있는 일
existing facility 기존 시설	outstanding speaker 뛰어난 연설가	upcoming festival 다가오는[곧 있을] 축제
lasting effect 지속되는 영향	remaining work 남은 일	

┌─ 과거분사 + 명사 ───┐
accomplished artist 뛰어난 예술가	designated area 지정 구역	preferred means 선호하는 수단
complicated system 복잡한 제도	detailed information 자세한 정보	experienced engineer 숙련된 기술자
damaged roads 파손된 도로	limited time 제한된 시간	proposed schedule 제안된 일정

▶ 감정 표현 분사
주로 감정을 유발하는 대상인 사물은 현재분사, 감정을 느끼는 사람은 과거분사와 어울려 쓰입니다.

amazing 놀라게 하는	amazed 놀란	satisfying 만족시키는	satisfied 만족하는
exciting 흥분시키는	excited 신난	motivating 동기 부여하는	motivated 의욕적인
surprising 놀라게 하는	surprised 놀란	disappointing 실망시키는	disappointed 실망한
interesting 흥미롭게 하는	interested 흥미로워하는	confusing 혼란스럽게 하는	confused 혼란스러워하는
fascinating 매료시키는	fascinated 매료된	exhausting 지치게 하는	exhausted 지친

The new play received **disappointing** reviews.　새 연극은 실망스러운 평가를 받았다.

Passengers were **disappointed** with the poor service.　승객들은 형편없는 서비스에 실망했다.

ETS 유형 연습

다음 문장의 빈칸에 들어갈 알맞은 말을 고르세요.

STEP 1

1. To report lost or ------- baggage, please visit Nextrair's baggage services booth.
   (A) damaged
   (B) damaging

2. The government has published regulations ------- owners to provide recycling services for tenants.
   (A) required
   (B) requiring

3. In March, the city's orchestra will present an ------- opera by talented newcomer Maria Cruz.
   (A) excited
   (B) exciting

4. The sales representative is ------- in negative feedback from his customers.
   (A) disappointing
   (B) disappointed

STEP 2

5. Because of his experience ------- international accounts, Mr. Ito will take charge of the overseas office.
   (A) supervisor
   (B) supervising
   (C) supervise
   (D) supervised

6. An ------- degree in economics is necessary for the senior analyst position at Liffler, Inc.
   (A) advancement
   (B) advancing
   (C) advances
   (D) advanced

7. The plan ------- by the Ministry of Tourism to reduce unnecessary fees has been very well received.
   (A) present
   (B) presents
   (C) presented
   (D) presenting

8. Any recommendations for the ------- contract negotiations may be shared with Mr. Li through next week.
   (A) upcoming
   (B) estimated
   (C) permanent
   (D) accurate

| 어휘 | 1 lost 잃어버린 2 regulation 규정, 규칙 tenant 세입자 3 present 보여주다, 소개하다 talented 재능 있는 newcomer 신입 4 sales representative 판매사원 5 account 거래, 계정 take charge of ~을 담당하다 overseas 해외의, 해외에 supervise 관리하다, 감독하다 6 degree 학위 senior 수석의, 상급의 position 직책 advanced 고급[상급]의 7 Ministry of Tourism 관광부 fee 수수료, 요금 8 negotiation 협상

③ 분사구문

분사구문이란 긴 부사절을 간단하게 축약해서 만든 구문을 말합니다.

Reviewing the document, Andy found an error.

▶ 분사구문이란?

〈접속사+주어+동사〉로 이루어진 부사절을 분사가 포함된 형태의 부사구로 축약시킨 구문을 의미하며, 문장의 앞과 뒤에 모두 위치할 수 있습니다.

▶ 분사구문 만들기

❶ 부사절 접속사를 생략 ↓ ❷ 부사절의 주어가 주절의 주어와 같을 경우 부사절의 주어 생략 ↓ ❸ 부사절의 동사를 분사(동사원형+-ing)로 변경	❶ ~~While~~ he reviewed the contract, Andy found a significant error. ↓ ❷ ~~While he~~ reviewed the contract, Andy found a significant error. ↓ ❸ ~~While he~~ reviewed the contract, Andy found a significant error. → **Reviewing** the contract, Andy found a significant error. 계약서를 검토하다가, 앤디는 중대한 오류를 발견했다.

LEVEL UP 정확한 의미 전달을 위해 접속사는 남겨 두기도 합니다.

You must wear eye protection **when working** with tools. 도구로 작업할 때는 반드시 보안경을 착용해야 합니다.
As discussed over the phone, your order will be delivered soon.
전화로 논의된 대로, 귀하께서 주문하신 물품이 곧 도착할 겁니다.
→ 〈as+p.p.〉는 '~된 대로'라는 의미의 관용구로, as mentioned(언급된 대로), as stated(명시된 대로) 등도 자주 쓰입니다.

▶ 분사구문의 다양한 의미

시간　**Arriving** at the hotel early, Ms. Lim had some time to prepare her speech.
　　　= When she arrived at the hotel early, ~. 호텔에 일찍 도착하자, 임 씨는 연설을 준비할 시간이 있었다.

이유　(**Being**) **upgraded** recently, the office computers were much faster.
　　　= As they were upgraded recently, ~. 최근 업그레이드되어서 사무실 컴퓨터들이 훨씬 빨라졌다.
　　　→ 수동태 분사구문에서 be동사는 being으로 바뀌는데, being은 생략될 수 있어서 p.p. 형태만 남을 수 있습니다.

동시상황　**Watching** the fashion show, the audience filled out an evaluation form.
　　　= As they watched the fashion show, ~. 패션쇼를 지켜보면서 관객들은 평가서를 작성했다.

ETS 유형 연습

다음 문장의 빈칸에 들어갈 알맞은 말을 고르세요.

정답과 해설 p.160

STEP 1

1. ------- near one of the tourist attractions in the city, the hotel attracts a lot of travelers.
   (A) Location
   (B) Located

2. ------- the draft of the contract, Mr. Kelvin found some errors in it.
   (A) Review
   (B) Reviewing

3. ------- all electrical devices, the facility manager left for the day.
   (A) Unplugging
   (B) Unplugged

4. ------- three decades ago, the exhibition hall needs to be renovated.
   (A) Constructing
   (B) Constructed

STEP 2

5. ------- a leading industry report, executives have decided to increase the manufacture of truck tires.
   (A) Citing
   (B) Cite
   (C) Cited
   (D) Cites

6. ------- in plain language, the magazine on health and nutrition is easy to read.
   (A) Written
   (B) Writing
   (C) Write
   (D) Have written

7. JK Electronics, Inc., expanded into the Asian market, ------- its market share in the international market.
   (A) increase
   (B) being increased
   (C) increasing
   (D) increasingly

8. When ------- for the ZJA conference, you must provide your membership number.
   (A) register
   (B) registers
   (C) registering
   (D) was registered

| 어휘 | 1 attract 끌어들이다   locate 위치시키다   2 draft 초안   contract 계약서   3 electrical device 전기 장치   leave for the day 퇴근하다   unplug 플러그를 뽑다   4 decade 10년   exhibition 전시   construct 건설하다   5 leading 주요한, 선두의   executive 임원, 중역   manufacture 생산, 제조   cite 인용하다   6 plain 쉬운   nutrition 영양   7 expand 확장하다   market share 시장 점유율   8 provide 제공하다   register for ~에 등록하다

ETS 실전 문제

1. New employees of Peachpower Software must attend a very ------- two-week training course when they are hired.
   (A) demands
   (B) demanded
   (C) demanding
   (D) demand

2. During their tour, the new interns were ------- with the efficiency of the factory operations.
   (A) conducted
   (B) discovered
   (C) promoted
   (D) impressed

3. The advertising team made an ------- recovery from a late start to finish the project a week ahead of schedule.
   (A) amaze
   (B) amazing
   (C) amazement
   (D) amazingly

4. Recent graduates apply for work at Harnum Corporation because it offers ------- opportunities for advancement.
   (A) outstand
   (B) to be outstood
   (C) outstood
   (D) outstanding

5. When ------- in combination with a maintenance package, the Auto Tech Computer includes a three-year warranty.
   (A) was purchasing
   (B) purchased
   (C) is purchased
   (D) purchases

6. Stormy weather in Lorraine led to power outages last night, ------- some residents without electricity.
   (A) will leave
   (B) leaving
   (C) have left
   (D) leaves

7. Staff who receive a reporter's question by e-mail should think about both form and content when ------- a response.
   (A) to formulate
   (B) formulating
   (C) formulated
   (D) to be formulating

8. Because the teams in Beijing and Lisbon must work together closely, e-mail is the ------- method of communication for this project.
   (A) prefer
   (B) preferred
   (C) preferably
   (D) preference

9. Because a flower market exists near the ------- site of a new Ayame Florist Shop, another location is being sought.
   (A) obliged
   (B) voluntary
   (C) deliberate
   (D) proposed

10. After nine ------- years at Kewlab, Inc., Ms. Rosen will resign as executive director to pursue a new business venture.
    (A) reward
    (B) rewards
    (C) rewarding
    (D) rewardingly

Questions 11-14 refer to the following article.

Fun Panda Coming to Richmond

RICHMOND (August 24)—Virginia is expected to see its first Fun Panda restaurant early next year. ------- in Singapore, the Asian fast-food chain started expanding to North America ten
       11.
years ago and quickly grew in popularity. It ------- has 53 locations throughout the United
                                              12.
States. However, there are no Fun Panda restaurants in the Richmond area; the one ------- to
                                                                                    13.
Richmond is almost 275 kilometers away in Raleigh, North Carolina.

The new Fun Panda will be located on Cooper Boulevard in a building that formerly housed Hometown Diner. ------- .
                 14.

11. (A) Based
    (B) Basing
    (C) To base
    (D) Having based

12. (A) mainly
    (B) now
    (C) fully
    (D) instead

13. (A) oldest
    (B) fastest
    (C) largest
    (D) closest

14. (A) An opening date has not yet been announced.
    (B) Asian food has recently grown in popularity in the United States.
    (C) Cooper Boulevard is home to several hotel chains.
    (D) Richmond is known for its wide variety of restaurant options.

UNIT 12 전치사와 접속사

무료 강의

1 전치사의 개념과 역할

전치사의 뒤에는 항상 명사, 대명사, 동명사가 옵니다.
He moved forward **with** a flag.

▶ 전치사의 개념

전치사는 명사 앞에 위치하여 시간, 장소, 자격 등 다양한 의미를 더해주는 말입니다.

at 2 o'clock 2시에　　　**in** the building 건물 안에　　　**as** a lawyer 변호사로서

▶ 전치사의 목적어

전치사 뒤에는 명사(구), 즉 명사, 대명사, 동명사 등이 위치하게 되는데 이들을 '전치사의 목적어'라고 합니다.

전치사 + 명사	This special offer is only **for** our patrons.
	이 특가 행사는 우리의 단골 손님만을 위한 것이다.
전치사 + 대명사	Please report any problems **to** me by e-mail.
	어떤 문제라도 제게 이메일로 말씀해 주세요.
전치사 + 동명사	Fill out the form completely **before** submitting it.
	제출하기 전에 양식을 완벽하게 작성하세요.

▶ 전치사의 역할

전치사와 명사(구)가 이루는 구를 전명구라고 하는데 문장에서 형용사, 부사의 역할을 합니다.

형용사 역할	명사 수식	The producer **of the new play** is Emily Silva. 새 연극의 제작자는 에밀리 실바다.
	보어	Our staff is **on duty** 24 hours a day. 우리 직원들은 하루 24시간 근무 중이다.
부사 역할	동사 수식	The equipment arrived **behind schedule**. 장비가 예정보다 늦게 도착했다.
	형용사 수식	Anita Shan is familiar **with the new system**. 아니타 샨은 새 시스템에 익숙하다.
	문장 수식	**In the end**, the two parties reached an agreement. 결국 양측은 합의에 이르렀다.

ETS 유형 연습

다음 문장의 빈칸에 들어갈 알맞은 말을 고르세요.

STEP 1

1. The video explains best practices ------- managing small-business finances.
   (A) to
   (B) for

2. Please provide the expiration date ------- your credit card.
   (A) of
   (B) has

3. Customers can speak with a representative by phone ------- normal business hours.
   (A) among
   (B) during

4. All passengers are responsible for ------- proper travel documents.
   (A) obtain
   (B) obtaining

STEP 2

5. Three major market areas lie ------- a five-hundred-mile radius of our main production plant.
   (A) good
   (B) well
   (C) high
   (D) within

6. We have enclosed the damaged merchandise together ------- a written request for a full refund.
   (A) in
   (B) by
   (C) from
   (D) with

7. ------- high registration numbers, school administrators plan to add more classes.
   (A) Because of
   (B) Otherwise
   (C) Therefore
   (D) Not only

8. Mr. Yamaguchi's train was delayed, forcing him to wait ------- the station for over two hours.
   (A) at
   (B) for
   (C) to
   (D) with

| 어휘 | 1 practice 사례, 관례   finance 재무, 재정   2 expiration date 유효기간   3 representative 대리인   4 be responsible for ~에 책임이 있다   proper 적절한   obtain 보유하고 있다   5 lie 놓여 있다   radius 반경, 범위   plant 공장   6 enclose 동봉하다   damaged 파손된   merchandise 상품   refund 환불   7 registration 등록   administrator 행정가, 관리자   8 force A to A가 (어쩔 수 없이) ~하게 만들다

2 전치사의 종류와 의미

전치사는 명사 앞에 위치하여 시간이나 장소, 수단, 목적, 이유 등 다양한 의미를 나타냅니다.

because of bad weather
= **due to** bad weather

▶ 시간 전치사

시점	in+월/계절/연도/morning on+날짜/요일 at+시각/noon	in the morning 아침에 on Friday 금요일에	in March 3월에 at four o'clock 4시에
	by (완료) ~까지 until (계속) ~까지	arrive by Friday 금요일까지 도착하다	stay until Friday 금요일까지 머무르다
	before=prior to ~ 전에 after ~ 후에	leave before 5 P.M. 5시 전에 떠나다	after the performance 공연 후에
기간	for+숫자 during+명사 ~ 동안	for three days 사흘 동안	during the presentation 발표 동안
	over the next[past]+기간 다음[지난] ~에 걸쳐	over the past 5 years 지난 5년에 걸쳐	
	throughout+명사 ~ 내내	throughout the summer 여름 내내	
	within+기간 ~ 이내에	within a week 일주일 이내에	

▶ 장소, 방향 전치사

장소	at+지점 in+공간 throughout+장소 ~ 곳곳에, ~ 도처에	at the station 역에 throughout the building 건물 곳곳에	in the city 도시에
	in front of ~ 앞에 behind ~ 뒤에 over=above ~ 위에 next to=beside ~의 옆에 near ~ 근처에 around ~ 주변에	in front of the entrance 출입문 앞에 over the floor 바닥 위쪽에 next to the printer 프린터 옆에 near the bus station 버스 정류장 근처에	behind the seat 좌석 뒤에 above the bed 침대 위에 beside the road 길 옆에 around the building 건물 주변에
	between+복수명사 (둘) 사이에 among+복수명사 (셋 이상) 사이에	between two nations 두 국가 사이에 among the trees 나무 사이에	
방향	to ~로, ~에 toward ~을 향해	be open to all 모두에게 열려 있다	toward the bus 버스를 향해
	from ~로부터	permission from the supervisor 관리자의 승인	

▶ 기타 전치사

수단	by ~함으로써 through+추상 수단 ~을 통해	by adjusting the volume 소리를 조절함으로써 through the use of tools 도구의 사용을 통해
자격	as+직업/자격 ~로서	known as a writer 작가로 알려져 있는
주제	about=on ~에 대해 =regarding, concerning	an article about music 음악에 대한 기사 questions regarding the interview 면접에 관한 질문
제외	except (for) ~을 제외하고	every day except Sunday 일요일을 제외하고 매일
첨가	in addition to=besides ~ 뿐만 아니라	in addition to developing new products 신제품을 개발하는 것 이외에도
이유	because of=due to ~ 때문에	because of the weather 날씨 때문에
양보	despite=in spite of ~에도 불구하고	resign despite many benefits 많은 혜택에도 불구하고 사임하다
목적	for+목적/이유 ~을 위해/~해서	for further information 추가 정보를 위해서
소지	with ~와 함께 without ~ 없이	with care 주의 깊게 without any other help 다른 도움 없이

ETS 유형 연습

다음 문장의 빈칸에 들어갈 알맞은 말을 고르세요.

정답과 해설 p.163

STEP 1

1. Please visit our Web site for more information ------- your new Brightstar camera.
   (A) about
   (B) of

2. Planning for the community's recycling event is expected to begin ------- July 12.
   (A) along
   (B) on

3. Vehicle sales reports must be submitted ------- 8:00 A.M. every Monday.
   (A) by
   (B) on

4. JHB Bank cannot process a loan application ------- the proper documentation.
   (A) without
   (B) along

STEP 2

5. For more information about group events, call the office ------- 9:00 A.M. and 5:00 P.M., Monday through Friday.
   (A) from
   (B) along
   (C) between
   (D) after

6. ------- the best efforts of Bromes Shirt Company staff, some customers have not received their orders on time.
   (A) Toward
   (B) Despite
   (C) Until
   (D) Before

7. The work environment is designed to encourage collaboration ------- coworkers.
   (A) among
   (B) throughout
   (C) until
   (D) besides

8. The city health department runs several free clinics for health professionals ------- the year.
   (A) concerning
   (B) throughout
   (C) before
   (D) around

| 어휘 | 2 planning 계획   recycling 재활용   3 vehicle 차량, 탈것   submit 제출하다   4 process 처리하다
loan application 대출 신청   documentation 서류   6 effort 노력   7 environment 환경   encourage 촉진하다
collaboration 협업   coworker 동료   8 run 운영하다, 작동하다   clinic 강습, 병원   health professional 의료 종사자
concerning ~에 관한

UNIT 12 | 전치사와 접속사   **217**

3 등위접속사와 상관접속사

등위접속사와 상관접속사는 문법적인 성격이 같은 말을 이어줍니다.

by car **or** on foot 등위접속사
either driving **or** walking 상관접속사

▶ 등위접속사

서로 같은 성격의 단어와 단어, 구와 구, 절과 절을 대등하게 연결하는 말입니다.

| and 그리고 | or 또는 | but/yet 그러나 | so 그래서 |

The article is **interesting and informative**. 그 기사는 흥미롭고 유익하다.
　　　　　　　단어(형용사)　단어(형용사)

You should make a payment **before or on** Thursday. 당신은 목요일 전 혹은 당일에 결제해야 한다.
　　　　　　　　　　　　단어(전치사)　단어(전치사)

Dr. Dorin **is on vacation but** still **keeps busy**. 도린 박사는 휴가 중이지만 여전히 바쁘다.
　　　　　동사구　　　　　　　　　동사구

It is cold outside, so you should wear a coat. 밖이 추우니까 코트를 입는 게 좋겠다.
　　　　절　　　　　　　　절

→ 접속사 so는 절과 절만 연결할 수 있고, 단어나 구를 연결하는 데는 쓸 수 없습니다.

▶ 상관접속사

두 단어 이상이 짝을 이루어 쓰이는 접속사를 상관접속사라고 합니다.

| both A and B A와 B 둘 다 | neither A nor B A도 B도 아닌 | not only A but (also) B A뿐만 아니라 B |
| either A or B A나 B 둘 중 하나 | not A but B A가 아니라 B | B as well as A A뿐만 아니라 B도 |

The lawyer finished **both** writing **and** proofreading the agreement.
변호사는 계약서 작성과 교정을 모두 마쳤다.

The company hopes to move their offices to **either** Hong Kong **or** Singapore.
그 회사는 사무실을 홍콩이나 싱가포르로 옮기고 싶어 한다.

Neither the shopkeeper **nor** the customer could remember the price.
가게 주인도, 손님도 가격을 기억할 수 없었다.

The soup **not only** tastes good **but** is good for your health as well.
그 수프는 맛있을 뿐 아니라 건강에도 좋다.

ETS 유형 연습

다음 문장의 빈칸에 들어갈 알맞은 말을 고르세요.

STEP 1

1. Ms. Ambani does not speak French, ------- she is fluent in Gujarati and Mandarin.
   (A) or
   (B) but

2. Mr. Yakamoto recommended ------- Mr. Ono and Ms. Simmons for promotions.
   (A) both
   (B) either

3. To get from Oslo to Bergen, Mr. Wu can either fly ------- take a train through the mountains.
   (A) and
   (B) or

4. Neither Mr. Tang ------- Ms. Tsuri attended the press conference on environmental policy.
   (A) and
   (B) nor

STEP 2

5. Ms. Choi is not only a good public speaker ------- also a talented writer.
   (A) both
   (B) if
   (C) nor
   (D) but

6. The career development seminars are open to both part-time ------- full-time employees.
   (A) and
   (B) or
   (C) not
   (D) to

7. Employees have the option of attending a training class ------- completing an online tutorial.
   (A) except
   (B) but
   (C) or
   (D) so

8. Majuri Furniture renewed its contract with us, ------- Lenora Lighting did not.
   (A) neither
   (B) but
   (C) nor
   (D) or

| 어휘 | 1 fluent 유창한   Gujarati 구자라트어   Mandarin 표준 중국어   2 recommend 추천하다   promotion 승진   4 attend 참석하다   press conference 기자회견   environmental policy 환경 정책   5 public speaker 연설가   talented 재능 있는   6 career development 경력 개발   part-time 시간제의, 시간제 근무의   full-time 전임의   7 option 선택 사항   complete 완료하다   tutorial 개별 지도   8 renew 갱신하다   contract 계약

ETS 실전 문제

1. Mr. Shim has been leading the sales team ------- January.
   (A) since
   (B) already
   (C) last
   (D) recently

2. Any Air-Fresh air conditioner will be repaired or replaced free of charge if it malfunctions ------- one year of the purchase date.
   (A) beneath
   (B) off
   (C) within
   (D) on

3. Ms. Jung has suggested that ------- Mr. Tesler or Ms. Sato attend the conference next month.
   (A) both
   (B) neither
   (C) as
   (D) either

4. Mayall Bank's security team protects clients' personal information ------- unauthorized access.
   (A) from
   (B) among
   (C) within
   (D) along

5. The best way to find out whether your business is entitled to a tax rebate is ------- the Clay County Web site.
   (A) through
   (B) beside
   (C) among
   (D) upon

6. Instructions for operating our new machinery will be provided to all employees ------- Monday's training session.
   (A) during
   (B) up
   (C) against
   (D) above

7. Today, shareholders of Lewis Ridge Mining will approve ------- reject the sale of its copper division to Caxias Metals.
   (A) and
   (B) or
   (C) as if
   (D) neither

8. The Jonasson Library will not open until noon on Monday, February 4, ------- necessary building maintenance.
   (A) due to
   (B) instead of
   (C) even though
   (D) now that

9. Electronic payments submitted after 4:00 P.M. on Friday will not be processed ------- Tuesday morning at the earliest.
   (A) into
   (B) since
   (C) until
   (D) while

10. ------- writing an introduction and an epilogue, the author asked a famous novelist to produce a preface for his book.
    (A) For example
    (B) Besides
    (C) In contrast to
    (D) If

Questions 11-14 refer to the following memo.

To: All employees
From: Patricio Mendoza, General Manager
Date: September 17
Subject: Customer engagement

Customer satisfaction studies show that when supermarket employees engage in conversations ------- them, customers find greater enjoyment in their shopping experience.
   11.
------- . Topics can include the weather, music, sports, and community events, among
12.
others. We seek to develop a reputation as the most helpful supermarket in town, and we are counting on you to help us reach this ------- . And to prove how much we value your
                                                                       13.
participation, beginning next month we ------- our friendliest employee of the month with a
                                          14.
$100 gift certificate.

11. (A) for
    (B) with
    (C) near
    (D) upon

12. (A) However, we disagree with the results of these studies.
    (B) A full list of our policies is available on our Web site.
    (C) Customer opinion polls should always be taken seriously.
    (D) Therefore, we encourage staff to spend more time talking to customers.

13. (A) goal
    (B) level
    (C) number
    (D) destination

14. (A) will be rewarding
    (B) will be rewarded
    (C) have been rewarding
    (D) have been rewarded

UNIT 13 부사절 접속사

무료 강의

❶ 시간·조건의 부사절 접속사

시간이나 조건 등을 의미하는 부사절 접속사로는 before, since, if, as long as 등이 있습니다.

Before I met you, my life was empty.
I'm happy **as long as** I have you.

▶ 부사절 접속사의 역할

〈접속사+주어+동사〉 덩어리가 문장 맨 앞이나 맨 뒤에서 수식어 역할을 하면 그것을 부사절이라고 하는데, 이런 부사절을 이끄는 접속사를 부사절 접속사라고 합니다.

All contracts must be reviewed thoroughly. + They(= all contracts) are signed.
　　　　　　완전한 절　　　　　　　　　　　　　　　완전한 절

All contracts must be reviewed thoroughly **before they are signed**.
모든 계약서들은 사인하기 전에 철저히 검토되어야 한다.　　시간을 나타내는 부사절

= **Before they are signed**, all contracts must be reviewed thoroughly.

→ 부사절은 문장 앞과 뒤 어디든 위치할 수 있습니다.

▶ 시간을 나타내는 접속사

when/as ~할 때	while ~하는 동안에	before ~하기 전에	after ~한 후에
as soon as ~하자마자	until ~할 때까지	since ~ 이래로 (지금까지)	by the time ~할 즈음에

Audience members are not allowed to take photos **after the concert starts**.
관객들은 공연이 시작한 후에는 사진을 찍으면 안 된다.

Stock prices have doubled **since the news was reported**. 그 소식이 보도된 이후로 주가는 두 배가 되었다.

→ before, after, since, until은 같은 의미의 전치사로도 쓰입니다.

▶ 조건을 나타내는 접속사

if 만약 ~라면	unless(= if not) ~가 아니라면	once 일단 ~하면
in case ~의 경우에 (대비하여)	provided that ~라면	as long as ~하는 한

If you are interested, an insurance agent will help you. 만약 관심 있으시면, 보험 설계사가 도와드릴 것입니다.

The class will be canceled **unless three people or more sign up**. 세 명 이상이 등록하지 않으면 수업은 취소됩니다.
　　　　　　　　= if three people or more don't sign up

ETS 유형 연습

다음 문장의 빈칸에 들어갈 알맞은 말을 고르세요.

STEP 1

1. Customers picking up prescriptions must show personal identification ------- they arrive at the Lillo Pharmacy counter.
   (A) when
   (B) during

2. The staff has been more productive ------- the new time-management software was installed.
   (A) if
   (B) since

3. Customers can write a check ------- they have two pieces of identification.
   (A) although
   (B) if

4. ------- you have registered with Select Software, you will receive a customer identification number.
   (A) Once
   (B) Next

STEP 2

5. ------- all the applications are received, the committee will determine a list of people to be interviewed.
   (A) About
   (B) Except
   (C) After
   (D) With

6. Gym memberships are automatically renewed on the client's anniversary date ------- a cancellation has been requested.
   (A) unless
   (B) although
   (C) few
   (D) just

7. Ultrafast Oil customers can relax in our lounge ------- waiting for their vehicles to be serviced.
   (A) since
   (B) while
   (C) yet
   (D) as

8. We will begin processing Mr. Vallejo's loan application ------- we receive the supporting documents.
   (A) just
   (B) once
   (C) upon
   (D) still

| 어휘 | 1 prescription 처방전 identification 신분증명서 pharmacy 약국 2 productive 생산적인 install 설치하다 3 write a check 수표를 발행하다 4 receive 받다 identification number 식별 번호 5 determine 확정하다, 결정하다 6 renew 갱신하다 anniversary 기념일 cancellation 취소 7 relax 휴식을 취하다 vehicle 차량 service (차 등을) 정비하다 8 process 처리하다 loan application 대출 신청 document 서류, 문서

2 이유·양보·기타의 부사절 접속사

이유나 양보, 목적은 because, although, so that 등으로 표현할 수 있습니다.

He used his phone secretly **so that** his mom wouldn't see.

▶ 이유를 나타내는 접속사

| because, as, since, now that ~하기 때문에 |

Dr. Logan was absent from the meeting **because his flight was delayed.**
로건 박사는 비행기가 연착하는 바람에 회의에 불참했다.

▶ 양보·대조를 나타내는 접속사

| though, although, even though, even if 비록 ~에도 불구하고 | while, whereas ~인 반면에 |

Although he had plans for a trip, Mr. Kim was too busy. 김 씨는 여행 계획이 있었지만, 너무 바빴다.
The 1st floor offices handle customer service, **while** the 2nd floor deals with marketing.
2층은 마케팅을 다루는 반면에 1층 사무실은 고객 서비스를 취급한다.

▶ 기타 접속사

| so that, in order that+주어+(can) ~하기 위해서, ~할 수 있도록 | so+형용사/부사+that 매우 ~해서 …하다 |

The company attended the job fair **so that they can find** competent applicants.
　　　　　　　　　　　　　　　= **in order that they can find** competent applicants.
　　　　　　　　　　　　　　　= **in order to find** competent applicants.
회사는 유능한 지원자를 찾기 위해서 취업 박람회에 참석했다.

The presentation was **so persuasive that** the clients signed another contract.
프레젠테이션이 아주 설득력 있어서 고객들은 다른 계약에도 서명했다.

▶ 전치사 vs. 접속사

접속사 뒤에는 〈주어+동사〉가 오지만 전치사 뒤에는 명사(구)가 옵니다.

	접속사+주어+동사	전치사+명사(구)/동명사(구)
이유 ~ 때문에 양보 ~에도 불구하고 시간 ~ 동안	because, as, since although, though, even though, even if while	because of, due to despite, in spite of during

The game was canceled (**because of** / ~~because~~) **the bad weather.** 궂은 날씨 때문에 경기가 취소되었다.
(**While** / ~~During~~) **you are** in the library, you must not eat. 도서관에 있는 동안, 먹으면 안 된다.

ETS 유형 연습

다음 문장의 빈칸에 들어갈 알맞은 말을 고르세요.

STEP 1

1. Mr. Jose has moved to the city ------- he is tired of the long commute to work.
   (A) because
   (B) whereas

2. ------- Ms. Tianen's team has been working diligently on the report, it is still not finished.
   (A) Even though
   (B) Only if

3. The product is ------- expensive that most shoppers are reluctant to buy it.
   (A) so
   (B) very

4. Aya Kodura maintained a rigorous practice schedule ------- her national tour.
   (A) during
   (B) while

STEP 2

5. Ms. Cho decided to visit the new laboratory in Busan ------- her colleagues were unable to join her.
   (A) rather than
   (B) regardless of
   (C) even though
   (D) wherever

6. The cancellation of Saturday's concert was ------- unexpected problems with the sound system.
   (A) because
   (B) as if
   (C) due to
   (D) unless

7. Mario D'Amico has been assigned to check the facts ------- Sean McCree types a draft of the report.
   (A) also
   (B) than
   (C) moreover
   (D) while

8. Birkert Financial's main office will open one hour late on Monday ------- a work crew can replace the carpet in the lobby.
   (A) according to
   (B) based on
   (C) so that
   (D) to allow

| 어휘 | 1 be tired of ~에 지치다   commute 통근(하다)   2 diligently 부지런히   only if ~해야만   3 be reluctant to ~하는 것을 꺼리다   4 maintain 유지하다, 관리하다   rigorous 엄격한, 정확한   5 laboratory 연구소   colleague 동료   6 unexpected 예상치 못한   7 assign (업무를) 맡다, 할당하다   draft 초안   8 main office 본사   work crew 작업팀   replace 교체하다

ETS 실전 문제

1. ------- our chief financial officer is away on business, the budget meeting has been rescheduled for Monday.
   (A) Since
   (B) Either
   (C) How
   (D) That

2. Cosimo's Grocery offers customers practical cooking tips ------- they can make the most of the foods they purchase.
   (A) in addition
   (B) so that
   (C) just as
   (D) in case

3. Varangia Marketing Services has become a leader in corporate advertising, ------- they have only been in business for four years.
   (A) owing to
   (B) before
   (C) even though
   (D) instead

4. Tenants may play musical instruments ------- the music does not disturb other residents in the building.
   (A) provided that
   (B) such as
   (C) in case of
   (D) owing to

5. Highway 28 is closed ------- construction is fully completed.
   (A) during
   (B) until
   (C) along
   (D) past

6. ------- several ideas have been suggested to expand Carlston City's public transportation system, not one is within budget.
   (A) Why
   (B) Whether
   (C) Although
   (D) Unless

7. The personnel department revised the vacation policy ------- many employees found the old version confusing.
   (A) unless
   (B) because
   (C) until
   (D) thus

8. ------- the cleanup campaign has ended, the large trash bin will be removed from the work area.
   (A) Even so
   (B) In particular
   (C) Now that
   (D) For instance

9. Ms. Vega's reimbursement request will be processed ------- her supervisor has signed the form.
   (A) once
   (B) alike
   (C) such as
   (D) sooner

10. ------- he arrives at the airport in the next ten minutes, Mr. Santini is going to have to take a later flight.
    (A) Regardless
    (B) While
    (C) Unless
    (D) Rather

Questions 11-14 refer to the following notice.

Attention Cleardale Apartments tenants:

Please be advised that the annual maintenance and cleaning of the boiler has been scheduled to take place on October 18. -------11.------- . The water supply for the entire building will be shut off during this time. -------12.-------, the laundry room will be closed.

We apologize for any inconvenience this -------13.------- . Thank you in advance for your cooperation -------14.------- we complete this important work.

Louis Verella, Building Manager

11. (A) The project will last from 10:00 A.M. to approximately 1:00 P.M.
    (B) We are seeking a few volunteers to pick up trash on the grass.
    (C) All overdue rental payments must be submitted by this date.
    (D) The new machine will be more powerful and reliable.

12. (A) Nevertheless
    (B) Elsewhere
    (C) Consequently
    (D) Alternatively

13. (A) caused
    (B) should have caused
    (C) cause
    (D) may cause

14. (A) so
    (B) also
    (C) as
    (D) that

UNIT 14 관계대명사

무료 강의

1 관계대명사의 개념과 종류

접속사와 대명사가 합쳐진 것이 관계대명사입니다.

They are watching a movie **which** is about a foreign planet.　　= **and + it**

▶ 관계대명사의 개념

관계대명사는 두 개의 문장을 하나로 만들 때 〈접속사＋대명사〉 기능을 하는 단어로, 관계대명사가 이끄는 절은 관계대명사 앞에 위치한 명사(선행사)를 수식하는 역할을 합니다.

We watched **a movie**. + **It** is about a foreign planet.　우리는 영화를 보았다. 그것은 외계 행성에 관한 영화다.

→ We watched a movie **and it** is about a foreign planet.
　→ 두 개의 문장을 하나로 만들 때는 반드시 접속사가 필요합니다.

→ We watched a movie **which** is about a foreign planet.　우리는 외계 행성에 관한 영화를 보았다.
　　　　　　　선행사

▶ 관계대명사의 종류

관계대명사절에서 관계대명사가 담당하는 역할(격)과 선행사의 종류에 따라 사용되는 관계대명사가 달라집니다.

	주격: 바로 뒤에 동사가 옴	**소유격**: 바로 뒤에 오는 명사를 수식	**목적격**: 뒤에 〈주어＋동사〉가 옴
사람 선행사	who, that	whose	who(m), that
사물 선행사	which, that	whose, of which	which, that

▶ 주격 관계대명사

관계대명사가 관계대명사절에서 주어로 쓰이면 주격 관계대명사 who/which/that을 씁니다.

Mr. Han (who / ~~which~~) is the owner of the café plans to open a new store.

카페 주인인 한 씨는 새 가게를 열 계획이다.

➜ 선행사 Mr. Han이 사람이므로 who 또는 that을 씁니다. 관계대명사절의 동사는 선행사와 수를 일치시키는데 Mr. Han이 단수명사이므로 who 뒤에 단수동사(is)가 옵니다.

ETS 유형 연습

다음 문장의 빈칸에 들어갈 알맞은 말을 고르세요.

STEP 1

1. Many people ------- were interviewed felt that they did not need a larger car.
   (A) whom
   (B) who

2. Around 2,000 people went to the job fair ------- was held last month.
   (A) which
   (B) whose

3. These boots are made of synthetic leather ------- is durable and easy to clean.
   (A) that
   (B) whom

4. The customs agent ------- inspects passports is also authorized to issue visitors' visas.
   (A) whose
   (B) who

STEP 2

5. Ms. Reston and Mr. Parnthong were two of the senior partners ------- visited the clients last week.
   (A) who
   (B) when
   (C) what
   (D) whose

6. Films-Now is a new Internet-streaming service ------- offers rewards for subscriber referrals.
   (A) whoever
   (B) such
   (C) that
   (D) where

7. Saturday's clearance sale will make room for next season's products, ------- will arrive very soon.
   (A) when
   (B) what
   (C) where
   (D) which

8. Employees who ------- trade shows should always have business cards ready to hand out to a potential client.
   (A) attendance
   (B) attends
   (C) attending
   (D) attend

| 어휘 | 2 job fair 취업 박람회   be held 열리다   3 be made of ~로 만들어지다   synthetic leather 합성피혁   durable 내구성 있는   4 customs 세관   inspect 검사하다   be authorized to ~할 수 있는 권한이 있다   issue 발행하다   5 senior partner (조합·합명 회사 따위의) 장, 사장   6 referral 추천   7 clearance sale 창고 정리 세일   make room for ~을 위한 공간을 마련하다   8 hand out 나눠주다   potential 잠재적인   attendance 참석

❷ 목적격 관계대명사와 소유격 관계대명사

관계대명사는 주격 외에도 소유격과 목적격이 있습니다.

People tend to buy clothes **whose** prices have decreased.
　　　　　　　　　　　　　소유격 관계대명사

▶ 목적격 관계대명사

관계대명사가 관계대명사절 안에서 목적어로 쓰이면 목적격 관계대명사 who(m)/which/that을 씁니다.

The information (which / ~~whom~~) you requested is confidential.

당신이 요구했던 정보는 기밀 사항입니다.

→ 타동사 requested의 목적어이자 선행사인 The information이 사물이므로 목적격 관계대명사 which나 that을 씁니다.

▶ 소유격 관계대명사

선행사(관계대명사 앞의 명사)가 관계대명사 뒤에 오는 명사를 소유하는 관계일 때 소유격 관계대명사 whose를 씁니다.

People tend to buy **clothes** (**whose** / ~~which~~) **prices have decreased**.

사람들은 가격이 떨어진 옷을 사는 경향이 있다.

▶ 관계대명사의 생략

❶ 〈주격 관계대명사+be동사〉 생략: 주격 관계대명사 뒤에 〈be+p.p.〉 또는 〈be+-ing〉 형태가 오면 관계대명사와 be동사가 함께 생략될 수 있습니다. 이런 경우, 분사가 명사를 뒤에서 수식하는 구조와 동일해집니다.

Anyone **(who is)** interested in the seminar must sign up by noon.

세미나에 관심 있는 사람은 정오까지 신청해야 한다.

→ 선행사(Anyone) 뒤에 오는 과거분사(interested)를 동사로 착각하지 않도록 주의해야 합니다.
　문장의 동사는 must sign up입니다.

❷ 목적격 관계대명사 생략

The technician **(that)** we met yesterday is experienced.

우리가 어제 만났던 기술자는 경험이 많다.

→ 명사(The technician) 뒤에 명사나 대명사(we)가 연달아 나온다면 중간에 목적격 관계대명사가 생략됐을 확률이 높습니다.

ETS 유형 연습

다음 문장의 빈칸에 들어갈 알맞은 말을 고르세요.

STEP 1

1. The tasks ------- Ms. Ogawa must carry out are outlined in her employment agreement.
   (A) who
   (B) that

2. Refunds will be given to all customers ------- orders are damaged in shipping.
   (A) which
   (B) whose

3. The book ------- ordered yesterday will be delivered tomorrow morning.
   (A) you
   (B) your

4. The file ------- to this e-mail must be examined carefully.
   (A) attaching
   (B) attached

STEP 2

5. The applicant ------- the professor recommended will come for an interview soon.
   (A) when
   (B) which
   (C) what
   (D) that

6. Akira Tsukada's novel, ------- title hasn't been finalized yet, will be released next year.
   (A) which
   (B) that
   (C) whose
   (D) whom

7. Paula Coe has been contracted to inspect the area ------- the Crinside Hotel to ensure compliance with regulations.
   (A) surround
   (B) surrounds
   (C) surrounded
   (D) surrounding

8. The quality-control procedures ------- in the contract must be reviewed by the head of engineering.
   (A) including
   (B) includes
   (C) included
   (D) include

| 어휘 | 1 task 업무 carry out 수행하다 outline 간략히 서술하다 2 damaged 파손된 4 examine 검토하다, 검사하다 attach 첨부하다 5 applicant 지원자 professor 교수 6 finalize 마무리 짓다 release 공개하다, 발표하다 7 contract (하청) 계약을 맺다 inspect 점검하다 compliance 준수 regulation 규정 surround 둘러싸다 8 procedure 절차 include 포함하다

UNIT 14 | 관계대명사 **231**

ETS 실전 문제

1. Many of the candidates ------- applied for the administrative assistant position at Ferber Systems were highly qualified.
   (A) which
   (B) what
   (C) who
   (D) when

2. Hemton House on Main Street, ------- served as Lunburgh's first schoolhouse, has been designated a historical landmark.
   (A) who
   (B) which
   (C) where
   (D) when

3. Factory personnel ------- job is to operate industrial machinery must attend a safety course once a year.
   (A) whose
   (B) they
   (C) that
   (D) these

4. Of all the business plans ------- by the marketing manager, Mr. Martin's idea is the most impressive.
   (A) review
   (B) reviewed
   (C) are reviewed
   (D) which reviewed

5. The Batami Financial Group provides expert consulting services ------- are based on economic research and analysis.
   (A) also
   (B) who
   (C) that
   (D) once

6. Skytown Airlines apologized to the passengers for the delays ------- experienced.
   (A) they
   (B) their
   (C) them
   (D) this

7. The keynote speaker was J. M. Lim, ------- research on wind power has helped shape the alternative energy industry.
   (A) whose
   (B) which
   (C) from
   (D) of

8. ZG Dental thanks all staff members who ------- marketing materials at last week's National Dentistry Expo in Pittsburgh.
   (A) distribute
   (B) distributes
   (C) distributed
   (D) distributing

9. Juanita is the most reliable employee ------- we have, so we can depend on her to handle this contract.
   (A) which
   (B) what
   (C) that
   (D) whose

10. The organization ------- donated the land for the park will also provide funds to build picnic shelters there.
    (A) that
    (B) likewise
    (C) whereas
    (D) has

Questions 11-14 refer to the following advertisement.

Living Room Concepts

Do you need new furniture? Are you looking to freshen up your living space? Living Room Concepts offers the best in comfort and luxury. Our chairs, loveseats, and sofas provide the ultimate relaxation experience. Check out our rugs, artwork, and ------- . These accessories
                                                                                                        11.
will add warmth and style. Request a free consultation with Michael Nathan, our in-house interior designer, ------- will help you choose furniture and fabrics to suit your space. ------- .
                              12.   **13.**
Visit our stores and ------- this advertisement to get 10 percent off your purchase! We have
                         14.
two locations in Wellington: 37 Crescent Highway and 145 Gosport Avenue.

---

11. (A) beds
    (B) lamps
    (C) appliances
    (D) countertops

12. (A) when
    (B) who
    (C) someone
    (D) everybody

13. (A) All he needs to get started is your room's dimensions.
    (B) This storewide sale ends soon, so hurry!
    (C) Delivery charges vary depending on the distance from our warehouse.
    (D) Mr. Nathan promotes efficient teamwork.

14. (A) publish
    (B) avoid
    (C) expect
    (D) mention

UNIT 15 명사절 접속사

무료 강의

1 명사절 접속사 that, whether, if

that, if, whether는 문장에서 명사 역할을 하는 절을 이끌 수 있습니다.

I am wondering **whether** you are available tomorrow.

▶ 명사절이란?

명사처럼 주어, 목적어, 보어 역할을 하는 절을 명사절이라고 하며, 문장에서 명사절을 이끄는 접속사를 명사절 접속사라고 합니다.

The notice says **that** the train will be 10 minutes late. 안내문에는 기차가 10분 연착된다고 나와 있다.
　　　　　　　문장의 동사 says의 목적어인 절(the train ~ late)을 that이 연결합니다.

▶ that | ~라는[하는] 것

주어　**That** the play got disappointing reviews **is** true. 그 연극이 실망스러운 평가를 받은 것은 사실이다.
　　　= **It** is true **that** the play got disappointing reviews.
　　　→ 주어가 that절처럼 긴 경우 주어를 뒤로 보내고 그 자리에 가주어 it을 대신 쓸 수 있습니다.

보어　The problem **is that** we need more staff. 문제는 우리에게 더 많은 직원이 필요하다는 것이다.

목적어　**Ensure that** your work area is clean. 당신의 작업 공간을 깨끗하게 하세요.

┌─ that절을 목적어로 취하는 빈출 동사 ──────────────────────────────┐
│ agree that ~에 동의하다　　　　ensure that ~을 보장하다　　　announce that ~을 발표하다 │
│ indicate that ~을 나타내다　　　confirm that ~을 확인하다　　　note that ~을 유념하다 │
└───┘

▶ whether / if | ~인지 아닌지, ~할지 안 할지

불확실한 사실을 전달할 때 사용되는 whether는 종종 뒤에 or not과 함께 쓰이며 whether 뒤에 주어를 생략하고 바로 to부정사를 쓸 수도 있습니다. if는 whether와 달리 동사 뒤에서 목적어절을 이끌 때만 씁니다.

(**Whether** / If) the city will widen the road hasn't been decided. 시가 도로를 확장할지는 결정되지 않았다.

Ms. Serena is considering (**whether** / if) to renew the contract. 세레나 씨는 계약을 갱신할지 말지를 고려 중이다.
　　　　　　　　　　　= whether or not to renew the contract

The survey will determine (**whether** / **if**) the cost is important (or not).
설문조사는 비용이 중요한지를 판가름할 것이다.

ETS 유형 연습

다음 문장의 빈칸에 들어갈 알맞은 말을 고르세요.

STEP 1

1. The committee's opinion is ------- we have to build a day-care center.
   (A) that
   (B) whether

2. Gladsock employees do not know ------- they will receive a bonus this year.
   (A) if
   (B) and

3. Please note ------- a copy of the contract for you to sign is included with this letter.
   (A) which
   (B) that

4. Hahm Plastic Corporation is currently deciding ------- to open new offices in Jeju City.
   (A) whether
   (B) if

STEP 2

5. ------- the rival company will file a lawsuit against Trolman, Inc., remains to be seen.
   (A) Wherever
   (B) Which
   (C) Whether
   (D) What

6. Sales representatives know ------- they should reach their quarterly sales targets.
   (A) about
   (B) what
   (C) that
   (D) it

7. It is difficult to determine ------- Mr. Thomson is the best person to lead the project.
   (A) whether
   (B) what
   (C) so that
   (D) for

8. The company's decision on whether or not ------- a candidate will depend on reference checks.
   (A) hire
   (B) hiring
   (C) to hire
   (D) will hire

| 어휘 | 1 committee 위원회   opinion 의견   day-care center 탁아 시설   2 receive 받다   3 note 유념하다   copy 한 부; 사본   contract 계약(서)   include 포함하다   4 currently 현재   5 file a lawsuit 소송을 제기하다   remain to be seen 두고 볼 일이다   6 sales representative 영업 사원, 판매 직원   quarterly 분기별, 분기의   7 determine 결정하다   8 depend on ~에 달려 있다   reference 추천(서)

❷ 의문사 형태의 명사절 접속사

의문사 who, what, how 등도 명사절 접속사로 쓸 수 있습니다.

He realized **how** socks disappear.

▶ 의문사

who, what, which, when, where, how, why와 같은 의문사도 명사절 접속사로 쓰입니다.

주어　**Who** will be in charge of the job **is** everyone's concern.　누가 그 업무를 담당할 것인지가 모두의 관심이다.
　　　　문장의 주어 역할

목적어　The workers will **choose how** they will receive payment.　직원들은 급여를 어떻게 받을지 선택할 것이다.
　　　　　　　　　동사 뒤 목적어 역할

　　　　We will talk **about what** is more important than the design.　우리는 무엇이 디자인보다 더 중요한지에 대해 논의할 것이다.
　　　　　　　　　전치사 뒤 목적어 역할

보어　Our main concern **is when** we release the new product.　우리의 주된 관심사는 언제 신제품을 출시하느냐이다.
　　　　　　　　　be동사 뒤 보어 역할

▶ what vs. that

what과 that은 둘 다 '~하는 것'으로 해석될 수 있지만, what 뒤에는 불완전한 절(빠진 문장 요소가 있는 절), that 뒤에는 완전한 절이 옵니다.

The accountants provided **what** the executives asked for.　회계사들은 임원이 요구하는 것을 제공했다.
　　　　　　　　　　that　　　불완전한 절

→ 전치사 for 뒤에 목적어가 없는 불완전한 절이 왔으므로 what을 씁니다.

The secretary confirmed **that** the flight was reserved.　비서는 항공편이 예약되었다는 것을 확인했다.
　　　　　　　　　　what　　　완전한 절

→ 참고로 명사절 접속사 that, if, whether, when, where, how, why 뒤에는 완전한 절이 오고,
　who, what, which 뒤에는 불완전한 절이 옵니다.

▶ 의문사의 활용

❶ 의문사+to부정사: 의문사 뒤에 주어와 동사 대신 간단히 to부정사가 나오는 형태가 문장에서 명사 역할을 하기도 합니다.

The interns are learning **how to use** the software.　인턴들은 그 소프트웨어를 어떻게 쓰는지 배우는 중이다.

❷ 의문사+-ever: 의문사 뒤에 -ever를 붙이면 '~(하)든지'라고 해석합니다.

| whoever 누가 ~든지 | whenever 언제 ~든지 | whatever 무엇을 ~든지 |
| wherever 어디서 ~든지 | however 어떻게/얼마나 ~든지 | whichever 어느 것을 ~든지 |

Whoever wins the game will receive a big prize.　게임에서 우승하는 사람은 누구든지 큰 상을 받을 것이다.

ETS 유형 연습

다음 문장의 빈칸에 들어갈 알맞은 말을 고르세요.

정답과 해설 p.172

STEP 1

1. The Personnel Manager has not decided ------- will be transferred to the Seoul office.
   (A) who
   (B) when

2. Most of the conference attendees do not understand ------- the presenter is saying now.
   (A) what
   (B) that

3. Free virus protection software is available to ------- does not have it yet.
   (A) anyone
   (B) whoever

4. At Neng Publishing Agency, clients are encouraged to write ------- they wish to express.
   (A) however
   (B) whatever

STEP 2

5. Tomorrow's session will train participants on ------- to prepare containers for overseas shipments.
   (A) what
   (B) how
   (C) that
   (D) then

6. The employee directory has a section that tells users ------- can answer questions about various departments.
   (A) if
   (B) how
   (C) who
   (D) he

7. Primo Publishing has not yet decided ------- they will introduce their new software's features.
   (A) which
   (B) who
   (C) what
   (D) when

8. ------- responding to the restaurant survey will receive a $10 gift certificate to the Rangely Café.
   (A) Whoever
   (B) Whose
   (C) Someone
   (D) Everyone

| 어휘 | 1 personnel 인사부   decide 결정하다   transfer 전근하다, 옮기다   2 attendee 참석자   presenter 발표자
3 protection 보호   available 이용 가능한   4 be encouraged to ~하도록 독려되다   express 표현하다
5 participant 참가자   overseas 해외의, 해외에   shipment 수송   6 directory 명부   section 부분, 부문
various 다양한, 여러 가지의   department 부서   7 introduce 소개하다, 도입하다   8 respond to ~에 응답하다

ETS 실전 문제

1. The study will determine ------- drilling new water wells in Nontock County will have a significant impact on groundwater levels.
   (A) whatever
   (B) while
   (C) whichever
   (D) whether

2. The instruction manual for the food processor indicates ------- it can be used for both grains and vegetables.
   (A) but
   (B) that
   (C) while
   (D) so

3. The board of directors is discussing ------- they will maintain their core technology.
   (A) who
   (B) which
   (C) how
   (D) what

4. The product development team cannot say ------- the new line of products will be released.
   (A) which
   (B) who
   (C) what
   (D) when

5. A report in the *Journal of the Agricultural Society* suggests that consumers are increasingly concerned about ------- their produce is grown.
   (A) it
   (B) where
   (C) what
   (D) that

6. *Jenkins Business Review* has asked thousands of people in a wide range of professions to describe ------- their jobs entail.
   (A) what
   (B) how
   (C) when
   (D) which

7. Please let senior management know by Friday ------- the sales team needs to reschedule its presentation.
   (A) whether
   (B) either
   (C) rather
   (D) yet

8. Investors are expressing uncertainty about ------- sales of Marandic Motors' new electric car will increase.
   (A) unless
   (B) whether
   (C) even if
   (D) in case

9. ------- arrives first to the grand opening of Dimkin's Ice Cream Shop will receive a free T-shirt.
   (A) Who
   (B) What
   (C) Whoever
   (D) That

10. The corporate officers have requested that Ms. Nguyen ------- all available options for reducing costs at the Hanoi factory.
    (A) to investigate
    (B) has investigated
    (C) investigate
    (D) is investigating

Questions 11-14 refer to the following press release.

FOR IMMEDIATE RELEASE   November 18

TREFFORD CITY — The City Waste Management Authority(CWMA) has teamed up with GDA Waste Solutions, a local recycling facility, to collect electronic waste for recycling.

This ------- allows residents to drop off old devices, such as mobile phones and laptop
    11.
computers, for pickup at the Community Center on Fir Street. ------- . Residents are asked
                                                          12.
not to leave items outside the center after it has closed. "The drop-off program is part of our new 'Clean City' campaign," said CWMA Director Lloyd Ingram. "Now it's time for residents to decide ------- to promote this campaign." To that end, a public meeting ------- next Thursday
       13.   **14.**
at 7 P.M., in Room B of City Hall, to seek community input on promotion ideas.

More information: www.cwma-ewaste.org

---

11. (A) modification
(B) partnership
(C) separation
(D) law

12. (A) These devices are not considered recyclable at this time.
(B) The written estimate will include the total repair costs.
(C) Items are accepted during the center's regular hours.
(D) The company's new products are more energy-efficient.

13. (A) what
(B) how
(C) unless
(D) whose

14. (A) was being held
(B) will be held
(C) has been held
(D) would have been held

UNIT 16 비교구문

무료 강의

1 비교급과 원급

비교급 = -er/more + than

The cheetah is fast**er than** the lion.

▶ 비교급

두 대상을 비교해서 어느 한쪽의 정도가 더하거나 덜함을 나타내는 비교급 구문은 〈형용사/부사의 비교급(-er/more/less)+than+비교 대상〉의 형태를 취합니다. 따라서 문장에 than이 나오면 앞에 형용사나 부사의 비교급이 나와야 합니다.

The actual cost will be **higher than** the estimate. 실제 비용은 견적보다 더 높을 것이다.

The CEO has donated **more generously than** last year. CEO는 작년보다 더 후하게 기부했다.

Recycled paper is **less expensive than** new paper. 재생지는 새 종이보다 덜 비싸다.

┌─ 비교급 강조 부사: 훨씬 더 ~한/하게 ─────
│ much, even, still, far, a lot
└─────────────────────────────

The department store was **much busier than** usual. 백화점은 평소보다 훨씬 더 부산했다.
~~very, more~~

▶ 원급 비교

두 대상이 동등함을 나타내며 〈as+형용사/부사의 원형+as A: A만큼 ~한/하게〉로 표현합니다.

Mobile games are as **popular** as computer games. 모바일 게임은 컴퓨터 게임만큼 인기 있다.
~~more popular, popularly~~

Your request will be addressed as **promptly** as possible. 귀하의 요청 사항이 가능한 신속하게 처리될 겁니다.
~~prompt~~

→ as ~ as 사이에 들어갈 품사를 고르는 문제는 앞의 as를 없애고 문장의 구조를 살펴서 빈칸에 적절한 품사를 고르면 됩니다.

▶ 비교급 관용 표현

no later than 늦어도 ~까지	no longer 더 이상 ~않다	as soon as possible 가능한 한 빨리
twice as ~ as 두 배 더 ~한	비교급+than expected 예상보다 더 ~한	more than ~이상
less than ~이하	rather than ~보다는 오히려	the 비교급 ~, the 비교급 ... ~하면 할수록 더 …하다

The nominations will be accepted **no later than** July 15. 늦어도 7월 15일까지만 후보 추천을 받을 것이다.

The new videos sold **better than expected**. 그 신작 비디오는 예상보다 더 잘 팔렸다.

ETS 유형 연습

다음 문장의 빈칸에 들어갈 알맞은 말을 고르세요.

정답과 해설 p.175

STEP 1

1. The new antivirus software is more powerful ------- the old version.
   (A) than
   (B) with

2. Red Badge Corporation is now ------- famous as its competitor, Talo Security.
   (A) very
   (B) as

3. Plastic is now a ------- more versatile construction material than it was in the past.
   (A) much
   (B) very

4. Reimbursements for medical expenses will be paid as ------- as possible.
   (A) quickly
   (B) quicker

STEP 2

5. Professional experience is ------- important as educational credentials for the editorial position.
   (A) as
   (B) so
   (C) much
   (D) more

6. Tomorrow's training is intended for employees who have been with the company for ------- one year.
   (A) rather than
   (B) less than
   (C) no longer
   (D) by far

7. Surveyed consumers responded even ------- to the product's new packaging than expected.
   (A) favorably
   (B) most favorable
   (C) more favorably
   (D) favorable

8. Ms. Chan has asked employees to submit their time sheets no ------- than 5:00 P.M.
   (A) late
   (B) later
   (C) lateness
   (D) latest

| 어휘 | 1 antivirus 바이러스 방지 2 competitor 경쟁자 3 versatile 다용도의 construction material 건축 자재 past 과거 4 reimbursement 상환, 변제 medical expenses 의료비 5 educational credential 학력 editorial 편집의 6 be intended for ~을 위해[대상으로] 마련되다 7 survey 설문조사를 하다; 설문조사 consumer 소비자 respond 반응하다, 응답하다 8 submit 제출하다 time sheet 근무 시간 기록표

❷ 최상급

최상급 = the + -est/most

Snow White is **the most beautiful** girl in the world.

▶ 최상급의 의미와 단서 표현

셋 이상의 대상들 중에서 정도나 수준이 가장 높다는 것을 나타낼 때 최상급을 씁니다. 형용사나 부사 뒤에 -est를 붙이거나 앞에 most를 쓰는데, 형용사일 경우에는 최상급 앞에 the나 소유격이 옵니다.

❶ **최상급 + in + 장소/분야/시간:** ~에서 가장 …한

Fairheed Inc. is one of **the oldest** companies **in the industry**.
~~the most oldest~~

페어히드 사는 업계에서 가장 오래된 기업 중 하나이다.

❷ **최상급 + of/among + 복수명사:** ~중에서 가장 …한

Yu Shang is **the most experienced of all the managers**.

유 생 씨는 전체 매니저들 중 가장 경험이 많은 사람이다.

❸ **최상급 + that + 주어 + have (ever) p.p.:** 지금까지 ~한 중에서 가장 …한

This is **the biggest** change **that we have ever experienced**.

이것은 우리가 지금까지 경험한 것 중에 가장 큰 변화이다.

> **LEVEL UP** 품사 문제는 항상 자리부터 확인하자.
> 보기에 형용사나 부사의 비교급, 최상급, 원급 등이 함께 나오더라도, 빈칸이 형용사 자리인지 부사 자리인지를 먼저 확인해야 합니다.
> It rains (**frequently** / ~~frequent~~ / ~~more frequent~~) these days. 요즘은 비가 자주 온다.

▶ 주의할 비교급, 최상급 형태

원급	비교급	최상급
good/well 좋은/잘	better 더 좋은/더 잘	best 최상의/가장 잘
bad 나쁜	worse 더 나쁜	worst 최악의
many/much 많은	more 더 많은	most 가장 많은
little 적은	less 더 적은	least 가장 적은

ETS 유형 연습

다음 문장의 빈칸에 들어갈 알맞은 말을 고르세요.

STEP 1

1. The NX 2016 model from AC Autos is one of the ------- cars in the world.
   (A) fast
   (B) fastest

2. Yesterday's festival featured some of the ------- performances that the Palace Theater has ever hosted.
   (A) most lively
   (B) lively

3. Among the candidates the manager has interviewed, Ms. Porwit is the ------- highly qualified.
   (A) so
   (B) most

4. Of the three presentations that were given, the one made by the Shanti Group was the -------.
   (A) impression
   (B) most impressive

STEP 2

5. Sorin's Lakeview Grill is the ------- restaurant that we've ever been to in the city of Swensen.
   (A) large
   (B) larger
   (C) largely
   (D) largest

6. Sunnydec Resort is reviewing proposals from several businesses, and it will choose the ------- bid.
   (A) most affordable
   (B) more affordable
   (C) affordably
   (D) affordability

7. Mayor Applebaum announced that the city is experiencing the ------- job market in a decade.
   (A) strengthen
   (B) strength
   (C) strongest
   (D) strong

8. Edwards & Sons Plumbing earned the ------- ratings for customer satisfaction in this year's survey.
   (A) higher
   (B) highest
   (C) more highly
   (D) most highly

| 어휘 | 2 feature ~을 특징으로 하다　host 주최하다　lively 활기찬　3 among ~ 중에서　candidate 후보자　highly 매우　qualified 적임의, 자격이 있는　6 proposal 제안(서)　bid 입찰 (가격)　affordable 가격이 적당한　7 decade 10년　strengthen 강화하다　strength 힘　strong 강한　8 earn (명성·평판 등을) 얻다　rating 평가, 순위　customer satisfaction 고객 만족

ETS 실전 문제

1. E-mailing the technology assistance office generally gets a ------- response than calling does.
   (A) quick
   (B) quicker
   (C) quickest
   (D) quickly

2. The general contractor expects Mountain Office Park to be ready for occupancy no ------- than next month.
   (A) late
   (B) later
   (C) latest
   (D) lately

3. Please contact Ms. Shridhar as ------- as possible about planning the spring clothing sale.
   (A) long
   (B) soon
   (C) highly
   (D) stated

4. Although no additional workers were scheduled, the inventory review was completed ------- than expected.
   (A) most rapidly
   (B) rapid
   (C) rapidly
   (D) more rapidly

5. Once the most recent update is installed, the phone's platform will ------- longer support this application.
   (A) not
   (B) none
   (C) no
   (D) nowhere

6. Architects' models of the proposed bridge are ------- easier to understand than their drawings alone.
   (A) very
   (B) much
   (C) so
   (D) too

7. ------- the three candidates for art director at CCAR, Mr. Shaw has the most experience.
   (A) Of
   (B) At
   (C) Yet
   (D) So

8. In your search for an architect, you could not hope to find a ------- designer than Ms. Lopez.
   (A) more accurately
   (B) most accurately
   (C) more accurate
   (D) most accurate

9. Ms. Ramos decided to take a position at Eta Banking ------- one at Neun Financial.
   (A) subsequently
   (B) moreover
   (C) rather than
   (D) in regard to

10. The newly released Nivido mobile phone is almost ------- as expensive as the company's other models.
    (A) double
    (B) two
    (C) second
    (D) twice

Questions 11-14 refer to the following advertisement.

If you are planning a party, conference, or any social event, use Inviting Designs. ------- We
are ------- to use than other card companies because of our extensive collection of premade
invitations. Planners in a rush can choose from these invitation ------- that are perfectly suited
to dozens of different occasions. Or, if you need a ------- touch, we can create a customized
package just for you. Whatever you need, call today and order Inviting Designs invitations
that your guests won't be able to ignore!

11. (A) We can help you invite all your guests with style.
    (B) A party is the best time to tell others about our service.
    (C) All of our invitations are made specifically for you.
    (D) We offer all the supplies you need to prepare for any event.

12. (A) easy
    (B) easier
    (C) easing
    (D) easiest

13. (A) templates
    (B) fonts
    (C) designers
    (D) enhancements

14. (A) typical
    (B) specialized
    (C) reusable
    (D) sensitive

UNIT 17 어휘 1: 명사/형용사

▶ 기출 어휘 – 명사 1 🔊 650_P5_01

동 동의어　반 반의어

advantage advantageous a. 유리한, 이로운 동 edge 우세, 강점	유리한 점, 이점 take advantage of ~을 활용하다	**character** characteristic n. 특징 동 figure 인물	인물; 성격 a fictional character 가상의 인물
appointment appoint v. 임명하다	약속, 임명 make an appointment 약속을 잡다	**choice** choose v. 선택하다 동 option 선택지, 선택권	선택(지), 선택권 our top choices 우리의 최상위 선택
approval approve v. 인정하다, 승인하다	인정, 승인 receive approval 승인을 받다	**compensation** compensate v. 보상하다	보상(금) receive compensation for overtime 초과 근무에 대해 보상받다
assistance assist v. 돕다 assistant n. 조수	도움, 지원 further assistance 추가적인 도움	**concern** concerned a. 걱정하는 concerning prep. ~에 관한	관심사, 걱정, 근심 have concerns about ~에 대해 걱정하다
authority authorize v. 인가하다, 권한을 부여하다	권한; 당국 have the authority to ~할 권한이 있다	**consideration** consider v. 고려하다	고려, 배려 thank you for your consideration. 배려해 주셔서 감사합니다.
badge	신분증, 배지 company identification badge 사원증	**contract**	계약(서); 계약하다 win a contract 계약을 따내다[수주하다]
benefit	혜택, 이익; 이익을 주다 membership benefits 회원 혜택	**contribution** contribute v. 공헌하다, 기여하다	기여, 공헌, 기부(금) contribution to the company 회사에 대한 기여
budget	예산 budget cuts 예산 삭감 a tight budget 빠듯한 예산	**debate**	토론, 논의; 토론하다, 논의하다 after lengthy debate 긴 논의 후에
candidate candidacy n. 출마, 후보(자격)	지원자, 후보자 qualified candidates 자격을 갖춘 지원자들	**defect** defective a. 결함 있는 동 flaw n. 결함, 결	결함, 결점 eliminate defects 결함을 제거하다
capacity	용량, 수용력, 능력 at full capacity 완전 가동하여	**demand**	요구, 수요; 요구하다 demand for organic food 유기농 식품에 대한 수요

ETS 유형 연습

다음 문장의 빈칸에 들어갈 알맞은 말을 고르세요.

STEP 1

1. Dietrich Dentistry asks patients to provide 24-hour notice to cancel a scheduled -------.
   (A) appointment
   (B) investment

2. ------- about the actual cost of the project have delayed the plans for expanding the arena.
   (A) Additions
   (B) Concerns

3. Kweon Accounting and Sunwoo Cleaning Services will renegotiate their current ------- before it expires.
   (A) authority
   (B) contract

4. All items shipped by Howeland Manufacturing are carefully inspected for possible -------.
   (A) defects
   (B) inquiry

STEP 2

5. Please thank the team at the Southfield office for their continued ------- to the Dewan merger project.
   (A) demonstrations
   (B) contributions
   (C) professions
   (D) ambitions

6. Ndori Industries received all the necessary ------- from the town council for the proposed construction project.
   (A) certainties
   (B) activities
   (C) intentions
   (D) approvals

7. The Minabet County Forestry Service has the ------- to close recreational areas early when necessary.
   (A) authority
   (B) consequence
   (C) significance
   (D) reaction

8. Marsden Manufacturing, Inc., is hiring temporary workers to address the present ------- for greater personnel resources.
   (A) measure
   (B) denial
   (C) demand
   (D) claim

| 어휘 | 2 actual 실제의 arena 경기장 addition 추가(물) 3 renegotiate 재협상하다 expire 만료되다 authority 권한; 당국 5 continued 지속된 demonstration 설명, 입증 profession 직업 ambition 야망 6 proposed 제안된 certainty 확실성 intention 의도 7 consequence 결과 significance 중요성 8 address (어려운 문제를) 다루다, 처리하다 measure 조치; 치수를 재다 denial 부정, 부인 claim 요구, 주장

기출 어휘 – 명사 2   650_P5_02

동 동의어   반 반의어

description describe v. 묘사하다	묘사, 설명 job description 직무 내용 기술서	**gain** 동 increase, rise 증가	증가, 이득; 얻다 financial gains 금전적 이득 gain work experience 업무 경험을 쌓다
development develop v. 개발하다	개발 research and development 연구 개발(R&D)	**industry** industrial a. 산업의, 공업의 industrialize v. 산업화하다, 공업화하다	산업, 공업 work in the food industry 음식업계에서 일하다
directions direct v. 길을 안내하다; 지시하다	길 안내; 사용법 directions to the branch 지사로 가는 길 (안내)	**inspection** inspector n. 검사관, 조사관 inspect v. 점검하다	검사, 점검, 검열 pass a safety inspection 안전 검사를 통과하다
distribution distribute v. 분배하다, 나눠주다	유통, 분배, 배부 an overseas distribution system 해외 유통 시스템 exclusive distribution rights 독점 유통권	**instructions** instruct v. 지시하다, 가르치다	설명(서), 지시 (사항) follow the instructions 설명서를 따르다
district	지역, 지구, 구역 the financial district 금융 지구	**investment** invest v. 투자하다 investor n. 투자자	투자(물) initial investment 초기 투자 a secure investment 안전한 투자
enrollment enroll v. 등록하다 동 registration 등록	등록 enrollment period 등록 기간	**maintenance** maintain v. 유지하다	유지보수, 관리 routine maintenance 정기 점검 under maintenance 유지보수 중인
estimate estimated a. 추정되는	견적(서); 견적을 내다 a free estimate 무료 견적	**malfunction** 반 function 기능; (제대로) 작동하다	오작동; 오작동하다 computer malfunction 컴퓨터 오작동
exhibit exhibition n. 전시회	전시(품); 전시하다 a museum exhibit 박물관 전시	**measure** measurement n. 측정; 치수	조치, 정책; 측정하다 effective measures 효과적인 조치 safety measures 안전 조치
expiration expire v. 만료되다	(기한 등의) 만료, 종료 expiration date 유효기간	**negotiation** negotiate v. 협상하다	협상, 협의 contract negotiation 계약 협상 after lengthy negotiation 오랜 협상 끝에
forecast 동 predict 예측하다	예상[예측], 예보; 예상[예보]하다 economic forecasts 경제 전망 forecast a heavy snowfall 폭설을 예보하다	**objection** object v. 반대하다	반대, 이의 the main objection to the plan 계획에 반대하는 주된 이유

ETS 유형 연습

다음 문장의 빈칸에 들어갈 알맞은 말을 고르세요.

정답과 해설 p.178

STEP 1

1. The assistant statistician's job ------- includes data collection, coding, and statistical analysis.
   (A) topic
   (B) description

2. Zumorito Tile Company offers a free DVD that provides step-by-step installation -------.
   (A) destinations
   (B) instructions

3. The study found that the biotechnology ------- is growing faster than other related fields.
   (A) equipment
   (B) industry

4. In yesterday's third-quarter financial statement, Vargas Industries reported a 15 percent ------- in value.
   (A) gain
   (B) advantage

STEP 2

5. For ------- to Pavella Testing Lab's corporate office, as well as a map, click on the link below.
   (A) experiments
   (B) directions
   (C) reviews
   (D) situations

6. Norhaven Associates, Inc., provides clients with expert market ------- for a three-year period.
   (A) industries
   (B) forecasts
   (C) penalties
   (D) refusals

7. Residents who have ------- to the plan for the community center's renovation can present their concerns at Monday night's meeting.
   (A) decisions
   (B) offenses
   (C) objections
   (D) installments

8. Teklind, Inc., implements strict security ------- to prevent unauthorized users from gaining access to confidential information.
   (A) consents
   (B) measures
   (C) angles
   (D) distances

| 어휘 | 1 statistician 통계학자   statistical analysis 통계 분석   **2** destination 목적지   **3** related 관련된
4 financial statement 재무제표   **5** corporate 회사의   situation 상황   **6** expert 전문적인   refusal 거절
7 decision 결정   offense 공격   installment 설치   **8** implement 시행하다   strict 엄격한   prevent 방지하다
unauthorized 권한이 없는, 무단의   access 접근   confidential 기밀의   consent 동의   angle 각도   distance 거리

기출 어휘 - 명사 3 🔊 650_P5_03

동 동의어   반 반의어

operation	작동, 작업	**regulation**	규정, 규칙
operator n. 기사, 운영자	joint operation 공동 작업 streamline operations 운영을 간소화하다	regulate v. 규제하다 동 rule 규칙	safety regulations 안전 규칙 meet regulations 규정을 준수하다

option	선택(권), 옵션	**replacement**	교체(품), 후임자
opt v. 선택하다	a wide range of options 폭넓은 선택권	replace v. 대신하다, 대체하다	replacement parts 교체 부품 train my replacement 후임자를 교육시키다

participation	참여, 참가	**reputation**	명성, 평판
participate v. 참여[참가]하다 participant n. 참가자	participation in the survey 설문 조사 참여	동 renown, fame 명성	build a reputation 명성을 쌓다

preference	선호, 우선권	**requirement**	필요 조건
prefer v. 선호하다 preferably ad. 되도록이면	food preference 음식 선호도	require v. 요구하다, 필요로 하다	meet the requirements 필요 조건을 충족시키다 job requirements 직무 자격 요건

presence	존재(감)	**reservation**	예약
present a. 있는, 존재하는	international presence 국제적 영향력	reserve v. 예약하다	make a reservation 예약하다 confirm a reservation 예약을 확인하다

priority	우선 사항, 우선 순위	**responsibility**	책임(감), 책무
prior to prep. ~ 전에	top priority 최우선 사항	responsible a. 책임이 있는	primary responsibilities 주요 책무 take responsibility for ~의 책임을 떠맡다

promotion	승진, 홍보, 촉진	**solution**	해결책
promote v. 승진시키다, 홍보하다 promotional a. 홍보용의	promotion to sales manager 영업 부장으로의 승진	solve v. 해결하다 동 answer 해답	find a solution 해결책을 찾다

proposal	제안, 기획안	**strategy**	전략, 계획
propose v. 제안하다	business proposal 사업 제안 reject the proposal 제안을 거절하다	strategic a. 전략적인 동 plan 계획	marketing strategy 마케팅 전략

purchase	구입(품), 구매; 구입하다, 구매하다	**submission**	제출, 제출물
purchaser n. 구입자, 구매자	all cosmetic purchases 모든 화장품 구매 purchase order 구입 주문서	submit v. 제출하다	review the submissions 제출물을 검토하다

questionnaire	설문지, 질문지	**warehouse**	창고
동 survey 설문지	fill out a questionnaire 설문지를 작성하다 complete a questionnaire 설문지를 완료하다	동 storage 저장고	warehouse logistics 창고 물류 warehouse inventory 창고 재고

ETS 유형 연습

다음 문장의 빈칸에 들어갈 알맞은 말을 고르세요.

STEP 1

1. Stafford Cable offers several payment ------, so customers can choose the most convenient way to pay their bills.
   (A) outcomes
   (B) options

2. Divard, Inc., is a small public relations firm dedicated to the ------ of promising new musicians.
   (A) promotion
   (B) application

3. ------ that are out of compliance with contest rules will be automatically disqualified.
   (A) Submissions
   (B) Consequences

4. Conference fees and travel costs will be paid by Direxco, but dining expenses are the participants' ------.
   (A) requirement
   (B) responsibility

STEP 2

5. Because of its ------ for outstanding customer service, Mei's Hair Salon is the most popular business of its kind in the area.
   (A) approval
   (B) estimation
   (C) probability
   (D) reputation

6. Because Legolos Company recognizes the importance of protecting customer information, it has made data privacy a high ------.
   (A) conformity
   (B) liability
   (C) priority
   (D) seniority

7. Because of anticipated demand, the Emerald Pond Inn recommends making ------ at least one month ahead of time.
   (A) reservations
   (B) suggestions
   (C) observations
   (D) exceptions

8. Airline safety ------ must be followed by passengers as well as crew members.
   (A) ceremonies
   (B) departments
   (C) regulations
   (D) constructions

| 어휘 | **1** outcome 결과 **2** public relations 홍보 dedicated to ~에 전념하는 promising 유망한 application 지원, 신청 **3** compliance 준수 disqualify 실격시키다 **4** expense 경비, 지출 requirement 필요 조건 **5** outstanding 우수한 estimation 판단, 평가 probability 가능성, 개연성 **6** recognize 인식하다, 인정해 주다 data privacy 자료 보호 conformity 부응, 따름 liability 책임 seniority 연공서열 **7** anticipated 예상되는 ahead of time 사전에 observation 관찰 exception 예외 **8** ceremony 의식 department 부서

기출 어휘 – 형용사 1 🔊 650_P5_04

동 동의어   반 반의어

accountable 동 responsible 책임이 있는	책임이 있는 be accountable for ~에 대한 책임이 있다 hold him accountable 그에게 책임을 묻다	**complimentary** compliment v. 칭찬(하다)	무료의, 칭찬의 complimentary tickets 무료 티켓
additional add v. 추가하다 addition n. 추가(물)	추가적인 additional workers 추가 직원들	**confidential** confidentiality n. 기밀성	기밀의, 비밀의 confidential information 기밀 정보
advanced advance v. 진보시키다, 전진하다	고급의, 진보된 advanced degree 고급 학위 advanced technology 첨단 기술	**considerable** 동 significant 상당한, 중요한	상당한, 많은 a considerable amount 상당한 양 considerable damage 상당한 피해
agreeable agree v. 동의하다	동의하는, (사람이) 성격이 좋은 be agreeable to the changes 변경 사항에 동의하다	**creative** creativity n. 창의성 동 innovative 혁신적인	창의적인 the most creative proposal 가장 창의적인 제안
alternative alternatively ad. 그렇지 않으면 alternate v. 번갈아 하다	대안의; 대안 alternative energy 대체 에너지	**critical** criticize v. 비판하다	비평의; 비판적인; 중대한 receive critical acclaim 호평을 받다 critical issues 중대한 문제
appropriate appropriately ad. 적절하게	적절한 wear appropriate gear 적절한 장비를 착용하다 appropriate permits 적절한 허가증	**dedicated** dedication n. 헌신, 공헌	헌신적인, 전념하는 dedicated employees 헌신적인 직원들
available availability n. 이용할 수 있음	이용 가능한 available for rental 임대 가능한	**dependent** depend v. 의존하다 반 independent 독립된, 독립적인	의존하는 be dependent upon ~에 의존하다 financially dependent 재정적으로 의존하는
aware awareness n. 인식 반 unaware 알지 못하는	알고 있는 be aware of customer needs 고객의 욕구를 알다	**detailed** details n. 세부사항	세부적인, 자세한 detailed information 자세한 정보
captivating captivate v. (마음 등을) 사로잡다	매력적인 a captivating performance 매력적인 공연	**eligible** 동 entitled, qualified 자격이 있는	자격이 있는, 적임의 be eligible for promotion 승진할 자격이 있다
competitive compete v. 경쟁하다 competition n. 경쟁	경쟁적인, 경쟁력 있는 competitive prices 경쟁력 있는 가격	**entire** entirely ad. 전적으로 동 whole 전체의, 완전한	전체의 the entire department 부서 전체 the entire organization 조직 전체

ETS 유형 연습

다음 문장의 빈칸에 들어갈 알맞은 말을 고르세요.

정답과 해설 p.180

STEP 1

1. The entertainment complex is ------- for private functions every weekend.
   (A) attractive
   (B) available

2. Your selection will arrive in seven to ten days and will be followed by ------- deliveries every six weeks.
   (A) thorough
   (B) additional

3. The street guide to Tompkinsville has been compiled from ------- national and local maps.
   (A) dependent
   (B) detailed

4. Edith Kozik's corporation guarantees that even temporary employees are ------- for paid holidays.
   (A) eligible
   (B) flexible

STEP 2

5. It is ------- that laboratory employees follow the instructions in this manual exactly as written.
   (A) particular
   (B) critical
   (C) substantial
   (D) immediate

6. *Global Flyways* is a ------- magazine provided as a courtesy to Olan Airlines passengers.
   (A) complimentary
   (B) variable
   (C) perpetual
   (D) subsequent

7. In keeping with her reputation for originality, Ms. Kwan submitted the most ------- proposal for the design of the new airport terminal.
   (A) hesitant
   (B) persistent
   (C) creative
   (D) pleasant

8. With a medieval castle overlooking its cobblestone streets, the ------- town of Ljubljana is a favorite tourist destination.
   (A) captivating
   (B) selective
   (C) implicit
   (D) sequential

| 어휘 | 1 attractive 매력적인   3 compile 편찬하다, 편집하다   4 corporation 기업   flexible 유연한   5 laboratory 실험실   particular 특별한   substantial 상당한   immediate 즉각적인   6 courtesy 서비스, 배려   variable 변하는   perpetual 끊임없이 계속되는   subsequent 차후의   7 in keeping with ~와 어울려   hesitant 망설이는   persistent 끈질긴   pleasant 즐거운   8 medieval 중세의   cobblestone 조약돌   selective 선택적인   implicit 암시된   sequential 순차적인

UNIT 17 | 어휘 1: 명사/형용사   **253**

기출 어휘 - 형용사 2 🔊 650_P5_05

동 동의어   반 반의어

exciting 동 thrilling 신나는	흥미진진한, 신나는 an exciting opportunity 흥미로운 기회	**punctual** punctually ad. 시간대로, 엄수하여	시간을 지키는[엄수하는] a punctual start at 9 o'clock 9시에 정확히 맞춘 시작
extensive extend v. 연장하다, 늘리다 extension n. 연장, 내선 전화	광범위한 extensive experience 광범위한 경험	**qualified** 동 eligible 자격이 있는 competent 능숙한	자격이 있는, 능력이 있는 qualified candidates 자격을 갖춘 지원자 highly qualified 고도로 숙련된
flexible	유연한, 융통성 있는 flexible schedule 유연한 일정 flexible working hours 탄력적 근무 시간	**reliable** rely v. 믿다, 의지하다	믿을 만한, 신뢰할 수 있는 reliable transportation 믿을 만한 교통 수단
genuine 동 sincere 진정한 authentic 진짜의	진실된, 진짜의 genuine interest 진정한 관심 genuine concern 진심 어린 걱정	**remaining** remain v. 남다	남은 remaining time 남은 시간
impressive impress v. 깊은 인상을 주다	인상적인, 뛰어난 impressive track record 뛰어난 실적[경력]	**significant** significantly ad. 상당하게	중요한, 상당한 significant changes 상당한 변화 a significant impact on ~에 대한 상당한 영향
innovative innovate v. 혁신하다 innovation n. 혁신	혁신적인 an innovative product 혁신적인 제품	**stable** stability n. 안정(감)	안정된, 안정적인 stable prices 안정적인 물가
local	그 지역의, 현지의; 현지인 local residents and businesses 지역 주민들과 기업	**substantial** 동 considerable 상당한	상당한, 실질적인 a substantial increase in sales 판매에서의 상당한 증가 a substantial amount of 막대한 양의
permanent 동 lasting 영속적인	영구적인 permanent residence 영구 거주지 a permanent position 정규직	**supplemental** supplement n. 보충(물)	추가적인 supplemental materials 보충 자료
personal 동 confidential 비밀[기밀]의	개인의, 사적인 personal information 개인 정보 personal belongings 개인 소지품	**thorough** thoroughly ad. 철저하게	철저한 thorough inspection 철저한 검사
potential potentially ad. 잠재적으로	잠재적인; 잠재력 potential customers 잠재 고객들	**valid** 동 effective 유효한 반 invalid 유효하지 않은	유효한 valid form of ID 유효한 신분증 valid for a year 1년간 유효한

ETS 유형 연습

다음 문장의 빈칸에 들어갈 알맞은 말을 고르세요.

STEP 1

1. ------- savings on the cost of building materials contributed to a growth in Minbrough Construction's revenue.
   (A) Virtual
   (B) Significant

2. Thanks to his fifteen years at Dulesse Tech, Mr. Duvarre has a ------- understanding of company policies.
   (A) thorough
   (B) last

3. Applicants for the dental assistant position must possess a license that is ------- in the state of New York.
   (A) valid
   (B) actual

4. Analysts characterize Westonville Financial as a ------- company because it has a long record of sustained profitability.
   (A) routine
   (B) stable

STEP 2

5. According to the firm's policy, staff should not use workplace e-mail accounts for ------- purposes.
   (A) entire
   (B) active
   (C) cautious
   (D) personal

6. Benningfield Farmhouse is the only ------- eighteenth-century building in downtown Wickhurst.
   (A) gradual
   (B) remaining
   (C) mutual
   (D) delayed

7. Widely praised by audiences and critics, *Nineteen Rainbows* is considered one of the year's most ------- films.
   (A) sufficient
   (B) ongoing
   (C) exciting
   (D) grateful

8. Many employment recruiters use social networking sites to help identify ------- candidates.
   (A) qualified
   (B) indefinite
   (C) concluding
   (D) spacious

| 어휘 | **1** contribute 기여하다 growth 증대 revenue 수익 virtual 가상의 **4** characterize 규정하다 sustained 지속적인 profitability 수익성 routine 일상적인 **5** account 계정 **6** farmhouse 농가 **7** audience 관객 critic 평론가 consider 간주하다 sufficient 충분한 ongoing 진행 중인 grateful 감사하는 **8** recruiter 모집자 identify 찾다 indefinite 무기한의 concluding 종결의 spacious 넓은

ETS 실전 문제

1. Scottish novelist Elsie Baxter has been praised for her highly imaginative -------.
   (A) characters
   (B) packagers
   (C) exercises
   (D) possibilities

2. Customers at Harry's Restaurant have the ------- of soup or salad to accompany any dinner.
   (A) wish
   (B) taste
   (C) choice
   (D) piece

3. The South Bay Maritime Museum is featuring an ------- on the history of shipbuilding in the region.
   (A) exhibit
   (B) advertisement
   (C) expression
   (D) indication

4. You will be notified by e-mail when the period for ------- in Chef Gomar's Culinary Academy begins.
   (A) appearance
   (B) enrollment
   (C) convenience
   (D) replacement

5. The management team has plans to increase the company's international ------- by opening a branch in Berlin.
   (A) expedition
   (B) evaluation
   (C) collection
   (D) presence

6. Winston Plumbing Company has been in ------- for more than 75 years.
   (A) statement
   (B) decision
   (C) ability
   (D) operation

7. At least 30 large cans of blue paint will be needed for the interior of the -------.
   (A) combination
   (B) warehouse
   (C) tent
   (D) party

8. The engineers discussed the problem for two hours but could not agree on a -------.
   (A) chance
   (B) trouble
   (C) solution
   (D) progress

9. Neltin Corporation takes ------- security measures to safeguard all customer data from unauthorized access.

   (A) appropriate
   (B) dependent
   (C) receptive
   (D) concerned

10. Trade magazine writers remain largely ------- of Airita's new technology and how it could drastically affect the market.

    (A) severe
    (B) indicative
    (C) subtle
    (D) unaware

11. The information you provide on this questionnaire is strictly ------- and will not be shared with any other vendors.

    (A) potential
    (B) concentrated
    (C) dedicated
    (D) confidential

12. The ------- organization has been invited to Mr. Olner's retirement party, so the group will be large.

    (A) attentive
    (B) solid
    (C) final
    (D) entire

13. On Thursday, the CEO held a press conference ------- plans to merge with Remini Financial Services.

    (A) except
    (B) versus
    (C) along
    (D) concerning

14. JQT Corporation's business goals cannot be fulfilled without ------- market research.

    (A) contented
    (B) convinced
    (C) reliable
    (D) right

15. Tomorrow's seminar begins at 9:00 A.M. sharp, so attendees should try to be -------.

    (A) punctual
    (B) advanced
    (C) instant
    (D) sudden

16. Stylists at Heather's Salon show a ------- passion for hair, beauty, and customer satisfaction.

    (A) trimmed
    (B) genuine
    (C) straight
    (D) hospitable

UNIT 18 어휘 2: 동사/부사

▶ 기출 어휘 - 동사 1 🔊 650_P5_06

동 동의어 반 반의어

accelerate acceleration n. 가속, 가속도	속도를 높이다, 가속화하다 accelerate the company's growth 회사의 성장 속도를 높이다	**attach** attachment n. 첨부 (파일)	첨부하다 attach a sample form 샘플 양식을 첨부하다
accept acceptance n. 수락	수락하다, 인정하다 accept a position 직책을 수락하다	**attend** attendance n. 참석 attention n. 주의, 주목	참석하다, 관심을 두다 attend a seminar 세미나에 참석하다
access accessible a. 접근 가능한	접근하다, 접속하다; 접근, 접속 access restricted areas 제한 구역에 접근하다	**attract** attraction n. 명소 attractive a. 매력적인 동 appeal to ~의 관심을 끌다; ~에 호소하다	끌어당기다 attract visitors 방문객을 끌어들이다
accommodate accommodation n. 숙박, 수용	수용하다 accommodate your request 당신의 요청 사항을 수용하다	**award** awardee n. 수상자	(상을) 주다, 수여하다; 상 award-winning 상을 받은, 수상한 award first prize to ~에게 일등상을 수여하다
accompany 동 go with 동행하다	동행하다 be accompanied by ~와 동행하다	**boost** 동 promote 촉진하다; 승진시키다	향상시키다, 촉진하다 boost sales 매출을 증가시키다 boost employee morale 직원 사기를 높이다
address 동 handle, deal with 다루다, 처리하다	연설하다; 다루다, 처리하다 address the audience 청중에게 연설하다 address a complaint 불만 사항을 처리하다	**collaborate** collaborative a. 공동의	협력하다, 공동 작업하다 collaborate to achieve a goal 목표를 달성하기 위해 협력하다
announce announcement n. 공지	알리다, 발표하다 announce a new policy 새로운 정책을 발표하다	**commend** commendation n. 칭찬, 찬사	칭찬하다, 기리다 be highly commended 높이 칭찬받다
apply application n. 지원, 신청 applicant n. 지원자	지원하다; (크림 등을) 바르다 apply for a job 일자리에 지원하다	**comply** compliance n. (법령의) 준수, 따름	따르다, 준수하다 comply with regulations 규정을 따르다
assess assessment n. 평가, 과제	평가하다, 산정하다 assess the team's performance 팀 실적을 평가하다	**confirm** confirmation n. 승인, 확인	확인하다 confirm a reservation 예약을 확인하다
assign assignment n. 과제, 임무	맡기다, 할당하다 assigned task 할당된 업무	**cooperate** cooperative a. 협조적인 cooperation n. 협동	협동하다 cooperate with each other 서로 협동하다

ETS 유형 연습

다음 문장의 빈칸에 들어갈 알맞은 말을 고르세요.

STEP 1

1. The mayor will ------- the issue of road improvement in today's speech.
   (A) educate
   (B) address

2. Employees who wish to ------- the sales exposition in London next month should let their managers know.
   (A) participate
   (B) attend

3. Executives from the two firms may soon be ready to ------- the terms of the proposed merger.
   (A) confirm
   (B) collaborate

4. The initial model produced by our contractors failed to ------- with the specifications we provided them.
   (A) approach
   (B) comply

STEP 2

5. Pawel Ltd. has ------- more than fifteen educational scholarships to local high school students this year.
   (A) entitled
   (B) allowed
   (C) awarded
   (D) appointed

6. How to ------- production of furniture at the Linderwood plant is the topic of the next supervisors' meeting.
   (A) appeal
   (B) notify
   (C) accelerate
   (D) subscribe

7. Eating establishments in the city are frequently ------- by inspectors to verify compliance with health and safety standards.
   (A) invested
   (B) assessed
   (C) conducted
   (D) conveyed

8. Delwar Cosmetics will ------- its partnership with Briggman Ltd. at next week's press conference.
   (A) consist
   (B) announce
   (C) issue
   (D) tell

| 어휘 | 1 improvement 개선 2 participate (in) 참가하다 3 executive 임원 terms 조건 merger 합병 collaborate 협력하다 4 initial 초기의 contractor 계약업자 fail to ~하지 못하다 specification 명세 사항 5 scholarship 장학금 entitle 자격을 주다 7 eating establishment 식당 inspector 검사관 verify 검증하다 compliance 준수 conduct 이행하다 convey 전달하다 8 partnership 제휴, 협력 press conference 기자회견

기출 어휘 - 동사 2 🔊 650_P5_07

동 동의어   반 반의어

create creative a. 창조적인, 창의적인 creation n. 창조, 창작(물)	창조하다, 만들어 내다 create a protective barrier 보호막을 만들다	**improve** improvement n. 향상, 개선	개선되다, 향상시키다 improve productivity 생산성을 향상시키다
deliver delivery n. 배달, 배송	배달하다, 배송하다 deliver products with care 제품을 주의해서 배달하다	**increase** 동 boost 향상시키다 surge 급증하다	증가하다, 증가시키다 increase prices 가격을 인상하다 increase productivity 생산성을 향상시키다
disclose 동 reveal 공개하다 divulge 누설하다	밝히다, 공개하다 disclose information 정보를 공개하다	**issue**	발행하다; 문제, 쟁점, 호 issue an invitation 초대장을 발행하다 social issues 사회 문제
distribute distribution n. 분배, 배급	나누다, 배포하다 distribute the work evenly 일을 고르게 분배하다	**negotiate** negotiation n. 협상	협상하다, 조정하다 negotiate a price 가격을 협상하다 negotiate the terms 조건을 협상하다
enclose enclosed a. 동봉된	동봉하다 the document is enclosed 문서가 동봉되다	**notify** notification n. 통지	알리다, 통보하다 notify Ms. Suh of her promotion 서 씨에게 승진을 통보하다
encourage encouragement n. 격려 encouraging a. 격려의, 유망한	격려하다, 고무하다 encourage employees 직원들을 격려하다	**occupy** occupied a. 사용 중인; (사람이) 바쁜	차지하다, 점유하다 occupy the position of manager 매니저 직위를 맡다
evaluate evaluation n. 평가 동 assess 평가하다	평가하다, 점검하다 evaluate employee performance 직원 성과를 평가하다	**offer** 동 serve, provide 제공하다	제안하다, 제공하다; 제안, 제공 offer a variety of appetizers 다양한 애피타이저를 제공하다 receive a job offer 일자리 제안을 받다
evolve evolution n. 진화, 발전	발전하다, 발달하다 evolve into a big city 대도시로 발전하다	**operate** operation n. 작동, 운영	작동하다, 운영하다 operate new machinery 새 장비를 작동하다
expand expansion n. 확장	확장하다, 확대하다 expand business 사업을 확장하다	**perform** performance n. 실적, 공연	수행하다, 공연하다 perform a task 업무를 수행하다
implement implementation n. 시행, 이행	시행하다, 이행하다 implement the new policies 새로운 정책을 실시하다	**permit** permission n. 허락	허락하다, 허용하다; 허가(증) photography is not permitted 사진촬영은 허용되지 않는다 obtain a building permit 건축 허가를 받다

ETS 유형 연습

다음 문장의 빈칸에 들어갈 알맞은 말을 고르세요.

STEP 1

1. Croydon Transport will always ------- your parcel on time.
   (A) exceed
   (B) deliver

2. Forming international partnerships is an effective way for a company to ------- its market.
   (A) expand
   (B) include

3. Leeworth's coffee subsidiary will ------- under the name of Genus Beans.
   (A) conduct
   (B) operate

4. The CEO of Argall Enterprises is expected to ------- a statement to the press later this week.
   (A) speak
   (B) issue

STEP 2

5. Heloglas plans to ------- its production of solar panels over the next five years.
   (A) notify
   (B) benefit
   (C) concern
   (D) increase

6. While all the programmers ------- well in their job interviews, Susan Trafford stood out from the rest.
   (A) treated
   (B) revealed
   (C) handled
   (D) performed

7. Anyone interested in mentoring a summer intern should ------- Sharmila Kumar in the human resources department.
   (A) acquaint
   (B) notify
   (C) respond
   (D) explain

8. Senior management ------- employees to submit ideas for increasing workplace satisfaction to the human resources department.
   (A) responds
   (B) excels
   (C) maintains
   (D) encourages

| 어휘 | 1 parcel 소포 on time 제시간에 exceed 초과하다 2 international 국제적인 effective 효과적인 3 subsidiary 자회사 4 statement 성명(서) press 언론 5 production 생산 solar panel 태양광 패널 6 stand out 돋보이다 7 acquaint 숙지시키다 8 senior management 고위 경영진 submit 제출하다 satisfaction 만족(도) respond 응답하다 excel 뛰어나다 maintain 유지하다

기출 어휘 - 동사 3 🔊 650_P5_08

동 동의어 반 반의어

possess	소유하다	**return**	돌아오다; 반송[반납]하다
possession n. 소유물, 소유권	possess a skill 기술을 보유하다		complete and return the form 양식을 작성하여 반송하다
동 own 소유하다 hold 소지하다, 유지하다			

present	제시하다, 소개하다; 현재의	**revise**	수정하다, 개정하다
동 give 제시하다 introduce 소개하다	present a boarding pass 탑승권을 제시하다	revision n. 수정, 검토	revise the contract 계약을 수정하다
			revise our policy 정책을 개정하다

prevent	막다, 예방하다	**sign**	서명하다; 표지판, 간판
prevention n. 예방	prevent staff from accessing the file 직원들이 그 파일을 열 수 없도록 막다	signature n. 서명	sign a contract 계약서에 서명하다
			traffic sign 교통 표지판

| **provide** | 제공하다 | **sponsor** | 후원자; 후원하다, 지원하다 |
| 동 supply 공급하다 | provide a replacement 교체품을 제공하다 | 동 patron 후원자 | sponsor a charity event 자선 행사를 후원하다 |

reach	이르다, 닿다; 연락을 취하다	**stimulate**	촉진하다, 활성화시키다
동 get in touch with ~와 연락을 취하다	reach our destination 우리의 목적지에 닿다	동 provoke 자극하다 encourage 장려하다	stimulate tourism 관광을 활성화시키다
	reach him by e-mail 그에게 이메일로 연락하다		

recruit	채용하다, 모집하다; 신입 사원	**suggest**	제안하다
동 hire 고용하다; 신입 사원	recruit volunteers 자원봉사자를 모집하다	suggestion n. 제안 동 propose 제안하다	suggest an alternative 대안을 제안하다
	recruit staff 직원을 채용하다		suggest a solution 해결책을 제안하다

| **register** | 등록하다, 기록하다 | **support** | 지지[지원]하다, 후원하다 |
| registration n. 등록 동 sign up, enroll 등록하다 | register for a workshop 워크숍에 등록하다 | supportive a. 지원하는 | support a proposal 제안을 지지하다 |

reject	거절하다, 반려하다	**transfer**	이동하다, 전송하다
rejection n. 거절	reject the offer 제안을 거절하다		transfer the data 데이터를 전송하다
			transfer a call 착신 전환하다

release	출시하다, 개봉하다	**undergo**	겪다, 경험하다
동 launch 출시하다	release new products 신제품을 출시하다	동 experience 경험하다 go through 겪다	undergo changes 변화를 겪다
	release a film 영화를 개봉하다		

| **reserve** | 예약하다, 보류하다 | **urge** | 권장하다, 촉구하다 |
| reserved a. 예약된 동 book 예약하다 | reserve a meeting room 회의실을 예약하다 | 동 encourage 권장하다, 격려하다 | be urged to warm up 준비 운동을 하도록 권장되다 |

ETS 유형 연습

다음 문장의 빈칸에 들어갈 알맞은 말을 고르세요.

정답과 해설 p.184

STEP 1

1. Meran Investments has ------- an agreement to purchase new headquarters.
   (A) labeled
   (B) signed

2. We require all visitors to ------- photo identification prior to entering the building.
   (A) notify
   (B) present

3. Team leaders should try to ------- workshop attendees from repeating one another's comments.
   (A) prevent
   (B) organize

4. To ------- the hotel fitness center, please use the staircase at the back of the main lobby.
   (A) reach
   (B) feature

STEP 2

5. Workshop participants may choose any seat in the auditorium except those in the front row, which are ------- for the presenters.
   (A) chaired
   (B) reserved
   (C) substituted
   (D) performed

6. To receive reimbursement for any business travel, employees must submit expense reports within 30 days of ------- from their trip.
   (A) working
   (B) flying
   (C) returning
   (D) conducting

7. The computer technicians ------- sales representatives with detailed instructions for accessing the client database.
   (A) offer
   (B) arrange
   (C) contribute
   (D) provide

8. All track-and-field athletes are ------- to warm up before jumping or sprinting.
   (A) addressed
   (B) regarded
   (C) urged
   (D) judged

| 어휘 | 1 agreement 계약(서)　headquarters 본사　label 라벨을 붙이다　2 prior to ~ 전에　3 attendee 참석자　organize 조직하다　5 auditorium 강당　presenter 발표자　chair 의장직을 맡다　substitute 대신하다, 대용하다　6 reimbursement 환급　submit 제출하다　expense 비용　7 arrange 배치하다, 준비하다　8 track-and-field athlete 육상 선수　sprint 전력 질주하다　regard 여기다　judge 판단하다

기출 어휘 - 부사 1 🔊 650_P5_09

동 동의어 반 반의어

accurately accurate a. 정확한	정확하게 describe accurately 정확하게 묘사하다	**effectively** effective a. 효과적인	효과적으로 communicate more effectively 더 효과적으로 소통하다
annually annual a. 매년의 동 yearly 매년	매년 be renewed annually 매년 갱신되다 be held annually 매년 개최되다	**exclusively** exclude v. 제외하다 exclusive a. 독점적인, 배타적인	독점적으로, 오로지 exclusively available 독점적으로 이용 가능한
automatically automatic a. 자동의	자동적으로, 기계적으로 download automatically 자동으로 다운로드하다	**finally** final a. 마지막의, 최종적인	마침내, 최종적으로 finally finish the report 마침내 보고서를 완성하다 finally sign the contract 마침내 계약서에 서명하다
briefly brief a. 간략한 v. 간략히 보고하다	잠시, 간략하게 visit briefly 잠시 방문하다	**formally** formal a. 정식의, 공식적인	정식으로, 공식적으로 formally announce the merger 합병을 공식 발표하다
closely close a. 가까운 ad. 가까이에	면밀히, 밀접하게 be monitored closely 면밀히 감시되다 analyze results closely 결과를 면밀히 분석하다	**frequently** frequent a. 잦은, 빈번한	종종, 자주 be frequently delayed 자주 지연되다
completely complete a. 완전한 v. 완료하다	완전히 completely new 완전히 새로운	**generally** general a. 일반적인 generalize v. 일반화하다	일반적으로, 대개, 보통 generally free on Wednesdays 일반적으로 수요일에 한가한
consistently consistent a. 지속적인	지속적으로, 일관되게 consistently positive reviews 지속적으로 긍정적인 평가	**highly** 동 extremely 매우, 극히	매우 highly recommended 강력히 추천되는 highly effective 매우 효과적인
conveniently convenient a. 편리한	편리하게, 용이하게 conveniently located 편리한 위치에 있는	**immediately** immediate a. 즉각적인, 직접의	즉시 immediately after purchase 구매 직후에 immediately upon receipt 수령 즉시
diligently diligent a. 부지런한, 근면한 diligence n. 근면, 성실	부지런히, 열심히, 애써 work diligently 부지런히 일하다	**increasingly** increase v. 증가하다 increasing a. 증가하는	점점 become increasingly popular 점점 더 인기 있어지다
dramatically dramatic a. 급격한	급격하게 dramatically increase 급격하게 증가하다	**intentionally** intentional a. 의도적인, 고의로 한 동 on purpose 고의로	의도적으로, 고의로 intentionally omit the information 의도적으로 정보를 삭제하다

ETS 유형 연습

다음 문장의 빈칸에 들어갈 알맞은 말을 고르세요.

정답과 해설 p.185

STEP 1

1. The revised work plan is scheduled to begin ------- and will be in effect for at least three months.
   (A) immediately
   (B) closely

2. Requests for new office equipment ------- take one month to process.
   (A) totally
   (B) generally

3. Mr. Loren worked for Kloss Fibers for one week before he was ------- introduced to his division manager.
   (A) currently
   (B) formally

4. Employees at Tihomir Toys work ------- to ensure the quality of the company's merchandise.
   (A) diligently
   (B) extremely

STEP 2

5. Please make sure that all sections of the form are filled out ------- for quick processing.
   (A) moderately
   (B) hardly
   (C) completely
   (D) highly

6. Customers who make cash withdrawals ------- may be interested in our new online banking service.
   (A) totally
   (B) hugely
   (C) greatly
   (D) frequently

7. The flash on the Yinkam camera activates -------, so the photographer does not need to turn it on.
   (A) potentially
   (B) ultimately
   (C) automatically
   (D) simultaneously

8. Dr. Saito's research project has been discontinued because it became ------- time-consuming and financially taxing.
   (A) poorly
   (B) thickly
   (C) increasingly
   (D) differently

| 어휘 | 1 be in effect 효력이 있다[발생하다] 2 totally 완전히 3 division manager 부서장 4 ensure 확보하다 extremely 극도로 5 moderately 적당하게 hardly 거의 ~않다 6 cash withdrawal 현금 인출 hugely 엄청나게, 크게 7 activate 작동하다 potentially 잠재적으로 ultimately 궁극적으로, 마침내 simultaneously 동시에 8 discontinue 중단하다 time-consuming 시간이 많이 걸리는 taxing 부담이 큰 poorly 형편 없이 thickly 두껍게

기출 어휘 - 부사 2 🔊 650_P5_10

동 동의어   반 반의어

jointly joint a. 공동의, 합동의	공동으로, 함께 jointly own 공동 소유하다 jointly developed 공동 개발된	**reasonably** reasonable a. 타당한, 합리적인	합리적으로, 적절하게 reasonably priced 합리적인 가격의 reasonably well 꽤 잘
later 동 afterward 후에	나중에; ~ 뒤의 one hour later 한 시간 뒤에 no later than 늦어도 ~까지	**recently** recent a. 최근의	최근에 recently renovated 최근에 보수된
noticeably noticeable a. 뚜렷한, 분명한	눈에 띄게, 두드러지게 noticeably higher 눈에 띄게 더 높은 noticeably reduced 눈에 띄게 줄어든	**respectively** respective a. 각각의	각각 receive 10 and 12 votes, respectively 각각 10표와 12표를 받다
particularly particular a. 특정한	특히 particularly busy in winter 겨울에 특히 바쁜	**seamlessly** 동 harmoniously 조화롭게	매끄럽게, 자연스럽게 seamlessly combine 매끄럽게 결합하다 blend seamlessly with ~와 자연스럽게 섞이다
periodically 동 regularly 정기적으로	정기적으로, 주기적으로 conduct inspections periodically 정기적으로 점검을 실시하다	**securely** secure a. 안전한, 확실한	확실하게, 단단히; 안전하게 securely fastened 단단히 고정된 stored securely 안전하게 보관된
predictably predictable a. 예측 가능한 동 as expected 예상대로	예상대로 predictably low occupancy rates 예상대로 낮은 점유율	**slightly** slight a. 약간의	약간 slightly different 약간 다른
previously previous a. 이전의	이전에, 미리 as previously scheduled 이전에 정해진 대로	**solely** sole a. 유일한 동 only 오직	오직, 단독으로 based solely on ~에만 근거한 used solely for ~만을 위해 사용되는
primarily primary a. 주요한	주로 focus primarily on marketing strategies 주로 마케팅 전략에 집중하다	**specifically** specific a. 구체적인	특별히, 명확하게 parking space specifically designated for the staff 직원들에게 특별히 지정 할당된 주차 공간
promptly prompt a. 신속한	신속하게, 지체 없이 arrive promptly 정시에 도착하다 act promptly 즉시 조치를 취하다	**steadily** steady a. 꾸준한, 안정적인 동 regularly 꾸준히	꾸준히 rise steadily 꾸준히 증가하다
rapidly rapid a. 신속한	빠르게, 신속하게 grow rapidly 급속히 성장하다	**temporarily** temporary a. 일시적인 동 briefly 잠시	일시적으로, 잠시 be temporarily closed 일시적으로 닫히다 temporarily out of service 일시적으로 이용 불가능한

ETS 유형 연습

다음 문장의 빈칸에 들어갈 알맞은 말을 고르세요.

STEP 1

1. Tyradex assembly-line workers are expected to do their jobs ------- but accurately.
   (A) fortunately
   (B) rapidly

2. The ------- formed client advisory division of the Mantar Corporation is now hiring financial specialists.
   (A) currently
   (B) recently

3. The latest digital edition of *Silvina Business Law* has an online review section that was not available -------.
   (A) professionally
   (B) previously

4. Volunteers are needed to take pictures at the company banquet, ------- those who have experience in event photography.
   (A) specifically
   (B) gradually

STEP 2

5. Total occupancy rates at beachfront hotels were ------- low last season because of the rainy weather that forecasters warned about.
   (A) predictably
   (B) carelessly
   (C) absently
   (D) smoothly

6. Sales have risen ------- in the hardware departments at all Vismet Supply stores.
   (A) steadily
   (B) personally
   (C) cheaply
   (D) noisily

7. It is essential to monitor your checking account balance ------- to avoid accidental overdrafts.
   (A) authentically
   (B) unusually
   (C) periodically
   (D) approximately

8. Mr. Defoe told the landscapers they could go home and finish the project -------.
   (A) almost
   (B) later
   (C) previously
   (D) exactly

| 어휘 | 1 fortunately 운 좋게   2 advisory 자문의   4 experience 경험   gradually 점차   5 occupancy rate 객실 이용률   forecaster 일기 예보관   carelessly 부주의하게   absently 무심코   6 hardware 장비, 철물   7 monitor 감시하다   checking account 당좌예금 계좌   balance 잔액   accidental 뜻하지 않은, 우연한   overdraft 초과 인출   authentically 진정으로   unusually 이례적으로   approximately 대략, 거의   8 landscaper 조경사

ETS 실전 문제

1. Exhibitions at the Koh Art Museum typically ------- between 60,000 and 100,000 visitors.
   (A) notice
   (B) inquire
   (C) direct
   (D) attract

2. Beata's Café, which serves traditional Polish fare, has opened in the South Street location formerly ------- by Keesport Bistro.
   (A) finalized
   (B) postponed
   (C) occupied
   (D) accompanied

3. Skaghill Fisheries have been ------- by local authorities for exceeding workplace safety guidelines.
   (A) proposed
   (B) commended
   (C) perceived
   (D) asserted

4. Ludlow Cat Clinic veterinarians are dedicated to ------- expert care for felines.
   (A) attending
   (B) committing
   (C) providing
   (D) entrusting

5. Officials attribute the ------- in service to a software upgrade that makes the system run faster.
   (A) exchange
   (B) relief
   (C) improvement
   (D) lift

6. The survey results ------- that employees are generally satisfied with their pension plan.
   (A) suggest
   (B) discover
   (C) believe
   (D) require

7. City officials hope that the newly opened art museum will ------- tourism.
   (A) defend
   (B) stimulate
   (C) prefer
   (D) negotiate

8. The Shady Oaks Lecture Series is ------- by several local organizations.
   (A) traded
   (B) sponsored
   (C) explored
   (D) achieved

9. Our experienced employees ------- the skills needed to accelerate growth in our division.
   (A) enlarge
   (B) benefit
   (C) contain
   (D) possess

10. This year alone, the V1X Auto Industry Awards will be given ------- to manufacturers of energy-efficient vehicles.
    (A) exceptionally
    (B) routinely
    (C) traditionally
    (D) exclusively

11. Through the years, Glenview Laboratory has ------- provided quality, cost-effective services to its customers.
    (A) broadly
    (B) formerly
    (C) consistently
    (D) repetitiously

12. To save time during Sunday's session, the roundtable discussion was ------- omitted from the conference schedule.
    (A) intentionally
    (B) arguably
    (C) commonly
    (D) vitally

13. Developed last December, Speedy Print's new emission-reduction strategy will ------- be implemented next month.
    (A) finally
    (B) recently
    (C) lastly
    (D) exactly

14. The employees at Greyfeld Industries are reviewed ------- before promotion decisions are made.
    (A) certainly
    (B) subsequently
    (C) densely
    (D) annually

15. Metta Electronics, Inc., has not sold its old building because it is waiting for an ------- that meets the asking price.
    (A) offer
    (B) expense
    (C) addition
    (D) incident

16. The inn is ------- located within walking distance of several restaurants and shops.
    (A) widely
    (B) quickly
    (C) gradually
    (D) conveniently

READING COMPREHENSION

PART 7

독해

INTRO
UNIT 19 편지/이메일
UNIT 20 회람/공지/광고/기사
UNIT 21 기타 양식
UNIT 22 복수 지문
PART 7 빈출 표현

 무료 강의

PART 7 독해

단일 지문 10개 / 복수 지문 5세트, 총 54문항

Part 7은 제시된 지문을 읽고 그에 따른 문제를 푸는 유형으로, 단일 지문이 총 29문항, 복수 지문이 총 25문항 출제됩니다.

▶ PART 7의 빈출 지문 유형과 질문을 익혀두자

1. 지문 유형: 편지, 이메일, 광고, 회람, 공지, 기사, 정보문, 기타 양식
2. 질문 유형: 주제·목적 찾기, 세부 내용 파악, Not/True, 추론, 문장 삽입, 동의어 찾기, 연계 추론

Questions 147-148 refer to the following e-mail. — ❶

To: Stephen Clayton <stephen@claytongym.com>
From: Amanda Palmer <apalmer@linkedmail.net>
Date: October 26
Subject: Fitness Center Membership

Dear Mr. Clayton,

This e-mail is in response to your letter of October 14, which stated that my membership at your fitness center will expire on October 31. **I wish to let you know that I have chosen not to renew it.** ······ ❸ 팔머 씨가 이메일을 발송한 이유

When I first became a member, the cost was $25 per month. Now the cost is $50 per month. Aside from **this significant increase in cost**, I have been dissatisfied with some of the services at the fitness center. **There never seems to be enough equipment available for use at peak hours during the day. In addition, many of the new aerobics classes that I registered for were canceled due to low attendance.** ······ ❻ 팔머 씨의 불만 사항

Sincerely,
Amanda Palmer

147. Why did Ms. Palmer send the e-mail? ······ ❷
   (A) **To explain why she will not renew her membership**
   (B) To recommend an increase in staff
   (C) To ask for information about the center ······ ❹
   (D) To report that a machine is not working

148. What is NOT one of Ms. Palmer's concerns? ······ ❺
   (A) Fitness equipment is sometimes unavailable.
   (B) Some aerobics classes were canceled.
   (C) The membership fees are too high. ······ ❼
   (D) **The fitness trainers are inexperienced.**

▶ PART 7 이렇게 풀자

❶ 지문의 종류를 읽는다.
이 글은 이메일이므로, 누가 누구에게 어떤 목적으로 보낸 이메일인지를 염두에 두고 문제 풀이에 임해야 합니다.
→ 아만다 팔머 씨가 스티븐 클레이튼 씨에게 보낸 이메일로, 제목(Subject: Fitness Center Membership)을 통해 헬스 클럽 회원권에 관련해 보낸 이메일임을 예상할 수 있습니다.

❷ 문제를 파악한다.
팔머 씨가 이메일을 보낸 이유는 무엇인가?
→ Why did ~ send the e-mail? / What is the purpose of the e-mail? / Why was the e-mail written? 등은 이메일을 보낸 목적을 묻는 문제입니다.

❸ 본문을 처음부터 읽는다.
문제 포인트와 관련된 내용이 나올 때까지 요약하며 읽습니다.
→ 팔머 씨는 자신의 회원권이 10월 31일자로 만료되는데, 회원권을 갱신하지 않기로 결정했다고 했습니다.

❹ 답이 나올 때까지 읽고 답한다.
(A) 회원권을 갱신하지 않는 이유를 설명하려고
→ 팔머 씨는 회원권을 갱신하지 않겠다고 했으니, (A)가 정답입니다.

❺ 다음 문제를 읽는다.
팔머 씨의 불만 사항이 아닌 것은 무엇인가?
→ Not 문제이므로, 지문에 언급된 내용과 선택지의 내용을 하나씩 대조해가며 문제를 풀어야 한다는 것을 예상할 수 있습니다.

❻ 본문을 이어서 읽는다.
두 번째 단락에 팔머 씨의 불만 사항이 조목조목 열거되어 있습니다.
→ 팔머 씨는 한 달에 25달러에서 50달러로 인상된 회비, 피크 시간대에는 이용할 수 없는 부족한 장비, 저조한 출석률로 인해 취소된 강좌에 대해 불만을 토로하고 있습니다.

❼ 답이 나올 때까지 읽고 답한다.
(D) 헬스 트레이너들의 경험이 부족하다.
→ 헬스 트레이너에 대한 언급은 없으므로 (D)가 정답입니다.

UNIT 19 편지 / 이메일

무료 강의

핵심 포인트 1 사내 편지/이메일에서는 업무 제안, 수리 및 행사 일정 등의 주제가 주로 다뤄지고 회사-외부인 편지/이메일에서는 감사, 불만, 제품 문의, 예약 확인 같은 내용이 자주 나옵니다.

핵심 포인트 2 글의 흐름은 '주제/목적 → 세부사항 → 요청/제안사항'의 순서로 전개되는 것이 일반적입니다.

빈출 질문
What is the purpose of the letter? 편지의 목적은 무엇인가?
Why was the e-mail written? 이메일은 왜 쓰였는가?
What are employees asked to do? 직원들은 무엇을 하도록 요청 받는가?
What was sent with the letter? 편지와 함께 발송된 것은 무엇인가?

▶ ETS 기출 예제 정답과 해설 p.188

받는 사람
Dear Mr. Osborn:

문제점
Aphrodite Sporting Goods (ASG) recently mailed you a copy of our summer catalogue, using the address we have on file for you. Unfortunately, the item was returned, marked "Undeliverable."

목적
We would like to get the catalogue to you. Given your order history, you might be interested in our new line of tennis equipment. If you could provide me your current mailing address, I will resend the catalogue along with some valuable coupons.

추가적인 세부 사항
We have also made improvements to our mail order service. We now provide online order tracking and no longer charge shipping on orders over $50. We hope to hear from you.

보낸 사람
Trang Minh Pham

Q What is the purpose of the e-mail?
(A) To explain how to get a refund
(B) To offer a gift card
(C) **To obtain contact information**
(D) To provide details about an order

STEP 2 단서 찾기
글의 목적은 주로 초반부에 제시되는 경우가 많지만, 글 전반에 걸쳐 제시되는 경우도 있으니 유의합니다.

목적을 담고 있는 빈출 표현
- I am writing (in regard to) ~
- I would like to ~
- This is to remind you that ~
- I'm pleased to ~
- Please ~

STEP 1 질문 파악: 목적 문제
What is the (main) purpose of ~? / Why was ~ sent? / Why was ~ written? 등은 목적을 묻는 문제입니다.

STEP 3 정답 찾기
카탈로그와 쿠폰을 받을 수 있는 주소를 요청하고 있으므로, 정답은 (C)입니다.

| 어휘 | equipment 장비   online order tracking 온라인 주문 추적 서비스   no longer 더 이상 ~않다   charge 청구하다

ETS 유형 연습

다음 지문을 읽고 문제를 풀어보세요.

1. **E-mail**

To: Ming Lai <mlai@azurewingimports.com.hk>
From: Marco Cerinza <mcerinza@cerinzajewellery.com.ph>
Subject: Information
Attachment: Cerinza1; Cerinza2

Dear Ms. Lai:

I have received my jewellery order. However, the ten watches I ordered were not in any of the packages. The watches are listed on the invoice but not on the packing list that was included in the first box. I have attached scans of both documents. Please let me know the status of the watches.

Sincerely,

Marco Cerinza

What is the purpose of the e-mail?

(A) To apologize for a mistake
(B) To inquire about missing items

2. **Letter**

Dear Ms. Gomez:

We anticipate an opening for a bilingual customer service associate in our sales department starting next month. Your application was retained from last year's search for our bilingual clerical pool. We are interested in learning whether you still have an interest and might be available to work full-time this year. If so, please contact me at 604-555-0009 by Friday, May 15th and I can supply you with further details.

Sincerely,

Pamela Finch

What qualification is required for the position?

(A) Experience in sales
(B) Fluency in two languages

| 어휘 | 1 package 소포   invoice 송장   packing 포장   apologize 사과하다   inquire 문의하다   missing 빠진
2 bilingual 두 개 언어를 구사하는   application 지원(서)   retain 보관하다, 유지하다   clerical 사무직의   pool 이용 가능한 인력   further details 추가 상세 사항   fluency 유창함

Questions 1-2 refer to the following e-mail.

To:	ayang@winklightmail.net
From:	hughes@knowltoninn.com
Date:	October 20
Subject:	Your stay

Dear Ms. Yang,

Thank you for choosing to stay at the Knowlton Inn. We are proud of the wonderful facilities at our inn, including our new state-of-the-art business center and our newly remodeled restaurant, Fresh Perspectives.

As a valued customer, your opinions are important to us. Please take a moment to fill out a brief survey at www.knowltoninn.com/guest_comments. If you do so by November 1, we will mail you a voucher for 25% off your next visit to Fresh Perspectives.

Thank you again for choosing the Knowlton Inn. I hope your stay was a pleasant one.

Harris Hughes, Manager
Knowlton Inn

1. Why did Mr. Hughes send the e-mail?
    (A) To confirm a reservation
    (B) To request feedback from a customer
    (C) To respond to a customer's complaint
    (D) To ask that payment be made

2. What is suggested about the Knowlton Inn?
    (A) It is located in a city's historic district.
    (B) Its Web site will soon be redesigned.
    (C) It has recently undergone changes.
    (D) It is noted for its reasonable pricing.

Questions 3-4 refer to the following letter.

May 26

Ken Izumu
Westlake Marching Band
5443 Wells Point Blvd.
Kingsland, Missouri 64160

Dear Mr. Izumu,

Congratulations! Your marching band has been selected to perform in the Kingsland summer parade. The parade will begin at 2:00 P.M. on Saturday, June 20. Please tell your musicians to arrive at the convention center no later than 1:30 P.M. Performers will gather near the south gate of the convention center to start and then head west on Main Street, past city hall, and toward the Joplin Bridge. The festivities will end at Perrywood Park, where shuttle buses back to the convention center will be available.

We look forward to seeing you there!

Sincerely,

Maryann Jones
Maryann Jones
Event Coordinator

3. Who most likely is Mr. Izumu?
   (A) A band leader
   (B) A bus driver
   (C) A convention center employee
   (D) A parade organizer

4. Where will the parade begin?
   (A) At city hall
   (B) Under the Joplin Bridge
   (C) In Perrywood Park
   (D) At the convention center

Questions 5-7 refer to the following e-mail.

To:	Jin-Hee Chang <jchang@bottlepress.co.uk>
From:	Lemar Jacobson <ljacobson@balogcentre.jm>
Date:	2 September
Subject:	Reaching out
Attachment:	Centre information

Dear Ms. Chang:

I am the director of the Balog Centre for Business Leadership in Kingston, Jamaica. — [1] —. I am writing to ask whether you might be interested in delivering a presentation at the centre about your latest research. We have dates available this year in November and next year in March and April. — [2] —. We would be happy to cover your airfare and provide a speaker's fee. — [3] —. Moreover, as our on-site guest house was completed last June, we can offer you free accommodation for two nights.

I have attached information about the centre and our presentation policies. — [4] —. I look forward to hearing from you.

Sincerely,

Lemar Jacobson

5. What is the purpose of the e-mail?
   (A) To issue an apology
   (B) To request a referral
   (C) To extend an invitation
   (D) To confirm a reservation

6. According to the e-mail, what happened in June?
   (A) Airfare rates changed.
   (B) An event was canceled.
   (C) Fees for rooms increased.
   (D) Construction on a building ended.

7. In which of the positions marked [1], [2], [3], and [4] does the following sentence best belong?

   "I am also responsible for programming a monthly guest speaker series at our centre."

   (A) [1]
   (B) [2]
   (C) [3]
   (D) [4]

Questions 8-10 refer to the following e-mail.

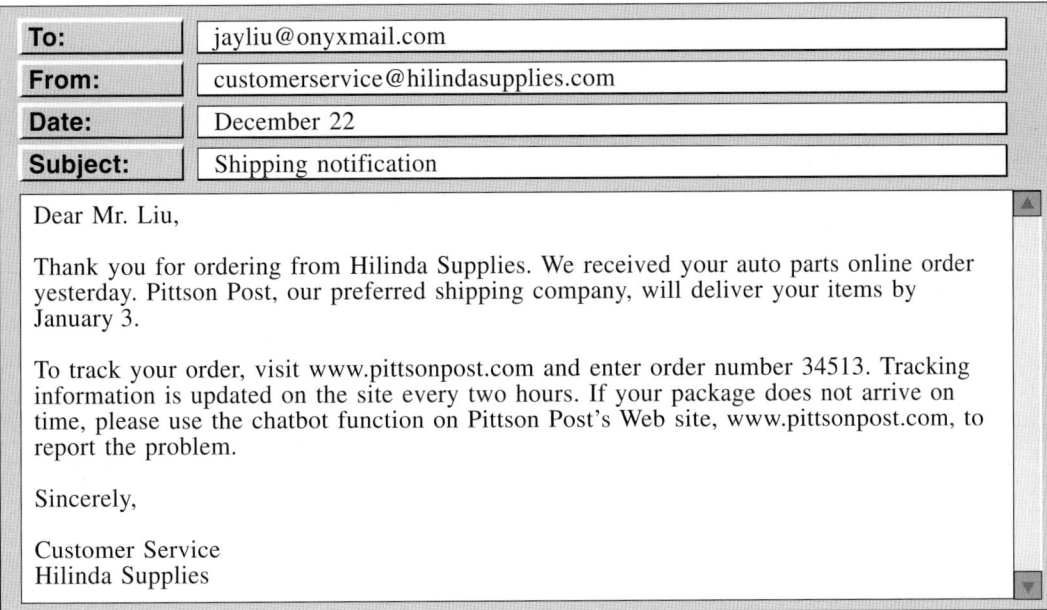

8. What is suggested about Hilinda Supplies?
   (A) It processes orders within two hours.
   (B) It has filled orders from Mr. Liu before.
   (C) It is located near Pittson Post's facilities.
   (D) It does business with Pittson Post regularly.

9. When did Mr. Liu place the order?
   (A) On December 21
   (B) On December 22
   (C) On January 3
   (D) On January 4

10. What is Mr. Liu asked to do if his package does not arrive on time?
    (A) Contact a delivery service
    (B) Visit a store in person
    (C) Call a Hilinda Supplies department
    (D) Reply to an e-mail from Pittson Post

Questions 11-13 refer to the following e-mail.

To:	Ferris Homaidi <f.homaidi@harpco.com>
From:	Marie Daalmans <m.daalmans@mgmttax.com>
Date:	November 10
Subject:	Following up

Dear Mr. Homaidi,

— [1] —. I hope you had a pleasant journey home from the conference this weekend. I wanted to follow up with a reminder about my firm's complimentary "Preparing for Year-End Payroll" webinar taking place on Wednesday, November 18, at 2:30 p.m. Our experts will explain how to deal with the end-of-year forms for payroll compliance. — [2] —. They will also share tips on how to keep your company's finances in order throughout the year. — [3] —.

Also, you mentioned that you might be interested in learning about our commercial tax-preparation services. We take pride in helping small businesses like yours navigate the process. — [4] —. Are you available for a call this Thursday afternoon, Friday morning, or any time early next week?

I look forward to hearing back from you.

Sincerely,

Marie Daalmans
MGMT Tax Consulting Group

11. What does Ms. Daalmans remind Mr. Homaidi about?

    (A) A free virtual presentation
    (B) A request for a job interview
    (C) A meeting that they previously scheduled
    (D) A packet of forms that need to be signed

12. What is indicated about Mr. Homaidi?

    (A) He is a professional tax preparer.
    (B) He owns a small business.
    (C) He frequently travels for work.
    (D) He was a speaker at a recent conference.

13. In which of the positions marked [1], [2], [3], and [4] does the following sentence best belong?

    "I would like to tell you more about what we have to offer."

    (A) [1]
    (B) [2]
    (C) [3]
    (D) [4]

Questions 14-17 refer to the following letter.

April 3

Kristen Cheon
304 Newport Road
Salyersville, KY 41465

Dear Ms. Cheon,

Thank you for purchasing our Brightstar 2200 streaming device. I am writing to follow up on the conversation you had with our support technician. We are sorry that you are having trouble setting up the device. The support team has determined the cause of the problem and provided the following instructions.

First, turn off and unplug the Brightstar 2200 and your television. In this envelope is a new HDMI cable. Please use it to connect the Brightstar 2200 to your television.

Next, turn on the Brightstar 2200 and wait for it to start up. Leave your television turned off until the start-up process is completed. You will know the device has rebooted when the small light stops blinking. This takes a few seconds.

Turn on your television. Your television and the Brightstar 2200 should now be linked. Once the television recognizes the Brightstar 2200, go into the Settings menu to set up your Internet connection.

Please call 606-555-0130 for more help. We promise to address any further issues promptly.

Best,

Karen Ng

Karen Ng, Customer Service Representative
Brightstar Streaming

---

14. What is the purpose of the letter?

(A) To introduce a new type of product
(B) To explain how to return a product
(C) To warn about a potential problem
(D) To explain how to fix a problem

15. What came with the letter?

(A) A new power cord
(B) A new HDMI cable
(C) A new streaming device
(D) A new television remote control

16. According to the instructions, when should Ms. Cheon turn on her television?

(A) As soon as she turns on the Brightstar 2200
(B) After setting up her Internet connection
(C) Before connecting the Brightstar 2200 to her television
(D) After a small light on the Brightstar 2200 stops blinking

17. The word "address" in paragraph 5, line 1, is closest in meaning to

(A) greet
(B) direct
(C) deal with
(D) speak about

UNIT 20 회람 / 공지 / 광고 / 기사

무료 강의

핵심 포인트 1 회람과 공지는 다수의 사람들에게 특정 사항을 알리는 글로, 일정이나 권장 사항 등을 주로 안내합니다.
핵심 포인트 2 광고는 상품 광고와 구인 광고로 나뉘는데, '광고 대상 → 세부사항 → 부가 정보나 연락처' 순서로 전개됩니다.
핵심 포인트 3 기사는 기업체의 확장, 사업가의 성공담, 지역 소식 등이 주를 이룹니다.

빈출 질문
What is being announced? 무엇이 발표되고 있는가?
What is the purpose of the notice? 공지의 목적은 무엇인가?
What are the employees asked to do? 직원들이 요청 받는 것은 무엇인가?
What is NOT a requirement? 필수 자격요건이 아닌 것은 무엇인가?
When will the policy change take effect? 변경된 정책은 언제부터 효력이 있는가?

▶ **ETS 기출 예제** 정답과 해설 p.193

Mantero City Community Center
Summer Cooking Classes

공지 목적 The Mantero City Community Center will offer the following cooking classes this summer:

Class	Date	Time	Cost
Soups and Appetizers	July 9	4:00 P.M.-6:00 P.M.	$20
Poultry and Meat Dishes	July 11	1:00 P.M.-3:00 P.M.	$35
Quick Pasta Dishes	July 13	9:00 A.M.-11:00 A.M.	$25

세부 사항 Classes will be held at the Mantero City Community Center, 3535 Springdale Boulevard, Mantero City. Registration will begin on July 1. To reserve a place, visit the administration office. Alternatively, you may send your information to Rosa Morales by fax at 928-555-0198 or by e-mail at rmorales@manterocc.net. Please include your name, the name of the class you wish to attend, and a telephone number.

STEP 2 단서 찾기
지문에 언급된 내용과 보기를 하나씩 확인해 봅니다. 보기에서는 지문의 내용을 다른 표현으로 바꾸어 제시하는 경우가 많으므로 주의해야 합니다.

- visit the administration office
  → (D) In person
- by fax at 928-555-0198
  → (C) By fax
- by e-mail at rmorales@manterocc.net
  → (A) By e-mail

STEP 1 질문 파악: Not/True 문제
(What is) NOT ~? / What is true about ~? / What is mentioned ~? 등은 사실 관계를 확인하는 문제입니다.

Q In what way are readers **NOT** instructed to respond?

(A) By e-mail
(B) By telephone
(C) By fax
(D) In person

STEP 3 정답 찾기
지문에 전화번호는 언급되어 있지 않으므로, 정답은 (B)입니다.

| 어휘 | poultry 가금류 hold 열다, 개최하다 registration 등록 reserve 예약하다 administration office 행정실
alternatively 그 대신에, 그렇지 않으면

ETS 유형 연습

다음 지문을 읽고 문제를 풀어보세요.

정답과 해설 p.193

1.

Advertisement

> # Jentel Premium Hooks
> ## Available at all sporting goods stores
>
> - Top-notch metals
> - Advanced technology
> - Versatile and reliable
> - Multiple sizes and styles
>
> Bass hooks, circle hooks, double hooks, fly hooks, jig hooks, and more!
>
> "Jentel Premium Hooks are the world's best!" —*Better Tackle Magazine*
> "Top ratings in our fishing-gear performance category" —*Sports Timer Gazette*

What is being advertised?

(A) A camping-gear store
(B) A type of fishing equipment

2.

Memo

> From: Eun Mi Ha, CEO
> To: All Employees
> Subject: January 10 Meeting
> Date: January 13
>
> We will be changing the regular work hours for most employees as part of our initiative to reduce energy costs. Since our energy costs are generally higher in the late afternoon, it will be to our advantage to perform more work in the morning. Therefore, beginning on Monday, February 24, the workday will officially start at 8:00 A.M. instead of 9:00 A.M., and it will end at 4:00 P.M. instead of 5:00 P.M. The last day of the old schedule will be Friday, February 21.

What are employees asked to do?

(A) Adjust their typical work schedules
(B) Switch to energy-efficient light bulbs

| 어휘 | **1** hook (낚시) 바늘 top-notch 최고의 advanced 선진의 versatile 다용도의 reliable 믿을 수 있는 multiple 다양한 rating 등급, 순위 gear 장비 performance 성능 equipment 장비 **2** regular 정규의 initiative 계획, 전략 to one's advantage ~에게 유리하게 workday (하루의) 근무 시간, 평일 officially 공식적으로 adjust 조정하다, 맞추다 typical 전형적인, 일반적인 energy-efficient 연료[에너지]가 적게 드는 light bulb 전구

ETS 실전 문제

Questions 1-2 refer to the following advertisement.

Deena's
www.deenas.com

For more than 40 years, Deena's has been the area's go-to destination for every item you might need for a holiday gathering, a birthday celebration, or any other social occasion—from costumes and colorful decorations to rental tables and chairs.

For large events, check out our featured product, now at a 10 percent discount:

Classic paper admission tickets in rolls of 100, 300, or 500

- Available in a variety of fonts, colors, sizes, and styles.
- Add your company or sponsor logo so that ticket holders remember your brand—fast turnaround for these special orders!

---

1. What kind of business is Deena's?

    (A) An event-planning agency
    (B) A uniform manufacturer
    (C) A catering company
    (D) A party-supply store

2. What does the advertisement indicate about the featured product?

    (A) It will be out of stock soon.
    (B) It is eligible for free delivery.
    (C) It can be customized.
    (D) It was recently redesigned.

Questions 3-5 refer to the following memo.

To: All staff
From: Stuart Wentworth, Vice President of Operations
Date: Monday, January 26
Subject: Winter storm

Because of the impending snowstorm, Zelman Architects will be closed tomorrow. The county Department of Transportation has requested that all nonemergency vehicles stay off the roads.

Employees are expected to work on assignments at home during regular business hours and to stay in touch with their department managers by e-mail. Managers should note that all end-of-month deadlines remain in effect.

The storm is expected to stop early Wednesday morning. To give the snowplow crews enough time to clear the parking areas, employees are asked to arrive no earlier than 10:30 A.M. on Wednesday. The usual Wednesday morning staff meetings will be moved to later in the day.

Thank you for your cooperation.

3. What is the purpose of the memo?
   (A) To explain a new policy
   (B) To remind staff about a new deadline
   (C) To request that employees work extended hours
   (D) To notify employees about an office closing

4. What are managers expected to do on Tuesday, January 27?
   (A) Attend a staff meeting in the afternoon
   (B) Arrive at work later than usual
   (C) Contact Mr. Wentworth about revised schedules
   (D) Maintain e-mail communication with staff

5. What is suggested about Zelman Architects?
   (A) It has a contract with the Department of Transportation.
   (B) It has several office locations.
   (C) It employs many people who commute by car.
   (D) It has had to postpone a special company event.

Questions 6-7 refer to the following job advertisement.

Loch Leman seeks a creative individual to work part-time developing graphics for our growing business. Applicants must have experience designing advertisements, menus, place mats, and signs. Please e-mail your CV, work samples, and a summary of your skills and experience or a link to your Web site to Jill Seamans, j.seamans@lochleman.co.uk.

6. In what industry does Loch Leman most likely operate?
   (A) Food service
   (B) Interior design
   (C) Computer programming
   (D) Restaurant construction

7. Who most likely would be a good candidate for the job?
   (A) A banking executive
   (B) A business analyst
   (C) A landscape designer
   (D) A graphic designer

Questions 8-10 refer to the following notice.

Thank you for your purchase of Meyer Almond Flour!

Congratulations on buying a Meyer Almond product made from delicious ground almonds. Meyer Almond Flour is different from our competitors' coarse almond-meal products that are made with almond skins intact. Our almonds are boiled briefly in water to remove their tough outer skins, then ground and sifted to make a light, tasty flour that is ideal for baking. Our almond flour is also good for you—it is rich in antioxidants, protein, and fiber. Generations of the Meyer family have been committed to creating high-quality almond products for decades. We hope you enjoy this special product. Please visit www.meyeralmond.com if you have any questions or comments.

---

8. Where would the notice most likely be found?

    (A) On a door in a factory
    (B) On a delivery vehicle
    (C) On the side of a package
    (D) On an office bulletin board

9. What is indicated about the Meyer Almond product?

    (A) It contains no almond skins.
    (B) It has a heavy, coarse texture.
    (C) It requires a long cooking time.
    (D) It comes with a money-back guarantee.

10. What is suggested about the Meyer Almond company?

    (A) It makes its products by hand.
    (B) It adds preservatives to its products.
    (C) It has been operating for many years.
    (D) It recently relocated to a larger facility.

Questions 11-13 refer to the following memo.

To: All staff
From: Neil Halderan, CEO, Halderan Financial, Inc.
Date: January 25
Subject: Job Search

As many of you are aware, we have recently conducted a thorough search for a new vice president of Halderan Financial, Inc. We are pleased to announce that Ms. Chieko Sakai has been appointed to the position.

Ms. Sakai served as the managing director of BRI Investment Group for the last five years. Before that, she was a senior sales representative at Welton Insurance Ltd. for three years; she attained the senior position after serving for two years as a junior sales representative for the same company. She has a bachelor of science degree in business and a master of business administration, both from Northmont University.

To welcome Ms. Sakai to Halderan Financial, we will be holding a reception at the Round House Restaurant on Broad Street between 5 and 7 P.M. on Friday, February 4, which all employees are invited to attend. Ms. Sakai assumed her new position today.

11. Why was the memo sent?
    (A) To explain a marketing plan
    (B) To announce a job opening
    (C) To arrange an employee orientation
    (D) To introduce a new employee

12. What is Ms. Sakai's current title?
    (A) Vice president
    (B) Managing director
    (C) Senior sales representative
    (D) Junior sales representative

13. What will happen on February 4?
    (A) A job interview will be conducted.
    (B) A university course will begin.
    (C) A gathering will be held.
    (D) A company will be sold.

Questions 14-17 refer to the following article.

Parks Department Invites Public Review of Plans

MIDLAWN (July 12)—The town's parks department released a draft of plans to redesign the west section of Midlawn Park this week. The need to improve the west section follows the recent expansion of the Midlawn Culture Center in the east section of the park. Outdoor gathering spaces with stone walkways and picnic tables were created around the perimeter of the culture center. — [1] —. To maintain a balance between the developed and the natural areas of the park, the parks department wants to keep the west side mostly green.

In a series of public meetings held earlier this month, representatives from the parks department presented potential ideas to enhance the park's west side. — [2] —.

A plan to construct a walkway over a scenic wetland received favorable reactions from meeting attendees. Several Midlawn residents suggested building an open-air pavilion that community members could reserve for celebratory events. However, this idea was not taken up by the parks department. — [3] —. Proposals to develop a softball or football field were likewise discounted.

The parks department has narrowed down its plans and is now soliciting online feedback from the community on its Web site. Residents are asked to review the plans and submit comments no later than noon on August 17 so that the parks department can review them before its business meeting later that evening. — [4] —.

14. Why is the parks department considering proposals for a section of Midlawn Park?

(A) To meet the needs of local sports teams
(B) To help preserve green space
(C) To increase the popularity of a culture center
(D) To meet municipal zoning regulations

15. What enhancement to the park's west side did some community members recommend?

(A) A nature center for visitor education
(B) A path for bicycles
(C) An enlarged parking area
(D) A structure for holding outdoor events

16. What is scheduled to happen on August 17 ?

(A) Park officials will appear at a news conference.
(B) Work on a renovation project will begin.
(C) Feedback on proposals will be discussed.
(D) The results of a survey will be announced online.

17. In which of the positions marked [1], [2], [3], and [4] does the following sentence best belong?

"In addition, the site now features an open-air theater."

(A) [1]
(B) [2]
(C) [3]
(D) [4]

UNIT 21 기타 양식

무료 강의

핵심 포인트 1 양식 지문은 단편 정보들로 구성되는 경우가 많으며, 비교적 단시간에 풀 수 있는 쉬운 유형입니다. 문제에서 요구하는 정보 위주로 검색하면서 푸는 것이 좋습니다.

핵심 포인트 2 문자 메시지/온라인 채팅은 주로 신속한 업무 처리를 위해 정보나 의견을 전달하는 내용이 나옵니다.

빈출 질문
What is scheduled for June 8? 6월 8일에는 무슨 일정이 잡혀 있는가?
Why did Ms. Alden receive free shipping? 알덴 씨는 왜 무료로 배송 받았는가?
At 10:08, what does Lopez mean when she writes, "Absolutely"?
10시 8분에 로페즈가 "물론이죠"라고 쓴 것은 무슨 의미인가?

▶ ETS 기출 예제 정답과 해설 p.197

말론 씨의 문제점

Paula Malone [8:53 A.M.]
Can you do me a favor? I'm scheduled to teach my exercise class at the gym at 9:00, and I'm going to be late. The train I'm on had a mechanical problem and left the station about 15 minutes behind schedule.

Martin Bileck [8:54 A.M.]
That's too bad. How can I help you?

말론 씨의 요청

Paula Malone [8:55 A.M.]
Would you either cancel the class or let the students know that I'll be there about 9:15?

STEP 2 단서 찾기
제시문의 주변 상황을 통해 문맥을 파악해야 합니다.

말론 씨: 수업을 취소하거나 학생들에게 자신이 9시 15분쯤에 도착할 것임을 알려 달라고 요청
빌렉 씨: 수키와 바꿔 수업 시간 변경 제안

빌렉 씨의 제안

Martin Bileck [8:57 A.M.]
Most of your students are already here, so I hate to cancel. Suki is also working today and is here early. I'll ask her to switch class with you, and you can teach the 10:00 class.

Paula Malone [8:58 A.M.]
That works out perfectly. Thanks.

STEP 1 질문 파악: 의도 파악 문제
문제를 읽고 지문에서 제시문의 위치를 확인합니다.

Q At 8:58 A.M., what does Ms. Malone most likely mean when she writes, "That works out perfectly"?

(A) She likes Mr. Bileck's idea.
(B) She likes exercising in the morning.
(C) She is excited about her new job.
(D) She is happy that she has the day off.

STEP 3 정답 찾기
수업 시간을 변경하여 10시에 수업을 할 수 있을 것이라는 빌렉 씨의 아이디어가 좋다는 의미이므로, 정답은 (A)입니다.

| 어휘 | gym 체육관   mechanical problem 기계적인 문제   behind schedule 예정보다 늦게   switch 바꾸다

ETS 유형 연습

다음 지문을 읽고 문제를 풀어보세요.

정답과 해설 p.198

1. **Sign**

Bosko and Sons
Quality roofing and siding

Additions and repairs

We service businesses and residences.

www.boskoandsons.com

Fully insured • Free estimates • License KE404

What kind of business is Bosko and Sons?

(A) A small-business consulting firm
(B) A construction company

2. **Form**

Aunt Amelia's Cakes
Home-style cakes, tarts, and more!

Thank you for your purchase. We value our customers' feedback. Please take the time to fill out the enclosed survey and return it in the addressed, postage-paid envelope we have provided. In return, we will send you a coupon for 20 percent off the price of your next purchase.

Rate the following on a scale of 1 to 5, with 5 being "excellent" and 1 being "poor."

Taste	1	2	3	4	**(5)**
Texture	1	2	3	4	**(5)**
Decoration (if applicable)	**(1)**	2	3	4	5
Overall appearance	**(1)**	2	3	4	5

What are customers asked to do?

(A) Pick up a cake
(B) Mail a form

| 어휘 | **1** quality 품질이 좋은 roofing 지붕 (공사) siding 외벽 마감(재) addition 추가 repair 수리 residence 주거지 insured 보험을 든 estimate 견적 license 라이선스 firm 회사 construction 건설 **2** value 소중히 여기다 fill out (서식을) 작성하다 addressed 주소가 적힌 postage-paid envelope (우편요금 지급필) 반송용 봉투 mail (우편으로) 보내다 form 서식, 양식

ETS 실전 문제

Questions 1-2 refer to the following receipt.

Congrani Coffee Co.
Store #10380, 7 Waterford Quay, Pipitea, Wellington
04-555-0128

Receipt number: 9374
Date: 10 June

Item	Quantity	Total ($)
Ciabatta roll	2	9.98
Iced raspberry mocha	1	3.45
Boxed tea	1	12.95
Gift card	1	20.00

Discounts:	Reward beverage	-3.45
Total:		**42.93**

Rewards number: 1028-493-02
Payment type: Credit Card XXXXXXXXXXXX0192
Cardholder name: Emilia Ocampo

---

1. What is indicated on the receipt?

    (A) One ciabatta roll costs $9.98.
    (B) Two gift cards were purchased.
    (C) Congrani Coffee Co. was closed on June 10.
    (D) Payment was made by credit card.

2. What reward was offered?

    (A) A box of tea
    (B) A free gift card
    (C) A complimentary drink
    (D) A discount on a future purchase

Questions 3-4 refer to the following form.

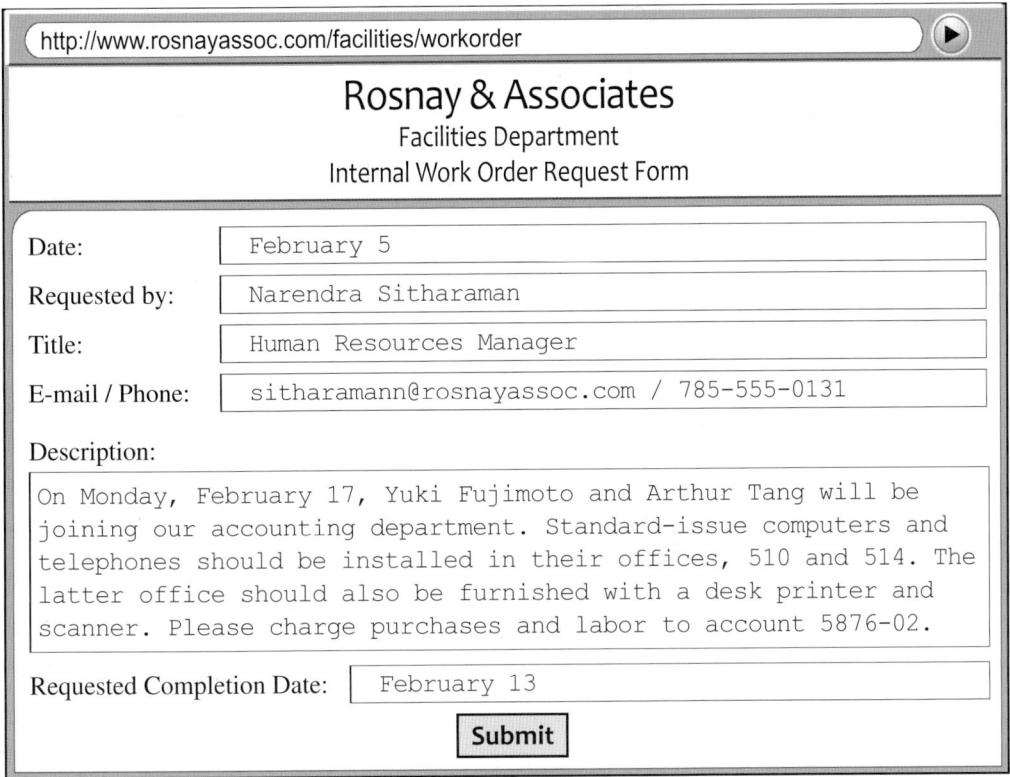

3. What most likely did Rosnay & Associates recently do?

   (A) They merged with an accounting firm.
   (B) They upgraded their computer system.
   (C) They hired additional employees.
   (D) They changed their purchasing process.

4. What is the order for?

   (A) Equipment setup
   (B) Furniture assembly
   (C) Printer repairs
   (D) Office cleaning

Questions 5-6 refer to the following text-message chain.

Amy Morro [2:17 P.M.]
Hi, Kevin. I'm at the office supply store. Name badges are currently being discounted. We seem to always need those. Should I grab some for the summer interns? We're preparing the materials for them soon, right?

Kevin Cho [2:18 P.M.]
Yes, that's right. And it's a good idea to buy those. The seven interns will be in the office in two weeks to start training, in fact.

Amy Morro [2:19 P.M.]
OK. It looks like other supplies are discounted as well. Do you need anything else, like envelopes, folders, or notepads?

Kevin Cho [2:20 P.M.]
Let me see.

Amy Morro [2:20 P.M.]
Sure.

Kevin Cho [2:22 P.M.]
I'm fine.

Amy Morro [2:23 P.M.]
OK, then. I should be back in the office in 30 minutes.

---

5. According to the writers, what will happen in two weeks?

   (A) Some coupons will expire.
   (B) Some interns will arrive.
   (C) A sales event will conclude.
   (D) A vacation period will begin.

6. At 2:22 P.M., what does Mr. Cho most likely mean when he writes, "I'm fine"?

   (A) He is not concerned about a project deadline.
   (B) He has enough staff on his work team.
   (C) He does not need any other office supplies.
   (D) He plans to visit a store later in the day.

Questions 7-9 refer to the following invoice.

Calden Company

From:
Calden Company
5 Extension Road
Mobile, Alabama 36606
T: 251-555-0152

To:
Landers Restaurant
71 W. Charles Street
Chapel Hill, NC 27515

Item Number	Description	Quantity	Unit Price	Subtotals
121-B	Salad plates (12/case)	4	$25.59	_____
782-A	Engraved soup spoons (12/pack)	4	$5.78	$23.12
78-K	Soup bowls (48/case)	1	$58.19	$58.19
59-C	Cloth napkins (12/pack)	8	$13.29	$106.32
193-W	5-quart stainless steel sauté pan with lid	3	$46.31	$138.93
			Total Cost	$326.56
			Shipping	$17.92
			Amount Due	$344.48

Note: The engraved spoons you ordered will be shipped separately, directly from one of our retail locations. The salad plates you ordered are currently out of stock and will not be available for 2–3 weeks. You will not be charged for that item until it is shipped, and the shipping charge for that item will be reduced by 50 percent.
We apologize for any inconvenience.

7. What most likely is Calden Company?
   (A) A regional catering service
   (B) An interstate shipping company
   (C) A chain of kitchen goods stores
   (D) An exclusive restaurant

8. What is indicated about Item 782-A?
   (A) It was mislabeled in the catalog.
   (B) It arrived damaged.
   (C) It is not available in the color requested.
   (D) It is being sent from a retail store.

9. What is indicated about the shipment of the items?
   (A) One item will be shipped at a discount.
   (B) One item could not be shipped due to bad weather.
   (C) Some items will be shipped overnight.
   (D) Some items were shipped to the wrong address.

Questions 10-12 refer to the following Web page.

https://www.eastbayuniversity.ac.uk/garden-ideas

A Growing Concern

It is once again the time of year to begin planning a home garden. — [1] —. Botanists here at East Bay University have shared some facts that may be helpful to those who are looking to conserve water this season.

- Tomatoes grow roots quickly and can draw moisture from deep in the ground when there is less water on the surface.

- — [2] —. Like tomatoes, melons also grow deep roots and can survive when the surface of the ground is dry, as long as they receive plenty of water early in the season.

- Beans are well adapted to dry conditions. Some varieties originated in desert areas and require little water when grown in other environments.

- Radishes, asparagus, Swiss chard, eggplant, mustard greens, and peppers are among those plants that can aid in the conservation of water. — [3] —.

The scientists also recommend planting vegetables with similar water needs together to ensure that each plant will receive an appropriate amount of water. — [4] —.

10. What does the Web page discuss?

    (A) A new research project at a university
    (B) Useful information for home gardeners
    (C) A profile of a local farmer
    (D) The history of a university's botany program

11. What plant group is mentioned as having grown in the desert?

    (A) Tomatoes
    (B) Melons
    (C) Beans
    (D) Radishes

12. In which of the positions marked [1], [2], [3], and [4] does the following sentence best belong?

    "That is because they require watering for just a brief length of time."

    (A) [1]
    (B) [2]
    (C) [3]
    (D) [4]

Questions 13-16 refer to the following online chat discussion.

Leila Ndidi (10:18 A.M.) Hi, Oscar and Yael. Are you planning to go to the tourism conference next month?

Oscar Bonmati (10:22 A.M.) Yes, I'll be there. What about you?

Yael Raso (10:22 A.M.) Yes. I'm looking forward to it.

Leila Ndidi (10:25 A.M.) I've just registered. I might take the train.

Oscar Bonmati (10:27 A.M.) Me too. Should we try to book the same one?

Leila Ndidi (10:28 A.M.) That sounds like a good plan. What about you, Yael?

Yael Raso (10:29 A.M.) Normally I'd want to take the train, but I'll be driving from my sister's house in Springfield.

Leila Ndidi (10:31 A.M.) That's nice that you'll have a chance to visit her before the conference. Please tell her that Oscar and I say hello.

Oscar Bonmati (10:33 A.M.) Yes, please do. By the way, I'm thinking that we could attend different sessions and then trade notes afterward. What do you think?

Yael Raso (10:34 A.M.) That's a great idea.

Oscar Bonmati (10:35 A.M.) Also, isn't there a conference discount code to use when booking the hotel? I'm having trouble finding it.

Leila Ndidi (10:36 A.M.) There is. I'll forward you the e-mail that mentions it right away.

Oscar Bonmati (10:37 A.M.) Thanks!

13. Why does Ms. Ndidi contact Mr. Bonmati and Ms. Raso?
    (A) To coordinate travel plans with them
    (B) To schedule a meeting with them
    (C) To ask them for help planning a conference
    (D) To ask for their notes on a conference session

14. At 10:28 A.M., what does Ms. Ndidi imply when she writes, "That sounds like a good plan"?
    (A) She will complete a conference registration form.
    (B) She is eager to see her colleagues.
    (C) She would like to take the same train as Mr. Bonmati.
    (D) She is happy that Ms. Raso can have a family visit.

15. What is suggested about Ms. Ndidi and Mr. Bonmati?
    (A) They live in Springfield.
    (B) They know Ms. Raso's sister.
    (C) They report directly to Ms. Raso.
    (D) They enjoy touring other countries.

16. What will Ms. Ndidi most likely do next?
    (A) Purchase train tickets
    (B) Make a hotel reservation
    (C) Drive to a conference venue
    (D) Send information to Mr. Bonmati

UNIT 22 복수 지문

핵심 포인트 1 복수 지문은 편지/이메일이 포함된 구성이 가장 일반적입니다.
핵심 포인트 2 문제를 풀기 전에 지문의 종류, 수신인/발신인 등을 훑으면서 각 지문들 간의 관계를 파악하는 것이 좋습니다.

▶ **ETS 기출 예제** 정답과 해설 p. 202

Calling all artists!

Are you an amateur or professional graphic artist? Relling Transit(RT) Center is holding its first ever logo contest. Logos that are related to bus or train travel will be accepted from August 2 to 22 at the RT Central Office, located at Relling Terminal. Thirty Finalists will be selected for display in the alcove at Union Street Station. From September 1 to 30, the public will be able to cast a ballot and vote on their favorite logo. Four prizes will be awarded.

First place: *Yellow pass.* Good for unlimited rides on the RT local train or bus for five days.
Second place: *Blue pass.* Good for unlimited rides on the RT local train for three days.
Third place: *Green pass.* Good for one round-trip ticket to any destination on the RT express train.
Fourth place: *Red pass.* Good for one round-trip ticket to any destination on an RT express bus.

STEP 3 두 지문 간의 연결 고리 찾기
5일간 유효한 패스는 옐로 패스입니다.

Dear Ms. Ivankova:

Congratulations on winning Relling Transit Center's Logo Contest. Enclosed is your prize. Please note that the pass does not have a definite start date. It is valid for any five-day period, beginning whenever you wish.

On behalf of Relling Transit Center, I would like to thank you for your contribution.

Sincerely,

Rita Rajwal
Community Relations Manager, Relling Transit Center

STEP 2 단서 찾기
이반코바 씨가 부상으로 받은 것은 5일짜리 패스입니다.

STEP 1 질문 파악
이반코바 씨가 받은 것을 묻는 문제입니다.

Q What did Ms. Ivankova receive?

(A) A yellow pass
(B) A blue pass
(C) A green pass
(D) A red pass

STEP 4 정답 찾기
이반코바 씨가 부상으로 받은 것은 5일짜리 패스라는 것과, 옐로 패스가 5일간 유효하다는 두 단서를 조합해 보면, 이반코바 씨가 받은 것은 옐로 패스이므로 정답은 (A)입니다.

| 어휘 | alcove 벽감(벽면을 들어가게 해서 만든 공간)   cast a ballot 투표를 하다   valid 유효한   on behalf of ~을 대표[대신]하여

Questions 1-2

Web page + Comment

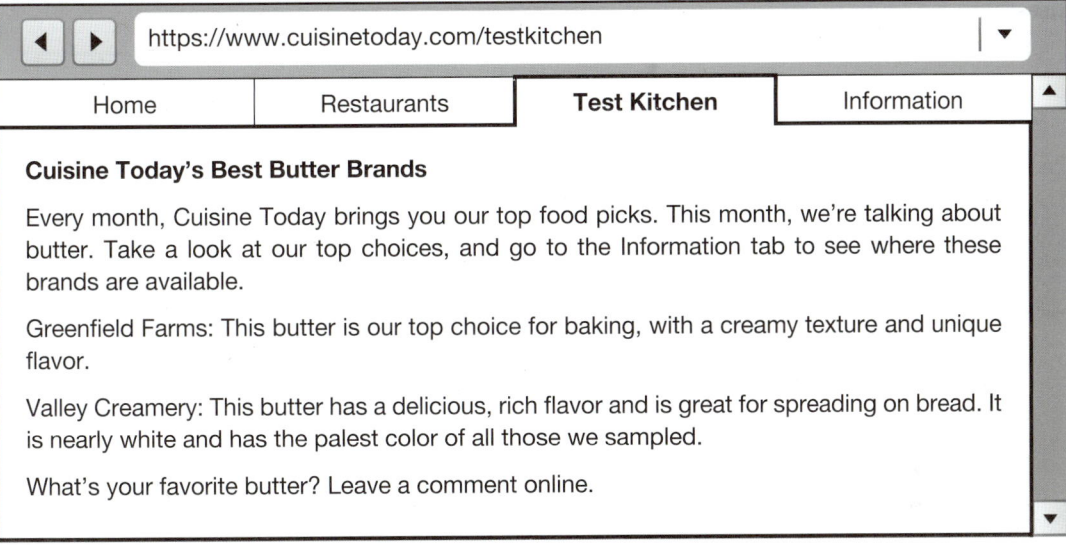

Cuisine Today's Best Butter Brands

Every month, Cuisine Today brings you our top food picks. This month, we're talking about butter. Take a look at our top choices, and go to the Information tab to see where these brands are available.

Greenfield Farms: This butter is our top choice for baking, with a creamy texture and unique flavor.

Valley Creamery: This butter has a delicious, rich flavor and is great for spreading on bread. It is nearly white and has the palest color of all those we sampled.

What's your favorite butter? Leave a comment online.

Commenter: Wataru Sano

I'm a professional cake designer, and I've used the Premium Farms brand of butter for a while. So I was curious to try the ones on your list. I needed to make a white cake, so I used the lightest-colored butter first, and I was very pleased with how it turned out. I then used the others and was happy with the results from all the brands on the list.
I have to add that I agree with your review of Greenfield Farms butter.

1. What can readers find on the Information tab?
   (A) Where brands on the list are sold
   (B) Prices of different brands of butter

2. What brand of butter from the list on the Web page did Mr. Sano try first?
   (A) Greenfield Farms
   (B) Valley Creamery

| 어휘 | pick 뽑힌 것   spread 바르다   pale (색깔이) 옅은   sample 사용해 보다   commenter 댓글 작성자, 논평자   curious 궁금한   review 논평

Questions 1-5 refer to the following letter and blog post.

Artland in the Heartland
4525 Queen Street
Kansas City, MO 64111
United States of America

August 8

Marcus Hamada
Rua Hilton Braga, 357
Rio de Janeiro - RJ, 22640-102
Brazil

Dear Mr. Hamada:

Thank you for your letter inquiring about our company. I am sorry to inform you that we are not hiring now. But we feel that the images you sent for our humorous card division are quite good. Should we need a full-time greeting card illustrator in the future, we will certainly reach out.

We wish you the best of luck in your career endeavors.

Sincerely,

Malina Rose

Malina Rose
Artland in the Heartland

The Magnificent Art of Marcus Hamada

by Yolanda Norris

September 19—As you, my readers, already know, I arrived in Brazil last weekend. The first thing I did was attend a street art festival in Rio de Janeiro, where I encountered the works of many exceptional local artists. The festival also showcased incredible artists from Spain, Mexico, the United States, England, and Israel. But most impressive was the work of a young local artist, Marcus Hamada, who was presenting his works to the public for the first time.

Mr. Hamada's work clearly appeals to many audiences. Visiting his booth were art dealers marveling at his large, colorful acrylic and oil paintings as well as families eyeing his modern, bright pastels. There were also young people perusing his amusing pen-and-ink illustrations, the kind seen on funny greeting cards. These delightful works were also transferred onto T-shirts, mugs, and other affordable souvenir-type items.

I have never seen such a diverse collection of works from one artist. I am looking forward to following Mr. Hamada's career.

1. What is the purpose of the letter?
   (A) To explain that a company has no job openings
   (B) To correct information in a job posting
   (C) To promote a company's products
   (D) To ask an artist to display his works

2. What type of business most likely is Artland in the Heartland?
   (A) A museum
   (B) An art gallery
   (C) A school of design
   (D) A greeting card manufacturer

3. What did Mr. Hamada most likely use to create the samples he sent to Ms. Rose?
   (A) Pastels
   (B) Oil paint
   (C) Pen and ink
   (D) Acrylic paint

4. In the blog post, the phrase "appeals to" in paragraph 2, line 1, is closest in meaning to
   (A) protects
   (B) attracts
   (C) requests
   (D) claims

5. What did Ms. Norris find most impressive about Mr. Hamada?
   (A) His use of bright colors
   (B) His ability to market his art
   (C) His wide variety of artistic creations
   (D) His popularity with younger audiences

Questions 6-10 refer to the following e-mail and online form.

To:	So-Hee Kang <skang@worldmail.com>
From:	Andrew Belle <abelle@invernessbank.co.uk>
Date:	13 December
Subject:	Help improve Inverness Bank

Dear Ms. Kang,

Our records show that you visited Inverness Bank's Glasgow branch on 6 December. Please let us know how we did by taking our survey at www.invernessbank.co.uk/survey. Use customer ID number 5851. You may also share your comments with one of my team members by e-mailing info@invernessbank.co.uk. Any information you provide will be reviewed at a future staff meeting.

Thank you in advance for your time.

Sincerely,

Andrew Belle

Inverness Bank Customer Satisfaction Survey—Customer ID 5851
Please indicate your responses to the following statements on a scale of 1 (strongly disagree) to 4 (strongly agree). Kindly add a comment to explain each of your responses.

1. The Inverness representative was personally engaging and had a friendly demeanour.

Comments: The bank teller who welcomed me, Julia, was polite and eager to help address my concern. However, as it was her first day on the job, she seemed a bit overwhelmed. She finally asked the branch manager to help solve my problem.

2. The Inverness representative listened to my needs and took the appropriate action to address them.

Comments: I needed help adding another layer of security to my bank account using the Inverness mobile app. The branch manager, Jim, apologised for the trouble and was able to show me how to secure my account. He also told me that I can call or e-mail him directly if I experience any issues.

3. I am likely to refer others to Inverness Bank.

Comments: After Jim's help, I now use the app to do my banking from home. Plus, if I need to visit a branch, your bank has many locations with extended hours, unlike most other banks.

6. What does Mr. Belle ask Ms. Kang to do?

(A) Provide some feedback
(B) Correct an error
(C) Confirm a recent transaction
(D) Visit a new bank branch

7. According to the e-mail, who most likely is Mr. Belle?

(A) A human resources specialist
(B) A Web site designer
(C) A customer service manager
(D) An Inverness Bank lawyer

8. What is suggested about a bank teller?

(A) She helped create Inverness Bank's mobile app.
(B) She is adjusting to a new work environment.
(C) She works most weekends.
(D) She recently opened her own account.

9. Why did Ms. Kang visit the Glasgow branch on December 6?

(A) To open a new bank account
(B) To complain about customer service
(C) To strengthen her account's security
(D) To attend an annual meeting

10. According to the online form, why might Ms. Kang recommend Inverness Bank?

(A) For its interest rates
(B) For its personal loans
(C) For its reputation
(D) For its convenience

Questions 11-15 refer to the following e-mail, advertisement, and review.

To:	Trina Chen
From:	Harold Lenbarr
Date:	November 1
Subject:	New items to shelve

Hi, Trina,

Please find the products below in the storage area and put them in the designated aisles of the store. Please complete this task by the end of the day tomorrow.

Aisle	Category	Item Number	Manufacturer; Description
2	Sandpaper	A222	Idley; various grits
3	Scissors	RJ283	Fifi's; gardening shears
4	Saws	D727	Coakley; crosscut saw
5	Screws	H01017	Jancon; Phillips-head steel

Thank you,

Harold

Lenbarr Hardware Store

One-Day Sale: November 3

Bottled Water Specials
Acardi Spa: $3.99 per case
Bluewell Pure: $5.99 per case
Tops Springtree: $7.99 per case
Wahl Mountain: $8.99 per case

Also on Sale:
10 percent off all fishing equipment and paint

교통

commuter 통근자
fine 벌금, 과태료
intersection 교차로
lane 길, 차선
parking garage 주차장
pedestrian 보행자
ramp 경사로
route 경로, 길
toll 통행료
traffic congestion 교통체증
undergo 겪다

행사

annual event 연례 행사
ceremony 의식, 예식
charity 자선 단체
conference 학회, 회의
drawing 추첨, 제비뽑기
facility 시설
gathering 모임, 집회
grand opening 개업식
host 주최하다
mark 기념하다(= celebrate)
present 소개하다, 제시하다

대회/전시

admission 입장(료)
competition 대회, 경쟁
critic 비평가
deadline 마감일
entry 출품(작)
exhibition 전시회
judge 심사위원
match 시합, 경기
notify 통지하다
showcase 전시하다
trade show 무역 박람회
venue 개최지, 장소

문화/예술

artifact 인공품, 공예품
artwork 예술 작품
author 작가
celebrity 유명인사, 명사
composer 작곡가
depict 묘사하다
aesthetic 미학적인, 예술적인
draft (원고) 초안
inspire 영감을 주다
sculpture 조각
unveil 공개하다, 발표하다
virtual 가상의, 실제에 가까운

PART 7 | 빈출 표현

경제

adverse effect 역효과, 부작용
analyze 분석하다
debt 빚
commerce 상업
expenditure 지출
figures 수치
investment 투자
lack 부족(하다)
market share 시장 점유율
quarter 분기
recession 불황(= downturn)
spokesperson 대변인

경영

aid 원조, 지원; 돕다
aspiring 장차 ~이 되려는
associate 제휴하다, 결합시키다; 사원
boost 북돋우다
competitor 경쟁자
corporation 기업, 법인
entrepreneur 기업가
executive 임원; 행정의
expand 확장하다
founder 설립자
morale 근로 의욕, 사기
motivate 동기를 부여하다

청구/결제

amount 양
balance 잔액
billing address 청구 주소
deposit 보증금, 선불금
estimate 견적(액); 어림잡다
expedite 신속히 처리하다
invoice 송장
measurement 치수, 측정
overdue 기한이 지난, 늦은
payment 지불(액)
recipient 수령인
reduction 할인, 축소

상품/서비스

appliance 전자제품
assemble 조립하다
beverage 음료
browse 둘러보다
custom-made 맞춤식의
diverse 다양한
manufacturer 제조업체
offering 제품, 서비스 (제공)
price tag 가격표
release 출시하다
specifications 명세서
state-of-the-art 최신식의

구인/구직

application 지원(서)
benefit 복지, 혜택
bilingual 두 개 언어를 구사하는
candidate 후보자
certified 공인된
résumé 이력서
cover letter 자기소개서
desirable 바람직한
deadline 마감일(= due date)
degree 학위
fluent 능숙한
hire 고용하다(= employ)
human resources 인사과
job opening 공석
preference 우대사항
applicant 지원자
perform a task 업무를 수행하다
permanent 정규직의
primary duty 주요 업무
proficiency 능숙함
qualified 자격을 갖춘
reference 추천서
relevant 관련된(= related)
replacement 교체, 후임자
required 필수적인
headquarters 본사

공사/건축

aim 목표; 겨냥하다
annex 부속 건물
interrupt 방해하다, 중단시키다
launch 시작하다
plumbing 배관 (작업)
procedure 절차
put into action 조치를 취하다
refurbish 재단장하다
repave (도로 등을) 재포장하다
restoration 복원, 복구
resume 재개하다

부동산

commercial 상업적인; 광고
flat 아파트
floor plan 평면도
fully-furnished 내부가 완비된
landlord 집주인
lease 임대하다
realtor 부동산 중개인
rent 임대료; 임대[임차]하다
residential 거주용의
separate 분리된
located ~에 위치한(= situated)
studio 원룸 형태의 공간
tenant 세입자

PART 7 | 빈출 표현

감사 / 축하

accomplished 뛰어난
achieve 달성하다
appreciate 감사히 여기다
award 수여하다
celebrate 축하하다
commitment 헌신, 약속
contribute 공헌하다
donation 기부
hold 열다, 개최하다
impressed 감명 받은
pleased 즐거운(= delighted, glad)
reason 이유

문제 / 사과

apology 사과
breakage 파손
cancel 취소하다
complaint 불평
concern 걱정, 염려; 관련되다
damaged 손상된
defective 결함 있는(= faulty)
exchange 교환; 교환하다
explain 설명하다
inconvenience 불편
postpone 미루다(= delay)
refund 환불; 환불하다

구매 / 주문

account 계정, 계좌
brochure 소책자(= booklet)
bulk 대량
clarify 명확히 하다
confirm 확인하다
include 포함하다
method 방법
parcel 소포
purchase 구매; 구매하다
receipt 영수증, 수령
respond 응답하다
status 상태, 지위
ship overnight 익일 배송하다

출장 / 여행

accommodations 숙박 시설
belongings 소지품
destination 목적지
book 예약하다
board 탑승하다
departure 출발
expense 비용
itinerary 여행 일정표
passport 여권
reservation 예약
round trip 왕복 여행
take off 이륙하다
jet lag 시차증(시차로 인한 피로)

From:	Seema Shah <s.shah@gopromail.com>
To:	OOS Customer Service <customerservice@ossieofficesupply.com>
Date:	August 22
Subject:	Missing order

Hi,

I am writing about invoice #08912. It was due to arrive today, but it is now the close of business, and it has not yet arrived. We have never had issues with getting our orders from your company on time before. Please let me know how I can find out when our order will arrive. If we will not get it before Friday, then I will have to cancel our order and make a trip to the store.

Thank you,

Seema Shah
Go Pro Executives, Office Manager

---

16. What does Mr. Goodwin ask members of the management team to do?

(A) Help to train a new employee
(B) Submit their teams' sales results
(C) Make edits to an article
(D) Review a return policy

17. Who will present on shipping companies?

(A) Ms. Park
(B) Ms. Lindt
(C) Mr. Goodwin
(D) Mr. Gomez

18. Which of Mr. Goodwin's suggestions did the group most likely approve?

(A) Free shipping
(B) Free returns
(C) A buy-one-get-one-free special
(D) A loyalty discount

19. What will a customer support representative most likely ask Ms. Shah to do?

(A) Visit Zip Ship's Web site
(B) Cancel an order
(C) Visit an Ossie Office Supply store
(D) Call the customer service number

20. When was Ms. Shah's delivery supposed to arrive?

(A) On June 14
(B) On July 2
(C) On August 18
(D) On August 22

Questions 16-20 refer to the following e-mails and invoice.

From:	Todd Goodwin <t.goodwin@ossieofficesupply.com>
To:	OOS Management Team <management@ossieofficesupply.com>
Date:	July 2
Subject:	Team meeting agenda
Attachment:	📎Kurminoff article

Hi, team.

Here is the agenda for today's management meeting. See you at 1 P.M.!

1. New-employee training schedule. Karen Park was hired this week and will begin training on July 8. Please look at your schedules before the meeting and come prepared to take a training shift.
2. Second quarter sales results. Julio Gomez will review our in-store sales. I will discuss our online sales.
3. Online sales. Please read the attached article about boosting online sales and come to the meeting prepared to discuss its ideas. We need to boost online sales, so I think we should consider offering free shipping or returns, a buy-one-get-one-free special, or a 10 percent loyalty discount for return customers.
4. Progress on finding a new shipping company. Last month on June 14, I presented on the results of a customer survey, which showed that customers want to be able to track their packages. They also want lower shipping rates. Julie Lindt will present on a few shipping companies for us to consider.

Todd Goodwin
Ossie Office Supply General Manager

From:	Ossie Office Supply <invoice@ossieofficesupply.com>
To:	Seema Shah <s.shah@gopromail.com>
Date:	August 18
Subject:	Invoice #08912

Thank you for your purchase from Ossie Office Supply! Please see your invoice below.

Item	Quantity	Unit Price	Total Price
Black Ballpoint Pens (8 pack)	10	$2.99	$29.90
Red Ballpoint Pens (8 Pack)	2	$2.99	$5.98
White printer paper (500 sheets)	20	$4.29	$85.80
		Subtotal	$121.68
		Discount: (10% off)	$12.17
		Tax: (5%)	$6.08
		Shipping: (express)	$10.00
		Pay this amount:	**$125.59**

Your online order can be revised or canceled up until it ships. If you need to make a change, please call (413) 555-0130. The progress of your shipment can be tracked on Zip Ship's Website using tracking number 0008971 (zipship.com/trackmypackage).

Store Review: Lenbarr Hardware Store
By Ann Avery

(November 10)—I love Lenbarr Hardware Store! It is a small, family-owned establishment with almost any item you can imagine, including the ones you would not expect to find at a hardware store. However, I often have to ask the shop assistant where the product is that I came in for since it never seems to be where I would ordinarily expect it.

For example, last Monday, I went in to buy a bottle of Hannon's model glue. Rather than in the arts and crafts section where I thought it would be, it was in the paint department, next to the sandpaper. And the Jancon Phillips-head steel screws I needed were with the beverages rather than with the hardware products.

Another reason why I regularly shop at Lenbarr is its daily bargains. Thus, on the day I visited, the store had a one-day sale on bottled water. I bought a case of Bluewell bottled water at less than half the price I usually pay!

So, while the store's layout is somewhat puzzling to me, I go there at least once a week since it generally has whatever I am looking for.

---

11. According to the e-mail, what is Item RJ283?

(A) A screw made by Jancon
(B) A saw made by Coakley
(C) A type of sandpaper
(D) A gardening tool

12. What is mentioned in the advertisement about the sale at Lenbarr Hardware Store?

(A) It lasts one week.
(B) It includes fishing equipment.
(C) It takes place every November.
(D) It features 10 percent off all hardware.

13. Where most likely did Ms. Avery find glue?

(A) Aisle 2
(B) Aisle 3
(C) Aisle 4
(D) Aisle 5

14. What does Ms. Avery indicate in the review about Lenbarr Hardware Store?

(A) Its organization is a bit confusing.
(B) It does not treat customers well.
(C) It does not stock enough goods.
(D) Its large size can be overwhelming.

15. What was the sale price of the bottled water that Ms. Avery bought?

(A) $3.99
(B) $5.99
(C) $7.99
(D) $8.99

ETS 토익 단기공략 650+

최신 개정판
무료 동영상 강의
LC
RC

정답과 해설

PART 1
LISTENING COMPREHENSION

UNIT 01 인물 중심 사진

1 1인 사진

ETS 유형 연습 본책 p.021

1 (B)   2 (D)   3 (A)   4 (B)

1

M-Cn

(A) He's installing lamps on a wall.
(B) He's kneeling to set up work supplies.
(C) He's cleaning a paintbrush in a sink.
(D) He's covering some windows with paper.

(A) 남자가 벽에 등을 설치하고 있다.
(B) 남자가 작업 물품을 준비하려고 무릎을 꿇고 있다.
(C) 남자가 싱크대에서 페인트붓을 씻고 있다.
(D) 남자가 몇몇 창문들을 종이로 덮고 있다.

해설 **1인 사진 - 실내 작업**
(A) **사진에 없는 명사를 이용한 오답:** 사진에 등(lamps)이 보이지 않는다.
(B) **정답:** 남자가 작업 물품을 준비하려고 무릎을 꿇고 있는(is kneeling) 모습이므로 정답이다.
(C) **사진에 없는 명사를 이용한 오답:** 사진에 싱크대(sink)가 보이지 않는다.
(D) **동작 묘사 오답:** 남자가 창문을 종이로 덮고 있는(is covering) 모습이 아니다.

어휘 install 설치하다   kneel 무릎을 꿇다   supplies 물품, 용품

2

M-Au

(A) A woman is exiting a restaurant.
(B) A woman is throwing some trash into a bin.
(C) A woman is serving a meal to some customers.
(D) A woman is clearing containers from a dining area.

(A) 여자가 식당을 나가고 있다.
(B) 여자가 쓰레기를 쓰레기통에 버리고 있다.
(C) 여자가 몇몇 손님들에게 식사를 제공하고 있다.
(D) 여자가 식사 공간에서 용기를 치우고 있다.

해설 **1인 사진 - 식당**
(A) **동작 묘사 오답:** 여자가 식당을 나가고 있는(is exiting) 모습이 아니다.
(B) **사진에 없는 명사를 이용한 오답:** 사진에 쓰레기통(bin)은 보이지 않는다.
(C) **사진에 없는 명사를 이용한 오답:** 사진에 손님들(customers)이 없다.
(D) **정답:** 여자가 용기를 치우고 있는(is clearing) 모습이므로 정답이다.

어휘 exit 나가다   bin 쓰레기통   serve (음식을) 제공하다   customer 고객   container 용기, 그릇

3

M-Cn

(A) She's putting money into a cashbox.
(B) She's holding a serving utensil.
(C) She's arranging food on paper plates.
(D) She's removing supplies from a vehicle.

(A) 여자가 현금보관함에 돈을 넣고 있다.
(B) 여자가 서빙 도구를 들고 있다.
(C) 여자가 종이 접시에 음식을 준비하고 있다.
(D) 여자가 차량에서 물품을 꺼내고 있다.

해설 **1인 사진 - 실외**
(A) **사진에 없는 명사를 이용한 오답:** 사진에 돈(money)과 현금보관함(cashbox)이 보이지 않는다.
(B) **정답:** 여자가 서빙 도구를 들고 있는(is holding) 모습이므로 정답이다.
(C) **사진에 없는 명사를 이용한 오답:** 사진에 음식(food)이 보이지 않는다.
(D) **동작 묘사 오답:** 여자가 차량에서 물품을 꺼내고 있는(is removing) 모습이 아니다.

어휘 cashbox 현금보관함   serving utensil 서빙 도구   arrange 준비하다, 마련하다   remove 옮기다, 치우다

4

W-Am

(A) The woman's pushing a display case in a hallway.
(B) The woman's walking past a display of books.
(C) The woman's piling up books on a counter.
(D) The woman's arranging merchandise on a rack.

(A) 여자가 복도에서 진열장을 밀고 있다.
(B) 여자가 책 진열대를 지나가고 있다.
(C) 여자가 카운터에 책을 쌓고 있다.
(D) 여자가 선반에 상품을 진열하고 있다.

해설 **1인 사진 - 서점**
(A) **동작 묘사 오답:** 여자가 진열장을 밀고 있는(is pushing) 모습이 아니다.
(B) **정답:** 여자가 책 진열대를 지나가고 있는(is walking past) 모습이므로 정답이다.
(C) **동작 묘사 오답:** 여자가 책을 쌓고 있는(is piling up) 모습이 아니다.
(D) **동작 묘사 오답:** 여자가 상품을 진열하고 있는(is arranging) 모습이 아니다.

어휘 display case 진열장 hallway 복도 pile (up) 쌓다 arrange 정리하다, 배열하다 merchandise 상품

② 2인 이상 사진

ETS 유형 연습 본책 p.023

1 (D)   **2** (C)   **3** (A)   **4** (B)

1

W-Br

(A) Two men are painting a wall.
(B) A man is plugging in a cord.
(C) A man is handing tools to his coworker.
(D) Both of the men are using tools.

(A) 두 남자가 벽을 페인트칠하고 있다.
(B) 한 남자가 코드를 꽂고 있다.
(C) 한 남자가 동료에게 공구를 건네고 있다.
(D) 두 남자 모두 공구를 사용하고 있다.

해설 **2인 사진 - 실외 작업**
(A) **동작 묘사 오답:** 두 남자가 벽을 칠하고 있는(are painting) 모습이 아니다.
(B) **동작 묘사 오답:** 사진에 코드(cord)가 보이지만 두 남자 모두 코드를 꽂고 있는(is plugging in) 모습이 아니다.
(C) **동작 묘사 오답:** 사진에 공구(tools)가 보이지만 동료에게 공구를 건네고 있는(is handing) 사람은 없다.
(D) **정답:** 두 사람 모두 공구를 사용하고 있는(are using tools) 모습이므로 정답이다.

어휘 hand 건네다 tool 공구 coworker 동료

2

M-Cn

(A) The woman is folding a newspaper in half.
(B) The woman is reading a sign on the wall.
(C) The man is raising a cup to his mouth.
(D) The man is leaning on a counter.

(A) 여자가 신문을 반으로 접고 있다.
(B) 여자가 벽에 걸린 표지판을 읽고 있다.
(C) 남자가 컵을 입 쪽으로 들어 올리고 있다.
(D) 남자가 카운터에 기대어 있다.

해설 **2인 사진 - 실내**
(A) **동작 묘사 오답:** 여자가 신문을 읽고 있는 모습이지 접고 있는(is folding) 모습이 아니다.
(B) **사진에 없는 명사를 이용한 오답:** 사진에 표지판(sign)이 없다.
(C) **정답:** 남자가 컵을 입 쪽으로 들어 올리고 있는(is raising) 모습이므로 정답이다.
(D) **동작 묘사 오답:** 사진에 카운터는 있지만 남자가 기대어 있는(is leaning) 모습은 아니다.

어휘 fold A in half A를 반으로 접다 raise 들어 올리다
lean on ~에 기대다

3

M-Cn

(A) The people are hiking outdoors.
(B) The people are gathering under a tent.
(C) Some of the people are cutting bushes.
(D) Some of the people are eating a snack.

(A) 사람들이 야외에서 하이킹을 하고 있다.
(B) 사람들이 텐트 아래에 모이고 있다.
(C) 몇몇 사람들이 덤불을 자르고 있다.
(D) 몇몇 사람들이 간식을 먹고 있다.

해설 **3인 이상 사진 - 야외**
(A) **정답:** 사람들이 하이킹하고 있는(are hiking) 모습이므로 정답이다.
(B) **사진에 없는 명사를 이용한 오답:** 사진에 텐트(tent)가 보이지 않는다.
(C) **동작 묘사 오답:** 사람들이 덤불을 자르고 있는(are cutting) 모습이 아니다.
(D) **동작 묘사 오답:** 사람들이 간식을 먹고 있는(are eating) 모습이 아니다.

어휘 hike 하이킹하다 gather 모이다, 모으다 bush 덤불

4

W-Am

(A) Some people are seated in a lobby.
(B) Some people are riding an escalator.
(C) Some people are standing on a balcony.
(D) Some people are walking down a staircase.

(A) 몇몇 사람들이 로비에 앉아 있다.
(B) 몇몇 사람들이 에스컬레이터를 타고 있다.
(C) 몇몇 사람들이 발코니 위에 서 있다.
(D) 몇몇 사람들이 계단을 걸어 내려가고 있다.

해설 **3인 이상 사진 - 에스컬레이터**
(A) **상태 묘사 오답**: 로비에 앉아 있는(are seated) 사람은 보이지 않는다.
(B) **정답**: 사람들이 에스컬레이터를 타고 있는(are riding) 모습이므로 정답이다.
(C) **상태 묘사 오답**: 발코니 위에 서 있는(are standing) 사람은 보이지 않는다.
(D) **사진에 없는 명사를 이용한 오답**: 사진에 에스컬레이터 외에 계단(staircase)은 보이지 않는다.

어휘 staircase 계단

ETS 실전 문제   본책 p.024

| 1 (A) | 2 (D) | 3 (C) | 4 (D) | 5 (C) | 6 (B) |
| 7 (B) | 8 (C) | 9 (C) | 10 (A) | 11 (D) | 12 (D) |

1

M-Cn

(A) She's working on her computer.
(B) She's setting a bag on the ground.
(C) She's plugging in a laptop computer.
(D) She's wiping off a tabletop.

(A) 여자가 컴퓨터로 작업하고 있다.
(B) 여자가 가방을 바닥에 놓고 있다.
(C) 여자가 노트북 컴퓨터 플러그를 꽂고 있다.
(D) 여자가 테이블 위를 닦고 있다.

해설 **1인 사진 - 실외 업무 장소**
(A) **정답**: 여자가 컴퓨터로 작업하고 있는(is working) 모습이므로 정답이다.
(B) **동작 묘사 오답**: 가방은 바닥에 이미 놓여 있지 여자가 놓고 있는(is setting) 모습이 아니다.
(C) **동작 묘사 오답**: 사진에 노트북 컴퓨터는 보이지만 여자가 플러그를 꽂고 있는(is plugging in) 모습은 아니다.
(D) **동작 묘사 오답**: 여자가 테이블을 닦고 있는(is wiping off) 모습이 아니다.

어휘 plug in ~의 플러그를 꽂다   wipe off ~을 닦다
tabletop 테이블 윗면[표면]

2

W-Am

(A) Some people are having a meal outside.
(B) Some people are painting a boat.
(C) Some people are fishing from a pier.
(D) Some people are gathered by the water.

(A) 몇몇 사람들이 밖에서 식사하고 있다.
(B) 몇몇 사람들이 배에 페인트를 칠하고 있다.
(C) 몇몇 사람들이 부두에서 낚시하고 있다.
(D) 몇몇 사람들이 물가에 모여 있다.

해설 **3인 이상 사진 - 물가**
(A) **동작 묘사 오답**: 밖에서 식사를 하고 있는(are having a meal) 사람은 보이지 않는다.
(B) **동작 묘사 오답**: 사진에 배는 있지만 배에 페인트를 칠하고 있는(are painting) 사람은 보이지 않는다.
(C) **동작 묘사 오답**: 부두에서 낚시하고 있는(are fishing) 사람은 보이지 않는다.
(D) **정답**: 사람들이 물가에 모여 있는(are gathered) 모습이므로 정답이다.

어휘 have a meal 식사하다   pier 부두

3

W-Br

(A) Some people are picking up trash from a street.
(B) Some people are repairing a railing.
(C) One of the men is playing a piano for onlookers.
(D) One of the men is selling street food.

(A) 몇몇 사람들이 거리에서 쓰레기를 줍고 있다.
(B) 몇몇 사람들이 난간을 수리하고 있다.
(C) 남자들 중 한 명이 구경꾼들을 위해 피아노를 치고 있다.
(D) 남자들 중 한 명이 길거리 음식을 팔고 있다.

해설 **3인 이상 사진 - 야외**
(A) **동작 묘사 오답**: 쓰레기를 줍고 있는(are picking up trash) 사람은 보이지 않는다.
(B) **동작 묘사 오답**: 난간을 수리하고 있는(are repairing a railing) 사람은 보이지 않는다.
(C) **정답**: 한 남자가 피아노를 치고 있는(is playing a piano) 모습이므로 정답이다.
(D) **사진에 없는 명사를 이용한 오답**: 사진에 길거리 음식(street food)은 보이지 않는다.

어휘 railing 난간   onlooker 구경꾼

4

W-Br

(A) A person is closing a cupboard door.
(B) A person is organizing food in a pantry.
(C) A person is stacking dinner plates on a shelf.
(D) A person is putting drinking glasses in a cupboard.

(A) 사람이 찬장 문을 닫고 있다.
(B) 사람이 식료품 저장실에서 식품을 정리하고 있다.
(C) 사람이 선반 위에 만찬용 접시를 쌓고 있다.
(D) 사람이 찬장에 유리컵을 넣고 있다.

해설 **1인 사진 - 주방**
(A) **동작 묘사 오답:** 사진에 찬장 문(cupboard door)은 보이지만 사람이 닫고 있는(is closing) 모습이 아니다.
(B) **사진에 없는 명사를 이용한 오답:** 사진에 음식(food)은 보이지 않는다.
(C) **사진에 없는 명사를 이용한 오답:** 사진에 만찬용 접시(dinner plates)는 보이지 않는다.
(D) **정답:** 사람이 찬장에 유리컵을 넣고 있는(is putting) 모습이므로 정답이다.

어휘 cupboard 찬장   pantry 식료품 저장실

5
M-Cn

(A) They're hammering nails into wooden beams.
(B) One of the men is riding up an escalator.
(C) One of the men is wearing a safety vest.
(D) They're digging a hole at a construction site.

(A) 사람들이 목재 기둥에 못을 박고 있다.
(B) 남자들 중 한 명이 에스컬레이터를 타고 올라가고 있다.
(C) **남자들 중 한 명이 안전 조끼를 입고 있다.**
(D) 사람들이 건설 현장에서 구멍을 파고 있다.

해설 **2인 사진 - 건설 현장**
(A) **동작 묘사 오답:** 사람들이 망치로 못을 박고 있는(are hammering) 모습이 아니다.
(B) **동작 묘사 오답:** 에스컬레이터를 타고 올라가고 있는(is riding up) 사람은 보이지 않는다.
(C) **정답:** 한 남자가 안전 조끼를 입고 있는(is wearing) 모습이므로 정답이다.
(D) **동작 묘사 오답:** 사람들이 구멍을 파고 있는(are digging) 모습이 아니다.

어휘 nail 못   beam 기둥, 들보   safety vest 안전 조끼

6
W-Am

(A) A woman is opening an umbrella.
(B) Customers are shopping in an open-air market.
(C) A vendor is reaching into a display case.
(D) Some people are bicycling through a market.

(A) 한 여자가 우산을 펴고 있다.
(B) **손님들이 노천 시장에서 쇼핑을 하고 있다.**
(C) 행상인이 진열장 안으로 손을 뻗고 있다.
(D) 몇몇 사람들이 자전거를 타고 시장을 지나가고 있다.

해설 **3인 이상 사진 - 노천 시장**
(A) **동작 묘사 오답:** 우산을 펴고 있는(is opening) 사람은 보이지 않는다.
(B) **정답:** 노천 시장(open-air market)에서 손님들이 쇼핑을 하고 있는(are shopping) 모습이므로 정답이다.
(C) **동작 묘사 오답:** 행상인이 진열장 안으로 손을 뻗고 있는(is reaching) 모습이 아니다.
(D) **동작 묘사 오답:** 자전거를 타고 있는(are bicycling) 사람은 보이지 않는다.

어휘 open-air market 노천 시장   vendor 행상인, 노점상   reach into ~ 안으로 손을 뻗다   display case 진열장

7
W-Br

(A) One of the women is disposing of her gloves.
(B) One of the women is extending her arm.
(C) A health-care worker is adjusting her uniform.
(D) A doctor is examining a patient's eyes.

(A) 여자들 중 한 명이 장갑을 버리고 있다.
(B) **여자들 중 한 명이 팔을 뻗고 있다.**
(C) 의료 종사자가 유니폼 매무새를 정돈하고 있다.
(D) 의사가 환자의 눈을 진찰하고 있다.

해설 **2인 사진 - 검사실**
(A) **동작 묘사 오답:** 한 여자가 장갑을 끼고 있는 상태지 버리고 있는(is disposing) 모습이 아니다.
(B) **정답:** 한 여자가 팔을 뻗고 있는(is extending) 모습이므로 정답이다.
(C) **동작 묘사 오답:** 의료 종사자가 유니폼 매무새를 정돈하고 있는(is adjusting) 모습이 아니다.
(D) **사진에 없는 명사를 이용한 오답:** 사진에 환자의 눈을 진찰하고 있는(is examining) 의사는 보이지 않는다.

어휘 dispose of ~을 버리다   extend (팔·다리 등을) 뻗다   health-care worker 의료 종사자   adjust (매무새 등을) 정돈하다   examine 진찰하다   patient 환자

8
M-Au

(A) One of the men is putting a guitar in a case.
(B) One of the men is leaning against a post.
(C) One of the men is wearing sunglasses.
(D) One of the men is taking off a jacket.

(A) 남자들 중 한 명이 기타를 케이스에 넣고 있다.
(B) 남자들 중 한 명이 기둥에 기대고 있다.
(C) **남자들 중 한 명이 선글라스를 쓰고 있다.**
(D) 남자들 중 한 명이 재킷을 벗고 있다.

해설 **3인 이상 사진 - 길거리 공연**
(A) **동작 묘사 오답:** 기타를 케이스에 넣고 있는(is putting) 사람은 보이지 않는다.

(B) **동작 묘사 오답:** 기둥에 기대고 있는(is leaning) 사람은 보이지 않는다.
(C) **정답:** 한 남자가 선글라스를 쓰고 있는(is wearing) 상태이므로 정답이다.
(D) **동작 묘사 오답:** 재킷을 벗고 있는(is taking off) 사람은 없다.

어휘 lean against ~에 기대다 post 기둥

9  W-Br

(A) She's closing the window shades.
(B) She's turning on the television.
(C) She's reading in an armchair.
(D) She's setting up a conference room.

(A) 여자가 창문 블라인드를 닫고 있다.
(B) 여자가 텔레비전을 켜고 있다.
(C) 여자가 안락의자에서 책을 읽고 있다.
(D) 여자가 회의실을 준비하고 있다.

해설 1인 사진 – 거실
(A) **동작 묘사 오답:** 여자가 창문 블라인드를 닫고 있는(is closing) 모습이 아니다.
(B) **동작 묘사 오답:** 여자가 텔레비전을 켜고 있는(is turning on) 모습이 아니다.
(C) **정답:** 여자가 안락의자에서 책을 읽고 있는(is reading) 모습이므로 정답이다.
(D) **장소 묘사 오답:** 사진 속 장소가 회의실(a conference room)이 아니다.

어휘 shade 블라인드, 차양 armchair 안락의자

10  M-Au

(A) A customer is examining some items.
(B) A customer is paying for some merchandise.
(C) A customer is closing a bottle.
(D) A customer is setting an item on the floor.

(A) 고객이 제품들을 살펴보고 있다.
(B) 고객이 상품 값을 지불하고 있다.
(C) 고객이 병을 닫고 있다.
(D) 고객이 바닥에 제품을 놓고 있다.

해설 1인 사진 – 마트
(A) **정답:** 고객이 제품들을 살펴보고 있는(is examining) 모습이므로 정답이다.
(B) **동작 묘사 오답:** 고객이 상품 값을 지불하고 있는(is paying) 모습이 아니다.
(C) **동작 묘사 오답:** 고객이 병을 닫고 있는(is closing) 모습이 아니다.
(D) **동작 묘사 오답:** 고객이 바닥에 제품을 놓고 있는(is setting) 모습이 아니다.

어휘 examine 살펴보다 merchandise 상품

11  M-Cn

(A) She's placing some clothing into a cart.
(B) She's looking at herself in a mirror.
(C) She's asking a sales associate for help.
(D) She's picking up an item of clothing.

(A) 여자가 옷을 카트에 넣고 있다.
(B) 여자가 거울 속의 자신을 보고 있다.
(C) 여자가 판매원에게 도움을 요청하고 있다.
(D) 여자가 옷 한 벌을 집어 들고 있다.

해설 1인 사진 – 의류 매장
(A) **사진에 없는 명사를 이용한 오답:** 사진에 카트(cart)가 보이지 않는다.
(B) **동작 묘사 오답:** 여자가 거울을 보고 있는(is looking at herself) 모습이 아니다.
(C) **사진에 없는 명사를 이용한 오답:** 사진에 판매원(sales associate)은 보이지 않는다.
(D) **정답:** 여자가 옷을 집어 들고 있는(is picking up) 모습이므로 정답이다.

어휘 place 놓다 sales associate 판매 사원

12  W-Am

(A) Some people are reading a menu in front of a restaurant.
(B) A worker is scooping some food onto a plate.
(C) A customer is paying at a register.
(D) A server is handing a customer a dish.

(A) 몇몇 사람들이 식당 앞에서 메뉴를 읽고 있다.
(B) 직원이 접시에 음식을 퍼 담고 있다.
(C) 고객이 계산대에서 지불하고 있다.
(D) 종업원이 손님에게 접시를 건네고 있다.

해설 3인 이상 사진 – 식당
(A) **동작 묘사 오답:** 사람들이 식당 앞에서 메뉴를 읽고 있는(are reading) 모습이 아니다.
(B) **동작 묘사 오답:** 접시에 음식이 이미 담겨 있는 상태지 직원이 음식을 퍼 담고 있는(is scooping) 모습이 아니다.
(C) **동작 묘사 오답:** 고객이 지불하고 있는(is paying) 모습이 아니다.
(D) **정답:** 종업원이 손님에게 접시를 건네고 있는(is handing) 모습이므로 정답이다.

어휘 scoop 푸다 register 계산대 hand 건네다

UNIT 02 사물/배경 중심 사진

1 사물/배경 사진 **2** 인물/사물 혼합 사진

ETS 유형 연습   본책 p.027

1 (A)   2 (B)   3 (B)   4 (A)

1

W-Am

(A) Some gardening equipment has been left outside.
(B) The wheel has been removed from a wheelbarrow.
(C) There's a rake leaning against a wall.
(D) There's a pile of wood under an archway.

(A) 몇몇 원예 장비들이 밖에 놓여 있다.
(B) 바퀴가 손수레에서 분리되어 있다.
(C) 갈퀴가 벽에 기대어져 있다.
(D) 나무 더미가 아치 길 아래에 있다.

해설 사물 사진 - 정원
(A) **정답:** 원예 장비들이 밖에 놓여 있는(has been left outside) 모습이므로 정답이다.
(B) **상태 묘사 오답:** 바퀴는 손수레에서 분리되어 있지(has been removed) 않다.
(C) **위치 묘사 오답:** 갈퀴는 손수레 위에 놓여 있다.
(D) **사진에 없는 명사를 이용한 오답:** 아치 길 아래에 나무 더미(pile of wood)가 보이지 않는다.

어휘 equipment 장비   remove 떼어내다   wheelbarrow 손수레   rake 갈퀴   a pile of ~ 더미   archway 아치 길

2

W-Br

(A) Pedestrians are crossing at an intersection.
(B) Trees are planted on both sides of a street.
(C) People are waiting to board a bus.
(D) Lines are being painted on a road.

(A) 보행자들이 교차로를 건너고 있다.
(B) 나무들이 도로 양쪽에 심어져 있다.
(C) 사람들이 버스에 타려고 기다리고 있다.
(D) 차선이 도로에 그려지고 있다.

해설 배경 사진 - 도로
(A) **사진에 없는 명사를 이용한 오답:** 사진에 보행자들(pedestrians)은 보이지 않는다.
(B) **정답:** 나무들이 도로 양쪽에(on both sides) 심어져 있는(are planted) 모습이므로 정답이다.
(C) **사진에 없는 명사를 이용한 오답:** 사진에 버스를 기다리고 있는(are waiting) 사람들은 보이지 않는다.
(D) **상황 묘사 오답:** 차선이 도로에 그려지고 있는(are being painted) 모습이 아니다.

어휘 pedestrian 보행자   intersection 교차로   board 탑승하다

3

M-Au

(A) Some pictures are stacked on the ground.
(B) Some artwork is arranged on a wall.
(C) A man is painting a picture.
(D) A man is hanging up a jacket.

(A) 몇몇 그림들이 바닥에 쌓여 있다.
(B) 몇몇 예술 작품이 벽에 배열되어 있다.
(C) 남자가 그림을 그리고 있다.
(D) 남자가 재킷을 걸고 있다.

해설 인물·사물 혼합 사진 - 매장
(A) **상태 묘사 오답:** 그림들은 벽에 걸려 있지 바닥에 쌓여 있지(are stacked) 않다.
(B) **정답:** 예술 작품이 벽에 배열되어 있는(is arranged on a wall) 모습이므로 정답이다.
(C) **동작 묘사 오답:** 남자가 그림을 그리고 있는(is painting) 모습이 아니다.
(D) **동작 묘사 오답:** 남자가 재킷을 걸고 있는(is hanging up) 모습이 아니다.

어휘 stack 쌓다   artwork 예술 작품   arrange 배열[배치]하다

4

W-Am

(A) Some cyclists are viewing a city from a distance.
(B) The city's skyline is obscured by clouds.
(C) Several people are leaning against a low wall.
(D) A woman is setting her helmet on a ledge.

(A) 자전거 타는 사람들이 멀리서 도시를 바라보고 있다.
(B) 도시의 스카이라인이 구름에 가려져 있다.
(C) 몇몇 사람들이 낮은 벽에 기대어 있다.
(D) 한 여자가 헬멧을 바위 턱에 놓고 있다.

해설 인물·사물 혼합 사진 - 자전거 하이킹
(A) **정답:** 자전거 타는 사람들이 멀리서 도시를 바라보고 있는(are viewing) 모습이므로 정답이다.
(B) **상태 묘사 오답:** 도시의 스카이라인이 구름에 가려져 있지(is obscured) 않다.
(C) **동작 묘사 오답:** 사람들이 벽에 기대어 있는(are leaning) 모습이 아니다.

(D) 동작 묘사 오답: 여자가 헬멧을 바위 턱에 놓고 있는(is setting) 모습이 아니다.

어휘 from a distance 멀리서   obscure 가리다, 흐리게 하다
ledge 바위 턱

ETS 실전 문제   본책 p.028

| 1 (D) | 2 (C) | 3 (D) | 4 (A) | 5 (A) | 6 (C) |
| 7 (A) | 8 (A) | 9 (D) | 10 (D) | 11 (A) | 12 (B) |

1
W-Br

(A) Some chairs are lined up next to a counter.
(B) A customer is ordering from a menu.
(C) Some light fixtures have been set on a table.
(D) A worker is pushing an empty cart.

(A) 몇몇 의자들이 카운터 옆에 줄지어 놓여 있다.
(B) 고객이 메뉴에서 주문하고 있다.
(C) 몇몇 조명들이 테이블 위에 놓여 있다.
(D) 직원이 빈 카트를 밀고 있다.

해설 인물·사물 혼합 사진 – 식당
(A) 상태 묘사 오답: 의자가 카운터 옆에 줄지어 놓여 있는 (are lined up) 모습이 아니다.
(B) 사진에 없는 명사를 이용한 오답: 사진에 고객 (customer)은 보이지 않는다.
(C) 위치 묘사 오답: 조명은 테이블 위(on a table)에 놓여 있지 않고 천장에 매달려 있다.
(D) 정답: 직원이 빈 카트를 밀고 있는(is pushing) 모습이므로 정답이다.

어휘 order 주문하다   light fixture 조명 (기구)

2
M-Au

(A) One of the people is closing an office door.
(B) One of the people is organizing books on a shelf.
(C) Some books are being stacked next to a box.
(D) Some cables have been scattered on the floor.

(A) 사람들 중 한 명이 사무실 문을 닫고 있다.
(B) 사람들 중 한 명이 선반에 책을 정리하고 있다.
(C) 몇몇 책들이 상자 옆에 쌓이고 있다.
(D) 몇몇 전선들이 바닥에 흩어져 있다.

해설 인물·사물 혼합 사진 – 사무실
(A) 동작 묘사 오답: 사진에 사무실 문(an office door)은 보이지만 문을 닫고 있는(is closing) 사람은 없다.
(B) 사진에 없는 명사를 이용한 오답: 사진에 선반(shelf)이 보이지 않는다.
(C) 정답: 여자에 의해 책들이 상자 옆에 쌓이고 있는(are being stacked) 모습이므로 정답이다.
(D) 위치 묘사 오답: 전선이 책상 위에 보이지만 바닥에(on the floor) 흩어져 있는지 알 수 없다.

어휘 organize 정리하다   stack 쌓다   scatter 흐트러뜨리다

3
W-Br

(A) Some patio umbrellas have been left open.
(B) Some benches are set up in a shaded area.
(C) Some blankets have been placed on the grass.
(D) Some bushes line the outside of a building.

(A) 몇몇 파라솔들이 펼쳐져 있다.
(B) 몇몇 벤치들이 그늘진 곳에 설치되어 있다.
(C) 몇몇 담요들이 잔디 위에 놓여 있다.
(D) 덤불이 건물 바깥에 줄지어 있다.

해설 배경 사진 – 실외 공간
(A) 상태 묘사 오답: 파라솔은 펼쳐져 있지(have been left open) 않다.
(B) 위치 묘사 오답: 벤치는 그늘진 곳에(in a shaded area) 놓여 있지 않다.
(C) 사진에 없는 명사를 이용한 오답: 사진에 담요 (blankets)가 보이지 않는다.
(D) 정답: 덤불(bushes)이 건물 바깥에 줄지어 있는(line the outside of a building) 모습이므로 정답이다.

어휘 shaded 그늘진   blanket 담요   bush 덤불

4
M-Au

(A) A bicycle is parked near a tree.
(B) A person is riding a bicycle.
(C) A lamppost is being taken down.
(D) One of the people is getting into a car.

(A) 자전거가 나무 근처에 주차되어 있다.
(B) 한 사람이 자전거를 타고 있다.
(C) 가로등이 철거되고 있다.
(D) 사람들 중 한 명이 차에 타고 있다.

해설 인물·사물 혼합 사진 – 길거리
(A) 정답: 자전거가 나무 근처에 주차되어 있는(is parked) 모습이므로 정답이다.
(B) 동작 묘사 오답: 자전거를 타고 있는(is riding) 사람은 없다.
(C) 상황 묘사 오답: 가로등(lamppost)이 철거되고 있는(is being taken down) 모습이 아니다.

(D) 동작 묘사 오답: 차에 타고 있는(is getting into a car) 사람은 보이지 않는다.

어휘 lamppost 가로등   take down 철거하다

5

W-Am

(A) A walkway runs alongside a body of water.
(B) A rock wall surrounds a group of trees.
(C) Some boats are sailing into a harbor.
(D) Some benches have been set up in a grassy area.

(A) 산책로가 물가를 따라 이어져 있다.
(B) 돌담이 나무 무리를 둘러싸고 있다.
(C) 몇몇 보트들이 항구로 들어가고 있다.
(D) 몇몇 벤치들이 잔디밭에 설치되어 있다.

해설 배경 사진 - 강변
(A) 정답: 산책로가 물가를 따라 이어져 있는(runs alongside) 모습이므로 정답이다.
(B) 상태 묘사 오답: 돌담이 나무 무리를 둘러싸고 있는(surrounds) 모습이 아니다.
(C) 사진에 없는 명사를 이용한 오답: 사진에 보트(boats)가 보이지 않는다.
(D) 사진에 없는 명사를 이용한 오답: 사진에 벤치(benches)가 보이지 않는다.

어휘 walkway 산책로, 보도   a body of water 강, 호수; 수역
harbor 항구   grassy 풀로 덮인

6

W-Am

(A) The keyboards on the desks are being replaced.
(B) The carpet is being vacuumed.
(C) None of the workstations are occupied.
(D) Some chairs have been stacked.

(A) 책상 위의 키보드들이 교체되고 있다.
(B) 카펫이 진공청소기로 청소되고 있다.
(C) 어떤 작업대도 사용되고 있지 않다.
(D) 몇몇 의자들이 쌓여 있다.

해설 사물 사진 - 컴퓨터실
(A) 상황 묘사 오답: 키보드가 교체되고 있는(are being replaced) 모습이 아니다.
(B) 상황 묘사 오답: 카펫이 청소되고 있는(is being vacuumed) 모습이 아니다.
(C) 정답: 작업대가 모두 비어 있는(None ~ are occupied) 모습이므로 정답이다.
(D) 상태 묘사 오답: 사진에 의자는 있지만 쌓여 있는(have been stacked) 모습이 아니다.

어휘 replace 교체하다   vacuum 진공청소기로 청소하다
workstation 작업대   occupy 사용하다   stack 쌓다

7

M-Cn

(A) Some ceiling lights have been turned on.
(B) Some chairs are facing a window.
(C) Some paintings are leaning against a piano.
(D) Some coats have been hung on a rack.

(A) 몇몇 천장 조명들이 켜져 있다.
(B) 몇몇 의자들이 창문을 향하고 있다.
(C) 몇몇 그림들이 피아노에 기대어져 있다.
(D) 몇몇 코트들이 걸이에 걸려 있다.

해설 사물 사진 - 실내 공간
(A) 정답: 천장에 있는 조명들이 켜져 있는(have been turned on) 모습이므로 정답이다.
(B) 사진에 없는 명사를 이용한 오답: 사진에 창문(window)이 보이지 않는다.
(C) 사진에 없는 명사를 이용한 오답: 사진에 그림(paintings)이 보이지 않는다.
(D) 사진에 없는 명사를 이용한 오답: 사진에 코트(coats)가 보이지 않는다.

어휘 ceiling 천장   face 향하다, 마주보다   rack 걸이, 선반

8

W-Am

(A) The door of a truck has been left open.
(B) Some tree branches are stacked next to a fence.
(C) A man is repairing the tire on a truck.
(D) Some leaves have been raked into a pile.

(A) 트럭 문이 열려 있다.
(B) 나뭇가지들이 울타리 옆에 쌓여 있다.
(C) 한 남자가 트럭의 타이어를 수리하고 있다.
(D) 나뭇잎들이 더미로 모아져 있다.

해설 인물·사물 혼합 사진 - 숲
(A) 정답: 트럭 문이 열려 있는(has been left open) 모습이므로 정답이다.
(B) 사진에 없는 명사를 이용한 오답: 사진에 울타리(fence)가 없다.
(C) 동작 묘사 오답: 남자가 타이어를 수리하고 있는(is repairing) 모습이 아니다.
(D) 상태 묘사 오답: 나뭇잎들이 갈퀴로 모아져 있는(have been raked) 모습이 아니다.

어휘 branch 나뭇가지   rake (갈퀴 따위로) 모으다

9

W-Br

(A) Some cars are passing through an intersection.
(B) Some cyclists have stopped in the middle of a road.
(C) A man is walking through a field.
(D) A man is waiting to cross the street.

(A) 차 몇 대가 교차로를 지나고 있다.
(B) 몇몇 자전거 타는 사람들이 도로 한가운데 멈춰 섰다.
(C) 한 남자가 들판을 가로질러 걷고 있다.
(D) 한 남자가 길을 건너려고 기다리고 있다.

해설 인물·사물 혼합 사진 – 도로
(A) 상태 묘사 오답: 차 몇 대가 보이지만 교차로를 지나고 (pass through) 있지 않다.
(B) 사진에 없는 명사를 이용한 오답: 사진에 자전거 타는 사람들(cyclists)은 보이지 않는다.
(C) 장소 묘사 오답: 사진 속 장소는 들판(field)이 아니다.
(D) 정답: 남자가 길을 건너려고 기다리고(is waiting to cross) 있는 모습이므로 정답이다.

어휘 field 들판

10

W-Br

(A) A rolled-up rug is standing in a corner.
(B) A tapestry has been hung up on a wall.
(C) There are some magazines scattered on the floor.
(D) There is a basket on a piece of furniture.

(A) 말아 놓은 깔개가 구석에 세워져 있다.
(B) 태피스트리가 벽에 걸려 있다.
(C) 몇몇 잡지들이 바닥에 흩어져 있다.
(D) 가구 위에 바구니가 있다.

해설 사물 사진 – 거실
(A) 상태 묘사 오답: 사진에 깔개(rug)는 보이지만 세워져 있는(is standing) 모습이 아니다.
(B) 사진에 없는 명사를 이용한 오답: 벽에 태피스트리(tapestry)가 보이지 않는다.
(C) 상태 묘사 오답: 잡지는 바닥에 흩어져 있지(scattered) 않다.
(D) 정답: 가구 위에(on a piece of furniture) 바구니가 있으므로 정답이다.

어휘 rolled-up 둥글게 말린 rug 깔개, 카펫
tapestry 태피스트리, 색실로 그림을 짜 넣은 직물
furniture 가구

11

W-Am

(A) Some trash bins have been placed side by side.
(B) Some leaves are gathered in a pile.
(C) A ladder is leaning against a roof.
(D) A sign has fallen onto the ground.

(A) 몇몇 쓰레기통들이 나란히 놓여 있다.
(B) 나뭇잎들이 무더기로 모아져 있다.
(C) 사다리가 지붕에 기대어져 있다.
(D) 표지판이 땅에 쓰러져 있다.

해설 배경 사진 – 공원
(A) 정답: 쓰레기통들이 나란히 놓여 있는(have been placed side by side) 모습이므로 정답이다.
(B) 사진에 없는 명사를 이용한 오답: 사진에 모아져 있는 나뭇잎들(leaves)이 보이지 않는다.
(C) 사진에 없는 명사를 이용한 오답: 사진에 사다리(ladder)가 보이지 않는다.
(D) 상태 묘사 오답: 표지판이 땅에 쓰러져 있는(has fallen onto the ground) 모습이 아니다.

어휘 trash bin 쓰레기통 side by side 나란히

12

M-Au

(A) One of the women is lifting a piece of luggage.
(B) One of the women is seated on a bench.
(C) A bus is driving down a road.
(D) A backpack has been propped against a suitcase.

(A) 여자들 중 한 명이 짐을 들어 올리고 있다.
(B) 여자들 중 한 명이 벤치에 앉아 있다.
(C) 버스가 도로를 주행하고 있다.
(D) 배낭이 여행가방에 기대어져 있다.

해설 인물·사물 혼합 사진 – 버스 터미널
(A) 동작 묘사 오답: 사진에 짐을 들어 올리고 있는(is lifting) 사람은 없다.
(B) 정답: 한 여자가 벤치에 앉아 있는(is seated) 모습이므로 정답이다.
(C) 상태 묘사 오답: 버스가 도로를 주행하고 있는(is driving) 모습이 아니다.
(D) 위치 묘사 오답: 배낭은 여행가방에 기대어져 있지(has been propped against) 않고 한 여자가 메고 있다.

어휘 luggage 짐 be propped against ~에 기대어져 있다

PART 2
LISTENING COMPREHENSION

UNIT 03 Who/What/Which 의문문

1 Who 의문문

ETS CHECK UP 본책 p.038

1 (C) 2 (B) 3 (C) 4 (A) 5 (C)

1 W-Br / M-Au
Who can bring the clients upstairs?
(A) They're available online.
(B) No, I'm afraid not.
(C) The receptionist is planning to.

누가 고객들을 위층으로 데려올 수 있죠?
(A) 그것들은 온라인에서 이용할 수 있어요.
(B) 아니요, 아니에요.
(C) 접수원이 할 예정이에요.

해설 고객 인솔자를 묻는 Who 의문문
(A) 관련 없는 오답: 질문과 상관없는 답변을 제시하고 있다.
(B) Yes/No 대답 불가 오답: 의문사 의문문에 Yes/No로 답변한 오답이다.
(C) 정답: 누가 고객들을 위층으로 데려올지 묻는 질문에 구체적인 직책(receptionist)으로 답하고 있으므로 정답이다.

어휘 upstairs 위층으로 available 이용할 수 있는 receptionist 접수원 plan to ~할 예정이다

2 M-Cn / W-Am
Who's getting the lunch order today?
(A) Sometime after three.
(B) Adam offered to go.
(C) On the top shelf.

오늘 주문한 점심은 누가 갖고 오죠?
(A) 3시 이후예요.
(B) 아담이 가겠다고 했어요.
(C) 맨 위 선반에요.

해설 점심을 가져올 사람을 묻는 Who 의문문
(A) 관련 없는 오답: Who 의문문이 아닌 When 의문문에 어울리는 대답이다.
(B) 정답: Who 의문문에 구체적인 이름(Adam)으로 답하고 있으므로 정답이다.
(C) 관련 없는 오답: Who 의문문이 아닌 Where 의문문에 어울리는 대답이다.

어휘 shelf 선반

3 W-Am / W-Br
Who came up with our new slogan?
(A) It went pretty well.
(B) This escalator goes down.
(C) Someone on the marketing team.

누가 우리 새 슬로건을 생각해 냈나요?
(A) 꽤 순조로웠어요.
(B) 이 에스컬레이터는 내려가요.
(C) 마케팅팀 팀원이요.

해설 슬로건을 고안한 사람을 묻는 Who 의문문
(A) 연상 작용 오답: 질문의 came에서 연상 가능한 went를 이용한 오답이다.
(B) 연상 작용 오답: 질문의 came과 up에서 연상 가능한 goes와 down을 이용한 오답이다.
(C) 정답: 새 슬로건을 생각해 낸 사람을 묻는 질문에 마케팅팀 팀원(Someone on the marketing team)이라고 특정 소속을 언급하고 있으므로 정답이다.

어휘 come up with 생각해 내다

4 M-Cn / W-Am
Who do you think we should offer the position to?
(A) I'm having a hard time deciding.
(B) Yes, I think we should.
(C) Leave it in the "off" position.

우리가 그 자리를 누구에게 제안해야 한다고 생각하세요?
(A) 전 결정하기 힘드네요.
(B) 네, 그래야 할 것 같아요.
(C) 그것을 "꺼짐" 위치에 두세요.

해설 적임자를 묻는 Who 의문문
(A) 정답: 누구에게 자리를 제안할지 묻는 질문에 결정하기 힘들다(I'm having a hard time deciding)는 불확실성 표현으로 응답하고 있으므로 정답이다.
(B) 단어 반복·Yes/No 대답 불가 오답: 질문의 think와 we should를 그대로 반복해 혼동을 유발하고, 의문사 의문문에 Yes/No로 답변한 오답이다.
(C) 단어 반복·유사 발음 오답: 질문의 position을 반복하고 offer와 부분적으로 발음이 유사한 off를 사용한 오답이다.

어휘 position 자리, 직위 have a hard time -ing ~하느라 힘든 시간을 보내다 decide 결정하다

5 W-Br / M-Cn
Who's managing the bookstore tomorrow?
(A) Mostly history and art books.
(B) At ten A.M.
(C) I just posted the staff schedule.

내일 서점 관리는 누가 하나요?
(A) 대부분 역사와 미술 서적이에요.
(B) 오전 10시예요.
(C) 방금 제가 직원 일정표를 올렸어요.

해설 서점 운영자를 묻는 Who 의문문
(A) 연상 작용 오답: 질문의 bookstore에서 연상 가능한 books를 이용한 오답이다.
(B) 관련 없는 오답: 시간을 묻는 When 의문문에 적합한 대답이다.
(C) 정답: 내일 서점 관리는 누가 하느냐는 질문에 '방금 직원 일정표를 올렸다'라고 우회적으로 답변한 정답이다.

어휘 post 올리다, 게시하다

❷ What / Which 의문문

✔ ETS CHECK UP 본책 p.039

| 1 (B) | 2 (A) | 3 (A) | 4 (B) | 5 (B) |

1 M-Au / W-Br
What happens at the weekly meetings?
(A) In the conference room.
(B) We get project updates.
(C) I was sitting near the front.

주간 회의에선 뭘 하죠?
(A) 회의실에서요.
(B) 프로젝트 관련 새 소식을 얻어요.
(C) 저는 앞쪽 가까이에 앉아 있었어요.

해설 회의에서 무엇을 하는지 묻는 What 의문문
(A) 연상 작용 오답: 질문의 meetings에서 연상 가능한 conference를 이용한 오답이다.
(B) 정답: 회의에서 무엇을 하는지 묻는 질문에 프로젝트 관련 새 소식(project updates)을 얻는다고 알려 주고 있으므로 정답이다.
(C) 관련 없는 오답: 질문과 상관없는 답변을 제시하고 있다.

어휘 front 앞쪽

2 W-Am / M-Cn
Which of these companies is accepting résumés?
(A) Only the first three on the list.
(B) Luca bought tickets already.
(C) No, she didn't receive it.

이 회사들 중 어느 곳에서 이력서를 받고 있나요?
(A) 목록에서 첫 세 군데만요.
(B) 루카는 이미 티켓을 샀어요.
(C) 아니요, 그녀는 그것을 못 받았어요.

해설 이력서 수락 회사를 묻는 Which 의문문
(A) 정답: 어느 회사에서 이력서를 받고 있는지 묻는 질문에 목록에서 첫 세 군데만(Only the first three on the list)이라며 구체적으로 응답하고 있으므로 정답이다.
(B) 관련 없는 오답: 질문과 상관없는 답변을 제시하고 있다.
(C) Yes/No 불가 오답: Which 의문문은 Yes/No 응답이 불가능하다.

어휘 accept 받아 주다 résumé 이력서

3 W-Am / M-Cn
What time does the train arrive?
(A) It should be here soon.
(B) Yes, I think it might rain.
(C) No, I won't have time.

기차가 몇 시에 도착하나요?
(A) 곧 올 거예요.
(B) 네, 비가 올 것 같아요.
(C) 아니요, 전 시간이 없을 거예요.

해설 기차 도착 시간을 묻는 What 의문문
(A) 정답: 기차 도착 시각을 묻는 질문에 곧 올 것이라고 대략적인 도착 시점을 알려주고 있으므로 정답이다.
(B) 유사 발음 오답: 질문의 train과 부분적으로 발음이 유사한 rain을 이용한 오답이다.
(C) 단어 반복 오답: 질문의 time을 반복 이용한 오답이다.

4 W-Am / W-Br
Which company developed this software?
(A) No, it's too difficult.
(B) I'll look it up.
(C) Quite recently.

어떤 회사가 이 소프트웨어를 개발했죠?
(A) 아니요, 그건 너무 어려워요.
(B) 제가 찾아볼게요.
(C) 꽤 최근에요.

해설 소프트웨어 개발 회사를 묻는 Which 의문문
(A) Yes/No 대답 불가 오답: Which 의문문을 포함한 대부분의 의문사 의문문은 Yes/No로 응답할 수 없다.
(B) 정답: 어떤 회사가 소프트웨어를 개발했는지 묻는 질문에 그 회사를 찾아보겠다(I'll look it up)고 우회적 응답을 하고 있으므로 정답이다.
(C) 관련 없는 오답: When 의문문에 대한 응답으로, 질문 후반부의 developed this software만 들으면 고를 수 있는 오답이다.

어휘 develop 개발하다 look up (자료·컴퓨터 등에서 정보를) 찾아보다

5 W-Br / M-Cn
What do you think of this month's budget?
(A) Yes, this month.
(B) Looks like we need money.
(C) Thanks, it was a gift.

이번 달 예산에 대해 어떻게 생각하십니까?
(A) 네, 이번 달이요.
(B) 돈이 필요할 것 같아요.
(C) 감사해요, 그건 선물이었어요.

해설 의견을 묻는 What 의문문
(A) 단어 반복 오답: 질문의 this month를 반복 이용한 오답이다.
(B) 정답: 예산에 대해 어떻게 생각하는지 묻는 질문에 대한 의견, 즉 사실상 예산이 부족하다는 의미를 간접적으로 전

달하고 있으므로 정답이다.
(C) 관련 없는 오답: 질문의 내용과 논리적으로 맞지 않다.

어휘 budget 예산

ETS 유형 연습
본책 p.040

1 (C) **2** (A) **3** (A) **4** (B) **5** (B)

---

1 M-Cn / W-Am

Who designed the floor plan?
(A) They're affordable.
(B) Only three floors.
(C) Mr. Bryson did.

누가 평면도를 설계했나요?
(A) 그것들은 가격이 적당해요.
(B) 단지 3개 층입니다.
(C) 브라이슨 씨가 했습니다.

해설 평면도 설계자를 묻는 Who 의문문
(A) 관련 없는 오답: Who 의문문인데, 가격에 대한 답을 하고 있으므로 논리적으로 맞지 않다.
(B) 단어 반복 오답: 질문의 floor를 반복한 오답이다.
(C) 정답: 누가 평면도를 설계했는지 묻는 질문에 대해 구체적인 이름(Mr. Bryson)으로 대답하고 있다.

어휘 floor plan (건물의) 평면도 affordable (가격이) 적당한

---

2 M-Au / W-Am

What's included in the rent?
(A) Electricity and water.
(B) On Atlantic Avenue.
(C) She lent me her bicycle.

임대료에 뭐가 포함되나요?
(A) 전기와 수도요.
(B) 애틀랜틱 대로에서요.
(C) 그녀는 제게 자전거를 빌려줬어요.

해설 임대료에 포함된 것을 묻는 What 의문문
(A) 정답: 임대료에 무엇이 포함되는지 묻는 질문에 전기와 수도(Electricity and water)라고 구체적으로 답변한 정답이다.
(B) 관련 없는 오답: 장소를 묻는 Where 의문문에 가능한 답변이다.
(C) 유사 발음 오답: 질문의 rent와 발음이 유사한 lent를 이용한 오답이다.

어휘 include 포함하다 electricity 전기

---

3 W-Br / M-Cn

Which carpet was replaced recently?
(A) The one in the hallway.
(B) Yes, I'd like to.
(C) Place it on the counter.

어떤 카펫이 최근에 교체되었죠?
(A) 복도에 있는 거요.
(B) 네, 그러고 싶어요.
(C) 카운터 위에 놓아주세요.

해설 최근 교체된 카펫을 묻는 Which 의문문
(A) 정답: 최근에 교체된 카펫을 묻는 질문에 복도에 있는 것(The one in the hallway)이라며 장소를 지칭해 구체적으로 응답하고 있다.
(B) Yes/No 대답 불가 오답: Which 의문문을 포함한 대부분의 의문사 의문문은 Yes/No로 응답할 수 없다.
(C) 관련 없는 오답: 질문과 상관없는 답변이다.

어휘 replace 교체하다 recently 최근에 hallway 복도 place 놓다

---

4 M-Cn / W-Br

What's the topic of today's seminar?
(A) In an hour.
(B) I'm not sure.
(C) No, on the bottom.

오늘 세미나의 주제는 무엇입니까?
(A) 한 시간 뒤에요.
(B) 잘 모르겠어요.
(C) 아니요, 바닥에요.

해설 세미나 주제를 묻는 What 의문문
(A) 관련 없는 오답: 시간을 묻는 When 의문문에 가능한 답변이다.
(B) 정답: 세미나의 주제를 묻는 질문에 모른다고 답변한 정답이다.
(C) Yes/No 대답 불가 오답: 의문사 의문문은 Yes/No로 대답할 수 없다.

---

5 W-Am / M-Au

Who's available to help me contact potential investors?
(A) A coupon for five percent off.
(B) I know Bianca is free this morning.
(C) Thousands of dollars.

제가 잠재적인 투자자들과 연락하는 걸 누가 도와주실 수 있나요?
(A) 5퍼센트 할인 쿠폰이에요.
(B) 비앙카가 오늘 오전에 한가하다고 알고 있어요.
(C) 수천 달러요.

해설 업무를 도와줄 사람을 묻는 Who 의문문
(A) 관련 없는 오답: 질문과 상관없는 답변을 제시하고 있다.
(B) 정답: 잠재적인 투자자들과 연락하는 걸 누가 도와줄 수 있는지 묻는 질문에, 구체적인 이름(Bianca)을 들어 답변하고 있으므로 정답이다.
(C) 관련 없는 오답: 금액을 묻는 How much 의문문에 어울리는 답변이다.

어휘 available 시간이 되는 potential 잠재적인 investor 투자자

ETS 실전 문제
본책 p.041

1 (B)	2 (A)	3 (B)	4 (B)	5 (A)
6 (B)	7 (A)	8 (C)	9 (A)	10 (C)
11 (B)	12 (B)	13 (B)	14 (C)	15 (A)
16 (B)	17 (C)	18 (B)	19 (A)	20 (A)
21 (B)	22 (A)	23 (B)	24 (C)	25 (A)

1 M-Cn / W-Br

Who's leading the new project?
(A) I already read that one.
(B) Ms. Azuma is.
(C) Several years ago.

새로운 프로젝트는 누가 이끌고 있나요?
(A) 그건 이미 읽었어요.
(B) 아즈마 씨요.
(C) 몇 년 전에요.

해설 프로젝트의 리더를 묻는 Who 의문문
(A) 유사 발음 오답: 질문의 leading과 부분적으로 발음이 비슷한 read를 이용한 오답이다.
(B) 정답: 프로젝트의 리더를 묻는 질문에 구체적으로 Ms. Azuma라는 사람 이름을 언급하므로 정답이다.
(C) 관련 없는 오답: Who 의문문이 아닌 When 의문문에 어울리는 대답이다.

2 M-Au / W-Am

What are you bringing to the office party?
(A) A cheese platter.
(B) I don't know if they did.
(C) No, I took the stairs.

사무실 파티에 무엇을 가져오실 건가요?
(A) 치즈 플래터요.
(B) 그들이 했는지 모르겠어요.
(C) 아니요, 저는 계단으로 왔어요.

해설 파티에 가져올 음식을 묻는 What 의문문
(A) 정답: 사무실 파티에 무엇을 가져올지 묻는 질문에 구체적인 음식의 종류(cheese platter)를 제시하고 있다.
(B) 인칭 오류·관련 없는 오답: 의문문에 they를 가리킬 만한 대상이 없고, 질문과 상관없는 답변을 제시하고 있다.
(C) 관련 없는 오답: 질문과 상관없는 답변이다.

3 W-Br / M-Cn

Which path do I take to get to the lake?
(A) Here, I'll take it.
(B) The one on the left.
(C) Swimming and boating.

호수에 가려면 어느 길로 가야 하나요?
(A) 자, 제가 받을게요.
(B) 왼쪽 길이요.
(C) 수영과 뱃놀이요.

해설 호수로 가는 길을 묻는 Which 의문문
(A) 단어 반복 오답: 질문의 take를 반복 이용한 오답이다.
(B) 정답: 호수에 가려면 어느 길로 가야 하는지 묻는 질문에 왼쪽에 있는 것(The one on the left)이라며 구체적으로 응답하고 있으므로 정답이다.
(C) 연상 작용 오답: 질문의 lake와 의미상 연결이 가능한 단어 swimming과 boating을 이용하여 혼동을 준 오답이다.

어휘 path 길 lake 호수 boating 뱃놀이

4 M-Cn / W-Br

What would you like on your cheeseburger?
(A) The table is only set for three.
(B) Lettuce, tomatoes, and onion.
(C) Yes, I'll have the soup.

치즈버거에 무엇을 넣어 드릴까요?
(A) 테이블이 세 명만을 위해 차려져 있어요.
(B) 양상추, 토마토 그리고 양파요.
(C) 네, 저는 수프를 먹을게요.

해설 버거에 넣을 내용물을 묻는 What 의문문
(A) 연상 작용 오답: 질문의 cheeseburger에서 연상 가능한 table을 이용한 오답이다.
(B) 정답: 치즈버거에 무엇을 넣을지 묻는 질문에 구체적인 재료의 이름을 제시하고 있으므로 정답이다.
(C) 연상 작용 오답·Yes/No 대답 불가 오답: 질문의 cheeseburger에서 연상 가능한 soup를 이용해 혼동을 주었고, 의문사 의문문에 Yes/No로 답변한 오답이다.

어휘 lettuce (양)상추

5 W-Am / M-Cn

Who's going to pick up the guest speakers for today's all-staff meeting?
(A) Andrey volunteered to do it.
(B) No, they weren't.
(C) That's an interesting idea.

오늘 전 직원 회의에 초청 연사를 누가 모셔 올 건가요?
(A) 안드레이가 자원해서 하기로 했어요.
(B) 아니요, 그들이 아니었어요.
(C) 흥미로운 아이디어네요.

해설 초청 연사를 데려올 사람을 묻는 Who 의문문
(A) 정답: 회의에 초청 연사를 누가 데려올 건지 묻는 질문에 구체적으로 Andrey라는 사람 이름을 언급하므로 정답이다.
(B) Yes/No 대답 불가 오답: 의문사 의문문에 Yes/No로 답변한 오답이다.
(C) 연상 작용 오답: 질문의 meeting에서 연상 가능한 idea를 이용한 오답이다.

어휘 volunteer 자원하다

6 W-Br / W-Am
What are your store's hours of operation?
(A) That's a great opportunity!
(B) We're open weekdays from nine to five.
(C) We don't have any more in stock.

여기 상점의 영업 시간이 어떻게 되나요?
(A) 아주 좋은 기회네요!
(B) 평일 9시부터 5시까지 엽니다.
(C) 더 이상 재고가 없어요.

해설 영업 시간을 묻는 What 의문문
(A) 관련 없는 오답: 질문 내용과 관련 없는 대답이다.
(B) 정답: 영업 시간을 묻는 질문에 구체적인 시간 표현인 weekdays from nine to five라고 대답하고 있다.
(C) 연상 작용 오답: 질문의 store에서 연상 가능한 stock을 이용한 오답이다.

어휘 hours of operation 영업 시간   opportunity 기회
weekdays 주중에, 평일에   in stock 재고로

7 M-Cn / M-Au
Who will the hotel hire to remodel the lobby?
(A) We just sent out a request for proposals.
(B) That never occurred to me before.
(C) Yes, the colors are appealing.

호텔에서 로비를 개조하는 데 누구를 고용할 건가요?
(A) 방금 입찰 요청서를 보냈어요.
(B) 그건 전에 생각해 본 적이 없어요.
(C) 네, 색상이 매력적이네요.

해설 특정 주체를 묻는 Who 의문문
(A) 정답: 호텔에서 로비 개조에 누구를 고용할지 묻는 질문에 방금 입찰 요청서를 보냈다며 아직 정해지지 않았음을 우회적으로 표현하고 있다.
(B) 관련 없는 오답: 질문과 상관없는 답변이다.
(C) 연상 작용 오답·Yes/No 대답 불가 오답: 질문의 remodel에서 연상 가능한 colors를 이용해 혼동을 주었고, 의문사 의문문에 Yes/No로 답변한 오답이다.

어휘 request for proposal 입찰 요청서
occur (생각이) 떠오르다   appealing 매력적인

8 M-Cn / M-Au
What time does the aquarium close?
(A) In the center of the room.
(B) I live on the first floor.
(C) At seven P.M. on weekdays.

몇 시에 수족관이 폐장하나요?
(A) 방 중앙에서요.
(B) 저는 1층에 살아요.
(C) 평일에는 오후 7시예요.

해설 수족관 폐장 시점을 묻는 What time 의문문
(A) 관련 없는 오답: 위치를 묻는 Where 의문문에 적합한 대답이다.
(B) 관련 없는 오답: 위치를 묻는 Where 의문문에 적합한 대답이다.
(C) 정답: 수족관이 폐장하는 시간을 묻는 질문에 평일에는 오후 7시라며 구체적인 시간을 알려주고 있으므로 정답이다.

9 W-Br / M-Cn
Who needs a parking permit?
(A) I don't drive.
(B) Food is not allowed in the library.
(C) No, the park is closed today.

누가 주차증이 필요하죠?
(A) 저는 운전 안 해요.
(B) 도서관에서는 음식이 허용되지 않습니다.
(C) 아니요, 공원은 오늘 문을 닫아요.

해설 특정 주체를 묻는 Who 의문문
(A) 정답: 주차증이 필요한 사람이 누구인지 묻는 질문에 자신은 운전을 하지 않는다고 하며 주차증이 필요 없다는 것을 우회적으로 답변하고 있다.
(B) 연상 작용 오답: 질문의 permit에서 연상 가능한 allowed를 이용한 오답이다.
(C) 유사 발음 오답: parking과 일부 발음이 비슷한 park를 이용한 오답이다.

어휘 permit 허가증   allow 허용하다

10 W-Am / M-Au
Which design was chosen for the company letterhead?
(A) The design team.
(B) Earlier this morning.
(C) We haven't decided yet.

회사 레터헤드에 어떤 디자인이 선정되었나요?
(A) 디자인팀이요.
(B) 오늘 아침 일찍요.
(C) 아직 결정하지 못했어요.

해설 선정된 디자인을 묻는 Which 의문문
(A) 단어 반복 오답: 질문의 design을 그대로 반복 이용한 오답이다.
(B) 관련 없는 오답: 시간을 묻는 When 의문문에 가능한 답변이다.
(C) 정답: 선정된 디자인을 묻는 질문에 아직 결정하지 않았다 (We haven't decided yet)는 불확실성 표현으로 응답하고 있으므로 정답이다.

어휘 letterhead 레터헤드(편지 맨 위에 인쇄한 회사명과 주소)
decide 결정하다

11 M-Au / M-Cn
Who'll be in charge of finalizing the contract with Parker Associates?
(A) Not until next month.
(B) That's Jin Hee's project.
(C) Just your signature.

파커 어소시어츠와의 계약 마무리 작업은 누가 맡나요?
(A) 다음 달은 돼야 해요.
(B) 그건 진희의 프로젝트예요.
(C) 서명만 하세요.

해설 담당 주체를 묻는 Who 의문문
(A) 관련 없는 오답: 시간을 묻는 When 의문문에 가능한 답변이다.
(B) 정답: 담당자를 묻는 Who 의문문에 구체적인 이름(Jin Hee)으로 답변한 정답이다.
(C) 연상 작용 오답: 질문의 contract에서 연상 가능한 signature를 이용한 오답이다.

어휘 be in charge of ~을 맡다   contract 계약
not until ~이 돼야 비로소   signature 서명

12 W-Am / M-Cn
What's the phone number for the pharmacy?
(A) A new medication.
(B) It's posted on the bulletin board.
(C) About ten.

약국 전화번호가 어떻게 되나요?
(A) 신약이에요.
(B) 게시판에 붙어 있어요.
(C) 10개 정도요.

해설 전화번호를 묻는 What 의문문
(A) 연상 작용 오답: 질문의 pharmacy에서 연상 가능한 medication을 이용한 오답이다.
(B) 정답: 약국의 전화번호를 묻는 질문에 게시판에 게시되어 있다(It's posted on the bulletin board)고 우회적 응답을 하고 있으므로 정답이다.
(C) 연상 작용 오답: 질문의 number에서 연상 가능한 ten을 이용한 오답이다.

어휘 pharmacy 약국   medication 약
bulletin board 게시판

13 W-Am / M-Au
Which of you approved this loan application?
(A) I can lend you some.
(B) John okayed it.
(C) It was hard to prove.

여러분 중에 누가 이 대출 신청을 승인하셨죠?
(A) 제가 좀 빌려드릴 수 있습니다.
(B) 존이 승인했어요.
(C) 그건 입증하기 어려웠어요.

해설 인물 선택을 묻는 Which 의문문
(A) 연상 작용 오답: 질문의 loan에서 연상 가능한 lend를 이용한 오답이다.
(B) 정답: 누가 했는지 묻는 Which 의문문에 John이라는 구체적인 인물로 응답하고 있으므로 정답이다.
(C) 유사 발음 오답: 질문의 approved와 부분적으로 발음이 유사한 prove를 이용한 오답이다.

어휘 approve 승인하다   loan 대출   application 신청
lend 빌려주다   okay 승인하다, 허락하다
prove 입증하다, 증명하다

14 W-Am / M-Au
Who was selected to work on the advertising project?
(A) A great success.
(B) It's a popular brand.
(C) I haven't heard.

누가 광고 프로젝트 일에 선정되었나요?
(A) 대성공이에요.
(B) 인기 있는 브랜드예요.
(C) 못 들었어요.

해설 선정된 사람을 묻는 Who 의문문
(A) 관련 없는 오답: 성공 정도를 묻는 How 의문문에 적합한 대답이다.
(B) 연상 작용 오답: 질문의 advertising에서 연상 가능한 brand를 이용한 오답이다.
(C) 정답: 선정된 사람이 누구인지 묻는 질문에, 아직 못 들었다(I haven't heard)는 우회적인 대답으로 불확실함을 표현하고 있으므로 정답이다.

어휘 select 선정하다   advertising 광고

15 W-Am / M-Cn
Which airline do you usually use?
(A) I haven't flown in quite a while.
(B) A new line of luggage.
(C) Your flight leaves from gate 31.

보통 어느 항공사를 이용하세요?
(A) 한동안 비행기를 안 탔어요.
(B) 새로운 여행 가방 라인이에요.
(C) 당신의 비행기는 31번 게이트에서 출발해요.

해설 이용하는 항공사를 묻는 Which 의문문
(A) 정답: 보통 어느 항공사를 이용하는지 묻는 질문에 한동안 비행기를 안 탔다며 답을 하기 어려움을 우회적으로 말하고 있다.
(B) 유사 발음 오답: 질문의 airline과 발음이 부분적으로 유사한 line을 이용한 오답이다.
(C) 연상 작용 오답: 질문의 airline에서 연상 가능한 flight와 gate를 이용한 오답이다.

어휘 luggage 여행 가방, 수하물

16 W-Am / M-Cn
What's the dress code in this office?
(A) Every day except Friday.
(B) We require business attire.
(C) It doesn't come in that size.

이 사무실은 복장 규정이 어떻게 되나요?
(A) 금요일을 제외하고 매일이요.
(B) 정장을 요구해요.
(C) 그 사이즈는 안 나와요.

해설 **복장 규정을 묻는 What 의문문**
(A) **관련 없는 오답:** 질문과 상관없는 답변이다.
(B) **정답:** 사무실에서의 복장 규정이 무엇인지 묻는 질문에 구체적인 복장 종류(business attire)를 제시하고 있다.
(C) **연상 작용 오답:** 질문의 dress에서 연상 가능한 size를 이용한 오답이다.

어휘 dress code 복장 규정 except ~을 제외한
attire 의상

17 M-Cn / W-Br
Who's going to introduce the speaker?
(A) About starting a business.
(B) In the auditorium.
(C) Isn't Mr. Sato doing it?

연사는 누가 소개하죠?
(A) 창업에 관해서요.
(B) 강당에서요.
(C) 사토 씨가 하는 거 아닌가요?

해설 **연사를 소개할 사람을 묻는 Who 의문문**
(A) **연상 작용 오답:** 질문의 speaker에서 연상 가능한 연설 주제(About starting a business)를 이용한 오답이다.
(B) **연상 작용 오답:** 질문의 speaker에서 연상 가능한 auditorium을 이용한 오답이다.
(C) **정답:** 누가 연사를 소개할지 묻는 질문에 대해 구체적인 이름(Mr. Sato)을 대며 되묻고 있으므로 정답이다.

어휘 start a business 사업을 시작하다 auditorium 강당

18 M-Cn / W-Br
Which factory makes the kitchen sets?
(A) Several stainless steel appliances.
(B) The one in Shelbyville.
(C) About 400 dollars.

어느 공장에서 주방 세트를 만드나요?
(A) 몇몇 스테인리스 기기요.
(B) 셸비빌에 있는 곳에서요.
(C) 400달러 정도요.

해설 **주방 세트 제조 공장을 묻는 Which 의문문**
(A) **연상 작용 오답:** 의미상 연결이 가능한 두 단어 factory와 stainless steel appliances를 이용한 오답이다.
(B) **정답:** 어느 공장에서 주방 세트를 만드는지 묻는 질문에 구체적인 위치(The one in Shelbyville)로 응답하고 있으므로 정답이다.
(C) **연상 작용 오답:** 질문의 kitchen sets에서 연상 가능한 제품의 가격 400 dollars를 이용한 오답이다.

어휘 appliance (가정용) 기기

19 W-Am / M-Cn
What happened to those files we worked on?
(A) John is reviewing them.
(B) Wednesday would work for me.
(C) Yes, they'll do it.

우리가 작업한 파일들은 어떻게 됐나요?
(A) 존이 검토하고 있어요.
(B) 전 수요일 괜찮아요.
(C) 네, 그들이 할 거예요.

해설 **파일이 어떻게 되었는지 묻는 What 의문문**
(A) **정답:** 작업한 파일들이 어떻게 됐는지 묻는 질문에 존이 가지고 있다고 우회적으로 답변한 정답이다.
(B) **단어 반복 오답:** 질문의 work를 반복 이용한 오답이다.
(C) **Yes/No 대답 불가 오답:** 의문사 의문문에 Yes/No로 대답할 수 없다.

어휘 review 검토하다

20 M-Cn / M-Au
Who should I tell if I need to leave early?
(A) Let your supervisor know.
(B) For a dentist appointment.
(C) About two o'clock.

일찍 퇴근하려면 누구에게 말해야 하나요?
(A) 당신 상사에게 알리세요.
(B) 치과 예약 때문에요.
(C) 2시쯤이요.

해설 **대상을 묻는 Who 의문문**
(A) **정답:** 누구에게 말해야 하는지 묻는 질문에 구체적인 인물(your supervisor)을 알려 주고 있으므로 정답이다.
(B) **연상 작용 오답:** 질문의 leave에서 연상 가능한 appointment를 이용하여 혼동을 유발하고, Why 의문문에 적절한 답변이다.
(C) **관련 없는 오답:** 시간을 묻는 When 의문문에 가능한 답변이다.

어휘 let A know A에게 알리다 supervisor 상사, 감독관
appointment (진료) 예약

21 M-Cn / W-Am
What kind of decoration would you like on the tables?
(A) No, there's no assembly required.
(B) Just some fresh flowers.
(C) Anywhere on the counter, please.

테이블에 어떤 장식을 원하시나요?
(A) 아니요, 조립은 필요 없어요.
(B) 그냥 싱싱한 꽃 몇 송이만요.
(C) 카운터 위 아무데나요.

해설 **장식 종류를 묻는 What 의문문**
(A) **Yes/No 대답 불가 오답:** 의문사 의문문에 Yes/No로 대답할 수 없다.
(B) **정답:** 테이블에 할 장식의 종류를 묻는 질문에 구체적인 품목인 fresh flowers라고 대답하고 있다.
(C) **관련 없는 오답:** 장소를 묻는 Where 의문문에 가능한 답변이다.

어휘 decoration 장식 assembly 조립 required 필요한

22 W-Am / M-Cn

Who's going to lead the training session today?
(A) One of the department coordinators.
(B) The train leaves in about an hour.
(C) Yes, it was quite entertaining.

오늘 교육은 누가 진행하나요?
(A) 부서 코디네이터 중 한 명이요.
(B) 기차가 약 한 시간 후에 출발해요.
(C) 네, 꽤 재미있었어요.

해설 교육 진행자를 묻는 Who 의문문
(A) 정답: 누가 교육을 진행하는지 묻는 질문에 부서 코디네이터 중 한 명(One of the department coordinators)이라고 특정 신분을 언급하고 있으므로 정답이다.
(B) 유사 발음 오답: 질문의 training과 부분적으로 발음이 비슷한 train을 이용한 오답이다.
(C) Yes/No 대답 불가 오답: 의문사 의문문에 Yes/No로 대답할 수 없다.

어휘 department 부서 coordinator 코디네이터
entertaining 재미있는

23 M-Au / W-Am

What are the delivery options for mailing this package?
(A) In the conference room.
(B) Overnight or three-day delivery.
(C) Let's shut the window.

이 소포를 부칠 때 배송 선택 사항이 어떻게 되나요?
(A) 회의실에서요.
(B) 익일 또는 3일 배송이에요.
(C) 창문을 닫읍시다.

해설 배송 방법을 묻는 What 의문문
(A) 관련 없는 오답: 장소를 묻는 Where 의문문에 가능한 답변이다.
(B) 정답: 소포의 배송 방법을 묻는 질문에 두 가지 선택 사항(Overnight or three-day delivery)을 제시하고 있다.
(C) 관련 없는 오답: 질문과 상관없는 답변이다.

어휘 delivery 배송 mail 부치다 overnight 익일 (배송)의

24 W-Br / W-Am

Who can help me find the stationery with company letterhead?
(A) We discussed the budget.
(B) The parking garage is full.
(C) The supply closet's by the office manager's desk.

누가 회사 레터헤드가 새겨진 문구류 찾는 일을 도와주실 수 있나요?
(A) 예산에 대해 논의했어요.
(B) 주차장이 만차예요.
(C) 물품 보관함은 사무실 관리자 책상 옆에 있어요.

해설 특정 주체를 묻는 Who 의문문
(A) 관련 없는 오답: 질문과 상관없는 답변이다.
(B) 관련 없는 오답: 질문과 상관없는 답변이다.
(C) 정답: 누가 문구류 찾는 일을 도와줄 수 있는지 묻는 질문에 물품을 찾을 수 있는 위치를 알려주는 답변으로 우회적인 도움을 주고 있다.

어휘 stationery 문구류 letterhead 레터헤드
discuss 논의하다 budget 예산
parking garage 주차장 supply closet 물품 보관함

25 W-Br / W-Am

Which of your dairy products are produced locally?
(A) All of them, I believe.
(B) That's too far away.
(C) The Glenside Grocery Store.

유제품 중 어떤 게 이 지역에서 생산되는 건가요?
(A) 전부 다일 거예요.
(B) 그건 너무 멀어요.
(C) 글렌사이드 식료품점요.

해설 여럿 중 하나를 고르는 Which 의문문
(A) 정답: 어떤 유제품이 이 지역에서 생산되는지를 묻는 질문에 전부 다(All of them)일 것이라고 대답하고 있으므로 정답이다.
(B) 관련 없는 오답: 유제품의 종류에 대한 질문과 의미상 어울리지 않는다.
(C) 연상 작용 오답: 질문의 dairy products(유제품)에서 연상 가능한 Grocery Store(식료품점)를 이용한 오답이다.

어휘 dairy product 유제품 produce 생산하다
locally 현지에서

UNIT 04 When/Where 의문문

1 When 의문문

ETS CHECK UP 본책 p.042

1 (C) **2** (C) **3** (A) **4** (A) **5** (C)

1 W-Am / M-Cn

When does the grocery store close?
(A) He bought fruit.
(B) Close the door, please.
(C) Soon, I think.

식료품점은 언제 문을 닫나요?
(A) 그는 과일을 샀어요.
(B) 문을 닫아 주세요.
(C) 곧 닫을 겁니다.

해설 폐점 시간을 묻는 When 의문문
(A) 연상 작용 오답: 질문의 grocery store에서 연상 가능

한 fruit을 이용한 오답이다.
(B) **단어 반복 오답**: 질문의 close를 반복 이용한 오답이다.
(C) **정답**: 식료품점 폐점 시간을 묻는 질문에 미래 부사 Soon을 사용해 곧 닫는다고 대답하고 있다.

어휘 grocery store 식료품점   close (상점 등이) 문을 닫다, (문·커튼 등을) 닫다   soon 곧, 머지않아

2 M-Cn / W-Br

When's your next dental checkup?
(A) A checking account.
(B) How long have you been here?
(C) **On Wednesday afternoon.**

다음 치과 검진은 언제인가요?
(A) 예금 계좌요.
(B) 여기 오신 지 얼마나 되셨죠?
(C) 수요일 오후요.

해설 검진 시점을 묻는 When 의문문
(A) **유사 발음 오답**: 질문의 checkup과 부분적으로 발음이 유사한 checking을 이용한 오답이다.
(B) **연상 작용 오답**: 질문의 When에서 연상 가능한 How long을 이용한 오답이다.
(C) **정답**: 다음 치과 검진 시점을 묻는 질문에 수요일 오후라며 구체적인 시점을 말하고 있으므로 정답이다.

어휘 checkup 검사   checking account 예금 계좌

3 M-Au / W-Am

When will the construction begin?
(A) On the south side of the building.
(B) Some new offices.
(C) **After the budget is approved.**

공사가 언제 시작되나요?
(A) 건물 남쪽에요.
(B) 새 사무실 몇 군데요.
(C) 예산이 승인된 후에요.

해설 공사 시작 시점을 묻는 When 의문문
(A) **연상 작용 오답**: 질문의 construction에서 연상 가능한 building을 사용한 오답으로, 장소를 묻는 Where 의문문에 어울리는 대답이다.
(B) **연상 작용 오답**: 질문의 construction에서 연상 가능한 new offices를 이용한 오답이다.
(C) **정답**: 공사가 언제 시작되는지 묻는 질문에 예산이 승인된 후(After the budget is approved)라는 우회적 표현으로 시점을 제시하고 있으므로 정답이다.

어휘 construction 공사   budget 예산   approve 승인하다

4 M-Cn / M-Au

When do we need to register for the sales seminar?
(A) **The deadline was last week.**
(B) About 30 euros.
(C) At the registration desk.

영업 세미나 등록은 언제 해야 하나요?
(A) 지난주가 마감일이었어요.
(B) 30유로 정도요.
(C) 등록 데스크에서요.

해설 등록 시점을 묻는 When 의문문
(A) **정답**: 언제 세미나에 등록해야 하는지 묻는 질문에 지난주가 마감일이었다며 이미 등록 시기가 지났다는 것을 우회적으로 전달하고 있다.
(B) **관련 없는 오답**: 가격을 묻는 How much 의문문에 가능한 답변이다.
(C) **파생어 오답**: 질문의 register와 파생어 관계인 registration을 이용한 오답이다.

어휘 register for ~에 등록하다   deadline 마감일   registration 등록

5 W-Am / M-Au

When will you have the results of the customer survey?
(A) Around twenty-five questions.
(B) He's our best customer.
(C) **We just sent it out today.**

고객 설문조사 결과는 언제 받으시나요?
(A) 약 25개 문항이에요.
(B) 그는 우리의 최고 고객이에요.
(C) 오늘 막 발송했어요.

해설 결과 획득 시점을 묻는 When 의문문
(A) **연상 작용 오답**: 의미상 연결이 가능한 두 단어 survey와 questions를 이용한 오답이다.
(B) **단어 반복 오답**: 질문에 사용된 customer를 그대로 반복 이용한 오답이다.
(C) **정답**: 고객 설문조사 결과를 받기까지 아직 멀었다는 것을 우회적으로 표현하고 있다.

어휘 survey (설문)조사   send out 보내다

❷ Where 의문문

✓ ETS CHECK UP 본책 p.043

1 (B)   2 (A)   3 (C)   4 (C)   5 (A)

1 W-Br / W-Am

Where did you store the extra name tags?
(A) Just last week.
(B) **They're in the closet.**
(C) The store was closed.

여분의 명찰은 어디에 보관하셨죠?
(A) 바로 지난주에요.
(B) 벽장 안에 있어요.
(C) 가게가 문을 닫았어요.

해설 보관 장소를 묻는 Where 의문문
(A) **관련 없는 오답**: 시간을 묻는 When 의문문에 적합한 대답이다.
(B) **정답**: 명찰의 보관 장소를 묻는 질문에 벽장(closet)이라

는 구체적인 장소를 언급하고 있다.
(C) 다의어 오답: 서로 다른 의미의 store를 반복 이용한 오답이다. 질문의 store는 '보관하다'라는 뜻의 동사이고, 보기의 store는 '가게'라는 뜻의 명사이다.

어휘 store 보관하다; 가게, 상점 closet 벽장

2 M-Au / M-Cn

Where will the conference be held next month?
(A) I'll send you all the information.
(B) In early May.
(C) The president of the company.

다음 달 컨퍼런스는 어디서 열리나요?
(A) 모든 정보를 보내드릴게요.
(B) 5월 초예요.
(C) 사장님께서요.

해설 회의 개최 장소를 묻는 Where 의문문
(A) **정답**: 컨퍼런스 개최 장소를 묻는 질문에 관련된 모든 정보를 보내주겠다며 우회적으로 답변하고 있다.
(B) **관련 없는 오답**: 시점을 묻는 When 의문문에 적합한 대답이다.
(C) **연상 작용 오답**: 질문의 conference에서 연상 가능한 company를 이용한 오답이다.

어휘 president 사장

3 W-Br / M-Cn

Where was Mr. Wagner yesterday?
(A) The whole department.
(B) No, that's tomorrow.
(C) With a client.

와그너 씨가 어제 어디에 있었나요?
(A) 부서 전체요.
(B) 아니요, 내일이에요.
(C) 고객과 함께 있었어요.

해설 과거 행방을 묻는 Where 의문문
(A) **관련 없는 오답**: 질문의 내용과 답변이 논리적으로 맞지 않다.
(B) **Yes/No 대답 불가 오답**: Where 의문문에는 Yes/No 답변이 불가능하다.
(C) **정답**: 와그너 씨가 어제 어디에 있었는지를 묻는 질문에 고객과 함께 있었다고 하므로 정답이다.

어휘 whole 전체의, 전부의 department 부서 client 고객

4 M-Au / W-Am

Where can I attend an evening course?
(A) Yes, attendance is required.
(B) It's a four-course meal.
(C) The university has some night classes.

어디에서 야간 과정을 들을 수 있죠?
(A) 네, 출석은 필수입니다.
(B) 그건 4코스 식사예요.
(C) 대학에 야간 수업이 좀 있어요.

해설 야간 과정을 들을 수 있는 장소를 묻는 Where 의문문
(A) **파생어 오답**: 질문의 attend와 파생어 관계인 attendance를 이용한 오답이다.
(B) **단어 반복 오답**: 질문의 course를 반복 이용한 오답이다.
(C) **정답**: 야간 과정을 들을 수 있는 곳을 묻는 질문에 대학교(university)라는 구체적인 장소를 언급하고 있으므로 정답이다.

어휘 attend 참석하다 evening course 야간 과정 attendance 참석, 출석 course (식사의 개별) 코스 meal 식사

5 W-Am / M-Cn

Where's the library branch going to be built?
(A) It hasn't been decided yet.
(B) The bill's been sent.
(C) Much larger than the old one.

도서관 분관을 어디에 지을 예정이죠?
(A) 아직 결정되지 않았어요.
(B) 청구서가 발송되었습니다.
(C) 예전 것보다 훨씬 더 큽니다.

해설 건립 장소를 묻는 Where 의문문
(A) **정답**: 도서관 분관의 건립 장소를 묻는 질문에 아직 결정되지 않았다(It hasn't been decided yet)는 불확실성 표현으로 응답하고 있으므로 정답이다.
(B) **유사 발음 오답**: 질문의 built와 유사한 발음인 bill을 이용한 오답이다.
(C) **연상 작용 오답**: 질문의 library branch와 built에서 연상할 수 있는 Much larger를 이용한 오답이다.

어휘 branch 분점, 지점 bill 청구서 much (비교급 강조어) 훨씬

ETS 유형 연습 본책 p.044

1 (A) 2 (C) 3 (B) 4 (A) 5 (A)

1 W-Am / M-Au

When will the renovations be done?
(A) They haven't given us a date.
(B) A new heating system.
(C) Through the side entrance.

개조 공사는 언제 끝날까요?
(A) 저희에게 날짜를 알려 주지 않았어요.
(B) 새로운 난방 장치요.
(C) 측면 출입구를 통해서요.

해설 공사 종료 시점을 묻는 When 의문문
(A) **정답**: 공사 종료 시점을 묻는 질문에 우리에게 날짜(date)를 알려 주지 않았다는 불확실성 표현으로 대답하고 있다.
(B) **연상 작용 오답**: renovations에서 연상 가능한 new와 heating system을 이용한 오답이다.
(C) **관련 없는 오답**: 질문 내용과 관련 없는 대답이다.

어휘 renovation 개조 공사   be done 끝나다(= be over)
give A a date A에게 날짜를 알려 주다
side entrance 측면 출입구

2 W-Am / W-Br
Where can I find more printer paper?
(A) No, it's not quite enough.
(B) By tomorrow evening.
(C) It's on sale at Greenville Office Supplies.

프린터 용지를 어디서 더 찾을 수 있나요?
(A) 아니요, 충분하지 않아요.
(B) 내일 저녁까지요.
(C) 그린빌 사무용품점에서 할인 중이에요.

해설 보관 장소를 묻는 Where 의문문
(A) Yes/No 대답 불가 오답: 의문사 의문문에 Yes/No로 답변한 오답이다.
(B) 관련 없는 오답: When 의문문에 어울리는 대답이다.
(C) 정답: 프린터 용지를 어디서 찾을 수 있는지 묻는 질문에 용지를 구할 수 있는 장소를 구체적으로 알려주고 있다.

어휘 quite 상당히, 완전히

3 M-Cn / W-Br
When will the software be updated?
(A) I really like that store.
(B) This morning sometime.
(C) No, it isn't.

소프트웨어는 언제 업데이트되나요?
(A) 그 가게가 정말 마음에 들어요.
(B) 오늘 오전 중으로요.
(C) 아니요, 그렇지 않아요.

해설 소프트웨어 업데이트 시점을 묻는 When 의문문
(A) 유사 발음 오답: 질문의 the software와 유사한 발음인 that store를 이용한 오답이다.
(B) 정답: 소프트웨어를 언제 업데이트하는지 묻는 질문에 구체적인 시기를 말하고 있으므로 정답이다.
(C) Yes/No 대답 불가 오답: 의문사 의문문에 Yes/No로 대답할 수 없다.

4 M-Cn / W-Br
When will the manager's seminar be held?
(A) During the second week of July.
(B) The conference room, downstairs.
(C) Yes, it's being organized now.

매니저 세미나는 언제 열립니까?
(A) 7월 두 번째 주 동안이에요.
(B) 아래층 회의실요.
(C) 네, 지금 준비 중입니다.

해설 시점을 묻는 When 의문문
(A) 정답: 매니저 세미나가 언제 열리는지에 대해 7월 두 번째 주 동안(During the second week of July)이라는 구체적인 시간을 언급하고 있다.

(B) 관련 없는 오답: 장소를 묻는 Where 의문문에 어울리는 대답이다.
(C) Yes/No 대답 불가 오답: When 의문문에 Yes/No로 대답할 수 없다.

5 M-Cn / W-Am
Where did you find this article?
(A) In yesterday's business section.
(B) It's about international trade.
(C) Yes, I have a newspaper subscription.

이 기사 어디서 보셨어요?
(A) 어제자 경제면에서요.
(B) 국제 무역에 관한 거예요.
(C) 네, 신문을 구독하고 있어요.

해설 기사의 출처를 묻는 Where 의문문
(A) 정답: 어디에서 기사를 보았는지 묻는 질문에 어제자 경제면(yesterday's business section)이라는 구체적인 정보를 제공하고 있으므로 정답이다.
(B) 관련 없는 오답: What 의문문에 어울리는 대답이다.
(C) 연상 작용·Yes/No 대답 불가 오답: 질문의 article에서 연상 가능한 newspaper를 이용해 혼동을 유발하고, 의문사 의문문에 Yes/No로 답변한 오답이다.

어휘 article 기사   business section (신문의) 경제면
international trade 국제 무역   subscription 구독

ETS 실전 문제 본책 p.045

1 (B)	2 (A)	3 (C)	4 (A)	5 (C)
6 (B)	7 (B)	8 (C)	9 (C)	10 (C)
11 (C)	12 (B)	13 (C)	14 (B)	15 (A)
16 (C)	17 (C)	18 (B)	19 (A)	20 (B)
21 (A)	22 (B)	23 (C)	24 (C)	25 (A)

1 W-Am / M-Cn
When should we discuss the sales figures?
(A) I've never shopped there before.
(B) What time are you available?
(C) It was a productive discussion.

언제 판매 수치에 대해 논의하는 것이 좋을까요?
(A) 거기서 한 번도 쇼핑해 본 적이 없어요.
(B) 언제 시간이 있으세요?
(C) 그것은 생산적인 논의였어요.

해설 시점을 묻는 When 의문문
(A) 연상 작용 오답: 질문의 sales에서 연상 가능한 shopped를 이용한 오답이다.
(B) 정답: 적당한 회의 시간을 묻는 When 의문문에 시간 표현으로 답하는 대신, 상대에게 편한 시간을 되묻고 있다.
(C) 파생어 오답: 질문의 discuss와 파생어 관계인 discussion을 이용한 오답이다.

어휘 sales figures 판매 수치 available 시간 여유가 있는, 이용 가능한 productive 생산적인 discussion 논의

2 W-Am / M-Cn
Where can I pay for these shirts?
(A) At the cashier on the first floor.
(B) They come in two colors.
(C) A full refund.

이 셔츠들은 어디서 계산할 수 있나요?
(A) 1층 계산대에서요.
(B) 두 가지 색상으로 나와요.
(C) 전액 환불이요.

해설 계산 장소를 묻는 Where 의문문
(A) 정답: 셔츠를 계산할 수 있는 곳을 묻는 Where 의문문에 1층 계산대라는 구체적인 위치를 언급하고 있으므로 정답이다.
(B) 연상 작용 오답: 질문의 shirts에서 연상 가능한 colors를 이용한 오답이다.
(C) 연상 작용 오답: 질문의 pay에서 연상 가능한 refund를 이용한 오답이다.

어휘 cashier 계산대, 출납원 refund 환불(금)

3 M-Cn / W-Br
When do you think we'll take the group photo?
(A) A good camera.
(B) I prefer working in groups.
(C) At around ten o'clock.

단체 사진은 언제 찍을 것 같나요?
(A) 좋은 카메라요.
(B) 저는 단체로 일하는 걸 선호합니다.
(C) 10시쯤에요.

해설 사진 촬영 시점을 묻는 When 의문문
(A) 연상 작용 오답: 질문의 photo에서 연상 가능한 camera를 이용한 오답이다.
(B) 단어 반복 오답: 질문의 group을 반복 이용한 오답이다.
(C) 정답: 단체 사진 촬영 시점을 묻는 질문에 10시쯤(around ten o'clock)이라는 시간 표현으로 대답하고 있으므로 정답이다.

어휘 around ~쯤, 약

4 W-Am / M-Cn
Where did you put our office supplies?
(A) They're in the closet.
(B) Several boxes.
(C) Yes, that's correct.

사무용품을 어디에 두셨나요?
(A) 벽장에 있어요.
(B) 여러 상자요.
(C) 네, 맞아요.

해설 보관 장소를 묻는 Where 의문문
(A) 정답: 사무용품을 보관한 장소를 묻는 질문에 벽장(in the closet)이라는 구체적인 위치를 제시하고 있다.
(B) 연상 작용 오답: 질문의 office supplies에서 연상 가능한 boxes를 이용한 오답이다.
(C) Yes/No 대답 불가 오답: 의문사 의문문에 Yes/No로 답변한 오답이다.

어휘 closet 벽장

5 W-Br / W-Am
When is the new engineer's first day?
(A) It's a short video, actually.
(B) My house was repainted last Wednesday.
(C) I'm working on the schedule now.

새로운 엔지니어는 첫 근무일이 언제인가요?
(A) 사실 그것은 짧은 영상이에요.
(B) 제 집은 지난 수요일에 다시 칠해졌어요.
(C) 지금 일정을 짜는 중이에요.

해설 새 직원의 첫 근무 시점을 묻는 When 의문문
(A) 관련 없는 오답: 질문과 상관없는 답변을 제시하고 있다.
(B) 연상 작용 오답: When 질문에서 연상 가능한 시점 last Wednesday를 이용한 오답이다.
(C) 정답: 새로운 엔지니어의 첫 근무일이 언제인지 묻는 질문에 지금 일정을 짜는 중이라며 아직 확정되지 않았다는 것을 우회적으로 표현하고 있다.

6 M-Au / W-Am
Where is tomorrow's presentation going to take place?
(A) Yes, it takes three days.
(B) In the company conference room.
(C) Oh, probably several copies.

내일 프레젠테이션은 어디에서 열리나요?
(A) 네, 3일 걸려요.
(B) 회사 회의실에서요.
(C) 아, 아마 여러 부일 걸요.

해설 장소를 묻는 Where 의문문
(A) Yes/No 대답 불가 오답: 장소를 묻는 Where 의문문에는 Yes/No로 대답할 수 없다.
(B) 정답: 프레젠테이션이 어디에서 열리는지 묻는 질문에 회사 회의실이라고 구체적인 장소를 알려주고 있다.
(C) 연상 작용 오답: 의미상 연결이 가능한 두 표현 presentation과 copies를 이용한 오답이다.

어휘 take place (행사 등이) 열리다 copy (서류 등의) 한 부

7 M-Au / W-Am
When will Mr. Stein's book be available?
(A) Two tickets, please.
(B) It'll be published this fall.
(C) He's not here.

스타인 씨의 책은 언제 시중에서 구할 수 있을까요?
(A) 표 두 장 주세요.
(B) 올가을에 출판될 겁니다.
(C) 그는 여기 없어요.

| 해설 | 시점을 묻는 When 의문문
(A) 관련 없는 오답: 개수를 묻는 How many 의문문에 적합한 대답이다.
(B) 정답: 언제 책을 구할 수 있을지에 대해 올가을(this fall)이라는 구체적인 시점으로 대답하고 있다.
(C) 인칭 오류 오답: 질문의 book에 대한 답변이 아닌 제3자 He로 대답한 오답이다.

어휘 available (시중에서) 구할 수 있는 publish 출판하다

8 M-Au / W-Br
Where do you want me to set up the microphones?
(A) I bought a new smartphone.
(B) It was a great concert!
(C) **Didn't you get my memo?**

마이크를 어디에 설치해 드리면 될까요?
(A) 새 스마트폰을 샀어요.
(B) 멋진 콘서트였어요!
(C) 제 메모를 못 받으셨나요?

해설 설치 장소를 묻는 Where 의문문
(A) 유사 발음 오답: microphones와 부분적으로 발음이 유사한 smartphone을 이용한 오답이다.
(B) 연상 작용 오답: 질문의 microphones에서 연상 가능한 concert를 이용한 오답이다.
(C) 정답: 마이크를 어디에 설치하면 될지 묻는 질문에 이미 메모를 통해 설치 장소를 전달했다는 것을 우회적으로 표현하고 있다.

어휘 microphone 마이크

9 W-Am / M-Cn
When was the last time you updated the company Web site?
(A) Use a different password.
(B) A more modern design.
(C) **It's been quite a while.**

당신이 회사 웹사이트를 마지막으로 업데이트한 게 언제였죠?
(A) 다른 암호를 사용하세요.
(B) 좀 더 현대적인 디자인이에요.
(C) 꽤 오래됐어요.

해설 업데이트 시점을 묻는 When 의문문
(A) 연상 작용 오답: 의미상 연결이 가능한 Web site와 password를 이용한 오답이다.
(B) 연상 작용 오답: 의미상 연결이 가능한 updated와 modern을 이용한 오답이다.
(C) 정답: 마지막으로 업데이트한 시점을 묻는 When 의문문에 꽤 오래됐다고 대략적인 시점으로 답한 정답이다.

10 W-Br / M-Cn
Where is the conference room on this floor?
(A) Yes, there are.
(B) The annual board meeting.
(C) **It's the third door on the left.** | 이 층에 회의실이 어디에 있나요?
(A) 네, 있어요.
(B) 연례 이사회 회의요.
(C) 왼쪽 세 번째 문이에요.

해설 위치를 묻는 Where 의문문
(A) Yes/No 대답 불가 오답: 의문사 의문문에 Yes/No로 대답할 수 없다.
(B) 연상 작용 오답: 질문의 conference에서 연상할 수 있는 meeting을 이용한 오답이다.
(C) 정답: 회의실이 어디에 있는지 묻는 질문에 the third door on the left라는 구체적인 위치를 언급하고 있으므로 정답이다.

어휘 annual 연례의 board meeting 이사회 회의

11 W-Am / M-Cn
When is the next shift starting?
(A) The last assignment.
(B) We're hiring a new chef.
(C) **This afternoon at two o'clock.**

다음 교대 근무는 언제 시작하나요?
(A) 마지막 임무요.
(B) 새로운 요리사를 채용 중이에요.
(C) 오늘 오후 2시에요.

해설 교대 근무 시간을 묻는 When 의문문
(A) 연상 작용 오답: 질문의 next shift에서 연상 가능한 last assignment를 이용한 오답이다.
(B) 유사 발음 오답: 질문의 shift와 부분적으로 발음이 유사한 chef를 이용한 오답이다.
(C) 정답: 교대 근무가 시작하는 시점을 묻는 질문에 오늘 오후 2시라는 구체적인 시점을 말하고 있으므로 정답이다.

어휘 shift (한 차례의) 교대 근무 assignment 임무

12 W-Br / M-Au
Where can I pick up my new identification badge?
(A) Sure, here's my contact information.
(B) **At the security desk in the lobby.**
(C) A black-and-white photograph.

제 새 신분증 배지를 어디에서 받을 수 있나요?
(A) 물론이죠, 여기 제 연락처예요.
(B) 로비에 있는 보안 데스크에서요.
(C) 흑백 사진이요.

해설 수령 장소를 묻는 Where 의문문
(A) Yes/No 대답 불가 오답: 의문사 의문문에 Yes에 해당하는 Sure로 대답할 수 없다.
(B) 정답: 새 신분증 배지를 받을 수 있는 장소를 묻는 질문에 로비에 있는 보안 데스크라는 구체적인 장소를 알려주고 있다.
(C) 연상 작용 오답: 의미상 연결이 가능한 두 표현 identification과 photograph를 이용한 오답이다.

어휘 identification badge 신분증 배지
    contact information 연락처 security 보안

13 W-Am / M-Cn
When should we expect to receive payment?
(A) Because of the price.
(B) With a credit card.
(C) By the end of the week.

우리는 언제 대금을 받을 수 있을까요?
(A) 가격 때문에요.
(B) 신용 카드로요.
(C) 이번 주 말까지요.

해설 대금 수령 시점을 묻는 When 의문문
(A) 연상 작용 오답: payment에서 연상 가능한 price를 이용한 오답이다.
(B) 연상 작용 오답: payment에서 연상 가능한 credit card를 이용한 오답이다.
(C) 정답: 언제 대금을 받을 수 있는지에 대해 이번 주 말까지(By the end of the week)라는 구체적인 시점을 언급하고 있다.

어휘 payment 대금, 지불 (금액)

14 M-Cn / W-Br
Where can I find Li's e-mail address?
(A) Today at five is good.
(B) Try the company directory.
(C) I'll pick up the mail.

리의 이메일 주소는 어디에 있나요?
(A) 오늘 5시가 좋아요.
(B) 회사 인명록을 보세요.
(C) 제가 우편물을 가져올게요.

해설 주소가 있는 곳을 묻는 Where 의문문
(A) 관련 없는 오답: 시간을 묻는 When 의문문에 가능한 답변이다.
(B) 정답: 이메일 주소가 어디에 있는지 묻는 질문에 회사 인명록(company directory)이라는 구체적인 정보를 제시하고 있으므로 정답이다.
(C) 단어 반복 오답: 질문의 mail을 반복 이용한 오답이다.

어휘 directory (이름·연락처 등을 적은) 인명록

15 W-Am / W-Br
Where can I make copies of these forms?
(A) In the copy room on the first floor.
(B) About 30 pages long.
(C) Let's get lunch now.

어디서 이 양식들을 복사할 수 있을까요?
(A) 1층 복사실에서요.
(B) 30쪽 분량 정도요.
(C) 이제 점심을 먹읍시다.

해설 서류 복사가 가능한 장소를 묻는 Where 의문문
(A) 정답: 양식을 복사할 수 있는 장소를 묻는 질문에 1층 복사실이라며 구체적으로 알려주고 있으므로 정답이다.
(B) 연상 작용 오답: 질문의 copies에서 연상 가능한 30 pages를 이용한 오답이다.
(C) 관련 없는 오답: 질문과 상관없는 답변이다.

어휘 form 양식

16 W-Br / M-Au
When will the board meeting be over?
(A) I'm sure it will.
(B) No, it didn't change.
(C) By four at the latest.

이사회 회의는 언제 끝나죠?
(A) 틀림없이 그럴 거예요.
(B) 아니요, 바뀌지 않았어요.
(C) 늦어도 4시에요.

해설 회의 종료 시간을 묻는 When 의문문
(A) 단어 반복 오답: 질문의 will을 반복 이용한 오답이다.
(B) Yes/No 대답 불가 오답: 의문사 의문문에 Yes/No로 대답할 수 없다.
(C) 정답: 회의가 끝나는 시간을 묻는 질문에 늦어도 4시까지라는 구체적인 시간 표현으로 대답하고 있다.

어휘 at the latest 늦어도

17 M-Au / M-Cn
Where can I rent commercial space downtown?
(A) The cost is reasonable.
(B) You can borrow it today.
(C) Try the Burnside building.

시내에서 상업공간을 빌릴 수 있는 곳이 어딘가요?
(A) 비용은 적당해요.
(B) 오늘 빌릴 수 있어요.
(C) 번사이드 빌딩을 알아보세요.

해설 임대 장소를 묻는 Where 의문문
(A) 연상 작용 오답: 의미상 연결이 가능한 두 표현 rent와 cost를 이용해서 혼동을 유발하는 오답이다.
(B) 연상 작용 오답: 질문의 rent에서 연상 가능한 borrow를 이용한 오답이다.
(C) 정답: 상업공간을 빌릴 수 있는 곳을 묻는 Where 의문문에 Burnside building이라는 구체적인 장소를 언급하고 있다.

어휘 commercial 상업의 reasonable 적당한 borrow 빌리다

18 W-Br / M-Cn
When will you finish designing the new Web site?
(A) I like that design too.
(B) The deadline is still being negotiated.
(C) It's at least twelve meters long.

새로운 웹사이트 디자인은 언제 끝내실 예정이세요?
(A) 저도 그 디자인이 좋아요.
(B) 마감일을 아직 협의 중이에요.
(C) 최소한 12미터예요.

해설 웹사이트 디자인 완료 시점을 묻는 When 의문문
(A) 파생어 오답: designing과 파생어 관계인 design을 이용한 오답이다.
(B) 정답: 새로운 웹사이트 디자인이 언제 끝나는지 묻는 질문에 마감일이 아직 결정되지 않았음을 우회적으로 답변하고 있다.
(C) 관련 없는 오답: 길이를 묻는 How long 의문문에 적합한 대답이다.

어휘 deadline 마감일 negotiate 협상하다 at least 최소한

19 W-Br / W-Am
Where will the training session be held?
(A) I'll check the e-mail Erika sent us.
(B) Safety procedures.
(C) Because of a schedule change.

교육 과정이 어디에서 진행되나요?
(A) 에리카가 우리에게 보낸 이메일을 확인해 볼게요.
(B) 안전 절차요.
(C) 일정 변경 때문이에요.

해설 장소를 묻는 Where 의문문
(A) 정답: 교육 과정이 어디에서 진행되는지를 묻는 질문에 자신도 잘 모르니 이메일을 한번 확인하겠다며 우회적으로 답하고 있다.
(B) 연상 작용 오답: 질문의 training session에서 연상 가능한 Safety procedures를 이용한 오답이다.
(C) 관련 없는 오답: 이유를 묻는 Why 의문문에 가능한 답변이다.

어휘 training session 교육 과정 be held (수업 따위가) 진행되다, (모임 따위가) 열리다 safety procedures 안전 절차

20 W-Am / M-Cn
When does Mr. Cho want to pick up his cake?
(A) I'll carry it to the car for you.
(B) He said he'd be in around three o'clock.
(C) For his colleagues.

조 씨는 언제 케이크를 찾아가실 건가요?
(A) 제가 그걸 차에 실어드릴게요.
(B) 3시쯤 오겠다고 하셨어요.
(C) 그의 동료들을 위해서요.

해설 회수 시점을 묻는 When 의문문
(A) 연상 작용 오답: 질문의 pick up his cake에서 연상 가능한 carry it을 이용한 오답이다.
(B) 정답: 케이크를 언제 찾을지를 묻는 질문에 3시쯤(around three o'clock)이라는 구체적인 시점을 언급하고 있다.
(C) 관련 없는 오답: 케이크를 사는 목적을 묻는 Why 의문문에 적합한 대답이다.

어휘 pick up ~을 찾으러[가지러] 가다 colleague 동료

21 M-Cn / M-Au
Where should we leave the cleaning supplies?
(A) Take them to the storeroom.
(B) No, she hasn't left yet.
(C) Tomorrow is fine.

청소용품은 어디에 두어야 하나요?
(A) 창고로 가져가세요.
(B) 아니요, 그녀는 아직 떠나지 않았어요.
(C) 내일 괜찮아요.

해설 보관 장소를 묻는 Where 의문문
(A) 정답: 청소용품을 둘 곳을 묻는 질문에 storeroom이라는 구체적인 장소를 제시하고 있으므로 정답이다.
(B) 다의어·Yes/No 대답 불가 오답: 질문의 leave(두다, 놓다)와 의미가 다른 leave(떠나다)의 과거형을 이용해 혼동을 유발하고, 의문사 의문문에 Yes/No로 답변한 오답이다.
(C) 관련 없는 오답: 질문과 상관없는 답변이다.

어휘 supplies 용품, 비품 storeroom 창고

22 W-Am / W-Br
When will the employee telephone directory be ready?
(A) Three hundred forty-six employees.
(B) I just have to update a few more phone numbers.
(C) The director's office.

직원 전화번호부는 언제 준비되나요?
(A) 직원 346명이요.
(B) 제가 전화번호 몇 개만 더 업데이트하면 돼요.
(C) 이사실이요.

해설 준비 시점을 묻는 When 의문문
(A) 단어 반복 오답: 질문의 employee를 반복 이용한 오답이다.
(B) 정답: 언제 직원 전화번호부가 준비될지에 대해 전화번호 몇 개만 업데이트하면 된다며 곧 준비될 것을 우회적으로 전달하고 있다.
(C) 유사 발음 오답: 질문의 directory와 부분적으로 발음이 유사한 director를 이용한 오답이다.

어휘 telephone directory 전화번호부 director 이사

23 M-Cn / W-Am
Where can I get a key for the hotel gym?
(A) Sometimes after work.
(B) A six-month membership.
(C) Oscar can give you one.

호텔 체육관 열쇠는 어디서 받을 수 있나요?
(A) 퇴근 후 가끔요.
(B) 6개월 회원제예요.
(C) 오스카가 하나 줄 거예요.

해설 열쇠 받는 곳을 묻는 Where 의문문
(A) 연상 작용 오답: 질문의 gym에서 연상 가능한 운동 시간 after work를 이용한 오답이다.
(B) 연상 작용 오답: 질문의 gym에서 연상 가능한 membership을 이용한 오답이다.
(C) 정답: 열쇠를 어디서 받을 수 있는지 묻는 질문에 오스카가 하나 줄 수 있다며 구체적인 정보를 제공하고 있으므로 정답이다.

24 W-Br / M-Cn
When do you think we'll hear if we've won the Jones account?
(A) I lost my accounting manual.
(B) One of our biggest clients.
(C) Ms. Watson might already know.

우리가 존스 거래 계약을 따냈는지에 관해 언제 듣게 될 것 같아요?
(A) 회계 편람을 잃어버렸어요.
(B) 우리 회사의 제일 큰 고객 중 하나예요.
(C) 왓슨 씨가 벌써 알고 있을지도 몰라요.

해설 정보 확인 시점을 묻는 When 의문문
(A) 파생어 오답: 질문에 언급된 account의 파생어인 accounting을 이용한 오답이다.
(B) 연상 작용 오답: 질문의 account에서 연상 가능한 clients를 이용한 오답이다.
(C) 정답: 소식을 언제 듣게 될지 묻는 질문에 왓슨 씨가 알고 있을지도 모른다(Ms. Watson might already know)는 우회적인 응답을 제시하고 있다.

어휘 win an account 거래 계약을 따내다
accounting manual 회계 편람

25 W-Br / W-Am
Where can I find an employee-referral form?
(A) I think they're in Jan's office.
(B) Seven job candidates.
(C) Thanks for letting me know.

직원 추천서는 어디에 있나요?
(A) 잰의 사무실에 있을 거예요.
(B) 입사 지원자 7명이에요.
(C) 알려 줘서 고마워요.

해설 추천서가 있는 곳을 묻는 Where 의문문
(A) 정답: 직원 추천서가 있는 곳을 묻는 질문에 잰의 사무실(Jan's office)이라는 구체적인 장소를 언급하고 있으므로 정답이다.
(B) 연상 작용 오답: 의미상 연결이 가능한 두 표현 employee와 job candidates를 이용한 오답이다.
(C) 관련 없는 오답: 추천서가 있는 곳을 묻는 질문에 적합하지 않다.

어휘 referral 추천서   job candidate 입사 지원자, 구직자

UNIT 05 Why/How 의문문

① Why 의문문

ETS CHECK UP   본책 p.046

1 (A)   2 (C)   3 (C)   4 (B)   5 (C)

1 M-Cn / W-Br
Why isn't Matt's contact information in the company directory?
(A) He just started working here.
(B) We went there directly.
(C) Yes, I saved it.

맷의 연락처 정보가 왜 회사 인명록에 없죠?
(A) 그는 이제 막 여기서 일을 시작했어요.
(B) 우리는 곧장 거기로 갔어요.
(C) 네, 제가 저장했어요.

해설 정보가 없는 이유를 묻는 Why 의문문
(A) 정답: 맷의 연락처 정보가 왜 없는지 묻는 질문에 이제 막 근무를 시작했다(just started working)는 이유를 제시하고 있다.
(B) 유사 발음 오답: 질문의 directory와 부분적으로 발음이 유사한 directly를 이용한 오답이다.
(C) Yes/No 대답 불가 오답: 의문사 의문문에 Yes/No로 대답할 수 없다.

어휘 contact information 연락처 정보   directly 곧장

2 W-Br / M-Cn
Why do we need three copies of the contract?
(A) During Wednesday's budget meeting.
(B) Yes, I gave them to Mr. Kim.
(C) Luisa and Diego also have to read it.

계약서가 왜 3부 필요한가요?
(A) 수요일 예산안 회의 때요.
(B) 네, 제가 김 씨에게 드렸어요.
(C) 루이사와 디에고도 읽어야 해요.

해설 사본이 필요한 이유를 묻는 Why 의문문
(A) 관련 없는 오답: 시점을 묻는 When 의문문에 적합한 대답이다.
(B) Yes/No 대답 불가 오답: 의문사 의문문에 Yes/No로 대답할 수 없다.
(C) 정답: 계약서 3부가 필요한 이유를 묻는 질문에 구체적인 이유를 언급하고 있으므로 정답이다.

어휘 contract 계약(서)

3 M-Cn / W-Br
Why are the technicians here?
(A) They should be here soon.
(B) No, at the escalator.
(C) To set up a new computer lab.

기술자들이 왜 여기에 와 있죠?
(A) 곧 여기 올 거예요.
(B) 아니요, 에스컬레이터에서요.
(C) 컴퓨터실을 새로 마련하기 위해서요.

해설 기술자들의 방문 이유를 묻는 Why 의문문
(A) **단어 반복 오답**: 질문의 here를 반복 이용한 오답이다.
(B) **Yes/No 대답 불가 오답**: 의문사 의문문에는 Yes/No로 대답을 할 수 없다.
(C) **정답**: 기술자들이 와 있는 이유를 묻는 질문에 구체적인 이유를 언급하고 있으므로 정답이다.

어휘 technician 기술자 set up 마련하다 lab 실험실, 연구실

4 W-Am / W-Br
Why were our expenses over budget last month?
(A) Maybe a less expensive brand.
(B) We had unexpected maintenance costs.
(C) Probably the one from December.

지난달에 지출이 예산을 초과한 이유는 뭔가요?
(A) 아마 덜 비싼 브랜드일 거예요.
(B) 예상치 못한 유지비가 있었어요.
(C) 아마 12월에서 나온 것 같아요.

해설 예산 초과 이유를 묻는 Why 의문문
(A) **파생어 오답**: 질문의 expenses와 파생어 관계인 expensive를 이용한 오답이다.
(B) **정답**: 왜 지출이 예산을 초과했는지에 대해 예상치 못한 유지비(unexpected maintenance costs)가 있었다는 이유를 제시하고 있다.
(C) **연상 작용 오답**: 질문의 month에서 연상 가능한 December를 이용한 오답이다.

어휘 expense 지출 budget 예산 expensive 비싼 unexpected 예상치 못한 maintenance cost 유지비

5 W-Am / W-Br
Why aren't these scarves included in the clearance sale?
(A) Through Sunday.
(B) Thirty percent off.
(C) Because we just got them in.

이 스카프들은 왜 재고정리 할인에 포함되지 않나요?
(A) 일요일까지요.
(B) 30퍼센트 할인이에요.
(C) 방금 입고되었거든요.

해설 이유를 묻는 Why 의문문
(A) **관련 없는 오답**: 기간을 묻는 질문에 가능한 답변이다.
(B) **연상 작용 오답**: 의미상 연결이 가능한 두 표현 clearance sale과 Thirty percent off를 이용한 오답이다.
(C) **정답**: Why 의문문에 이유의 접속사 Because로 구체적인 이유를 제시하고 있다.

어휘 clearance sale 재고정리 할인

② How 의문문

ETS CHECK UP 본책 p.047

1 (A) **2** (C) **3** (C) **4** (B) **5** (B)

1 W-Br / M-Cn
How do I get to the doctor's office?
(A) It's at the end of the street.
(B) Because Mr. Hong has just arrived.
(C) I'm not feeling very well.

병원에는 어떻게 가나요?
(A) 도로 끝에 있어요.
(B) 홍 씨가 방금 도착했거든요.
(C) 몸이 좀 안 좋네요.

해설 방법을 묻는 How 의문문
(A) **정답**: 병원에 어떻게 가는지에 대해 도로 끝(end of the street)에 있다는 구체적인 위치를 언급하고 있다.
(B) **관련 없는 오답**: 이유를 묻는 Why 의문문에 적합한 대답이다.
(C) **연상 작용 오답**: 의미상 연결이 가능한 두 표현 doctor's office와 not feeling very well을 이용한 오답이다.

2 M-Au / W-Am
How was your stay at the hotel?
(A) I'm sorry, I can't.
(B) Near Fourth Avenue.
(C) I enjoyed it.

호텔에서 머무시는 동안 어떠셨나요?
(A) 죄송합니다만 저는 할 수 없어요.
(B) 4번가 근처요.
(C) 좋았습니다.

해설 의견을 묻는 How 의문문
(A) **관련 없는 오답**: 질문의 내용과 논리적으로 맞지 않다.
(B) **관련 없는 오답**: 장소를 묻는 Where 의문문에 가능한 답변이다.
(C) **정답**: 호텔에 대한 의견을 묻는 질문에 긍정의 내용으로 답하고 있으므로 정답이다.

어휘 stay 머무름, 방문

3 M-Cn / W-Br
How long have you been gardening?
(A) No, she's been working here a long time.
(B) A landscaping project.
(C) For about two years now.

얼마나 오래 정원을 가꾸셨나요?
(A) 아니요, 그녀는 여기서 오랫동안 일했어요.
(B) 조경 프로젝트예요.
(C) 이제 2년쯤 됐어요.

해설 기간을 묻는 How long 의문문
(A) **Yes/No 대답 불가 오답**: 의문사 의문문에 Yes/No로 답변한 오답이다.

(B) **연상 작용 오답**: 질문의 gardening에서 연상 가능한 landscaping을 이용한 오답이다.
(C) **정답**: 얼마나 오래 정원을 가꾸었는지 묻는 질문에 약 2년 동안(For about two years)이라는 구체적인 기간으로 대답하고 있다.

어휘 garden 정원을 가꾸다 landscaping 조경

4 W-Br / M-Au
How much is this umbrella?
(A) It's going to rain.
(B) Fifteen euros.
(C) It won't take long.

이 우산은 얼마인가요?
(A) 비가 올 거예요.
(B) 15유로입니다.
(C) 오래 걸리지 않을 거예요.

해설 가격을 묻는 How much 의문문
(A) **연상 작용 오답**: 질문의 umbrella에서 연상 가능한 rain을 이용한 오답이다.
(B) **정답**: 우산 가격을 묻는 질문에 구체적인 가격(Fifteen euros)을 제시하고 있다.
(C) **관련 없는 오답**: How long does it take ~? 등 기간을 묻는 의문문에 어울리는 대답이다.

5 M-Au / W-Am
How often do you charge your phone?
(A) Cash only, please.
(B) At least once a day.
(C) In my wallet.

얼마나 자주 휴대전화를 충전하세요?
(A) 현금만 받아요.
(B) 적어도 하루에 한 번이요.
(C) 제 지갑 안에요.

해설 빈도를 묻는 How often 의문문
(A) **연상 작용 오답**: 질문의 charge(충전하다)를 의미가 다른 charge(요금을 청구하다)로 연상한 후, charge에서 연상 가능한 cash를 이용한 오답이다.
(B) **정답**: 빈도를 묻는 질문에 적어도 하루에 한 번(At least once a day)이라는 구체적인 빈도를 언급하고 있다.
(C) **관련 없는 오답**: 위치를 묻는 Where 의문문에 어울리는 대답이다.

어휘 charge 충전하다 at least 최소한 wallet 지갑

ETS 유형 연습
본책 p.048

| 1 (C) | 2 (B) | 3 (B) | 4 (C) | 5 (B) |

1 M-Cn / W-Br
Why should we sign up for a bus tour of the city?
(A) At the corner of Maple and Third Street.
(B) Yes, the bank is open.
(C) Because the clients haven't been here before.

우리가 왜 시내버스 투어를 신청해야 하나요?
(A) 메이플 가와 3번가 모퉁이에서요.
(B) 네, 은행이 영업 중이에요.
(C) 고객들이 전에 여기 와 본 적이 없어서요.

해설 이유를 묻는 Why 의문문
(A) **관련 없는 오답**: 위치를 묻는 Where 의문문에 적합한 대답이다.
(B) **Yes/No 대답 불가 오답**: 의문사 의문문에 Yes/No로 대답할 수 없다.
(C) **정답**: 투어에 신청해야 하는 이유를 묻는 질문에 고객들이 전에 여기 와 본 적이 없다(the clients haven't been here before)는 구체적인 이유를 언급하고 있으므로 정답이다.

어휘 sign up for ~을 신청하다 client 고객

2 W-Br / M-Cn
How do I register for the conference?
(A) To demonstrate our new model.
(B) Just fill out this form.
(C) I'd prefer the elevator.

컨퍼런스에 어떻게 등록하나요?
(A) 우리 새 모델을 시연하려고요.
(B) 이 양식을 작성하시면 돼요.
(C) 저는 엘리베이터가 좋아요.

해설 등록 방법을 묻는 How 의문문
(A) **관련 없는 오답**: 이유를 묻는 Why 의문문에 적합한 대답이다.
(B) **정답**: 컨퍼런스 등록 방법을 묻는 질문에 대해 양식을 작성하라(fill out this form)는 구체적인 방법을 제시하고 있다.
(C) **유사 발음 오답**: 질문의 for와 부분적으로 발음이 유사한 prefer를 이용한 오답이다.

어휘 register for ~에 등록하다 demonstrate 시연하다 fill out 작성하다 prefer 선호하다

3 W-Am / M-Cn
How many workshops is the company offering this summer?
(A) I brought my toolbox.
(B) I don't know yet.
(C) OK, I'll go there now.

회사에서 이번 여름에 몇 번의 워크숍을 제공하나요?
(A) 제가 공구 상자를 가져왔어요.
(B) 아직 모르겠어요.
(C) 좋아요, 지금 갈게요.

해설 워크숍 횟수를 묻는 How many 의문문
  (A) 관련 없는 오답: 질문과 상관없는 답변을 제시하고 있다.
  (B) 정답: 회사에서 몇 번의 워크숍을 제공하는지 묻는 질문에 아직 모른다고 대답하고 있다.
  (C) Yes/No 대답 불가 오답: How many 의문문에 Yes에 해당하는 OK로 대답할 수 없다.

어휘 toolbox 공구 상자

4 M-Cn / W-Br

Why is the store closed so early today?
(A) No, it isn't very close.
(B) Yes, I got up at six today.
(C) It's a national holiday.

오늘 가게가 왜 이렇게 일찍 문을 닫았죠?
(A) 아니요, 별로 가깝지 않아요.
(B) 네, 저는 오늘 6시에 일어났어요.
(C) 오늘은 국경일이에요.

해설 이유를 묻는 Why 의문문
  (A) 유사 발음 오답: 질문의 closed와 발음이 유사한 close를 이용한 오답이다.
  (B) 단어 반복·Yes/No 대답 불가 오답: 질문의 today를 반복 사용해 혼동을 유발하고, 이유를 묻는 Why 의문문에 Yes/No로 답변한 오답이다.
  (C) 정답: 왜 가게가 일찍 문을 닫았는지에 대해 국경일(national holiday)이라는 이유를 제시하고 있다.

어휘 closed 문을 닫은 close 가까운
  national holiday 국경일

5 M-Cn / W-Br

How much does this tea kettle cost?
(A) With milk and sugar, please.
(B) Oh, you should ask a sales associate.
(C) I lost my key.

이 찻주전자는 얼마예요?
(A) 우유와 설탕을 넣어 주세요.
(B) 아, 영업사원에게 물어보세요.
(C) 열쇠를 잃어버렸어요.

해설 가격을 묻는 How much 의문문
  (A) 연상 작용 오답: 질문의 tea에서 연상 가능한 milk and sugar를 이용한 오답이다.
  (B) 정답: 찻주전자 가격을 묻는 질문에 영업사원에게 물어보라는 우회적 답변을 하고 있으므로 정답이다.
  (C) 유사 발음 오답: 질문의 tea와 발음이 유사한 key를 이용한 오답이다.

어휘 kettle 주전자 sales associate 영업사원

ETS 실전 문제

본책 p.049

1 (C)	2 (B)	3 (A)	4 (A)	5 (B)
6 (C)	7 (C)	8 (C)	9 (C)	10 (A)
11 (A)	12 (C)	13 (B)	14 (B)	15 (C)
16 (C)	17 (A)	18 (A)	19 (C)	20 (A)
21 (A)	22 (B)	23 (C)	24 (C)	25 (B)

1 W-Am / M-Cn

Why did Ms. Tong put boxes of used equipment in the lobby?
(A) You'll need some scissors.
(B) The stairway is next to the elevator.
(C) Because they're being picked up today.

통 씨는 왜 로비에 중고 장비가 든 상자를 놔두셨나요?
(A) 가위가 필요하실 거예요.
(B) 계단은 엘리베이터 옆에 있어요.
(C) 오늘 수거될 거라서요.

해설 이유를 묻는 Why 의문문
  (A) 연상 작용 오답: 질문의 boxes에서 연상 가능한 scissors를 이용한 오답이다.
  (B) 연상 작용 오답: 질문의 lobby에서 연상 가능한 stairway와 elevator를 이용한 오답이다.
  (C) 정답: Why 의문문에 접속사 Because로 구체적인 이유를 말하고 있으므로 정답이다.

어휘 equipment 장비 stairway 계단
  pick up ~을 찾으러[가지러] 가다

2 W-Br / M-Au

How was the movie you decided to watch?
(A) A famous action hero.
(B) I understand why the director won an award.
(C) Oh, that's a nice watch.

보기로 했던 영화는 어땠어요?
(A) 유명한 액션 히어로예요.
(B) 그 감독이 상을 받은 이유를 알겠어요.
(C) 오, 멋진 시계네요.

해설 의견을 묻는 How 의문문
  (A) 연상 작용 오답: 질문의 movie에서 연상 가능한 action hero를 이용한 오답이다.
  (B) 정답: 영화가 어땠는지 묻는 질문에 감독이 상을 받은 이유를 알겠다며 긍정의 대답을 우회적으로 표현하고 있다.
  (C) 다의어 오답: 질문의 watch(보다)와 품사와 의미가 다른 watch(시계)를 이용한 오답이다.

어휘 director 감독 award 상

3 W-Br / M-Au
Why has the carpet been removed from the lobby?
(A) Because they're putting in a wood floor.
(B) The local furniture store.
(C) Sure, I'll keep the key.

왜 로비에 있던 카펫이 치워졌나요?
(A) 나무 바닥을 깔 거라서요.
(B) 지역 가구 매장이요.
(C) 네, 열쇠를 가지고 있을게요.

해설 이유를 묻는 Why 의문문
(A) 정답: Why 의문문에 접속사 Because로 구체적인 이유를 대고 있으므로 정답이다.
(B) 연상 작용 오답: 질문의 carpet에서 연상 가능한 furniture를 이용한 오답이다.
(C) Yes/No 대답 불가 오답: Why 의문문에 Yes에 해당하는 Sure로 대답할 수 없다.

어휘 remove 치우다

4 W-Br / W-Am
How's the construction of the new office building coming along?
(A) It's almost finished.
(B) He's coming in a few days.
(C) Luke designed it.

새 사무실 빌딩 건축은 어떻게 진행되고 있나요?
(A) 거의 다 끝났어요.
(B) 그는 며칠 후에 와요.
(C) 루크가 설계했어요.

해설 건축 진행 상황을 묻는 How 의문문
(A) 정답: 건축이 어떻게 진행되고 있는지 묻는 질문에 '거의 다 끝났다'라는 대답은 자연스러운 연결이므로 정답이다.
(B) 단어 반복 오답: 질문의 coming을 그대로 반복 이용한 오답이다.
(C) 연상 작용 오답: 질문의 construction에서 연상 가능한 designed를 이용한 오답이다.

어휘 construction 건축 come along 진행되다

5 M-Cn / W-Am
Why are you asking about my availability this afternoon?
(A) Yes, it's an expensive phone.
(B) There are mistakes in your contract.
(C) Is he a reporter for the magazine?

왜 오늘 오후에 제가 시간이 되는지 물어보시나요?
(A) 네, 그것은 비싼 전화기예요.
(B) 당신의 계약서에 오류가 있어요.
(C) 그는 그 잡지의 기자인가요?

해설 질문의 이유를 묻는 Why 의문문
(A) Yes/No 대답 불가 오답: 의문사 의문문에 Yes/No로 대답할 수 없다.
(B) 정답: 오늘 오후에 시간이 되는지를 묻는 이유로 계약서에 오류가 있음을 제시하고 있다.
(C) 인칭 오류·관련 없는 오답: Why 의문문에 he를 가리킬 만한 대상이 없고, 질문과 상관없는 답변을 하고 있다.

어휘 availability 시간 가능 여부 contract 계약(서)

6 W-Br / M-Au
How soon can we announce the staff promotions?
(A) There's enough room.
(B) Oh, that's wonderful news.
(C) At the next meeting.

직원 승진을 얼마나 빨리 발표할 수 있을까요?
(A) 충분한 공간이 있어요.
(B) 오, 그거 좋은 소식이군요.
(C) 다음 회의에서요.

해설 시점을 묻는 How soon 의문문
(A) 관련 없는 오답: 질문의 내용과 논리적으로 맞지 않다.
(B) 연상 작용 오답: 질문의 staff promotions에서 연상 가능한 wonderful news를 이용한 오답이다.
(C) 정답: 진급자 명단 발표 시점을 묻는 질문에 next meeting이라는 구체적인 시점으로 응답하고 있다.

어휘 announce 발표하다 promotion 승진
room 공간, 자리

7 W-Br / M-Au
Why isn't the San Diego manufacturing plant operational yet?
(A) Please water them twice a week.
(B) I thought he transferred to a different company.
(C) Because some of the equipment just arrived last week.

샌디에이고 제조 공장은 왜 아직 가동하지 않나요?
(A) 일주일에 두 번 물을 주세요.
(B) 저는 그가 다른 회사로 이직한 줄 알았어요.
(C) 일부 장비가 지난주에야 도착했거든요.

해설 이유를 묻는 Why 의문문
(A) 연상 작용 오답: 질문의 plant(공장)와 의미가 다른 plant(식물)를 연상한 후, plant에서 의미상 연상 가능한 water를 이용한 오답이다.
(B) 인칭 오류 오답: 의문문에 he를 가리킬 만한 대상이 없다.
(C) 정답: Why 의문문에 접속사 Because로 구체적인 이유를 말하고 있으므로 정답이다.

어휘 manufacturing 제조 plant 공장 operational 가동되는 transfer 옮기다 equipment 장비

8 M-Au / W-Br

How many times have you relocated for work?
(A) Yes, I live in Madrid now.
(B) You should make twenty-five signs.
(C) This is my second move.

직장 때문에 몇 번이나 이사하셨나요?
(A) 네, 저는 지금 마드리드에 살고 있어요.
(B) 표지판 25개를 만들어야 해요.
(C) 이번이 두 번째 이사예요.

해설 이사 횟수를 묻는 How many 의문문
(A) **Yes/No 대답 불가 오답**: 의문사 의문문에 Yes/No로 대답할 수 없다.
(B) **연상 작용 오답**: 질문의 How many times에서 연상 가능한 twenty-five를 이용한 오답이다.
(C) **정답**: 횟수를 묻는 질문에 이번이 두 번째 이사(second move)라는 구체적인 횟수를 언급하고 있다.

어휘 relocate 이사하다

9 M-Au / W-Br

Why weren't you at work yesterday?
(A) Unfortunately, it was.
(B) A five percent increase.
(C) Because I was sick.

어제 왜 출근을 안 하셨나요?
(A) 유감스럽게도 그랬어요.
(B) 5퍼센트 인상이에요.
(C) 몸이 안 좋았어요.

해설 결근 이유를 묻는 Why 의문문
(A) **인칭 오류 오답**: 질문과 관련 없는 it으로 답변하고 있다.
(B) **관련 없는 오답**: 인상폭을 묻는 How much 의문문에 적합한 대답이다.
(C) **정답**: 어제 출근하지 않은 이유를 묻는 질문에 몸이 안 좋았다며 구체적인 이유를 제시하고 있다.

어휘 unfortunately 유감스럽게도

10 M-Cn / M-Au

How do I log in to my e-mail account?
(A) We'll have to assign you a password.
(B) He doesn't work in accounting.
(C) No, it's only temporary.

제 이메일 계정으로 어떻게 로그인하죠?
(A) 저희가 비밀번호를 할당해 드려야 해요.
(B) 그는 회계부에서 근무하지 않아요.
(C) 아니요, 임시일 뿐이에요.

해설 로그인 방법을 묻는 How 의문문
(A) **정답**: 로그인하는 방법을 묻는 질문에 비밀번호를 할당할 것(assign you a password)이라는 우회적인 대답을 하고 있다.
(B) **유사 발음 오답**: 질문의 account와 발음이 비슷한 accounting을 이용한 오답이다.
(C) **Yes/No 대답 불가 오답**: 방법을 묻는 How 의문문에는 Yes/No로 대답할 수 없다.

어휘 account 계정 assign 배정하다 accounting 회계(과) temporary 임시의

11 W-Am / M-Cn

Why was the finance department's meeting postponed?
(A) Oh, I didn't realize it was.
(B) The funds are for charity.
(C) Let's meet in the lobby.

경리부 회의가 왜 연기되었나요?
(A) 아, 그런 줄 몰랐어요.
(B) 자선을 위한 기금이에요.
(C) 로비에서 만나요.

해설 회의 연기 이유를 묻는 Why 의문문
(A) **정답**: 회의가 연기된 이유를 묻는 질문에 연기된지 몰랐다고 답변한 정답이다.
(B) **연상 작용 오답**: 의미상 연결이 가능한 두 단어 finance와 funds를 이용해서 혼동을 유발하는 오답이다.
(C) **파생어 오답**: 질문의 meeting과 파생어 관계인 meet을 이용한 오답이다.

어휘 finance department 경리부 postpone 연기하다 realize 알다 charity 자선

12 W-Am / M-Cn

How do you think the press conference went?
(A) No, press the button on the left side.
(B) They say Aruba is a good holiday destination.
(C) I arrived too late because of traffic.

기자 회견이 어떻게 진행되었다고 생각하세요?
(A) 아니요, 왼쪽 버튼을 누르세요.
(B) 아루바가 좋은 휴양지라고 하더군요.
(C) 차가 막혀서 너무 늦게 도착했어요.

해설 의견을 묻는 How 의문문
(A) **다의어·Yes/No 대답 불가 오답**: 질문의 press(언론)와 의미가 다른 press(누르다)를 이용하여 혼란을 유발하고, 의문사 의문문에 Yes/No로 대답한 오답이다.
(B) **관련 없는 오답**: 질문과 상관없는 답변이다.
(C) **정답**: 기자 회견이 어땠는지 묻는 질문에 차가 막혀서 너무 늦게 도착했다며 모른다는 말을 우회적으로 답변하고 있다.

어휘 press conference 기자 회견 destination 목적지 traffic 교통(량)

13 W-Br / M-Au

How many market surveys were conducted last year?
(A) Head of the marketing team.
(B) More than we expected.
(C) Yes, after next year.

작년에 시장조사가 몇 번 실시되었나요?
(A) 마케팅팀 팀장이요.
(B) 우리가 예상했던 것보다 더 많았어요.
(C) 네, 내년 이후예요.

해설 시장조사 건수를 묻는 How many 의문문
(A) 파생어 오답: 질문의 market과 파생어 관계인 marketing을 이용한 오답이다.
(B) 정답: 시장조사가 몇 번 실시되었는지를 묻는 질문에 예상보다 많았다며 대략적으로 답변한 정답이다.
(C) 단어 반복·Yes/No 대답 불가 오답: 질문의 year를 그대로 반복해 혼동을 유발하고, 의문사 의문문에 Yes/No로 답변한 오답이다.

어휘 market survey 시장조사 conduct 실시하다

14 W-Br / M-Au

Why didn't we see Mr. Kimura at the grand opening?
(A) Yes, he's finishing that paperwork now.
(B) Because he had to go to California.
(C) Yes, wear your uniform.

왜 개업식에서 키무라 씨가 보이지 않았죠?
(A) 네, 그는 지금 서류 작업을 마무리하고 있어요.
(B) 그는 캘리포니아에 가야 했거든요.
(C) 네, 유니폼을 착용하세요.

해설 개업식에 키무라 씨가 보이지 않은 이유를 묻는 Why 의문문
(A) Yes/No 대답 불가 오답: 의문사 의문문에 Yes/No로 대답할 수 없다. Yes/No로 대답할 수 있는 제안을 나타내는 Why don't we나 Why don't you 의문문과 착각하지 않도록 유의해야 한다.
(B) 정답: 개업식에서 키무라 씨가 보이지 않은 이유를 묻는 질문에 그가 캘리포니아에 가야 했다며 구체적인 이유를 제시하고 있다.
(C) Yes/No 대답 불가 오답: 의문사 의문문에 Yes/No로 대답할 수 없다.

15 M-Au / W-Am

How many sweaters do we have left?
(A) The office is on the right.
(B) Yes, in the top drawer.
(C) We have about twenty on the shelves.

스웨터가 몇 장 남아 있죠?
(A) 사무실은 오른쪽에 있어요.
(B) 네, 맨 위 서랍이요.
(C) 선반에 20개 정도 있어요.

해설 스웨터 개수를 묻는 How many 의문문
(A) 연상 작용 오답: 질문의 left와 다의어 관계인 '왼쪽'을 뜻하는 left에서 연상 가능한 right를 이용한 오답이다.
(B) Yes/No 대답 불가 오답: 의문사 의문문은 Yes/No로 대답할 수 없다.
(C) 정답: 스웨터가 몇 장 남아 있는지 묻는 질문에 선반에 20개 정도 있다고 구체적인 개수로 대답하고 있다.

어휘 drawer 서랍 shelf 선반

16 W-Am / W-Am

Why did Louisa decide to retire this year?
(A) Because she needs new tires.
(B) These are very good reasons.
(C) I have no idea.

루이자는 왜 올해 은퇴하기로 결정했죠?
(A) 그녀는 새 타이어가 필요하기 때문이에요.
(B) 매우 좋은 이유들이네요.
(C) 모르겠어요.

해설 은퇴 이유를 묻는 Why 의문문
(A) 유사 발음 오답: retire와 발음이 일부 유사한 tires를 이용한 오답이다.
(B) 연상 작용 오답: 질문의 Why에서 연상 가능한 reasons를 이용한 오답이다.
(C) 정답: 이유를 묻는 질문에 모르겠다고 답변한 정답이다.

어휘 retire 은퇴하다

17 W-Am / M-Cn

Why's everybody waiting in front of the building?
(A) There was a safety drill.
(B) Twenty minutes or more.
(C) No, I'm pretty sure they're all there.

왜 다들 건물 앞에서 기다리고 있죠?
(A) 안전 훈련이 있었어요.
(B) 20분 이상이요.
(C) 아니요, 분명 그들 모두 거기 있을 거예요.

해설 건물 앞에서 기다리는 이유를 묻는 Why 의문문
(A) 정답: 왜 다들 건물 앞에서 기다리고 있는지에 대해 안전 훈련(safety drill)이라는 이유를 제시하고 있다.
(B) 연상 작용 오답: 질문의 waiting에서 연상 가능한 Twenty minutes를 이용한 오답이다.
(C) Yes/No 대답 불가 오답: 의문사 의문문에 Yes/No로 대답할 수 없다.

어휘 in front of ~ 앞에 safety 안전 drill 훈련

18 M-Au / W-Am

How often does the coffee machine need to be cleaned?
(A) Once a week, I think.
(B) At the coffee shop.
(C) No, I didn't clean it.

커피 머신은 얼마나 자주 청소해야 하나요?
(A) 일주일에 한 번일 걸요.
(B) 커피숍에서요.
(C) 아니요, 전 청소하지 않았어요.

해설 빈도를 묻는 How often 의문문
(A) 정답: 빈도를 묻는 질문에 일주일에 한 번(Once a week)이라는 구체적인 빈도를 언급하고 있다.
(B) 단어 반복 오답: 질문의 coffee를 그대로 반복 이용한 오답이다.

(C) 단어 반복·Yes/No 대답 불가 오답: 질문의 clean을 반복해 혼동을 유발하고, 의문사 의문문에 Yes/No로 답변한 오답이다.

19 W-Am / M-Au

Why does the office look so empty this afternoon?
(A) I'll see you in the morning.
(B) Because her office is next to mine.
(C) A lot of people left early.

오늘 오후에 사무실이 왜 이렇게 비어 보이죠?
(A) 아침에 봐요.
(B) 그녀의 사무실이 내 사무실 옆이라서요.
(C) 많이들 일찍 퇴근했어요.

해설 사무실이 비어 보이는 이유를 묻는 Why 의문문
(A) 연상 작용 오답: 질문의 afternoon에서 연상 가능한 morning을 이용한 오답이다.
(B) 단어 반복·연상 작용 오답: 질문의 office를 반복하고 Why에서 연상 가능한 Because를 이용한 오답이다.
(C) 정답: 사무실이 비어 보이는 이유를 묻는 질문에 많은 사람들이 일찍 퇴근했다는 이유로 대답하고 있다.

어휘 empty 빈

20 M-Cn / W-Br

How was the brainstorming session this morning?
(A) It went very well.
(B) OK, I'll keep that in mind.
(C) Yes, I have some in my desk drawer.

오늘 아침 브레인스토밍 회의는 어땠나요?
(A) 아주 잘 됐어요.
(B) 알겠습니다, 명심할게요.
(C) 네, 제 책상 서랍에 몇 개 있어요.

해설 의견을 묻는 How 의문문
(A) 정답: 회의가 어땠는지 묻는 질문에 긍정의 내용으로 답하므로 정답이다.
(B) Yes/No 대답 불가 오답: How 의문문에 Yes에 해당하는 OK로 대답할 수 없다.
(C) Yes/No 대답 불가 오답: 의견을 묻는 How 의문문에는 Yes/No로 대답할 수 없다.

어휘 go well 잘 (진행)되다 keep in mind 명심하다

21 W-Br / M-Cn

Why do you need to reschedule your appointment?
(A) Something came up unexpectedly.
(B) I'm not disappointed.
(C) On Friday morning.

왜 약속 일정을 변경해야 하죠?
(A) 예기치 못하게 일이 생겼어요.
(B) 저는 실망하지 않았어요.
(C) 금요일 오전에요.

해설 일정 변경 이유를 묻는 Why 의문문
(A) 정답: 왜 약속을 조정해야 하는지에 대해 예기치 못한 일이 발생했다는 이유를 제시하고 있다.
(B) 유사 발음 오답: 질문의 appointment와 부분적으로 발음이 비슷한 disappointed를 이용한 오답이다.
(C) 연상 작용 오답: 질문의 reschedule에서 연상 가능한 Friday morning을 이용한 오답이다.

어휘 reschedule (일정을) 변경하다, 조정하다
come up (일 등이) 생기다

22 W-Br / W-Am

How long have you been employed at this organization?
(A) About thirty kilometers from here.
(B) Since it was founded.
(C) Yes, they're very organized.

이 단체에 얼마나 오래 근무하셨나요?
(A) 여기서 30킬로미터 정도예요.
(B) 창립부터요.
(C) 네, 그들은 아주 체계적이에요.

해설 근무 기간을 묻는 How long 의문문
(A) 연상 작용 오답: 질문의 long에서 연상 가능한 thirty kilometers를 이용한 오답이다.
(B) 정답: 근무 기간을 묻는 질문에 창립 때부터(Since it was founded)라고 응답하고 있으므로 정답이다.
(C) 파생어·Yes/No 대답 불가 오답: 질문의 organization과 파생어 관계인 organized를 사용해 혼동을 유발하고, 의문사 의문문에 Yes/No로 답변한 오답이다.

어휘 employ 고용하다 organization 단체 found 창립하다
organized 체계적인

23 M-Au / W-Br

Why does Ms. Yamada want access to the laboratory?
(A) Yes, I went there yesterday.
(B) On her way to the office.
(C) To conduct a research project.

야마다 씨는 왜 실험실을 사용하고 싶어 하죠?
(A) 네, 저는 어제 거기 갔었어요.
(B) 사무실로 가는 도중에요.
(C) 연구 프로젝트를 수행하기 위해서요.

해설 실험실 사용 이유를 묻는 Why 의문문
(A) Yes/No 대답 불가 오답: 이유를 묻는 Why 의문문에는 Yes/No로 대답할 수 없다.
(B) 관련 없는 오답: 실험실 사용(access to the laboratory)을 원하는 이유와 관련 없는 대답이다.
(C) 정답: 실험실을 사용하고 싶어 하는 이유를 묻는 질문에 to부정사를 써서 연구 프로젝트를 수행하기 위해서(To conduct a research project)라는 목적을 제시하고 있다.

어휘 access 사용 권한, 접근 laboratory 실험실

24 M-Au / W-Am

How many interviews do we have scheduled today?
(A) No, I don't have time this week.
(B) I enjoyed the talk.
(C) Two, actually.

오늘 면접이 몇 건 잡혀 있나요?
(A) 아니요. 이번 주에는 제가 시간이 없어요.
(B) 대화가 즐거웠어요.
(C) 사실 두 건이에요.

해설 면접 횟수를 묻는 How many 의문문
(A) Yes/No 대답 불가 오답: 의문사 의문문에 Yes/No로 대답할 수 없다.
(B) 연상 작용 오답: 질문의 interviews에서 연상 가능한 talk를 이용한 오답이다.
(C) 정답: 횟수를 묻는 질문에 두 건이라는 구체적인 횟수를 언급하고 있다.

25 W-Br / M-Au

Why was the time of the morning news program changed?
(A) Sorry, I only have yesterday's paper.
(B) To make room for another show.
(C) Do you need extra time?

아침 뉴스 프로그램 시간이 왜 바뀌었나요?
(A) 죄송해요. 저한테 어제 신문밖에 없네요.
(B) 다른 프로그램을 위해 자리를 마련하려고요.
(C) 시간이 더 필요하신가요?

해설 시간 변경 이유를 묻는 Why 의문문
(A) 연상 작용 오답: 질문의 news에서 연상 가능한 paper를 이용한 오답이다.
(B) 정답: 뉴스 프로그램 시간이 왜 바뀌었는지 묻는 질문에 대해 구체적인 이유를 제시하고 있으므로 정답이다.
(C) 단어 반복 오답: 질문의 time을 그대로 반복 이용한 오답이다.

어휘 room 자리, 공간

UNIT 06 일반/선택 의문문

① 일반 의문문

ETS CHECK UP 본책 p.050

| 1 (C) | 2 (C) | 3 (A) | 4 (A) | 5 (A) |

1 W-Br / M-Cn

Do you want to see a play tomorrow night?
(A) Forty-five dollars.
(B) I just saw her.
(C) I'd love to.

내일 밤에 연극 보실래요?
(A) 45달러예요.
(B) 방금 그녀를 봤어요.
(C) 좋아요.

해설 의견을 묻는 조동사(Do) 의문문
(A) 관련 없는 오답: 가격을 묻는 질문에 가능한 답변이다.
(B) 단어 반복 오답: 질문에 언급된 see의 과거형인 saw를 반복 이용한 오답이다.
(C) 정답: 내일 밤에 연극을 볼 것인지 묻는 질문에 긍정적으로 대답하고 있다.

2 M-Au / W-Am

Was the advertising team informed about the leadership change?
(A) The game will be televised.
(B) Let me check my wallet.
(C) It's not official yet.

광고팀이 지도부 변경에 대해 통보를 받았나요?
(A) 경기는 TV로 중계될 거예요.
(B) 지갑을 확인해 볼게요.
(C) 아직 공식적인 건 아니에요.

해설 통보 여부를 묻는 Be동사 의문문
(A) 연상 작용 오답: 질문의 team에서 연상 가능한 game을 이용한 오답이다.
(B) 연상 작용 오답: 질문의 change를 잔돈으로 오해할 경우 연상 가능한 wallet을 이용한 정답이다.
(C) 정답: 지도부 변경에 대해 광고팀이 통보를 받았는지 묻는 질문에 변경이 아직 공식적인 건 아니라며 우회적인 대답으로 정보의 불확실함을 표현하고 있다.

어휘 leadership 지도부, 대표직 official 공식적인

3 M-Cn / W-Br

Has the gallery received our shipment of artwork?
(A) Yes, they just confirmed it.
(B) I prefer this painting.
(C) That's a good idea.

화랑에서 우리가 보낸 미술품을 받았나요?
(A) 네, 그들이 방금 확인해 줬어요.
(B) 전 이 그림이 더 좋아요.
(C) 좋은 생각이에요.

해설 완료 여부를 묻는 조동사(Have) 의문문
(A) 정답: 화랑이 미술품을 받았는지 묻는 질문에, 긍정의 대답인 Yes로 응답하며 뒤에 이어지는 내용도 자연스러우므로 정답이다.
(B) 연상 작용 오답: 질문의 gallery와 artwork에서 연상 가능한 painting을 이용한 오답이다.
(C) 관련 없는 오답: 상대방의 의견이나 제안에 동의하는 말이므로 질문에 적합하지 않다.

어휘 receive 받다 shipment 배송(품)
confirm (받았음을) 확인하다 prefer 선호하다

4 M-Au / W-Am

Does the chef use local ingredients?
(A) There aren't many farms in the area.
(B) A reservation for six.
(C) Dessert is included.

그 요리사는 현지 재료를 사용하나요?
(A) 이 지역에는 농장이 많지 않아요.
(B) 6명 예약이에요.
(C) 후식이 포함되어 있어요.

해설 현지 재료 사용 여부를 묻는 조동사(Does) 의문문
(A) 정답: 요리사가 현지 재료를 사용하는지 묻는 질문에 이 지역에는 농장이 많지 않다며 우회적으로 부정의 의미를 전달하고 있다.
(B) 연상 작용 오답: 질문의 chef에서 식당 예약을 연상하게 하는 reservation을 이용한 오답이다.
(C) 연상 작용 오답: 질문의 chef에서 연상 가능한 dessert를 이용한 오답이다.

5 W-Am / M-Au

Do you know what kind of car you'd like to lease?
(A) Something small and fuel efficient.
(B) It's due at the end of the month.
(C) I got stuck in traffic.

어떤 차를 빌리고 싶으세요?
(A) 작고 연비가 좋은 거요.
(B) 월말에 만기가 돼요.
(C) 차가 막혔어요.

해설 원하는 종류를 묻는 What kind of 간접 의문문
(A) 정답: 원하는 차량의 종류를 묻는 what kind of 의문문에 구체적인 사항(small and fuel efficient)으로 답변한 정답이다.
(B) 연상 작용 오답: 질문의 lease에서 연상 가능한 임대 만기 시점 at the end of the month로 응답한 오답이다.
(C) 연상 작용 오답: 질문의 car에서 연상 가능한 traffic을 이용한 오답이다.

어휘 lease 빌리다   fuel efficient 연비가 좋은   due 만기인   stuck in traffic 차가 막히는

② 선택 의문문

◆ETS CHECK UP   본책 p.051

| 1 (B) | 2 (C) | 3 (C) | 4 (C) | 5 (A) |

1 M-Cn / W-Am

Does Henry speak Spanish or Italian?
(A) They are European.
(B) He speaks both.
(C) It was a long speech.

헨리 씨는 스페인어를 하나요, 아니면 이탈리아어를 하나요?
(A) 그들은 유럽인이에요.
(B) 그는 둘 다 해요.
(C) 그것은 긴 연설이었어요.

해설 구사하는 언어를 묻는 선택 의문문
(A) 연상 작용 오답: 질문의 Spanish와 Italian에서 연상 가능한 European(유럽인)을 이용한 오답이다.
(B) 정답: both를 사용해 두 가지 선택 사항(스페인어/이탈리아어)을 모두 선택한 정답이다.
(C) 연상 작용 오답: 질문의 speak에서 연상 가능한 speech를 이용한 오답이다.

어휘 Spanish 스페인어; 스페인의   Italian 이탈리아어; 이탈리아의   European 유럽인; 유럽의   speech 연설

2 M-Cn / W-Br

Are you presenting your research today or tomorrow?
(A) Lots of data.
(B) I need an accounting job.
(C) Tomorrow at 10 A.M.

오늘 연구를 발표하시나요, 아니면 내일 하시나요?
(A) 많은 데이터요.
(B) 저는 회계 관련 일자리가 필요해요.
(C) 내일 오전 10시에요.

해설 발표 시점을 묻는 선택 의문문
(A) 연상 작용 오답: 질문의 research에서 연상 가능한 data를 이용한 오답이다.
(B) 관련 없는 오답: 질문과 상관없는 답변이다.
(C) 정답: 연구를 발표할 시점으로 오늘과 내일 중 내일을 선택해 응답한 것이므로 정답이다.

어휘 present 발표하다   research 연구   accounting 회계

3 W-Am / W-Br

Would you like this shirt or a smaller one?
(A) Yes, just a little.
(B) Is there another caller?
(C) What sizes do you have?

이 셔츠로 하시겠어요, 아니면 더 작은 걸로 하시겠어요?
(A) 네, 아주 조금요.
(B) 전화를 건 사람이 또 있나요?
(C) 어떤 사이즈가 있나요?

해설 옷 사이즈를 묻는 선택 의문문
(A) 연상 작용·Yes/No 대답 불가 오답: 질문의 smaller에서 연상 가능한 little을 사용해 혼동을 유발하고, 선택 의문에 Yes/No로 대답한 오답이다.
(B) 연상 작용 오답: 질문의 or와 one에서 연상 가능한 another를 이용한 오답이다.
(C) 정답: 사이즈를 선택해야 하는 상황에서 자연스럽게 되묻는 질문이다.

어휘 caller 전화를 건 사람

4 W-Am / W-Br

Do you want my home or work phone number?
(A) She leaves work at five.
(B) It's 52 Broad Street.
(C) Whichever one I can reach you at.

제 집 전화번호를 알려드릴까요, 아니면 직장 전화번호를 알려드릴까요?
(A) 그녀는 5시에 퇴근해요.
(B) 브로드 가 52번지예요.
(C) 어느 쪽이든 제가 연락할 수 있는 것으로요.

해설 **선호하는 정보를 묻는 선택 의문문**
(A) **단어 반복·인칭 오류 오답**: 질문의 work를 반복 사용한 오답이며, 질문에 She를 가리킬 만한 대상이 없다.
(B) **관련 없는 오답**: 장소를 묻는 Where 의문문에 어울리는 대답이다.
(C) **정답**: 두 가지 상황을 제시한 선택 의문문에 둘 중 한 가지를 고르는 대신 어느 쪽이든 괜찮다고 대답하고 있다.

어휘 leave work 퇴근하다 whichever 어느 쪽이든
reach 연락이 닿다

5 W-Am / M-Au

Should we reserve the conference room for one hour or two?
(A) It's a long presentation.
(B) No, he wasn't.
(C) Thanks for your help with my project.

회의실을 한 시간 동안 예약해야 할까요, 아니면 두 시간을 해야 할까요?
(A) 발표가 길어요.
(B) 아니요, 그는 아니었어요.
(C) 제 프로젝트를 도와주셔서 감사합니다.

해설 **회의실 예약 시간을 묻는 선택 의문문**
(A) **정답**: 두 가지 선택 사항 one hour와 two hours 중 발표가 길다는 대답으로 후자를 우회적으로 선택하여 적절히 답변한 정답이다.
(B) **인칭 오류·Yes/No 대답 불가 오답**: 의문문에 he를 가리킬 만한 대상이 없고, 선택 의문문에는 Yes/No로 대답할 수 없다.
(C) **연상 작용 오답**: 질문의 conference에서 연상 가능한 project를 이용한 오답이다.

어휘 reserve 예약하다

ETS 유형 연습   본책 p.052

1 (A)   2 (C)   3 (C)   4 (C)   5 (B)

1 W-Am / M-Au

Are these instructions clear?
(A) No, could you repeat them?
(B) It's already clean.
(C) He's a good teacher.

이 설명이 알아듣기 쉬운가요?
(A) 아니요, 한 번 더 반복해 주시겠어요?
(B) 그것은 이미 깨끗해요.
(C) 그는 좋은 교사예요.

해설 **이해 여부를 묻는 Be동사 의문문**
(A) **정답**: 설명이 쉬운지 묻는 질문에 부정의 뜻(No)을 나타낸 뒤, 한 번 더 설명해 달라고 요청하고 있다.
(B) **유사 발음 오답**: 질문의 clear와 발음이 비슷한 clean을 이용한 오답이다.
(C) **연상 작용 오답**: 질문의 instructions에서 연상 가능한 teacher를 이용한 오답이다.

어휘 instructions 설명, 설명서 clear 알아듣기 쉬운, 분명한
repeat 반복하다

2 M-Cn / W-Am

Will the next shipment be by air or by truck?
(A) A free magazine subscription.
(B) I already have a truck.
(C) Our supplier handles that.

다음 수송은 항공편으로 할 건가요, 아니면 트럭으로 할 건가요?
(A) 무료 잡지 구독이요.
(B) 저에게 이미 트럭이 있어요.
(C) 그건 우리 공급업체에서 처리해요.

해설 **수송 방식을 묻는 선택 의문문**
(A) **관련 없는 오답**: 질문 내용과 관련 없는 대답이다.
(B) **단어 반복 오답**: 질문에 언급된 truck을 반복 이용한 오답이다.
(C) **정답**: 두 가지 선택 사항 by air와 by truck 중에서 선택하는 대신 공급업체에서 배송을 처리한다고 제3의 선택 사항을 제시하며 적절히 답변한 정답이다.

어휘 shipment 배송 subscription 구독
supplier 공급업체 handle 처리하다

3 M-Cn / W-Am

Are you giving your presentation in the small conference room?
(A) No, a member of the board.
(B) In the top drawer.
(C) I need a room with a projector.

작은 회의실에서 발표를 하실 건가요?
(A) 아니요, 이사회 구성원이요.
(B) 맨 위 서랍에요.
(C) 프로젝터가 있는 방이 필요해요.

해설 **장소 사용 여부를 묻는 Be동사 의문문**
(A) **연상 작용 오답**: 질문의 presentation과 conference에서 연상 가능한 board(이사회)를 이용한 오답이다.
(B) **관련 없는 오답**: 위치를 묻는 Where 의문문에 가능한 답변이다.
(C) **정답**: 작은 회의실에서 발표를 할 것인지 묻는 질문에 Yes를 생략한 채 프로젝터가 있는 방이 필요하다며 장소를 사용하는 이유를 밝히고 있다.

어휘 board 이사회   projector 프로젝터, 영사기

4 W-Br / M-Cn
Should we review our notes today, or is tomorrow OK?
(A) They got great reviews.
(B) Yes, I noticed.
(C) It doesn't matter to me.

우리가 기록을 오늘 검토해야 하나요, 아니면 내일 해도 되나요?
(A) 그들은 좋은 평가를 받았어요.
(B) 네, 저도 알아차렸어요.
(C) 저는 상관없어요.

해설 검토 시점을 묻는 선택 의문문
(A) 다의어 오답: 서로 다른 의미의 review를 반복 이용한 오답이다. 질문의 review는 '검토하다'라는 동사이고, 보기의 reviews는 '평가, 비평'이라는 명사이다.
(B) 유사 발음 오답: 질문의 notes와 발음이 유사한 noticed를 이용한 오답이다.
(C) 정답: 오늘 아니면 내일이 좋은지 묻는 질문에 언제라도 상관없다고 응답하고 있다.

어휘 review 검토하다; 평가, 비평   notice 알아차리다   matter 중요하다, 문제가 되다

5 M-Au / W-Br
Do your employees receive an annual bonus?
(A) The manual arrived today.
(B) Yes, every December.
(C) That job is still open.

당신 직원들은 연간 보너스를 받나요?
(A) 설명서가 오늘 도착했어요.
(B) 네, 매년 12월에요.
(C) 그 자리는 아직 충원되지 않았어요.

해설 보너스 지급 여부를 묻는 조동사(Do) 의문문
(A) 유사 발음 오답: 질문의 annual과 부분적으로 발음이 유사한 manual을 이용한 오답이다.
(B) 정답: 보너스를 받는다는 뜻으로 Yes라고 말한 후 구체적인 지급 시점을 덧붙이고 있다.
(C) 연상 작용 오답: 질문의 employees에서 연상 가능한 job을 이용한 오답이다.

어휘 receive 받다   annual 연간의

ETS 실전 문제
본책 p.053

1 (C)	2 (A)	3 (A)	4 (C)	5 (A)
6 (A)	7 (A)	8 (B)	9 (B)	10 (B)
11 (C)	12 (B)	13 (A)	14 (B)	15 (A)
16 (C)	17 (C)	18 (B)	19 (B)	20 (C)
21 (A)	22 (B)	23 (A)	24 (C)	25 (C)

1 M-Cn / W-Br
Will you be at your desk all day today?
(A) Yes, he is on vacation.
(B) At the tech service department.
(C) No, I have several meetings.

오늘 하루 종일 자리에 계실 건가요?
(A) 네, 그는 휴가 중이에요.
(B) 기술 서비스 부서에서요.
(C) 아니요, 회의가 여러 개 있어요.

해설 자리에 있을지 묻는 조동사(Will) 의문문
(A) 인칭 오류 오답: 질문의 주어가 you인데 보기의 주어는 he이므로 논리적으로 맞지 않다.
(B) 관련 없는 오답: 질문과 상관없는 답변을 제시하고 있다.
(C) 정답: 오늘 종일 자리에 있을지 묻는 질문에 No로 대답한 후, 회의가 여러 개 있다고 구체적인 정보를 제공하고 있으므로 정답이다.

어휘 on vacation 휴가 중인

2 W-Br / M-Cn
Do you want to answer another question or go on to the next topic?
(A) We can move ahead.
(B) Around nine forty-five.
(C) At the retirement party.

다른 질문에 답변하시겠어요, 아니면 다음 주제로 넘어가시겠어요?
(A) 다음으로 넘어가 보죠.
(B) 9시 45분쯤이요.
(C) 은퇴식에서요.

해설 둘 중 하나를 고르는 선택 의문문
(A) 정답: 다른 질문에 답변할지 아니면 다음 주제로 넘어갈지 묻자 다음으로 넘어가 보자며 후자를 선택하여 답변하고 있다.
(B) 관련 없는 오답: 시간을 묻는 What time 의문문에 가능한 답변이다.
(C) 관련 없는 오답: 질문과 상관없는 답변이다.

어휘 ahead 앞으로   around ~쯤, 약   retirement 은퇴

3 M-Cn / W-Am
Do I need to attend the safety training?
(A) Yes, it's a requirement.
(B) I'll put it in the safe.
(C) The company headquarters.

제가 안전교육에 참석해야 하나요?
(A) 네, 요구 사항이에요.
(B) 제가 금고에 넣을게요.
(C) 회사 본사요.

해설 의무 사항을 묻는 조동사(Do) 의문문
(A) 정답: 안전교육에 참석해야 하는지 묻는 질문에 요구 사항이라고 적절히 대답하고 있다.
(B) 유사 발음 오답: 질문의 safety와 부분적으로 발음이 유사한 safe를 이용한 오답이다.

(C) 관련 없는 오답: 질문과 상관없는 답변이다.

어휘 requirement 요구 사항 safe 금고
headquarters 본부

4 W-Am / M-Cn
Will you be here tomorrow, or are you working at the branch office?
(A) Because there's a lot to do.
(B) Yes, they liked the work.
(C) I'm here all week.

내일 여기 오실 거예요, 아니면 지사에서 일하실 거예요?
(A) 할 일이 많아서요.
(B) 네, 그들은 작품을 마음에 들어 했어요.
(C) 전 일주일 내내 여기 있어요.

해설 근무할 장소를 묻는 선택 의문문
(A) 관련 없는 오답: 이유를 묻는 Why 의문문에 적합한 대답이다.
(B) 다의어 오답: 질문의 working과 의미가 다른 work(작품, 작업)를 이용한 오답이다.
(C) 정답: 두 가지 선택 사항 be here tomorrow와 working at the branch office 중 계속 여기에 있을 것이라고 전자를 선택하여 대답하고 있다.

5 M-Cn / W-Br
Is there a stapler I can borrow?
(A) Yes, I have one right here.
(B) Tomorrow is Saturday.
(C) I won it at a fair.

제가 빌릴 수 있는 스테이플러가 있나요?
(A) 네, 여기 하나 있어요.
(B) 내일은 토요일이에요.
(C) 박람회에서 그걸 땄어요.

해설 스테이플러가 있는지 묻는 Be동사 의문문
(A) 정답: 빌릴 수 있는 스테이플러가 있는지 묻는 질문에, Yes라고 긍정 응답한 후 여기 하나 있다고 덧붙이고 있으므로 정답이다.
(B) 관련 없는 오답: 질문 내용과 관련 없는 대답이다.
(C) 관련 없는 오답: Where 의문문에 어울리는 대답이다.

어휘 fair 박람회

6 M-Au / W-Am
Should we take the group photo indoors or outdoors?
(A) Outdoors would be better.
(B) A bank statement.
(C) A small part in a movie.

단체 사진을 실내에서 찍을까요, 아니면 야외에서 찍을까요?
(A) 야외가 더 좋겠어요.
(B) 은행 명세서요.
(C) 영화에서 작은 배역이요.

해설 촬영 장소를 묻는 선택 의문문
(A) 정답: 실내 촬영과 야외 촬영 중 야외 촬영을 선택해 응답한 것이므로 정답이다.
(B) 관련 없는 오답: 질문 내용과 관련 없는 대답이다.
(C) 연상 작용 오답: 질문의 group photo에서 연상 가능한 movie를 이용한 오답이다.

어휘 indoors 실내에서 outdoors 야외에서
bank statement 은행 명세서

7 M-Au / W-Br
Will you be checking any baggage for today's flight?
(A) Yes, I have one suitcase.
(B) A one-way flight.
(C) No, I bring food from home.

오늘 비행기에 짐을 부치실 건가요?
(A) 네, 여행 가방이 하나 있어요.
(B) 편도 비행이요.
(C) 아니요, 전 집에서 음식을 가져와요.

해설 짐을 부칠 것인지 묻는 조동사(Will) 의문문
(A) 정답: 오늘 비행기에 짐을 부칠지 묻는 질문에 Yes로 대답한 후, 여행 가방이 하나 있다(I have one suitcase)고 구체적인 정보를 제공하고 있으므로 정답이다.
(B) 단어 반복 오답: 질문의 flight를 반복 이용한 오답이다.
(C) 관련 없는 오답: 질문과 상관없는 답변을 제시하고 있다.

어휘 baggage 짐 one-way 편도의

8 M-Au / W-Br
Do you want Amy Shimizu to present first, or should I?
(A) Yes, it's a nice day.
(B) Let's start with Amy.
(C) Wasn't it on Second Avenue?

에이미 시미즈가 먼저 발표할까요, 아니면 제가 먼저 할까요?
(A) 네, 날씨가 좋네요.
(B) 에이미부터 시작합시다.
(C) 2번가에 있지 않았나요?

해설 발표 순서를 묻는 선택 의문문
(A) Yes/No 대답 불가 오답: 선택 의문문에는 Yes/No로 대답할 수 없다.
(B) 정답: 먼저 발표할 사람으로 에이미와 질문자 중 에이미를 선택해 응답한 것이므로 정답이다.
(C) 연상 작용 오답: 의미상 연결이 가능한 두 표현 first와 Second를 이용한 오답이다.

어휘 present 발표하다

9 M-Au / W-Br
Did you go sightseeing when you were in Switzerland?
(A) That would be great.
(B) I was too busy.
(C) The Metropolitan Hotel.

스위스에 있을 때 관광을 하셨나요?
(A) 그거 좋겠어요.
(B) 너무 바빴어요.
(C) 메트로폴리탄 호텔이요.

해설 과거의 사건을 묻는 조동사(Did) 의문문
(A) **관련 없는 오답**: 과거의 사건을 묻는 질문과는 의미상 어울리지 않는다.
(B) **정답**: 스위스에 있을 때 관광을 했는지 묻는 질문에 No를 생략한 채 바빴다고 관광을 하지 못한 이유를 우회적으로 밝히고 있다.
(C) **연상 작용 오답**: 질문의 sightseeing에서 연상 가능한 Hotel을 이용한 오답이다.

어휘 go sightseeing 관광하러 다니다

10 M-Au / W-Br

Are you interested in renting a place in the city or farther out of town?
(A) The rental price includes all utilities.
(B) Somewhere near my office would be best.
(C) It was a very interesting location.

시내에 있는 집을 임차하시겠어요, 아니면 더 멀리 시내에서 떨어진 집을 임차하시겠어요?
(A) 임대료에는 공공요금이 전부 포함돼요.
(B) 제 사무실 근처 어디면 가장 좋겠어요.
(C) 아주 관심이 가는 장소였어요.

해설 임차할 집의 위치를 묻는 선택 의문문
(A) **유사 발음 오답**: 질문의 place와 발음이 유사한 price를 이용한 오답이다.
(B) **정답**: 시내와 외곽 중 어느 곳에 집을 임차할지 묻는 질문에 둘 중에서 선택하는 대신 사무실 근처로 하면 좋겠다고 답변한 정답이다.
(C) **파생어 오답**: 질문에 언급된 interested와 파생어 관계인 interesting을 이용한 오답이다.

어휘 farther 더 멀리 utility (수도·전기·가스 등) 공공요금

11 M-Au / W-Br

Will we need to make changes to the budget?
(A) Here's your change.
(B) I couldn't make it yesterday.
(C) I think this is fine.

우리가 예산을 수정해야 할까요?
(A) 잔돈 여기 있습니다.
(B) 저는 어제 참석할 수 없었어요.
(C) 이것도 괜찮다고 생각해요.

해설 의견을 묻는 조동사(Will) 의문문
(A) **다의어 오답**: 서로 다른 의미의 change를 반복 이용한 오답이다. 질문의 change는 '수정, 변경'의 의미이고, 보기의 change는 '잔돈'의 의미이다.
(B) **단어 반복 오답**: 질문에 사용된 단어 make를 그대로 반복 이용한 오답이다.
(C) **정답**: 조동사 의문문에 No를 생략하고, 수정할 필요 없이 현재 예산도 괜찮다고 답변한 정답이다.

어휘 change 수정, 변경; 잔돈 budget 예산(안)
make it 참석하다, (시간에 맞게) 도착하다

12 W-Am / M-Au

Will you be walking or driving to work tomorrow?
(A) A new set of keys.
(B) My car is still with the mechanic.
(C) He works in marketing.

내일 걸어서 출근할 건가요, 아니면 운전할 건가요?
(A) 새로운 열쇠 세트요.
(B) 제 차가 아직 정비소에 있어요.
(C) 그는 마케팅 쪽에서 일해요.

해설 출근 방법을 묻는 선택 의문문
(A) **관련 없는 오답**: 질문과 상관없는 답변이다.
(B) **정답**: 내일 걸어서 출근할지 아니면 운전해서 갈지 묻자 차가 아직 정비소에 있다며 걸어서 출근해야 한다는 것을 우회적으로 표현하고 있다.
(C) **단어 반복 오답**: 질문의 work와 품사가 다른 works를 이용한 오답이다.

어휘 mechanic 정비사

13 M-Au / W-Br

Are you going to enlarge the text size in the slide deck?
(A) I've already sent it to the client.
(B) Do you have a receipt?
(C) A variety of design templates.

슬라이드의 글자 크기를 키우실 건가요?
(A) 이미 고객에게 그것을 보냈어요.
(B) 영수증이 있으신가요?
(C) 다양한 디자인 서식이요.

해설 글자 크기 조정 여부를 묻는 Be동사 의문문
(A) **정답**: 슬라이드의 글자 크기를 키울지 묻는 질문에 이미 고객에게 보냈다며 더 이상 조정할 수 없음을 우회적으로 표현하고 있다.
(B) **관련 없는 오답**: 질문 내용과 관련 없는 대답이다.
(C) **연상 작용 오답**: 의미상 연결이 가능한 두 표현 slide deck와 design templates를 이용한 오답이다.

어휘 enlarge 확대하다 slide deck 프레젠테이션 슬라이드 (모음) receipt 영수증 a variety of 다양한 template 서식

14 W-Br / M-Cn

Should we try to find this book at the store, or just buy it online?
(A) I put them all up on the top shelf.
(B) It'll be hard to find in a local shop.
(C) The author has written several books.

이 책을 매장에서 찾아볼까요, 아니면 그냥 온라인으로 살까요?
(A) 전부 책꽂이 맨 위에 올려놓았어요.
(B) 그걸 지역 매장에서는 찾기 힘들 거예요.
(C) 저자는 책을 여러 권 썼어요.

해설 책 구매 장소를 묻는 선택 의문문
(A) **연상 작용 오답**: 질문의 book에서 연상 가능한 shelf를 이용한 오답이다.
(B) **정답**: 매장에서의 구입과 온라인 구입 중 지역 매장에서는 찾기 힘들 것이라며 간접적으로 온라인 구입을 선택해 응답한 것이므로 정답이다.
(C) **단어 반복 오답**: 질문의 book을 반복 이용한 오답이다.

어휘 shelf 책꽂이, 선반

15 M-Cn / M-Au
Did Ms. Yang give you a copy of the sales report?
(A) Yes, but I haven't looked at it yet.
(B) I'll see if the room is free.
(C) Oh, is it on sale?

양 씨가 판매 보고서 사본을 줬나요?
(A) 네, 하지만 아직 안 봤어요.
(B) 방이 비어 있는지 확인할게요.
(C) 아, 할인 중인가요?

해설 판매 보고서를 받았는지 묻는 조동사(Did) 의문문
(A) **정답**: 양 씨가 판매 보고서를 주었는지 묻는 질문에 우선 Yes라고 대답한 뒤 아직 보지는 못했다고 덧붙이고 있다.
(B) **연상 작용 오답**: 질문의 sales에서 연상 가능한 free(비어 있는; 무료의)를 이용한 오답이다.
(C) **단어 반복 오답**: 질문의 sales를 sale로 반복 이용한 오답이다.

16 M-Cn / M-Au
Do I need a special pass to view this film screening, or is it open to the public?
(A) No, it's at the same time.
(B) Yes, maybe a larger screen.
(C) Everyone's welcome to attend.

이 영화 상영을 보려면 특별 출입증이 필요하나요, 아니면 일반인에게 공개되나요?
(A) 아니요. 동시예요.
(B) 네, 아마 더 큰 화면이요.
(C) 누구나 참석하셔도 돼요.

해설 영화 상영 공개 여부를 묻는 선택 의문문
(A) **Yes/No 대답 불가 오답**: 선택 의문문에 Yes/No로 대답할 수 없다.
(B) **파생어·Yes/No 대답 불가 오답**: 질문의 screening과 파생어 관계인 screen을 이용해 혼동을 유발하고, 선택 의문문에 Yes/No로 답변한 오답이다.
(C) **정답**: 영화 상영을 보기 위해 특별 출입증이 필요한지 또는 모두에게 공개된 것인지 묻자 누구나 참석해도 된다며 후자를 선택하여 답변하고 있다.

어휘 film screening 영화 상영

17 M-Cn / W-Am
Is there a bus stop nearby?
(A) Four tickets, please.
(B) No, I haven't.
(C) There's one across the street.

근처에 버스 정류장이 있나요?
(A) 티켓 네 장 주세요.
(B) 아니요, 저는 안 했어요.
(C) 길 건너에 하나 있어요.

해설 근처 버스 정류장의 유무를 묻는 Be동사 의문문
(A) **관련 없는 오답**: How many 의문문에 어울리는 답변이다.
(B) **관련 없는 오답**: 질문 내용과 관련 없는 대답이다.
(C) **정답**: 근처에 버스 정류장이 있는지 묻는 질문에 길 건너에 하나 있다는 구체적인 정보를 제공하고 있으므로 정답이다.

18 W-Am / W-Br
Do you want to sit in the cafeteria or on the patio outside?
(A) This is very good coffee.
(B) Let's stay indoors.
(C) Pizza and a soda, please.

카페테리아 안에 앉을까요, 아니면 바깥 테라스에 앉을까요?
(A) 이건 아주 좋은 커피네요.
(B) 실내에 있죠.
(C) 피자와 탄산음료 주세요.

해설 둘 중 하나를 고르는 선택 의문문
(A) **연상 작용 오답**: 질문의 cafeteria에서 연상 가능한 coffee를 이용한 오답이다.
(B) **정답**: 두 가지 선택 사항 in the cafeteria와 on the patio outside 중 실내를 뜻하는 부사 indoors로 전자를 선택하여 대답하고 있다.
(C) **연상 작용 오답**: cafeteria에서 연상 가능한 pizza와 soda를 이용한 오답이다.

어휘 cafeteria 카페테리아, 간이식당 patio 테라스 indoors 실내에 soda 탄산음료

19 M-Cn / W-Br
Are you interested in joining the employee fitness center?
(A) Three times a week.
(B) Yes, a membership fee.
(C) I'll think about it.

직원 헬스클럽에 가입하시겠어요?
(A) 일주일에 세 번이에요.
(B) 네, 회비요.
(C) 생각해 볼게요.

해설 가입 여부를 묻는 Be동사 의문문
(A) **관련 없는 오답**: 빈도를 묻는 How often 의문문에 적합한 대답이다.

(B) **연상 작용 오답**: 질문의 fitness center에서 연상 가능한 membership fee를 이용한 오답이다.
(C) **정답**: 가입 여부를 묻는 질문에 생각해 보겠다며 확답을 미루고 있다.

20 M-Cn / W-Br

Do you want me to send Mr. Foster an e-mail or give him a call?
(A) It's on the Web site.
(B) Yes, I know him.
(C) Do you have his phone number?

포스터 씨에게 이메일을 보낼까요, 아니면 전화를 할까요?
(A) 웹사이트에 있어요.
(B) 네, 아는 사람이에요.
(C) 그분 전화번호를 아세요?

해설 연락 방법을 묻는 선택 의문문
(A) **연상 작용 오답**: 질문의 e-mail에서 연상 가능한 Web site를 이용한 오답이다.
(B) **단어 반복·Yes/No 대답 불가 오답**: 질문의 him을 그대로 반복해 혼동을 유발하고, 선택 의문문에 Yes/No로 답변한 오답이다.
(C) **정답**: 이메일과 전화 중 어느 방법으로 연락할지 묻는 질문에 대해 전화번호를 아는지 되물어보며 우회적으로 전화 걸기를 선택하고 있다.

21 M-Au / W-Br

Will the office renovations be finished soon?
(A) Yes—sometime this week.
(B) Extra chairs in the supply closet.
(C) There's a coffee machine in the break room.

사무실 보수 공사가 곧 끝날까요?
(A) 네, 이번 주 중으로요.
(B) 물품 보관함에 있는 여분의 의자요.
(C) 휴게실에 커피 머신이 있어요.

해설 공사 완료 여부를 묻는 조동사(Will) 의문문
(A) **정답**: 사무실 보수 공사가 곧 끝날지 묻는 질문에 Yes로 대답한 후, 이번 주 중(sometime this week)이라고 구체적인 정보를 제공하고 있으므로 정답이다.
(B) **연상 작용 오답**: 질문의 office에서 연상 가능한 chairs와 supply closet을 이용한 오답이다.
(C) **연상 작용 오답**: 질문의 office에서 연상 가능한 break room을 이용한 오답이다.

어휘 renovation 수리   supply closet 물품 보관함

22 M-Cn / W-Br

Should I fold the newsletters in half, or leave them unfolded?
(A) I've only read half of it.
(B) I usually fold them.
(C) She'll leave the file with you.

회보를 반으로 접을까요, 아니면 펼쳐진 채로 놔둘까요?
(A) 반밖에 읽지 않았어요.
(B) 전 보통 접어요.
(C) 그녀가 서류를 당신에게 맡길 겁니다.

해설 회보를 접을지 여부를 묻는 선택 의문문
(A) **단어 반복 오답**: 질문에 사용된 half를 반복 이용한 오답이다.
(B) **정답**: 두 가지 선택 사항(반으로 접는 것/펼치는 것) 중 질문의 fold를 그대로 반복 사용해 접는 것을 선호함을 드러내고 있다.
(C) **인칭 오류 오답**: 질문과 관련 없는 제3자 She로 답변하고 있다.

어휘 fold 접다   newsletter 회보   in half 반으로
unfold 펼치다

23 M-Au / W-Am

Are you registered for the seminar on nutrition or the one on fitness?
(A) I'm hoping to go to both.
(B) Yes, it's very healthy.
(C) In the fitting room.

영양 세미나에 등록하셨나요, 아니면 운동 세미나에 등록하셨나요?
(A) 둘 다 가고 싶어요.
(B) 네, 건강에 아주 좋아요.
(C) 탈의실에요.

해설 등록한 세미나를 묻는 선택 의문문
(A) **정답**: both를 사용해 두 가지 선택 사항(영양 세미나/운동 세미나)을 모두 선택한 정답이다.
(B) **Yes/No 대답 불가 오답**: 선택 의문문에 Yes/No로 대답할 수 없다.
(C) **유사 발음 오답**: 질문의 fitness와 부분적으로 발음이 동일한 fitting을 이용한 오답이다.

어휘 register for ~에 등록하다   nutrition 영양
healthy 건강에 좋은, 건강한

24 M-Au / M-Cn

Has the budget estimate changed since we last discussed it?
(A) An interesting discussion.
(B) The financial department.
(C) Not that I know of.

우리가 지난번 논의한 이후로 예산 추정치가 변경되었나요?
(A) 흥미로운 토론이에요.
(B) 경리부요.
(C) 제가 아는 바로는 아니에요.

해설 변경 여부를 묻는 조동사(Have) 의문문
(A) **파생어 오답**: 질문의 discussed와 파생어 관계인 discussion을 이용한 오답이다.
(B) **연상 작용 오답**: 질문의 budget에서 연상 가능한 financial을 이용한 오답이다.

(C) 정답: 변경 사항이 있었는지를 묻는 질문에 변경 없음을 표현하고 있다.

어휘 budget 예산 estimate 추정치

25 W-Br / W-Am

Should we give our clients the tour of our facilities this afternoon or this evening?
(A) Yes, the business school faculty.
(B) Several large tour buses.
(C) Our dinner reservation is at seven.

고객들에게 우리 시설 견학을 오늘 오후에 해 드릴까요, 아니면 오늘 저녁에 할까요?
(A) 네, 경영대 교수진이에요.
(B) 대형 관광 버스 여러 대요.
(C) 저녁 식사 예약이 7시에 있어요.

해설 견학 시간을 묻는 선택 의문문
(A) Yes/No 대답 불가 오답: 선택 의문문에는 Yes/No로 대답할 수 없다.
(B) 단어 반복 오답: 질문의 tour를 반복 이용한 오답이다.
(C) 정답: 두 가지 선택 사항(오늘 오후 견학 진행/오늘 저녁 견학 진행) 중 저녁 식사 예약이 7시에 있다는 대답으로 전자를 우회적으로 선택한 정답이다.

어휘 facility 시설 faculty 교수진

UNIT 07 부정/부가 의문문

1 부정 의문문

ETS CHECK UP 본책 p.054

1 (C) 2 (C) 3 (A) 4 (B) 5 (A)

1 W-Br / M-Au

Shouldn't the drywall have been delivered by now?
(A) I've already seen that movie.
(B) Towels are in the locker room.
(C) The truck is on its way.

지금쯤 석고보드가 배송되었어야 하지 않나요?
(A) 이미 그 영화를 봤어요.
(B) 수건은 탈의실에 있어요.
(C) 트럭이 오는 중이에요.

해설 배송이 완료되었어야 하는지를 묻는 부정 의문문
(A) 관련 없는 오답: 질문과 상관없는 답변이다.
(B) 유사 발음 오답: 질문의 drywall과 발음이 비슷한 Towels를 이용한 오답이다.
(C) 정답: 지금쯤 석고보드가 배송되었어야 하는지 묻는 질문에 트럭이 오는 중이라며 배송 상태에 대해 설명하고 있으므로 정답이다.

어휘 drywall 석고보드 locker room 라커룸[탈의실] on one's way 오는[가는] 도중인

2 M-Cn / W-Br

Shouldn't we have dinner soon?
(A) No, on the second shelf.
(B) A train delay.
(C) I am getting hungry.

우리 곧 저녁 먹어야 하지 않나요?
(A) 아니요, 두 번째 선반에 있어요.
(B) 열차 지연이요.
(C) 배가 고파오긴 하네요.

해설 식사를 할지 묻는 부정 의문문
(A) 관련 없는 오답: 질문과 상관없는 답변이다.
(B) 연상 작용 오답: 질문의 soon에서 반대의 의미로 연상 가능한 delay를 이용한 오답이다.
(C) 정답: 곧 저녁을 먹어야 할지 묻는 질문에 배가 고파온다며 우회적으로 긍정의 의미를 전달하고 있다.

어휘 delay 지연

3 M-Cn / W-Am

Aren't we offering a free-ticket promotion next week?
(A) Actually, it's the following week.
(B) He's certainly the most qualified.
(C) I took it to the office.

다음 주에 무료 티켓 판촉을 제공하는 것 아닌가요?
(A) 실은 그 다음 주예요.
(B) 확실히 그 사람이 가장 적임자예요.
(C) 제가 그걸 사무실로 가져갔어요.

해설 행사 계획을 확인하는 부정 의문문
(A) 정답: 다음 주에 티켓 판촉을 제공하는지를 확인하는 질문에 그 다음 주(it's the following week)라고 잘못된 정보를 정정하고 있다.
(B) 인칭 오류 오답: 의문문에 He를 가리킬 만한 대상이 없으므로 오답이다.
(C) 유사 발음 오답: 질문의 offering과 부분적으로 발음이 유사한 office를 이용한 오답이다.

어휘 promotion 판촉, 홍보 qualified 적임의

4 W-Br / M-Au

Shouldn't the roof be inspected for potential leaks?
(A) It was released last week.
(B) Can you recommend someone to do it?
(C) Next to the inspection station.

누수 가능성이 있는지 지붕을 점검해야 하지 않을까요?
(A) 그건 지난주에 개봉했어요.
(B) 할 사람을 추천해 주실래요?
(C) 검사소 옆이에요.

해설 점검해야 하는지를 묻는 부정 의문문
(A) 유사 발음 오답: 질문의 leaks와 부분적으로 발음이 유사한 released를 이용한 오답이다.
(B) 정답: 누수 가능성에 대해 지붕을 점검해야 하는지 묻는

질문에 점검할 사람을 추천해 줄 수 있는지 되묻고 있다.
(C) 파생어 오답: 질문의 inspected와 파생어 관계인 inspection을 이용한 오답이다.

어휘 inspect 점검하다　potential 가능성이 있는, 잠재적인
leak 누수　release 개봉하다　recommend 추천하다

5 W-Br / M-Au
Isn't Alonso moving into an apartment in the city?
(A) I haven't talked to him in a while.
(B) These parts need to be counted.
(C) The ticket booth closes at eleven P.M.

알론소는 시내 아파트로 이사하는 거 아닌가요?
(A) 한동안 그와 이야기를 못했어요.
(B) 이 부품들을 세어야 해요.
(C) 매표소는 오후 11시에 문을 닫아요.

해설 이사 여부를 확인하는 부정 의문문
(A) 정답: 알론소가 시내 아파트로 이사하지 않는지 묻는 질문에 한동안 그와 이야기를 못했다(I haven't talked to him in a while)는 우회적인 응답을 통해 불확실함을 나타내고 있으므로 정답이다.
(B) 유사 발음 오답: 질문의 apartment와 부분적으로 발음이 유사한 parts를 이용한 오답이다.
(C) 관련 없는 오답: 질문과 상관없는 답변이다.

어휘 in a while 한동안

❷ 부가 의문문

◆ ETS CHECK UP　본책 p.055

| 1 (B) | 2 (B) | 3 (C) | 4 (A) | 5 (A) |

1 M-Au / W-Br
That meeting was called by Ms. Romero, wasn't it?
(A) No, it's on the left.
(B) I believe so.
(C) Sure, I'll add your report to the agenda.

그 회의는 로메로 씨가 소집한 거죠, 아닌가요?
(A) 아니요, 왼쪽에 있어요.
(B) 그런 것 같아요.
(C) 물론이죠, 당신의 보고서를 안건에 추가해 드릴게요.

해설 로메로 씨의 회의 소집 여부를 확인하는 부가 의문문
(A) 관련 없는 오답: 질문과는 어울리지 않는 위치 관련 답변이다.
(B) 정답: 로메로 씨가 회의를 소집한 것인지 확인하는 질문에 그런 것 같다(I believe so)고 긍정하는 의미의 대답을 하고 있다.
(C) 연상 작용 오답: 의미상 연결이 가능한 두 표현 meeting과 agenda를 이용한 오답이다.

어휘 call 소집하다　agenda 안건

2 W-Br / M-Au
That photocopy machine is broken, isn't it?
(A) He's a member of the board.
(B) You're right—it needs to be replaced.
(C) I prefer working in the mornings.

저 복사기 고장 났죠, 그렇죠?
(A) 그는 이사회 일원이에요.
(B) 맞아요, 교체해야 해요.
(C) 저는 오전에 일하는 게 더 좋아요.

해설 고장 여부를 확인하는 부가 의문문
(A) 인칭 오류 오답: 질문과 관련 없는 제3자 He로 답변하고 있다.
(B) 정답: 복사기의 고장 여부를 확인하는 질문에 먼저 You're right로 긍정 응답을 한 후, 교체되어야 한다(it needs to be replaced)고 부연 설명하고 있으므로 정답이다.
(C) 관련 없는 오답: 질문과 상관없는 답변을 제시하고 있다.

어휘 photocopy machine 복사기　board 이사회
replace 교체하다

3 W-Am / M-Au
You drive to work every day, don't you?
(A) Yes, I take the bus.
(B) I'm a research worker.
(C) Only occasionally.

매일 자가용으로 출근하죠, 그렇지 않나요?
(A) 네, 저는 버스를 타요.
(B) 저는 연구원이에요.
(C) 가끔만요.

해설 자가용 출퇴근 여부를 확인하는 부가 의문문
(A) Yes/No를 혼동하여 쓴 오답: No가 와야 뒤에 오는 말과 논리적으로 부합된다.
(B) 파생어 오답: 질문의 work와 파생어 관계인 worker를 이용한 오답이다.
(C) 정답: 출근을 자가용으로 하는지 확인하는 질문에 Yes는 생략하고 빈도(가끔)를 언급한 정답이다.

어휘 drive to work 자가용으로 출근하다
research 연구, 조사　occasionally 가끔

4 W-Br / M-Au
You used to own that furniture store, didn't you?
(A) Yes, but I sold it last year.
(B) Two coffee tables.
(C) The technicians are on their way.

당신이 그 가구점을 운영했었죠, 그렇지 않나요?
(A) 네, 그렇지만 작년에 팔았어요.
(B) 커피 테이블 두 개요.
(C) 기술자들이 오는 중이에요.

해설 가구점 운영 여부를 확인하는 부가 의문문
(A) 정답: 가구점을 운영했었는지 묻는 질문에 Yes라고 긍정한 후, 그렇지만 작년에 팔았다고 덧붙이고 있다.

(B) 연상 작용 오답: 질문의 furniture에서 연상 가능한 coffee tables을 이용한 오답이다.
(C) 유사 발음 오답: 질문의 own과 발음이 유사한 on을 이용한 오답이다.

어휘 technician 기술자

5 W-Am / M-Au
You're meeting Monica tomorrow, aren't you?
(A) She hasn't confirmed it yet.
(B) No, we didn't.
(C) Yes, it's more reliable.

내일 모니카를 만날 거죠, 그렇죠?
(A) 그녀가 아직 확실히 알려 주지 않았어요.
(B) 아니요, 우리는 그러지 않았어요.
(C) 네, 그것이 더 믿을 만하네요.

해설 일정을 확인하는 부가 의문문
(A) 정답: 일정을 확인하는 질문에 대해 아직 상대가 확답하지 않았다고 대답하고 있으므로 정답이다.
(B) 시제 오류 오답: 내일 일정을 묻고 있으므로 미래 시제로 답해야 적절하다.
(C) 관련 없는 오답: 부가 의문문에 Yes로 답할 수 있으나, 이어지는 내용이 어울리지 않아 오답이다.

어휘 confirm 확인해 주다, 사실임을 보여 주다
reliable 믿을 수 있는

ETS 유형 연습
본책 p.056

| 1 (C) | 2 (C) | 3 (C) | 4 (B) | 5 (B) |

1 W-Br / M-Cn
My car will be ready today, won't it?
(A) I read it yesterday.
(B) All new tires.
(C) It depends on how busy we are.

제 차가 오늘 준비되겠죠, 그렇죠?
(A) 전 어제 읽었어요.
(B) 모두 새 타이어예요.
(C) 저희가 얼마나 바쁜지에 달려 있어요.

해설 준비 여부를 확인하는 부가 의문문
(A) 유사 발음 오답: 질문의 ready와 발음이 유사한 read it을 이용한 오답이다.
(B) 연상 작용 오답: 질문의 car에서 연상 가능한 tires를 이용한 오답이다.
(C) 정답: 차의 준비 여부를 확인하는 질문에 얼마나 바쁜지에 달려 있다고 대답하고 있으므로 정답이다.

어휘 depend on ~에 달려 있다

2 W-Br / M-Au
Isn't the inspector coming tomorrow?
(A) A building permit.
(B) Sure, I can carry those.
(C) No, he postponed until Friday.

내일 검사관이 오지 않나요?
(A) 건축 허가서요.
(B) 물론이죠, 제가 그것들을 들고 갈 수 있어요.
(C) 아니요, 그분이 금요일로 연기했어요.

해설 검사관 방문 일정을 확인하는 부정 의문문
(A) 연상 오류 오답: 질문의 inspector에서 연상 가능한 permit을 이용한 오답이다.
(B) 인칭 오류 오답: 의문문에 those가 가리킬 만한 대상이 없으므로 오답이다.
(C) 정답: 검사관이 내일 방문하는지를 확인하는 질문에 No로 부정한 후, 그가 금요일로 연기했다며 부연 설명을 덧붙이고 있다.

어휘 inspector 검사관 permit 허가증 postpone 연기하다

3 W-Am / M-Cn
You don't need to use the copier now, do you?
(A) Yes, this is good coffee.
(B) I already have some, thanks.
(C) No, I just finished with it.

지금 복사기 쓸 일 없죠, 그렇죠?
(A) 네, 이 커피 맛있네요.
(B) 이미 몇 개 가지고 있어요, 고마워요.
(C) 없어요. 방금 다 끝냈어요.

해설 상대방의 동의를 구하는 부가 의문문
(A) 유사 발음 오답: 질문의 copier와 발음이 유사한 coffee를 이용한 오답이다.
(B) 관련 없는 오답: 질문 내용과 관련 없는 대답이다.
(C) 정답: 지금 복사기를 쓰지 않을 거냐고 묻는 질문에 방금 사용을 마쳤다(I just finished with it)고 쓸 일이 없다는 것을 우회적으로 표현하고 있다.

어휘 copier 복사기 finish 끝마치다

4 W-Br / M-Au
Hasn't the warehouse floor been repaired?
(A) Thanks for the offer.
(B) The funding was just approved.
(C) I have one of those.

창고 바닥이 수리되지 않았나요?
(A) 제안해 주셔서 감사합니다.
(B) 자금이 방금 승인되었어요.
(C) 저도 그것들 중 하나를 갖고 있어요.

해설 수리 여부를 확인하는 부정 의문문
(A) 관련 없는 오답: 질문과 상관없는 답변이다.
(B) 정답: 창고 바닥이 수리되었는지를 확인하는 질문에 자금이 방금 승인되었다며 아직 수리 전임을 우회적으로 나타내고 있다.

(C) 관련 없는 오답: 질문과 상관없는 답변이다.

어휘 warehouse 창고 repair 수리하다 offer 제안 funding 자금 approve 승인하다

5 W-Am / M-Au

That building's still under construction, isn't it?
(A) Maybe the site manager.
(B) Yes, it's due to be finished in October.
(C) Yes, it's on level six.

그 건물은 여전히 공사 중인 거죠, 그렇죠?
(A) 아마 현장 소장이요.
(B) 네, 10월에 완공 예정이에요.
(C) 네, 6층에 있어요.

해설 공사 진행 여부를 확인하는 부가 의문문
(A) **연상 작용 오답**: 질문의 construction에서 연상 가능한 site manager를 이용한 오답이다.
(B) **정답**: 공사가 여전히 진행 중인지 확인하는 질문에 Yes라는 긍정적인 응답을 한 후, 10월에 완공 예정(due to be finished in October)이라며 상황에 적합한 부연 설명을 하고 있다.
(C) **연상 작용 오답**: 질문의 building에서 연상 가능한 level을 이용한 오답이다.

어휘 under construction 공사 중인 site manager 현장 소장 be due to ~할 예정이다 level 층

ETS 실전 문제 (본책 p.057)

1 (A)	2 (C)	3 (A)	4 (A)	5 (A)
6 (C)	7 (B)	8 (A)	9 (B)	10 (B)
11 (A)	12 (A)	13 (A)	14 (C)	15 (B)
16 (A)	17 (A)	18 (B)	19 (C)	20 (B)
21 (A)	22 (A)	23 (B)	24 (B)	25 (A)

1 W-Br / W-Am

The recycling bins are in the loading area, aren't they?
(A) I saw them in the storage room.
(B) This is very comfortable furniture.
(C) He uses plastic utensils.

재활용통은 적재 구역에 있는 거죠?
(A) 창고에서 그것들을 봤어요.
(B) 이것은 아주 편안한 가구입니다.
(C) 그는 플라스틱 도구를 사용해요.

해설 위치 정보를 확인하는 부가 의문문
(A) **정답**: 재활용통이 적재 구역에 있는지 묻는 질문에 No는 생략하고 통이 실제로 있는 위치를 언급하고 있으므로 정답이다.
(B) **관련 없는 오답**: 질문과 상관없는 답변이다.
(C) **연상 작용 오답**: 질문의 recycling bins에서 연상 가능한 plastic을 이용한 오답이다.

어휘 recycling bin 재활용통 loading 적재 storage room 창고 utensil (주방) 도구

2 M-Cn / W-Am

Won't construction of the greenhouse take a long time?
(A) A ten-dollar fee.
(B) The furniture is well constructed.
(C) No, it's a short project.

온실 건설에 오랜 시간이 걸리지 않을까요?
(A) 요금 10달러요.
(B) 가구가 잘 짜였네요.
(C) 아니요, 단기 프로젝트예요.

해설 온실 건설 기간을 확인하는 부정 의문문
(A) **관련 없는 오답**: 가격을 묻는 How much 의문문에 가능한 답변이다.
(B) **파생어 오답**: 질문의 construction과 파생어 관계인 constructed를 이용한 오답이다.
(C) **정답**: 부정 의문문에 대한 답변은 긍정이면 Yes, 부정이면 No로 대답한다. No로 부정한 후, 단기 프로젝트라는 설명을 덧붙이고 있으므로 정답이다.

어휘 construction 건설 greenhouse 온실 fee 요금 construct 구성하다

3 W-Am / M-Au

Haven't you already been to that exhibition?
(A) I didn't see everything last time.
(B) No, I put it in the bin.
(C) I'd like to visit Egypt.

그 전시회에 이미 가보지 않았나요?
(A) 지난번에 전부 다 보지 못했어요.
(B) 아니요, 쓰레기통에 넣었어요.
(C) 저는 이집트를 방문하고 싶어요.

해설 전시회 방문 경험을 확인하는 부정 의문문
(A) **정답**: 전시회에 가봤는지 확인하는 질문에 Yes를 생략하고, (가봤지만) 다 관람하지는 못했다는 추가 정보로 답변한 정답이다.
(B) **유사 발음 오답**: 질문의 been과 발음이 유사한 bin을 이용한 오답이다.
(C) **연상 작용 오답**: 의미상 연결이 가능한 두 표현 have been to와 visit을 이용한 오답이다.

어휘 exhibition 전시(회) bin 통, 쓰레기통

4 M-Au / W-Am

Shouldn't we purchase more ink for the printer?
(A) It is getting low, isn't it?
(B) On the bottom of each page.
(C) She put them in alphabetical order.

프린터용 잉크를 더 사야 하지 않을까요?
(A) 점점 줄어들고 있긴 하죠?
(B) 각 페이지 하단에요.
(C) 그녀는 그것들을 알파벳순으로 배열했어요.

해설 잉크 구매를 제안하는 부정 의문문
(A) 정답: 잉크를 더 구입해야 하는지 제안하는 질문에 Yes를 생략하고, 점점 줄어들고 있는지 확인하며 제안에 동의하고 있다.
(B) 연상 작용 오답: 질문의 printer에서 연상 가능한 page를 이용한 오답이다.
(C) 인칭 오류 오답: 질문과 관련 없는 제3자 She로 답변하고 있다.

어휘 purchase 구매하다   order 순서

5 M-Cn / W-Br
The loan officer is on his break now, right?
(A) Yes, but he'll be back soon.
(B) In the other cabinet.
(C) Isn't it already rented?

대출 담당자가 지금 휴식 중인 거죠?
(A) 네, 하지만 곧 돌아올 거예요.
(B) 다른 수납장에 있어요.
(C) 이미 임대되지 않았나요?

해설 담당자의 부재를 확인하는 부가 의문문
(A) 정답: 대출 담당자가 휴식 중인지 확인하는 질문에 긍정으로 대답한 후, 하지만 곧 돌아올 것이라고 부연 설명하고 있으므로 정답이다.
(B) 관련 없는 오답: 위치를 묻는 Where 의문문에 가능한 답변이다.
(C) 연상 작용 오답: 질문의 loan에서 연상 가능한 rented를 이용한 오답이다.

어휘 loan officer 대출 담당자   on (one's) break 휴식 중인

6 W-Br / M-Au
Ms. Germain has an appointment scheduled with the clients, doesn't she?
(A) I don't subscribe to that channel.
(B) There's a snack shop on the fifth floor.
(C) Yes, I believe so.

제르매인 씨는 고객들과 약속이 잡혀 있어요, 그렇죠?
(A) 저는 그 채널을 구독하지 않아요.
(B) 5층에 간식 가게가 있어요.
(C) 네, 그런 것 같아요.

해설 일정을 확인하는 부가 의문문
(A) 연상 작용 오답: 질문의 scheduled에서 연상 가능한 channel을 이용한 오답이다.
(B) 관련 없는 오답: 질문과 상관없는 답변이다.
(C) 정답: 제르매인 씨가 고객들과 약속이 있는지 확인하는 질문에 먼저 Yes라고 긍정 응답을 한 후, 그런 것 같다고 일관되게 말하고 있으므로 정답이다.

어휘 appointment (공식적인) 약속
subscribe to ~을 구독하다

7 W-Br / M-Au
The art museum is open late tonight, isn't it?
(A) Several new exhibitions.
(B) No, only on Fridays.
(C) I don't think it's far away.

미술관은 오늘 밤 늦게까지 문을 열죠, 그렇죠?
(A) 몇 개의 새로운 전시회예요.
(B) 아니요, 금요일만요.
(C) 멀지 않은 것 같아요.

해설 문을 여는지 확인하는 부가 의문문
(A) 연상 작용 오답: 질문의 museum에서 연상 가능한 exhibitions를 이용한 오답이다.
(B) 정답: 오늘 밤 늦게까지 미술관이 문을 여는지 확인하는 질문에 부정하면서 금요일만 그렇다는 추가 정보를 제시하고 있다.
(C) 관련 없는 오답: 질문과 상관없는 답변을 제시하고 있다.

8 W-Br / M-Cn
Isn't the Thai restaurant closed for renovations?
(A) I'll call them.
(B) About fifteen euros.
(C) A bottle of water, please.

태국 음식점은 보수 공사로 문을 닫지 않았나요?
(A) 제가 전화해 볼게요.
(B) 약 15유로요.
(C) 물 한 병 주세요.

해설 문을 닫았는지 확인하는 부정 의문문
(A) 정답: 음식점이 보수 공사로 문을 닫았는지 확인하는 질문에 전화해 보겠다며 확실히 모른다는 것을 우회적으로 표현하고 있다.
(B) 관련 없는 오답: 가격을 묻는 How much 의문문에 적합한 대답이다.
(C) 연상 작용 오답: 질문의 restaurant에서 연상 가능한 a bottle of water를 이용한 오답이다.

어휘 renovation 보수

9 W-Br / W-Am
We should go to lunch before our tour, shouldn't we?
(A) The tour guide was knowledgeable.
(B) I'd prefer to eat on the bus.
(C) Yes, they volunteer there regularly.

우리 투어하기 전에 점심 먹으러 가야 하지 않을까요?
(A) 여행 가이드는 아는 것이 많았어요.
(B) 저는 버스에서 먹고 싶어요.
(C) 네, 그들은 거기서 정기적으로 자원봉사해요.

해설 점심식사 동행을 제안하는 부가 의문문
(A) 단어 반복 오답: 질문의 tour를 반복 이용한 오답이다.
(B) 정답: 투어하기 전에 점심을 먹으러 갈지를 묻는 질문에 버스에서 먹고 싶다며 우회적으로 거절하고 있다.
(C) 관련 없는 오답: 부가 의문문에 Yes로 답할 수 있으나, 이어지는 내용이 어울리지 않아 오답이다.

어휘 knowledgeable 아는 것이 많은 volunteer 자원봉사하다 regularly 정기적으로

10 M-Au / W-Br

Haven't you seen the results of the customer surveys?
(A) Several months of research.
(B) Why, was there a problem?
(C) Please call customer service for help.

고객 설문조사 결과를 못 보셨나요?
(A) 수개월간의 연구예요.
(B) 왜요, 문제가 있었나요?
(C) 고객 서비스에 전화해 도움을 받으세요.

해설 결과를 봤는지 확인하는 부정 의문문
(A) 연상 작용 오답: 질문의 results와 surveys에서 연상 가능한 research를 이용한 오답이다.
(B) 정답: 설문조사 결과를 봤는지 확인하는 질문에 문제가 있었는지 되묻고 있다.
(C) 단어 반복 오답: 질문의 customer를 그대로 반복 이용한 오답이다.

어휘 survey (설문)조사 research 연구

11 W-Am / M-Au

Don't you think we should take a short break?
(A) OK, but just ten minutes.
(B) He can fix it.
(C) It's pretty tall.

우리 잠깐 쉬어야 할 것 같지 않아요?
(A) 좋아요, 하지만 딱 10분만요.
(B) 그가 고칠 수 있어요.
(C) 그건 꽤 높아요.

해설 쉬는 시간을 제안하는 부정 의문문
(A) 정답: 잠깐 쉬자는 제안에 대해 먼저 수락을 한 후, 휴식 시간으로 ten minutes를 언급하고 있다.
(B) 연상 작용 오답: 질문의 break를 '고장나다'로 생각할 때 연상 가능한 fix를 이용한 오답이다.
(C) 연상 작용 오답: 질문의 short에서 반의어로 연상 가능한 tall을 이용한 오답이다.

어휘 break 휴식 fix 고치다, 수리하다 pretty 꽤, 매우

12 M-Cn / M-Au

The new interns have had a tour of the facilities, haven't they?
(A) I believe they just finished.
(B) A map of the city center.
(C) Pick up your name tag here.

새로 온 인턴들이 시설을 둘러봤죠, 그렇죠?
(A) 제 생각에 막 끝낸 것 같아요.
(B) 도심 지도예요.
(C) 여기 명찰 가져가세요.

해설 견학 여부를 확인하는 부가 의문문
(A) 정답: 신입 인턴들이 시설을 둘러봤는지 확인하는 질문에 방금 끝냈을 것(I believe they just finished)이라고 말하고 있다.
(B) 연상 작용 오답: tour에서 연상 가능한 map과 city를 이용한 오답이다.
(C) 관련 없는 오답: 질문과 상관없는 답변이다.

어휘 facility 시설

13 W-Am / W-Br

Didn't we go over the building specifications already?
(A) We should do it again now that everyone's here.
(B) He only designs large office buildings.
(C) It was working yesterday.

설계 명세서는 이미 검토하지 않았나요?
(A) 이제 모두 왔으니 다시 해야죠.
(B) 그는 대형 사무용 빌딩만 설계해요.
(C) 어제는 작동했는데요.

해설 검토 여부를 확인하는 부정 의문문
(A) 정답: 설계 명세서를 이미 검토하지 않았는지 묻는 질문에 Yes를 생략하고 (이미 했지만) 모두 모였으니 다시 해야 한다고 답변한 정답이다.
(B) 단어 반복 오답: 질문의 building을 반복 이용한 오답이다.
(C) 인칭 오류 오답: 질문의 주어가 we인데 보기의 주어는 It 이므로 논리적으로 맞지 않다.

어휘 building specifications 설계 명세서

14 W-Br / W-Am

This shirt isn't available in medium, is it?
(A) When are you available next week?
(B) Sure, I'll adjust the height.
(C) No, we don't have any more in that size.

이 셔츠는 중간 사이즈가 없네요, 그렇죠?
(A) 다음 주 언제 시간이 되시나요?
(B) 네, 높이를 조정할게요.
(C) 네, 그 사이즈는 더 이상 없어요.

해설 제품의 유무를 확인하는 부가 의문문
(A) 단어 반복 오답: 질문의 available을 그대로 반복 이용한 오답이다.
(B) 연상 작용 오답: 질문의 medium에서 연상 가능한 height를 이용한 오답이다.
(C) 정답: 중간 사이즈의 셔츠가 있는지 확인하는 질문에 No 라고 부정 답변을 한 후, 그 사이즈는 더 이상 없다고 일관된 내용을 덧붙이고 있으므로 정답이다.

어휘 adjust 조정하다 height 높이

15 M-Au / W-Br

Wasn't Ms. Ross supposed to order more food containers?
(A) Some paper bags.
(B) Did you check the storage room?
(C) No, there aren't.

로스 씨가 더 많은 음식 용기를 주문하기로 하지 않았나요?
(A) 종이 봉투 몇 개요.
(B) 창고를 확인해 보셨나요?
(C) 아니요, 없어요.

해설 용기 주문 여부를 확인하는 부정 의문문
(A) 연상 작용 오답: 질문의 food containers에서 연상 가능한 paper bags를 이용한 오답이다.
(B) 정답: 로스 씨가 더 많은 음식 용기를 주문했는지 확인하는 질문에 창고를 확인해 보았는지 되물으며 용기가 있을 수 있는 장소를 제안하고 있다.
(C) 관련 없는 오답: 질문과 상관없는 답변을 제시하고 있다.

어휘 be supposed to ~하기로 되어 있다   container 용기   storage room 창고

16 M-Cn / M-Au

You made extra copies of the agenda, didn't you?
(A) Oh, but I forgot to bring them.
(B) Thanks for doing that.
(C) No, the exit's on the left.

그 안건을 여분으로 복사하셨죠, 그렇죠?
(A) 아, 그런데 깜박 잊고 안 가져왔어요.
(B) 그렇게 해주셔서 고마워요.
(C) 아니요, 출구는 왼쪽에 있어요.

해설 추가 복사 여부를 확인하는 부가 의문문
(A) 정답: 안건을 여분으로 복사했는지 확인하는 질문에 복사는 했지만 가져오는 걸 잊었다(I forgot to bring them)고 하고 있으므로 정답이다.
(B) 관련 없는 오답: 여분의 복사를 했는지 확인하는 질문에 감사 인사를 하는 것은 전혀 관련이 없는 대답이다.
(C) 유사 발음 오답: 질문의 extra와 발음이 비슷한 exit를 이용한 오답이다.

어휘 make a copy of ~을 복사하다   agenda 안건, 의제   exit 출구   on the left 왼쪽에

17 W-Br / M-Au

Isn't Mr. Kim going to help us prepare the budget?
(A) No, he's leaving soon.
(B) A new travel policy.
(C) It was repaired yesterday.

김 씨가 예산 준비 작업을 도와주실 거 아닌가요?
(A) 아니요, 그는 곧 나갈 거예요.
(B) 새로운 출장 정책이요.
(C) 어제 수리되었어요.

해설 사실을 확인하는 부정 의문문
(A) 정답: 김 씨가 작업을 도와줄지 확인하는 질문에 No라고 부정한 후, 그가 곧 나갈 것이라고 도와주지 못하는 이유를 덧붙이고 있으므로 정답이다.
(B) 연상 작용 오답: 의미상 연결이 가능한 두 표현 budget과 travel policy를 이용한 오답이다.
(C) 유사 발음 오답: 질문의 prepare와 부분적으로 발음이 유사한 repaired를 이용한 오답이다.

어휘 budget 예산   policy 정책   repair 수리하다

18 M-Cn / M-Au

Aren't you attending the employee awards ceremony tomorrow?
(A) The position has been filled.
(B) That event's next week.
(C) Two hundred people attended.

내일 직원 시상식에 참석 안 하시나요?
(A) 그 자리는 충원되었어요.
(B) 그 행사는 다음 주예요.
(C) 200명이 참석했어요.

해설 시상식 참석을 확인하는 부정 의문문
(A) 연상 작용 오답: 질문의 employee에서 연상 가능한 position을 이용한 오답이다.
(B) 정답: 내일 시상식에 참석할 것인지 묻는 질문에 시상식은 다음 주라고 잘못된 정보를 정정한 정답이다.
(C) 단어 반복 오답: 질문의 attend를 반복 이용한 오답이다.

어휘 awards ceremony 시상식   fill (공석에) 충원하다

19 W-Am / W-Br

You returned the merchandise at the checkout counter, didn't you?
(A) I counted them twice.
(B) I turned it on this morning.
(C) No, I had to speak with the manager.

계산대에서 제품을 반품하셨죠, 그렇죠?
(A) 제가 두 번 셌어요.
(B) 제가 오늘 아침에 켰어요.
(C) 아니요, 매니저와 얘기해야 했어요.

해설 반품 여부를 확인하는 부가 의문문
(A) 유사 발음 오답: 질문의 counter와 발음이 유사한 counted를 이용한 오답이다.
(B) 유사 발음 오답: 질문의 returned와 부분적으로 발음이 유사한 turned를 이용한 오답이다.
(C) 정답: 제품을 계산대에서 반품했는지 확인하는 질문에 대해 먼저 No로 부정 답변을 한 후, 매니저와 얘기해야 했다(I had to speak with the manager)며 이유를 제시하고 있으므로 정답이다.

어휘 merchandise 제품   checkout counter 계산대

20 M-Au / W-Am
Doesn't Luis work at the Prague branch?
(A) To the sales manager.
(B) Yes, since September.
(C) I'll find it later.

루이스는 프라하 지사에서 일하지 않나요?
(A) 영업부장에게요.
(B) 네, 9월부터요.
(C) 제가 나중에 찾아볼게요.

해설 **근무지를 확인하는 부정 의문문**
(A) 연상 작용 오답: 질문의 work와 branch에서 연상 가능한 sales manager를 이용한 오답이다.
(B) 정답: 루이스가 프라하 지사에서 일하지 않느냐는 질문에 Yes라고 답한 후 9월부터 일했다는 추가 정보를 덧붙이고 있다.
(C) 관련 없는 오답: 질문과 상관없는 답변이다.

21 W-Am / M-Au
We've just ordered several new fax machines, haven't we?
(A) Yes, we should get them tomorrow.
(B) They should be in alphabetical order.
(C) The facts I reported were correct.

우리가 좀 전에 새 팩스기 몇 대를 주문했죠, 그렇죠?
(A) 네, 내일 받게 될 거예요.
(B) 그것들은 알파벳 순서대로 돼 있어야 해요.
(C) 제가 보고한 사실들은 정확했어요.

해설 **주문 여부를 확인하는 부가 의문문**
(A) 정답: 주문했는지 확인하는 질문에 Yes로 답한 뒤, 내일 받을 것이라는 부가 정보도 제공한 정답이다.
(B) 다의어 오답: 서로 다른 의미의 order를 반복 이용한 오답이다. 질문의 order는 '주문하다'라는 동사이고, 보기의 order는 '순서'라는 명사이다.
(C) 유사 발음 오답: 질문의 fax와 발음이 비슷한 facts를 사용해 혼동을 유발하는 오답이다.

어휘 in alphabetical order 알파벳 순서로   correct 정확한

22 W-Br / M-Au
They haven't finished repairing Atley Street yet, have they?
(A) No, it's still closed to traffic.
(B) An old pair of shoes.
(C) May I have another?

아직 애틀리 가 보수가 끝나지 않았죠, 그렇죠?
(A) 네, 아직 교통이 통제되고 있어요.
(B) 낡은 신발 한 켤레요.
(C) 하나 더 주시겠어요?

해설 **보수 완료를 확인하는 부가 의문문**
(A) 정답: 애틀리 가 보수가 끝났는지 확인하는 질문에 대해 먼저 No로 부정 답변을 한 후, 교통이 아직 통제되고 있다(it's still closed to traffic)고 부연 설명한 것이므로 정답이다.
(B) 유사 발음 오답: 질문의 repairing과 부분적으로 발음이 유사한 pair를 이용한 오답이다.
(C) 단어 반복 오답: 질문의 have를 그대로 반복 이용한 오답이다.

어휘 repair 보수하다

23 M-Cn / W-Am
Haven't you been in contact with the landscaping company?
(A) By the garden.
(B) I'm waiting for a response.
(C) Yes, I wear contact lenses.

조경 회사와 연락하지 않았나요?
(A) 정원 옆에요.
(B) 대답을 기다리고 있어요.
(C) 네, 전 콘택트렌즈를 껴요.

해설 **회사와의 연락을 확인하는 부정 의문문**
(A) 연상 작용 오답: 질문의 landscaping에서 연상 가능한 garden을 이용한 오답이다.
(B) 정답: 조경 회사와의 연락을 확인하는 질문에 대답을 기다리고 있다고 현재 상황을 설명하며 간접적으로 대답하고 있다.
(C) 다의어 오답: 서로 다른 의미의 contact를 반복 이용한 오답이다. 질문의 contact는 '연락'이라는 뜻이고, 보기의 contact는 lenses와 결합하여 '콘택트렌즈'라는 뜻이다.

어휘 in contact with ~와 연락하는   landscaping 조경   response 대답, 응답

24 M-Cn / W-Am
The hotel has a wireless Internet connection, doesn't it?
(A) A reservation for two nights.
(B) Of course—and it's free for guests.
(C) On a connecting flight.

호텔에 무선 인터넷이 연결되어 있죠, 그렇죠?
(A) 2박 예약이요.
(B) 물론이죠—게다가 고객에게는 무료예요.
(C) 연결 비행편에서요.

해설 **무선 인터넷 연결을 확인하는 부가 의문문**
(A) 연상 작용 오답: 의미상 연결이 가능한 두 표현 hotel과 A reservation for two nights를 이용해서 혼동을 유발하는 오답이다.
(B) 정답: 호텔에 무선 인터넷이 연결되어 있는지를 확인하는 질문에 Of course라는 긍정적인 응답을 한 후, 고객에게 무료(it's free for guests)라는 추가 정보를 제시하고 있으므로 정답이다.
(C) 파생어 오답: 질문의 connection과 파생어 관계인 connecting을 이용한 오답이다.

어휘 connection 연결   reservation 예약

25 M-Au / W-Am
Shouldn't we add more images to the brochure?
(A) No, I think we have enough already.
(B) I'm sorry, but we don't sell those anymore.
(C) By adjusting the brightness.

안내책자에 이미지를 좀 더 추가해야 하지 않을까요?
(A) 아니요, 이미 충분하다고 생각해요.
(B) 죄송하지만 더 이상 그것들을 팔지 않아요.
(C) 밝기를 조정해서요.

해설 이미지 추가를 제안하는 부정 의문문
(A) 정답: 안내책자에 이미지를 더 추가해야 하는지 제안하는 질문에 No라고 부정한 후, 이미 충분히 있다고 생각한다며 이유를 덧붙이고 있다.
(B) 관련 없는 오답: 질문과 상관없는 답변이다.
(C) 연상 작용 오답: 의미상 연결이 가능한 두 표현 images와 brightness를 이용한 오답이다.

어휘 brochure 안내책자   adjust 조정하다   brightness 밝기

UNIT 08 요청·제안 의문문 / 평서문

1 요청·제안 의문문

ETS CHECK UP 본책 p.058
1 (B)   2 (A)   3 (C)   4 (B)   5 (C)

1 M-Au / W-Am
Can I help you carry those books?
(A) Here's my library card.
(B) No, thanks—it's OK.
(C) Several new chairs in the lobby.

그 책들을 옮기는 것을 도와드릴까요?
(A) 여기 제 도서관 카드요.
(B) 아니요, 감사하지만 괜찮습니다.
(C) 로비에 새 의자 몇 개요.

해설 제안을 나타내는 조동사(Can) 의문문
(A) 연상 작용 오답: 질문의 books에서 연상 가능한 library를 이용한 오답이다.
(B) 정답: 책 옮기는 것을 돕겠다는 제안에 No라고 거절한 뒤 괜찮다고 적절히 답변한 정답이다.
(C) 관련 없는 오답: 질문과 상관없는 답변이다.

2 M-Au / W-Br
Would you mind taking notes for me at the seminar?
(A) I wasn't planning on going.
(B) Thanks, I'll sit here instead.
(C) As soon as you can.

저를 위해 세미나에서 메모해 주시겠어요?
(A) 전 갈 계획이 없었어요.
(B) 고마워요, 전 대신 여기 앉을게요.
(C) 최대한 빨리요.

해설 요청을 나타내는 Would you mind 의문문
(A) 정답: 세미나에서 메모해 주겠냐는 요청에 갈 계획이 없었다며 우회적으로 거절하고 있다.
(B) 관련 없는 오답: 질문과 상관없는 답변을 제시하고 있다.
(C) 관련 없는 오답: 기한을 묻는 질문에 가능한 답변이다.

3 W-Am / M-Cn
Can I borrow a hammer?
(A) The bank just closed.
(B) Two cans of tomato soup, please.
(C) I left my tools at home.

망치를 빌릴 수 있을까요?
(A) 은행이 방금 문을 닫았어요.
(B) 토마토 수프 두 캔 주세요.
(C) 연장을 집에 두고 왔어요.

해설 요청을 나타내는 조동사(Can) 의문문
(A) 연상 작용 오답: 질문의 borrow에서 연상 가능한 bank를 이용한 오답이다.
(B) 다의어 오답: 질문의 can을 반복 이용한 오답으로, 질문의 Can은 '할 수 있다'라는 뜻의 조동사이고, 보기의 can은 '통조림, 캔'이라는 뜻의 명사이다.
(C) 정답: 망치를 빌릴 수 있을지에 대해 연장을 집에 두고 왔다며 우회적으로 부정의 의미를 전달하고 있다.

어휘 tool 연장

4 M-Au / W-Br
Wouldn't you like to join the team for dinner?
(A) All payment options are available.
(B) The budget report has to be finished tomorrow.
(C) An additional fifteen percent off.

팀과 함께 저녁 식사를 하지 않으시겠어요?
(A) 모든 결제 방식이 가능합니다.
(B) 내일까지 예산 보고서를 끝내야 해요.
(C) 추가 15퍼센트 할인이요.

해설 제안을 나타내는 부정 의문문
(A) 관련 없는 오답: 질문과 상관없는 답변이다.
(B) 정답: 팀과 함께 저녁 식사를 하자는 제안에 내일까지 예산 보고서를 끝내야 한다며 우회적으로 거절하고 있다.
(C) 관련 없는 오답: 할인율을 묻는 How much 의문문에 가능한 답변이다.

어휘 payment 결제   option 선택(할 수 있는 것)   available 이용 가능한   budget 예산   additional 추가의

5 M-Cn / M-Au
Why don't we ride together to the conference?
(A) Unfortunately, I don't have an extra one.
(B) Because I already signed for them.
(C) Good idea—I'd be happy to pick you up.

회의장까지 차로 같이 가지 않으실래요?
(A) 아쉽게도 저한테 여분이 없어요.
(B) 제가 이미 서명했거든요.
(C) 좋은 생각이에요—제가 데리러 갈게요.

해설 제안을 나타내는 Why don't we 의문문
(A) **단어 반복 오답**: 질문의 don't를 그대로 반복 이용한 오답이다.
(B) **관련 없는 오답**: 질문과 상관없는 답변이다.
(C) **정답**: 우선 Good idea로 동의한 후, 자신이 데리러 가겠다며 다시 제안한 정답이다.

어휘 unfortunately 아쉽게도, 안타깝게도
sign for (우편물 등을 수령했다는 의미로) 서명하다

② 평서문

ETS CHECK UP 본책 p.059

1 (A)　**2** (C)　**3** (B)　**4** (A)　**5** (C)

1 M-Au / W-Br
I just bought a new telephone.
(A) How do you like it?
(B) A twenty percent discount.
(C) I haven't called yet.

저는 막 새 전화기를 샀어요.
(A) 어때요?
(B) 20퍼센트 할인이요.
(C) 아직 전화하지 않았어요.

해설 사실을 전달하는 평서문
(A) **정답**: 새 물건을 구매했다는 말에, 물건에 대한 의견을 물음으로써 답변한 정답이다.
(B) **연상 작용 오답**: 의미상 연결이 가능한 두 단어 bought 와 discount를 이용한 오답이다.
(C) **연상 작용 오답**: 의미상 연결이 가능한 두 단어 telephone 과 called를 이용한 오답이다.

2 W-Br / W-Am
I can't find the paper you asked me to sign.
(A) Do I turn at the stop sign?
(B) A recently published paper.
(C) I left it on your desk.

서명해 달라고 요청하신 서류를 찾을 수가 없어요.
(A) 정지 표지판에서 꺾어야 하나요?
(B) 최근에 출판된 논문이요.
(C) 당신 책상 위에 두었어요.

해설 사실을 전달하는 평서문
(A) **다의어 오답**: 평서문의 sign을 다른 의미로 사용한 오답으로, 평서문의 sign은 '서명하다'를, 보기의 sign은 '표지판'을 뜻한다.
(B) **단어 반복 오답**: 평서문의 paper를 반복 이용한 오답이다.
(C) **정답**: 서류를 찾을 수 없다는 말에 서류가 있는 구체적인 위치를 알려주고 있으므로 정답이다.

어휘 paper 서류, 논문

3 W-Br / M-Cn
Let's take a break for a few minutes.
(A) I took care of a few.
(B) I wish I could.
(C) No, I didn't break it.

우리 몇 분만 휴식을 취하죠.
(A) 제가 몇 가지를 처리했어요.
(B) 할 수만 있다면 그러고 싶어요.
(C) 아니요, 제가 고장내지 않았어요.

해설 제안 사항을 전달하는 평서문
(A) **단어 반복 오답**: 제안문의 a few를 반복 이용한 오답이다.
(B) **정답**: 휴식을 취하자는 제안에 상황상 할 수 없다는 부정의 의미를 전달하고 있다. 〈I wish + 가정법〉 구문으로 '~했으면 좋겠는데'라는 뜻으로 현재의 사실에 반대되는 소망을 표현한다는 점에 유의한다.
(C) **다의어 오답**: 평서문의 break를 반복 이용한 오답으로, 제안문의 break는 '휴식'을, 보기의 break는 '고장내다'를 뜻한다.

어휘 take a break 휴식을 취하다

4 W-Am / M-Cn
Let's find out if Mr. Gao wants to manage this account.
(A) OK, I'll ask him.
(B) On the kitchen counter.
(C) That shirt is ten percent off.

가오 씨가 이 계정을 관리하고 싶어 하는지 알아봅시다.
(A) 좋아요, 제가 물어볼게요.
(B) 주방 조리대 위에요.
(C) 그 셔츠는 10퍼센트 할인해요.

해설 제안 사항을 전달하는 평서문
(A) **정답**: 가오 씨가 계정을 관리하고 싶어 하는지 알아보자는 제안에 OK라고 긍정 응답을 한 후, 그에게 물어보겠다며 구체적인 실행 방안을 제시하고 있다.
(B) **유사 발음·관련 없는 오답**: 평서문의 account와 발음이 비슷한 counter를 이용한 오답으로, Where 의문문에 어울리는 답변이다.
(C) **관련 없는 오답**: 평서문 내용과 관련 없는 대답이다.

어휘 find out 알아내다

5 M-Au / W-Br
I'd like to see your speech for the awards ceremony.
(A) Because the client is not available.
(B) A dynamic speaker.
(C) It's not until next month.

당신의 시상식 연설문을 보고 싶네요.
(A) 고객이 시간이 안 되어서요.
(B) 역동적인 연설자예요.
(C) 그건 다음 달에 있어요.

051

해설 희망 사항을 전달하는 평서문
(A) **관련 없는 오답**: 질문과 상관없는 답변이다.
(B) **연상 작용 오답**: 평서문의 speech에서 연상 가능한 speaker를 이용한 오답이다.
(C) **정답**: 시상식 연설문을 보고 싶다는 말에 시상식이 다음 달에 있으며 연설문이 아직 준비되지 않았다는 것을 우회적으로 표현하고 있다.

어휘 awards ceremony 시상식   available 시간이 되는   dynamic 역동적인

ETS 유형 연습
본책 p.060

1 (C) **2** (B) **3** (C) **4** (A) **5** (B)

1 M-Au / W-Am
My computer won't start.
(A) We began at six thirty.
(B) Yes, I want to be early.
(C) Maybe it's not plugged in.

컴퓨터가 안 켜져요.
(A) 우리는 6시 30분에 시작했어요.
(B) 네, 저는 일찍 도착하고 싶어요.
(C) 아마도 플러그가 안 꽂혀 있나 봐요.

해설 사실을 전달하는 평서문
(A) **연상 작용 오답**: 평서문의 start에서 연상 가능한 began을 이용한 오답이다.
(B) **유사 발음 오답**: 평서문의 won't와 발음이 비슷한 want를 이용한 오답이다.
(C) **정답**: 컴퓨터가 켜지지 않는다는 말에 가능할 법한 이유를 대고 있다.

어휘 start 시작하다, (컴퓨터 등이) 켜지다
plug in 플러그를 꽂다

2 W-Am / M-Au
Let's have Dr. Lu review the financial statements.
(A) Yes, I do.
(B) That's a good idea.
(C) No, there's no room left.

루 박사에게 재무제표를 검토하게 합시다.
(A) 네, 맞아요.
(B) 좋은 생각이네요.
(C) 아니요, 남는 공간이 없어요.

해설 제안 사항을 전달하는 평서문
(A) **관련 없는 오답**: 평서문과 상관없는 답변이다.
(B) **정답**: 루 박사에게 재무제표를 검토하게 하자는 제안에 좋은 생각이라며 찬성의 의미를 표현하고 있다.
(C) **관련 없는 오답**: 제안문과 상관없는 답변이다.

어휘 financial statement 재무제표

3 M-Au / W-Am
Everyone in the department is going to tonight's basketball game.
(A) What was the final score?
(B) I didn't buy a ticket.
(C) Put the trash in the basket.

부서 전원이 오늘 밤 농구 경기에 갈 거예요.
(A) 최종 점수는 몇 점이었어요?
(B) 저는 표를 안 샀어요.
(C) 쓰레기는 바구니에 넣으세요.

해설 정보를 전달하는 평서문
(A) **연상 작용 오답**: 평서문의 basketball game에서 연상 가능한 final score를 이용한 오답이다.
(B) **정답**: 부서 전원이 오늘 밤 농구 경기에 간다는 말에 자신은 표를 사지 않았다며 같이 갈 수 없다는 것을 우회적으로 표현하고 있다.
(C) **파생어 오답**: 평서문의 basketball과 파생어 관계인 basket을 이용한 오답이다.

어휘 department 부서

4 M-Au / W-Br
Can you cover my shift for me on Friday?
(A) I'm already filling in for Hiroki.
(B) The storage cabinet is locked.
(C) Yes, some colorful furniture covers.

금요일에 저 대신 근무해 주실 수 있을까요?
(A) 저는 이미 히로키를 대신하기로 했어요.
(B) 보관함이 잠겨 있어요.
(C) 네, 컬러풀한 가구 커버 몇 개요.

해설 요청을 나타내는 조동사(Can) 의문문
(A) **정답**: 금요일에 대신 근무해 줄 수 있는지 묻는 질문에 이미 히로키를 대신하기로 했다며 거절하는 답변을 우회적으로 표현하고 있다.
(B) **관련 없는 오답**: 질문과 상관없는 답변이다.
(C) **다의어 오답**: 질문의 cover를 반복 이용한 오답으로, 질문의 cover는 '대신하다', 보기의 cover는 '덮개'를 뜻한다.

어휘 cover 대신하다; 덮개   fill in for ~을 대신하다
storage 보관

5 M-Au / M-Cn
Could you give me a ride to the airport?
(A) No, I didn't give him any.
(B) Sure, what time is your flight?
(C) About twenty minutes.

저 좀 공항까지 태워 주실 수 있나요?
(A) 아니요, 그에게 아무것도 주지 않았어요.
(B) 물론이죠, 몇 시 비행기죠?
(C) 20분쯤이요.

해설 요청을 나타내는 조동사(Could) 의문문
(A) 단어 반복 오답: 질문의 give를 반복 이용한 오답이다.
(B) 정답: 요청하는 질문에 수락한다는 긍정의 의미를 전달한 후 구체적인 내용을 되묻고 있다.
(C) 관련 없는 오답: How long 의문문에 어울리는 대답이다.

어휘 give a ride[lift] (탈것에) 태워 주다 flight 비행, 항공편

ETS 실전 문제 본책 p.061

1 (B)	2 (A)	3 (A)	4 (B)	5 (C)
6 (B)	7 (B)	8 (B)	9 (C)	10 (B)
11 (C)	12 (C)	13 (A)	14 (A)	15 (A)
16 (B)	17 (C)	18 (B)	19 (B)	20 (C)
21 (B)	22 (B)	23 (A)	24 (B)	25 (A)

1 M-Au / M-Cn

I can't figure out this new e-mail software.
(A) At the post office.
(B) Me neither.
(C) He made a mistake.

전 이 새 이메일 소프트웨어를 이해할 수 없어요.
(A) 우체국에서요.
(B) 저도 마찬가지예요.
(C) 그가 실수했어요.

해설 도움을 요청하는 평서문
(A) 연상 작용 오답: 평서문의 mail에서 연상 가능한 post office를 이용한 오답이다.
(B) 정답: 새 이메일 소프트웨어를 이해할 수 없다는 말에, 자신도 마찬가지라고 맞장구를 치고 있으므로 정답이다.
(C) 인칭 오류 오답: 관련 없는 제3자 He로 답변하고 있다.

어휘 figure out 이해하다

2 M-Au / W-Am

Could you go to the board meeting in the morning?
(A) Sure, what time is it?
(B) She doesn't have any more left.
(C) It started raining before noon.

아침에 이사회 회의에 참석하실 수 있나요?
(A) 물론이죠, 몇 시인가요?
(B) 그녀에게 더 이상 여분이 없어요.
(C) 정오 전에 비가 내리기 시작했어요.

해설 요청을 나타내는 조동사(Could) 의문문
(A) 정답: 요청하는 질문에 Sure로 긍정의 의미를 전달한 후 실행을 위한 구체적인 정보를 묻고 있으므로 정답이다.
(B) 인칭 오류 오답: 질문의 주어가 you인데 보기의 주어는 She이므로 논리적으로 맞지 않다.
(C) 연상 작용 오답: 질문의 morning에서 연상 가능한 noon을 이용한 오답이다.

어휘 board meeting 이사회 회의

3 W-Br / M-Au

Our new marketing campaign was very successful.
(A) Give my congratulations to the team.
(B) My favorite market is nearby.
(C) No, by the end of the quarter.

우리 새 마케팅 캠페인은 대성공이었어요.
(A) 팀에게 제가 축하한다고 전해 주세요.
(B) 제가 가장 좋아하는 시장이 근처에 있어요.
(C) 아니요, 분기 말까지요.

해설 의견을 전달하는 평서문
(A) 정답: 새 마케팅 캠페인이 대성공이었다는 말에 대해 축하를 전해 달라고 답변한 정답이다.
(B) 유사 발음 오답: 평서문의 marketing과 일부 발음이 유사한 market을 이용한 오답이다.
(C) 관련 없는 오답: 기간 관련 질문에 가능한 답변이다.

어휘 successful 성공적인 nearby 인근의 quarter 분기

4 M-Cn / W-Am

Could you work the late shift for me on Friday night?
(A) He prefers to walk.
(B) I'll be on vacation.
(C) A revised company policy.

금요일 밤에 저 대신 야간 근무를 해 주실 수 있나요?
(A) 그는 걷는 것을 선호해요.
(B) 저는 휴가 중일 거예요.
(C) 개정된 회사 정책이요.

해설 요청을 나타내는 조동사(Could) 의문문
(A) 유사 발음·인칭 오류 오답: 질문의 work와 발음이 유사한 walk를 사용하고, 관련 없는 제3자 He로 답변한 오답이다.
(B) 정답: 금요일 밤에 대신 근무해 줄 수 있는지에 대한 질문에 자신이 휴가 중일 것이라며 우회적으로 부정의 의미를 전달하고 있다.
(C) 연상 작용 오답: 질문의 work에서 연상 가능한 company를 이용한 오답이다.

어휘 shift (한 차례의) 교대 근무 revise 수정하다

5 M-Au / W-Am

All of the candidates for the internship are highly qualified.
(A) Please mark it on the calendar.
(B) The entrance is around the corner.
(C) It'll be difficult to choose one, won't it?

인턴 지원자들 모두 자격을 충분히 갖추고 있어요.
(A) 일정표에 표시하세요.
(B) 입구는 모퉁이를 돌면 있어요.
(C) 한 사람을 고르기가 힘들겠어요, 그렇죠?

해설 의견을 전달하는 평서문
(A) **유사 발음 오답**: 평서문의 candidates와 부분적으로 발음이 유사한 calendar를 이용한 오답이다.
(B) **관련 없는 오답**: 평서문과 상관없는 답변을 제시하고 있다.
(C) **정답**: 인턴 지원자들 모두가 자격을 충분히 갖추고 있다는 의견에 맞장구를 치며 답변한 정답이다.

어휘 candidate 지원자 highly qualified 자격을 충분히 갖춘 entrance 입구

6 W-Am / W-Br
I think we're going to need more chairs for this afternoon's meeting.
(A) I'll do it tomorrow morning.
(B) **There should be some in the lounge.**
(C) They all have copies of the agenda.

오늘 오후 회의에 의자가 더 필요할 것 같아요.
(A) 제가 내일 아침에 할게요.
(B) 휴게실에 좀 있을 거예요.
(C) 그들 모두 안건 사본을 갖고 있어요.

해설 필요 사항을 전달하는 평서문
(A) **연상 작용 오답**: 의미상 연결이 가능한 두 단어 afternoon과 morning을 이용한 오답이다.
(B) **정답**: 회의에 의자가 더 필요할 것이라는 말에, 휴게실(lounge)에 좀 있을 것이라고 정보를 제공하고 있다.
(C) **연상 작용 오답**: 의미상 연결이 가능한 두 단어 meeting과 agenda를 이용한 오답이다.

7 M-Au / W-Br
I can give you a tour of the gallery if you're interested.
(A) The new financial consultant.
(B) **My friend will be here in a few minutes.**
(C) An invoice from the travel agency.

관심 있으시면 제가 갤러리를 안내해드릴게요.
(A) 새로 온 재무 상담사요.
(B) 제 친구가 몇 분 뒤에 올 거예요.
(C) 여행사에서 온 청구서요.

해설 제안을 나타내는 평서문
(A) **관련 없는 오답**: 평서문과 상관없는 답변이다.
(B) **정답**: 갤러리를 안내해 주겠다는 제안에, 친구가 올 예정이라며 우회적으로 거절하고 있다.
(C) **연상 작용 오답**: 평서문의 tour에서 연상 가능한 travel을 이용한 오답이다.

어휘 consultant 상담사 invoice 청구서

8 M-Cn / M-Au
Ms. Espinoza is going to the retirement party.
(A) Just some refreshments.
(B) **Great—when is it?**
(C) No, I can't.

에스피노자 씨는 은퇴 기념식에 갈 예정이에요.
(A) 그냥 다과 조금이요.
(B) 잘됐네요, 언제인가요?
(C) 아니요, 저는 못 가요.

해설 사실을 전달하는 평서문
(A) **연상 작용 오답**: 질문의 party에서 연상 가능한 refreshments를 이용한 오답이다.
(B) **정답**: 에스피노자 씨가 은퇴 기념식에 갈 예정이라는 말에, 잘됐다며 기념식이 언제인지 구체적인 정보를 되묻고 있다.
(C) **인칭 오류 오답**: 평서문 내용과 관련 없는 I로 답변하고 있다.

어휘 retirement 은퇴 refreshments 다과

9 W-Am / W-Br
I forgot to bring my sunglasses today.
(A) A chance of rain.
(B) No, I'll have a glass of water.
(C) **I have an extra pair in my car.**

오늘 선글라스를 가져오는 걸 깜빡했어요.
(A) 비가 올 가능성이요.
(B) 아니요, 물 한 잔 주세요.
(C) 제 차에 여분이 하나 있어요.

해설 사실을 전달하는 평서문
(A) **연상 작용 오답**: 평서문의 sunglasses의 sun에서 연상 가능한 rain을 이용한 오답이다.
(B) **유사 발음 오답**: 평서문의 sunglasses와 부분적으로 발음이 유사한 glass를 이용한 오답이다.
(C) **정답**: 오늘 선글라스를 가져오는 것을 깜빡했다는 말에, 여분이 하나 있다며 빌려주겠다는 의도를 우회적으로 표현하고 있다.

어휘 chance 가능성

10 W-Br / M-Cn
Why don't you join us for dinner tonight?
(A) No, they haven't yet.
(B) **Thanks, but I have other plans.**
(C) To attach some new parts.

오늘 밤 우리와 같이 저녁 식사하는 게 어때요?
(A) 아니요, 그들은 아직 안 했어요.
(B) 고맙지만 다른 계획이 있어요.
(C) 새 부품들을 붙이기 위해서요.

해설 제안을 나타내는 Why don't you 의문문
(A) **인칭 오류·시제 오류 오답**: 질문의 주어가 you인데 보기의 주어는 they이므로 논리적으로 맞지 않으며, 시제도 맞지 않다.
(B) **정답**: 저녁 식사를 함께 하자는 제안에 다른 계획(other plans)이 있다며 거절하고 있다.
(C) **관련 없는 오답**: 질문 내용과 관련 없는 대답이다.

어휘 attach 붙이다 part 부품

11 M-Au / M-Cn
I'm not sure how to raise my computer monitor.
(A) OK, with a larger screen.
(B) I can probably lower the price.
(C) Here, let me give you a hand.

컴퓨터 모니터를 어떻게 올려야 할지 모르겠어요.
(A) 좋아요, 더 큰 화면으로요.
(B) 어쩌면 가격을 낮출 수 있을 거예요.
(C) 자, 제가 도와드릴게요.

해설 도움을 요청하는 평서문
(A) **연상 작용 오답**: 평서문의 computer monitor에서 연상 가능한 screen을 이용한 오답이다.
(B) **연상 작용 오답**: 평서문의 raise에서 연상 가능한 반의어 lower를 이용한 오답이다.
(C) **정답**: 컴퓨터 모니터를 어떻게 올려야 할지 모르겠다는 말에 도와주겠다고 대답하고 있다.

어휘 raise 올리다 give A a hand A를 도와주다

12 W-Br / M-Cn
Would you like to join us in the cafeteria for lunch today?
(A) Just a chicken sandwich, please.
(B) In an adjoining building.
(C) Sorry, I have other plans.

오늘 우리와 구내식당에 점심 먹으러 가실래요?
(A) 그냥 치킨 샌드위치만 주세요.
(B) 인접한 건물에서요.
(C) 죄송해요, 다른 계획이 있어요.

해설 제안을 나타내는 Would you like 의문문
(A) **연상 작용 오답**: cafeteria와 lunch에서 연상 가능한 chicken sandwich를 이용한 오답이다.
(B) **유사 발음 오답**: 질문의 join과 부분적으로 발음이 유사한 adjoining을 이용한 오답이다.
(C) **정답**: 함께 점심을 먹으러 가자는 제안에 다른 계획(other plans)이 있다며 거절하고 있다.

어휘 adjoining 인접한

13 M-Au / W-Br
I wonder if the client has arrived at the airport.
(A) Let me check.
(B) Yes, that is wonderful.
(C) No, the hotel is nearby.

고객이 공항에 도착했는지 궁금하네요.
(A) 제가 확인해 볼게요.
(B) 네, 아주 훌륭하네요.
(C) 아니요, 호텔은 근처에 있어요.

해설 간접적 질문을 나타내는 평서문
(A) **정답**: 고객이 공항에 도착했는지 알고 싶다고 간접적으로 질문하는 말에, 확인해 보겠다고 답변한 정답이다.
(B) **유사 발음 오답**: 일부 발음이 유사한 두 단어 wonder와 wonderful을 이용한 오답이다.
(C) **연상 작용 오답**: 의미상 연결이 가능한 두 단어 airport와 hotel을 이용한 오답이다.

어휘 wonder if ~인지 궁금하다 nearby 인근의

14 M-Cn / W-Am
Can you describe the hiring process in more detail?
(A) Sure, what more would you like to know?
(B) Yes, he's a great addition to our team.
(C) A very thorough job description.

채용 절차를 좀 더 자세히 설명해 주시겠어요?
(A) 물론이죠, 어떤 걸 더 알고 싶으세요?
(B) 네, 그는 우리 팀에 아주 좋은 보강이에요.
(C) 아주 빈틈없는 직무기술서요.

해설 요청을 나타내는 조동사(Can) 의문문
(A) **정답**: 채용 절차를 더 자세히 설명해 달라는 요청에 우선 Sure라고 수락한 후 세부적인 사항을 묻고 있다.
(B) **인칭 오류 오답**: 질문과 관련 없는 제3자 he로 답변하고 있다.
(C) **연상 작용 오답**: 질문의 hiring process에서 연상 가능한 job description을 이용한 오답이다.

어휘 describe 설명하다 hiring process 채용 절차
addition 보강 thorough 빈틈없는
job description 직무기술서

15 M-Cn / W-Br
I'm looking for someone to review my presentation before the board meeting.
(A) Feel free to send it to me.
(B) He missed today's deadline.
(C) The meeting should last an hour.

이사회 회의 전에 프레젠테이션을 검토해 줄 사람을 찾고 있어요.
(A) 부담 갖지 마시고 저한테 보내세요.
(B) 그는 오늘 기한을 넘겼어요.
(C) 회의는 1시간 걸릴 거예요.

해설 도움을 요청하는 평서문
(A) **정답**: 프레젠테이션을 검토할 사람을 찾고 있다는 말에 자신이 봐 주겠다고 답변하고 있다.
(B) **인칭 오류 오답**: 평서문에 He를 가리킬 만한 대상이 없으므로 오답이다.
(C) **단어 반복 오답**: 평서문의 meeting을 그대로 반복 이용한 오답이다.

어휘 review 검토하다 board meeting 이사회 회의
feel free to 부담 없이 ~하다 last (시간이) 걸리다, 지속되다

16 M-Cn / W-Am
Would you like me to set up the chairs in the conference room?
(A) Ji-Mi Kwon uses our corporate account.
(B) We've decided to meet in my office.
(C) It costs ten dollars.

제가 회의실에 의자를 준비해 놓을까요?
(A) 권지미 씨는 우리 회사 계정을 사용해요.
(B) 우리는 제 사무실에서 만나기로 했어요.
(C) 비용은 10달러예요.

해설 제안을 나타내는 Would you like me to 의문문
(A) 관련 없는 오답: 질문과 상관없는 답변이다.
(B) 정답: 회의실에 의자를 준비해 놓겠다는 제안에 자신의 사무실에서 만나기로 했다며 우회적으로 거절하고 있으므로 정답이다.
(C) 관련 없는 오답: How much 질문에 어울리는 답변이다.

어휘 corporate 회사의   account 계정

17   W-Am / M-Cn
Would you like to give a presentation on your latest findings?
(A) Do you have the key?
(B) The laboratory is down the hall.
(C) What day were you thinking of?

최근 연구 결과에 대해 발표하시겠어요?
(A) 열쇠를 갖고 있나요?
(B) 연구실은 복도 지나서 있어요.
(C) 무슨 요일을 생각하고 있었나요?

해설 제안을 나타내는 Would you like to 의문문
(A) 관련 없는 오답: 발표를 제안하는 질문과 의미상 어울리지 않는다.
(B) 연상 작용 오답: 질문의 findings에서 연상 가능한 laboratory를 이용한 오답이다.
(C) 정답: 연구 결과에 대해 발표할 것인지 묻는 질문에 무슨 요일에 발표하면 좋을지 되묻고 있다.

어휘 findings (연구 등의) 결과   laboratory 연구실

18   W-Am / W-Br
I'll need the complete inventory by five today.
(A) No, I only have two.
(B) That shouldn't be a problem.
(C) I've finished reading that story.

오늘 5시까지 완성된 재고 목록이 필요해요.
(A) 아니요, 저는 두 개밖에 없어요.
(B) 문제없습니다.
(C) 그 이야기를 다 읽었어요.

해설 요청을 전달하는 평서문
(A) 연상 작용 오답: 평서문의 five라는 숫자에서 연상 가능한 two를 이용한 오답이다.
(B) 정답: 5시까지 완전한 물품 목록이 필요하다는 말에, 아무 문제가 없을 것이라고 긍정적으로 답하고 있다.
(C) 연상 작용 오답: 질문의 complete에서 연상 가능한 finish를 이용한 오답이다.

어휘 inventory 물품 목록, 재고(품)

19   M-Au / W-Am
Can you please provide a list of the audio equipment that needs to be replaced?
(A) About a hundred dollars each.
(B) I'll leave it on your desk.
(C) Where's the electrical outlet?

교체해야 할 오디오 장비 목록을 주시겠어요?
(A) 각각 100달러 정도예요.
(B) 당신 책상 위에 둘게요.
(C) 전기 콘센트는 어디 있나요?

해설 요청을 나타내는 조동사(Can) 의문문
(A) 관련 없는 오답: 가격을 묻는 질문에 가능한 답변이다.
(B) 정답: 목록을 요청하는 질문에 수락한다는 의미로 구체적인 정보를 주고 있다.
(C) 연상 작용 오답: 질문의 audio equipment에서 연상 가능한 electrical outlet을 이용한 오답이다.

어휘 equipment 장비   replace 교체하다
electrical outlet 전기 콘센트

20   M-Cn / W-Br
The interns started working in the laboratory this morning.
(A) A few new microscopes.
(B) The furniture store.
(C) Don't they have to complete some paperwork first?

인턴들이 오늘 아침에 실험실에서 근무를 시작했어요.
(A) 새 현미경 몇 개요.
(B) 가구점이요.
(C) 그들은 먼저 서류 작업부터 끝내야 하지 않나요?

해설 사실을 전달하는 평서문
(A) 연상 작용 오답: 평서문의 laboratory에서 연상 가능한 microscopes를 이용한 오답이다.
(B) 관련 없는 오답: Where 의문문에 어울리는 대답이다.
(C) 정답: 인턴들이 오늘 아침에 실험실에서 근무를 시작했다는 말에 그들이 서류 작업부터 끝내야 하지 않냐고 되물으며 업무 절차를 확인하고 있다.

어휘 microscope 현미경   complete 완료하다
paperwork 서류 작업

21   M-Cn / W-Am
I'd like to change my appointment time.
(A) Sorry, I have no change.
(B) The dentist could see you tomorrow.
(C) Thanks, I'm glad you like it.

제 예약 시간을 바꾸고 싶어요.
(A) 미안하지만 잔돈이 없어요.
(B) 치과 선생님께서 내일 진료를 보실 수 있어요.
(C) 고마워요, 좋아하신다니 다행입니다.

해설	요청을 나타내는 평서문

(A) **다의어 오답**: 평서문의 change(변경하다)와 다른 의미로 쓰인 change(잔돈)를 이용한 오답이다.
(B) **정답**: 예약 시간 변경을 원한다는 말에 가능한 날짜로 답변하고 있다.
(C) **단어 반복 오답**: 평서문의 like를 반복 이용한 오답이다.

어휘 appointment 예약, (공식적인) 약속

22 M-Cn / W-Am

You should announce the date for the employee luncheon soon.
(A) No, he hasn't been here long.
(B) I'm planning to do that today.
(C) The usual catering company.

직원 오찬 날짜를 곧 발표하셔야 해요.
(A) 아니요, 그는 여기 온 지 오래되지 않았어요.
(B) 오늘 할 계획이에요.
(C) 평소 이용하던 음식 공급 회사요.

해설	필요 사항을 전달하는 평서문

(A) **인칭 오류 오답**: 평서문과 관련 없는 제3자 he로 답변하고 있다.
(B) **정답**: 직원 오찬 날짜를 곧 발표해야 한다는 말에, 오늘 그럴 계획이라고 대답하고 있다.
(C) **연상 작용 오답**: 의미상 연결이 가능한 luncheon과 catering을 이용한 오답이다.

어휘 luncheon 오찬 usual 평소의 catering 음식 공급

23 W-Am / M-Au

There's a safety inspection scheduled for Thursday.
(A) My calendar says they're coming on Friday.
(B) The score is tied.
(C) Five dollars per person.

목요일에 안전 검사가 예정되어 있어요.
(A) 제 일정표에는 금요일에 온다고 되어 있는데요.
(B) 점수가 동점이에요.
(C) 인당 5달러예요.

해설	정보를 전달하는 평서문

(A) **정답**: 목요일에 안전 검사가 예정되어 있다는 말에 자신은 금요일로 알고 있다고 잘못된 정보를 정정하고 있다.
(B) **관련 없는 오답**: 질문과 상관없는 답변이다.
(C) **관련 없는 오답**: How much 의문문에 어울리는 대답이다.

어휘 inspection 검사 tied 동점인

24 W-Am / W-Br

Could I speak to you about applying for a job here?
(A) Some full-time lab technicians.
(B) I'll be free in a few minutes.
(C) There are about fifty employees.

이곳 입사 지원에 대해 얘기 좀 할 수 있을까요?
(A) 정규직 실험실 기사 몇 명이요.
(B) 몇 분 후면 시간이 돼요.
(C) 직원 약 50명이 있어요.

해설	요청을 나타내는 조동사(Could) 의문문

(A) **연상 작용 오답**: 의미상 연결이 가능한 두 표현 applying for a job과 full-time lab technicians를 이용한 오답이다.
(B) **정답**: 입사 지원에 대해 이야기할 수 있는지 묻는 질문에 몇 분 후에 가능하다고 답변하고 있다.
(C) **연상 작용 오답**: 의미상 연결이 가능한 두 단어 job과 employees를 이용한 오답이다.

어휘 apply for ~에 지원하다 technician 기사
employee 직원

25 W-Am / W-Br

Our department's holding a reception for the new investors this Friday.
(A) Oh, I'll be out of town.
(B) About 50 words.
(C) His office is on the fourth floor.

우리 부서에서 이번 금요일에 신규 투자자를 위한 환영회를 개최합니다.
(A) 아, 저는 출장 중일 거예요.
(B) 약 50단어요.
(C) 그의 사무실은 4층에 있어요.

해설	정보를 전달하는 평서문

(A) **정답**: 금요일에 신규 투자자를 위한 환영회를 개최한다는 말에 자신은 출장 중일 것이라며 참석할 수 없다는 것을 우회적으로 표현하고 있다.
(B) **관련 없는 오답**: 개수를 묻는 How many 의문문에 어울리는 대답이다.
(C) **연상 작용 오답**: 의미상 연결이 가능한 department와 office를 이용한 오답이다.

어휘 reception 환영회 investor 투자자

PART 3
LISTENING COMPREHENSION

UNIT 09 주제·목적 문제 / 화자·장소 문제

① 주제·목적 문제

ETS 유형 연습 본책 p.071

1 (C)   2 (B)   3 (B)   4 (B)

[1] M-Au / W-Br

M Hello, **I'm calling to place an order for a set of headphones** I saw in your catalog.
W All right, I can help you with that. Can you give me the product code for those?
M I have the catalog right here—if you can give me a moment, I'll check it and see.

남 안녕하세요. 카탈로그에서 본 헤드폰을 한 세트 주문하려고 전화 드렸어요.
여 네, 그거라면 제가 도와드릴 수 있어요. 제품 코드를 알려 주시겠어요?
남 카탈로그를 지금 가지고 있어요. 잠시 시간을 주시면 확인해 볼게요.

어휘 place an order 주문하다   product code 제품 코드

Q 남자는 왜 전화를 하는가?
(A) 계좌를 개설하려고   (B) 오류를 신고하려고
(C) 주문하려고   (D) 물건을 반품하려고

해설 전체 내용 – 전화 이유
전화한 이유나 목적을 묻는 질문은 대화의 앞 부분에 I'm calling to라고 밝히는 부분을 잘 들어야 한다. 첫 대사에서 남자가 헤드폰을 주문하기 위해(place an order for a set of headphones) 전화했다는 것을 알 수 있으므로 정답은 (C)이다.

어휘 open an account 계좌를 개설하다

[2] M-Au / W-Am

M **I got a bill from the electric company** in the mail today. It's so expensive!
W Mine is too. I guess that's because I've been using the air conditioner so much in this hot weather.
M So have I, but **I still don't think I should have been billed this much.** Maybe I should call the electric company and find out if the rates have gone up.

남 오늘 전기 회사의 청구서를 우편으로 받았는데요. 요금이 너무 많이 나왔어요!
여 저도 그래요. 이렇게 더운 날씨에 에어컨을 너무 많이 틀어서 그런 것 같아요.
남 그건 저도 마찬가지죠. 하지만 그래도 **이렇게 많이 나왔을 것 같진 않은데요.** 전기 회사에 전화해서 요금이 올랐는지 알아봐야겠어요.

어휘 bill 청구서; 청구서를 보내다   electric company 전기 회사   in the mail 우편으로   air conditioner 에어컨

Q 화자들은 무엇에 대해 이야기하고 있는가?
(A) 전화 요금   **(B) 전기 요금**
(C) 일기 예보   (D) 고장 난 에어컨

해설 전체 내용 – 대화 주제
남자가 첫 대사에서 전기 회사의 청구서를 받았는데 요금이 너무 많이 나왔다(I got a bill from the electric company in the mail today. It's so expensive!)고 하자 여자가 자기도 많이 나왔다고 맞장구를 친 후 전기 요금과 관련한 대화가 이어지므로 (B)가 정답이다.

어휘 weather report 일기 예보   broken 고장 난

[3] M-Cn / W-Br

M **I'm calling to speak with someone about opening a new savings account.** Is this something I can do over the phone?
W Unfortunately, to open an account, you'll have to come to the bank with two forms of identification. Would you like to make an appointment to see an account manager?
M No, I'll just stop by when I can.

남 새 예금 계좌를 개설하는 것에 대해 문의하려고 전화했습니다. 전화로 계좌 개설을 할 수 있나요?
여 안타깝지만, 계좌를 개설하려면 신분증 두 가지를 지참하셔서 은행으로 오셔야 합니다. 계좌 담당자를 만날 약속을 잡으시겠어요?
남 아니요, 시간이 날 때 들르겠습니다.

어휘 savings 예금   identification 신분증   stop by 들르다

Q 남자는 왜 전화를 하는가?
(A) 연락처 정보를 수정하려고
(B) 새 계좌를 개설하려고
(C) 대출을 신청하려고
(D) 분실된 카드를 신고하려고

해설 전체 내용 – 남자가 전화한 이유
전화를 건 사람인 남자의 대사에 주목하면, 새 예금 계좌를 개설하는 것에 대해 문의(I'm calling to speak with someone about opening a new savings account)하고 있으므로 정답은 (B)이다.

어휘 contact information 연락처 정보   apply for 신청하다
      loan 대출   lost 분실된

[4] M-Au / W-Br

M Ms. Johnson, I'm planning the company's cafeteria menu for next month, and I'd like to add some vegetarian options to what I'll be cooking. Would that be OK with you?
W That'd be fine. I'm sure there will be requests for vegetarian dishes.
M I have some excellent recipes for vegetarian meals. I can make a few for you to sample.

남 존슨 씨, 다음 달 회사 구내식당 메뉴를 계획 중인데, 제가 요리할 음식에 채식 옵션을 추가하려고 해요. 괜찮으시겠어요?
여 좋아요. 분명 채식 요리를 달라는 요청이 있을 거예요.
남 저한테 채식 식단을 위한 훌륭한 요리법들이 좀 있어요. 시식하실 수 있도록 제가 몇 개 만들게요.

어휘 vegetarian 채식의   sample 시식하다

Q 화자들은 주로 무엇에 관해 이야기하고 있는가?
  (A) 워크숍 개최   (B) 메뉴 만들기
  (C) 여행 계획   (D) 지원서 검토

해설 전체 내용 – 대화 주제
남자의 첫 번째 대사에서 구내식당 메뉴에 채식 옵션을 추가하려 한다(I'm planning the company's cafeteria menu for next month, and I'd like to add some vegetarian options to what I'll be cooking)고 한 후 여자의 의견을 물었고 이에 여자가 괜찮다고 답하면서 관련 대화를 이어가고 있으므로 정답은 (B)이다.

어휘 organize 계획하다   application 지원(서)

Paraphrasing 대화의 add some vegetarian options to what I'll be cooking → 보기의 Creating a menu

❷ 화자·장소 문제

ETS 유형 연습   본책 p.073

1 (B)   2 (C)   3 (B)   4 (A)

[1] M-Au / W-Br

M I was here for last night's performance, and I think I left my jacket on the back of my seat. I was sitting in the last row of the theater.
W I'll have to check. Can you describe what the jacket looks like?
M It's dark blue and has a pocket on the left side.

남 어젯밤 공연을 보러 이곳에 왔다가 제 좌석 뒤에 재킷을 두고 온 것 같아요. 극장 마지막 줄에 앉아 있었는데요.
여 제가 확인해 봐야 할 것 같은데요. 그 재킷 모양을 설명해 주시겠어요?
남 짙은 파란색이고 왼쪽에 주머니가 하나 있습니다.

어휘 performance 공연   row 줄, 열   describe 묘사하다

Q 화자들은 어디에 있는 것 같은가?
  (A) 식당   (B) 극장
  (C) 경기장   (D) 쇼핑 센터

해설 전체 내용 – 대화 장소
대화 장소를 묻는 질문으로 대화 첫 부분을 잘 들어야 한다. 첫 대사에 장소 관련 표현인 here, performance, theater가 언급되므로 화자들이 극장에 있음을 알 수 있다. 따라서 정답은 (B)이다.

[2] M-Au / W-Am

M Thanks for meeting with me, Ms. Breton. I'm a fan of your cooking show and really like your recipes.
W That's great. And how would I fit in?
M I want to feature your recipes on our Web site. Here are some photographs of the meals we've planned in the past for you to look at.

남 만나 주셔서 감사합니다, 브레튼 씨. 저는 선생님 요리 프로그램의 팬이고 선생님의 조리법을 정말 좋아합니다.
여 기쁘군요. 제가 어떤 식으로 참여하게 될까요?
남 저희 웹사이트에 선생님의 레시피를 소개하고 싶습니다. 예전에 저희가 계획했던 식단 사진을 몇 장 가져왔으니 한번 보시죠.

어휘 recipe 조리법   fit in (역할, 위치 등에) 어울리다, 적합하다   feature 다루다, 포함하다

Q 여자는 누구인 것 같은가?
  (A) 슈퍼마켓 주인
  (B) 음식 평론가
  (C) 요리사
  (D) 사진작가

해설 전체 내용 – 여자의 신분
첫 대사에서 남자가 여자에게 본인이 그녀의 요리 프로그램의 팬이고 그녀의 조리법을 정말 좋아한다(I'm a fan of your cooking show and really like your recipes)고 말하는 것으로 보아 여자가 요리사임을 알 수 있다. 따라서 정답은 (C)이다.

어휘 owner 주인   critic 평론가

[3] M-Au / W-Am

M Hi, this is Larry from Millwood Automotive Repairs. I'm replacing a couple of large tires on a truck. I'm calling to see whether your warehouse stocks them. The model number on the tires is RCL forty-four.
W I'm afraid we don't have it in stock right now. I could order it for you, and it would be delivered directly to you in three working days. Does that work?
M Not really.

남 안녕하세요, 밀우드 자동차 정비소 래리예요. 제가 지금 트럭에 있는 큰 타이어 두 개를 교체하고 있는데요. 그쪽 창고에 비축해 둔 타이어가 있는지 알아보려고 전화했어요. 타이어의 모델 번호는 RCL 44예요.
여 죄송하지만 당장은 재고가 없어요. 제가 주문해 드릴 수 있는데, 영업일로 3일 후에 바로 그쪽으로 배송돼요. 그럼 될까요?
남 곤란한데요.

어휘 repair 수리, 정비 replace 교체하다 warehouse 창고 stock 비축하다 deliver 배송하다 directly 바로

Q 남자는 어디에서 일하는가?
(A) 렌터카 업체   **(B) 자동차 정비소**
(C) 급송 서비스 업체   (D) 운전면허증 사무소

해설 전체 내용 – 남자의 근무 장소
남자의 첫 번째 대사(Hi, this is Larry from Millwood Automotive Repairs)에서 남자가 밀우드 자동차 정비소의 래리라고 말하고 있고 이어지는 대화 내용도 자동차 수리에 필요한 부속품에 관한 것이므로 정답은 (B)이다.

어휘 driver's license 운전면허증

[4] M-Cn / W-Am

M Hello, I'd like to purchase a ticket for the 3 o'clock train to Chicago.
W Unfortunately, sir, that train's already full. Here's a copy of the daily train schedule.
M Hmmm... if I wait for the 3:40 train, I'll have time to buy some souvenirs before leaving.

남 안녕하세요, 시카고행 3시 기차표를 한 장 사고 싶습니다.
여 안타깝게도 그 기차는 이미 만석입니다. 여기 일일 기차 시간표를 한 부 드릴게요.
남 음… 제가 3시 40분 기차를 기다리면, 출발하기 전에 기념품을 살 시간이 있겠네요.

어휘 unfortunately 안타깝게도 souvenir 기념품, 선물

Q 대화는 어디에서 일어나고 있는가?
(A) 기차역   (B) 공항
(C) 버스 터미널   (D) 렌터카 대리점

해설 전체 내용 – 대화 장소
남자의 첫 대사에서 장소 관련 키워드인 ticket과 train이 나오며, 표를 사고 싶다고 말하고 있으므로, 대화가 이루어지는 장소는 기차역임을 알 수 있다. 따라서 정답은 (A)이다.

어휘 agency 대리점, 대행사

ETS 실전 문제   본책 p.074

1 (C)	2 (A)	3 (D)	4 (D)	5 (C)	6 (D)
7 (B)	8 (D)	9 (C)	10 (C)	11 (A)	12 (D)
13 (B)	14 (A)	15 (C)	16 (A)	17 (C)	18 (C)
19 (C)	20 (B)	21 (A)	22 (C)	23 (A)	24 (C)

[1-3] W-Am / M-Au

W ¹Since our organic soaps have been so popular, I've been thinking we should expand our bath product line.
M ¹How about adding shampoo bars? ²They don't need to be packaged in plastic containers, so they would demonstrate to our customers our company's commitment to the environment.
W Right. Customers can help decide on the scents for the shampoo bars. ³I could create a survey and ask them what they would like their shampoo to smell like.
M ³Can you do that now?

여 ¹우리 유기농 비누가 굉장히 인기가 많아서, 목욕 용품 라인을 확장해야 한다고 생각하고 있어요.
남 ¹샴푸 바를 추가하는 건 어때요? ²플라스틱 용기에 포장할 필요가 없어서 우리 회사가 환경을 위해 헌신하고 있다는 것을 고객들에게 보여줄 수 있을 거예요.
여 좋아요. 고객들이 샴푸 바의 향을 결정하는 걸 도와줄 수도 있어요. ³설문조사를 만들어서 샴푸에서 어떤 향이 나기를 원하는지 물어볼 수 있겠어요.
남 ³지금 해 줄 수 있어요?

어휘 expand 확장하다 package 포장하다 container 용기 demonstrate 보여주다 commitment 헌신 environment 환경 scent 향

1 화자들은 무엇에 관해 이야기하고 있는가?
(A) 신입 직원 모집   (B) 출장 경비 절감
(C) 신제품 개발   (D) 회사 로고 업데이트

해설 전체 내용 – 대화 주제
대화 초반부에 여자가 목욕 용품 라인 확장(I've been thinking we should expand our bath product line)을 제안하고 있고, 남자도 샴푸 바를 추가하자(How about adding shampoo bars?)는 의견을 내고 있다. 이로 보아 화자들은 새로 출시할 제품에 대한 아이디어를 구상하고 있다는 것을 알 수 있으므로 정답은 (C)이다.

어휘 recruit 모집하다 reduce 줄이다 expense 경비

2 남자에 따르면, 회사에 중요한 것은 무엇인가?
   (A) 환경 지속 가능성   (B) 고객 충성도
   (C) 작업장 안전   (D) 직무 개발

해설 세부 내용 – 회사에 중요한 것
남자가 첫 대사에서 샴푸 바는 플라스틱 용기에 포장할 필요가 없어서 회사가 환경을 위해 헌신하고 있다는 것을 고객들에게 보여줄 수 있을 것(They don't need to be packaged in plastic containers, so they would demonstrate to our customers our company's commitment to the environment)이라고 한 말을 통해 회사는 환경 보존을 중시하고 있다는 것을 알 수 있다. 따라서 정답은 (A)이다.

어휘 sustainability 지속 가능성 loyalty 충성(심)

3 여자는 다음에 무엇을 할 것 같은가?
   (A) 경쟁사의 가격 조사
   (B) 포장 디자인 공모전 개최
   (C) 업계 전문가와 상의
   (D) 고객을 위한 설문조사 작성

해설 세부 내용 – 여자가 다음에 할 일
여자가 두 번째 대사에서 설문조사를 만들어서 샴푸에서 어떤 향이 나기를 원하는지 고객에게 물어볼 수 있겠다(I could create a survey and ask them what they would like their shampoo to smell like)고 제안하자 남자가 지금 해 줄 수 있는지(Can you do that now?) 묻고 있으므로 정답은 (D)이다.

어휘 research 조사하다 competitor 경쟁자 launch 시작하다 consult 상의하다 industry 산업 expert 전문가

[4-6] W-Br / M-Cn

W Hello. ⁴I'm calling to find out the name of a new song that you played yesterday. Do you have a playlist?
M Well, ⁵I'm only a receptionist for the radio station, but I can find out for you. What can you tell me about the song?
W Oh, it played in the segment from nine A.M. to ten A.M. It had a lot of drumming in it.
M Ah, yes. ⁶That was by Yuliya Maksim, and it was from her new album. But I don't know the name of the song offhand. I'll find out for you.

여 안녕하세요. ⁴어제 틀었던 신곡의 제목을 알고 싶어서 전화했어요. 재생 목록이 있나요?
남 음, ⁵저는 단지 라디오 방송국의 접수원이긴 하지만, 알아봐 드릴 수는 있어요. 그 노래에 대해 무엇을 알려주실 수 있을까요?
여 아, 오전 9시에서 10시 사이 구간에 재생되었어요. 드럼 연주가 많이 들어 있었고요.
남 아, 네. ⁶그건 율리야 막심의 곡이고 그녀의 새 앨범에 수록된 거예요. 그런데 노래 제목을 곧바로 모르겠네요. 제가 찾아보겠습니다.

어휘 receptionist 접수원 segment 부분 offhand (확인해 보지 않고) 바로

4 여자는 왜 전화를 하고 있는가?
   (A) 음악 축제에 대해 문의하려고
   (B) 일자리에 지원하려고
   (C) 대회에 참가하려고
   (D) 노래 제목을 찾으려고

해설 전체 내용 – 전화를 하는 이유
첫 대사에서 여자가 어제 틀었던 신곡의 제목을 알고 싶어서 전화했다(I'm calling to find out the name of a new song that you played yesterday)고 전화한 이유를 밝히고 있으므로 정답은 (D)이다.

어휘 apply for ~에 지원하다 enter 참가하다

Paraphrasing 대화의 name → 보기의 title

5 남자는 어디에서 일하는가?
   (A) 음반 가게   (B) 녹음 스튜디오
   (C) 라디오 방송국   (D) 연예 기획사

해설 전체 내용 – 남자의 근무 장소
남자가 첫 대사에서 자신을 라디오 방송국의 접수원(I'm only a receptionist for the radio station)이라고 소개했으므로 정답은 (C)이다.

어휘 agency 대행사, 단체

6 율리야 막심은 누구인 것 같은가?
   (A) 행사 진행자   (B) 음향 엔지니어
   (C) 아나운서   (D) 음악가

해설 세부 내용 – 율리야 막심의 신분
남자가 마지막 대사에서 여자가 찾는 노래가 율리야 막심의 곡이고 그녀의 새 앨범에 수록된 것(That was by Yuliya Maksim, and it was from her new album)이라고 한 말을 통해 율리야 막심이 음악가임을 알 수 있다. 따라서 정답은 (D)이다.

어휘 coordinator 진행자

[7-9] W-Br / M-Cn

W ⁷Welcome to the skilled-trades job fair! Please sign in here. So, what type of job are you looking for?
M Well, ⁸I have extensive training and experience as an electrician. But I recently moved here from another state and would like to work closer to my new home.

W   Oh, there are multiple companies seeking electricians here. And many are offering hiring bonuses. **9Here is a map of the job fair.** It shows where all the companies' booths are located on this floor.

여   **7**숙련직 취업 박람회에 오신 것을 환영합니다! 여기 서명해 주세요. 어떤 종류의 직장을 찾고 계신가요?
남   음, **8**저는 전기 기사로서 폭넓은 훈련과 경험을 갖고 있습니다. 하지만 최근에 제가 다른 주에서 여기로 이사를 와서 새 집에서 가까운 곳에서 일하고 싶어요.
여   아, 이곳에 전기 기사를 구하는 회사가 여러 군데 있어요. 그리고 많은 곳에서 채용 보너스를 제공하고 있고요. **9**여기 취업 박람회 지도가 있어요. 이 층에 있는 모든 회사의 부스 위치가 표시되어 있어요.

어휘   skilled-trades 숙련된 기술직   job fair 취업 박람회
sign in (입장하기 위해) 서명하다   extensive 폭넓은
electrician 전기 기사   state 주   booth 부스

7   남자는 어떤 종류의 행사에 참석하고 있는가?
(A) 신입 직원 오리엔테이션
(B) 취업 박람회
(C) 안전 교육
(D) 시상식

해설   **전체 내용 - 대화 장소**
첫 대사에서 여자가 남자에게 숙련직 취업 박람회에 온 것을 환영한다(Welcome to the skilled-trades job fair!)고 했으므로 정답은 (B)이다.

어휘   new-hire 신입 직원   awards ceremony 시상식

8   남자의 직업은 무엇인가?
(A) 건축가   (B) 기차 운전사
(C) 자동차 정비사   (D) 전기 기사

해설   **전체 내용 - 남자의 직업**
남자가 자신이 전기 기사로서 폭넓은 훈련과 경험을 갖고 있다(I have extensive training and experience as an electrician)고 했으므로 정답은 (D)이다.

어휘   occupation 직업   architect 건축가
mechanic 정비사

9   여자는 남자에게 무엇을 주는가?
(A) 주차권   (B) 식사 이용권
(C) 층 지도   (D) 프로그램 시간표

해설   **세부 내용 - 여자가 주는 것**
마지막 대사에서 여자가 여기 취업 박람회 지도가 있다(Here is a map of the job fair)며 남자에게 지도를 건네주고 있으므로 정답은 (C)이다.

[10-12]   W-Am / M-Cn

W   Ji-Soo, **10thanks for meeting to discuss your performance review.** You received high ratings in every area.
M   Thank you. That's because giving good patient care is very important to me. And **11I really enjoy working with the doctors and nurses here.**
W   It certainly shows. Do you have questions about your performance review?
M   Actually, I did notice that I didn't get credit for taking the hospital's required training courses. I have all my completion certificates.
W   Excellent. **12Could you please send those certificates to me?** We need all that information so that our records are accurate.

여   지수, **10**업무 평가를 논의하기 위해 만나 주셔서 감사합니다. 모든 영역에서 높은 평가를 받으셨어요.
남   감사합니다. 환자를 잘 보살피는 것은 저에게 매우 중요한 일이라서요. **11**저는 여기 의사와 간호사분들과 함께 일하는 것이 정말 즐겁습니다.
여   확실히 그렇게 보이네요. 업무 평가에 대해 질문이 있나요?
남   실은, 병원에서 요구하는 교육 과정을 이수한 것에 대해 인정을 받지 못했다는 걸 알게 되었습니다. 저에게 모든 수료증이 있습니다.
여   좋습니다. **12**그 수료증들을 저에게 보내 주실 수 있을까요? 기록이 정확하려면 우리는 모든 정보가 필요하거든요.

어휘   performance review 업무 평가   rating 평가
patient 환자   certainly 확실히   completion certificate 수료증   accurate 정확한

10   화자들은 무엇에 관해 이야기하고 있는가?
(A) 면접 일정   (B) 고객 불만
(C) 업무 평가   (D) 컨퍼런스 발표

해설   **전체 내용 - 대화 주제**
첫 대사에서 여자가 업무 평가를 논의하기 위해 만나 줘서 감사하다(thanks for meeting to discuss your performance review)며 대화의 주제를 언급하고 있으므로 정답은 (C)이다.

11   화자들은 어디에서 일할 것 같은가?
(A) 병원   (B) 호텔
(C) 법률 사무소   (D) 채용 센터

해설   **전체 내용 - 근무 장소**
남자가 첫 대사에서 여기 의사와 간호사들과 함께 일하는 것이 정말 즐겁다(I really enjoy working with the doctors and nurses here)고 한 것으로 보아 화자들이 병원에서 근무하고 있다는 것을 알 수 있다. 따라서 정답은 (A)이다.

12 여자는 남자에게 무엇을 해 달라고 요청하는가?
(A) 정책 검토
(B) 이메일 회신
(C) 장비 설치
(D) 서류 제공

해설 **세부 내용 – 여자가 요청하는 것**
마지막 대사에서 여자가 남자에게 수료증들을 본인에게 보내 줄 수 있을지(Could you please send those certificates to me?) 묻고 있으므로 정답은 (D)이다.

어휘 review 검토하다 equipment 장비

Paraphrasing 대화의 send those certificates
→ 보기의 Provide some documents

[13-15] W-Br / M-Cn

W Sorry, Shahid, but do you have a minute? **13 I have to submit the receipts from my last business trip so I can get reimbursed for travel expenses.** I haven't used the company's new system, though.
M Sure, I can help you. You can find the reimbursement request form online, and then you have to attach electronic versions of your receipts when you submit it. It's better than the old system **14 because you'll get your reimbursement processed much more quickly.**
W OK, great. **13,15 I only have paper copies of the receipts, but I'll go scan them into computer files and upload them to the request form.**

여 샤히드, 죄송하지만 잠깐 시간 되세요? **13 지난번 출장 영수증을 제출해야 제 출장 경비를 환급 받을 수 있어요.** 그런데 전 회사의 새로운 시스템을 사용해 본 적이 없어요.
남 물론이죠. 도와드릴게요. 환급 요청서는 온라인에 있고, 제출 시 전자 영수증을 첨부해야 해요. **14 환급이 훨씬 더 빨리 처리되기 때문에 예전 시스템보다 나아요.**
여 그렇군요. 좋네요. **13,15 종이 영수증 사본만 가지고 있는데 스캔해서 컴퓨터 파일로 요청서에 올릴게요.**

어휘 submit 제출하다 receipt 영수증 reimburse 환급하다 expense 비용 attach 첨부하다 process 처리하다

13 대화는 주로 무엇에 관한 것인가?
(A) 여행 준비
(B) 비용 영수증 제출
(C) 사업대출 신청
(D) 컴퓨터 수리

해설 **전체 내용 – 대화 주제**
여자가 남자에게 환급을 위해 출장 영수증을 제출해야 한다(I have to submit the receipts from my last business trip so I can get reimbursed for travel expenses)며 도움을 요청하는 말로 대화가 시작되어, 영수증 스캔본을 환급 요청서에 올리겠다(I only have paper copies of the receipts, but I'll go scan them into computer files and upload them to the request form)는 내용으로 이어지고 있다. 따라서 정답은 (B)이다.

어휘 arrangement 준비 apply for ~을 신청하다

14 남자의 말에 따르면, 왜 새로운 시스템이 더 나은가?
(A) 결제 처리가 빠르다.
(B) 운영비가 적게 든다.
(C) 온라인으로 일정을 관리한다.
(D) 보증서가 포함되어 있다.

해설 **세부 내용 – 새로운 시스템이 더 나은 이유**
남자의 대사에 주목하면, 환급 절차가 더 빨라서(because you'll get your reimbursement processed much more quickly) 예전 시스템보다 더 좋다고 하므로 정답은 (A)이다.

어휘 payment 결제 operate 운영하다 warranty 보증(서)

Paraphrasing 대화의 much more quickly
→ 보기의 faster

15 여자는 다음에 무엇을 할 것 같은가?
(A) 약속시간 변경
(B) 다른 동료와 상의
(C) 전자문서 생성
(D) 은행 거래내역서 수정

해설 **세부 내용 – 여자가 다음에 할 일**
대화 마지막에 여자가 문서를 스캔해서 컴퓨터 파일로 올릴 것(I only have paper copies of the receipts, but I'll go scan them into computer files and upload them to the request form)이라고 하므로 정답은 (C)이다.

어휘 appointment 약속 colleague 동료 correct 수정하다 bank statement 은행 거래내역서

Paraphrasing 대화의 scan them into computer files
→ 보기의 Create electronic documents

[16-18] W-Br / M-Cn

W **16 I'm here for my appointment with Marcus—for a shampoo and haircut.**
M Oh, **17 I'm so sorry, but Marcus just called. His car broke down, so he won't be able to make your appointment.** Would you like to reschedule or try another hair stylist?
W I can come back on another day. Is Marcus free tomorrow at noon?
M Tomorrow's his day off. But **18 he can fit you in on Wednesday at that time.**
W **18 Sounds good.** Thanks.

063

여	**16**마커스 선생님과 샴푸랑 헤어컷 약속이 있어서 왔어요.
남	아, **17**정말 죄송하지만 마커스 선생님이 방금 전화했는데요. 차가 고장 나서 약속을 못 지킬 것 같아요. 예약을 다시 잡아드릴까요, 아니면 다른 헤어 스타일리스트한테 하시겠어요?
여	다른 날 다시 올게요. 마커스 선생님은 내일 정오에 시간이 되시나요?
남	내일은 마커스 선생님이 쉬는 날이에요. 하지만 **18**수요일 같은 시간대에는 될 것 같아요.
여	**18**좋아요. 감사합니다.

어휘 break down 고장 나다   reschedule 일정을 변경하다
day off 휴일   fit A in 시간을 내어 A를 만나다

16 대화는 어디에서 이루어지고 있는가?
(A) 미용실   (B) 진료소
(C) 의류 매장   (D) 사진관

해설 전체 내용 – 대화 장소
첫 대사에서 마커스 선생님과 샴푸와 헤어컷 약속이 있어서 왔다(I'm here for my appointment with Marcus—for a shampoo and haircut)고 하므로 여자가 미용실에 찾아온 손님임을 알 수 있다. 따라서 정답은 (A)이다.

17 마커스는 왜 약속을 지킬 수 없는가?
(A) 자격증이 만료되었다.
(B) 필요한 용품을 찾을 수 없었다.
(C) 차가 고장 났다.
(D) 아파서 집에 있다.

해설 세부 내용 – 마커스가 약속을 지킬 수 없는 이유
남자가 첫 번째 대사에서 마커스 선생님의 차가 고장 나서 약속을 못 지킬 것 같다(His car broke down, so he won't be able to make your appointment)고 하므로 (C)가 정답이다.

어휘 certification 자격증   expire 만료되다   supplies 용품

> Paraphrasing 대화의 His car broke down
> → 보기의 His car is not working

18 여자는 언제 다시 올 것 같은가?
(A) 오늘 오후 늦게   (B) 내일
(C) 수요일   (D) 토요일

해설 세부 내용 – 여자의 재방문 시기
대화 후반부에서 남자가 마커스 선생님이 수요일 같은 시간대에는 될 것 같다(he can fit you in on Wednesday at that time)고 하자 여자가 좋다(Sounds good)고 대답하고 있다. 따라서 여자가 수요일에 다시 올 예정임을 알 수 있으므로 정답은 (C)이다.

[19-21] M-Au / W-Br

M Hi. **19**I'm calling about obtaining my employee ID card. I was just hired to work in the marketing department, and I was told to contact you.
W That's correct. **20**Have you completed the ID application form yet?
M Yes, I have.
W Great. **20**Be sure to bring that with you. I can schedule an appointment for you to have your picture taken next week. What time works best for you?
M Hmm. How about Wednesday at nine A.M.?
W Sure. And just so you know, we recently moved. **21**You can find directions to our new office on the employee Web site. See you next week.

남	안녕하세요. **19**제 직원 신분증 발급과 관련해 전화 드렸습니다. 이제 막 마케팅 부서에서 근무하도록 채용되었는데, 당신께 연락하라고 들었습니다.
여	맞아요. **20**신분증 신청서는 작성하셨나요?
남	네, 했습니다.
여	좋아요. **20**반드시 지참하시고요. 다음 주에 사진을 찍을 수 있도록 예약해 드릴게요. 몇 시가 가장 좋은가요?
남	음. 수요일 오전 9시는 어떤가요?
여	좋아요. 그리고 참고로, 저희가 최근에 이전을 했어요. **21**새 사무실로 오는 길 안내는 직원 웹사이트에서 확인하실 수 있어요. 다음 주에 뵙겠습니다.

어휘 obtain 얻다   complete 작성하다   application form 신청서   schedule 일정을 잡다   directions (길) 안내

19 남자는 왜 전화를 하고 있는가?
(A) 일자리에 지원하려고
(B) 투어 일정을 세우려고
(C) 신분증을 요청하려고
(D) 스포츠 클럽에 가입하려고

해설 전체 내용 – 전화를 하는 이유
첫 대사에서 남자가 직원 신분증 발급과 관련해 전화했다(I'm calling about obtaining my employee ID card)고 했으므로 정답은 (C)이다.

어휘 arrange ~ 일정을 세우다   identification card 신분증

> Paraphrasing 대화의 obtaining my employee ID card
> → 보기의 request an identification card

20 여자는 남자에게 무엇을 가져오라고 말하는가?
(A) 할인 쿠폰   (B) 작성한 양식
(C) 입장권   (D) 추천서 목록

해설 **세부 내용 – 여자의 요구 사항**
여자가 남자에게 신분증 신청서를 작성했는지(Have you completed the ID application form yet?)를 확인하며 반드시 지참하라(Be sure to bring that with you)고 하고 있다. 이를 통해 여자가 남자에게 작성이 완료된 신분증 신청서를 가져오라는 것임을 알 수 있으므로 정답은 (B)이다.

어휘 admission 입장

21 여자는 웹사이트에서 무엇을 찾을 수 있다고 하는가?
(A) 길 안내
(B) 사진
(C) 근무 시간
(D) 일자리

해설 **세부 내용 – 여자가 웹사이트에서 찾을 수 있다고 하는 것**
마지막 대사에서 여자가 새 사무실로 오는 길 안내를 직원 웹사이트에서 확인할 수 있다(You can find directions to our new office on the employee Web site)고 하므로 정답은 (A)이다.

[22-24] 3인 대화 M-Au / M-Cn / W-Am

> M1 **22**There have been complaints that the conveyor belt is moving slowly. Alessandro, you're the supervisor on the floor. What do you think?
> M2 **22**I think we should look into repairing it. It's only about five years old.
> W Yes, **23**I'm concerned about costs, so trying to repair it is a good idea. We don't want to exceed our budget this year.
> M2 OK, I'll contact maintenance.
> W Great. **24**Please e-mail us when you have some information.
>
> 남1 **22**컨베이어 벨트가 느리게 움직인다는 불평이 있어요. 알레산드로, 작업장 관리자이신데, 어떻게 생각하세요?
> 남2 **23**수리를 알아봐야 할 것 같네요. 아직 5년 정도밖에 안 됐거든요.
> 여 그래요. **23**비용이 걱정되니 고쳐 보는 게 좋겠네요. 올해 예산을 초과하지 않았으면 하잖아요.
> 남2 네, 정비 팀에 연락해 볼게요.
> 여 좋아요. **24**소식이 있으면 우리에게 이메일로 보내 주세요.

어휘 conveyor belt 컨베이어 벨트 supervisor 관리자 exceed 초과하다 maintenance 정비, 유지 관리

22 화자들은 무엇에 관해 이야기하고 있는가?
(A) 연례 검사
(B) 새로운 소프트웨어 프로그램
(C) 장비 기능 불량
(D) 직원 근무 일정

해설 **전체 내용 – 대화 주제**
첫 대사에서 첫 번째 남자가 컨베이어 벨트가 느리게 움직인다는 불평이 있다(There have been complaints that the conveyor belt is moving slowly)고 하자, 두 번째 남자가 수리를 알아봐야 할 것 같다(I think we should look into repairing it)고 대답한 것을 통해 장비의 기능 불량 문제에 대해 논의 중임을 알 수 있다. 따라서 정답은 (C)이다.

어휘 annual 연례의, 매년의 inspection 검사 malfunctioning 기능 불량의, 오작동하는 equipment 장비

> Paraphrasing 대화의 conveyor belt
> → 보기의 equipment
> 대화의 moving slowly → 보기의 Malfunctioning

23 여자는 무엇을 걱정하는가?
(A) 예산 초과
(B) 고객 만족
(C) 직원 부족
(D) 생산 지연

해설 **세부 내용 – 여자의 걱정거리**
대화 중반부에서 여자가 비용이 걱정되니 고쳐 보는 게 좋겠다(I'm concerned about costs, so trying to repair it is a good idea)고 하고, 올해 예산을 초과하지 않았으면 한다(We don't want to exceed our budget this year)고 하므로 정답은 (A)이다.

어휘 satisfy 만족시키다 shortage 부족 delay 지연

24 여자는 무엇을 요청하는가?
(A) 평면도
(B) 명단
(C) 이메일을 통한 최신 소식
(D) 회사 정책

해설 **세부 내용 – 여자의 요청 사항**
마지막 대사에서 여자가 소식이 있으면 이메일로 보내 달라(Please e-mail us when you have some information)고 요청하고 있으므로 정답은 (C)이다.

UNIT 10 세부 사항 문제 / 문제점·걱정거리 문제

1 세부 사항 문제

ETS 유형 연습
본책 p.077

1 (C)   2 (A)   3 (A)   4 (C)

[1] M-Au / W-Br

> M Susan, could you reschedule my nine o'clock client tomorrow?
> W Sure, Mr. Miller. When is the earliest you could see him?
> M The mechanic told me that my car should be ready by ten. So, let's say eleven.
> W OK, I'll ask him to come in at eleven.

남	수잔, 내일 9시 고객 약속을 다시 잡아 줄래요?
여	알겠습니다. 밀러 씨. 그분을 만날 수 있는 가장 빠른 시간이 언제인가요?
남	정비공이 10시까지는 차가 준비될 거라고 했어요. **그러니 11시로 합시다.**
여	알겠습니다. 그분에게 11시에 오시라고 요청할게요.

어휘 reschedule 일정을 변경하다   mechanic 정비공

Q 남자는 내일 고객들을 언제부터 만나기 시작할 것인가?
(A) 오전 9시   (B) 오전 10시
(C) 오전 11시   (D) 오후 1시

해설 세부 내용 – 남자가 고객들을 만날 시각
여자가 약속을 조정하기 위해서 언제 가장 빨리 고객을 만날 수 있는지 묻자, 남자가 11시로 하자(let's say eleven)고 답한다. 따라서 정답은 (C)이다. (B)의 오전 10시는 차 수리가 끝나 남자가 차를 가지고 갈 수 있는 시각이다.

---

[2] W-Am / M-Au

W	Luis, I didn't see you at the supervisors' meeting, but there's good news for factory employees.
M	What's the news?
W	**The company's going to start providing shuttle bus service to and from the Metrorail station.**
M	**I'm happy to hear that.**

여	루이스, 당신을 관리자 회의에서 못 봤는데, 공장 직원들에게 좋은 소식이 있어요.
남	무슨 소식인가요?
여	회사에서 메트로레일 역을 오가는 셔틀버스 서비스를 제공할 예정이에요.
남	기쁜 소식이네요.

어휘 supervisor 관리자   to and from ~로 오가는

Q 남자는 무엇을 알고 기뻐하는가?
(A) 새로운 교통 수단 선택권이 생길 것이다.
(B) 근무 일정이 변경되었다.
(C) 직원들이 급여 인상을 받을 것이다.
(D) 추가 휴가가 제공될 것이다.

해설 세부 내용 – 남자가 기뻐하는 것
대화 중반부에서 여자가 회사에서 메트로레일 역을 오가는 셔틀버스 서비스를 제공할 예정(The company's going to start providing shuttle bus service to and from the Metrorail station)이라는 소식을 전하자 남자가 I'm happy to hear that이라고 대답하므로 정답은 (A)이다.

어휘 transportation 교통 수단   salary 급여   increase 인상   award 주다

Paraphrasing   대화의 shuttle bus service
→ 보기의 transportation option

---

[3] M-Cn / W-Br

M	Divya, I have a question about the client appreciation banquet. Do you know how many people we can invite this year?
W	**I'm still waiting to get a confirmation from the South York Hotel** that we can use their ballroom. If it's available, we can host as many clients as we like.
M	Oh, OK. Please let me know as soon as possible.

남	디비야, 고객 감사 연회에 대해 질문이 있어요. 올해는 몇 명이나 초청할 수 있는지 아세요?
여	사우스 요크 호텔의 연회장을 사용할 수 있는지 **아직 호텔 측 확답을 기다리고 있어요.** 만약 그 연회장을 사용할 수 있다면 우리가 원하는 만큼 고객들을 많이 초청할 수 있어요.
남	아, 알겠습니다. 가능한 한 빨리 알려 주세요.

어휘 appreciation 감사   banquet 연회   confirmation 확인   host 주최하다

Q 여자는 왜 남자의 질문에 답할 수 없는가?
(A) 호텔로부터 연락을 받지 못했다.
(B) 인터넷에 접속할 수 없다.
(C) 행사 예산이 제공되지 않았다.
(D) 이사가 출장을 갔다.

해설 세부 내용 – 여자가 남자의 질문에 답할 수 없는 이유
여자가 아직 호텔 측 확답을 기다리고 있다(I'm still waiting to get a confirmation from the South York Hotel)고 하므로 정답은 (A)이다.

---

[4] W-Br / M-Cn

W	Hello, Mr. Wilson? This is Susan Chung—a reporter for the local newspaper. **I'm following up on a report that you have plans to redevelop the vacant Claremont property site.**
M	I lead a community group that wants to convert the Claremont property into the biggest park in the city. Local residents and businesses are really excited about this possibility.
W	I imagine you'll need to take your proposal to the city.
M	That's right.

여	저 안녕하세요, 윌슨 씨? 저는 지역 신문 기자 수잔 정입니다. **당신이 비어 있는 클레어몬트 부동산 부지를 재개발하려는 계획이라는 보도에 대해 후속 취재하고 있어요.**
남	저는 클레어몬트 부동산을 시에서 가장 큰 공원으로 바꾸려는 지역 단체를 이끌고 있어요. 지역 주민들과 기업들은 이 가능성에 대해 무척 설레하고 있어요.
여	당신이 제안서를 시로 가져가셔야 할 것 같군요.
남	맞아요.

어휘 local 지역의 follow up 후속 취재하다 redevelop 재개발하다 property 부동산 community 지역 convert A into B A를 B로 바꾸다 resident 주민 possibility 가능성 proposal 제안(서)

Q 남자는 클레어몬트 부동산에 대해 무엇이라고 말하는가?
(A) 그의 업체와 가깝다.
(B) 역사적인 건물이 있다.
(C) 재개발하기를 희망한다.
(D) 팔기로 결정했다.

해설 세부 내용 – 남자가 부동산에 대해 한 말
여자는 남자가 계획하는 클레어몬트 부동산 부지 재개발 보도에 대해 후속 취재를 하고 있다(I'm following up on a report that you have plans to redevelop the vacant Claremont property site)고 했고, 남자는 해당 장소를 시에서 가장 큰 공원으로 바꾸려는 지역 단체를 이끌고 있다(I lead a community group that wants to convert the Claremont property into the biggest park in the city)고 설명하고 있으므로 정답은 (C)이다.

② 문제점·걱정거리 문제

ETS 유형 연습   본책 p.079

1 (A)   2 (C)   3 (A)   4 (C)

[1] 3인 대화 M-Au / M-Cn / W-Am

M1 We've moved all the kitchen furniture in. Now let's work on the living room stuff.
M2 That sounds good, but **I think this couch is going to be too wide to get through the door.** Maybe we can remove the legs on it?
M1 Hm. That should work.
W Sorry to bother you, but will you have everything set up in the house by this evening?

남1 주방 가구는 다 옮겼어요. 이제 거실 물건을 작업하죠.
남2 좋은 생각이긴 한데, 이 소파가 너무 넓어서 문을 통과하지 못할 것 같아요. 다리를 떼어내 볼까요?
남1 음. 그럼 되겠네요.
여 방해해서 죄송하지만 오늘 저녁까지 집안의 모든 것들을 정리해 주실 수 있나요?

어휘 couch 소파 bother 귀찮게 하다

Q 남자들은 어떤 문제를 논의하고 있는가?
(A) 가구가 너무 크다.
(B) 프로젝트가 지연되었다.
(C) 일부 장비가 손상되었다.
(D) 일부 업그레이드가 승인되지 않았다.

해설 세부 내용 – 남자들의 문제점
두 번째 남자가 소파가 너무 넓어서 문을 통과하지 못할 것 같다(I think this couch is going to be too wide to get through the door)고 문제를 제기하며 첫 번째 남자와 해결책을 논의하고 있다. 따라서 (A)가 정답이다.

어휘 delay 지연시키다 damage 손상시키다 approve 승인하다

Paraphrasing 대화의 couch → 보기의 A piece of furniture

[2] W-Br / M-Au

W Hi, I'm having trouble with my printer. The problem is, um, **every time I try to print a document on both sides of the paper, the paper gets stuck** in the machine.
M I'm sorry to hear that. Unfortunately, we can't offer technical support over the phone.
W I guess I'll bring it back to the store this afternoon.

여 안녕하세요, 제 프린트기에 문제가 있어요. 문제는, 음, 양면으로 서류를 프린트하려고 하면 매번 종이가 기계에 걸려요.
남 그렇다니 죄송합니다. 안타깝게도 저희는 전화상으로 기술 지원을 제공해드릴 수 없습니다.
여 제가 오늘 오후에 매장으로 가져가 봐야겠네요.

어휘 every time ~할 때마다 document 서류 get stuck 걸리다 technical support 기술 지원

Q 여자는 어떤 문제를 언급하는가?
(A) 매장을 찾을 수 없다.
(B) 프로그램을 설치할 수 없다.
(C) 서류를 인쇄할 수 없다.
(D) 잉크 카트리지를 교체할 수 없다.

해설 세부 내용 – 여자의 문제점
여자가 종이가 프린트기에 끼어서 인쇄를 할 수 없다(every time I try to print a document on both sides of the paper, the paper gets stuck in the machine)고 했으므로 정답은 (C)이다.

어휘 locate ~의 정확한 위치를 찾다 install 설치하다

[3] 3인 대화 W-Am / M-Cn / M-Au

W **I'm worried about the production rate on assembly line number three.** The machine that seals the mobile phone boxes isn't running as fast as it should.
M1 Oh, we've had trouble with that machine in the past. Instead of having it repaired again, I think we'd better just replace it.

M2 I agree. But we should try to get a new one put in as soon as possible, or we might have to shut down that assembly line.

여 3번 조립라인의 생산 속도 때문에 걱정이에요. 휴대폰 상자를 밀봉하는 기계가 정상적으로 빠르게 작동하지 않아요.
남1 아, 이전에도 그 기계에 문제가 있었어요. 또 수리하는 대신 그냥 교체하는 게 나을 것 같아요.
남2 맞아요. 하지만 가능한 한 빨리 새것을 들여놓지 않으면, 그 조립라인을 중단시켜야 할지도 몰라요.

어휘 production rate 생산 속도 assembly line 조립라인 seal 밀봉하다 run 작동하다 have trouble with ~에 문제가 있다 put in 들여놓다, 설치하다 shut down (기계를) 멈추다, 정지시키다

Q 여자는 무엇을 걱정하는가?
(A) 생산 속도
(B) 직원 가용성
(C) 실내 온도
(D) 배송비

해설 세부 내용 – 여자의 걱정거리
여자가 3번 조립라인의 생산 속도 때문에 걱정(I'm worried about the production rate on assembly line number three)이라고 했으므로 정답은 (A)이다.

[4] M-Cn / W-Br

M Hello? Ms. Reed?
W Hello, Mr. Park. Could you possibly get me another blueprint? I can't find the drawings for the front entrance.
M Certainly. It'll take some time to print the plan, though. If you come by my office around three o'clock, I'll have it ready for you by then.

남 안녕하세요? 리드 씨?
여 안녕하세요, 박 씨. 설계도를 한 부 더 줄 수 있나요? 정문 도면을 못 찾겠어요.
남 물론이죠. 그런데 설계도를 출력하는 데 시간이 조금 걸릴 겁니다. 3시쯤 제 사무실에 들르면 그때까지 준비해 놓을게요.

어휘 blueprint 설계도, 청사진 drawing 도면 front entrance 정문 come by ~에 들르다

Q 리드 씨는 어떤 문제를 언급하는가?
(A) 송장이 불완전하다.   (B) 사무실이 닫혔다.
(C) 문서가 없다.   (D) 치수가 부정확하다.

해설 세부 내용 – 문제점
여자(Ms. Reed)가 정문 도면을 못 찾겠다(I can't find the drawings for the front entrance)고 했으므로 정답은 (C)이다.

ETS 실전 문제   본책 p.080

1 (B)	2 (C)	3 (C)	4 (D)	5 (C)	6 (B)
7 (B)	8 (C)	9 (D)	10 (C)	11 (B)	12 (A)
13 (C)	14 (D)	15 (D)	16 (D)	17 (B)	18 (A)
19 (B)	20 (C)	21 (D)	22 (C)	23 (D)	24 (B)

[1-3] W-Br / M-Au

W Thanks for coming on the podcast, Pablo. I'm thrilled to hear about your new film. 1 This documentary about a picturesque fishing village in Scotland is a big shift from the comedy films you typically make.
M Well, it was a project I'd wanted to do ever since visiting this beautiful village a few years ago and learning about its history. 2 One challenging thing, however, was the weather. We wanted to mainly film outside, but it rained during most days of filming.
W Wow. But the attention must be great for local businesses. 3 I read in a newspaper article that now that the film is out, visitors from all over the world are flocking to the area.

여 팟캐스트에 나와 주셔서 감사합니다. 파블로 씨. 당신의 새 영화에 대해 듣게 되어 정말 좋네요. 1 스코틀랜드의 한 그림 같은 어촌에 대한 이 다큐멘터리는 보통 제작하시던 코미디 영화에서 큰 변화인데요.
남 음, 몇 년 전에 이 아름다운 마을을 방문하고 그곳의 역사에 대해 알게 된 이후로 꼭 해보고 싶었던 프로젝트였어요. 하지만 2 날씨가 힘든 점이었어요. 주로 야외 촬영을 하길 원했는데 촬영일 대부분에 비가 왔거든요.
여 오, 그래도 이 관심이 현지 업체들에게 참 좋을 것 같습니다. 3 영화가 나오고 나서 세계 각지의 방문객들이 이 지역으로 몰려들고 있다고 신문 기사에서 읽었어요.

어휘 thrilled 아주 신이 난 picturesque 그림 같은 shift 변화 typically 보통 challenging 힘든 mainly 주로 attention 관심 flock (많은 수가) 모이다

1 남자의 새 영화는 이전 영화들과 어떻게 다른가?
(A) 특수 효과를 사용한다.
(B) 다큐멘터리이다.
(C) 시나리오 작가가 다르다.
(D) 출연진이 더 적다.

해설 세부 내용 – 남자의 새 영화가 전작들과 다른 점
여자가 스코틀랜드의 한 그림 같은 어촌에 대한 다큐멘터리는 남자가 보통 제작하던 코미디 영화에서 큰 변화(This documentary about a picturesque fishing village in Scotland is a big shift from the comedy films you typically make)라고 언급하고 있다. 따라서 정답은 (B)이다.

어휘 | special effect 특수 효과   screenwriter 시나리오 작가   cast 출연진

2 남자가 어려웠다고 말하는 것은 무엇인가?
(A) 오디션을 진행하는 것
(B) 예산을 맞추는 것
(C) 열악한 날씨에 촬영하는 것
(D) 개봉일을 맞추는 것

해설 | 세부 내용 – 남자가 어려웠다고 말하는 것
남자가 날씨가 힘든 점(One challenging thing, however, was the weather)이었다며 주로 야외 촬영을 하길 원했는데 촬영일 대부분에 비가 왔다(We wanted to mainly film outside, but it rained during most days of filming)고 토로하고 있으므로 정답은 (C)이다.

어휘 | conduct (특정 활동을) 진행하다   budget 예산   release 개봉

3 여자는 촬영 장소에 대해 무엇을 읽었다고 말하는가?
(A) 우연히 발견되었다.
(B) 배경 소음이 많았다.
(C) 관광지가 되었다.
(D) 예약하기가 비쌌다.

해설 | 세부 내용 – 여자가 촬영 장소에 대해 읽은 것
마지막 대사에서 여자는 영화가 나오고 나서 세계 각지의 방문객들이 촬영 지역으로 몰려들고 있음을 신문에서 읽었다(I read in a newspaper article that now that the film is out, visitors from all over the world are flocking to the area)고 했으므로 정답은 (C)이다.

어휘 | discover 발견하다   by accident 우연히   background 배경   tourist destination 관광지   reserve 예약하다

Paraphrasing 대화의 visitors from all over the world are flocking to the area → 보기의 become a tourist destination

---

[4-6] M-Cn / W-Br

M   Hello, Ms. Sanchez? This is Hugo Simon calling from Scottsdale Park. **⁴You reserved the park's north pavilion next Saturday for a company picnic, right?**

W   Yes, that's right. I reserved the pavilion and the surrounding picnic area from noon until three P.M. that day. Is there a problem?

M   **⁵We've been making some repairs to that pavilion's roof and I'm afraid they won't be completed by next Saturday.** You can postpone the event until the following Saturday, or if you can't change the date— there is another smaller picnic area at the park you could reserve.

W   **⁶Hmm, I think I'd like to reschedule the event.** We really need the bigger space. Please reserve the pavilion for me for the following Saturday instead.

남   여보세요, 산체스 씨? 저는 스코츠데일 공원의 휴고 사이먼이에요. ⁴다음 주 토요일 회사 야유회를 위해 공원 북쪽 대형 천막을 예약하셨죠?

여   예, 맞아요. 그날 정오부터 오후 3시까지 대형 천막과 주변 소풍 구역을 예약했어요. 문제가 있나요?

남   ⁵대형 천막 지붕을 수리하고 있는데 다음 주 토요일까지 끝낼 수 없을 것 같아요. 그 다음 주 토요일로 행사를 연기하시거나, 날짜를 변경할 수 없다면 공원에 또 다른 작은 소풍 구역을 예약할 수 있어요.

여   ⁶흠, 행사 일정을 다시 잡아야 할 것 같네요. 우린 정말 더 넓은 공간이 필요해요. 대형 천막을 그 다음 주 토요일로 대신 예약해 주세요.

어휘 | pavilion 대형 천막, 가건물   surrounding 주변의   repairs 수리 작업   postpone 연기하다   reschedule 일정을 변경하다

4 화자들은 어떤 행사를 논의하고 있는가?
(A) 영화제
(B) 착공식
(C) 강연 시리즈
(D) 소풍

해설 | 세부 내용 – 논의되는 행사
남자는 여자에게 회사 야유회를 위해 공원 북쪽 대형 천막을 예약(You reserved the park's north pavilion next Saturday for a company picnic, right?)한 사실을 확인한 후, 행사 장소와 관련된 문제를 논의하고 있다. 따라서 정답은 (D)이다.

어휘 | groundbreaking ceremony 착공식

5 남자는 어떤 문제를 언급하는가?
(A) 일기예보가 나쁘다.
(B) 건축허가증이 발급되지 않았다.
(C) 구조물을 보수하고 있다.
(D) 초청 연사가 올 수 없다.

해설 | 세부 내용 – 문제점
문제가 있는지를 묻는 여자의 질문에 남자가 천막 지붕 공사가 토요일까지 끝나지 않을 것 같다(We've been making some repairs to that pavilion's roof and I'm afraid they won't be completed by next Saturday)고 했다. 따라서 정답은 (C)이다.

어휘 | weather forecast 일기예보   permit 허가증   issue 발급하다   unavailable 시간이 없는, 만날 수 없는

Paraphrasing 대화의 making some repairs to that pavilion's roof → 보기의 A structure is being repaired.

6 여자는 무엇을 하기로 결정하는가?
(A) 환불 요청
(B) 행사 일정 변경
(C) 다른 장소 예약
(D) 관리자와 대화

해설 세부 내용 – 여자의 결정 사항
여자의 마지막 대사에서 행사 일정 조정을 원한다(I'd like to reschedule the event)는 것을 알 수 있다. 따라서 정답은 (B)이다.

어휘 refund 환불   venue 장소   supervisor 관리자

[7-9] M-Au / W-Br

M Hi! **7 Welcome to Vitale Fashions! We have the latest styles for the best prices.** How can I help you?
W I'm looking for a new dress for a company banquet next week.
M **8 I have good news. Our dresses recently went on sale.** We're offering up to a 50 percent discount on some of them.
W That's great! I really like this one with the floral pattern, but I don't have time to try it on.
M Well, our store offers a 30-day return policy on all items, even those on sale. So, **9 if you don't like how it fits, you can bring it back with the receipt.**

남 안녕하세요! **7 비탈레 패션에 오신 것을 환영합니다!** 저희는 최고의 가격으로 최신 스타일을 갖추고 있습니다. 무엇을 도와드릴까요?
여 다음 주 회사 연회에서 입을 새 드레스를 찾고 있어요.
남 **8 좋은 소식이 있습니다.** 저희 드레스가 최근 할인에 들어갔어요. 일부 드레스는 최대 50퍼센트까지 할인해드리고 있어요.
여 굉장하네요! 이 꽃무늬 드레스가 정말 마음에 드는데 입어볼 시간이 없어요.
남 음, 저희 매장은 모든 상품에 대해 30일 반품 정책을 제공하고 있는데, 심지어 할인 제품에도요. 그래서 **9 입은 게 마음에 들지 않으시면 영수증과 함께 반품하실 수 있어요.**

어휘 latest 최신   banquet 연회   up to 최대
floral 꽃무늬의   return 반품   fit (모양·크기가) 맞다

7 대화는 어디에서 이루어지고 있는 것 같은가?
(A) 꽃 가게   **(B) 의류 매장**
(C) 세탁소   (D) 식당

해설 전체 내용 – 대화 장소
첫 대사에서 남자가 비탈레 패션에 온 것을 환영한다(Welcome to Vitale Fashions!)며 최고의 가격으로 최신 스타일을 갖추고 있다(We have the latest styles for the best prices)고 했다. 따라서 정답은 (B)이다.

8 남자는 어떤 좋은 소식을 공유하는가?
(A) 영업 시간이 연장되었다.
(B) 두 번째 지점이 개점했다.
(C) 일부 상품이 할인되었다.
(D) 새로운 배송품이 최근에 도착했다.

해설 세부 내용 – 남자가 전하는 소식
대화 중반부에서 남자가 좋은 소식이 있다(I have good news)며 드레스가 최근 할인에 들어갔다(Our dresses recently went on sale)고 안내하고 있으므로 정답은 (C)이다.

어휘 extend 연장하다   shipment 배송물

Paraphrasing 대화의 on sale → 보기의 discounted

9 남자는 여자가 무엇을 할 수 있다고 말하는가?
(A) 신용카드 결제
(B) 우수 고객 프로그램 가입
(C) 배달 신청
(D) 상품 반품

해설 세부 내용 – 여자가 할 수 있다고 남자가 말하는 것
남자가 마지막 대사에서 입은 게 마음에 들지 않으면 영수증과 함께 반품할 수 있다(if you don't like how it fits, you can bring it back with the receipt)고 했으므로 정답은 (D)이다.

어휘 credit card 신용카드

[10-12] W-Am / M-Cn

W Good morning. Anything I can help you with today? I'm Adeola, the store manager.
M Yes, **10 I recently remodeled my kitchen**, and I want to purchase some new kitchenware products. But **11 I don't see any of the brands I like.**
W Our store is under new corporate ownership, and many of our long-standing brands have been replaced with new ones.
M Oh. It's disappointing to hear that.
W You know, you're not the first shopper to express this feeling. I like the older brands myself.
M Well, what's a good cookware option here? I don't recognize these names.
W I really like Belco. **12 I'll get a brochure for you to look over.**

여 좋은 아침입니다. 오늘 제가 도와드릴 일이 있을까요? 저는 매장 매니저 아데올라입니다.
남 네, **10 최근에 제 주방을 개조해서** 새 주방용품을 사고 싶어요. 하지만 **11 제가 좋아하는 브랜드가 하나도 보이지 않네요.**
여 저희 매장이 새로운 기업 소유 체제에 속하게 되어, 오래된

저희 브랜드 중 다수가 새 브랜드로 교체되었어요.
남 아. 그 말을 들으니 실망이네요.
여 그런 기분을 표현하신 손님이 고객님이 처음은 아닙니다. 저도 기존 브랜드를 좋아하거든요.
남 그럼. 여기서 괜찮은 조리기구 옵션은 어떤 게 있나요? 이 이름들은 잘 모르겠네요.
여 저는 벨코를 정말 좋아해요. 12살펴보실 수 있게 안내책자를 갖다드릴게요.

어휘 purchase 구매하다 kitchenware 주방용품 corporate 기업의 ownership 소유(권) long-standing 오래된 replace 교체하다 express 표현하다 cookware 조리기구 brochure 안내책자 look over 살펴보다

10 남자가 최근에 한 일은 무엇인가?
(A) 요리 수업을 들었다.
(B) 직장에서 승진을 했다.
(C) 개조 프로젝트를 완료했다.
(D) 새 아파트로 이사했다.

해설 세부 내용 – 남자가 최근에 한 일
남자가 첫 대사에서 최근에 주방을 개조했다(I recently remodeled my kitchen)고 했으므로 정답은 (C)이다.

어휘 earn 얻다 promotion 승진 complete 완료하다 renovation 개조

Paraphrasing 대화의 remodeled → 보기의 renovation

11 남자는 왜 실망하는가?
(A) 일부 가격이 올랐다.
(B) 특정 브랜드의 상품이 제공되지 않는다.
(C) 매장의 영업시간이 바뀌었다.
(D) 위치가 불편하다.

해설 세부 내용 – 남자가 실망한 이유
남자가 첫 대사에서 자신이 좋아하는 브랜드가 하나도 보이지 않는다(I don't see any of the brands I like)고 불평하고 있으므로, 매장에 그가 원하는 브랜드 제품이 없다는 점에 실망했다는 것을 알 수 있다. 따라서 정답은 (B)이다.

어휘 certain 특정한 inconvenient 불편한

12 여자는 무엇을 하겠다고 제안하는가?
(A) 안내책자 제공
(B) 피드백 보고
(C) 할인 적용
(D) 특별 주문

해설 세부 내용 – 여자의 제안 사항
마지막 대사에서 여자가 남자에게 안내책자를 가져다주겠다(I'll get a brochure for you to look over)고 하고 있으므로 정답은 (A)이다.

[13-15] M-Au / W-Br

M Shiori, 13we're getting our delivery of Magali Bertrand's new book tomorrow.
W OK. 13It'll probably sell very well. That order was for 100 copies, right?
M Yes. 14Could you set up a display after it arrives?
W 14No problem. And I'll come up with a list of specific books for the display right now.
M Thanks. 15I'd like to look over that list before we close for the day.

남 시오리, 13내일 마갈리 베르트랑의 새 책을 배송 받을 거예요.
여 알겠습니다. 13아마 아주 잘 팔릴 거예요. 그 주문은 100부였죠, 그렇죠?
남 네. 14도착하면 진열을 해 줄 수 있나요?
여 14그럼요. 지금 바로 진열을 위한 구체적인 도서 목록을 준비하겠습니다.
남 고마워요. 15오늘 마감하기 전에 그 목록을 살펴봤으면 해요.

어휘 copy (책·신문 등의) 한 부 set up ~을 놓다, 준비하다 specific 특정한

13 화자들은 어디에서 근무하는 것 같은가?
(A) 텔레비전 스튜디오   (B) 전자제품 매장
(C) 서점   (D) 인쇄소

해설 전체 내용 – 근무 장소
대화 초반부에서 남자가 내일 마갈리 베르트랑의 새 책을 배송 받을 것(we're getting our delivery of Magali Bertrand's new book tomorrow)이라고 하자, 여자가 아마 아주 잘 팔릴 것(It'll probably sell very well)이라고 대답한 것을 통해 화자들은 도서를 판매하는 서점에서 근무하는 것을 알 수 있다. 따라서 정답은 (C)이다.

어휘 electronics 전자제품

14 여자는 어떤 업무를 맡았는가?
(A) 예산 확정   (B) 구직자 면접
(C) 다과 주문   **(D) 진열 구성**

해설 세부 내용 – 여자가 맡은 업무
남자가 두 번째 대사에서 책이 도착하면 진열을 해 줄 수 있을지(Could you set up a display after it arrives?) 묻자 여자가 No problem으로 그렇다고 대답하고 있으므로 정답은 (D)이다.

어휘 task 업무 assign 배정하다 finalize 확정하다 budget 예산 job candidate 구직자 refreshments 다과

Paraphrasing 대화의 set up a display
→ 보기의 Creating a display

071

15 하루가 끝날 무렵 남자는 무엇을 하기를 기대하는가?
(A) 발표
(B) 허가증 신청
(C) 배송 일정 잡기
(D) 목록 검토

해설 세부 내용 - 남자가 오늘 중으로 할 일
마지막 대사에서 남자가 오늘 마감하기 전에 목록을 살펴봤으면 한다(I'd like to look over that list before we close for the day)고 했으므로 정답은 (D)이다.

어휘 announcement 발표 apply for ~을 신청하다 review 검토하다

Paraphrasing 대화의 look over → 보기의 Review

[16-18] W-Br / M-Au

W **16** Elm Road Pharmacy, how can I help you?
M Hi. I just heard from a neighbor about your prescription delivery service. I have a question about it, though.
W Sure, what is it?
M I'm interested, but **17** I'm worried about the cost.
W Actually, it's free of charge.
M Great, I'll sign up tonight. Also, **18** could you check on the medication I ordered? I was wondering if it was in yet.
W **18** Let me look that up for you. What's your name?

여 **16** 엘름 로드 약국입니다. 무엇을 도와드릴까요?
남 안녕하세요. 방금 이웃한테 처방약 배달 서비스에 대해 들었어요. 그런데 궁금한 게 있어요.
여 네, 무엇인가요?
남 관심은 있는데 **17** 비용이 걱정이에요.
여 실은 무료예요.
남 잘됐네요, 오늘 밤에 등록할게요. 그리고 **18** 제가 주문한 약도 확인해 주시겠어요? 들어왔나 해서요.
여 **18** 찾아볼게요. 성함이 어떻게 되시죠?

어휘 pharmacy 약국 prescription 처방(약) medication 약

---

16 여자는 어디에서 일하는가?
(A) 우체국
(B) 식당
(C) 컴퓨터 수리점
(D) 약국

해설 전체 내용 - 여자의 근무 장소
여자는 Elm Road Pharmacy라는 약국 이름을 정확히 언급하며 전화를 받고 있으므로 정답은 (D)이다.

17 남자는 무엇을 염려하는가?
(A) 영업시간
(B) 서비스 요금
(C) 분실물
(D) 송장의 오류

해설 세부 내용 - 남자의 걱정거리
남자가 두 번째 대사에서 비용이 걱정된다(I'm worried about the cost)고 했으므로 정답은 (B)이다.

어휘 fee 요금   invoice 송장, 청구서

Paraphrasing 대화의 the cost → 보기의 Fees for a service

18 여자는 다음에 무엇을 할 것 같은가?
(A) 주문 확인
(B) 동료와 대화
(C) 주소 확인
(D) 휴식

해설 세부 내용 - 여자가 다음에 할 일
주문한 약을 확인해달라는 남자의 요청(could you check on the medication I ordered?)에 여자는 찾아보겠다(Let me look that up for you)고 했으므로 정답은 (A)이다.

어휘 verify 확인하다

Paraphrasing 대화의 the medication I ordered → 보기의 an order

[19-21] 3인 대화 M-Au / W-Am / M-Cn

M1 Ms. Mutinda, did you enjoy the city tour?
W Yes, thanks for recommending it yesterday.
M1 Sure. **19** Is there anything else we can do to make your stay at our hotel more enjoyable?
W **20** I'm still waiting for the airline to deliver my other suitcase—but I've been out all morning. Could you check?
M1 My shift just started—let me ask. Andrey, **20** did Ms. Mutinda's luggage arrive?
M2 Unfortunately, no.
W OK. I'll call the airline again. But I'm almost out of clean clothes. **21** Do you offer laundry service?
M2 Yes. There's a laundry bag in the room closet that you can fill and place outside your door.

남1 무틴다 씨, 시티 투어는 즐거우셨나요?
여 네, 어제 추천해 주셔서 감사합니다.
남1 네. **19** 저희 호텔에서 더 즐겁게 지내실 수 있도록 저희가 할 수 있는 일이 또 있을까요?
여 **20** 아직 항공사에서 다른 여행 가방을 배달해 주기를 기다리는 중인데 제가 아침 내내 밖에 있었네요. 확인해 주실 수 있나요?
남1 제가 지금 막 근무를 시작해서 물어보겠습니다. 안드레이 씨, **20** 무틴다 씨의 짐이 도착했나요?
남2 안타깝게도, 도착하지 않았어요.
여 알겠습니다. 항공사에 다시 전화해야겠어요. 그런데 깨끗한 옷이 거의 다 떨어졌어요. **21** 세탁 서비스를 제공하시나요?
남2 네. 객실 옷장 안에 있는 세탁 가방을 채우셔서 문밖에 두시면 됩니다.

어휘 enjoyable 즐거운 luggage 짐, 수하물
unfortunately 안타깝게도 be out of ~이 바닥나다
fill 채우다

19 남자들은 어디에서 근무하는 것 같은가?
(A) 백화점 (B) 호텔
(C) 여행사 (D) 헬스장

해설 전체 내용 - 남자들의 근무 장소
첫 번째 남자가 여자에게 호텔에서 더 즐겁게 지낼 수 있도록 해줄 수 있는 일이 또 있을지(Is there anything else we can do to make your stay at our hotel more enjoyable?) 묻는 것으로 보아 남자들은 호텔에서 근무하고 있음을 알 수 있다. 따라서 정답은 (B)이다.

20 화자들이 주로 논의하고 있는 문제는 무엇인가?
(A) 취소된 관광 (B) 지연된 항공편
(C) 누락된 수하물 (D) 손상된 소포

해설 전체 내용 - 주된 문제점
여자가 두 번째 대사에서 아직 항공사에서 다른 여행 가방을 배달해 주기를 기다리는 중인데 아침 내내 자신이 밖에 있었다(I'm still waiting for the airline to deliver my other suitcase—but I've been out all morning)며 확인해 줄 수 있는지(Could you check?) 물었고, 첫 번째 남자가 두 번째 남자에게 무틴다 씨의 짐이 도착했는지(did Ms. Mutinda's luggage arrive?)를 확인하고 있다. 이를 통해 화자들이 항공사로부터 누락된 여자의 가방에 대해 논의하고 있음을 알 수 있으므로 정답은 (C)이다.

어휘 canceled 취소된 delayed 지연된 missing 빠진
damaged 손상된 parcel 소포

21 여자는 어떤 서비스에 대해 묻는가?
(A) 음식 (B) 세탁
(C) 인터넷 (D) 교통수단

해설 세부 내용 - 여자가 문의하는 서비스
대화 후반부에서 여자가 세탁 서비스를 제공하는지(Do you offer laundry service?)를 묻고 있으므로 정답은 (B)이다.

[22-24] W-Br / M-Au

W Hi, Jinyu. I wanted to let you know **22 the engineering team will need you to prepare a press release next week.** We've just made a major breakthrough in our batteries for electric vehicles.

M OK. I'm happy to do that. What kind of breakthrough will we be announcing to the press?

W Well, **23 electric car batteries are generally very large and take up a lot of space. Our new battery technology allows us to build much smaller batteries without a reduction**

in storage capacity.

M That's exciting! **24 Can you meet on Monday to explain the technology in more detail?**

W Yes, but **24 you'll also want to invite Asako and Tariq. They understand the project best.**

여 안녕하세요, 진유. **22** 엔지니어링 팀에서 다음 주에 보도 자료 준비를 당신에게 요청했다는 것을 알려드리고 싶어요. 우리가 전기차 배터리 분야에서 중대한 혁신을 이뤄냈어요.

남 네, 기꺼이 하겠습니다. 언론에 어떤 혁신을 발표할 예정인가요?

여 음, **23** 전기차 배터리는 일반적으로 매우 크고 공간을 많이 차지해요. 우리의 새로운 배터리 기술은 저장 용량의 감소 없이 훨씬 더 작은 배터리를 만들 수 있게 해 줘요.

남 대단하네요! **24** 월요일에 만나서 그 기술에 대해 좀 더 상세하게 설명해 주실 수 있나요?

여 네, 하지만 **24** 아사코와 타릭도 초대하는 게 좋을 거예요. 그들이 프로젝트를 가장 잘 이해하고 있거든요.

어휘 press release 보도 자료 major 중대한
breakthrough 혁신, 큰 발전 storage 저장
capacity 용량

22 엔지니어링 팀에서 남자에게 요청한 것은?
(A) 원자재 주문 (B) 연구원 채용
(C) 보도 자료 작성 (D) 특허 등록

해설 세부 내용 - 엔지니어링 팀에서 남자에게 요청한 일
여자가 첫 대사에서 엔지니어링 팀에서 보도 자료 준비를 남자에게 요청했다(the engineering team will need you to prepare a press release next week)고 알려 주고 있으므로 정답은 (C)이다.

어휘 raw material 원자재 researcher 연구원
register 등록하다 patent 특허

Paraphrasing 대화의 prepare a press release
→ 보기의 Write a press release

23 새로운 배터리에 있어 중요한 점은 무엇인가?
(A) 생산 비용이 저렴하다.
(B) 교체가 간단하다.
(C) 환경 친화적인 소재를 이용한다.
(D) 공간을 덜 차지한다.

해설 세부 내용 - 새 배터리의 중요한 점
대화 중반부에서 여자가 전기차 배터리는 일반적으로 매우 크고 공간을 많이 차지하는데 자사의 새로운 배터리 기술은 저장 용량의 감소 없이 훨씬 더 작은 배터리를 만들 수 있게 해 준다(electric car batteries are generally very large and take up a lot of space. Our new battery technology allows us to build much smaller batteries without a reduction in storage capacity)고 하고 있으므로 정답은 (D)이다.

어휘 significant 중요한   inexpensive 비싸지 않은
replace 교체하다   environmentally friendly 환경 친화적인   material 재료

24 아사코와 타릭은 왜 회의에 참석해야 하는가?
(A) 새로운 과제를 받기 위해
(B) 전문 지식을 제공하기 위해
(C) 발표를 연습하기 위해
(D) 새로운 정책에 대해 논의하기 위해

해설 세부 내용 - 아사코와 타릭이 회의에 참석해야 하는 이유
대화 후반부에서 남자가 월요일에 만나서 기술에 대해 좀 더 상세하게 설명해 줄 수 있는지(Can you meet on Monday to explain the technology in more detail?) 묻자 여자가 아사코와 타릭도 초대하는 게 좋겠다(you'll also want to invite Asako and Tariq)며 그들이 프로젝트를 가장 잘 이해하고 있다(They understand the project best)고 대답한다. 따라서 정답은 (B)이다.

어휘 assignment 과제   expertise 전문 지식   policy 정책

> Paraphrasing 대화의 understand the project best
> → 보기의 expertise

UNIT 11   요청·제안 문제 / 다음에 할 일 문제

1 요청·제안 문제

ETS 유형 연습
본책 p.083

1 (D)   2 (A)   3 (C)   4 (D)

[1] M-Cn / W-Am

M Hello, my name is Fred Kane, and I'm calling from the Clearsea Electronics Company. I'd like to transfer ten thousand dollars from our short-term savings account to our long-term account.
W No problem, sir. What's the account number that you're transferring from?
M The account number is 67843.

남 안녕하세요, 저는 프레드 케인이라고 하는데, 클리어시 일렉트로닉스 사에서 전화드립니다. 저희 단기 보통 예금 계좌에서 장기 예금 계좌로 1만 달러를 이체하고 싶습니다.
여 알겠습니다. 어떤 계좌번호에서 이체하시겠습니까?
남 계좌번호는 67843입니다.

어휘 transfer 이체하다   short-term 단기의   savings account 보통 예금   long-term 장기의

Q 여자는 무엇을 요청하는가?
(A) 주소   (B) 비밀번호
(C) 전화번호   **(D) 계좌번호**

해설 세부 내용 - 여자가 요청하는 것
여자의 요청 사항에 대한 문제이므로 여자의 대사에서 정답의 단서를 찾아야 한다. 여자는 남자에게 어떤 계좌에서 이체할 것인지 계좌번호를 묻고(What's the account number that you're transferring from?) 있다. 따라서 정답은 (D)이다.

[2] W-Am / M-Au

W Do you want to try lunch at the new restaurant near the ice cream shop?
M Oh, I went there last week and I wasn't very impressed. There were too many people and there wasn't enough space between the tables.
W Really? That's too bad.

여 아이스크림 가게 근처에 새로 생긴 식당에서 점심 먹을래요?
남 아, 지난주에 거기 가봤는데 별로였어요. 사람이 너무 많은데다 테이블 간격도 좁았어요.
여 정말요? 아쉽네요.

어휘 impressed 좋은 인상을 받은   space 공간, 자리

Q 여자는 어디에 가자고 제안하는가?
(A) 식당   (B) 커피숍
(C) 아이스크림 가게   (D) 회사 구내식당

해설 세부 내용 - 여자의 제안 장소
대화를 시작하면서 여자가 아이스크림 가게 근처에 새로 생긴 식당에 가자(Do you want to try lunch at the new restaurant near the ice cream shop?)고 하므로 정답은 (A)이다.

[3] W-Br / M-Cn

W Hi, I'm Petra Barlow. I have an interview for a position in the accounting department here at Houseman Incorporated.
M Hello, Ms. Barlow. Let me check in the computer. While I do that, would you put on this visitor's badge so it's easy to see?
W Yes, of course.

여 안녕하세요, 저는 페트라 발로우입니다. 이곳 하우스맨 사의 경리부서 자리에 취업 면접이 있습니다.
남 안녕하세요, 발로우 씨. 제가 컴퓨터로 확인해 볼게요. 그동안에, 이 방문자 배지를 잘 보이게 착용해 주시겠어요?
여 네, 알겠습니다.

어휘 accounting department 경리부서
put on 착용하다

Q 남자가 여자에게 요청하는 것은 무엇인가?
(A) 로비에서 기다리기
(B) 지원서 업데이트
(C) 배지 착용
(D) 사진이 붙은 신분증 제시

해설 세부 내용 – 남자의 요청 사항
남자가 여자에게 방문자 배지를 잘 보이게 착용해 달라(would you put on this visitor's badge so it's easy to see?)고 요청했으므로 정답은 (C)이다.

[4] W-Br / M-Cn

W Did you have a chance to look at the draft of the new book cover?
M Yes, I looked it over, and I think it's really good. I do have one suggestion though.
I think our publishing company's logo is very small compared to the other information. How about making it larger so people can see it better?
W That's a good idea.

여 새 책 표지의 초안을 볼 기회가 있었나요?
남 네, 훑어봤는데 아주 좋은 것 같아요. 하지만 한 가지 제안할 게 있어요. 우리 출판사 로고가 다른 정보에 비해 너무 작은 것 같아요. 사람들이 더 잘 볼 수 있도록 더 크게 만들면 어떨까요?
여 좋은 생각이에요.

어휘 have a chance to ~할 기회가 있다 draft 초안, 원고 look over ~을 훑어보다 suggestion 제안 though 하지만 publishing company 출판사 compared to ~와 비교하여

Q 남자는 로고에 대해 어떤 제안을 하는가?
(A) 위치 정하기
(B) 사진 추가하기
(C) 색을 바꾸기
(D) 크기를 늘리기

해설 세부 내용 – 남자의 제안 사항
남자가 제안을 나타내는 How about ~?을 사용하여 로고를 키우자(How about making it larger so people can see it better?)고 했으므로 정답은 (D)이다.

어휘 fix 정하다 add 추가하다

❷ 다음에 할 일 문제

ETS 유형 연습
본책 p.085

1 (D)　2 (B)　3 (D)　4 (B)

[1] M-Cn / W-Br

M I'm calling to thank you and your company for the great job you did catering for our business luncheon last week.
W Oh, don't thank me. Your event was planned by my colleague, Nadia.
M If Nadia's in the office, I'd like to tell her myself.
W Actually, she's out today. But I can put you through to her voice mail so that you can leave her a message.

남 지난주 저희 비즈니스 오찬 때 출장 음식 조달 서비스를 아주 잘해 주셔서 당신과 당신 회사에 고마움을 전하고자 전화를 드립니다.
여 아, 저한테 고마워하지 마세요. 그 행사는 제 동료인 나디아 씨가 계획했던 겁니다.
남 나디아 씨가 사무실에 있으면, 제가 직접 이야기하고 싶습니다.
여 실은, 나디아 씨는 오늘 사무실에 안 나옵니다. 하지만 메시지를 남기실 수 있도록 그녀의 음성 사서함으로 연결해드릴 수 있습니다.

어휘 catering (출장) 음식 조달, 음식 공급 colleague 동료 put A through to (전화로) A를 ~로 연결시키다

Q 남자는 다음에 무엇을 할 것 같은가?
(A) 약속 잡기　(B) 추천서 제공하기
(C) 상품 구입하기　(D) 메시지 남기기

해설 세부 내용 – 남자가 다음에 할 일
대화 마지막에 여자가 나디아 씨에게 메시지를 남길 수 있도록 음성 사서함으로 연결시켜 줄 수 있다(I can put you through to her voice mail so that you can leave her a message)고 했으므로 정답은 (D)이다.

[2] W-Br / M-Cn

W I hear that we've had some unhappy customers recently.
M In fact, I've just been talking with one of them. Our driver picked her up on time, but there was heavy traffic on the way to the airport, and she nearly missed her flight.
W We should probably take a look at roadwork scheduled in the area.
M And we have some other issues to consider as well. Look at the rest of these comments— we'll need to decide what to do.

여 최근에 불만을 제기한 고객들이 몇 명 있다는 이야기를 들었어요.
남 사실은 방금 그 고객들 중 한 명과 이야기를 하고 있었습니다. 우리 기사가 제때 고객을 태우긴 했지만, 공항으로 가는 길이 너무 막혀서 하마터면 비행기를 놓칠 뻔했다는군요.

여 아마도 지역 내 도로공사 일정을 살펴봐야겠어요.
남 그리고 또 생각해 볼 다른 문제도 있습니다. **나머지 이 의견들을 보세요. 저희가 어떻게 할지 결정을 해야 해요.**

어휘 on time 제때에 heavy traffic 교통 체증
on the way to ~로 가는 길에 nearly 하마터면
roadwork 도로공사 consider 고려하다 as well 또한

Q 화자들은 다음에 무엇을 할 것인가?
(A) 연료 가격 보기
(B) 고객 불만 사항 검토
(C) 직원 채용 일정 업데이트
(D) 교육 프로그램 준비

해설 세부 내용 – 다음에 할 일
대화 마지막에 남자가 여자에게 나머지 이런 의견들을 보고 어떻게 할지 결정을 해야 한다(Look at the rest of these comments—we'll need to decide what to do)고 했다. 이 말은 화자들이 고객 불만 사항을 검토하겠다는 의미이므로 정답은 (B)이다.

[3] W-Am / M-Cn

W I have a potential renter on the phone. Since I'm really busy today, I was going to ask Steven to show the apartment, but he isn't answering his phone.
M I noticed he forgot his mobile phone on his desk there. I might have some free time this afternoon to show the client the third-floor apartment.
W That would be great. OK, **I'll put the call through to you now.**

여 임차하려는 사람이 전화했어요. 제가 오늘 너무 바빠서 스티븐 씨에게 아파트 안내를 부탁하려 했는데 전화를 안 받네요.
남 보니까 저기 책상 위에 휴대폰을 놓고 갔더라고요. 제가 오늘 오후에 시간이 있으니까 고객에게 3층 아파트를 보여 줄 수 있을 거 같아요.
여 잘됐네요. 좋아요. **지금 전화를 연결해 드릴게요.**

어휘 potential 잠재적인 put a call through 전화를 연결하다

Q 여자는 다음에 무엇을 하겠다고 하는가?
(A) 파일 업데이트   (B) 계약 체결
(C) 가격 논의   **(D) 전화 연결**

해설 세부 내용 – 여자가 다음에 할 일
화자가 다음에 할 일은 주로 대화 후반부에 나온다. 고객에게 대신 아파트를 보여줄 수 있다는 남자의 제안에 여자는 마지막 대사에서 지금 고객과 전화를 연결해 주겠다(I'll put the call through to you now)고 했으므로 정답은 (D)이다.

어휘 sign a contract 계약을 체결하다

Paraphrasing 대화의 put the call through to you
→ 보기의 Transfer a call

[4] W-Am / M-Au

W Thanks for agreeing to photograph the house my agency is putting on the market! Your photos should improve the chances of a fast sale.
M I hope so. **Have you confirmed with the decorator that he can be on-site that day?**
W No, but **I'll do that this afternoon.**

여 저희 중개업소에서 시장에 내놓을 집을 촬영하는 데 동의해 주셔서 감사합니다! 당신의 사진이 빠른 판매 가능성을 높여줄 거예요.
남 그러면 좋겠네요. **그날 장식업자가 현장에 올 수 있는지 확인하셨나요?**
여 아니요. 그렇지만 **오늘 오후에 할게요.**

어휘 agency 중개업소 chance 가능성 decorator 장식가 on-site 현장에

Q 여자는 오늘 오후에 무엇을 하겠다고 말하는가?
(A) 유지보수 요청서 제출   **(B) 장식업자에게 연락**
(C) 가구 배치   (D) 전단지 만들기

해설 세부 내용 – 여자가 오후에 할 일
남자가 장식업자가 현장에 올 수 있는지 확인했는지(Have you confirmed with the decorator that he can be on-site that day?) 묻자 여자는 오늘 오후에 하겠다(I'll do that this afternoon)고 대답하고 있다. 따라서 여자가 오늘 오후에 장식업자에게 연락할 것임을 알 수 있으므로 정답은 (B)이다.

어휘 file 제출하다 maintenance 유지보수
flyer (광고용) 전단지

ETS 실전 문제   본책 p.086

1 (B)	2 (D)	3 (C)	4 (C)	5 (D)	6 (A)
7 (D)	8 (B)	9 (A)	10 (D)	11 (C)	12 (B)
13 (D)	14 (B)	15 (A)	16 (B)	17 (A)	18 (C)
19 (D)	20 (B)	21 (C)	22 (A)	23 (C)	24 (D)

[1-3] W-Am / M-Au

W Our community center's baseball team has been doing well so far. Ticket sales have exceeded our expectations.
M Yes, the community really comes out to support the team when it plays against teams from other towns. **[1] What the players need is some high-quality coaching so that they**

can improve their skills.
W We'd have to raise more money to hire a good coach. **2 How about getting a few more companies to sponsor the team?**
M Sounds good. **3 We should target some additional local businesses in the area. I'll run a search and come up with a list.**

여 우리 주민 센터 야구팀이 지금까지 잘해 오고 있습니다. 티켓 판매가 우리 기대 이상이에요.
남 네, 지역 주민들이 다른 지역 팀을 상대로 경기를 할 때 정말 많이 응원을 하러 와 주고 있어요. **1 선수들에게 필요한 것은 실력을 향상시켜 줄 높은 수준의 코칭이에요.**
여 좋은 코치를 고용하려면 자금을 더 마련해야 할 것 같아요. **2 팀을 후원할 회사를 몇 곳 더 구하는 게 어떨까요?**
남 좋아요. **3 우리 지역 현지 업체를 추가로 겨냥해야 할 것 같아요. 제가 알아보고 명단을 만들게요.**

어휘 exceed 넘어서다 expectation 기대 raise (자금 등을) 모으다 sponsor 후원하다 target 겨냥하다 search 조사, 검색

1 남자가 팀의 발전을 위해 필요하다고 말하는 것은?
(A) 더 넓은 야구장   (B) 높은 수준의 코칭
(C) 추가 선수   (D) 새로운 장비

해설 세부 내용 – 남자가 팀의 발전을 위해 필요하다고 말하는 것
남자가 첫 대사에서 선수들에게 필요한 것은 실력을 향상시켜 줄 높은 수준의 코칭(What the players need is some high-quality coaching so that they can improve their skills)이라고 했으므로 정답은 (B)이다.

어휘 field (스포츠를 하는) ~장 athlete (운동) 선수 equipment 장비

2 여자는 무엇을 제안하는가?
(A) 시 공무원에게 연락   (B) 일정 변경
(C) 여러 도시를 여행   (D) 더 많은 후원사 유치

해설 세부 내용 – 여자의 제안 사항
여자가 두 번째 대사에서 팀을 후원할 회사를 몇 곳 더 구하는 게 어떨지(How about getting a few more companies to sponsor the team?) 물으며 후원사를 추가로 유치해 보자고 제안하고 있으므로 정답은 (D)이다.

어휘 city official 시 공무원 attract 유치하다, 끌어 모으다 sponsor 후원사

Paraphrasing 대화의 getting a few more companies to sponsor the team → 보기의 Attracting more sponsors

3 남자는 무엇을 하겠다고 말하는가?
(A) 구인 공고 작성   (B) 선수들과 대화
(C) 현지 사업체 물색 (D) 워크샵 준비

해설 세부 내용 – 남자의 할 일
남자가 마지막 대사에서 우리 지역 현지 업체를 추가로 겨냥해야 할 것 같다(We should target some additional local businesses in the area)면서 알아보고 명단을 만들겠다(I'll run a search and come up with a list)고 했으므로 정답은 (C)이다.

어휘 organize 준비하다, 조직하다

Paraphrasing 대화의 run a search → 보기의 Search for

[4-6] W-Br / M-Au

W Alan, **4 the farm workers are almost ready to start making this year's batch of fresh apple juice for our customers to buy during the annual tours of the farm.** Is everything ready?
M Well, I think we're going to need a lot more bottles than last year, since our apple crop this year is so much bigger than usual. I hope we have enough to bottle all the juice.
W I don't think we have a lot of bottles in stock. **5 Could you place an order for some more bottles today?**
M **6 I can't take care of that today, since I'm making a delivery to the market,** but I'll be sure to do it first thing tomorrow.

여 앨런, **4 농장 일꾼들은 고객들이 연례 농장 견학 시 살 수 있는 신선한 햇사과 주스를 만들 준비가 거의 다 됐어요.** 모든 준비가 다 되었나요?
남 음, 올해 사과 수확량이 평년보다 훨씬 많아서 작년보다 병이 훨씬 더 많이 필요할 것 같아요. 주스를 전부 병에 담기에 충분한 양이 있으면 좋겠어요.
여 병 재고가 많지 않은 것 같은데요. **5 오늘 병을 더 주문해 주겠어요?**
남 **6 오늘은 제가 시장으로 배송을 나가니까 그 일을 처리할 수 없지만,** 내일 꼭 제일 먼저 할게요.

어휘 batch 묶음, 다발 annual 연례의 crop 수확량 in stock 재고가 있는 take care of ~을 처리하다 delivery 배송

4 화자들은 어디에서 일하는가?
(A) 국립공원   (B) 여행사
(C) 농장   (D) 시장

해설 전체 내용 – 근무 장소
첫 대사에서 여자가 남자에게 고객들이 연례 농장 견학 시 살 수 있는 햇사과 주스를 만들 준비가 거의 되었다(the farm workers are almost ready to start making this year's batch of fresh apple juice for our customers to buy during the annual tours of the

farm)고 말한 후, 사과 수확에 관한 대화가 이어지고 있다. 따라서 정답은 (C)이다.

5 여자는 남자에게 무엇을 요청하는가?
(A) 진열품 배열　　　　(B) 상자 하차
(C) 연락처 목록 업데이트　**(D) 물품 주문**

해설 세부 내용 – 여자의 요청 사항
여자의 요청 사항에 대한 질문이므로 여자의 대사에서 정답의 단서를 찾아야 한다. 여자는 두 번째 대사에서 병을 더 주문해 달라(Could you place an order for some more bottles today?)고 남자에게 요청하고 있으므로 정답은 (D)이다.

어휘 supplies 물품

> **Paraphrasing** 대화의 place an order for some more bottles → 보기의 Order supplies

6 남자는 왜 오늘 일을 완료할 수 없다고 말하는가?
(A) 배달을 해야 한다.
(B) 추가 정보가 필요하다.
(C) 도와줄 사람이 없다.
(D) 날씨가 안 좋다.

해설 세부 내용 – 남자가 오늘 일을 완료할 수 없는 이유
남자는 마지막 대사에서 시장으로 배송을 나가서 오늘 그 일을 처리할 수 없다(I can't take care of that today, since I'm making a delivery to the market)고 말하고 있으므로 정답은 (A)이다.

[7-9] W-Am / M-Cn

W　Hello, Mr. Ross. Thanks for coming in. **7We're so glad you decided to accept our offer for the truck-driver position.**
M　I'm excited to be working here. I have a friend who's driven a delivery truck for this logistics company for years, and he said this is a great place to work.
W　I'm happy to hear that. **8It's very important to us that our employees are satisfied with their jobs.**
M　I'm anxious to meet the team I'll be working on.
W　Well, **9first I have some paperwork for you to fill out.** Here's a pen you can use.

여　안녕하세요, 로스 씨. 와 주셔서 감사합니다. 7우리 트럭 운전기사 자리에 대한 제안을 수락해 주셔서 매우 기쁩니다.
남　여기서 일하게 되어 설렙니다. 수년간 이 물류 회사에서 배송 트럭을 운전해 온 친구가 있는데, 여기가 일하기 좋은 곳이라고 하더군요.
여　그 말을 들으니 기쁘네요. 8직원들이 자기 일에 만족하는 것은 저희에게 매우 중요합니다.
남　제가 함께 일할 팀 어서 만나고 싶습니다.

여　음. 9먼저 작성해야 할 서류가 몇 가지 있어요. 여기 이 펜을 쓰시면 됩니다.

어휘 accept 수락하다　logistics 물류　satisfied 만족하는　anxious 간절히 바라는　fill out 작성하다

7 남자는 어떤 일을 하도록 고용되었는가?
(A) 고객 불만 처리　　(B) 신제품 개발
(C) 전기 장비 수리　　**(D) 트럭 운전**

해설 세부 내용 – 남자가 고용된 일
여자가 첫 대사에서 남자에게 트럭 운전기사 자리에 대한 제안을 수락해 줘서 매우 기쁘다(We're so glad you decided to accept our offer for the truck-driver position)고 했으므로 정답은 (D)이다.

어휘 handle 처리하다　complaint 불만　electrical 전기의

8 여자에 따르면, 회사에 중요한 것은 무엇인가?
(A) 팀워크　　　　　　**(B) 직원 만족**
(C) 환경 지속 가능성　(D) 혁신

해설 세부 내용 – 회사에 중요한 것
대화 중반에 여자가 직원들이 자기 일에 만족하는 것이 회사에 매우 중요하다(It's very important to us that our employees are satisfied with their jobs)고 했으므로 정답은 (B)이다.

어휘 satisfaction 만족　environmental 환경의　sustainability 지속 가능성　innovation 혁신

9 남자는 다음에 무엇을 할 것 같은가?
(A) 서류 작성　　　(B) 신분증 수령
(C) 시설 견학　　　　(D) 발표 준비

해설 세부 내용 – 남자가 다음에 할 일
마지막 대사에서 여자가 남자에게 먼저 작성해야 할 서류가 몇 가지 있다(first I have some paperwork for you to fill out)고 했으므로 정답은 (A)이다.

어휘 identification 신원 확인　badge 표　facility 시설

> **Paraphrasing** 대화의 fill out → 보기의 Complete

[10-12] W-Br / M-Cn

W　**10Thanks for offering to help me prepare this report on potential sites for our new branch store.** I have a lot of information about three possible buildings, and I want to be sure it's presented clearly.
M　Well, **11I like the graphs you've made with the information for each location.** They make it easy to see the cost of rent and other expenses and what other businesses are in the area.
W　**11Yes, I'm pleased with the way those**

turned out. And I plan to include charts comparing the information for each location.

M That's a good idea. And I have another suggestion. You only have a few photographs of the sites. **12 I think you should include more of them in your report.**

여 **10**새 지점이 들어설 후보지에 대한 보고서 준비를 도와주겠다고 해서 고마워요. 저에게 가능한 건물 세 곳에 대한 정보가 많이 있는데, 명확하게 제시되어 있는지 확인하고 싶어요.

남 음, **11**각 입지의 정보로 만든 그래프가 마음에 들어요. 그래프를 통해 임대료와 기타 비용들, 그 지역에 있는 다른 업체들을 쉽게 볼 수 있네요.

여 **11**맞아요, 저도 그래프가 이렇게 나와서 만족해요. 그리고 각 입지의 정보를 비교하는 차트도 포함할 계획이에요.

남 좋은 생각이에요. 그런데 또 제안할 게 있어요. 장소 사진이 몇 장만 있네요. **12**보고서에 사진을 더 넣어야 할 것 같아요.

어휘 potential 후보 물망에 있는, 가능성 있는 possible 가능한 present 제시하다 location 입지 expense 비용 turn out (결과가 어떤 식으로) 나오다 compare 비교하다 suggestion 제안

10 보고서는 무엇에 관한 것인가?
(A) 대출 신청   (B) 소프트웨어 업데이트
(C) 개정된 채용 계획 **(D) 가능한 업체 입지**

해설 세부 내용 - 보고서의 주제
여자의 첫 번째 대사에서 새 지점이 들어설 후보지에 대한 보고서 준비를 도와주겠다고 해서 고맙다(Thanks for offering to help me prepare this report on potential sites for our new branch store)고 했으므로 정답은 (D)이다.

어휘 revised 개정된

Paraphrasing 대화의 potential sites for our new branch store → 보기의 Possible business locations

11 여자는 무엇이 마음에 든다고 말하는가?
(A) 시가 변동
(B) 숙련된 직원을 쓸 수 있음
(C) 일부 정보의 제시
(D) 일부 비용 절감

해설 세부 내용 - 여자가 마음에 들어하는 점
남자의 첫 번째 대사에서 각 입지의 정보로 만든 그래프가 마음에 든다(I like the graphs you've made with the information for each location)고 했고, 여자도 그래프가 그렇게 나와서 만족한다(Yes, I'm pleased with the way those turned out)고 동의했으므로 정답은 (C)이다.

어휘 availability 쓸 수 있음, 구할 수 있음

Paraphrasing 대화의 the graphs you've made with the information, the way those turned out
→ 보기의 The presentation of some information

12 남자는 무엇을 제안하는가?
(A) 컨설턴트 채용   **(B) 더 많은 사진 포함**
(C) 발표 일정 변경   (D) 제품 시연 요청

해설 세부 내용 - 남자의 제안 사항
마지막 대사에서 남자는 사진이 몇 장밖에 없으니 보고서에 사진을 더 넣어야 할 것(I think you should include more of them in your report)이라고 제안했으므로 정답은 (B)이다.

어휘 hire 채용하다 demonstration 시연

[13-15] M-Au / W-Br

M Hello, Janice. **13 I have two tickets to the Hampton Symphony Orchestra's concert next Friday night**, and it turns out I can't go. Since you mentioned your friend will be visiting from out of town, I thought you might be interested in going with her.

W That's very kind, Patrick. I like that orchestra, but **14 we actually already have plans to attend a hockey game that night.** You know, you could post a notice about the tickets on the bulletin board in the kitchen—one of our coworkers might want them.

M Yes, you're absolutely right. **15 I'll put a notice up now.** Lots of people go by that board—I'm sure someone will be interested.

남 안녕하세요, 재니스. **13**다음 주 금요일 밤 햄프턴 교향악단 연주회 표가 두 장 있는데, 갈 수가 없게 됐어요. 외지에서 친구가 온다고 하셨으니, 친구와 함께 가고 싶으실 것 같아서요.

여 마음 써주셔서 고마워요, 패트릭. 그 교향악단을 좋아하지만, **14**실은 그날 밤에 이미 하키 경기를 관람할 계획이에요. 탕비실 게시판에 표에 대한 공지를 붙이세요. 동료들 중 누군가 표를 원할지도 모르니까요.

남 그래요, 맞는 얘기예요. **15**지금 공지를 붙일게요. 많은 사람들이 게시판 앞을 지나다니니까 틀림없이 관심 있는 사람이 있을 거예요.

어휘 bulletin board 게시판 coworker 동료

13 남자는 어떤 표를 가지고 있다고 말하는가?
(A) 도시 관광   (B) 미술 전시회
(C) 야구 경기   **(D) 음악 콘서트**

해설 세부 내용 - 표의 종류
남자가 첫 대사에서 교향악단 연주회 표가 두 장 있다(I have two tickets to the Hampton Symphony

Orchestra's concert next Friday night)고 했으므로 정답은 (D)이다.

Paraphrasing 대화의 the Hampton Symphony Orchestra's concert → 보기의 A music concert

14 여자는 왜 표를 원하지 않는다고 말하는가?
(A) 그날 밤 야근할 계획이다.
(B) 다른 행사에 참석할 것이다.
(C) 휴가를 떠날 것이다.
(D) 다른 종류의 행사를 선호한다.

해설 **세부 내용 – 여자가 표를 원하지 않는 이유**
여자는 이미 하키 경기를 관람할 계획(we actually already have plans to attend a hockey game that night)이라고 했으므로 정답은 (B)이다.

Paraphrasing 대화의 attend a hockey game → 보기의 be at a different event

15 남자는 다음에 무엇을 하겠는가?
(A) 게시판에 정보 게시   (B) 고객과 점심 모임 참석
(C) 스포츠 경기 준비   (D) 환불 요청 전화

해설 **세부 내용 – 남자가 다음에 할 일**
게시판에 표에 대한 공지를 붙이라는 여자의 제안에 남자는 지금 공지를 붙일 것(I'll put a notice up now)이라고 했으므로 정답은 (A)이다.

Paraphrasing 대화의 put a notice up → 보기의 Place information on a bulletin board

[16-18] W-Br / M-Au

W You've reached Taylor Waste Services. How can I help you?
M Hi. **16**I'm the new owner of Sparkton Electronics on Seventh Avenue. **17**I recently discovered several old laptops and printers the previous owner left behind in the storeroom. Is there a way I can recycle these?
W Absolutely. In fact, we have a drop-off location for recycling electronics on Burton Street, just a few blocks from your store.
M Oh, that's great. I can let my customers know about that location, too. They might want to recycle their old equipment when they buy something new here.
W Actually, we have several drop-off locations around the city. **18**I can send you a map that shows them all.

여 테일러 폐기물 서비스입니다. 무엇을 도와드릴까요?
남 안녕하세요. **16**저는 7번가에 있는 스파크턴 전자의 새 주인입니다. **17**제가 최근에 이전 주인이 창고에 두고 간 오래된 노트북 컴퓨터와 프린터를 발견했어요. 이것들을 재활용할 수 있는 방법이 있을까요?
여 물론입니다. 사실 버튼 가에 전자 제품 재활용을 위한 저희 수거 장소가 있는데, 귀하의 매장에서 불과 몇 블록 거리에 있습니다.
남 오, 잘됐네요. 제 고객들에게도 그 장소를 알려줄 수 있겠네요. 고객들이 새 제품을 구입할 때 헌 장비를 재활용하고 싶어 할 수도 있거든요.
여 사실 도시 곳곳에 저희 수거 장소가 몇 군데 있습니다. **18**제가 모든 위치가 표시된 지도를 보내드릴 수 있어요.

어휘 owner 주인 discover 발견하다 previous 이전의 storeroom 창고 recycle 재활용하다 drop-off 내려주는 곳 equipment 장비

16 남자는 어떤 종류의 사업체를 소유하고 있는가?
(A) 영화 제작 스튜디오
(B) 전자 제품 매장
(C) 행사 기획 서비스
(D) 광고 회사

해설 **세부 내용 – 남자가 소유한 업체**
남자가 첫 대사에서 자신이 7번가에 있는 스파크턴 전자의 새 주인(I'm the new owner of Sparkton Electronics on Seventh Avenue)이라고 전자 제품 매장을 소유하고 있음을 밝히고 있으므로 정답은 (B)이다.

어휘 advertising 광고 firm 회사

17 남자는 여자에게 무엇에 대해 묻는가?
(A) 물품 재활용   (B) 수리
(C) 컨설턴트 채용   (D) 회의 장소 변경

해설 **세부 내용 – 남자의 문의 사항**
남자가 첫 대사에서 최근에 이전 주인이 창고에 두고 간 오래된 노트북 컴퓨터와 프린터를 발견했다(I recently discovered several old laptops and printers the previous owner left behind in the storeroom)면서 이것들을 재활용할 수 있는 방법이 있을지(Is there a way I can recycle these?)를 여자에게 묻고 있으므로 정답은 (A)이다.

어휘 repair 수리 consultant 상담가

18 여자는 남자에게 무엇을 보내주겠다고 제안하는가?
(A) 환불금   (B) 시간표
(C) 지도   (D) 계약서

해설 **세부 내용 – 여자가 보내준다고 제안하는 것**
마지막 대사에서 여자가 남자에게 모든 수거 장소가 표시된 지도를 보내줄 수 있다(I can send you a map that shows them all)고 했으므로 정답은 (C)이다.

어휘 refund 환불(금) contract 계약(서)

[19-21] 3인 대화 W-Am / M-Cn / W-Br

W1 Hey, folks! I have an update for you. **19 The driver who is delivering our fleet of new rental cars just called.** He's on his way, but he said he's stalled at the Northside Bridge.

M **20 I read about that bridge in an article on my phone this morning.** It said the bridge is closed for repairs. Sabine, you normally take that bridge to work, don't you?

W2 Yes, I went by the bridge this morning. **21 Tell the driver to take Meldon Road instead.**

W1 OK. I'll call him back and let him know.

여1 안녕하세요, 여러분! 여러분을 위한 업데이트가 있어요. **19우리의 새 렌터카를 운송 중인 기사님이 방금 전화했어요.** 지금 오는 중인데 노스사이드 다리에서 오도가도 못하고 있다네요.

남 **20오늘 아침 휴대전화로 그 다리에 대한 기사를 읽었어요.** 다리가 보수 작업 때문에 폐쇄되었다고 했어요. 사빈 씨, 보통 그 다리로 출근하시죠?

여2 네, 오늘 아침에 그 다리 옆을 지나갔어요. **21 기사님께 대신에 멜던 로를 타라고 전해주세요.**

여1 알겠어요. 다시 전화해서 말씀드릴게요.

어휘 fleet (회사 소유의) 차량 on one's way 가는 중인 stalled 오도가도 못하는, 정지된 normally 평소에 instead 대신에

19 화자들은 무엇이 배송되기를 기대하고 있는가?
(A) 휴대전화 부품
(B) 사무용 가구
(C) 건축 자재
(D) 차량

해설 세부 내용 – 배송될 물건
대화 초반부에 첫 번째 여자가 새 렌터카를 운송 중인 기사님이 방금 전화했다(The driver who is delivering our fleet of new rental cars just called)고 한 것으로 보아 화자들은 새 렌터카가 배송되기를 기다리고 있다는 것을 알 수 있다. 따라서 정답은 (D)이다.

어휘 part 부품 material 재료 vehicle 차량

Paraphrasing 대화의 rental cars → 보기의 vehicles

20 남자는 어떻게 문제에 대해 이미 알고 있는가?
(A) 회의에 참석했다.
(B) 기사를 읽었다.
(C) 라디오 방송을 들었다.
(D) 텔레비전 프로그램을 시청했다.

해설 세부 내용 – 남자의 문제 파악 경위
대화 초반부에서 첫 번째 여자가 전하는 문제 상황에 대해 남자가 오늘 아침 휴대전화로 그 다리에 대한 기사를 읽었다(I read about that bridge in an article on my phone this morning)고 했으므로 정답은 (B)이다.

어휘 broadcast 방송

21 사빈은 운전사에게 무엇을 하라고 제안하는가?
(A) 내비게이션 이용
(B) 정보 센터에 연락
(C) 대안인 길로 가기
(D) 주유를 위해 정차

해설 세부 내용 – 사빈이 운전사에게 제안하는 것
두 번째 여자(사빈)는 기사에게 대신에 멜던 로를 타라고 전해 달라(Tell the driver to take Meldon Road instead)고 하고 있다. 이는 기사에게 대안 노선으로 갈 것을 제안하는 것이므로 정답은 (C)이다.

어휘 alternate 대안의 route 길 fuel 연료

Paraphrasing 대화의 take Meldon Road instead
→ 보기의 Take an alternate route

[22-24] M-Cn / W-Am

M Hello. **22 I'm staying in Room 400, and I was woken up this morning by loud hammering sounds outside.** I'm on vacation and was really hoping to be able to sleep a bit later today.

W I'm very sorry, sir. **23 There's construction going on in the building next to our hotel until next Friday.** We've already spoken to them about starting later in the morning.

M Well, just in case they don't start later, I think I'd prefer to switch to a room on the other side of the hotel.

W Certainly. **24 Let me check if we have any other rooms available.**

남 여보세요. **22저는 400호실에 머물고 있는데, 오늘 아침 밖에서 들리는 망치 소리가 시끄러워서 잠을 깼어요.** 휴가 중인데 오늘은 제발 늦잠 좀 잘 수 있었으면 했거든요.

여 대단히 죄송합니다. **23호텔 옆 건물에서 다음 주 금요일까지 공사가 진행되고 있어요.** 저희가 이미 그들에게 아침 늦게 시작해 달라고 이야기를 했습니다.

남 음, 혹시 늦게 시작하지 않을 경우에 대비해서, 호텔 반대편에 있는 방으로 바꾸고 싶어요.

여 물론이죠. **24빈 방이 있는지 확인해 보겠습니다.**

어휘 construction 공사 just in case 혹시 ~할 경우에 대비해서

22 여자는 어디서 일하고 있는 것 같은가?
(A) 호텔
(B) 건축회사
(C) 영화관
(D) 식당

해설 전체 내용 – 여자의 근무 장소
대화 맨 처음에 남자가 여자에게 400호실에 머물고 있는데, 아침에 망치 소리에 잠을 깼다(I'm staying in Room 400, and I was woken up this morning by loud hammering sounds outside)며 불편 사항을 알리고 있

다. 이를 통해 여자가 호텔에서 근무한다는 것을 알 수 있으므로 정답은 (A)이다.

어휘 architectural 건축의

23 무엇이 문제를 일으키고 있는가?
(A) 개장 지연 (B) 청구서 오류
(C) 건설공사 소음 (D) 숙련된 인력 부족

해설 세부 내용 – 문제의 원인
소음에 대한 문제를 알리는 남자의 말에 여자는 다음 주 금요일까지 호텔 옆 건물에서 공사가 있다(There's construction going on in the building next to our hotel until next Friday)고 하므로 정답은 (C)이다.

어휘 incorrect 틀린 noise 소음 shortage 부족

24 여자는 다음에 무엇을 하겠는가?
(A) 매니저에게 말하기 (B) 확인 이메일 보내기
(C) 할인된 요금 제시 **(D) 사용 가능한 방 확인**

해설 세부 내용 – 여자가 다음에 할 일
호텔 반대편에 있는 방으로 바꾸고 싶다는 남자의 말에 여자는 빈 방이 있는지 알아보겠다(Let me check if we have any other rooms available)고 하므로 정답은 (D)이다.

어휘 reduced 할인된 rate 요금

> **Paraphrasing** 대화의 check if we have any other rooms available → 보기의 Check for an available room

---

UNIT 12 의도 파악 문제

❶ 의도 파악 문제 – 목적

ETS 유형 연습   본책 p.089

1 (D)   2 (C)   3 (D)   4 (C)

[1] M-Cn / W-Br

M Hello. Domani Real Estate. Alberto speaking. How may I help you?
W Hi. I'm starting a new job in Brazelton next month, and I'd like to rent an apartment downtown.
M OK. What type of apartment are you looking for?
W One with three bedrooms. Oh, and I really like to cook in my free time.

남 안녕하세요. 도마니 부동산 알베르토입니다. 무엇을 도와드릴까요?
여 안녕하세요. 다음 달부터 브라젤턴에서 새 직장을 다닐

예정인데, 시내의 아파트를 빌리고 싶어요.
남 알겠습니다. 어떤 종류의 아파트를 찾고 계신가요?
여 침실 세 개짜리 아파트요. 아, 그리고 저는 여가 시간에 요리하는 걸 정말 좋아해요.

어휘 free time 여가 시간

Q 여자는 왜 "저는 여가 시간에 요리하는 걸 정말 좋아해요"라고 말하는가?
(A) 직업적 배경을 설명하려고
(B) 영양에 관한 걱정을 표현하려고
(C) 초대를 거절하려고
(D) 선호 사항을 내비치려고

해설 세부 내용 – 화자의 의도
남자가 어떤 종류의 아파트를 찾고 있는지(What type of apartment are you looking for?) 묻는 말에 침실 세 개짜리 아파트(One with three bedrooms)라고 답한 뒤 "저는 여가 시간에 요리하는 걸 정말 좋아해요"라고 덧붙인 것은 살고 싶은 아파트에 대한 선호 사항을 내비치려는 의도이다. 따라서 정답은 (D)이다.

어휘 describe 설명하다, 묘사하다 background 배경 express 표현하다 concern 걱정 nutrition 영양 decline 거절하다 indicate 내비치다

[2] W-Am / M-Cn

W Hello. Can I still buy a ticket for the 9:05 train to Amsterdam? It's not too late, is it?
M I'm sorry. The train leaves in one minute. However, there are trains at 10:50 A.M. and 12:30 P.M. There are seats available on both.
W I'll take the first one.

여 안녕하세요. 암스테르담행 9시 5분 기차표를 아직 살 수 있을까요? 너무 늦지는 않았죠?
남 죄송합니다. 기차가 1분 뒤 출발합니다. 하지만, 오전 10시 50분과 오후 12시 30분에 기차가 있습니다. 둘 다 이용 가능한 좌석이 있습니다.
여 첫 번째 것을 탈게요.

어휘 available 이용할 수 있는 both 둘 다

Q 남자는 왜 "기차가 1분 뒤 출발합니다"라고 말하는가?
(A) 빠른 결정을 재촉하려고
(B) 이른 출발을 알리려고
(C) 표를 구입하지 못하게 하려고
(D) 여자가 제시간에 도착했음을 확인시켜 주려고

해설 세부 내용 – 화자의 의도
여자가 9시 5분 기차표 구입이 늦지 않았는지 묻자, 남자는 기차가 1분 뒤 출발한다고 한다. 기차가 곧 출발하면 표를 구입하더라도 탈 수 없는 상황으로 볼 수 있고, 남자가 다른 출발 시간 정보도 알려 주고 있으므로 표를 구입하지 못하게 하려는 의도임을 알 수 있다. 따라서 정답은 (C)이다.

어휘 urge 재촉하다 decision 결정 announce 알리다

departure 출발   deny 못하게 하다, 거부하다
assure 확인시키다

[3] M-Au / W-Am

M This is Jacob from the landscaping company. I'm afraid we won't be able to start working on your garden tomorrow.
W I'm going to be out of town for two weeks starting this Thursday. I wanted to give you a key to the gate, so you'd be able to keep working while I'm gone.
M OK. Then what if I come by tomorrow anyway, just to pick up the key?
W If you wouldn't mind. I'll be at home until ten-thirty in the morning.

남 조경업체의 제이콥입니다. 죄송하지만 내일 고객님 댁의 조경 작업을 시작할 수 없을 것 같아요.
여 제가 이번 주 목요일부터 2주간 지방에 갈 예정입니다. 제가 없는 동안 작업하실 수 있게 대문 열쇠를 드리려고 했어요.
남 알겠습니다. 그럼 제가 열쇠를 가지러 내일 잠깐 들를까요?
여 괜찮으시다면요. 저는 오전 10시 30분까지는 집에 있을 거예요.

어휘 landscaping 조경   be out of town 타지로 나가다   come by 들르다   pick up 찾아오다

Q 여자는 왜 "괜찮으시다면요"라고 말하는가?
 (A) 해결책을 제안하려고
 (B) 허가를 요청하려고
 (C) 불만을 제기하려고
 (D) 제안을 수락하려고

해설 세부 내용 – 화자의 의도
남자가 내일 들러 열쇠를 받으면 어떨지(what if I come by tomorrow anyway, just to pick up the key?) 물어보자 여자는 "괜찮으시다면요"라고 대답하고 있다. 이 대답은 남자의 제안을 수락하려는 의도로 볼 수 있으므로 정답은 (D)이다.

어휘 solution 해결책

[4] W-Br / M-Au

W Hi, Ilya. I have been trying to save a document to the company server for the past five minutes, but it hasn't been working at all.
M Did you try restarting your computer?
W Oh yeah, I always forget to do that. So, are you planning to attend the meeting about management training opportunities at two?
M That meeting is at two o'clock. Maybe I can finish the budget report later.

여 안녕하세요, 일리야. 지난 5분 동안 회사 서버에 문서를 저장하려고 애썼지만 전혀 안 되고 있어요.
남 컴퓨터를 재시작해 보셨나요?
여 그렇네요, 전 항상 그걸 깜빡하네요. 자, 2시에 경영 교육 기회에 관한 회의에 참석하실 계획이세요?
남 회의가 2시군요. 아마 예산 보고서는 나중에 끝낼 수 있을 것 같네요.

어휘 restart 재시작하다   attend 참석하다   training 교육   opportunity 기회

Q 남자는 왜 "회의가 2시군요"라고 말하는가?
 (A) 여자에게 회의 시작 시간을 상기시키려고
 (B) 여자에게 회의에 참석하라고 하려고
 (C) 회의 시간에 대한 실망을 표현하려고
 (D) 회의 준비에 대한 도움을 요청하려고

해설 세부 내용 – 화자의 의도
여자가 2시에 경영 교육 기회에 관한 회의에 참석할 계획인지(are you planning to attend the meeting about management training opportunities at two?) 묻자, 남자는 "회의가 2시군요"라고 재차 언급한 후 예산 보고서 작업이 늦어질 것 같다(Maybe I can finish the budget report later)고 덧붙이고 있다. 남자가 덧붙인 말을 통해 2시 회의 때문에 보고서 작성을 미루어야 한다는 사실에 실망을 표현하려는 의도로 볼 수 있으므로 정답은 (C)이다.

어휘 remind 상기시키다   disappointment 실망   preparation 준비

② 의도 파악 문제 – 문맥상 의미

ETS 유형 연습   본책 p.091

1 (C)   2 (A)   3 (C)   4 (C)

[1] M-Cn / W-Br

M I just noticed they started some construction work in the lobby.
W It's just regular renovation work—to improve the lobby's overall appearance.
M Oh, OK…. It was time for something like that.
W I heard the crews will even put up antique photos showing the company's foundation ceremony—more than a century ago.

남 방금 알았는데, 로비에서 공사를 시작했네요.
여 그냥 로비의 전체적인 외관을 개선하기 위한 정기 보수 공사예요.
남 아, 그렇군요… 그럴 때가 되긴 했죠.
여 작업자들이 100년도 더 지난 회사 창립식을 보여 주는 옛날 사진도 걸어둘 거예요.

어휘 regular 정기적인   improve 개선하다   overall 전체적인   appearance 외관   put up 게시하다   antique 오래된, 골동품인   foundation ceremony 창립식

Q 남자가 "그럴 때가 되긴 했죠"라고 말할 때 무엇을 의미하는가?
(A) 작업 마감시한이 걱정스럽다.
(B) 회의를 더 자주 열고 싶다.
(C) 프로젝트가 바람직하다고 생각한다.
(D) 특별 행사를 열고 싶다.

해설 세부 내용 – 화자의 의도
앞서 언급된 공사가 로비의 전체적인 외관을 개선하기 위한 정기 보수 공사(It's just regular renovation work—to improve the lobby's overall appearance)라는 말에 "그럴 때가 되긴 했죠"라고 남자가 말한 것은 프로젝트가 바람직하다는 의미이다. 따라서 정답은 (C)이다.

[2] W-Am / M-Cn

W   Ryan, I need your help at the loading dock. I know you have some deliveries to make, but can you help unload it?
M   Asher's Automotive Repair Shop is starting a big job today. I was just about to drop off these parts.
W   It won't take more than an hour to unload the shipment.

여   라이언, 하역장에서 당신의 도움이 필요해요. 배달 일이 있다는 건 알고 있지만, 하역 작업을 도와줄 수 있을까요?
남   애셔 자동차 수리점에서 오늘 큰 작업을 시작해요. 방금 이 부품들을 배달하려던 참이었어요.
여   화물을 내리는 데 한 시간 이상은 안 걸릴 거예요.

어휘 loading dock 하역장   automotive 자동차의   unload (짐을) 내리다   drop off 배달하다

Q 남자가 "방금 이 부품들을 배달하려던 참이었어요"라고 말할 때 무엇을 의미하는가?
(A) 도울 시간이 없다.
(B) 주문 취소에 대해 몰랐다.
(C) 인쇄된 송장이 필요하다.
(D) 오늘 분량의 작업을 거의 끝냈다.

해설 세부 내용 – 화자의 의도
배달 일이 있다는 건 알고 있지만 하역 작업을 도와달라는(I know you have some deliveries to make, but can you help unload it?) 여자의 말에, 애셔 자동차 수리점에서 오늘 큰 작업을 시작한다(Asher's Automotive Repair Shop is starting a big job today)고 답하며 "방금 이 부품들을 배달하려던 참이었어요"라고 남자가 말한 것은 중요한 배송을 나가야 하므로 여자를 도울 시간이 없다는 의미이다. 따라서 정답은 (A)이다.

어휘 unaware 알지 못하는   cancellation 취소   invoice 송장

[3] W-Br / M-Cn

W   Adem, our blog was featured on the *Marketing Milestones* radio show!
M   That's great. I hope more people will read the blog now.
W   Do you think now would be a good time to start a podcast? There's a lot of interest these days in innovating marketing using AI technology. I bet it would be popular.
M   I have so many responsibilities right now.

여   아뎀, 우리 블로그가 〈마케팅 마일스톤〉 라디오 쇼에 나왔어요!
남   잘됐네요. 이제 더 많은 사람들이 블로그를 읽으면 좋겠네요.
여   지금이 팟캐스트를 시작하기에 좋은 시기일까요? 요즘 AI 기술을 활용한 마케팅 혁신에 관심이 많잖아요. 인기가 있을 거라 장담해요.
남   지금은 제가 업무가 아주 많아요.

어휘 feature ~을 특집으로 하다, 포함하다   interest 관심, 흥미   bet 장담하다, 분명하다

Q 남자가 "지금은 제가 업무가 아주 많아요"라고 말할 때 무엇을 암시하는가?
(A) 도움을 원한다.
(B) 자신이 승진에 고려되어야 한다.
(C) 일을 할 시간이 없다.
(D) 기한을 연장하고 싶어 한다.

해설 세부 내용 – 화자의 의도
여자가 지금이 팟캐스트를 시작하기에 좋은 시기일지(Do you think now would be a good time to start a podcast?) 묻는 말에 "지금은 제가 업무가 아주 많아요"라고 남자가 말한 것은 지금 당장은 업무가 많아 새로운 일에 할애할 시간이 없다는 의미이므로 정답은 (C)이다.

어휘 assistance 도움   promotion 승진   task 일   extend 연장하다

[4] W-Am / M-Au

W   We'll have to delay some of the renovations we've asked you to do.
M   Do you know which parts of the project you'd like to put off?
W   Well, I know we talked about adding a library wing—but that's very expensive. So, if we don't make that addition, that's all we may need to cut.
M   You know, that's not a bad idea. Let's see how much you'd save if I take the library out of the renovation proposal.

여   저희가 부탁드린 보수공사 중 일부를 미뤄야겠어요.
남   어떤 공사를 연기하고 싶은 건가요?
여   음, 저희가 부속 도서관을 추가하는 것에 대해 이야기했었는데

그 공사가 비용이 너무 많이 들어요. **그래서 그것만 추가하지 않으면 다른 삭감은 필요 없을 것 같아요.**

남 그래요, **그게 나쁜 생각은 아니네요.** 보수공사 계획에서 도서관을 빼면 얼마나 절약하게 되는지 알아보죠.

어휘 delay 미루다, 연기하다 renovation 보수, 개조 put off 연기하다 wing 부속 건물 addition 추가 save 절약하다 proposal 계획, 제안

Q 남자가 "그게 나쁜 생각은 아니네요"라고 말할 때 무엇을 의미하는가?
(A) 몇 가지 제안을 더 듣고 싶다.
(B) 원래 계획을 선호한다.
(C) 제안된 해결책에 동의한다.
(D) 더 좋은 생각이 있다.

해설 세부 내용 – 화자의 의도
도서관을 추가하지 않으면 다른 삭감은 필요 없을 것 같다(if we don't make that addition, that's all we may need to cut)는 여자의 말에 남자는 "그게 나쁜 생각은 아니네요"라고 응답했다. 즉, 남자는 여자의 제안에 동의한다는 의미이므로 정답은 (C)이다.

ETS 실전 문제
본책 p.092

1 (B)	2 (A)	3 (D)	4 (D)	5 (A)	6 (B)
7 (D)	8 (A)	9 (C)	10 (B)	11 (D)	12 (B)
13 (B)	14 (D)	15 (A)	16 (C)	17 (A)	18 (B)
19 (D)	20 (B)	21 (C)	22 (A)	23 (D)	24 (B)

[1-3] M-Cn / W-Am

M Yan Li, **[1,2] what do you think of developing a larger battery for our newest mirrorless camera? I know it would increase the size of the camera, but it would solve the issue of low battery life.**

W Well, I just got the results of the most recent customer survey, and **our customers want a compact design.**

M OK, I see. I think I'd like to review the results of that survey. Where can I find them?

W Actually, **[3] I'm preparing a report on the survey results, and I'm going to present it at the team meeting tomorrow.**

남 얀 리, **[1,2]** 최신 미러리스 카메라용으로 더 큰 배터리를 개발하는 것에 대해 어떻게 생각하세요? 카메라가 커질 거란 건 알지만, 배터리 수명이 짧은 문제는 해결될 거예요.

여 음, 방금 최신 고객 설문조사 결과를 받았는데, 우리 고객들은 소형 디자인을 원해요.

남 그렇군요, 알겠어요. 그 조사 결과를 검토하고 싶어요. 어디서 찾을 수 있나요?

여 실은 **[3]** 제가 조사 결과에 대한 보고서를 준비하고 있는데,

내일 팀 회의에서 발표할 거예요.

어휘 mirrorless camera 미러리스 카메라(반사경을 제거한 카메라) increase 늘리다 survey (설문)조사 result 결과

1 회사는 무엇을 판매하는가?
(A) 계산기   (B) 카메라
(C) 노트북 컴퓨터   (D) 주방기기

해설 전체 내용 – 회사가 판매하는 제품
남자의 첫 대사에서 자사의 최신 카메라용으로 더 큰 배터리를 개발하는 것에 대한 의견을 묻는(what do you think of developing a larger battery for our newest mirrorless camera?) 것으로 보아 회사가 판매하는 제품은 카메라임을 알 수 있다. 따라서 정답은 (B)이다.

어휘 appliance 기기

2 여자는 왜 "우리 고객들은 소형 디자인을 원해요"라고 말하는가?
(A) 제안을 거부하려고
(B) 놀라움을 표현하려고
(C) 안심시키려고
(D) 도움을 요청하려고

해설 세부 내용 – 화자의 의도
더 큰 배터리 개발을 제안하며, 카메라의 사이즈는 커지지만 배터리의 짧은 수명 문제를 해결할 것(what do you think of developing a larger battery for our newest mirrorless camera? I know it would increase the size of the camera, but it would solve the issue of low battery life)이라는 남자의 말에 "우리 고객들은 소형 디자인을 원해요"라고 여자가 말한 것은 그 제안이 바람직하지 않다는 의미이다. 따라서 정답은 (A)이다.

어휘 reassurance 안심

3 여자는 내일 무엇을 할 것인가?
(A) 고객 만나기
(B) 이미지 선택하기
(C) 이메일로 보고서 보내기
(D) 발표하기

해설 세부 내용 – 여자가 내일 할 일
질문의 키워드인 tomorrow에 유의하여 지문을 들으면, 대화 맨 마지막에서 여자가 내일 팀 회의에서 조사 결과에 대한 보고서를 발표할 예정(I'm preparing a report on the survey results, and I'm going to present it at the team meeting tomorrow)임을 알 수 있다. 따라서 정답은 (D)이다.

Paraphrasing 대화의 present it → 보기의 Make a presentation

[4-6] M-Cn / W-Am

M Hi, Amal. I heard you attended an orchestra concert with Miguel over the weekend. How was it? **4 I heard it's long… about two hours, right? Is it worth checking out?**

W Two hours wasn't enough!

M Really? Hmm… **5 I've been busy for the last month working on the product design presentation**, so I haven't had a lot of time. I'd like to see it with a friend.

W Actually, Angie wanted to see it with us, but she felt a little sick that day. **6 Maybe you should ask her to go with you?** She should be at her desk now.

남 안녕하세요, 아말. 주말에 미구엘과 오케스트라 연주회에 갔다고 들었어요. 어땠어요? 4제가 듣기로는 길다는데… 두 시간 정도 맞죠? 볼만한 가치가 있나요?

여 두 시간으로 충분하지 않았어요!

남 정말요? 흠… 5지난달에 제품 디자인 발표 준비를 하느라 너무 바빠서 시간이 많이 없었어요. 친구와 함께 보고 싶네요.

여 실은, 앤지가 우리와 함께 보고 싶어 했는데, 그날 몸이 조금 아팠어요. 6그녀에게 같이 가자고 하는 건 어때요? 지금 그녀는 자리에 있을 거예요.

어휘 worth -ing ~할 가치가 있는 product 제품

4 여자가 "두 시간으로 충분하지 않았어요"라고 말할 때 무엇을 암시하는가?
(A) 마감일이 연장되었다.
(B) 프로젝트가 예상보다 오래 걸렸다.
(C) 그녀는 행사에 늦게 도착했다.
(D) 공연이 즐거웠다.

해설 세부 내용 - 화자의 의도
남자가 오케스트라 연주회가 두 시간 정도로 긴데 볼만한지 (I heard it's long... about two hours, right? Is it worth checking out?) 묻자, 여자는 "두 시간으로 충분하지 않았어요"라고 답하고 있다. 즉, 연주회가 지루하지 않고 즐거웠음을 추론할 수 있으므로 정답은 (D)이다.

어휘 deadline 마감일 extend 연장하다 expect 예상하다. 기대하다 event 행사 performance 공연, 성과

5 남자는 왜 바빴는가?
(A) 발표 준비를 했다.
(B) 안내 책자를 디자인했다.
(C) 고객 의견을 보고했다.
(D) 성과를 평가했다.

해설 세부 내용 - 남자가 바빴던 이유
남자가 제품 디자인 발표 작업 때문에 지난달에 바빴다(I've been busy for the last month working on the product design presentation)고 했으므로 정답은 (A)이다.

어휘 brochure 안내 책자, 팸플릿 comment 의견, 논평

6 여자는 남자에게 무엇을 하라고 제안하는가?
(A) 일찍 도착하기 **(B) 동료를 초대하기**
(C) 신제품을 시험하기 (D) 약을 추천하기

해설 세부 내용 - 여자의 제안 사항
여자가 마지막 대사에서 앤지에게 함께 가자고 말해 보라고(Maybe you should ask her to go with you?) 했고, 그녀가 자리에 있을 거라고 했으므로 앤지가 동료임을 추측할 수 있다. 따라서 정답은 (B)이다.

어휘 medicine 약

[7-9] M-Cn / W-Br

M Hmm. **7 It looks like your luggage is 23 kilograms. That's over the weight limit.**

W Oh, but **8 I thought the weight limit for business class was 32 kilograms.**

M That's true—but your seat is in the main cabin.

W Really? I asked my assistant to book a seat in business class. In any case, I need everything in my luggage for my trip. What can I do?

M Well, usually there's an extra fee for overweight baggage. But since you're only a few kilograms over, I'll waive the fee. **9 You can proceed to the gate.**

남 흠. 7고객님의 짐이 23kg인 것 같습니다. 무게 제한을 초과하셨네요.

여 아, 그런데 8비즈니스 클래스의 무게 제한은 32kg인 줄 알았는데요.

남 맞습니다. 하지만 고객님 좌석은 일반석에 있습니다.

여 그래요? 제 비서에게 비즈니스 클래스석을 예약해 달라고 했는데요. 어쨌든, 여행을 위해 제 가방 속에 있는 게 전부 다 필요해요. 어떻게 하면 되죠?

남 음, 보통 중량 초과 수하물에는 추가 요금이 부과돼요. 하지만 불과 몇 kg 초과한 것뿐이니 제가 요금을 면제해드릴게요. 9탑승구로 이동하시면 됩니다.

어휘 luggage 짐 main cabin 일반석 in any case 어쨌든 fee 요금 overweight 중량 초과의 baggage 짐 waive 면제하다 proceed 이동하다, 나아가다 gate 탑승구

7 여자는 어떤 문제를 겪고 있는가?
(A) 티켓을 잃어버렸다.
(B) 보너스 포인트를 사용할 수 없다.
(C) 항공편이 지연되었다.
(D) 짐이 너무 무겁다.

해설 전체 내용 - 여자의 문제점
첫 대사에서 남자가 여자에게 짐이 23kg인 것 같다(It looks like your luggage is 23 kilograms)며 무게 제한을 초과했다(That's over the weight limit)고 문제점을 지적했다. 따라서 정답은 (D)이다.

어휘 access 이용하다 delay 지연시키다

Paraphrasing 대화의 over the weight limit
→ 보기의 too heavy

8 남자는 왜 "고객님 좌석은 일반석에 있습니다"라고 말하는가?
(A) 잘못된 추측을 바로잡으려고
(B) 길을 안내하려고
(C) 요청을 신속하게 처리하려고
(D) 찬성을 표현하려고

해설 세부 내용 – 화자의 의도
비즈니스 클래스의 무게 제한은 32kg인 줄 알았다(I thought the weight limit for business class was 32 kilograms)는 여자의 말에, 남자가 "고객님 좌석은 일반석에 있습니다"라고 말한 것은 여자가 좌석을 잘못 알고 있음을 알려주려는 의도이므로 정답은 (A)이다.

어휘 correct 바로잡다 assumption 추측
directions (길) 안내 expedite 신속히 처리하다
express 표현하다

9 여자는 다음에 무엇을 할 것 같은가?
(A) 요금 지불하기
(B) 새로운 좌석 요청하기
(C) 탑승구로 걸어가기
(D) 관리자와 이야기하기

해설 세부 내용 – 여자가 다음에 할 일
마지막 대사에서 남자가 여자에게 탑승구로 이동하면 된다(You can proceed to the gate)고 했으므로 정답은 (C)이다.

Paraphrasing 대화의 proceed to the gate
→ 보기의 Walk to a gate

[10-12] M-Au / W-Br

M When should we be leaving the office?
W Hmm… in about an hour, I think. **¹⁰That should give us plenty of time to catch our flight at two P.M.**
M OK… **¹¹but we can't afford to miss the meeting with the investors in Janville.** Our company really needs their financial support at the moment.
W Don't worry, Charles—we have enough time. **¹²Have you prepared copies of the presentation for each of the attendees?**
M Actually, I just got a call from Janville—we'll have Internet access at all times. They'll e-mail us log-on instructions.
W Oh… that's good to know.

남 언제 사무실에서 나가야 할까요?
여 흠… 약 한 시간 뒤에요. ¹⁰그러면 오후 2시 비행기를 탈 수 있는 시간이 충분할 거예요.
남 그렇군요… ¹¹하지만 장빌에서 열리는 투자자 미팅은 놓치면 안 돼요. 우리 회사는 지금 그들의 재정 지원이 절실하게 필요해요.
여 걱정 마세요, 찰스. 시간은 충분해요. ¹²각 참석자에게 줄 발표 사본은 준비하셨나요?
남 실은, 방금 장빌에서 전화가 왔어요. 우린 언제든 인터넷에 접속할 수 있어요. 그들이 로그인 지침을 이메일로 보낼 거예요.
여 오… 잘됐네요.

어휘 can't afford to ~할 여유가 없다, ~할 형편이 안 된다
investor 투자자 financial 재정의 access 접속
instructions 지침

10 화자들은 오후 2시에 어디에 있어야 하는가?
(A) 사무실   (B) 공항
(C) 기차역   (D) 컨벤션 센터

해설 세부 내용 – 2시에 있어야 할 장소
여자가 첫 번째 대사에서 2시 비행기를 타기에 충분한 시간일 것(That should give us plenty of time to catch our flight at two P.M.)이라고 했으므로 정답은 (B)이다.

11 화자들은 장빌에서 무엇을 할 것인가?
(A) 조사 실시   (B) 세미나에서 발표
(C) 시설 점검   (D) 투자자들 만나기

해설 세부 내용 – 장빌에서 할 일
남자가 두 번째 대사에서 장빌에서 열리는 투자자 미팅은 놓치면 안 된다(we can't afford to miss the meeting with the investors in Janville)고 했으므로 정답은 (D)이다.

어휘 inspect 점검하다 facility 시설

Paraphrasing 대화의 meeting with the investors
→ 보기의 Meet with investors

12 남자가 "우린 언제든 인터넷에 접속할 수 있어요"라고 말할 때 무엇을 의미하는가?
(A) 인터넷 제공업체를 바꿨다.
(B) 복사할 필요가 없다.
(C) 여자는 서비스가 나쁘다고 불평하면 안 된다.
(D) 여자는 온라인으로 과제를 완료할 수 있다.

해설 세부 내용 – 화자의 의도
여자가 각 참석자에게 줄 발표 사본을 준비했는지(Have you prepared copies of the presentation for each of the attendees?) 묻자, 남자는 "우린 언제든 인터넷에 접속할 수 있어요"라고 답하고 있다. 즉, 여자에게 복사본을 준비할 필요가 없음을 알리려고 한 말임을 알 수 있으므로 정답은 (B)이다.

어휘 assignment 과제

[13-15] W-Br / M-Au

W Hi, Koji. I just came from the meeting with Melson Incorporated. And, guess what. **13They signed a contract with us!**

M That's great! But that means **14we'll need to fill the open position for a computer programmer on our software development team quickly.** Let's talk about the top candidates we're considering.

W Well, I guess it's between Raquel and Marina.

M I think we should offer the position to Marina. She performed better overall in the technical interview.

W That's true, but I have a concern. She'll need to use Denix for this software development project, and **15she said she's not very familiar with that programming language.**

M Well, she's learned more than five already.

여 안녕하세요, 코지. 저는 방금 멜슨 사와 회의를 하고 왔어요. 그리고, 무슨 일이 있었냐면요. **13그들이 우리와 계약을 체결했어요!**

남 잘됐군요! **14그렇다면 이제 소프트웨어 개발팀의 비어 있는 컴퓨터 프로그래머 자리를 빨리 충원해야 하겠어요.** 현재 고려 중인 상위 후보들에 대해 이야기해 봅시다.

여 음, 라켈과 마리나 중에서 택해야 하겠군요.

남 저는 마리나에게 이 자리를 제안해야 한다고 생각해요. 그녀가 기술 면접에서 전반적으로 더 나았어요.

여 그렇긴 한데, 한 가지 걱정이 있어요. 이번 소프트웨어 개발 프로젝트에 데닉스를 사용해야 하는데, **15그녀는 그 프로그래밍 언어는 잘 모른다고 했어요.**

남 뭐, 그녀는 이미 다섯 개 이상을 배웠잖아요.

어휘 contract 계약 fill 채우다 candidate 후보자 consider 고려하다 overall 전반적으로 perform (업무 등을) 수행하다 concern 걱정 familiar 잘 아는

13 여자는 어떤 좋은 소식을 전하는가?
(A) 제품 출시 일정이 잡혔다.
(B) 계약이 체결되었다.
(C) 일부 비용이 절감되었다.
(D) 일부 고객 평가가 긍정적이었다.

해설 세부 내용 – 여자가 전하는 소식
첫 대사에서 여자가 멜슨 사와 계약을 체결했다(They signed a contract with us!)며 기뻐하고 있으므로 정답은 (B)이다.

어휘 launch 출시 reduce 줄이다 review 평가 positive 긍정적인

14 화자들은 어떤 업체에서 근무하는 것 같은가?
(A) 마케팅 회사 (B) 백화점
(C) 의류 생산업체 **(D) 소프트웨어 개발 회사**

해설 전체 내용 – 근무 장소
남자가 첫 대사에서 소프트웨어 개발팀에 비어 있는 컴퓨터 프로그래머 자리를 빨리 충원해야겠다(we'll need to fill the open position for a computer programmer on our software development team quickly)고 하므로, 화자들이 소프트웨어 개발 회사에서 일한다는 것을 알 수 있다. 따라서 정답은 (D)이다.

어휘 manufacturer 생산 회사 developer 개발 회사

15 남자는 왜 "그녀는 이미 다섯 개 이상을 배웠잖아요"라고 말하는가?
(A) 안심시키려고
(B) 급여 인상을 권고하려고
(C) 놀라움을 표현하려고
(D) 교육 요청을 거절하려고

해설 세부 내용 – 화자의 의도
마리나가 데닉스라는 프로그래밍 언어는 잘 모른다고 했다(she said she's not very familiar with that programming language)며 우려를 나타내는 여자에게 남자가 "그녀는 이미 다섯 개 이상을 배웠잖아요"라고 말하는 것은 마리나가 데닉스도 잘 배울 것이라고 여자를 안심시키려는 의도임을 알 수 있다. 따라서 정답은 (A)이다.

어휘 reassurance 안심시키는 말 recommend 권고하다 pay raise 급여 인상 reject 거절하다

[16-18] M-Cn / W-Am

M **16I finished creating a 3-D model of the museum building.** Once it's approved, then the construction phase can begin.

W Thanks. Hmm. Although, **16didn't the client want a large circular window above the front entrance?**

M That wasn't in the sketches they gave us. Did they mention it during our meeting? I didn't hear anything about it.

W **17They decided to add it after that meeting and sent some modified drawings.** I'll send them to you. Um, **18is there any chance you could have a revised model finished by Tuesday?**

M I'm going to a professional-development seminar next week.

남 **16박물관 건물의 3D 모형 제작을 끝냈습니다.** 승인이 나면 공사 단계를 시작할 수 있을 거예요.

여 고마워요. 흠, 그런데 **16고객이 정문 위에 큰 원형 창을 원하지 않았나요?**

남 우리에게 준 스케치에는 그게 없었어요. 그들이 회의 중에 언급했었나요? 그 부분에 대해 전 아무것도 듣지 못했어요.

여 **17회의 후에 그걸 추가하기로 결정하고 수정된 도면을 보냈어요.** 제가 보내 줄게요. 음, **18화요일까지 수정 모형을 완성할 수 있을까요?**

남 저는 다음 주에 전문성 개발 세미나에 갈 예정이에요.

어휘 approve 승인하다 phase 단계 circular 원형의 entrance 출입구 modified 수정된 revised 수정된

16 화자들은 어떤 산업에 종사하는 것 같은가?
(A) 조경 (B) 관광
(C) 건축 (D) 텔레비전

해설 전체 내용 - 근무 업종
대화 초반부에서 남자가 박물관 건물의 3D 모형 제작을 끝냈다(I finished creating a 3-D model of the museum building)고 하자 여자가 고객이 정문 위에 큰 원형 창을 원하지 않았었는지(didn't the client want a large circular window above the front entrance?) 확인하는 내용을 통해 화자들이 건축업에 종사하고 있음을 알 수 있다. 따라서 정답은 (C)이다.

17 여자는 남자에게 무엇을 보내겠다고 말하는가?
(A) 업데이트된 도면 (B) 회의록
(C) 비용 견적서 (D) 비디오 녹화물

해설 세부 내용 - 여자가 남자에게 보내겠다고 하는 것
여자가 두 번째 대사에서 고객들이 회의 후에 원형 창문을 추가하기로 결정하고 수정된 도면을 보냈다(They decided to add it after that meeting and sent some modified drawings)며 자신이 그것을 보내 주겠다(I'll send them to you)고 했으므로 정답은 (A)이다.

어휘 estimate 견적서

Paraphrasing 대화의 modified → 보기의 Updated

18 남자가 "저는 다음 주에 전문성 개발 세미나에 갈 예정이에요"라고 말할 때 무엇을 암시하는가?
(A) 곧 자격증을 받을 것이다.
(B) 일을 끝내려면 추가 시간이 필요하다.
(C) 여자가 참석하기를 원한다.
(D) 진급을 희망한다.

해설 세부 내용 - 화자의 의도
여자가 화요일까지 수정 모형을 완성할 수 있을지(is there any chance you could have a revised model finished by Tuesday?) 묻는 말에 남자가 "다음 주에 전문성 개발 세미나에 갈 예정이에요"라고 말한 것은 세미나 일정 때문에 작업을 완수하려면 시간이 더 필요하다는 의미이다. 따라서 정답은 (B)이다.

어휘 certificate 자격증 additional 추가의 task 일 promotion 진급

[19-21] M-Au / W-Br

M Hi, Sakura. **19** I have all the new accounting guidelines ready. I e-mailed them to our team members this morning.
W Great. And we need to find a safe way to get rid of the old paper guidelines, since they contain sensitive information. I think we should shred the pages. **20** Could you make sure all the hard copies are destroyed?
M Of course! What should we do with the binders once the pages are removed?
W **21** Let's donate them to a secondhand shop. We usually donate to that one in Midtown.
M I have a client meeting in Midtown this afternoon. It'll be on the way.
W Perfect. Thanks!

남 안녕하세요, 사쿠라. **19** 새로운 회계 지침이 모두 준비되었어요. 오늘 아침에 팀원들에게 이메일로 보냈습니다.
여 좋습니다. 그리고 기존의 종이 지침 문서에 민감한 정보가 포함되어 있어서 안전하게 폐기할 방법을 찾아야 해요. 그 종이 문서를 파쇄해야 할 것 같습니다. **20** 모든 인쇄본이 파기되도록 해 줄 수 있나요?
남 물론입니다! 종이 문서를 제거하고 나서 바인더들은 어떻게 할까요?
여 **21** 중고 가게에 기부합시다. 보통 미드타운에 있는 중고 가게에 기부하고 있어요.
남 제가 오늘 오후에 미드타운에서 고객 미팅이 있어요. 가는 길에 있겠네요.
여 완벽해요. 고마워요!

어휘 accounting 회계 guideline 지침 get rid of ~을 제거하다 sensitive 민감한 shred 파쇄하다 remove 제거하다 donate 기부하다 secondhand 중고의 on the way 가는 길에

19 남자는 오늘 아침에 무엇을 했는가?
(A) 작업 공간을 정리했다.
(B) 발표를 했다.
(C) 행사 초대장을 인쇄했다.
(D) 지침을 이메일로 보냈다.

해설 세부 내용 - 남자가 아침에 한 일
첫 대사에서 남자가 새로운 회계 지침이 모두 준비되었으며 오늘 아침에 팀원들에게 이메일로 보냈다(I have all the new accounting guidelines ready. I e-mailed them to our team members this morning)고 했으므로 정답은 (D)이다.

어휘 organize 정리하다 workspace 작업 공간

20 여자는 남자에게 무엇을 하라고 요청하는가?
(A) 신입 직원 교육
(B) 일부 문서 파기
(C) 식당 예약
(D) 공급업체 계약서에 서명

해설 세부 내용 - 여자의 요청 사항
여자가 첫 대사에서 남자에게 모든 인쇄본이 파기되도록 해 줄 수 있는지(Could you make sure all the hard copies are destroyed?)를 요청하고 있으므로 정답은 (B)이다.

어휘 reservation 예약   vendor 공급업체

Paraphrasing 대화의 hard copies → 보기의 documents

21 남자는 왜 "제가 오늘 오후에 미드타운에서 고객 미팅이 있어요"라고 말하는가?
(A) 도움을 요청하려고
(B) 지연에 대해 설명하려고
(C) 업무를 수행하겠다고 제안하려고
(D) 일정에 대해 불평하려고

해설 세부 내용 – 화자의 의도
바인더들을 중고 가게에 기부하자(Let's donate them to a secondhand shop)며 보통 미드타운에 있는 중고 가게에 기부를 하고 있다(We usually donate to that one in Midtown)고 가게 위치를 알려주는 여자의 말에, 남자가 "제가 오늘 오후에 미드타운에서 고객 미팅이 있어요"라고 말하는 것은 자신이 물건을 가게로 가져가겠다는 의미이다. 따라서 정답은 (C)이다.

어휘 assistance 도움   delay 지연   complain 불평하다

[22-24] M-Au / W-Am

M **22Congratulations on your promotion to sales manager**, Ms. Kim. You really deserve it.
W Thank you. I heard that you'll be handling some of my previous duties, including client accounts.
M Yes. Right now, I'm working on the Tryger Technology account.
W Tryger Technology is a valuable client. They place the most orders for the microchips we produce.
M I know. **23,24I'm concerned about maintaining the same level of customer service you provided.**
W Just keep in mind they like to be informed regularly about our products.
M That's good to know.

남 김 부장님, 22영업 부장으로 승진하신 것을 축하드립니다. 정말 그럴 만하세요.
여 고마워요. 고객 계정을 포함한 저의 예전 업무 일부를 담당할 거라고 들었어요.
남 네. 지금은 트라이거 테크놀로지 계정을 맡고 있어요.
여 트라이거 테크놀로지는 소중한 고객이죠. 우리가 생산하는 마이크로칩에 대한 주문량이 가장 많아요.
남 알고 있습니다. 23,24부장님이 제공하셨던 고객 서비스와 같은 수준을 유지할 수 있을지 걱정이 되네요.
여 그들이 우리 제품에 대해 정기적으로 정보를 받고 싶어 한다는 점만 기억하세요.
남 좋은 정보네요.

어휘 deserve (마땅히) ~ 받을 만하다   handle 담당하다   previous 이전의   duty 업무   valuable 소중한   be concerned about ~에 대해 걱정하다   maintain 유지하다   inform 정보를 주다, 알리다   regularly 정기적으로

22 남자는 왜 여자를 축하하는가?
(A) 최근에 승진했다.
(B) 기사를 발표했다.
(C) 학위 과정을 마쳤다.
(D) 신제품을 개발했다.

해설 세부 내용 – 남자가 여자를 축하하는 이유
남자가 첫 대사에서 여자에게 영업 부장으로 승진한 것을 축하한다(Congratulations on your promotion to sales manager)고 했으므로 정답은 (A)이다.

어휘 degree program 학위 과정

23 남자는 무엇을 걱정하는가?
(A) 마감 기한을 맞추는 것
(B) 예산을 초과하지 않는 것
(C) 물품이 소진되는 것
(D) 좋은 고객 서비스를 제공하는 것

해설 세부 내용 – 남자의 걱정거리
대화 후반부에서 남자가 여자가 제공하던 고객 서비스와 같은 수준을 유지할 수 있을지 걱정이 된다(I'm concerned about maintaining the same level of customer service you provided)고 했으므로 정답은 (D)이다.

어휘 budget 예산   run out of ~을 소진하다, ~이 바닥나다

Paraphrasing 대화의 maintaining the same level of customer service you provided → 보기의 Providing good customer service

24 여자는 왜 "그들이 우리 제품에 대해 정기적으로 정보를 받고 싶어 한다"라고 말하는가?
(A) 불평을 하려고
(B) 조언을 하려고
(C) 회사 정책을 설명하려고
(D) 작업에 대한 도움을 받으라고 제안하려고

해설 세부 내용 – 화자의 의도
여자가 제공하던 고객 서비스와 같은 수준을 유지할 수 있을지 걱정(I'm concerned about maintaining the same level of customer service you provided)이라는 남자의 말에, 여자가 "그들이 우리 제품에 대해 정기적으로 정보를 받고 싶어 한다"라고 말한 것은 남자에게 조언을 제공하려는 의도이므로 정답은 (B)이다.

어휘 complaint 불평   describe 설명하다   policy 정책

UNIT 13　시각 정보 문제

① 시각 정보 문제 - 표·그래프

ETS 유형 연습　　　　　　　　　　본책 p.095

1 (D)　　2 (C)　　3 (C)

[1] 대화 + 청구서 W-Br / M-Cn

W May I have the key card to your room so I can begin processing your checkout?
M I actually misplaced it. Sorry about that. My name's Eric Peterson. I was in room 615.
W So… I will have to add an extra miscellaneous charge of seven dollars to your bill for the key card.

여 체크아웃 처리를 시작할 수 있도록 키 카드를 주시겠어요?
남 실은 어디 뒀는지 잊어버렸어요. 죄송해요. 제 이름은 에릭 피터슨이에요. 615호에 있었어요.
여 그렇다면… 키 카드 때문에 청구서에 별도로 기타 요금 7달러를 추가해야 해요.

어휘 process 처리하다　misplace 둔 곳을 잊어버리다　miscellaneous 기타의

고객명:	에릭 피터슨
숙박료:	95달러
공항간 교통비:	15달러
식당 요금:	45달러(두 끼)
기타:	20달러

Q 시각 정보에 따르면, 청구서에서 어떤 요금이 바뀌겠는가?
(A) 95달러　　(B) 15달러
(C) 45달러　　**(D) 20달러**

해설 세부 내용 - 시각 정보
마지막 대사에서 여자가 키 카드 때문에 청구서에 기타 요금 7달러를 추가해야 할 것(I will have to add an extra miscellaneous charge of seven dollars to your bill for the key card)이라고 했다. 그리고 표를 보면 기타에 20달러로 표시되어 있으므로 정답은 (D)이다.

[2] 대화 + 시간표 W-Am / M-Cn

W And now, for the next part of your training, I'm going to teach you how to record the results of the water tests.
M OK—and the water that flows through this facility is tested at several stages, right?
W Right. That way, we can ensure that it meets our water-treatment plant's quality standards.
M That makes sense.

여 이제 교육의 다음 부분으로, 수질 검사 결과를 기록하는 방법을 가르쳐드리겠습니다.
남 알겠습니다. 이 시설을 통과해 흐르는 물은 여러 단계에서 검사를 받는 거죠?
여 맞습니다. 그 방식으로 우리 정수 처리장의 품질 기준을 충족하게 할 수 있습니다.
남 그렇겠네요.

어휘 record 기록하다　result 결과　flow 흐르다　facility 시설　stage 단계　meet 충족시키다　water-treatment plant 정수 처리장

교육 시간표	
오전 8시	시설 견학
오전 9시 30분	샘플 수집
오전 10시 30분	**검사 결과 기록**
정오	직원 점심
오후 1시 30분	안전 프로토콜 학습

Q 시각 정보에 따르면, 대화가 이루어지는 것 같은 시간은 언제인가?
(A) 오전 8시　　　　(B) 오전 9시 30분
(C) 오전 10시 30분　(D) 오후 1시 30분

해설 세부 내용 - 시각 정보
첫 대사에서 여자가 이제 교육의 다음 부분으로 수질 검사 결과를 기록하는 방법을 가르쳐 주겠다(And now, for the next part of your training, I'm going to teach you how to record the results of the water tests)고 했다. 그리고 시간표를 보면 검사 결과 기록은 오전 10시 30분에 한다고 나와 있으므로 정답은 (C)이다.

[3] 대화 + 라벨 M-Cn / W-Br

M Is there a yogurt that's low in calories but also has a lot of protein?
W Here's one of our most popular brands of blueberry yogurt. See, there's a lot of protein…
M Mmm—nice! But my doctor told me I shouldn't eat a lot of sweet foods—and it would put me over the daily amount he recommended. That's more than 30 grams!
W In that case, I'd suggest buying a plain version of this yogurt.

남 칼로리는 낮지만 단백질은 풍부한 요거트가 있을까요?
여 가장 인기 있는 블루베리 요거트 브랜드 중 하나가 이겁니다. 보시면 단백질이 풍부합니다….
남 음… 좋네요! 하지만 담당 의사가 단 음식은 많이 먹지 말라고 했는데, 이건 의사의 하루 권장량을 초과할 것 같아요. 30그램이 넘네요!
여 그렇다면 이 요거트의 플레인 맛을 구입하시길 권해드려요.

어휘 low in calories 칼로리가 낮은　protein 단백질　sweet 달콤한　plain (설탕이나 과일 등이) 첨가되지 않은

영양 정보	
1회 제공량 : 200그램	
칼로리:	150
	1회분당 함량
지방	5그램
단백질	11그램
당분	**32그램**
나트륨	40밀리그램

Q 시각 정보에 따르면, 남자는 어떤 성분에 우려를 나타내는가?
(A) 지방 (B) 단백질
(C) 당분 (D) 나트륨

해설 세부 내용 – 시각 정보
남자의 두 번째 대사에서 담당 의사가 단 음식은 많이 먹지 말라고 했는데 이것은 하루 권장량을 초과하는 것(my doctor told me I shouldn't eat a lot of sweet foods—and it would put me over the daily amount he recommended)이라며 30그램이 넘는다(That's more than 30 grams!)고 했다. 그리고 표를 보면 당분(Sugar)이 32 grams로 표시되어 있으므로 정답은 (C)이다.

❷ 시각 정보 문제 – 지도·기타

ETS 유형 연습 본책 p.097

1 (B) 2 (B) 3 (B)

[1] 대화 + 광고 공간 가격 W-Br / M-Au

> **W** *Latest Fashion Magazine*, sales department. How may I help you?
> **M** Hi. I've been a fan of your fashion magazine for some time, and now I'd like to place an advertisement for my business in it.
> **W** Thank you! What size ad are you looking for?
> **M** **I'd like to go with the quarter page** and make it a recurring ad each month.
>
> 여 〈레이티스트 패션 매거진〉 영업부입니다. 무엇을 도와드릴까요?
> 남 안녕하세요. 오랫동안 귀사의 패션 잡지의 팬이었는데요, 이제 제 회사 광고를 잡지에 게재하고 싶습니다.
> 여 감사합니다! 어떤 크기의 광고를 고려하고 계시나요?
> 남 **1/4 페이지로 진행하고 싶고** 매달 정기 광고로 하려고요.

어휘 advertisement 광고 quarter 4분의 1 recurring 반복되어 발생하는

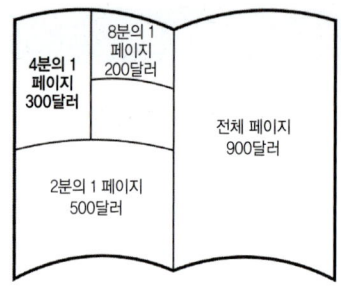

Q 시각 정보에 따르면, 남자는 한 달에 얼마를 지불할 것인가?
(A) 200달러 **(B) 300달러**
(C) 500달러 (D) 900달러

해설 세부 내용 – 시각 정보
남자가 두 번째 대사에서 1/4 페이지로 진행하고 싶다(I'd like to go with the quarter page)고 했다. 그리고 광고 공간 가격표를 보면 1/4 페이지는 300달러라고 나와 있으므로 정답은 (B)이다.

[2] 대화 + 지도 W-Am / M-Au

> **W** Excuse me, do you know where I can find an elevator here in the train station? I usually take the elevator at the Edgemont Street exit when I'm traveling with luggage, but there's a sign saying that exit is closed.
> **M** The Edgemont Street exit is closed due to construction, but **the Waverly Street exit is open, and it also has an elevator.**
> **W** Thank you, I'll go there.
>
> 여 실례지만 여기 기차역에서 엘리베이터를 어디서 찾을 수 있는지 아시나요? 저는 보통 짐을 가지고 이동할 때는 엣지몬트 가 출구에 있는 엘리베이터를 타는데, 그 출구가 폐쇄되었다는 표지판이 있네요.
> 남 엣지몬트 가 출구는 공사로 인해 폐쇄되었지만, **웨이버리 가 출구는 열려 있고 거기도 엘리베이터가 있어요.**
> 여 고맙습니다. 거기로 갈게요.

어휘 construction 공사

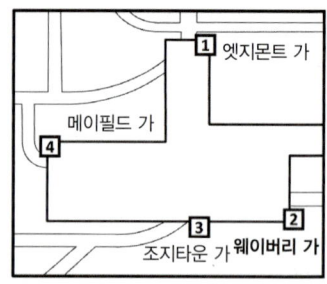

Q 시각 정보에 따르면, 여자는 어느 출구로 가겠는가?
(A) 1번 출구 **(B) 2번 출구**
(C) 3번 출구 (D) 4번 출구

해설 **세부 내용 - 시각 정보**
시각 정보가 지도임을 먼저 파악한다. 남자가 웨이버리 가 출구는 열려 있고 엘리베이터가 있다(the Waverly Street exit is open, and it also has an elevator)고 설명하자 여자는 거기로 가겠다(I'll go there)고 대답했다. 지도를 보면 웨이버리 가 출구는 2번 출구이므로 정답은 (B)이다.

[3] **대화 + 배치도 M-Au / W-Br**

M Hello, I'd like to register for this year's garden show.
W We have four types of vendor booths. I suggest one of the "Elite" locations.
M I will take one of the spots directly across from the food court. I'm guessing there'll be a lot of foot traffic there. Do I need to pay now?
W Just a deposit.

남 안녕하세요, 올해 정원 전시회에 등록하고 싶은데요.
여 네 가지 종류의 판매용 부스가 있습니다. "엘리트" 구역 중 한 곳을 추천합니다.
남 식당가 바로 맞은편에 있는 자리 중 하나로 할게요. 제 생각에 그쪽에 유동 인구가 많을 것 같아요. 지금 돈을 내야 하나요?
여 보증금만요.

어휘 register for ~에 등록하다 garden show 정원 전시회 vendor 판매상, 판매회사 spot 자리 directly 바로 across from ~의 맞은편에 food court 식당가, 푸드코트 foot traffic 유동 인구 deposit 보증금

Q 시각 정보에 따르면, 남자는 어떤 종류의 부스를 예약하는가?
(A) 엘리트   (B) 골드
(C) 브론즈   (D) 실버

해설 **세부 내용 - 시각 정보**
시각 정보가 배치도임을 먼저 파악한다. 남자가 두 번째 대사에서 식당가 바로 맞은편에 있는 자리 중 하나를 선택하겠다(I will take one of the spots directly across from the food court)고 했다. 배치도에서 식당가 맞은편 부스는 Gold이므로 정답은 (B)이다.

ETS 실전 문제   본책 p.098

1 (D) 2 (A) 3 (B) 4 (B) 5 (A) 6 (D)
7 (B) 8 (A) 9 (C) 10 (A) 11 (B) 12 (C)

[1-3] **대화 + 일정표 W-Br / M-Cn**

W ¹I've had such a busy morning. The ads we've been running on social media have really worked to bring in more customers. We've had three more small-business loan applications this morning.
M I'm busy with several car-loan applications myself. ²It's a good thing the bank will be hiring a new loan officer to help us with the workload. Speaking of—here's the interview schedule I made for us.
W These times look good. Oh, ³except Tuesday afternoon. I'm leaving the office early that day to pick up a friend at the airport.
M That's fine. ³I can do that one on my own.

여 ¹정말 바쁜 오전이었어요. 소셜 미디어에서 진행한 광고가 더 많은 고객을 유치하는 데 정말 효과가 있었어요. 오늘 오전에 소규모 사업 대출 신청이 세 건 더 있었어요.
남 저도 여러 자동차 대출 신청 때문에 바쁘네요. ²은행에서 업무량을 감당하는 걸 도와줄 새로운 대출 담당자를 채용한다니 다행이에요. 말이 나온 김에 여기 제가 만든 면접 시간표예요.
여 이 시간들은 괜찮아 보이네요. 아, ³화요일 오후는 빼고요. 공항에 친구를 마중 나가야 해서 그날 일찍 퇴근할 예정이에요.
남 괜찮아요. ³그 건은 저 혼자서 할 수 있어요.

어휘 run 진행하다 bring in 유치하다 loan 대출 application 신청 workload 업무량 on one's own 혼자서

면접 일정

지원자	면접 시간
오가와 씨	월요일 오전 10시
³이 씨	화요일 오후 2시
제브린 씨	목요일 오전 11시
알바레즈 씨	금요일 오후 3시

1 왜 화자들의 사업이 최근에 바쁜가?
(A) 새 지점이 문을 열었다.
(B) 새 제품이 출시되었다.
(C) 일부 가격이 인하되었다.
(D) 광고 캠페인이 성공적이었다.

해설 **세부 내용 - 사업이 바쁜 이유**
첫 대사에서 여자가 정말 바쁜 오전이었다며 소셜 미디어에서 진행한 광고가 더 많은 고객을 유치하는 데 정말 효과가 있었다(I've had such a busy morning. The ads

we've been running on social media have really worked to bring in more customers)고 한 것으로 보아 광고 효과로 고객이 많아져 바빠졌다는 것을 알 수 있다. 따라서 정답은 (D)이다.

어휘 branch 지점 launch 출시하다 reduce 인하다, 줄이다

> Paraphrasing 대화의 have really worked to bring in more customers → 보기의 has been successful

2 화자들은 어디에서 근무하는가?
(A) 은행   (B) 공항
(C) 자동차 대리점   (D) 소프트웨어 회사

해설 전체 내용 - 화자들의 근무 장소
화자들이 대출 신청 건으로 바쁘다고 했고, 은행에서 업무량을 감당하는 걸 도와줄 새로운 대출 담당자를 채용해서 다행 (It's a good thing the bank will be hiring a new loan officer to help us with the workload)이라는 남자의 대사를 통해 화자들은 은행 직원이라는 것을 알 수 있다. 따라서 정답은 (A)이다.

3 시각 정보에 따르면, 남자는 어느 지원자를 혼자서 면접할 것인가?
(A) 오가와 씨   (B) 이 씨
(C) 제브린 씨   (D) 알바레즈 씨

해설 세부 내용 - 시각 정보
대화 후반부에 여자가 화요일 오후에는 공항에 친구를 마중 나가야 해서 일찍 퇴근할 예정(except Tuesday afternoon. I'm leaving the office early that day to pick up a friend at the airport)이라고 했고, 남자가 그 건은 자기 혼자서 할 수 있다(I can do that one on my own)고 했다. 그리고 면접 일정표를 보면 화요일에 면접을 볼 지원자는 이 씨이므로 정답은 (B)이다.

[4-6] 대화 + 지도 M-Cn / W-Am

M Good afternoon. How can I help you?
W Hi. ⁴I'm in town for a business conference and was hoping to visit the museum tomorrow afternoon. I read online that some renovations are being done, so I was wondering whether you're open.
M Yes, we are. ⁵We're completely redoing our Local Artists Showcase, so it's temporarily closed. But all the other exhibits are open.
W Oh, that's great!
M And just so you know, ⁶we're offering a twenty percent discount on admission while the work is being done.
남 안녕하세요. 무엇을 도와드릴까요?
여 안녕하세요. ⁴저는 비즈니스 컨퍼런스 때문에 이곳에 왔는데 내일 오후에 미술관을 방문하고 싶어요. 온라인에서 보수 공사가 진행 중이라는 글을 읽었는데, 운영 중인지 알고 싶습니다.
남 네, 운영합니다. ⁵저희는 지역 예술가 전시를 완전히 새 단장 중이라 그곳은 임시 휴장입니다. 하지만 다른 전시는 모두 관람 가능합니다.
여 오, 다행이네요!
남 그리고 참고로, ⁶공사가 진행되는 동안 입장료를 20퍼센트 할인해드리고 있습니다.

어휘 renovation 보수, 개조 wonder 궁금해하다
completely 완전히 redo 새로 하다, 다시하다
temporarily 일시적으로 exhibit 전시 admission 입장(료) sculpture 조각 permanent 상설의, 영구적인

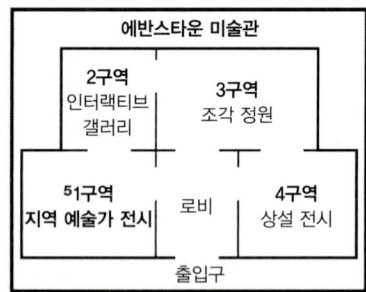

4 여자는 왜 이 도시에 있는가?
(A) 친구를 방문하려고   (B) 컨퍼런스에 참석하려고
(C) 면접을 보려고   (D) 검사를 수행하려고

해설 세부 내용 - 여자의 도시 방문 이유
여자가 첫 대사에서 비즈니스 컨퍼런스 때문에 이곳에 왔다(I'm in town for a business conference)고 밝혔으므로 정답은 (B)이다.

어휘 attend 참석하다 conduct (특정 활동을) 수행하다
inspection 검사

5 시각 정보에 따르면, 박물관의 어느 구역이 폐쇄되었는가?
(A) 1구역   (B) 2구역
(C) 3구역   (D) 4구역

해설 세부 내용 - 시각 정보
대화 중반에 남자가 미술관에서 지역 예술가 전시를 완전히 새 단장 중이라 그곳은 임시 휴장(We're completely redoing our Local Artists Showcase, so it's temporarily closed)이라고 했다. 그리고 지도를 보면 지역 예술가 전시는 1구역이므로 정답은 (A)이다.

6 남자는 무엇이 제공되고 있다고 말하는가?
(A) 매시간마다 진행되는 투어
(B) 무료 주차
(C) 카탈로그
(D) 할인

해설 세부 내용 - 남자가 말하는 제공 서비스
마지막 대사에서 남자가 공사가 진행되는 동안 입장료를 20퍼센트 할인해 주고 있다(we're offering a twenty

percent discount on admission while the work is being done)고 했으므로 정답은 (D)이다.

[7-9] 대화 + 면접 일정표 W-Am / M-Cn

W You've reached Winning Web Designs, Incorporated. How can I help you?
M Hi. My name's Lorenzo Ross. **7 I have an upcoming interview scheduled for the data analyst position.**
W Hi, Lorenzo. Let me check our calendar for that information. Yes, your interview's on April fifteenth at nine A.M.
M **8 Sorry, but I do need to change that. I have a conflicting appointment with a dentist.**
W Well, looking at the calendar, we still have some time slots on April thirteenth, fourteenth, and fifteenth.
M **9 Any time in the afternoon on April fourteenth would work for me.**

여 위닝 웹디자인 사로 전화 주셨습니다. 무엇을 도와드릴까요?
남 안녕하세요. 제 이름은 로렌조 로스입니다. **7 저는 데이터 분석가 자리에 곧 면접이 잡혀 있습니다.**
여 안녕하세요, 로렌조 씨. 정보 확인을 위해 일정표를 확인해 보겠습니다. 네, 4월 15일 오전 9시에 면접이 있으시네요.
남 **8 죄송하지만 제가 일정을 변경해야 해요. 치과 진료 예약과 일정이 겹쳐서요.**
여 음, 일정표를 보니 4월 13일, 14일, 15일에 아직 시간대가 남아 있네요.
남 **9 4월 14일 오후 아무 때나 괜찮아요.**

어휘 upcoming 곧 있을 position 일자리, 직책 calendar 일정표 conflicting 겹치는 time slot 시간대

	4/13	**9 4/14**	4/15
오전 9시	시간 1	시간 2	로렌조 로스
오전 10시	이페 조	카비 구	일리야 아슬란
9 오후 2시	비벡 라지	**9 시간 3**	시간 4

7 남자는 어느 직책에 지원하는가?
(A) 주방장   (B) 데이터 분석가
(C) 인사 관리자   (D) 웹사이트 디자이너

해설 세부 내용 – 남자가 지원하는 직책
대화 초반부에 남자가 데이터 분석가 자리에 곧 면접이 잡혀 있다(I have an upcoming interview scheduled for the data analyst position)고 했으므로 정답은 (B)이다.

8 남자는 왜 면접 일정을 다시 잡아야 하는가?
(A) 치과 예약이 있다.   (B) 차를 수리해야 한다.
(C) 프로젝트 마감일이 있다. (D) 휴가를 갈 예정이다.

해설 세부 내용 – 남자가 면접 일정을 다시 잡아야 하는 이유
대화 중반부에서 남자가 일정을 변경해야 한다(Sorry, but I do need to change that)면서 치과 진료 예약과 일정이 겹친다(I have a conflicting appointment with a dentist)고 이유를 말하고 있으므로 정답은 (A)이다.

9 시각 정보에 따르면, 남자는 어느 시간대를 선택할 것 같은가?
(A) 시간 1   (B) 시간 2
(C) 시간 3   (D) 시간 4

해설 세부 내용 – 시각 정보
마지막 대사에서 남자가 4월 14일 오후 아무 때나 괜찮다(Any time in the afternoon on April fourteenth would work for me)고 했고, 표를 보면 4월 14일 오후 2시에 시간 3이 있으므로 정답은 (C)이다.

[10-12] 대화 + 옵션 목록 W-Br / M-Cn

W Joshua, come look at this. **10 I found the cause of the water leak.** It looks like yesterday's cold weather froze the water in the pipe under the kitchen sink, and it burst.
M Hmm. **10 Sounds like we'll have to replace the entire pipe for this customer.** What type of pipe is it?
W Hold on, **11 I need to turn on the flashlight on my mobile phone to get a better look.** OK. This is a type M pipe. I don't think we have that one in the truck.
M But **12 isn't there a home-improvement store nearby? We could go there and buy one.**

여 조슈아, 이것 좀 와서 봐요. **10 물이 새는 원인을 찾았어요.** 어제 추운 날씨에 주방 싱크대 밑 파이프에 있던 물이 얼어서 터진 것 같아요.
남 음. **10 이 고객을 위해 전체 파이프를 교체해야 할 것 같군요.** 어떤 종류의 파이프인가요?
여 잠시만요. **11 휴대폰 손전등을 켜야 더 잘 보일 것 같아요.** 됐어요. M 타입 파이프예요. 우리 트럭에는 없는 것 같은데요.
남 그런데 **12 근처에 집수리 용품점이 있지 않나요? 거기 가서 하나 사면 될 것 같은데요.**

어휘 leak 샘, 누출 freeze 얼리다; 얼다 burst 터지다 replace 교체하다 entire 전체의 flashlight 손전등 home-improvement store 집수리 용품점, 철물점

10 화자들은 누구일 것 같은가?
(A) 배관공 (B) 전기 기사
(C) 일기 예보관 (D) 컴퓨터 기술자

해설 **전체 내용 – 화자의 직업**
여자는 첫 대사에서 물이 새는 원인을 찾았다(I found the cause of the water leak)고 했고, 남자는 고객을 위해 전체 파이프를 교체해야 할 것 같다(Sounds like we'll have to replace the entire pipe for this customer)고 한 것으로 보아 정답은 (A)이다.

11 시각 정보에 따르면, 여자는 어떤 휴대전화 옵션을 사용했는가?
(A) 옵션 1 (B) 옵션 2
(C) 옵션 3 (D) 옵션 4

해설 **세부 내용 – 시각 정보**
여자가 두 번째 대사에서 휴대폰 손전등을 켜야 더 잘 보일 것 같다(I need to turn on the flashlight on my mobile phone to get a better look)고 했고, 표를 보면 손전등은 옵션 2로 표시되어 있으므로 정답은 (B)이다.

12 남자는 무엇을 하는 것을 제안하는가?
(A) 사진 촬영 (B) 일정 확인
(C) 상점 방문 (D) 소프트웨어 업데이트

해설 **세부 내용 – 남자의 제안 사항**
남자가 마지막 대사에서 근처에 집수리 용품점이 있지 않는지(isn't there a home-improvement store nearby?) 물으면서, 가서 파이프를 사자(We could go there and buy one)고 했으므로 정답은 (C)이다.

PART 4
LISTENING COMPREHENSION

UNIT 14 전화 메시지

ETS 기출 예제
본책 p.108

안녕하세요, 클라크 씨. **1** 저는 워튼 기차역 분실물 관리소의 로저입니다. **2** 승객 한 분이 오늘 아침 귀하의 지갑을 습득해서 저희에게 주셨습니다. 지갑을 찾으러 오실 때, **3** 안내원에게 조회 번호를 제시하셔야 합니다. 5492번입니다. 역에 오실 때 이 번호를 꼭 기억하세요. 이 정보를 제시하지 않으면 지갑을 돌려드릴 수 없습니다.

어휘 lost property 분실물 wallet 지갑 retrieve 되찾다 attendant 안내원 reference 조회 present 제시하다

ETS 유형 연습
본책 p.109

1 (A) **2** (B) **3** (A) **4** (B) **5** (B) **6** (B)

[1-2] 전화 메시지 W-Br

1 I'm calling with an update on our regional office in Medford. As you know, we need to have a **new air-conditioning system** installed for the building. I received bids from three companies, and luckily, they're all within our budget. But **2** I think we should give the contract to the Classion Company. They've been in business for over twenty years and have done several installations in commercial properties like ours.

1 메드포드 지사에 대한 최신 정보를 드리고자 전화했습니다. 아시다시피, 건물에 새로운 냉방 시스템을 설치해야 합니다. 회사 세 곳으로부터 입찰을 받았고, 다행히 모두 예산 내에 있습니다. 하지만 **2** 클래션 사에 계약을 줘야 할 것 같습니다. 이 회사는 20년 넘게 사업을 해왔고 우리와 같은 상업용 부동산에 여러 번 설치를 해왔습니다.

어휘 regional office 지사 install 설치하다 bid 입찰 installation 설치 commercial 상업의 property 부동산

1 메드포드 지사에서 어떤 종류의 작업이 이루어질 것인가?
(A) 냉방 시스템이 설치될 예정이다.
(B) 지붕이 수리될 예정이다.

해설 **세부 내용 – 메드포드 사무실에 이루어질 작업**
지문 초반부에서 메드포드 지사에 대한 최신 정보를 공유하기 위해 전화했고(I'm calling with an update on our regional office in Medford) 건물에 새로운 냉방 시스템을 설치해야 한다(we need to have a new air-

conditioning system installed for the building)고 했으므로 정답은 (A)이다.

어휘 take place 일어나다   repair 수리하다

2   화자는 왜 클래션 사를 고용하기를 선호하는가?
    (A) 합리적인 가격을 청구한다.
    (B) 경험이 풍부하다.

해설 **세부 내용 – 클래션 사 고용을 선호하는 이유**
클래션 사에 계약을 줘야 할 것 같다(I think we should give the contract to the Classion Company)며, 이 회사는 20년 넘게 사업을 해왔고 상업용 부동산에 여러 번 설치를 해왔다(They've been in business for over twenty years and have done several installations in commercial properties like ours)고 한 것으로 보아 풍부한 경험 때문에 선호하는 것을 알 수 있다. 따라서 정답은 (B)이다.

어휘 charge 청구하다   reasonable 합리적인

[3-4] **전화 메시지 + 평면도 W-Am**

I'm calling because one of the apartment units has a leaky faucet. ³Could you come fix it later this afternoon or tomorrow morning? ⁴It's the one the Garcia family lives in... you know... the corner apartment on the third floor, right next to the stairwell? Their phone number is 555-0148. Please call them directly to arrange a time to make the repair.

아파트 중 한 가구에 수도꼭지가 새서 전화드려요. ³이따 오늘 오후에나 내일 오전에 와서 고쳐 주시겠어요? ⁴가르시아 가족이 사는 곳인데… 그러니까… 계단통 바로 옆 3층 모퉁이 아파트 아시죠? 전화번호는 555-0148이에요. 직접 전화해서 수리 시간을 잡아 주세요.

어휘 leaky 새는   faucet 수도꼭지   fix 수리하다
stairwell 계단통   directly 직접   arrange (미리) 정하다

3   누구를 위한 메시지인 것 같은가?
    (A) 수리공   (B) 부동산 중개업자

해설 **전체 내용 – 메시지의 대상**
지문 초반부에서 수도꼭지가 샌다며 오늘 오후나 내일 오전에 와서 고쳐 주겠는지(Could you come fix it later this afternoon or tomorrow morning?) 묻는 것으로 보아 청자는 수리공임을 알 수 있다. 따라서 정답은 (A)이다.

어휘 real estate 부동산

4   시각 정보에 따르면, 가르시아 가족은 어느 아파트에 사는가?
    (A) 3-A   **(B) 3-B**

해설 **세부 내용 – 시각 정보**
질문의 키워드인 Garcia family에 주목한다. 지문에서 계단통 바로 옆에 있는 3층 모퉁이 아파트(the corner apartment on the third floor, right next to the stairwell)라고 했는데, 시각 정보에서 모퉁이 아파트 중 계단통 바로 옆은 3-B이므로 정답은 (B)이다.

[5-6] **전화 메시지 M-Cn**

Hi, Ivan. I have some bad news. ⁵We had to change the location of the awards dinner next Friday night. Unfortunately, ⁶some water pipes burst in the kitchen at the Millson Conference Center, and the repair work will take over a week to complete. I was able to book a new venue across town at Tulip Hall. It's farther away, but it's our only option.

안녕하세요, 이반. 나쁜 소식이 있어요. ⁵다음 주 금요일 밤에 열릴 시상식 만찬 장소를 바꿔야 했어요. 안타깝게도, ⁶밀슨 컨퍼런스 센터의 주방 수도관이 터져서 수리 작업이 끝나는 데 일주일 이상이 걸릴 거예요. 도시 반대편에 있는 튤립 홀에서 새 행사장을 예약할 수 있었어요. 더 멀지만 그곳이 우리의 유일한 선택지예요.

어휘 awards dinner 시상식 만찬   unfortunately 안타깝게도   water pipe 수도관   burst 터지다   repair 수리   complete 완료하다   book 예약하다   venue 행사장   farther 더 멀리

5   화자는 왜 전화를 하고 있는가?
    (A) 메뉴를 확정하려고
    (B) 행사 장소 변경을 알리려고

해설 **전체 내용 – 전화의 목적**
화자는 다음 주 금요일 밤에 열릴 시상식 만찬 장소를 바꿔야 했다(We had to change the location of the awards dinner next Friday night)며 행사 장소 변경을 알리고 있으므로 정답은 (B)이다.

어휘 finalize 확정하다   announce 알리다

Paraphrasing   지문의 location → 보기의 venue

6   화자는 밀슨 컨퍼런스 센터에 대해 무엇을 말하는가?
    (A) 수상했다.
    (B) 수리가 진행 중이다.

해설 **세부 내용 – 밀슨 컨퍼런스 센터에 관해 언급한 것**
밀슨 컨퍼런스 센터의 주방 수도관이 터져서 수리 작업이 끝나는 데 일주일 이상이 걸릴 것(some water pipes burst in the kitchen at the Millson Conference Center, and the repair work will take over a week to complete)이라고 언급하고 있으므로 정답은 (B)이다.

어휘 receive 받다   undergo 겪다

ETS 실전 문제
본책 p.110

1 (B) 2 (D) 3 (C) 4 (C) 5 (B) 6 (A)
7 (D) 8 (B) 9 (A) 10 (B) 11 (C) 12 (D)
13 (A) 14 (B) 15 (D) 16 (D) 17 (B) 18 (A)
19 (B) 20 (D) 21 (A)

[1-3] 전화 메시지 W-Am

Good afternoon, Mr. Popova. **1 I'm calling regarding your request to have your electricity service transferred.** To confirm the information you provided— **2 you are moving out of your current address on October fifteenth and have provided 381 Deacon Street as your new address.** At this time, **3 you're enrolled in paperless billing, and your account is set to automatic bill pay.** If you wish these settings to apply to your new home, no further action is required. **3 If you wish to make changes, contact me at 555-0109.**

안녕하세요, 포포바 씨. **1** 전기 서비스를 이전해달라고 하신 요청 건으로 전화 드렸습니다. 제공하신 정보를 확인하자면, **2** 10월 15일에 현재 주소에서 이사하시고 새 주소로 디콘 가 381번지를 알려주셨습니다. 현재 **3** 고객님께서는 종이 없는 청구서에 등록해 계시고 계정은 자동 납부로 설정되어 있습니다. 이러한 설정을 새 주소지에 적용하시려면 추가 조치가 필요하지는 않습니다. **3** 변경을 원하시면 555-0109로 연락 주십시오.

어휘 transfer 이전하다, 옮기다 confirm 확인하다 current 현재의 enroll in ~에 등록하다 paperless 종이를 쓰지 않는 billing 청구서 발부 apply 적용하다 further 추가의

1 화자는 어디에서 일하는 것 같은가?
(A) 인터넷 서비스 공급업체 (B) 전기 회사
(C) 신문사 (D) 은행

해설 전체 내용 - 근무 장소
화자는 전기 서비스 이전을 요청한 건으로 전화를 했다(I'm calling regarding your request to have your electricity service transferred)고 했으므로 전기 서비스 업체 직원임을 알 수 있다. 따라서 정답은 (B)이다.

어휘 provider 공급업체

2 청자는 10월 15일에 무엇을 할 것인가?
(A) 새 직장 시작 (B) 휴가 떠나기
(C) 구독 취소 (D) 새로운 위치로 이사

해설 세부 내용 - 청자가 할 일
청자가 10월 15일에 현재 주소에서 이사하고 새 주소로 디콘 가 381번지를 알려줬다(you are moving out of your current address on October fifteenth and have provided 381 Deacon Street as your new address)고 했으므로 정답은 (D)이다.

어휘 vacation 휴가 subscription 구독

Paraphrasing 지문의 moving out of your current address → 보기의 Move to a new location

3 청자는 왜 전화번호로 전화를 걸겠는가?
(A) 인쇄된 일정표를 요청하려고
(B) 서비스에 대한 피드백을 제공하려고
(C) 계정에 변화를 주려고
(D) 추가 정보를 요청하려고

해설 세부 내용 - 청자가 전화를 걸 이유
현재 고객이 종이 없는 청구서에 등록해 있고 계정은 자동 납부로 설정되어 있다(you're enrolled in paperless billing, and your account is set to automatic bill pay)고 했고, 마지막 문장에서 변경을 원하면 555-0109로 연락하라(If you wish to make changes, contact me at 555-0109)고 했다. 따라서 계정 설정을 변경하려는 경우에 주어진 전화번호로 전화를 할 것이므로 정답은 (C)이다.

어휘 additional 추가의

[4-6] 전화 메시지 W-Br

Hello, I'm calling from Seattle Shuttle Services. This message is for Jackson Bailey. Mr. Bailey, **4,5 I'm calling to confirm your reservation for a one-way shuttle bus for three people today at four-fifteen P.M., from Jackson Telecommunications to the international terminal at Seattle Airport. 6 The total charge for this service is 65 dollars, and we do ask that you pay the bus driver when you board the shuttle.** Thanks, and we'll see you at four-fifteen.

안녕하세요. 시애틀 셔틀 서비스입니다. 잭슨 베일리 씨께 드리는 메시지입니다. 베일리 씨, **4,5** 오늘 오후 4시 15분에 잭슨 통신에서 시애틀 공항 국제선 터미널까지 가는 편도 셔틀버스를 세 분 예약하신 걸 확인하려 전화 드립니다. **6** 이 서비스의 총 요금은 65달러인데, 셔틀버스에 탑승할 때 버스 기사에게 지불해 주실 것을 요청합니다. 고맙습니다. 그럼 4시 15분에 뵐게요.

어휘 reservation 예약 charge 요금 board 타다

4 여자는 왜 전화를 하고 있는가?
(A) 항공편 예약 일정을 조정하려고
(B) 고객에게 지연을 통보하려고
(C) 교통편 상세 사항을 확인하려고
(D) 운전 길 안내를 제공하려고

해설 전체 내용 - 전화의 목적
오후 4시 15분에 잭슨 통신에서 시애틀 공항 터미널까지 가는 셔틀버스를 예약한 것을 확인하려 전화한다(I'm calling to confirm your reservation for a one-way shuttle bus for three people today at four-fifteen

P.M., from Jackson Telecommunications to the international terminal at Seattle Airport)고 하므로 정답은 (C)이다.

어휘 notify 통보하다 transportation 교통(편)

5 셔틀버스는 몇 시에 잭슨 통신에 도착할 것인가?
(A) 오후 3시 15분 **(B) 오후 4시 15분**
(C) 오후 5시 15분 (D) 오후 6시 15분

해설 세부 내용 – 셔틀 버스가 도착하는 시간
질문의 키워드인 Jackson Telecommunications에 초점을 맞춰 메시지를 듣는다. 오늘 오후 4시 15분에 잭슨 통신에서 시애틀 공항 터미널까지 가는 셔틀버스를 예약한 것을 확인하려 전화한다(I'm calling to confirm your reservation for a one-way shuttle bus for three people today at four-fifteen P.M., from Jackson Telecommunications to the international terminal at Seattle Airport)고 하므로 정답은 (B)이다.

6 청자는 무엇을 요청받는가?
(A) 기사에게 지불하기
(B) 신분증을 제시할 준비하기
(C) 체크인을 위한 시간 여유 두기
(D) 승객 수 확인하기

해설 세부 내용 – 청자에 대한 요청 사항
셔틀버스에 탑승할 때 버스 기사에게 서비스 비용을 지불해달라(The total charge for this service is 65 dollars, and we do ask that you pay the bus driver when you board the shuttle)고 요청하므로 정답은 (A)이다.

어휘 identification 신분증 passenger 승객

> **Paraphrasing** 지문의 pay the bus driver
> → 보기의 Give payment to the driver

[7-9] 전화 메시지 M-Au

7 I'm calling from Casella Bag Company. We really enjoy your videos about products and tips for frequent air travelers. I'm calling to ask whether you'd be interested in reviewing our newest travel bags and accessories on your channel. We make a line of carry-on luggage that sells well in some markets, but we're a new company. **8 It's challenging to reach a wide audience**, and, well, your videos are very popular. In addition to sending a free set for you to review, we'd also like to provide a second set. **9 We think you could give it out as a prize to one of your lucky viewers.**

7 카셀라 가방 회사에서 전화 드립니다. 저희는 자주 비행하는 여행객들을 위한 제품 및 조언에 관한 귀하의 영상이 정말 좋아요. 귀하 채널에서 저희의 최신 여행 가방과 액세서리를 리뷰하는 것에 관심이 있는지 여쭤보려고 전화 드립니다. 일부 마켓에서 잘 팔리는 기내용 가방 라인을 제작하고 있지만, 저희는 신생 회사입니다. 8 넓은 고객층에 접근하는 것이 힘든데, 음, 귀하의 영상이 인기가 아주 좋잖아요. 리뷰할 수 있도록 무료 세트를 하나 보내드리는 것 외에, 두 번째 세트도 제공해드리려고 해요. 9 이것을 행운의 시청자 중 한 분께 경품으로 나눠 주시면 좋을 것 같습니다.

어휘 tip 조언 frequent 잦은, 빈번한 carry-on (luggage) 기내용 가방 challenging 힘든 audience 관객 give out 나눠 주다 prize 경품

7 화자의 회사에서 무엇을 판매하는가?
(A) 조리기구 (B) 의류
(C) 보석 **(D) 여행 가방**

해설 전체 내용 – 회사의 판매 제품
첫 문장에서 카셀라 가방 회사(I'm calling from Casella Bag Company)라고 화자의 회사가 언급되었으므로 정답은 (D)이다.

8 화자가 "귀하의 영상이 인기가 아주 좋잖아요"라고 말할 때, 무엇을 의미하는가?
(A) 청자는 여행을 계속해야 할 것이다.
(B) 청자는 많은 사람들에게 다가갈 수 있다.
(C) 청자는 일부 장비를 업그레이드해야 한다.
(D) 청자는 연예 에이전트와 이야기해야 한다.

해설 세부 내용 – 의도 파악
앞서 넓은 고객층에 접근하는 것이 힘들다(It's challenging to reach a wide audience)고 말한 뒤, "귀하의 영상이 인기가 아주 좋잖아요"라고 말한 것은 청자의 동영상은 시청자가 많으니 많은 사람들에게 쉽게 다가갈 수 있다는 의미이다. 따라서 정답은 (B)이다.

어휘 equipment 장비

9 화자는 무엇을 하라고 권하는가?
(A) 경품 나눠 주기 (B) 시설 둘러보기
(C) 상담가와 만나기 (D) 시연을 시청하기

해설 세부 내용 – 화자의 권고 사항
두 번째 가방 세트를 시청자 중 한 사람에게 경품으로 주면 좋을 것 같다(We think you could give it out as a prize to one of your lucky viewers)고 했으므로 정답은 (A)이다.

어휘 facility 시설 demonstration 시연

[10-12] 전화 메시지 M-Cn

Hello. **10 This is Jim from Thompsonville Garage** with a message for Gloria Blanton. The reason the seat belt in your car won't tighten properly is because the mechanism that retracts it is broken. **11 That part can't be fixed, so I have to replace it.** It's going to cost two hundred dollars for the replacement part and one hundred dollars for labor. **12 I'll need you to approve this charge before I start fixing the car, so please call me back as soon as you can.** Thank you.

안녕하세요. **10**전 톰슨빌 정비소 짐인데 글로리아 블랜턴 씨에게 전할 말이 있어요. 차의 안전벨트가 제대로 조이지 않는 이유는 오므리는 기계 장치가 고장 났기 때문이에요. **11**그 부품은 고칠 수 없으니 교체해야 합니다. 교체 부품은 200달러, 인건비는 100달러입니다. **12**제가 차를 수리하기 전에 이 요금을 승인해 주셔야 하니 가능한 한 빨리 전화 주세요. 감사합니다.

어휘 garage 정비소 seat belt 안전벨트 tighten 조이다 properly 제대로 retract 오므리다, 집어넣다 replace 교체하다 labor 일, 노동 approve 승인하다

10 화자는 누구인 것 같은가?
 (A) 전기 기사   **(B) 자동차 정비사**
 (C) 목수   (D) 전화 수리공

해설 전체 내용 – 화자의 신분
대개 인물을 소개할 때는 '이름＋직업[신분]', '직업[신분]＋이름', 또는 '이름＋from＋소속 회사[부서]'로 언급한다. 여기서는 '이름＋from＋소속 회사[부서]'의 형식(Jim from Thompsonville Garage)으로 화자의 신분을 밝히고 있으므로 정답은 (B)이다.

어휘 mechanic 정비사 carpenter 목수

11 화자는 무엇을 해야 한다고 하는가?
 (A) 다른 점포에 연락   (B) 보증금 받기
 (C) 고장 난 부품 교체 (D) 동료와 상의

해설 세부 내용 – 해야 할 일
기계 장치 하나가 고장났다며 그 부품을 수리할 수 없어서 교체해야 한다(That part can't be fixed, so I have to replace it)고 밝히고 있으므로 정답은 (C)이다.

어휘 deposit 보증금

12 청자는 왜 다시 전화해야 하는가?
 (A) 약속을 잡으려고
 (B) 배송 시간을 확인하려고
 (C) 부서장과 이야기하려고
 (D) 요금을 승인하려고

해설 세부 내용 – 다시 전화해야 하는 이유
화자가 차를 수리하기 전에 요금 승인을 받아야 하니 전화해 달라(I'll need you to approve this charge before I start fixing the car, so please call me back as soon as you can)고 요청하고 있으므로 정답은 (D)이다.

어휘 appointment 약속 authorize 승인하다

Paraphrasing 지문의 approve this charge
→ 보기의 authorize a charge

[13-15] 전화 메시지 W-Am

Hello, Mr. Klein. **13 I'm returning your call.** I'm sorry to hear that your driver did not arrive at the scheduled time. **14 She should have called you when she was stuck in traffic due to road construction.** We would appreciate it if you could go to our Web site and log an incident report. That way, **15 I'll be able to generate an e-card for a complimentary ride good for one year.** We hope you will continue to ride with us.

안녕하세요. 클라인 씨. **13**회신 전화 드립니다. 운전기사가 예정된 시간에 도착하지 못했다니 유감입니다. **14**기사가 도로 공사 때문에 교통체증에 갇혔을 때 고객님께 전화를 드렸어야 합니다. 웹사이트로 방문하셔서 사고 보고서를 작성해 주시면 감사하겠습니다. 그렇게 하시면, **15**1년 동안 유효한 무료 승차용 전자카드를 만들어 드릴 수 있습니다. 저희 승차 서비스를 계속 이용해 주시기를 바랍니다.

어휘 stuck 갇힌 construction 공사 appreciate 고마워하다 log 일지에 작성하다 incident 사고, 사건 generate 만들어 내다 complimentary 무료의 ride 승차 good 유효한

13 화자는 왜 전화를 하고 있는가?
 (A) 불만 사항에 대응하려고
 (B) 취업 제안을 거절하려고
 (C) 서비스 이용 가능성을 확인하려고
 (D) 예약을 변경하려고

해설 전체 내용 – 전화의 목적
지문 초반부에서 화자가 회신 전화를 한다(I'm returning your call)고 했고, 운전기사가 예정된 시간에 도착하지 못했다니 유감(I'm sorry to hear that your driver did not arrive at the scheduled time)이라고 한 것으로 보아 고객이 전화하여 제기한 불만 사항에 대해 회신 전화를 걸어 대응하고 있다는 것을 알 수 있다. 따라서 정답은 (A)이다.

어휘 respond to ~에 대응하다 complaint 불평 decline 거절하다 availability 이용 가능성 reservation 예약

14 화자는 어떤 문제를 언급하는가?
 (A) 운전기사가 잘못된 주소로 갔다.
 (B) 운전기사가 도로 공사로 인해 늦었다.
 (C) 양식이 정확하게 작성되지 않았다.
 (D) 양식이 제때 제출되지 않았다.

해설 세부 내용 – 문제점
기사가 도로 공사 때문에 교통체증에 갇혔을 때 고객에게 전화를 했어야 한다(She should have called you when she was stuck in traffic due to road construction)며 기사가 도로 공사로 인해 늦어진 문제에 대해 언급하고 있으므로 정답은 (B)이다.

어휘 roadwork 도로 공사 fill out 작성하다 accurately 정확히 submit 제출하다 on time 제때, 정시에

Paraphrasing 지문의 stuck in traffic due to road construction → 보기의 delayed by roadwork

15 청자는 무엇을 받을 것인가?
(A) 수정된 계약서 (B) 회사 정책
(C) 할인된 티켓 (D) 무료 승차

해설 **세부 내용 – 청자가 받을 것**
화자는 1년 동안 유효한 무료 승차용 전자카드를 만들어 줄 수 있다(I'll be able to generate an e-card for a complimentary ride good for one year)고 하고 있으므로 정답은 (D)이다.

어휘 revised 수정된 contract 계약(서) policy 정책, 방침

[16-18] 전화 메시지 M-Au

Hi, it's Pierre. **16 I'm calling to let you know I'm going to be late for work.** I'm on the bus, but a construction crew just started to close off some lanes on the highway, so the traffic's very slow. I know what you're thinking... **17 Why did they decide to start the repairs now? It's rush hour.** Anyway, **18 I was supposed to give a presentation about market growth at this morning's staff meeting. Since I won't make it to the office in time, could you do it?** The notes are on my desk—they're fairly straightforward.

안녕하세요, 저 피에르예요. **16 회사에 늦는다고 알리려고 전화했어요.** 버스에 탔는데, 공사 인부들이 방금 일부 고속도로 차선을 차단하기 시작해서 차가 꽉 막혔어요. 무슨 생각하는지 알아요… **17 왜 지금 정비를 시작하기로 결정했을까요? 출퇴근 시간이잖아요.** 아무튼 **18 제가 오늘 오전 직원 회의에서 시장 성장에 대해 발표하기로 되어 있었어요. 제가 제시간에 사무실에 도착하지 못하니까, 당신이 해줄 수 있나요?** 메모들은 제 책상 위에 있어요. 꽤 간단합니다.

어휘 construction 공사 lane 차선 repair 정비 be supposed to ~하기로 되어 있다 growth 성장 make it in time 제시간에 도착하다 fairly 꽤 straightforward 간단한

16 화자는 누구에게 전화하고 있는 것 같은가?
(A) 가족 (B) 친구
(C) 고객 (D) 동료

해설 **전체 내용 – 청자의 신분**
화자가 회사에 늦는다고 알려 전화한다(I'm calling to let you know I'm going to be late for work)고 말하는 것으로 보아 청자는 화자의 직장 동료임을 알 수 있다. 따라서 정답은 (D)이다.

17 화자가 "출퇴근 시간이잖아요"라고 말할 때, 무엇을 암시하는가?
(A) 업무 일정이 바뀌었다.
(B) 공사 시간을 잘못 잡았다.
(C) 제안이 효과가 없을 것이다.
(D) 버스가 붐빈다.

해설 **세부 내용 – 화자의 의도**
지문 중반부에서 왜 지금 정비를 시작하기로 결정했는지(Why did they decide to start the repairs now?) 의문을 품은 다음, "출퇴근 시간이잖아요"라고 이어서 말한 것은 수리 공사를 하기에 안 좋은 시간대라는 의미이다. 따라서 정답은 (B)이다.

어휘 crowded 붐비는

18 화자는 청자에게 무엇을 요청하는가?
(A) 발표하기 (B) 약속 잡기
(C) 소포 부치기 (D) 선물 구입하기

해설 **세부 내용 – 화자의 요청 사항**
화자가 사무실에 제시간에 도착하지 못하니 오전 직원 회의에서 시장 성장에 대한 발표를 대신 해달라고 청자에게 요청(I was supposed to give a presentation about market growth at this morning's staff meeting. Since I won't make it to the office in time, could you do it?)하고 있으므로 정답은 (A)이다.

[19-21] 전화 메시지 + 메모 M-Cn

Hi, Tunji. **19 I just finished scouting some indoor and outdoor locations where we can shoot the new movie.** There are four locations that I recommend for filming. I'd like you and the director to take a closer look at them, so **20 I'll send you some photos of the locations this afternoon.** I'm sure you'll notice that **21 one of the locations is really far away from the studio—300 kilometers.** But it matches the aesthetics of the movie really well, so I think it's worth the cost to move all the equipment there.

안녕하세요, 툰지. **19 새 영화를 촬영할 수 있는 실내외 장소 발굴을 막 끝냈어요.** 촬영 장소로 제가 추천하는 곳이 네 군데 있어요. 당신과 감독님이 이 장소들을 더 자세히 봤으면 해서, **20 오늘 오후에 장소 사진을 몇 장 보낼게요. 21 이 장소들 중 한 곳은 스튜디오에서 아주 멀리 300km나 떨어져 있다는 점**을 알게 되실 텐데요. 그렇지만 이곳이 영화의 미학적 요소와 정말 잘 맞아서, 모든 장비를 거기로 옮기는 비용을 부담할 가치가 있다고 봅니다.

어휘 scout 발굴하다 shoot 촬영하다 filming 촬영 match (스타일 등이) 맞다 aesthetics 미학 worth ~의 가치가 있는 equipment 장비 residential 주거용의

장소
• ²¹스포츠 경기장, 300km 거리
• 실내 쇼핑몰, 15km 거리
• 시내 중심, 120km 거리
• 주거용 주택, 50km 거리

19 화자는 어떤 산업에서 일하는 것 같은가?
(A) 건축 (B) 영화
(C) 운송 (D) 부동산

해설 전체 내용 – 화자의 근무 업종
새 영화를 촬영할 수 있는 실내외 장소 발굴을 막 끝냈다(I just finished scouting some indoor and outdoor locations where we can shoot the new movie)고 한 것으로 보아 화자는 영화 촬영과 관련된 일을 하고 있다는 것을 알 수 있다. 따라서 정답은 (B)이다.

어휘 architecture 건축 shipping 운송 real estate 부동산

20 화자는 청자에게 무엇을 보낼 것인가?
(A) 평면도 (B) 일정표
(C) 영수증 (D) 사진

해설 세부 내용 – 화자가 보낼 것
오늘 오후에 장소 사진을 몇 장 보내겠다(I'll send you some photos of the locations this afternoon)고 했으므로 정답은 (D)이다.

어휘 floor plan 평면도 itinerary 일정표 receipt 영수증

21 시각 정보에 따르면, 화자는 어느 장소를 언급하는가?
(A) 스포츠 경기장 (B) 실내 쇼핑몰
(C) 시내 중심 (D) 주거용 주택

해설 세부 내용 – 시각 정보
촬영 장소 후보 중 한 곳은 스튜디오에서 300km나 떨어져 있다(one of the locations is really far away from the studio—300 kilometers)고 했다. 그리고 메모에서 300km 거리에는 스포츠 경기장이 있다고 나와 있으므로 정답은 (A)이다.

UNIT 15 공지 / 안내 / 회의

ETS 기출 예제   본책 p.112

¹비행기 승무원 교육 수료를 축하드립니다! 이제 첫 번째 업무 과제를 할 준비가 되셨습니다. ²여러분 모두 배정받고 싶은 공항 목록을 제출하셨는데요. 제가 여러분의 선호를 검토하여 이번 주까지 위치를 배정하겠습니다. 하지만 떠나기 전에 ³단체 사진을 찍을 테니, 방 앞쪽으로 나와 주세요. 사진은 회사 내부 웹사이트에 올리겠습니다.

어휘 flight attendant 비행기 승무원 assignment 과제 submit 제출하다 assign 배정하다 internal 내부의

ETS 유형 연습   본책 p.113

1 (A)   **2** (A)   **3** (A)   **4** (B)   **5** (A)   **6** (B)

[1-2] 공지 M-Cn

¹Our office building will be undergoing some repairs Saturday morning and, uh, the electricity will be off for about three hours. For any of you planning to come in on Saturday, power should be restored by one o'clock. ²I'll notify you by e-mail once the work's done.

¹저희 사무실 건물이 토요일 아침에 보수 공사를 할 예정이라, 음, 대략 3시간 동안 전기가 차단될 것입니다. 토요일에 출근할 직원들께 말씀드리자면 1시까지는 전기가 복구될 것입니다. ²작업이 완료되면 제가 이메일로 알려드리겠습니다.

어휘 office building 사무실 건물 undergo 겪다, 거치다 electricity 전기 be off 끊기다 power (공급되는) 전기 restore 복구하다 notify 알리다, 통지하다

1 화자는 어떤 문제점을 언급하는가?
(A) 건물에 전기가 들어오지 않을 것이다.
(B) 컴퓨터 몇 대가 교체될 것이다.

해설 세부 내용 – 문제점
사무실 건물이 토요일 아침에 보수 공사를 할 예정이고, 대략 3시간 동안 전기가 차단될 것(Our office building will be undergoing some repairs Saturday morning and, uh, the electricity will be off for about three hours)이라고 했으므로 정답은 (A)이다.

2 화자는 무엇을 할 것이라고 말하는가?
(A) 동료들에게 메시지 전송
(B) 팀장들과 만남

해설 세부 내용 – 화자가 할 일
작업이 완료되면 이메일로 알려 주겠다(I'll notify you by e-mail once the work's done)고 했으므로 정답은 (A)이다.

[3-4] 회의 W-Am

I want to talk about a big change coming to our restaurant soon. ³We're going to start a new fixed-price menu. Basically, our diners will have a special four-course meal that we select, instead of the diners choosing what they want from a full menu. OK, now one last thing. The new aprons have arrived. ⁴Please pick up your apron from the stockroom before the dinner shift starts.

곧 우리 레스토랑에 큰 변화가 생기는 것에 대해 이야기하겠습니다. ³우리는 새로운 정가 메뉴를 시작하려고 합니다. 기본적으로 식사 손님들은 전체 메뉴에서 자신이 원하는 것을 고르는 대신 우

리가 선택하는 특별 4코스 식사를 하게 될 겁니다. 자, 이제 마지막으로 한 가지만 더요. 새 앞치마가 도착했습니다. **4저녁 근무 시간이 시작되기 전에 창고에서 앞치마를 챙기세요.**

> **어휘** fixed-price 정가의 basically 기본적으로
> diner 식사하는 손님 apron 앞치마 stockroom 창고
> shift (한 차례의) 교대 근무

3 화자는 주로 무엇을 이야기하고 있는가?
  (A) 메뉴 변경   (B) 신규점 개점

해설 전체 내용 - 회의 주제
지문 초반부에서 새로운 정가 메뉴를 시작하려고 한다(We're going to start a new fixed-price menu)며 메뉴에 생길 변화에 대해 설명하고 있으므로 정답은 (A)이다.

4 화자에 따르면, 창고에서 무엇을 가져갈 수 있는가?
  (A) 기구   **(B) 앞치마**

해설 세부 내용 - 창고에서 가져갈 수 있는 것
저녁 근무 시간이 시작되기 전에 창고에서 앞치마를 챙기라(Please pick up your apron from the stockroom before the dinner shift starts)고 했으므로 정답은 (B)이다.

> **어휘** utensil (주방) 기구

[5-6] 안내 M-Cn

> Ladies and gentlemen, I'm sorry to announce that **5tonight's football game will be postponed by one hour**, due to heavy rain conditions. **6We expect to start at six P.M.** In the meantime, we encourage you to visit the food stands, which are now open. Please note there are no refunds, but you can exchange your ticket for a future game by visiting the box office next to the main gate.
>
> 신사 숙녀 여러분, 유감스럽게도 폭우로 **5오늘 밤 축구 경기가 한 시간 연기됨**을 알려드립니다. **6경기는 오후 6시에 시작될 것으로 예상됩니다.** 그동안 현재 영업 중인 매점에 다녀오시는 것을 권장합니다. 환불은 되지 않는다는 점에 유의하세요. 다만 정문 바로 옆 매표소를 방문하시면 차후 경기를 관람할 수 있는 입장권으로 교환은 가능합니다.

> **어휘** postpone 연기하다 due to ~ 때문에 conditions (특정 시기의) 날씨 in the meantime 그동안에
> food stand 매점 refund 환불

5 안내 방송의 목적은 무엇인가?
  (A) 일정 변경 알리기
  (B) 행사장 길 안내

해설 전체 내용 - 안내 방송의 목적
지문 초반부에 폭우로 오늘 밤 축구 경기가 한 시간 연기될 것(tonight's football game will be postponed by one hour)이라고 하므로 정답은 (A)이다.

6 경기는 언제 시작될 것인가?
  (A) 오후 1시   **(B) 오후 6시**

해설 세부 내용 - 경기 시작 시각
보기에 시간이 제시되어 있으므로 숫자가 언급되는 부분에 초점을 맞춰 들어야 한다. 경기가 오후 6시에 시작할 예정(We expect to start at six P.M.)이라고 하므로 정답은 (B)이다.

ETS 실전 문제   본책 p.114

1 (C)	2 (A)	3 (D)	4 (B)	5 (B)	6 (C)
7 (A)	8 (C)	9 (A)	10 (C)	11 (B)	12 (A)
13 (B)	14 (C)	15 (D)	16 (D)	17 (A)	18 (B)
19 (B)	20 (C)	21 (A)			

[1-3] 공지 W-Br

> Attention, all workers in Area G. **1We've just halted the assembly line** because **2several barrels of paint have been spilled in the area.** For safety reasons, the paint will have to be cleaned up before work can continue. **3Workers in Area G should report to the staff room immediately.** We've already contacted maintenance workers to take care of the problem, so it should be resolved within an hour. We'll let you know when things are back to normal.
>
> G구역에 있는 직원 전원에게 알립니다. **2해당 구역에 페인트가 여러 통 쏟아져서 1방금 조립 라인을 중지했습니다.** 안전상의 이유로, 작업을 계속하기 전에 페인트를 닦아야 합니다. **3G구역 직원은 즉시 직원실로 가십시오.** 이미 정비담당 직원들에게 연락해 문제를 처리하도록 했으므로 1시간 이내에 해결될 겁니다. 상황이 정상으로 돌아오면 알려드리겠습니다.

> **어휘** halt 중지하다 assembly 조립 barrel 통 spill 쏟다
> safety 안전 continue 계속되다 report to ~로 가다
> immediately 즉시 maintenance 정비 take care of
> ~을 처리하다 resolve 해결하다 normal 정상

1 공지가 어디에서 나오고 있을 것 같은가?
  (A) 페인트 가게   (B) 우체국
  (C) 제조 공장   (D) 공사 현장

해설 전체 내용 - 장소
공지가 이루어지고 있는 장소를 묻는 질문으로 주로 도입부에 단서가 제시된다. 지문 초반에 조립 라인을 중지했다(We've just halted the assembly line)고 하므로 공장에서 공지가 나온다는 것을 알 수 있다. 따라서 정답은 (C)이다.

> **어휘** manufacturing 제조 construction 공사, 건축

2 무엇이 문제를 일으켰는가?
(A) 페인트가 쏟아졌다.   (B) 기계가 꼼짝도 안 한다.
(C) 소포가 배달되지 않았다.   (D) 제품이 파손되었다.

해설 **세부 내용 – 문제의 원인**
조립 라인을 중지한 이유로 페인트가 쏟아진 것(several barrels of paint have been spilled in the area)을 지목하므로 정답은 (A)이다.

어휘 **jammed** (막히거나 걸려서) 꼼짝도 하지 않는

3 청자들이 무엇을 하라고 지시받는가?
(A) 기계 끄기   (B) 관리자와 면담
(C) 해당 구역 청소   (D) 직원실로 가기

해설 **세부 내용 – 청자들에 대한 지시 사항**
G구역 직원은 즉시 직원실로 가라(Workers in Area G should report to the staff room immediately)고 하므로 정답은 (D)이다.

어휘 **supervisor** 관리자, 상사

Paraphrasing 지문의 report to the staff room
→ 보기의 Go to the staff room

[4-6] 회의 M-Cn

⁴I want to extend a special thank-you to the baristas for working so hard since our shop opened. Customers are delighted with both the coffee and our service. We're getting lots of great reviews. Also, ⁵I'm excited to announce we'll be expanding our menu selection to offer pastries soon. We just signed a contract with the Pavlov Pastry Company. ⁶I'd like to get your opinions on which of their pastries might sell best. Here are some samples—let me know what you think.

⁴우리 가게가 문을 연 이후로 열심히 일해 준 바리스타분들께 특별히 감사 말씀을 전하고 싶습니다. 고객들은 우리의 커피와 서비스 둘 다에 만족하고 있습니다. 우리는 훌륭한 후기를 많이 받고 있습니다. 또한, ⁵곧 메뉴 선택지를 늘려 페이스트리를 제공할 예정이라는 소식을 발표하게 되어 기쁩니다. 우리는 최근에 파블로브 페이스트리 회사와 계약을 맺었습니다. ⁶그들의 페이스트리 중 어떤 것이 가장 잘 팔릴지에 대한 여러분의 의견을 듣고 싶습니다. 여기 몇 가지 샘플이 있으니 여러분의 생각을 알려주세요.

어휘 **extend** 주다, 베풀다   **delighted** 아주 즐거워하는
review 후기   **expand** 확장하다   **contract** 계약
sell 팔리다

4 회의가 어디에서 열리는 것 같은가?
(A) 식품 가공 시설   (B) 커피숍
(C) 컨퍼런스 센터   (D) 슈퍼마켓

해설 **전체 내용 – 장소**
회의가 이루어지고 있는 장소를 묻는 질문으로 주로 도입부에 단서가 제시된다. 시작 부분에서 가게가 문을 연 이후로 열심히 일해 준 바리스타들에게 고맙다고 전하고 싶고 고객들이 커피와 서비스에 만족하고 있다(I want to extend a special thank-you to the baristas for working so hard since our shop opened. Customers are delighted with both the coffee and our service)고 하므로 정답은 (B)이다.

어휘 **food processing** 식품 가공   **facility** 시설

5 화자는 무엇이 기쁘다고 말하는가?
(A) 새로운 장소로 이전하는 것
(B) 선택지를 늘리는 것
(C) 일부 장비를 교체하는 것
(D) 주차 구역을 추가하는 것

해설 **세부 내용 – 화자가 기쁜 점**
곧 메뉴 선택지를 늘려 페이스트리를 제공할 예정이라는 소식을 발표하게 되어 기쁘다(I'm excited to announce we'll be expanding our menu selection to offer pastries soon)고 했으므로 정답은 (B)이다.

어휘 **replace** 교체하다   **equipment** 장비

6 화자는 청자들에게 무엇을 요청하는가?
(A) 근무 일정 확인   (B) 진열대 설치
(C) 피드백 제공   (D) 작업 공간 청소

해설 **세부 내용 – 화자의 요청 사항**
페이스트리 중 어떤 것이 가장 잘 팔릴지에 대한 의견을 듣고 싶고 샘플에 대한 생각을 알려달라(I'd like to get your opinions on which of their pastries might sell best. Here are some samples—let me know what you think)고 요청하고 있으므로 정답은 (C)이다.

어휘 **display** 진열

Paraphrasing 지문의 opinions → 보기의 feedback

[7-9] 공지 M-Au

Before we open for business this morning, ⁷I have a quick reminder about the recent change in the store's recycling policy. When you unpack merchandise from the boxes, you need to bring all the packaging material to the recycling area as usual. But now you also have to separate the plastic wrap from the cardboard boxes and place these materials into different containers. The city's recycling company asked all businesses to follow this procedure, and ⁸we must comply with the city's new rule. ⁹Thursday will still be the pick-up day, so make sure that all items have been sorted by then.

오늘 아침 개업하기 전에, ⁷매장 재활용 정책의 최근 변경 사항에 대해 간단히 상기시켜드리고자 합니다. 상자에서 제품을 개봉할 때

는 평소처럼 모든 포장재를 재활용 구역에 갖다 둬야 합니다. 하지만 이제는 판지 상자에서 비닐 포장지를 분리해 이 재료들을 서로 다른 용기에 넣어야 합니다. 시의 재활용 회사는 모든 업체에게 이 절차를 따르도록 요청했고, 8우리는 시의 새로운 규정을 따라야 합니다. 9수거일은 여전히 목요일이므로 그때까지 반드시 모든 품목을 분류하도록 하십시오.

어휘 reminder 상기시키는 것 recycling 재활용 merchandise 제품 as usual 평소처럼 separate 분리하다 procedure 절차 comply with ~을 따르다, 지키다 sort 분류하다

---

7 공지의 주요 주제는 무엇인가?
(A) 재활용 정책   (B) 재고 관리 절차
(C) 직원 급여대장   (D) 컴퓨터 유지보수

해설 **전체 내용 – 공지의 주제**
지문 초반부에서 매장 재활용 정책의 최근 변경 사항에 대해 간단히 상기시켜 주겠다(I have a quick reminder about the recent change in the store's recycling policy)고 하므로 정답은 (A)이다.

어휘 inventory 재고 (관리) payroll 급여대장, 급여명부 maintenance 유지보수

8 회사는 왜 변경을 하는가?
(A) 수익을 증대하려고
(B) 신입 사원을 유치하려고
(C) 지역 법률을 준수하려고
(D) 신기술을 활용하려고

해설 **세부 내용 – 변경 이유**
시의 재활용 회사가 모든 업체에게 변경 사항을 따르도록 요청했다고 한 후, 시의 새 규정을 따라야 한다(we must comply with the city's new rule)고 했으므로 정답은 (C)이다.

어휘 revenue 수익 take advantage of ~을 활용하다

> **Paraphrasing** 지문의 city's new rule
> → 보기의 local laws

9 화자에 따르면, 목요일에 무슨 일이 일어나는가?
(A) 폐기물이 수거될 것이다.
(B) 기계가 정비될 것이다.
(C) 직원들이 급여를 받을 것이다.
(D) 발주가 처리될 것이다.

해설 **세부 내용 – 목요일에 있을 일**
질문의 키워드인 Thursday가 언급되는 마지막 문장에서 목요일에 재활용 쓰레기가 수거된다(Thursday will still be the pick-up day, so make sure that all items have been sorted by then)는 것을 알 수 있으므로 정답은 (A)이다.

어휘 discarded 폐기된 supply order (물품을 보내 달라는) 발주 process 처리하다

[10-12] 안내 M-Cn

May I have your attention, please? **10 This announcement is for passengers on the nine thirty A.M. train to Munich.** **11 We are sorry to announce that this train has been delayed indefinitely because of unexpected maintenance issues.** All passengers should report to the ticketing counter to receive instructions for other transportation options or to receive a refund. **12 Please be prepared to show your ticket at the counter.** We apologize for the inconvenience.

주목해 주시겠습니까? 10뮌헨으로 가는 오전 9시 30분 열차의 승객들을 위한 안내 방송입니다. 11예기치 못한 정비 문제로 인해 해당 열차가 무기한 지연되었음을 알려드리게 되어 유감입니다. 모든 승객 여러분은 다른 교통편에 대한 설명을 듣거나 환불을 받기 위해 발권 카운터로 이동해 주시기 바랍니다. 12카운터에서 표를 보여주실 수 있도록 준비해 주세요. 불편을 드려 죄송합니다.

어휘 attention 주목 passenger 승객 delay 지연시키다 indefinitely 무기한으로 unexpected 예기치 못한 maintenance 정비 report to ~로 가다, ~로 출두하다 instructions 설명, 지시 transportation 교통수단 inconvenience 불편

---

10 청자들은 어디에 있을 것 같은가?
(A) 여객선 터미널   (B) 스포츠 경기장
(C) 기차역   (D) 공항

해설 **전체 내용 – 안내 방송 장소**
지문 초반부에서 뮌헨으로 가는 오전 9시 30분 열차의 승객들을 위한 안내 방송(This announcement is for passengers on the nine thirty A.M. train to Munich)이라고 하는 것으로 보아 기차역에 있는 승객들을 대상으로 하는 방송임을 알 수 있다. 따라서 정답은 (C)이다.

어휘 stadium 경기장

11 화자는 무엇을 안내하는가?
(A) 충성 고객 할인   (B) 예기치 못한 지연
(C) 건축 정책   (D) 카페 개점

해설 **전체 내용 – 안내 방송 주제**
예기치 못한 정비 문제로 인해 열차가 무기한 지연되었음을 알리게 되어 유감(We are sorry to announce that this train has been delayed indefinitely because of unexpected maintenance issues)이라고 했으므로 정답은 (B)이다.

어휘 loyalty 충성, 단골 policy 정책

12 청자들은 무엇을 보여줄 준비를 해야 하는가?
(A) 표   (B) 가방
(C) 쿠폰   (D) 신분증

해설 **세부 내용 - 청자들이 준비할 것**
카운터에서 표를 보여줄 수 있도록 준비할 것(Please be prepared to show your ticket at the counter)을 요청하고 있으므로 정답은 (A)이다.

어휘 identification 신분증

[13-15] 회의 M-Cn

Good morning. **13 I called this meeting so we can review some important procedures.** Currently, **14 forecasters are predicting unusually low temperatures for Friday**, so there's a risk of water pipes bursting. **15 We're the company responsible for making sure our customers have safe, clean drinking water at all times.** All technicians should ensure that their company vehicles are ready to go out for service calls. Our communications office has already started sending out e-mail alerts to customers explaining how to protect their water pipes.

좋은 아침입니다. 13몇 가지 중대 절차를 되새기려고 이 회의를 소집했습니다. 현재, 14기상 캐스터들이 금요일에 이상 저온을 예측하고 있으며, 이에 따라 수도관이 터질 위험이 있습니다. 15우리는 고객들이 항상 안전하고 깨끗한 식수를 마시도록 할 책임이 있는 회사입니다. 모든 기술자는 서비스 호출 시 회사 차량을 출동시킬 준비를 확실히 해야 합니다. 우리의 통신실은 이미 고객들에게 수도관을 보호하는 방법을 설명하는 이메일 알림을 발송하기 시작했습니다.

어휘 currently 현재 forecaster 기상 캐스터 predict 예측하다 unusually 평소와 달리 risk 위험 burst 터지다 ensure 확실히 하다 vehicle 차량

13 회의의 목적은 무엇인가?
(A) 신입 사원 환영
(B) 절차 재검토
(C) 장비 업그레이드 일정 예약
(D) 신제품 라인 발표

해설 **전체 내용 - 회의 목적**
몇 가지 중대 절차를 되새기려고 회의를 소집했다(I called this meeting so we can review some important procedures)고 했으므로 정답은 (B)이다.

14 화자는 금요일에 대해 무엇을 말하는가?
(A) 관리자가 은퇴한다.
(B) 고객이 방문한다.
(C) 추운 날씨가 예상된다.
(D) 설문 조사 결과가 발표된다.

해설 **세부 내용 - 금요일에 대해 말하는 것**
질문의 키워드인 Friday가 언급되는 문장(forecasters are predicting unusually low temperatures for Friday)에서 기상 캐스터들이 금요일에 이상 저온을 예측하고 있다고 했으므로 정답은 (C)이다.

Paraphrasing 지문의 unusually low temperatures
→ 보기의 Cold weather

15 청자들은 어디에서 근무할 것 같은가?
(A) 텔레비전 방송국 (B) 집수리 용품점
(C) 부동산 중개업소 **(D) 수도 회사**

해설 **전체 내용 - 청자들의 근무 장소**
화자가 우리는 고객들이 항상 안전하고 깨끗한 식수를 마시도록 할 책임이 있는 회사(We're the company responsible for making sure our customers have safe, clean drinking water at all times)라고 했으므로 청자들은 물을 관리하는 회사에서 근무한다는 것을 유추할 수 있다. 따라서 정답은 (D)이다.

어휘 home-improvement store 집수리 용품점, 철물점 real estate agency 부동산 중개업소

[16-18] 공지 W-Am

Hello, everyone. **16 Thanks for attending the annual Brindale Music Festival.** Before the show begins, I have a few announcements. Due to the very hot weather conditions today, we have set up some water stations throughout the concert grounds. **17 These stations can be found under the green tents and will be serving free water throughout the event.** Also, remember that **18 at six P.M. some members of today's performing bands will be available near the south stage to sign autographs.** Now, please welcome our first band, the Wilson Seven, to the stage.

안녕하세요, 여러분. 16매년 열리는 브린데일 뮤직 페스티벌에 참석해 주셔서 감사합니다. 쇼가 시작되기 전에, 몇 가지 공지 사항이 있어요. 오늘 날씨가 무척 더워서, 콘서트장 곳곳에 식수대를 몇 군데 설치했습니다. 17이 식수대들은 녹색 텐트에서 찾을 수 있으며 행사 내내 무료 식수를 제공합니다. 또한 18오후 6시에 오늘 공연하는 밴드의 몇몇 멤버들을 남쪽 무대 근처 사인회에서 만나볼 수 있다는 점 기억하세요. 자, 이제 첫 번째 밴드인 윌슨 세븐을 무대로 맞이해 주세요.

어휘 annual 연례의 due to ~ 때문에 water station 식수대 throughout 곳곳에 perform 공연하다 autograph 사인

16 이 공지의 청중은 누구일 것 같은가?
(A) 조리사 (B) 정비사
(C) 음악가 집단 **(D) 콘서트 참석자**

해설 **전체 내용 - 청자의 신분**
화자가 브린데일 뮤직 페스티벌에 참가해 줘서 고맙다(Thanks for attending the annual Brindale Music Festival)고 말하며 청자들을 환영하는 것으로 보아 청자들은 콘서트 참석자임을 알 수 있다. 따라서 정답은 (D)이다.

어휘 attendee 참석자

17 청자들은 왜 녹색 텐트를 방문하도록 권유받는가?
(A) 물을 얻으려고
(B) 식품을 구입하려고
(C) 일정을 확인하려고
(D) 티셔츠를 얻으려고

해설 세부 내용 - 녹색 텐트 방문 권유 이유
식수대들은 녹색 텐트에서 찾을 수 있으며 행사 내내 무료 식수를 제공한다(These stations can be found under the green tents and will be serving free water throughout the event)고 하므로 녹색 텐트를 방문하도록 권유받는 이유는 물을 얻기 위해서라는 것을 알 수 있다. 따라서 정답은 (A)이다.

Paraphrasing 지문의 be serving free water
→ 보기의 get water

18 여자에 따르면, 오후 6시에 무슨 일이 있겠는가?
(A) 대회 우승자가 발표될 것이다.
(B) 공연자가 사인을 할 것이다.
(C) 장비를 점검할 것이다.
(D) 청소가 시작될 것이다.

해설 세부 내용 - 특정 시점에 있을 일
오후 6시에 밴드 몇몇 멤버들을 남쪽 무대 근처 사인회에서 만나볼 수 있다(at six P.M. some members of today's performing bands will be available near the south stage to sign autographs)고 알리고 있으므로 정답은 (B)이다.

[19-21] 공지 + 매장 안내도 M-Au

Attention, shoppers. **19 A customer has found and turned in a mobile phone.** If you're missing your phone, please come to the customer service desk to claim it. Also, **20 we're installing new shelving in the area where we usually display the granola bars, so they've been temporarily moved to an area near the checkout registers.** We apologize for any inconvenience. Finally, we want to remind you that **21 we close at two o'clock this afternoon. That's to give our employees some extra time to enjoy today's holiday.** Thank you for shopping at Greenville Grocery.

쇼핑객 여러분께 알립니다. 19고객 한 분께서 휴대전화를 발견해 제출하셨습니다. 휴대전화를 분실하신 경우, 고객 서비스 데스크로 오셔서 받아 가시기 바랍니다. 또한, 20평소 그래놀라 바를 진열하는 구역에 새로운 선반을 설치하고 있어, 계산대 근처 구역으로 임시로 이동하였습니다. 불편을 끼쳐드려 죄송합니다. 마지막으로 21오늘 오후 2시에 영업을 종료한다는 점을 다시 한번 알려드립니다. 이는 저희 직원들에게 오늘 휴일을 즐길 수 있는 시간을 더 주기 위해서입니다. 그린빌 식료품점에서 쇼핑해 주셔서 감사합니다.

어휘 turn in 제출하다 miss 분실하다 claim 요구하다 install 설치하다 shelving 선반 temporarily 일시적으로 checkout register 계산대 inconvenience 불편 aisle 통로 frozen 냉동된 beverage 음료 condiment 조미료

식료품점 안내도

통로	제품
1	냉동 식품
2	음료, 차, 커피
20 3	시리얼, 그래놀라 바
4	스낵, 조미료

19 고객은 어떤 물품을 발견했는가?
(A) 자동차 열쇠   (B) 휴대전화
(C) 지갑   (D) 신분증

해설 세부 내용 - 고객이 발견한 물품
한 고객이 휴대전화를 발견해 제출했다(A customer has found and turned in a mobile phone)고 했으므로 정답은 (B)이다.

20 시각 정보에 따르면, 어느 통로가 보수 중인가?
(A) 1번 통로   (B) 2번 통로
(C) 3번 통로   (D) 4번 통로

해설 세부 내용 - 시각 정보
평소 그래놀라 바를 진열하는 구역에 새로운 선반을 설치하고 있어 계산대 근처 구역으로 임시로 이동했다(we're installing new shelving in the area where we usually display the granola bars, so they've been temporarily moved to an area near the checkout registers)고 했다. 그리고 식료품점 안내도를 살펴보면 그래놀라 바는 3번 통로에 있으므로 정답은 (C)이다.

어휘 renovation 보수, 개조

21 가게는 왜 문을 일찍 닫는가?
(A) 휴일이다.
(B) 재고 조사가 진행될 것이다.
(C) 가게에서 비공개 행사가 열릴 것이다.
(D) 일시적으로 인력이 부족하다.

해설 세부 내용 - 가게가 일찍 문 닫는 이유
가게가 오늘 오후 2시에 영업을 종료한다(we close at two o'clock this afternoon)고 했고, 이는 직원들에게 오늘 휴일을 즐길 수 있는 시간을 더 주기 위해서(That's to give our employees some extra time to enjoy today's holiday)라고 했으므로 정답은 (A)이다.

어휘 take inventory 재고 조사를 하다 private 비공개의, 사적인 staffing 인력 shortage 부족

UNIT 16 광고/방송/보도

ETS 기출 예제
본책 p.116

> ¹오크 트리 어패럴은 최신 정장 패션으로 남성분들을 최고의 모습으로 꾸며 드린다는 명성을 쌓아 왔습니다. ²고객분들이 계속 재방문하시는 것은 저희 직원들의 개인 맞춤 서비스 때문입니다. 그리고 이제 더 나은 서비스를 제공하기 위해 ³문을 더 오래 열어 두려고 합니다. 다음 주부터 매일 아침 9시부터 저녁 9시까지 문을 엽니다. 들어오셔서 저희가 시에서 고객 만족 1위에 오른 이유를 알아보세요.
>
> **어휘** reputation 명성 individualized 개인 맞춤의 customer satisfaction 고객 만족

ETS 유형 연습
본책 p.117

1 (B) **2** (A) **3** (B) **4** (A) **5** (B) **6** (B)

[1-2] 방송 M-Au

> ¹This weekend's weather will be warm and sunny—perfect for attending the annual Summerton Jazz Extravaganza. You won't want to miss it. There'll be lots of talented musicians performing on three stages. ²To see the list of performers and showtimes, visit the Summerton social media page.
>
> ¹이번 주말 날씨는 따뜻하고 화창해서 매년 열리는 서머튼 재즈 쇼에 참석하기에 완벽할 것입니다. 놓치고 싶지 않을 것입니다. 세 개의 무대에서 여러 재능 있는 뮤지션들이 공연을 할 것입니다. ²공연자 목록과 공연 시간을 확인하려면 서머튼 소셜 미디어 페이지를 방문하세요.
>
> **어휘** extravaganza 화려한 쇼 miss 놓치다 talented 재능 있는 stage 무대

1 이번 주말에 무엇이 일어날 것인가?
(A) 미술관 개관 (B) 음악 축제

해설 세부 내용 – 주말에 일어날 일
이번 주말 날씨는 따뜻하고 화창해서 매년 열리는 서머튼 재즈 쇼에 참석하기에 완벽할 것(This weekend's weather will be warm and sunny—perfect for attending the annual Summerton Jazz Extravaganza)이라고 했으므로 이번 주말에 재즈 음악 행사가 개최된다는 것을 알 수 있다. 따라서 정답은 (B)이다.

Paraphrasing 지문의 Jazz Extravaganza
→ 보기의 music festival

2 화자는 왜 소셜 미디어를 확인하라고 권하는가?
(A) 일정표를 보려고
(B) 행사에 자원 봉사하려고

해설 세부 내용 – 소셜 미디어 확인을 권하는 이유
공연자 목록과 공연 시간을 확인하려면 서머튼 소셜 미디어 페이지를 방문하라(To see the list of performers and showtimes, visit the Summerton social media page)고 했으므로 정답은 (A)이다.

어휘 volunteer 자원 봉사하다

[3-4] 광고 + 리스트 W-Br

> Buy a Mishu E-reader today and discover the reading revolution. Mishu customers can carry more than three thousand books on one device! ³The model with the largest display size even has an application installed for video chatting. ⁴Visit the Mishu Web site "Customer Feedback" section to read for yourself what our customers are saying about their devices.
>
> 오늘 미슈 전자책 단말기를 구매하셔서 독서의 혁명을 발견하세요. 미슈 고객께서는 장치 하나에 3천 권이 넘는 책을 가지고 다닐 수 있습니다! ³화면이 가장 큰 모델에는 비디오 채팅을 위한 애플리케이션도 설치되어 있습니다. ⁴저희 고객들이 자신의 장치에 대해 뭐라고 하는지 직접 읽어 보시려면 미슈 웹사이트의 '고객 의견'란을 방문하세요.
>
> **어휘** discover 발견하다 revolution 혁명 carry 가지고 다니다, 휴대하다 device 장치, 기구 application 애플리케이션(응용 프로그램) install 설치하다

미슈 전자책 단말기

모델	화면 크기
PT-250	15센티미터
DX-16	16센티미터
DX-32	17센티미터
³DX-64	18센티미터

3 시각 정보에 따르면, 어떤 전자책 단말기에 비디오 채팅용 애플리케이션이 있는가?
(A) PT-250 (B) DX-64

해설 세부 내용 – 시각 정보
질문의 키워드인 app for video chatting에 주목한다. 비디오 채팅 애플리케이션을 탑재한 모델은 화면이 가장 크다(The model with the largest display size even has an application installed for video chatting)고 했는데, 시각 정보에서 화면이 가장 큰 모델을 찾아보면 DX-64이므로 정답은 (B)이다.

4 화자는 미슈 웹사이트 방문객들이 무엇을 할 수 있다고 하는가?
(A) 고객 평가 읽기 (B) 제품 구매

해설 세부 내용 – 고객들이 웹사이트에서 할 수 있는 것
질문의 키워드인 Web site에 주목한다. '고객 의견'란에서 미슈 고객의 의견을 읽어볼 수 있다(Visit the Mishu Web site "Customer Feedback" section to read for

yourself what our customers are saying about their devices)고 했으므로 정답은 (A)이다.

[5-6] 보도 W-Br

At a press conference today, the governor announced that a new hospital will be built in Starks County. **5** The governor emphasized that the hospital will create over 300 jobs—helping to boost the local employment rate. **6** After the break, I'll talk with some local citizens of Starks County. They've raised concerns that the proposed site for the project will have a negative impact on wildlife in the area.

오늘 기자 회견에서, 주지사는 스탁스 카운티에 새로운 병원을 지을 것이라고 발표했습니다. **5**주지사는 병원 신설로 300개 이상의 일자리가 생겨서 지역 취업률을 신장하는 데 기여할 거라고 강조했습니다. **6**광고 후에, 스탁스 카운티 시민들과 이야기를 나누어 볼 텐데요. 그들은 병원 프로젝트를 위해 제안된 부지가 지역 야생 동물에게 부정적인 영향을 끼칠 거라는 우려를 제기한 바 있습니다.

어휘 press conference 기자 회견 governor 주지사, 장관 county 카운티(자치군) emphasize 강조하다 boost 신장시키다 employment rate 취업률 raise (안건 등을) 제기하다 concern 우려, 걱정거리 negative 부정적인

5 주지사는 프로젝트의 어떤 장점을 언급했는가?
(A) 출퇴근 시간 단축
(B) 지역의 더 많은 일자리

해설 세부 내용 - 주지사의 언급 사항
주지사가 병원 신설로 지역에 300개 이상의 일자리가 생겨, 지역 취업률을 신장하는 데 기여할 것(The governor emphasized that the hospital will create over 300 jobs—helping to boost the local employment rate)이라고 말했다고 하므로 정답은 (B)이다.

6 광고 후에 누구를 인터뷰할 것인가?
(A) 주지사   **(B) 지역 주민들**

해설 세부 내용 - 인터뷰 대상
질문의 키워드인 after the break가 언급되는 후반부에서 지역 주민들과 이야기를 나눠 보겠다(I'll talk with some local citizens of Starks County)고 하므로 지역 주민을 인터뷰할 것임을 알 수 있다. 따라서 정답은 (B)이다.

ETS 실전 문제   본책 p.118

1 (A)	2 (A)	3 (B)	4 (C)	5 (B)	6 (C)
7 (B)	8 (A)	9 (D)	10 (D)	11 (C)	12 (B)
13 (A)	14 (B)	15 (D)	16 (B)	17 (C)	18 (D)
19 (A)	20 (C)	21 (D)			

[1-3] 광고 W-Br

Looking to establish healthier habits this year? **1** Ocean Springs is the newest and most modern fitness complex in the area, situated just outside Wellington on Rutherford Avenue. Members benefit from exercising in peaceful surroundings while still being just a short trip from downtown. But **2** what we think you'll appreciate most is the heated outdoor pool, open year-round! **3** Visit our Web site now to experience a virtual tour of our facilities. Start your new year off right by joining us at Ocean Springs!

올해 더 건강한 습관을 확립할 계획인가요? **1**오션 스프링스는 웰링턴 외곽의 러더포드 가에 위치한, 이 지역에서 가장 새롭고 현대적인 피트니스 단지입니다. 회원들은 도심에서 가까운 거리에 있으면서도 평화로운 환경에서 운동하는 혜택을 누립니다. 하지만 **2**가장 높이 평가하실 점은 연중 운영되는 야외 온수 수영장입니다! **3**지금 웹사이트를 방문하셔서 저희 시설을 가상으로 둘러보세요. 오션 스프링스와 함께 새해를 제대로 시작해 보세요!

어휘 look to ~할 계획이다 establish 확립하다 complex 단지 situated 위치한 benefit 혜택을 받다 surroundings 환경 appreciate 높이 평가하다, 인정하다 virtual 가상의 facility 시설

1 무엇이 광고되고 있는가?
(A) 피트니스 센터   (B) 아파트 단지
(C) 호텔   (D) 놀이공원

해설 전체 내용 - 광고되는 것
오션 스프링스는 이 지역에서 가장 새롭고 현대적인 피트니스 단지(Ocean Springs is the newest and most modern fitness complex in the area)라며 피트니스 센터를 광고하고 있으므로 정답은 (A)이다.

어휘 amusement park 놀이공원

Paraphrasing 지문의 fitness complex → 보기의 fitness center

2 화자에 따르면, 청자들은 오션 스프링스의 어떤 점을 가장 높이 평가하겠는가?
(A) 야외 수영장   (B) 셀프 커피 바
(C) 저렴한 가격   (D) 편리한 주차

해설 세부 내용 - 시설에 대해 가장 높이 평가할 만한 점
고객이 가장 높이 평가할 점은 연중 운영되는 야외 온수 수영장(what we think you'll appreciate most is the heated outdoor pool, open year-round)이라고 했으므로 정답은 (A)이다.

어휘 affordable (가격이) 저렴한 convenient 편리한

3 화자는 청자들에게 온라인으로 무엇을 하라고 제안하는가?
(A) 안내 책자 다운로드   (B) 가상 투어하기
(C) 방문 일정 잡기   (D) 후기 읽기

해설 세부 내용 – 온라인으로 하라고 제안한 것
웹사이트를 방문해서 시설을 가상으로 둘러보라(Visit our Web site now to experience a virtual tour of our facilities)고 제안하고 있으므로 정답은 (B)이다.

어휘 brochure 안내 책자   review 후기

[4-6] 방송 M-Au

Channel Seven News has learned that the city of Midway will soon begin purchasing a percentage of its electricity from **4 a wind farm currently under construction in Oklahoma.** **5 The main benefit of the wind energy project is that residents will notice a reduction in their utility bills.** We interviewed the head of the Sustainability Commission to learn more. **6 Tune in tonight at eight o'clock to hear what he has to say about the timeline for this project.**

채널 세븐 뉴스는 미드웨이 시가 **4** 현재 오클라호마에서 건설 중인 풍력 발전소에서 일정 비율의 전기를 구매하기 시작할 것이라는 소식을 입수했습니다. **5** 이 풍력 에너지 프로젝트의 주요 이점은 주민들이 공과금의 감소를 체감할 것이라는 점입니다. 우리는 더 많은 것을 알아보기 위해 지속 가능성 위원회의 책임자를 인터뷰했습니다. **6** 이 프로젝트의 일정에 대해 그가 하는 이야기를 들으시려면 오늘 밤 8시에 채널을 맞춰 주십시오.

어휘 purchase 구매하다   percentage 비율   wind farm 풍력 발전소   benefit 이점   resident 주민   reduction 감소   utility bill 공과금   sustainability 지속 가능성   timeline 일정   tune in 채널을 맞추다

4 현재 무엇을 건설 중인가?
(A) 터널   (B) 다리
(C) 풍력 발전소   (D) 태양광 발전소

해설 세부 내용 – 건설 중인 것
지문의 첫 문장에서 현재 오클라호마에서 건설 중인 풍력 발전소(a wind farm currently under construction in Oklahoma)에 대해 언급하고 있으므로 정답은 (C)이다.

어휘 solar farm 태양광 발전소

5 지역 주민들은 프로젝트로부터 어떻게 이익을 얻을 것인가?
(A) 도시의 거리가 더 깨끗해질 것이다.
(B) 서비스가 덜 비쌀 것이다.
(C) 더 많은 일자리가 추가될 것이다.
(D) 출퇴근 시간이 줄어들 것이다.

해설 세부 내용 – 프로젝트의 이익
풍력 에너지 프로젝트의 주요 이점은 주민들이 공과금의 감소를 체감할 것(The main benefit of the wind energy project is that residents will notice a reduction in their utility bills)이라고 했으므로 정답은 (B)이다.

어휘 commuting time 출퇴근 시간

Paraphrasing 지문의 a reduction in their utility bills
→ 보기의 A service will be less expensive

6 청자들은 어떻게 더 많은 정보를 알 수 있는가?
(A) 웹사이트 방문   (B) 소식지 신청
(C) 인터뷰 시청   (D) 주민 회의 참석

해설 세부 내용 – 추가 정보 확보 방법
프로젝트의 일정에 대해 지속 가능성 위원회의 책임자가 하는 이야기를 들으려면 오늘 밤 8시에 채널을 맞추라(Tune in tonight at eight o'clock to hear what he has to say about the timeline for this project)고 했으므로 정답은 (C)이다.

어휘 sign up for ~을 신청하다   newsletter 소식지

[7-9] 뉴스 보도 M-Cn

Good morning. **7 This is Raj Kumar for Radio 97, reporting live from Cityside Beach.** As you may have heard, this season's first migrating humpback whales have arrived in our area. **8 The arrival of the whales is good news for local business owners, who should see larger-than-normal crowds purchasing tickets for whale-watching tours and generally spending time—and money—at the beach.** Since there will be increased traffic in local waters, let's remind ourselves of some basic safety rules for boaters. We have with us this morning, Marjorie Kelley, from the local Office of Boating Safety. **9 Marjorie, what things should people be cautious of when they are out on the water?**

안녕하세요. **7** 라디오 97의 라즈 쿠마르가 시티사이드 해변에서 생방송으로 전합니다. 들으셨지만, 올 시즌 첫 번째로 이주하는 혹등고래들이 우리 지역에 도착했습니다. **8** 고래들의 도착은 지역 업주들에게 좋은 소식이죠. 고래 관찰 투어를 위한 표를 구입해서 대체로 해변에서 시간을 보내고 돈을 쓰는 사람이 평소보다 많아지니까요. 지역 해역의 교통량이 증가할 예정이므로, 배를 타는 사람을 위한 기본적인 안전 수칙을 상기합시다. 오늘 아침에는 지역 선박 안전국의 마조리 켈리 씨를 모셨습니다. **9** 마조리, 사람들이 물 위에 있을 때 주의해야 할 점은 무엇인가요?

어휘 migrate 이주하다, 이동하다   humpback whale 혹등고래   purchase 구입하다   increased 증가된   remind 상기시키다   be cautious of ~을 주의하다

7 화자는 누구인 것 같은가?
(A) 해양생물학자   (B) 뉴스 기자
(C) 지역 공무원   (D) 선장

해설 **전체 내용 - 화자의 신분**
지문 초반부에서 라디오 97의 라즈 쿠마르가 시티사이드 해변에서 생방송으로 전한다(This is Raj Kumar for Radio 97, reporting live from Cityside Beach)고 하므로 정답은 (B)이다.

8 화자에 따르면, 업주들은 무엇을 기대할 수 있는가?
(A) 고객 증가   (B) 에너지 비용 절감
(C) 세율 인상   (D) 주차 제한 감소

해설 **세부 내용 - 업주들이 기대할 수 있는 것**
고래 투어 덕분에 해변에서 시간을 보내고 돈을 쓰는 사람이 많아지기 때문에 고래들의 도착은 지역 업주들에게 좋은 소식(The arrival of the whales is good news for local business owners, who should see larger-than-normal crowds purchasing tickets for whale-watching tours and generally spending time—and money—at the beach)이라고 하므로 정답은 (A)이다.

어휘 reduction 절감   restriction 제한

> **Paraphrasing** 지문의 larger-than-normal crowds
> → 보기의 An increase in customers

9 마조리 켈리는 무엇을 논의할 것 같은가?
(A) 도로 상태   (B) 사업 기회
(C) 야생동물 보호   (D) 선박 안전

해설 **세부 내용 - 마조리 켈리가 논의할 것**
선박안전국의 마조리에게 물 위에 있을 때 주의할 점이 무엇인지(Marjorie, what things should people be cautious of when they are out on the water?) 묻는 것으로 보아 선박 안전을 이야기할 것임을 알 수 있다. 따라서 정답은 (D)이다.

어휘 conservation 보호

> **Paraphrasing** 지문의 be cautious of when they are out on the water → 보기의 Boating safety

[10-12] 광고 M-Au

> Whether you're preparing for a graduation, a wedding, or an important work presentation, Fairhill One helps you look your best. **10** Fairhill One offers formal wear and business attire in a variety of fabrics, styles, and colors. We can even help select the perfect look for you! **11** Simply book a complimentary fashion consultation at any of our locations. A fashion adviser will handpick outfits best suited to your style. Once your order is ready, it will ship right to your door. **12** Tell the sales associate at checkout that you heard this ad to receive ten percent off your purchase at Fairhill One.

졸업식, 결혼식, 또는 중요한 업무 프레젠테이션을 준비 중이든, 페어힐 원은 고객님이 최고로 보일 수 있도록 도와드립니다. **10** 페어힐 원은 다양한 소재, 스타일, 색상의 정장 및 비즈니스 복장을 제공합니다. 고객님께 가장 완벽하게 어울리는 스타일을 고르시는 걸 도와드릴 수도 있습니다! **11** 저희 지점 어디서든 무료 패션 상담을 예약하세요. 패션 상담사가 고객님의 스타일에 가장 적합한 의상을 직접 골라드립니다. 주문 상품이 준비되는 즉시 고객님 댁으로 바로 배송해드립니다. **12** 계산하실 때 판매원에게 이 광고를 들었다고 말씀하시고 페어힐 원 구매 제품에 10퍼센트 할인을 받으세요.

어휘 graduation 졸업식   formal wear 정장   attire 복장
fabric 원단   complimentary 무료의   consultation 상담
handpick 직접 고르다, 엄선하다   suited 적합한
checkout 계산대

10 어떤 종류의 업체가 광고되고 있는가?
(A) 꽃가게   (B) 미용실
(C) 행사 기획사   (D) 의류 매장

해설 **전체 내용 - 광고되는 업체**
페어힐 원은 다양한 소재, 스타일, 색상의 정장 및 비즈니스 복장을 제공한다(Fairhill One offers formal wear and business attire in a variety of fabrics, styles, and colors)고 구체적으로 언급하고 있으므로 정답은 (D)이다.

> **Paraphrasing** 지문의 formal wear and business attire
> → 보기의 clothing

11 업체에서 무엇을 무료로 제공할 수 있는가?
(A) 제품 샘플   (B) 우수 고객 카드
(C) 개인 맞춤 상담   (D) 빠른 배송

해설 **세부 내용 - 무료 제공 서비스**
페어힐 원 지점 어디서든 무료 패션 상담을 예약하라(Simply book a complimentary fashion consultation at any of our locations)고 하므로 정답은 (C)이다.

어휘 expedited 신속한

> **Paraphrasing** 지문의 complimentary → 질문의 free of charge

12 청자들은 어떻게 할인을 받을 수 있는가?
(A) 특별 코드 사용
(B) 계산할 때 광고를 언급
(C) 일정 금액 지출
(D) 고객 추천

해설 **세부 내용 - 할인 받는 방법**
계산할 때 판매원에게 이 광고를 들었다고 말하고 페어힐 원 구매 제품에 10퍼센트 할인을 받으라(Tell the sales associate at checkout that you heard this ad to receive ten percent off your purchase at Fairhill One)고 하므로 정답은 (B)이다.

어휘 certain 일정한   referral 추천, 소개

[13-15] 팟캐스트 M-Cn

This is Chen, your home decorating expert. **13 This week, I'll be discussing some factors to consider when redecorating your house or apartment.** I speak from experience when I say that **14 once you decide to redecorate, you'll feel eager to go out and buy new furniture and home décor right away. But remember, returning items is an inconvenience.** This is especially true when they're big, like a sofa! So, in a few minutes, I'll share some helpful advice on how to choose the right look for your space. **15 First, though, I want to answer some questions listeners posted about last week's episode.**

여러분의 집 꾸미기 전문가 첸입니다. **13 이번 주에는 주택이나 아파트를 다시 꾸밀 때 고려해야 할 요소들에 대해 이야기해 보겠습니다.** 제 경험을 바탕으로 말씀드리자면 **14 일단 다시 꾸미기로 결심이 서면 당장 새 가구와 집안 장식 용품을 사러 나가고 싶어질 텐데요. 하지만 기억하세요, 반품은 번거로운 일입니다.** 특히 소파처럼 덩치가 큰 경우에는 정말 그렇습니다! 잠시 후 여러분의 공간에 딱 맞는 스타일을 선택하는 방법에 대해 도움이 되는 조언을 공유하겠습니다. **15 하지만 먼저, 지난주 에피소드에 대해 청취자분들이 남겨 주신 질문에 답변부터 하겠습니다.**

어휘 expert 전문가　factor 요소　eager to 간절히 ~하고 싶어하는　post 게시하다

13 팟캐스트의 주제는 무엇인가?
(A) 실내 장식　　　(B) 건축
(C) 여행 사진　　　(D) 재정 관리

해설 전체 내용 - 팟캐스트의 주제
지문 초반부에서 주택이나 아파트를 다시 꾸밀 때 고려해야 할 요소들에 대해 이야기하겠다(This week, I'll be discussing some factors to consider when redecorating your house or apartment)면서 팟캐스트의 주제에 대해 언급하고 있으므로 정답은 (A)이다.

어휘 interior 실내　architecture 건축

> **Paraphrasing** 지문의 redecorating your house or apartment → 보기의 Interior decorating

14 화자는 왜 "반품은 번거로운 일입니다"라고 말하는가?
(A) 지연을 설명하려고
(B) 주의를 주려고
(C) 불만을 정당화하려고
(D) 정책 변경을 권고하려고

해설 세부 내용 - 화자의 의도
제시문 앞에서 집을 다시 꾸미기로 결심이 서면 당장 새 가구와 집안 장식 용품을 사러 나가고 싶어질 것(once you decide to redecorate, you'll feel eager to go out and buy new furniture and home décor right away)이라고 말한 뒤, 하지만 기억하라(But remember)고 당부하면서 "반품은 번거로운 일"이라고 하고 있다. 이는 계획 없이 무작정 쇼핑부터 하는 것에 대해 주의를 주려는 의도임을 알 수 있으므로 정답은 (B)이다.

어휘 caution 주의　justify 정당화하다　complaint 불평　recommend 권고하다　policy 정책

15 화자는 다음에 무엇을 하겠다고 말하는가?
(A) 게스트 인터뷰
(B) 향후 주제 발표
(C) 후원자에게 감사 표하기
(D) 질문에 답변

해설 세부 내용 - 다음에 할 일
마지막 문장에서 먼저 지난주 에피소드에 대해 청취자들이 남긴 질문에 답변부터 하겠다(First, though, I want to answer some questions listeners posted about last week's episode)고 했으므로 정답은 (D)이다.

어휘 announce 발표하다　sponsor 후원자, 광고주

[16-18] 뉴스 보도 W-Br

Welcome to Business News on Channel 10. **16 This is Pamela Shaw, reporting to you live from Phillip's Car Dealership, right here in our city.** Now, **17 a new article about car sales was published yesterday in the *National Automobile Association Magazine*,** which explains that the sale of used cars has gone up consistently over the last five years. While this may be surprising to some, many of the customers interviewed in the article said they thought a well-maintained used vehicle could provide a better value for their money than a brand-new car. **18 I'm now going to speak with the owner of Phillip's Car Dealership** to get his reactions and find out how he thinks this trend may influence the industry.

채널 10 경제 뉴스에 오신 걸 환영합니다. **16 저는 파멜라 쇼입니다. 우리 시에 있는 바로 이곳 필립 자동차 영업소에서 생방송으로 전해 드립니다.** 자, **17 어제 발간된 〈전국 자동차 협회지〉에 자동차 판매에 관한 새로운 기사가 실렸는데,** 지난 5년 동안 중고차 판매가 꾸준히 증가했다고 합니다. 놀라시는 분도 있겠지만, 기사에서 인터뷰한 많은 고객이 정비가 잘 된 중고차가 새 차보다 가성비가 좋다고 생각한다고 말했는데요. **18 저는 이제 필립 자동차 영업소 주인과 이야기를 나누면서** 그의 반응을 들어보고 이 추세가 업계에 어떤 영향을 미치리라 생각하는지 알아보겠습니다.

어휘 article 기사　publish 발간하다　consistently 꾸준히　maintain 정비하다　value for one's money 가성비, 돈에 합당한 가치　influence 영향을 미치다

16 화자는 어디에 있는가?
(A) 텔레비전 스튜디오　　(B) 자동차 영업소
(C) 주차장　　　　　　　(D) 시청

해설 **전체 내용 – 장소**
지문 초반부에서 시에 있는 필립 자동차 영업소에서 생방송으로 전한다(This is Pamela Shaw, reporting to you live from Phillip's Car Dealership, right here in our city)고 했으므로, 화자가 자동차 영업소에 있음을 알 수 있다. 따라서 정답은 (B)이다.

17 화자에 따르면, 어제 무슨 일이 있었는가?
(A) 계약이 체결되었다.
(B) 신제품이 판매에 들어갔다.
(C) 기사가 실렸다.
(D) 건설 공사가 시작되었다.

해설 **세부 내용 – 어제 있었던 일**
질문의 키워드인 yesterday를 그대로 언급하며, 자동차 판매에 관한 새로운 기사가 잡지에 실렸다(a new article about car sales was published yesterday in the *National Automobile Association Magazine*)고 밝히고 있으므로 정답은 (C)이다.

18 화자는 다음에 무엇을 할 것인가?
(A) 과정 시연
(B) 상품 검토
(C) 견학
(D) 인터뷰 실시

해설 **세부 내용 – 다음에 할 일**
마지막 문장에서 필립 자동차 영업소 주인과 이야기를 나누겠다(I'm now going to speak with the owner of Phillip's Car Dealership)고 했으므로 정답은 (D)이다.

어휘 demonstrate 시연하다

> **Paraphrasing** 지문의 speak with the owner
> → 보기의 Conduct an interview

[19-21] 방송 + 일정표 W-Am

It's just been announced that ¹⁹**the annual Country Music Festival will be held at historic Hutch Stadium**! This year's lineup of musicians is the largest ever! If you're attending, please be aware that repairs are being made to all the stadium entrances this summer. While one entrance is being repaired, the others will remain open. So, ²⁰**during the music festival, the Orchard Street entrance will not be available.** ²¹**For more information, download the Hutch Stadium mobile app to view details of the city's improvement plan for the stadium.**

¹⁹연례 컨트리 음악 축제가 역사적인 허치 경기장에서 열린다고 발표되었습니다! 올해의 뮤지션 구성은 역대 최대 규모입니다! 참석할 예정이라면, 올 여름 모든 경기장 출입구가 보수 중이라는 점을 염두에 두십시오. 출입구 하나가 보수되는 동안, 나머지 출입구들은 열려 있을 예정입니다. 따라서, ²⁰음악 축제 동안 오차드 가 입구는 이용할 수 없습니다. ²¹자세한 정보를 원하시면 허치 경기장 모바일 앱을 다운로드하셔서 경기장에 대한 시의 개선 계획 세부 사항을 확인하세요.

어휘 lineup 구성 entrance 출입구 improvement 개선

출입구 폐쇄

출입구	월
지하철역	5월
브릿지 가	6월
²⁰오차드 가	**7월**
스테이디엄 가	8월

19 화자는 어떤 행사를 이야기하고 있는가?
(A) 음악 축제
(B) 공휴일 기념 행사
(C) 개회식
(D) 스포츠 행사

해설 **전체 내용 – 행사 종류**
첫 문장에서 컨트리 음악 축제가 허치 경기장에서 열린다(the annual Country Music Festival will be held at historic Hutch Stadium)고 알리고 있으므로 정답은 (A)이다.

어휘 celebration 기념 행사 ceremony 기념식

20 시각 정보에 따르면, 언제 행사가 열리는가?
(A) 5월   (B) 6월
(C) 7월   (D) 8월

해설 **세부 내용 – 시각 정보**
음악 축제 동안 오차드 가 입구는 이용할 수 없다(during the music festival, the Orchard Street entrance will not be available)고 했고, 일정표를 보면 오차드 가 출입구는 7월에 폐쇄되므로 정답은 (C)이다.

21 청자들은 어떻게 추가 정보를 확인할 수 있는가?
(A) 웹사이트 방문
(B) 팟캐스트 청취
(C) 직원과 대화
(D) 모바일 애플리케이션 다운로드

해설 **세부 내용 – 추가 정보 확인 방법**
자세한 정보를 원하면 허치 경기장 모바일 앱을 다운로드해서 경기장에 대한 시의 개선 계획 세부 사항을 확인하라(For more information, download the Hutch Stadium mobile app to view details of the city's improvement plan for the stadium)고 했으므로 정답은 (D)이다.

어휘 agent 직원, 대리인

UNIT 17 인물 / 강연 / 설명

ETS 기출 예제
본책 p.120

¹안녕하세요, 여러분. 올해의 건축 학회를 즐기고 계시길 바랍니다. 저는 당사 뉴웨이브 프린터의 신제품을 소개하려고 여기 왔습니다. 자, 여러분 모두 소프트웨어 프로그램을 사용해 고객에게 건축 구상을 보여주는 모형을 만들어 보셨을 텐데요. ²저희 신제품 3D 프린터 레플리콘 3000으로, 전문가급의 프레젠테이션 모형을 만드는 시중에서 가장 정확한 도구를 경험하게 되실 겁니다. ³제가 레플리콘 3000으로 만든 모형을 몇 개 보여드리고 싶은데요. 결과가 얼마나 정밀한지 알 수 있으실 겁니다.

어휘 architecture 건축   experience 경험하다
accurate 정확한   precise 정밀한   outcome 결과

ETS 유형 연습
본책 p.121

1 (B) **2** (B) **3** (B) **4** (B) **5** (B) **6** (B)

[1-2] 강연 M-Au

¹**If you're new to travel photography, don't worry.** As an award-winning photojournalist who has worked all over the world, I'm here to share with you some easy ways to take an awesome photo. Even when traveling, the basic principles still apply. Above all, ²**I recommend that you keep lighting in mind. It makes a significant difference in the quality of the image you're capturing.**

¹여행 사진을 처음 접해본다 하더라도 걱정 마세요. 전 세계에서 활동한 수상 경력이 있는 보도 사진작가로서 근사한 사진을 찍을 수 있는 쉬운 방법 몇 가지를 여러분에게 공유하고자 합니다. 여행 중일 때조차 기본 원칙은 여전히 적용됩니다. 무엇보다 ²조명을 염두에 둘 것을 권합니다. 조명은 여러분이 포착하는 이미지의 질에 커다란 차이를 만듭니다.

어휘 award-winning 수상 경력이 있는   photojournalist 보도 사진가   principle 원칙   apply 적용되다   lighting 조명   significant 커다란   quality 질   capture 포착하다

1 강연은 어떤 종류의 사진에 대한 것인가?
(A) 패션   (B) 여행

해설 전체 내용 - 강연에서 다루는 사진의 종류
여행 사진을 처음 접해본다 하더라도 걱정 말라(If you're new to travel photography, don't worry)고 한 뒤 관련 내용을 이어가고 있으므로, 강연은 여행 사진에 대해 다룬다는 것을 알 수 있다. 따라서 정답은 (B)이다.

2 화자에 따르면, 사진작가가 좋은 사진을 찍는 데 무엇이 도움이 되는가?
(A) 자동 초점   (B) 광원

해설 세부 내용 - 좋은 사진 촬영에 도움이 되는 것
무엇보다 조명을 염두에 둘 것을 권한다(I recommend that you keep lighting in mind)고 했고, 조명은 이미지의 질에 커다란 차이를 만든다(It makes a significant difference in the quality of the image you're capturing)고 한 것으로 보아 정답은 (B)이다.

어휘 automated 자동의   focus 초점   source 원천

Paraphrasing 지문의 lighting → 보기의 light source

[3-4] 연설 W-Am

³**I feel truly honored by this award for employee of the year here at Flint and Gray Banking.** At the beginning of the year, I was asked to develop a mobile application for our account holders. After ten months of trial and error, we are now able to release a fully functioning application to our users. But I couldn't have done it without my team of programming specialists. ⁴**They all did a fabulous job.** So for that, please join me in giving them a warm round of applause.

³이곳 플린트 앤 그레이 은행에서 이렇게 올해의 직원상을 받게 되어 정말 영광입니다. 저는 올해 초, 계좌 소유자들을 위한 모바일 앱을 개발하라는 요청을 받았습니다. 10개월의 시행착오를 겪은 후, 이제 저희는 완전한 기능을 갖춘 앱을 이용자들에게 출시할 수 있게 되었습니다. 하지만 프로그래밍 전문가들로 구성된 저희 팀이 없었다면 이 일을 해낼 수 없었을 것입니다. ⁴그들 모두 멋진 일을 해냈습니다. 그러므로 저와 함께 그들에게 따뜻한 박수갈채를 보내주시기 바랍니다.

어휘 honored 영광으로 생각하는, 명예로운
account holder 계좌 소유자   trial and error 시행착오
release 출시하다   fully functioning 완전한 기능을 갖춘
specialist 전문가   applause 박수갈채

3 연설의 목적은 무엇인가?
(A) 회사를 발족하려고   (B) 수상하려고

해설 전체 내용 - 연설의 목적
플린트 앤 그레이 은행에서 올해의 직원 상을 받게 되어 영광(I feel truly honored by this award for employee of the year here at Flint and Gray Banking)이라고 했으므로 정답은 (B)이다.

어휘 inaugurate 발족하다, 시작하다

4 화자는 왜 "저희 팀이 없었다면 이 일을 해낼 수 없었을 것입니다"라고 말하는가?
(A) 그녀는 업무를 수행할 기술이 없다.
(B) 동료들에게 고마움을 표하고 싶어 한다.

해설 세부 내용 – 화자의 의도

화자가 수상 소감 도중 "저희 팀이 없었다면 이 일을 해낼 수 없었을 것입니다"라고 말한 후, 그들 모두 멋진 일을 해냈다(They all did a fabulous job)며 팀원들에게 고마움을 전하고 있다. 따라서 정답은 (B)이다.

어휘 competitor 경쟁사 flexible 유연한 process 처리하다 paycheck 급여

Paraphrasing 지문의 pay employees who live abroad → 보기의 processes international paychecks

[5-6] 설명 M-Cn

⁵Thanks for stopping by our booth. This is my company's first time at this trade show. Momentum Online helps businesses like yours search for and manage new staff. Our Web site allows employers to browse résumés from talented professionals in a variety of specialties. But ⁶unlike other Internet-based employment services, our company provides a platform that even makes it possible to pay employees who live abroad. Successful companies and skilled freelancers are already benefiting from our services.

⁵저희 부스에 들러 주셔서 감사합니다. 저희 회사는 이번 산업 박람회에 처음 참석합니다. 모멘텀 온라인은 귀사와 같은 사업체가 새로운 직원을 찾고 관리하는 데 도움을 드립니다. 저희 웹사이트는 고용주들로 하여금 다양한 전문 분야의 재능 있는 전문가들의 이력서를 열람할 수 있게 해줍니다. 하지만 ⁶다른 인터넷 기반 고용 서비스들과 달리, 저희 회사는 해외에 거주하는 직원에게 급여를 지급하는 것까지 가능하게 해주는 플랫폼을 제공합니다. 성공적인 기업과 숙련된 프리랜서들이 저희 서비스로부터 이미 혜택을 누리고 있습니다.

어휘 trade show 산업 박람회 employer 고용주 browse 훑어보다 specialty 전문 분야 employment 고용 abroad 해외에 benefit 혜택을 보다

5 담화는 어디에서 이루어지고 있는가?
(A) 기자 회견   **(B) 산업 박람회**

해설 전체 내용 – 담화 장소

지문 초반부에서 저희 부스에 들러 주어 감사하다(Thanks for stopping by our booth)면서, 이번 산업 박람회에 처음 참석한다(This is my company's first time at this trade show)고 한 것으로 보아 산업 박람회에서 설명을 하고 있다는 것을 알 수 있다. 따라서 정답은 (B)이다.

어휘 press conference 기자 회견

6 업체는 경쟁사와 어떻게 다른가?
(A) 유연한 근무 일정을 허용한다.
(B) 국제간 급여를 처리한다.

해설 세부 내용 – 경쟁사와의 차이점

다른 인터넷 기반 고용 서비스들과 달리 해외에 거주하는 직원의 급여 지급을 가능하게 해주는 플랫폼을 제공한다(unlike other Internet-based employment services, our company provides a platform that even makes it possible to pay employees who live abroad)고

했으므로 정답은 (B)이다.

어휘 competitor 경쟁사 flexible 유연한 process 처리하다 paycheck 급여

Paraphrasing 지문의 pay employees who live abroad → 보기의 processes international paychecks

ETS 실전 문제   본책 p.122

1 (B)	2 (D)	3 (C)	4 (B)	5 (B)	6 (D)
7 (B)	8 (D)	9 (A)	10 (B)	11 (C)	12 (C)
13 (B)	14 (D)	15 (A)	16 (B)	17 (D)	18 (A)
19 (C)	20 (A)	21 (B)			

[1-3] 인물 소개 W-Am

¹Hello and welcome to Health Talk on WKD radio. I'm your host Stephanie Ross, and ²today we'll be talking to sleep specialist Dr. Louisa Meyer. Dr. Meyer has written many groundbreaking articles on the science of sleep and has recently published a book on sleep habits. ³She's here to tell us about the fascinating findings on child and adult sleep patterns that she discusses in her new book. Welcome to the program, Dr. Meyer.

¹안녕하세요? WKD 라디오의 헬스 토크에 오신 것을 환영합니다. 저는 진행자 스테파니 로스이고 ²오늘은 수면 전문가 루이자 마이어 박사님과 이야기를 나누겠습니다. 마이어 박사님은 수면 과학에 관한 획기적인 기사를 많이 썼고 최근 수면 습관에 관한 책을 출간했습니다. ³박사님은 새 책에서 논한 아동과 성인의 수면 패턴에 대한 흥미진진한 발견에 대해 이야기하시기 위해 이곳에 오셨습니다. 마이어 박사님, 프로그램에 잘 오셨습니다.

어휘 host (TV·라디오 프로의) 진행자 groundbreaking 획기적인 recently 최근에 adult 성인

1 인터뷰는 어디에서 진행되고 있는 것 같은가?
(A) 진료소   **(B) 라디오 방송국**
(C) 출판사   (D) 텔레비전 스튜디오

해설 전체 내용 – 인터뷰 장소

지문 첫 문장에서 WKD 라디오의 헬스 토크에 온 것을 환영한다(Hello and welcome to Health Talk on WKD radio)고 하므로 정답은 (B)이다.

2 마이어 박사의 전문 분야는 무엇인가?
(A) 알레르기 치료   (B) 운동 과학
(C) 영양 보충제   **(D) 수면 연구**

해설 세부 내용 – 마이어 박사의 전문 분야

지문 초반부에서 마이어 박사가 수면 전문가(today we'll be talking to sleep specialist Dr. Louisa Meyer)

해설 　전체 내용 - 화자의 신분
화자는 콜드웰 가 23번지 주민들을 대신해 법적 대리 서비스를 제공하기 위해 플로레스 앤 호프만 법률 사무소에서 왔다(I'm here from the law firm of Flores and Hoffman to provide legal representation for my clients, the residents of 23 Caldwell Street)고 했으므로 정답은 (B)이다.

어휘 　accountant 회계사　architect 건축가

5　화자는 건축 프로젝트의 어떤 문제점을 언급하는가?
(A) 많은 허가가 필요할 수 있다.
(B) 현지 규정을 위반할 수 있다.
(C) 이웃이 항의했다.
(D) 비용이 원래 예산을 초과했다.

해설 　세부 내용 - 건축 프로젝트의 문제점
시 규정은 건물과 부지 경계선 사이에 5피트의 공간이 있어야 한다는 것을 명시하고 있으며 이는 건축 계획에 지장을 줄 수 있다(a town regulation specifies that there must be a five-foot space between the building and the property line, which would interfere with the building plan)고 했으므로 건축 계획과 마을 규정이 상충된다는 것을 알 수 있다. 따라서 정답은 (B)이다.

어휘 　permit 허가(증)　violate 위반하다　exceed 초과하다

6　화자는 다음에 무엇을 할 것 같은가?
(A) 질문에 응답하기
(B) 몇몇 고객에게 연락하기
(C) 새로운 비용 예상치 공유하기
(D) 이미지 보여주기

해설 　세부 내용 - 다음에 할 일
지문 후반부에서 위에서 바라본 부지의 모습을 보여줄 텐데 이 시각 자료가 도움이 될 것 같다(Let me show you what it looks like from above—I think the visual will be helpful)고 했으므로 정답은 (D)이다.

어휘 　respond 응답하다　projection 예상

Paraphrasing　지문의 visual → 보기의 image

라는 것이 언급되었으므로 정답은 (D)이다.

어휘 　treatment 치료　exercise 운동　nutritional 영양의　supplement 보충제, 보조식품

3　마이어 박사는 오늘 무엇에 관해 이야기할 것인가?
(A) 자신이 한 여행
(B) 자신이 받은 상
(C) 자신이 쓴 책
(D) 자신이 시작한 재단

해설 　세부 내용 - 마이어 박사가 이야기할 내용
마이어 박사는 새 책에서 논한 아동과 성인의 수면 패턴에 대한 발견에 대해 이야기하기 위해 이곳에 왔다(She's here to tell us about the fascinating findings on child and adult sleep patterns that she discusses in her new book)고 하므로 정답은 (C)이다.

어휘 　foundation 재단

[4-6] 설명 M-Cn

Good afternoon, members of the Springfield Town Council. ⁴I'm here from the law firm of Flores and Hoffman to provide legal representation for my clients, the residents of 23 Caldwell Street. They would like to build a garage on their property. However, ⁵a town regulation specifies that there must be a five-foot space between the building and the property line, which would interfere with the building plan. My clients are requesting an exception to allow the garage to be built. A forest runs directly alongside the property, so the change would not affect any neighbors. ⁶Let me show you what it looks like from above—I think the visual will be helpful. One moment.

안녕하세요, 스프링필드 시의회 여러분. ⁴저는 우리 고객인 콜드웰 가 23번지 주민들을 대신해 법적 대리 서비스를 제공하려고 플로레스 앤 호프만 법률 사무소에서 왔습니다. 그들은 자신의 부지에 차고를 짓기를 원합니다. 그러나 ⁵시 규정은 건물과 부지 경계선 사이에 5피트의 공간이 있어야 한다는 것을 명시하고 있으며, 이는 건축 계획에 지장을 줄 수 있습니다. 제 고객들은 차고를 건설할 수 있도록 예외를 요청하고 있습니다. 숲이 부지 바로 옆에 이어져 있어 해당 변경이 이웃에게 영향을 주지 않을 것입니다. ⁶위에서 바라본 모습을 보여드릴 텐데 이 시각 자료가 도움이 될 것 같습니다. 잠시만요.

어휘 　council 의회　legal 법적인　representation 대리　resident 주민　garage 차고　property 부동산　regulation 규정　specify 명시하다　interfere with ~에 지장을 주다　exception 예외　alongside 옆에　affect 영향을 미치다　visual 시각 자료

4　화자는 누구인 것 같은가?
(A) 회계사
(B) 변호사
(C) 엔지니어
(D) 건축가

[7-9] 워크숍 W-Br

⁷I'd like to begin this workplace safety training session by welcoming you to Kingston Tool Manufacturers. You may have operated similar machinery at previous workplaces, but procedures may vary. So, ⁸during the first part of today's training, you'll watch an instructional video on our company's safety procedures. After that, I'll take you to the factory floor to introduce you to your supervisors. ⁹They will demonstrate how to operate the machinery you'll be using in your specific area.

7 킹스턴 툴 제조사에 오신 것을 환영하며 이번 작업장 안전 교육을 시작하겠습니다. 이전 작업장에서 유사한 기계를 작동해봤을 수도 있겠지만 절차는 다를 수 있습니다. 그래서 8오늘 교육의 첫 부분에서는 우리 회사의 안전 절차에 관한 교육 영상을 시청하겠습니다. 그 후, 공장 작업장으로 여러분을 데리고 가서 관리자들을 소개하겠습니다. 9그들은 여러분이 지정된 구역에서 사용할 기계를 어떻게 작동하는지 시연할 겁니다.

어휘 operate 작동하다 similar 유사한 previous 이전의
procedure 절차 instructional 교육용의 floor 작업장
supervisor 관리자 demonstrate 시연하다

7 화자는 누구에게 연설하는 것 같은가?
(A) 장비 납품업체 **(B) 공장 직원**
(C) 이사회 (D) 잠재 고객

해설 **전체 내용 – 청자의 신분**
청자가 누구인지 찾기 위해서는 앞부분을 잘 들어야 한다. 첫 문장에서 킹스턴 툴 제조사에 온 것을 환영하며 이번 작업장 안전 교육을 시작하겠다(I'd like to begin this workplace safety training session by welcoming you to Kingston Tool Manufacturers)고 한 것으로 보아, 공장 직원들이 대상임을 알 수 있다. 따라서 정답은 (B)이다.

어휘 address 연설하다 supplier 납품업체
potential 잠재적인

8 화자에 따르면, 청자들은 처음에 무엇을 할 것인가?
(A) 사진 찍기 (B) 설문조사서 작성
(C) 간호사 만나기 **(D) 영상 보기**

해설 **세부 내용 – 청자들이 처음 할 일**
교육의 첫 부분에서 회사의 안전 절차에 관한 영상을 볼 것(during the first part of today's training, you'll watch an instructional video on our company's safety procedures)이라고 말하고 있으므로 정답은 (D)이다.

9 관리자들은 무엇을 할 것인가?
(A) 기계 작동 시연 (B) 연간 예산 심의
(C) 근무 성적 제출 (D) 특수 의류 배부

해설 **세부 내용 – 관리자들이 할 일**
지문 후반부에서 관리자들이 기계 작동을 시연할 것(They will demonstrate how to operate the machinery you'll be using in your specific area)이라고 밝히고 있으므로 정답은 (A)이다.

어휘 performance record 근무 성적 distribute 배부하다

Paraphrasing 지문의 how to operate the machinery
→ 보기의 machinery operation

[10-12] 인물 소개 W-Am

Welcome to Afternoon Edition. Today, 10 we'll be talking to education expert Dr. Catherine Hoffman about her recent research on the reading habits of young people worldwide. 11 One of her findings is that young people, aged 13 to 18, are more likely to read online sources than printed materials. Dr. Hoffman also found that schools have been spending more money on computers and e-reading materials as a result. 12 At the end of the week, she'll receive an award from the Brooklite Institute for her 20 years of work in the field of international education. So, thank you for joining us, Dr. Hoffman, and welcome to Afternoon Edition.

애프터눈 에디션에 오신 것을 환영합니다. 오늘은 10교육 전문가 캐서린 호프만 박사와 함께 전 세계 청소년들의 독서 습관에 관한 최근 연구에 대해 이야기하겠습니다. 11박사님의 연구 결과 중 하나는 13세에서 18세 청소년들이 인쇄물보다 온라인 자료를 더 많이 읽는다는 것입니다. 또한 호프만 박사는 학교들이 결과적으로 컴퓨터와 전자독서 교재에 더 많은 돈을 쓰고 있다는 것을 발견했습니다. 12이번 주말, 박사님은 국제 교육 분야에서 20년 동안의 공로로 브룩라이트 연구소에서 수상하실 예정입니다. 호프만 박사님, 함께해 주셔서 감사하고 애프터눈 에디션에 오신 것을 환영합니다.

어휘 expert 전문가 research 연구 institute 연구소

10 호프만 박사는 어느 분야에서 일하고 있는가?
(A) 사업 **(B) 교육**
(C) 의학 (D) 공학

해설 **전체 내용 – 호프만 박사가 일하고 있는 분야**
교육 전문가 캐서린 호프만 박사와 함께 전 세계 청소년들의 독서 습관에 관한 최근 연구에 대해 이야기하겠다(we'll be talking to education expert Dr. Catherine Hoffman about her recent research on the reading habits of young people worldwide)고 했으므로 정답은 (B)이다.

11 13세에서 18세 사이의 청소년들에 관해 무엇이 언급되는가?
(A) 어른보다 전자제품을 더 많이 산다.
(B) 방과후 프로그램에 자주 참가한다.
(C) 온라인 읽기 자료를 선호한다.
(D) 이전 세대 청소년보다 더 건강하다.

해설 **세부 내용 – 청소년들에 관해 언급된 것**
호프만 박사의 연구 결과 중 하나는 13세에서 18세 청소년들이 인쇄물보다 온라인 자료를 더 많이 읽는다는 것(One of her findings is that young people, aged 13 to 18, are more likely to read online sources than printed materials)이라고 했으므로 정답은 (C)이다.

어휘 participate in ~에 참가하다 prefer 선호하다
previous 이전의 generation 세대

Paraphrasing 지문의 more likely to read online sources → 보기의 prefer online reading sources

12 주말에 호프만 박사는 무엇을 할 것인가?
(A) 보고서 공개 (B) 컨퍼런스 주최
(C) 수상 (D) 새로운 일 시작

해설 세부 내용 – 호프만 박사가 주말에 할 일
주말에 박사는 교육 분야에서 일한 공로로 브룩라이트 연구소에서 수상할 예정(At the end of the week, she'll receive an award from the Brooklite Institute for her 20 years of work in the field of international education)이라고 했으므로 정답은 (C)이다.

[13-15] 강연 M-Au

> Thanks for attending this class offered by the city Parks Department. I'm Jingdao Tong, and **¹³I'll be teaching you about the flowers, grasses, and trees native to our region.** Of course, **¹⁴this class was designed to be held outdoors, but because of the rain, we'll be staying here in the visitor center.** But don't worry! I have a slideshow that includes close-up photographs of the plants we'll be discussing. **¹⁵It's just going to take me a few minutes to get the computer set up for the slideshow.** In the meantime, why don't you get to know one another?
>
> 시 공원 관리부에서 제공하는 이 수업에 참석해 주셔서 감사합니다. 저는 징다오 통이며 ¹³우리 지역 고유의 꽃, 풀, 나무에 대해 가르쳐드릴 거예요. 당연히 ¹⁴이 수업은 야외에서 열릴 계획이었는데, 비 때문에 여기 방문자 센터에서 진행하게 되었습니다. 하지만 걱정 마세요! 우리가 이야기할 식물들의 근접 사진이 포함된 슬라이드쇼가 있어요. ¹⁵슬라이드쇼를 위해 컴퓨터를 준비하는 데 몇 분 정도 걸릴 거예요. 그동안 서로에 대해서 알아보는 게 어떨까요?

어휘 attend 참석하다 offer 제공하다 native to ~ 고유의 region 지역 outdoors 야외에서 close-up 근접한 in the meantime 그동안에 one another 서로

13 수업은 주로 무엇에 대한 것인가?
(A) 자연 사진 **(B) 토종 식물**
(C) 날씨 패턴 (D) 캠핑 기술

해설 전체 내용 – 강의 주제
지문 초반부에서 우리 지역 고유의 꽃, 풀, 나무에 대해 가르쳐줄 것(I'll be teaching you about the flowers, grasses, and trees native to our region)이라고 수업 주제에 대해 공지하고 있으므로 정답은 (B)이다.

Paraphrasing 지문의 flowers, grasses, and trees → 보기의 plants

14 오늘 수업은 무엇이 다른가?
(A) 한 시간 일찍 끝난다.
(B) 촬영된다.
(C) 대체 교사가 진행한다.
(D) 실내에서 진행된다.

해설 세부 내용 – 수업의 다른 점
원래 수업이 야외에서 열릴 계획이었는데 비 때문에 방문자 센터에서 진행하게 되었다(this class was designed to be held outdoors, but because of the rain, we'll be staying here in the visitor center)고 했으므로 정답은 (D)이다.

어휘 film 촬영하다 substitute 대리자 indoors 실내에서

Paraphrasing 지문의 in the visitor center → 보기의 indoors

15 화자는 다음에 무엇을 할 것인가?
(A) 장비 준비하기 (B) 그룹을 둘씩 나누기
(C) 출석 부르기 (D) 소책자 나눠주기

해설 세부 내용 – 다음에 할 일
지문 후반부에서 화자가 슬라이드쇼를 위해 컴퓨터를 준비하는 데 몇 분 정도 걸릴 것(It's just going to take me a few minutes to get the computer set up for the slideshow)이라고 했으므로 정답은 (A)이다.

어휘 equipment 장비 divide 나누다 attendance 출석 distribute 나눠주다, 배포하다 booklet 소책자

[16-18] 설명 M-Au

> Hello, and **¹⁶welcome to this instructional video, where I will demonstrate how to assemble our new sofa model, the GL-300.** It's fairly easy, and it takes less than twenty minutes. **¹⁷All the tools you need should be right in the box.** Please check that you received those tools before you start the assembly. Good? OK, let's continue. Carefully open the compressed bags and remove the seat cushions from them. Then, **¹⁸you'll need to pick up the seat box and turn it over. You may want to ask a friend to help you with this step**—the seat box is quite heavy.
>
> 안녕하세요. ¹⁶이 설명 영상을 찾아 주신 것을 환영하며 여기서 저희의 새로운 소파 모델 GL-300의 조립 방법을 보여드리겠습니다. 조립은 상당히 간단하며 20분도 채 걸리지 않습니다. ¹⁷필요한 모든 도구는 상자 안에 들어 있을 겁니다. 조립을 시작하기 전에 이 도구들을 받았는지 확인해 주세요. 확인했나요? 좋습니다. 계속 진행해보죠. 압축된 가방을 조심스럽게 열어 시트 쿠션을 꺼내세요. 그 다음, ¹⁸시트 박스를 들어서 뒤집어 주셔야 합니다. 이 단계에서 친구에게 도와달라고 요청하는 게 좋을 거예요. 시트 박스가 꽤나 무겁거든요.

> 어휘 instructional 교육용의 demonstrate 보여주다
> assemble 조립하다 fairly 상당히 assembly 조립
> compressed 압축된 remove 꺼내다, 내보내다

16 시연 영상은 청자들에게 무엇을 하는 방법을 보여줄 것인가?
(A) 천장 선풍기 설치 **(B) 소파 조립**
(C) 컴퓨터 조립 (D) 샤워실 타일 깔기

> 해설 **세부 내용 - 시연 영상의 내용**
> 설명 영상에서 새로운 소파 모델 GL-300의 조립 방법을 보여주겠다(welcome to this instructional video, where I will demonstrate how to assemble our new sofa model, the GL-300)고 했으므로 정답은 (B)이다.

> 어휘 install 설치하다 ceiling 천장 tile 타일을 깔다

17 화자는 청자들에게 무엇을 상자에서 찾을 수 있다고 말하는가?
(A) 설명서 (B) 송장
(C) 쿠폰 **(D) 도구**

> 해설 **세부 내용 - 상자의 내용물**
> 조립을 위해 필요한 모든 도구는 상자 안에 들어 있을 것(All the tools you need should be right in the box)이라고 했으므로 정답은 (D)이다.

> 어휘 manual 설명서 invoice 송장

18 화자가 친구의 도움을 받으라고 제안하는 것은 무엇인가?
(A) 부속물 들어 올리기 (B) 테스트 수행
(C) 면적 측정 (D) 설명서 읽기

> 해설 **세부 내용 - 친구의 도움을 받으라는 것**
> 시트 박스를 들어서 뒤집을 때 친구에게 도와달라고 요청하는 게 좋을 것(you'll need to pick up the seat box and turn it over. You may want to ask a friend to help you with this step)이라고 했으므로 정답은 (A)이다.

> 어휘 lift 들어 올리다 conduct (특정 활동을) 수행하다
> measure 측정하다 instructions 설명(서)

> **Paraphrasing** 지문의 pick up the seat box
> → 보기의 Lifting a part

[19-21] 연설 + 표 W-Br

> ¹⁹**As mayor of Bloomville**, I've called this press conference to announce the city's decision about how we'll be allocating the remaining funds in this year's budget. We researched the costs of doing various projects, and it looks like we'll have enough money to fund only one project: ²⁰**adding bike lanes to the main roadways.** I know how popular the library expansion was, but uh, unfortunately, we'll have to delay that until a later time. ²¹**I'm now ready to take any questions you have about the budget or about the project itself.**

> ¹⁹블룸빌의 시장으로서, 올해 예산에서 남은 자금을 어떻게 할당할 것인지에 대한 시의 결정을 발표하기 위해 이번 기자회견을 소집했습니다. 저희가 다양한 프로젝트 실행 비용을 조사해 보니 단 하나의 프로젝트에만 자금을 충분히 지원할 수 있을 것 같은데, ²⁰주요 도로에 자전거 도로를 추가하는 것입니다. 도서관 확장을 얼마나 원했는지 알고 있습니다만, 아쉽게도 그것은 다음으로 미뤄야겠습니다. ²¹이제 예산이나 프로젝트 자체에 대한 여러분의 질문을 받겠습니다.

> 어휘 mayor 시장 call 소집하다 press conference 기자회견 allocate 할당하다, 배정하다 remaining 남은
> fund 자금; 자금을 대다 bike lane 자전거 도로 roadway 도로, 차도 expansion 확장

프로젝트	비용
²⁰**자전거 도로**	**1백만 달러**
도서관 확장	2백만 달러
주차용 건물	2백 5십만 달러
주민 회관	3백만 달러

19 화자는 누구인 것 같은가?
(A) 회계사 (B) 사업가
(C) 시 공무원 (D) 건축가

> 해설 **전체 내용 - 화자의 신분**
> 맨 처음에 화자가 자신을 블룸빌의 시장(mayor of Bloomville)이라고 소개했으므로 정답은 (C)이다.

> 어휘 official (고위) 공무원

20 시각 정보에 따르면, 선정된 프로젝트의 비용은 얼마이겠는가?
(A) 1백만 달러 (B) 2백만 달러
(C) 2백 5십만 달러 (D) 3백만 달러

> 해설 **세부 내용 - 시각 정보**
> 주요 도로에 자전거 도로를 추가하는(adding bike lanes to the main roadways) 프로젝트에 자금을 지원할 것이라고 했다. 그리고 표에서 자전거 도로 프로젝트에 1백만 달러의 비용이 드는 것으로 나와 있으므로 정답은 (A)이다.

21 화자는 다음에 무엇을 하겠는가?
(A) 비디오 상영 **(B) 추가 정보 제공**
(C) 도서관 방문 (D) 시상

> 해설 **세부 내용 - 다음에 할 일**
> 지문 마지막에서 예산이나 프로젝트에 대한 질문을 받겠다 (I'm now ready to take any questions you have about the budget or about the project itself)고 했으므로 정답은 (B)이다.

UNIT 18 여행 / 견학 / 관람

ETS 기출 예제
본책 p.124

1 고대사 박물관에 오신 것을 환영합니다. 저는 여러분의 가이드입니다. 지금 저희는 이집트 갤러리에 있습니다. 특이한 유물이 많이 전시되어 있죠. **2** 몇 분께서 책과 영화에서 들은 몇몇 유명한 채색 가면을 볼 수 있는지 벌써 물어보셨는데요. 저희 예술 보존 전문가가 말했듯이, 그 물건들은 빛에 의해 쉽게 손상됩니다. 하지만 **3** 가면에 대해 더 알고 싶으시면, 기념품점에서 멋진 책을 구입하실 수 있습니다.

어휘 unusual 특이한 artifact (인공) 유물 conservation 보존 expert 전문가

ETS 유형 연습
본책 p.125

1 (B) 2 (A) 3 (B) 4 (A) 5 (B) 6 (A)

[1-2] 관람 W-Am

1 We will now be entering the gallery named Gold Hall. For this next part of our tour, I ask that you please refrain from taking pictures. **1** The first painting, here on our right, is *The Look*, arguably the most famous painting by Esmeralda Blanchard. What exactly is the woman in the painting looking at? Well, if you guessed the gardener by the pond, you are correct. Historians have recently confirmed this through a letter Blanchard wrote to her sister. You can read more about the correspondence in **2** *Blanchard's Gaze*, a souvenir book which is available in the gift shop.

1 이제 골드 홀이라는 관에 들어갑니다. 지금 견학부터는, 사진 촬영을 삼가주실 것을 요청합니다. **1** 여기 우리 오른쪽에 있는 첫 번째 그림은 에스메랄다 블랜차드의 가장 유명한 그림이라고 할 수 있는 <더 룩>입니다. 그림에 있는 여자는 정확히 무엇을 보고 있나요? 연못 옆 정원사라고 추측했다면, 여러분이 맞습니다. 블랜차드가 자신의 자매에게 쓴 편지를 통해 사학자들이 최근 이것을 확인했습니다. **2** <블랜차드의 시선>에서 그 편지에 대해 더 읽어 볼 수 있으며, 이 기념 도서는 기념품점에서 구매 가능합니다.

어휘 refrain from ~을 삼가다 arguably 주장하건대, 거의 틀림없이 historian 사학자 confirm 확인하다 correspondence 편지, 서신 souvenir 기념품, 선물

1 화자는 어디에서 일하는 것 같은가?
(A) 사진 스튜디오   (B) 미술관

해설 **전체 내용 – 화자의 근무 장소**

첫 문장에서 gallery가 언급되었고, 이어서 에스메랄다 블랜차드의 가장 유명한 그림(The first painting, here on our right, is *The Look*, arguably the most famous painting by Esmeralda Blanchard)에 대해 이야기하고 있으므로 화자는 미술관에서 근무한다는 것을 알 수 있다. 따라서 정답은 (B)이다.

2 <블랜차드의 시선>은 무엇인가?
(A) 책   (B) 그림

해설 **세부 내용 – 특정 대상의 정체**

편지에 대해서는 <블랜차드의 시선>에서 더 읽을 수 있다고 했고, 그것이 기념 도서(a souvenir book)라고 했으므로 정답은 (A)이다.

[3-4] 견학 M-Cn

Welcome to Danmere Tea Company's factory tour. **3** The first thing we'll do on our tour is visit the interactive Introduction Hall, where you'll have the chance to handle a selection of tea leaves of various textures. Then we'll see the process of tea production on the factory floor, and finally—in our new Danmere Tasting Room—**4** you'll get to sample a wide range of tea drinks. Trust me… you won't be able to go through all of them. I encourage you to walk around and see all the offerings before making your choices. Now, if everyone is ready, let's begin the tour.

댄미어 차 회사의 공장 견학에 오신 걸 환영합니다. **3** 우리가 견학에서 가장 먼저 할 일은 상호작용형 안내관 방문으로, 그곳에서 여러분은 다양한 감촉의 찻잎을 만져볼 수 있는 기회를 가져볼 겁니다. 그리고 나서 우리는 작업 현장에서 차의 생산 과정을 보게 될 것이며, 마지막으로 새로 마련된 댄미어 시음방에서 **4** 다양한 종류의 차를 시음할 겁니다. 저를 믿으세요… 여러분은 그걸 전부 다 경험할 수는 없을 겁니다. 선택을 하시기 전에 돌아다니면서 제공되는 것을 모두 구경하시길 권해드립니다. 이제 모두 준비가 되셨으면 견학을 시작하겠습니다.

어휘 interactive 상호작용의 introduction 안내 handle (손으로) 만지다 texture 감촉, 질감 process 과정 production 생산 a wide range of 다양한 go through ~을 경험하다 encourage 권하다 offering 제공되는 것 make one's choice 선택하다

3 청자들은 무엇을 가장 먼저 할 것인가?
(A) 차 생산 과정을 보기
(B) 찻잎의 질감을 만져보기

해설 **세부 내용 – 먼저 할 일**

지문 초반부에서 가장 먼저 할 일을 언급하고 있다. 상호작용형 안내관에서 다양한 감촉의 찻잎을 만져볼 수 있을 것(The first thing we'll do on our tour is visit the interactive Introduction Hall, where you'll have the chance to handle a selection of tea leaves of various textures)이라고 했으므로 정답은 (B)이다.

4 화자가 "여러분은 그걸 전부 다 경험할 수는 없을 겁니다"라고 말할 때, 무엇을 암시하는가?
(A) 많은 종류의 제품이 있다.
(B) 몇몇 제품은 아주 비싸다.

해설 세부 내용 – 화자의 의도

제시문이 나온 문맥을 살펴보면, 다양한 종류의 차를 시음할 것인데(you'll get to sample a wide range of tea drinks) 전부 다 경험할 수는 없다고 하고 있다. 따라서 매우 많은 종류의 차가 있음을 유추할 수 있으므로 정답은 (A)이다.

[5-6] 여행 M-Cn

Welcome to beautiful Thompson Lake. Please be advised that **5 our boat tour lasts approximately two hours.** We'll make one stop to give everyone a chance to walk around and get refreshments. **6 There's a gift shop and a café near the dock where we're stopping.** We'll stay for 30 minutes and then resume the tour promptly. Please be sure to remain close to the boat dock, so you can hear me announce when we're ready to go.

아름다운 톰슨 호수에 오신 것을 환영합니다. **5 우리 보트 투어는 약 2시간 동안 진행된다**는 것을 참고하세요. 여러분께 둘러보시고 다과를 드실 시간을 드리기 위해 한 번 정차할 예정입니다. **6 정차하는 선착장 근처에 기념품점과 카페가 있습니다.** 30분간 머무른 후 곧바로 투어를 재개하겠습니다. 출발 준비가 되면 안내 방송을 들을 수 있도록 보트 선착장 근처에 대기해 주세요.

어휘 last (~동안) 지속되다 approximately 대략 refreshments 다과 resume 재개하다 promptly 곧바로 dock 선착장

5 담화는 어디에서 이루어지고 있는 것 같은가?
(A) 비행기   (B) 보트

해설 전체 내용 – 장소

보트 투어가 약 2시간 동안 진행된다고(our boat tour lasts approximately two hours)고 안내하는 것으로 보아 정답은 (B)이다.

6 화자에 따르면, 청자들은 무엇을 할 기회가 있는가?
(A) 음식 및 선물 쇼핑
(B) 라이브 음악 듣기

해설 세부 내용 – 청자들이 할 수 있는 것

정차할 선착장 근처에 기념품점과 카페가 있다(There's a gift shop and a café near the dock where we're stopping)고 했으므로, 청자들은 다과와 선물을 살 수 있다는 것을 알 수 있다. 따라서 정답은 (A)이다.

ETS 실전 문제
본책 p.126

1 (A)	2 (D)	3 (C)	4 (A)	5 (C)	6 (D)
7 (C)	8 (D)	9 (A)	10 (D)	11 (B)	12 (C)
13 (B)	14 (C)	15 (B)	16 (D)	17 (C)	18 (A)
19 (C)	20 (A)	21 (D)			

[1-3] 여행 M-Cn

Welcome to today's walking tour of historic Avila City. **1 On this tour, we'll visit the city's most famous buildings and I'll talk about their different architectural styles.** You're probably already wondering about Morales Avenue, where we're standing right now. You can definitely see the difference in construction materials and styles from one side of the street to the other— the buildings on this side are clearly older than the buildings on the other side. That's because **2 instead of Morales Avenue, there used to be a wall here.** This wall surrounded the old city and marked its outer limits. But as the population grew, it had to be knocked down to make room for new housing. At the end of this tour, **3 we'll visit the history museum where we will see a model of what the city looked like before it expanded.**

오늘 유서 깊은 아빌라 시 도보 투어에 오신 것을 환영합니다. **1 이번 투어에서 도시의 가장 유명한 건물들을 방문해 건물들의 다양한 건축 양식에 대해 이야기하겠습니다.** 여러분은 아마 우리가 지금 서 있는 모랄레스 가에 대해 벌써 궁금하실 겁니다. 길 한쪽과 반대쪽의 건축 자재와 스타일의 차이가 확연히 보일 텐데요. 이쪽에 있는 건물들이 반대쪽 건물들보다 분명 더 오래되었습니다. **2 이곳에 모랄레스 가 대신에 벽이 있었기** 때문입니다. 이 벽은 옛 도시를 에워싸 경계를 표시했습니다. 그러나 인구가 증가하면서, 새 주택을 위한 공간을 마련하려고 벽을 허물어야만 했죠. 투어 마지막에 **3 역사 박물관을 방문해 도시가 확장되기 전에 어떤 모습이었는지 모형을 보겠습니다.**

어휘 historic 유서 깊은 architectural 건축의 definitely 확연히 construction 건축 surround 에워싸다 population 인구 knock down 허물다 room 공간 expand 확장되다

1 화자에 따르면, 투어의 주된 초점은 무엇인가?
(A) 건축 양식   (B) 지역 요리
(C) 문학계 인물   (D) 전통 농업

해설 전체 내용 – 투어의 초점

투어에서 도시의 건물들을 방문해 다양한 건축 양식에 대해 이야기할 것(On this tour, we'll visit the city's most famous buildings and I'll talk about their different architectural styles)이라고 했으므로 정답은 (A)이다.

어휘 cuisine 요리 literary 문학의 figure 인물

2 화자는 모랄레스 가에 대해 무엇을 말하는가?
(A) 유명한 작가가 한때 그곳에 살았다.
(B) 연례 축제의 장소이다.
(C) 차량 출입이 금지된다.
(D) 한때 도시 벽이 있었다.

해설 세부 내용 - 모랄레스 가에 대해 말한 것
지문 중반부에 이곳에 모랄레스 가 대신 벽이 있었다(instead of Morales Avenue, there used to be a wall here)고 했으므로 정답은 (D)이다.

Paraphrasing 지문의 there used to be a wall here
→ 보기의 A city wall used to stand there

3 화자에 따르면, 청자들이 박물관에서 무엇을 할 수 있는가?
(A) 단편 영화 시청
(B) 기념품 구입
(C) 재현된 도시 보기
(D) 강의 참석

해설 세부 내용 - 박물관에서 할 수 있는 것
역사 박물관을 방문해 도시가 확장되기 전에 어떤 모습이었는지 모형을 보겠다(we'll visit the history museum where we will see a model of what the city looked like before it expanded)고 했으므로 재현된 도시를 볼 수 있음을 알 수 있다. 따라서 정답은 (C)이다.

어휘 reproduction 재현, 재건

Paraphrasing 지문의 model of what the city looked like → 보기의 reproduction of the city

[4-6] 관람 W-Br

Welcome to tonight's tour of the Windemore Palace. ⁴This tour is unique because it's the only way visitors can see what the palace looks like after dark. As we visit the gardens and palace interior, you'll see what a magical place it is at night. ⁵Please avoid flash photography because the bright light interferes with the tour experience. ⁶Our tour will end at the gift shop where you will have the opportunity to purchase souvenirs. If you stop in, you'll receive complimentary tea and snacks to enjoy while you shop.

오늘밤 윈드모어 궁전 투어에 오신 것을 환영합니다. ⁴이 투어가 특별한 이유는 방문객들이 해가 진 뒤 궁전의 모습을 볼 수 있는 유일한 방법이기 때문입니다. 정원과 궁전 내부를 둘러보며 이곳이 밤에 얼마나 신비로운지 감상하실 수 있습니다. ⁵밝은 빛은 투어를 즐기는 데 방해가 되므로 플래시 촬영은 삼가 주세요. ⁶투어는 기념품점에서 마무리되며 그곳에서 기념품을 구입하실 기회가 있습니다. 기념품점을 방문하시면 쇼핑하시는 동안 무료 차와 간식을 즐길 수 있습니다.

어휘 palace 궁전 interior 실내 avoid 삼가다, 피하다 interfere with ~에 방해가 되다 opportunity 기회 complimentary 무료의

4 화자에 따르면, 투어의 독특한 점은 무엇인가?
(A) 야간에 진행된다.
(B) 원예 정보가 포함되어 있다.
(C) 마술 쇼로 마무리된다.
(D) 1년에 한 번만 열린다.

해설 세부 내용 - 투어의 독특한 점
투어가 특별한 이유는 해가 진 뒤 궁전의 모습을 볼 수 있기 때문(This tour is unique because it's the only way visitors can see what the palace looks like after dark)이라고 했으므로 정답은 (A)이다.

어휘 take place 열리다 gardening 원예 occur 일어나다

Paraphrasing 지문의 after dark → 보기의 at night

5 화자는 무엇을 삼가야 한다고 말하는가?
(A) 전시물 만지기
(B) 영상 녹화
(C) 플래시를 이용해 사진 촬영
(D) 큰 소리로 말하기

해설 세부 내용 - 요청 사항
밝은 빛은 투어를 즐기는 데 방해가 되므로 플래시 촬영을 삼가 달라(Please avoid flash photography because the bright light interferes with the tour experience)고 요청하고 있으므로 정답은 (C)이다.

어휘 display 전시물 record 녹화하다

Paraphrasing 지문의 flash photography
→ 보기의 Taking photos with a flash

6 화자는 청자들이 어디에서 다과를 받을 수 있다고 말하는가?
(A) 정원 (B) 접수처
(C) 구내 식당 (D) 기념품점

해설 세부 내용 - 다과 수령 장소
투어의 마지막 장소인 기념품점에서 기념품을 구입할 수 있다(Our tour will end at the gift shop where you will have the opportunity to purchase souvenirs)면서 방문하면 무료 차와 간식을 즐길 수 있다(If you stop in, you'll receive complimentary tea and snacks to enjoy while you shop)고 안내하므로 정답은 (D)이다.

[7-9] 관람 M-Cn

⁷Welcome to the Delta National Aquarium! We hope you enjoy your day here. For your convenience, ⁸storage lockers are now available to all visitors for only one dollar. Just stop by the customer service desk to pick up a key.

While you're over there, check out the Goldfish Café. Special children's meals are now available. And finally, a reminder that ⁹**our aquatic show will begin in just 15 minutes.** Come see the dolphins—don't miss this exciting show!

⁷델타 국립 수족관에 오신 것을 환영합니다! 여러분이 이곳에서 즐거운 하루를 보내기를 바랍니다. 편의를 위해, ⁸**모든 방문객은 이제 물품 보관함을 단 1달러에 이용할 수 있습니다.** 고객 서비스 데스크에 들러 열쇠만 받으시면 됩니다. 거기 가신 김에, 금붕어 카페도 가보세요. 이제 어린이 특별 메뉴도 주문 가능합니다. 그리고 마지막으로, ⁹**15분 있으면 수중 쇼가 시작된다**는 점을 다시 알려드립니다. 오셔서 돌고래를 보세요. 이 신나는 쇼를 놓치지 마세요!

어휘 convenience 편의 storage locker 물품 보관함 available 이용할 수 있는

7 어디에서 들리는 안내 방송일 것 같은가?
(A) 연회장 (B) 쇼핑 센터
(C) 수족관 (D) 미술관

해설 **전체 내용 - 장소**
안내 방송이 이루어지고 있는 장소를 묻는 질문으로 주로 도입부에 단서가 제시된다. 시작 부분에서 델타 국립 수족관(Delta National Aquarium)에 온 것을 환영한다고 했으므로 정답은 (C)이다.

8 화자에 따르면, 방문객들은 고객 서비스 데스크에서 무엇을 할 수 있는가?
(A) 복권 응모 (B) 건물 지도 받기
(C) 회원 가입 **(D) 보관함 대여**

해설 **세부 내용 - 고객 서비스 데스크에서 할 수 있는 일**
물품 보관함(storage lockers) 이용에 대해 언급한 후, 고객 서비스 데스크에 들러 열쇠를 받으라(Just stop by the customer service desk to pick up a key)고 했으므로 정답은 (D)이다.

어휘 raffle (기금 모금 등을 위한) 복권

Paraphrasing 지문의 storage lockers are now available, pick up a key → 보기의 Rent a locker

9 화자는 15분 후에 무슨 일이 일어날 것이라고 말하는가?
(A) 쇼가 시작된다.
(B) 카페에서 점심 식사를 제공하기 시작한다.
(C) 사전 예매 티켓이 판매된다.
(D) 투어 그룹이 모인다.

해설 **세부 내용 - 미래에 있을 일**
질문의 키워드인 in fifteen minutes에 주목한다. 15분 뒤에 수중 쇼가 시작될 것(our aquatic show will begin in just 15 minutes)이라고 했으므로 정답은 (A)이다.

어휘 advance ticket 사전 예매 티켓

Paraphrasing 지문의 our aquatic show will begin → 보기의 A show will start

[10-12] 여행 W-Br

¹⁰**We've reached the observation deck of Ridley Tower. And what a great panoramic scene we have of Port Hollister!** From the north side of the tower here, you can see all the major landmarks of our city, such as the dome of the art museum and the National Sports Stadium. And then, from the south side, you will see the harbor area and the bridge to the nearby island. We're very lucky because ¹¹**the weather is so good today.** Normally that island is covered in clouds this time of year, and you can't see it from the tower. So, have a look around and enjoy yourselves, but ¹²**please return here, to this bench, in half an hour.**

¹⁰우리는 리들리 타워 전망대에 도착했습니다. 파노라마로 펼쳐진 홀리스터 항의 전경이 정말 멋지네요! 이곳 타워 북쪽에서는, 미술관 돔과 국립체육관 등 우리 도시의 주요 랜드마크를 모두 볼 수 있습니다. 그리고 남쪽에서는 항구 지역과 근처 섬으로 가는 다리가 보일 것입니다. 우리는 정말 운이 좋네요. ¹¹오늘 날씨가 정말 좋거든요. 보통 이맘때면 저 섬은 구름에 덮여 있어서 타워에서 보이지 않아요. 자, 주위를 둘러보고 즐기시고 ¹²30분 후에 여기, 이 벤치로 돌아오세요.

어휘 reach 도착하다 observation deck 전망대 port 항구 normally 보통

10 담화의 주제는 무엇인가?
(A) 스포츠 경기의 점수 (B) 미술 전시회의 내용
(C) 보트 경로 **(D) 타워에서 바라본 풍경**

해설 **전체 내용 - 담화의 주제**
리들리 타워 전망대에 도착했다(We've reached the observation deck of Ridley Tower)고 이야기를 시작한 후 파노라마로 펼쳐진 홀리스터 항의 전경이 멋지다(And what a great panoramic scene we have of Port Hollister!)고 하면서 타워에서 보이는 전망에 대한 이야기를 이어가고 있다. 따라서 정답은 (D)이다.

11 화자에 의하면, 오늘따라 특이한 점은 무엇인가?
(A) 표가 반값이다. **(B) 하늘이 맑다.**
(C) 다리가 폐쇄되었다. (D) 섬이 붐빈다.

해설 **세부 내용 - 오늘 특이한 점**
질문의 키워드인 today에 대해 언급한 부분에 주목한다. 오늘 날씨가 좋다(the weather is so good today)고 한 후, 보통은 구름에 덮여 타워에서 섬이 보이지 않는다(Normally that island is covered in clouds this time of year, and you can't see it from the tower)고 했으므로 (B)가 정답이다.

어휘 crowded 붐비는

Paraphrasing 지문의 the weather is so good → 보기의 The sky is clear

12 청자들은 30분 후에 무엇을 할 것인가?
(A) 버스에 탑승 (B) 방에서 나가기
(C) 벤치에서 만나기 (D) 헤드셋 반납

해설 세부 내용 – 미래에 할 일
지문 마지막에 30분 후에 벤치로 돌아오라(please return here, to this bench, in half an hour)고 했으므로 정답은 (C)이다.

Paraphrasing 지문의 return here, to this bench
→ 보기의 Meet at a bench

[13-15] 견학 M-Cn

Hello, everyone, and welcome to Patel's Ice Cream Factory! **13 I hope you all enjoyed the ice cream sample you were given in the reception lobby.** That's our most popular flavor—chocolate hazelnut. My name's John, and I'll be showing you around our factory today. **14 I'll also be teaching you about the French pot method, which is the method we use to produce our ice cream.** It involves making each batch by hand in small pots. In the past, for sanitation reasons, we couldn't show visitors this part of the production process. But **15 last month, we finished building a special viewing room that makes it possible to watch the production safely behind large glass windows.**

안녕하세요, 여러분. 파텔 아이스크림 공장에 오신 것을 환영합니다! **13 환영 로비에서 받으신 아이스크림 샘플을 즐기셨기를 바랍니다.** 그것은 저희의 가장 인기 있는 초콜릿 헤이즐넛 맛입니다. 제 이름은 존이며, 오늘 여러분께 저희 공장을 안내해드릴 겁니다. **14 저는 여러분께 프렌치 팟 방식에 대해서도 가르쳐드릴 건데, 이것은 저희가 아이스크림을 생산하는 데 사용하는 방법입니다.** 여기에는 작은 냄비에 1회분을 만드는 수작업이 포함됩니다. 과거에는 위생상의 이유로 방문객들에게 이 생산 공정을 보여드릴 수 없었습니다. 하지만 **15 지난달, 저희는 대형 유리창 뒤에서 안전하게 생산을 관람할 수 있는 특별한 관람실을 완공했습니다.**

어휘 reception 환영, 접수 flavor 맛 method 방법 produce 생산하다 involve 포함하다 batch 한 회분 sanitation 위생 process 과정 viewing room 관람실

13 청자들은 환영 로비에서 무엇을 받았는가?
(A) 인쇄된 조리법 (B) 제품 샘플
(C) 할인 쿠폰 (D) 입장권

해설 세부 내용 – 로비에서 받은 것
청자들에게 환영 로비에서 받은 아이스크림 샘플을 즐겼기 바란다(I hope you all enjoyed the ice cream sample you were given in the reception lobby)고 했으므로 정답은 (B)이다.

어휘 recipe 조리법 entry 입장

14 화자는 청자들이 무엇을 배우게 될 것이라고 말하는가?
(A) 회사의 역사 (B) 다가오는 마케팅 캠페인
(C) 생산 과정 (D) 안전 절차

해설 세부 내용 – 청자들이 배울 것
화자가 아이스크림을 생산하는 데 사용하는 프렌치 팟 방식에 대해 가르쳐 줄 것(I'll also be teaching you about the French pot method, which is the method we use to produce our ice cream)이라고 안내하고 있으므로 청자들은 아이스크림 생산 과정에 대해 배울 예정임을 알 수 있다. 따라서 정답은 (C)이다.

어휘 upcoming 다가오는 procedure 절차

Paraphrasing 지문의 method we use to produce
→ 보기의 production process

15 화자에 따르면, 최근에 무슨 일이 일어났는가?
(A) 협상 (B) 개조 공사
(C) 이전 (D) 합병

해설 세부 내용 – 최근에 일어난 일
지난달 대형 유리창 뒤에서 생산을 관람할 수 있는 특별한 관람실을 완공했다(last month, we finished building a special viewing room that makes it possible to watch the production safely behind large glass windows)고 했으므로 정답은 (B)이다.

어휘 negotiation 협상 renovation 개조 relocation 이전 merger 합병

Paraphrasing 지문의 building a special viewing room → 보기의 renovation

[16-18] 견학 M-Au

Good morning, volunteers. Welcome to our wildlife preserve. **16 You're here to help with environmental conservation efforts.** This includes tasks like testing water quality and monitoring animals. Before we begin today, **17 I overheard some of you saying that we don't provide any training for our volunteers.** Actually, each of you will be assigned a mentor. Now, we're going on a short tour of the preserve. **18 Please remember to take notes as we walk around.** We'll talk about everything you see afterwards.

자원 봉사자 여러분, 안녕하세요. 야생동물 보호구역에 오신 것을 환영합니다. **16 여러분은 환경보전 활동을 도와주러 오셨는데요.** 여기에는 수질 검사, 동물 관찰 같은 일이 포함됩니다. 오늘 시작하기 전에, **17 제가 우연히 들었는데, 여러분 중 몇 분이 우리가 자원봉사자들을 위한 어떠한 교육도 제공하지 않는다고 말하더군요.** 사실, 여러분 각자에게 멘토가 배정될 예정입니다. 자, 보호구역을 잠깐 둘러보겠습니다. **18 돌아다닐 때 메모하는 것을 잊지 마세요.** 봤던 모든 것에 대해서 나중에 이야기할 겁니다.

> 어휘 volunteer 자원 봉사자 preserve 보호구역 environmental 환경의 conservation 보전 effort 활동, 노력 overhear 우연히 듣다 assign 배정하다 afterwards 나중에

16 청자들은 어떤 종류의 자원봉사를 할 것인가?
(A) 예술 교육   (B) 보건 서비스
(C) 지역 개발   (D) 환경보전

해설 **전체 내용 - 자원 봉사 종류**
지문 초반부에서 청자들이 환경보전 활동을 도와주러 왔다(You're here to help with environmental conservation efforts)고 했으므로 정답은 (D)이다.

17 화자는 왜 "여러분 각자에게 멘토가 배정될 예정입니다"라고 말하는가?
(A) 제안을 거절하려고   (B) 피드백을 요청하려고
(C) 정보를 바로잡으려고   (D) 참여를 권장하려고

해설 **세부 내용 - 화자의 의도**
제시문이 나온 문맥을 살펴보면, 자원 봉사자들을 위한 어떠한 교육도 제공하지 않는다고 몇몇 사람들이 말하는 것을 들었다(I overheard some of you saying that we don't provide any training for our volunteers)고 한 후, 사실은 모두에게 멘토가 배정될 것이라고 밝힌 것으로 보아, 몇몇 사람들의 말과 달리 교육이 있다는 사실을 알리려고 한 말임을 알 수 있다. 따라서 정답은 (C)이다.

어휘 reject 거절하다   correct 바로잡다
encourage 권장하다

18 화자는 청자들에게 무엇을 상기시키는가?
(A) 메모하기   (B) 보안경 착용
(C) 면책동의서 서명   (D) 설명서 읽기

해설 **세부 내용 - 상기 사항**
보호구역을 돌아다니며 메모하는 것을 잊지 말라(Please remember to take notes as we walk around)고 했으므로 정답은 (A)이다.

어휘 waiver 면책동의서

[19-21] 관람 + 안내 책자 W-Am

Welcome to the Megahurst Art Gallery. You've chosen a very exciting time to visit our museum because **19 we just joined the Greater European Art Union.** Our membership in this union means our galleries will regularly feature new exhibits from private and public art collections around Europe. To see a complete list of where our various exhibits are from, take a look in your brochure. Also, notice that **20 there is a twenty percent off coupon in your brochure** that you can use at the Megahurst food court or gift shop. **21 Now, let's start our tour and enter the first exhibit, which is on loan to us from the Amsterdam Collection.** Please, follow me.

메가허스트 미술관에 오신 것을 환영합니다. 저희 미술관을 방문하기에 아주 좋은 때를 선택하셨는데, **19 저희가 최근 대 유럽 미술 협회에 가입했기** 때문입니다. 저희가 이 협회에 가입함으로써, 유럽 전역의 개인 및 공공 미술 소장품으로 구성된 새로운 전시들을 정기적으로 선보일 수 있게 되었습니다. 다양한 전시품들이 어디에서 왔는지 완전한 목록을 보려면, 안내 책자를 참고해주세요. 또한, 메가허스트 푸드 코트나 기념품점에서 사용할 수 있는 **20 20퍼센트 할인 쿠폰이 안내 책자에 있다**는 것도 알아두시기 바랍니다. **21 이제 관람을 시작하며 첫 번째 전시에 들어갈 텐데, 이 전시는 암스테르담 컬렉션에서 대여한 것입니다.** 저를 따라오세요.

어휘 union 협회, 연합   regularly 정기적으로   feature 출연시키다   exhibit 전시(품); 전시하다   private 개인 소유의   complete 완전한   on loan 대여한, 빌린

전시	전시품 출처
회화 업적	포르투갈 재단
현대 인쇄술	애커 가문
스위스 사진	베른 대학교
21 네덜란드 조각	암스테르담 컬렉션

19 메가허스트 미술관은 최근에 무엇을 했는가?
(A) 새 지점을 열었다.
(B) 미술 수업을 제공하기 시작했다.
(C) 미술 단체에 가입했다.
(D) 사진 촬영을 금지했다.

해설 **세부 내용 - 미술관이 최근에 한 일**
미술관이 최근에 대 유럽 미술 협회에 가입(we just joined the Greater European Art Union)했다고 했으므로 정답은 (C)이다.

20 안내 책자에 무엇이 포함되어 있는가?
(A) 할인 쿠폰   (B) 레스토랑 메뉴
(C) 행사 일정표   (D) 회원 신청서

해설 **세부 내용 - 안내 책자에 포함된 것**
질문의 키워드인 brochure에 주목하면, 20퍼센트 할인 쿠폰이 있다(there is a twenty percent off coupon in your brochure)고 했으므로 정답은 (A)이다.

21 시각 정보에 따르면, 투어 그룹은 어떤 전시를 먼저 방문할 것인가?
(A) 회화 업적   (B) 현대 인쇄술
(C) 스위스 사진   (D) 네덜란드 조각

해설 **세부 내용 - 시각 정보**
암스테르담 컬렉션에서 대여한 전시를 첫 번째로 볼 것(Now, let's start our tour and enter the first exhibit, which is on loan to us from the Amsterdam Collection)이라고 했고, 시각 정보에 암스테르담 컬렉션은 네덜란드 조각 전시로 나와 있으므로 정답은 (D)이다.

PART 5&6 READING COMPREHENSION

UNIT 01 문장의 구성 요소

❶ 주어와 동사

ETS 유형 연습 본책 p.137

| 1 (A) | 2 (B) | 3 (B) | 4 (A) | 5 (D) | 6 (B) |
| 7 (D) | 8 (D) |

1 (A)
번역 새 전자 노트패드의 주 기능은 인터넷 사용이다.
해설 빈칸은 be동사 is의 주어 자리이므로 명사 (A) function이 정답이다.

2 (B)
번역 이 씨는 최근에 회사의 주요 생산 시설 견학을 수행했다.
해설 빈칸은 문장의 동사가 필요한 자리이므로 과거 동사인 (B) conducted가 정답이다. to부정사인 (A) to conduct는 동사 역할을 할 수 없으므로 오답이다.

3 (B)
번역 배송품은 열흘 이내에 수령될 것으로 예상된다.
해설 빈칸은 동사 should be expected의 주어 자리이자 of the shipment의 수식을 받는 명사 자리이므로 명사 (B) Receipt가 정답이다.

4 (A)
번역 동봉된 설문서를 작성해서 저희 사무실로 반송해 주십시오.
해설 주어 없이 Please로 시작하는 명령문이므로 동사원형 (A) complete가 정답이다.

5 (D)
번역 계약 협상 동안 이무라 씨는 자신이 뛰어난 협상가라는 것을 입증했다.
해설 빈칸은 주어 she와 동격을 나타내는 주격 보어 자리이고, 앞에 부정관사 an과 형용사 excellent가 있으므로 명사 자리이다. 따라서 명사 (D) negotiator가 정답이다.

6 (B)
번역 카펫 설치는 사무용 가구를 옮기는 대로 완료될 수 있다.
해설 빈칸은 can be completed의 주어 자리이자 of the carpet의 수식을 받으면서 정관사 The 뒤에 오는 명사 자리이므로 명사 (B) installation이 정답이다. 명사 (C) installers(설치하는 사람)는 의미상 적합하지 않다.

7 (D)
번역 온라인 쇼핑객들은 제품이 웹사이트에 보이는 이미지와 외관상 다를 수 있다는 점에 유의해야 한다.
해설 빈칸이 조동사 may 뒤에 있으므로 동사원형 (D) differ가 정답이다.

8 (D)
번역 케인 씨는 이사회 회의 일정을 변경해 달라고 요청했다.
해설 빈칸은 동사 requested의 목적어 역할을 하는 that절에서 동사 be의 주어 자리이자 앞의 board와 복합명사 구조를 이루어 '이사회 회의'라는 의미가 되어야 자연스러우므로 (D) meeting이 정답이다.

❷ 목적어

ETS 유형 연습 본책 p.139

| 1 (B) | 2 (B) | 3 (B) | 4 (B) | 5 (C) | 6 (A) |
| 7 (D) | 8 (B) |

1 (B)
번역 시립 도서관은 6월 30일까지 중고책 기부를 받을 것이다.
해설 빈칸은 동사 will accept의 목적어 자리이므로 명사 (B) donations가 정답이다.

2 (B)
번역 지역 예술가들은 매주 토요일 아침마다 자신들의 수제 창작품을 판매한다.
해설 빈칸은 동사 sell의 목적어 자리이자 their handmade의 수식을 받는 명사 자리이므로 명사 (B) creations가 정답이다.

3 (B)
번역 마틴 씨는 일정이 맞지 않아 기획 회의를 연기하기로 결정했다.
해설 빈칸은 동사 has decided의 목적어 자리이므로 the planning meeting을 목적어로 취하면서 명사 역할을 할 수 있는 to부정사 (B) to postpone이 정답이다.

4 (B)
번역 며칠 동안 고온을 유지한 후에 어제 기온이 마침내 조금 떨어졌다.
해설 빈칸은 동사 fell 뒤에서 동사를 수식하는 수식어 자리이므로 부사 (B) slightly가 정답이다.

5 (C)
번역 CEO인 도널드 파라조는 국제 금융 언론에 합병 제안에 대한 간략한 성명서를 발표했다.
해설 빈칸은 동사 issued의 목적어 자리이자 a brief의 수식을 받는 명사 자리이므로 명사 (C) statement가 정답이다.

6 (A)

번역 전기 자동차는 배터리 수명이 개선되면 더 널리 수용될 것으로 예상된다.

해설 빈칸은 to부정사 to gain의 목적어 자리이자 비교급 형용사 wider의 수식을 받는 명사 자리이므로 명사 (A) acceptance가 정답이다. 나머지는 품사상 부적합하다.

7 (D)

번역 사무용품을 주문하기 전에 관리자로부터 서면 승인을 받는 것을 기억하세요.

해설 빈칸은 to부정사 to obtain의 목적어 자리이자 형용사 written의 수식을 받는 명사 자리이므로 명사 (D) authorization이 정답이다. 나머지는 품사상 빈칸에 들어갈 수 없다.

8 (B)

번역 올리버 씨는 옷감이 어떤 모양인지 보여 주려고 고객들에게 견본을 줬다.

해설 빈칸은 to부정사의 목적어 자리이다. show는 〈show+간접목적어+직접목적어〉의 구조를 취한다. 따라서 동사의 간접목적어 자리이므로 목적격 인칭대명사인 (B) them이 정답이다.

③ 보어

ETS 유형 연습
본책 p.141

1 (A) 2 (A) 3 (B) 4 (B) 5 (D) 6 (D)
7 (A) 8 (D)

1 (A)

번역 선 푸즈 사는 중국 내 가공식품 판매의 선두기업이 되었다.

해설 빈칸은 동사 has become의 주어인 Sun Foods, Inc.와 동일한 대상을 나타내는 주격 보어 자리이자 부정관사 a 뒤의 명사 자리이므로 명사 (A) leader가 정답이다.

2 (A)

번역 추 씨는 뛰어난 영업 실적으로 상을 받아서 매우 기뻤다.

해설 빈칸은 be동사 was의 주어인 Ms. Chu를 보충하는 주격 보어 자리이자 부사 extremely의 수식을 받는 형용사 자리이므로 형용사 (A) happy가 정답이다.

3 (B)

번역 무게가 가볍기 때문에 최신형 애퓨라지 진공 청소기는 운반하기 쉽다.

해설 빈칸은 be동사 is의 주어 the latest Apurage vacuum cleaner를 보충하는 주격 보어 자리이므로 형용사 (B) easy가 정답이다. 명사 보어는 주어와 동일한 대상을 나타내므로, 명사 (A) ease(용이함)는 의미상 적합하지 않다.

4 (B)

번역 전문가들은 이스트사이드 테크놀로지 사의 주식 안정성에 대해 여전히 낙관적이다.

해설 빈칸은 동사 remain의 주어인 Experts를 보충하는 주격 보어 자리이므로 형용사 (B) optimistic이 정답이다.

5 (D)

번역 이노우에 씨는 다음 주에 예산안을 마무리 지을 수 있을 것이라고 확신한다.

해설 빈칸은 be동사 is와 that절 사이에서 주어 Ms. Inoue를 보충 설명하는 주격 보어 자리이므로 형용사 (D) positive가 정답이다. 명사 보어는 주어와 동일한 대상을 나타내는데, (A) positivity(확실함)와 (B) positives(긍정적인 것)는 주어와 동일한 대상이 아니고, 부사 (C) positively(긍정적으로)는 품사상 적합하지 않다.

6 (D)

번역 탄탄한 경력 때문에 사카이 씨는 셀리나 리걸 어소시에이츠를 이끌어 갈 인물로 자연스럽게 선택되었다.

해설 빈칸은 be동사 was의 주어 Ms. Sakai와 동일한 대상을 나타내는 주격 보어 자리이자 a natural의 수식을 받는 명사 자리이므로 명사 (D) choice가 정답이다.

7 (A)

번역 자격을 갖춘 의료 인력에 대한 경쟁이 최근 들어 치열해졌다.

해설 빈칸은 has become의 주어인 The competition을 보충 설명하는 주격 보어 자리이므로 형용사 (A) intense가 정답이다. 명사 보어는 주어와 동일한 대상을 나타내는데, 명사 (B) intensity(강렬함)는 주어와 동일한 대상이 아니다.

8 (D)

번역 많은 직원들이 새로운 컴퓨터 프로그램이 상당히 유익하다고 보고했다.

해설 빈칸은 접속사 that이 이끄는 명사절에서 have found의 목적어인 the new computer program을 보충하는 목적격 보어 자리이므로 형용사인 (D) beneficial이 정답이다. 명사 목적격 보어는 목적어와 동일한 대상을 나타내므로, 명사 (A) benefit은 의미상 적합하지 않다.

ETS 실전 문제
본책 p.142

1 (C) 2 (B) 3 (A) 4 (A) 5 (B) 6 (D)
7 (C) 8 (A) 9 (C) 10 (C) 11 (C) 12 (D)
13 (C) 14 (A)

1 (C)

번역 출장 여행객은 비행기 기내용 가방에 대한 요건을 모두 충족하는 여행 가방을 구매해야 한다.

해설 앞에 정관사가 있고 뒤에 전치사 for가 있으므로 빈칸에는 명사가 들어가야 한다. 따라서 명사인 (C) requirements가 정답이다.

어휘 meet 충족시키다   carry-on 기내용 가방
requirement 요건

2 (B)

번역 앰플로노 산업의 최신 제품은 휴대전화와 경량 태블릿 컴퓨터를 결합한 것이다.

해설 빈칸은 be동사 is의 보어 자리이자 부정관사 a 뒤의 명사 자리이므로 명사 (B) combination이 정답이다.

어휘 latest 최신의   lightweight 경량의   combine 결합하다
combination 결합

3 (A)

번역 파인 리지 호텔의 주요 매력은 근사한 시골 경관이다.

해설 앞에 정관사 The와 형용사 main이 있으므로 빈칸에는 명사가 들어가야 한다. 또한 be동사의 단수형인 is의 주어 자리이므로 단수명사인 (A) appeal이 정답이다. (B) appeals는 복수명사이고, (C) appealed는 과거동사, (D) appealing(매력적인)은 형용사이므로 빈칸에 부적합하다.

어휘 stunning 근사한   countryside 시골   appeal 매력

4 (A)

번역 펠튼 엔지니어링 회의 주최자들은 제라드 와일리 박사를 올해의 기조 연설자로 모시게 되어 기쁩니다.

해설 빈칸은 be동사 are의 주어 자리이자 명사 Conference와 복합명사 구조를 이루는 명사 자리이므로 복수 명사 (A) organizers가 정답이다.

어휘 keynote speaker 기조 연설자   organizer 주최자

5 (B)

번역 포커스 그룹 구성원들 사이에서는 샐러드 드레싱이 충분히 달다는 데 의견이 일치한다.

해설 빈칸은 that 명사절에서 be동사 is의 주어인 명사 the salad dressing을 보충 설명하는 주격 보어 자리이자 부사 enough의 수식을 받는 형용사 자리이므로 형용사 (B) sweet이 정답이다. 최상급 형용사 (D) sweetest는 주로 정관사 the가 앞에 붙는다.

어휘 consensus 의견 일치   focus group 포커스 그룹
(시장조사를 위해 각계각층에서 뽑은 사람들)
sweeten 달게 하다

6 (D)

번역 키비 크래프트 오븐을 처음 사용하기 전에 사용 설명서를 참고하세요.

해설 주어 없이 Please로 시작하는 명령문이므로 동사원형 (D) consult가 정답이다.

어휘 owner's manual 사용 설명서   for the first time 처음으로   consult 참고하다, 상담하다

7 (C)

번역 적당한 지원자가 발견되면 지체 없이 일자리를 제안하는 것이 남궁 컨설팅의 정책이다.

해설 빈칸은 to부정사 to make의 목적어이면서 job과 복합명사 구조를 이루는 명사 자리이므로 명사 (C) offer가 정답이다. 부정관사 a 뒤의 명사 자리이므로 복수형인 (A) offerings(매물)는 적합하지 않다.

어휘 policy 정책   delay 지체   applicant 지원자
job offer 일자리 제안

8 (A)

번역 경리부는 청구 시스템을 개선하기 위한 예산 견적 초안을 제출했다.

해설 빈칸은 동사구 has submitted의 목적어 자리로, budget과 복합명사 구조를 이루며 initial 앞의 부정관사 an과 사용할 수 있는 명사가 와야 한다. 따라서 셀 수 있는 명사의 단수형인 (A) estimate이 정답이다.

어휘 submit 제출하다   initial 최초의   budget 예산
estimate 견적   estimation 판단, 평가

9 (C)

번역 맥더피 클리너즈 앤 테일러즈는 정장의 전문적인 수선으로 알려져 있다.

해설 빈칸은 전치사 for의 목적어 역할을 하는 자리이자, 소유격 its와 형용사 expert의 수식을 받는 명사 자리이므로 명사 (C) alterations가 정답이다.

어휘 expert 전문적인   formal wear 정장   alter 변경하다
alteration 수선, 변경   alterable 변경 가능한

10 (C)

번역 때때로 직원들은 문제를 해결하기 위해 위험을 감수하고 새로운 방식을 시도하도록 격려가 필요하다.

해설 빈칸은 동사 need의 목적어 자리이자 뒤의 to부정사구 to take risks and try new ways의 수식을 받는 명사 자리이므로 명사 (C) encouragement가 정답이다.

어휘 risk 위험   solve 해결하다   encouragement 격려

[11-14] 이메일

수신: 직원 〈employees@braffordtech.com〉
발신: 조안나 스파츠 〈joanna.spatz@braffordtech.com〉
날짜: 9월 5일
제목: 카멜라 바드를 위한 파티

안녕하세요, 여러분.

아시다시피, 우리 영업 사원 중 한 명인 카멜라 바드가 몇 달 전 **11 승진했습니다**. 새로운 역할의 일환으로 그녀에게 **12 더 많은 영업 책임이 주어졌습니다**. 이 새로운 임무로 그녀는 여기저기 이동

하며 지난 4주를 보내야 했습니다. 비록 한동안 카메라를 보지 못했지만 그녀는 여전히 여기 사무실에서 브래포드 테크 가족의 일원입니다. **13그러므로** 저는 그녀의 새로운 역할을 축하하고 2주 뒤 사무실로 돌아올 때 그녀의 귀환을 환영하기 위해 파티를 준비하고 있습니다. **14기여해 주실 수 있는 게 있다면 알려주세요.** 도움을 주시면 감사하겠으며, 여러분 모두 참석하실 수 있기를 바랍니다.

조안나 스파츠

어휘 sales representative 영업 사원 responsibility 책임 duty 임무 on the road 이동 중인 organize 준비하다

11 (C)

해설 빈칸 뒤 문장에서 새로운 역할 때문에 그녀에게 더 많은 영업 책임이 주어졌다(As part of her new role, she was given increased sales responsibilities)고 했으므로, 빈칸은 '카메라 바드가 승진했다'는 내용이 되어야 자연스럽다. 따라서 (C) promoted가 정답이다. (A) honored(영광을 주다), (B) featured(주연을 시키다), (D) discovered(발견하다)는 의미상 어울리지 않는다.

12 (D)

해설 빈칸은 동사 was given의 목적어 역할을 하는 명사구 sales responsibilities를 수식하는 형용사 자리이고, '증가한 영업 책임이 주어졌다'는 의미가 되어야 하므로 형용사 (D) increased가 정답이다. 참고로, 4형식 동사인 give가 수동태로 쓰일 때 간접목적어가 문장의 주어가 되면 직접목적어는 동사 뒤에 남는다.

13 (C)

해설 빈칸 앞 문장에서 한동안 카메라를 보지 못했지만 여전히 사무실의 일원이라고 했고, 빈칸 뒤에서는 그녀의 귀환을 환영하는 파티를 준비하고 있다고 했다. 따라서 '그러므로, 따라서'라는 의미로 앞뒤 내용의 인과관계를 나타내는 (C) therefore가 정답이다. (A) also(또한), (B) then(그 다음에), (D) nevertheless(그럼에도 불구하고)는 의미상 적합하지 않다.

14 (A)

번역 (A) 기여해 주실 수 있는 게 있다면 알려주세요.
(B) 회사는 올해 축하할 일이 많습니다.
(C) 카메라는 브래포드 테크에서 6년 이상 근무했습니다.
(D) 우리는 올해 안에 카메라가 사무실로 돌아오기를 바랍니다.

해설 빈칸 앞 문장에서 동료를 위한 파티를 준비 중(I am therefore organizing a party to celebrate her new role and welcome her back to the office when she returns in two weeks)이라고 했고, 빈칸 뒤 문장에서는 도움을 주면 감사하겠다(I would appreciate the help)는 말을 하고 있다. 따라서 빈칸에는 파티 준비에 대해 도움을 요청하는 (A)가 정답이다.

어휘 contribute 기여하다

UNIT 02 명사

1 명사의 역할과 자리

ETS 유형 연습
본책 p.145

1 (B) 2 (B) 3 (B) 4 (A) 5 (A) 6 (A)
7 (A) 8 (A)

1 (B)
번역 다양한 기념품을 그 선물가게에서 볼 수 있다.
해설 빈칸은 부정관사 A 뒤의 명사 자리이므로 명사 (B) variety가 정답이다. 참고로, A variety of souvenirs가 문장의 주어이다.

2 (B)
번역 주문서 하단에 서명을 포함시키는 것을 잊지 마세요.
해설 빈칸은 to부정사 to include의 목적어 자리이자 소유격 your 뒤의 명사 자리이므로 명사 (B) signature가 정답이다.

3 (B)
번역 공연 중 카메라 작동은 금지된다.
해설 빈칸은 be동사 is의 주어 자리이자 정관사 The 뒤의 명사 자리이므로 명사 (B) operation이 정답이다.

4 (A)
번역 안전 때문에 건설 현장에 들어가는 사람은 누구나 안전모를 써야 한다.
해설 빈칸은 전치사 of의 목적어 자리이므로 명사 (A) safety가 정답이다.

5 (A)
번역 지난달 보고서에 따르면 이번 분기에 소매 판매는 두 배로 증가할 것으로 예상된다.
해설 빈칸은 전치사 According to의 목적어 자리이고 앞에 소유격 last month's가 있으므로 명사가 들어가야 한다. 따라서 명사 (A) report가 정답이다. (B) to report는 to부정사, (C) reported는 과거동사/과거분사, (D) reportedly는 부사로 소유격 뒤 명사 자리에 들어갈 수 없다.

6 (A)
번역 서한에 서명하기 전 6번째 단락을 철저히 검토해야 한다.
해설 빈칸은 동사 should be made의 주어 자리이자 A thorough의 수식을 받는 명사 자리이므로 명사 (A) revision이 정답이다.

7 (A)

번역 리치브룩 미술관은 매우 귀중한 그림 한 점을 소장품으로 갖고 있다.

해설 빈칸은 동사 has의 목적어 자리이자 형용사 valuable의 수식을 받는 명사 자리이므로 명사 (A) drawing이 정답이다.

8 (A)

번역 구미코 세키네 씨는 5월 3일에 수채화 기법을 시연해 보일 것이다.

해설 빈칸은 동사 give의 목적어 자리이며, 그 앞에 셀 수 있는 명사의 단수형과 결합하는 부정관사 a가 있다. 따라서 셀 수 있는 명사의 단수형인 (A) demonstration이 정답이다.

② 셀 수 있는 명사와 셀 수 없는 명사

ETS 유형 연습   본책 p.147

| 1 (A) | 2 (B) | 3 (A) | 4 (A) | 5 (D) | 6 (C) |
| 7 (B) | 8 (A) |

1 (A)

번역 최고의 영업사원들은 잠재적인 구매자들과 신뢰를 먼저 확립한다.

해설 빈칸 앞에 셀 수 있는 명사의 단수형과 결합하는 부정관사 a가 있으므로 단수명사 (A) sense가 정답이다.

2 (B)

번역 전화로 접수된 주문에는 3달러의 수수료가 추가된다.

해설 order는 셀 수 있는 명사여서 앞에 부정관사 an이 붙거나 복수형을 써야 하므로 (B) orders가 정답이다. 참고로, orders 뒤의 과거분사 received가 orders를 꾸미는 구조로 'orders received by telephone'은 '전화로 접수된 주문'이라고 해석한다.

3 (A)

번역 리베라 씨는 고위 경영직 직위에 이제 막 임명되었다.

해설 senior management 앞에 부정관사 a가 있으므로 단수명사 (A) position이 정답이다. 여러 개의 명사가 나열되는 경우, 마지막에 나오는 명사와 한정사를 일치시킨다.

4 (A)

번역 스타 운송은 지난달에 새로운 사무용 가구를 주문했다.

해설 new office 앞에 부정관사 a가 없으므로 셀 수 없는 명사인 (A) furniture가 정답이다. 셀 수 있는 명사인 (B) desk가 정답이 되려면 new office 앞에 a가 있거나 복수형인 desks가 되어야 한다.

5 (D)

번역 관리자들은 전체 주문량을 채울 수 있을 때까지 선적을 미루기로 결정했다.

해설 빈칸은 to부정사 to delay의 목적어 자리이다. 앞에 부정관사 a(n)이 없는 것으로 보아 셀 수 없는 명사 자리이므로 '선적'이라는 의미의 셀 수 없는 명사 (D) shipment가 정답이다. (A) ship(배)과 (C) shipper(선적회사)는 부정관사 a가 필요한 셀 수 있는 명사이다.

6 (C)

번역 이번 분기 들어 지금까지 소형차의 지역 매출은 산업 분석가들의 예측을 웃돌았다.

해설 빈칸은 소유격 analysts'(분석가들의)의 수식을 받는 명사 자리이므로 명사 (C) predictions가 정답이다.

7 (B)

번역 D & Y 뷰티 코퍼레이션은 내년에 적어도 한 군데의 해외 지사를 추가할 계획이다.

해설 빈칸은 to부정사 to add의 목적어 자리이자 one과 결합하는 셀 수 있는 명사의 단수형 자리이므로 셀 수 있는 명사의 단수형인 (B) location이 정답이다.

8 (A)

번역 평균적으로 우리 직원들은 약 6년간 회사에 근무한다.

해설 빈칸은 전치사 On의 목적어 자리로, On과 결합하여 '평균적으로, 보통'이라는 의미를 나타내는 명사 (A) average가 정답이다. 전치사 뒤에는 명사와 동명사가 올 수 있지만 뒤에 목적어가 없으므로 능동 형태의 현재분사인 (C) averaging은 들어갈 수 없다.

③ 한정사의 개념과 종류

ETS 유형 연습   본책 p.149

| 1 (A) | 2 (B) | 3 (A) | 4 (B) | 5 (A) | 6 (C) |
| 7 (B) | 8 (B) |

1 (A)

번역 전임 사장 존 켄덜 씨에 대한 몬토야 씨의 전기는 많은 논란거리다.

해설 빈칸 뒤에 셀 수 없는 명사 debate가 있으므로 셀 수 없는 명사와 결합하는 한정사 (A) much가 정답이다. (B) many 뒤에는 셀 수 있는 명사의 복수형이 와야 한다.

2 (B)

번역 신형 불린 스포츠카에는 지난해 모델과 구별되는 몇 가지 특징이 있다.

해설 빈칸 앞에 셀 수 있는 명사의 복수형과 결합하는 한정사

several이 있으므로 셀 수 있는 명사의 복수형인 (B) features가 정답이다.

3 (A)
번역 불가피한 갈등 때문에, 칸 씨는 화상회의를 목요일까지 미룰 것이다.

해설 빈칸은 형용사 unavoidable의 수식을 받는 명사 자리이자 형용사 앞에 부정관사 an이 있으므로 셀 수 있는 명사의 단수형인 (A) conflict가 정답이다.

4 (B)
번역 모서 여행사는 일부 항공편을 할인가로 제공한다.

해설 빈칸 뒤에 셀 수 있는 명사의 복수형인 flights가 있으므로 셀 수 있는 명사의 복수형과 결합하는 한정사 (B) some이 정답이다. (A) much 뒤에는 셀 수 없는 명사가 와야 한다.

5 (A)
번역 프로토콜이 수정된 후 처음 몇 달간 생산성이 23퍼센트 증가했다.

해설 빈칸은 first와 함께 명사 months를 수식하는 형용사 자리로, 문맥상 '처음 몇 달간'이라는 의미가 되어야 자연스러우므로 정답은 (A) few이다. (B) small(작은)과 (C) high(높은)는 months를 수식하는 말로 어울리지 않고 (D) late(늦은)은 first와 의미가 상충되므로 적절하지 않다.

6 (C)
번역 자동차 생산 공장을 찾는 방문객은 반드시 보안 검문소에 등록해야 한다.

해설 빈칸은 동사 must register의 주어 자리이며, 그 앞에 셀 수 있는 명사의 복수형과 결합하는 한정사 All이 있다. 따라서 셀 수 있는 명사의 복수형인 (C) visitors가 정답이다.

7 (B)
번역 이번 달에 패터슨 인더스트리얼 솔루션즈의 사장은 많은 중요 계약서에 서명했다.

해설 빈칸은 형용사 important의 수식을 받는 명사 자리이다. 또한 앞에 셀 수 있는 명사의 복수형과 결합하는 한정사 a number of가 있으므로 빈칸에는 셀 수 있는 명사의 복수형인 (B) contracts가 와야 한다.

8 (B)
번역 지원자들 대부분은 회사 본사에서 유급 인턴 연수를 완료했다.

해설 빈칸 앞에 셀 수 있는 명사의 복수형과 결합하는 한정사 Most가 있으므로 셀 수 있는 명사의 복수형인 (B) applicants가 정답이다.

ETS 실전 문제 본책 p.150

1 (B)	2 (C)	3 (C)	4 (C)	5 (A)	6 (A)
7 (C)	8 (A)	9 (C)	10 (D)	11 (B)	12 (D)
13 (A)	14 (C)				

1 (B)
번역 콜비 사는 고객층에 대한 정보를 더 많이 수집한 후에 잠재 투자자들에게 사업 계획을 제시할 것이다.

해설 빈칸은 전치사 to의 목적어 자리이면서 형용사 potential의 수식을 받는 명사 자리이므로 명사 (B) investors가 정답이다. 명사 역할을 하는 동명사 (A) investing(투자, 투자하는 것)은 의미상 적합하지 않다.

어휘 customer base 고객층   potential 잠재적인   investor 투자자

2 (C)
번역 놀이공원 놀이기구 운영자들은 근무 시간이 시작될 때마다 안전 수칙 점검 목록을 검토해야 한다.

해설 빈칸에는 명사구 work period를 수식하는 것이 와야 한다. 빈칸 뒤의 work period가 단수명사이므로 단수명사와 결합하는 한정사 (C) every가 정답이다. (A) always는 부사라서 품사상 적합하지 않고, (B) whose도 한정사로 쓸 수 있지만 '누구의'라는 의미이고, (D) all은 복수 가산명사와 함께 쓴다.

어휘 amusement park 놀이공원   ride 놀이기구   operator 운영자   review 검토하다   safety-protocol 안전 수칙   period 기간

3 (C)
번역 카시스 화랑은 모든 지원자에게 전시 제안서를 제출하기 전에 지침을 꼼꼼하게 읽도록 권장한다.

해설 빈칸 앞에 셀 수 있는 명사의 단수형과 결합하는 every가 있으므로 셀 수 있는 명사이자 앞의 encourages와 결합하여 '모든 지원자에게 권장하다'의 의미를 나타내는 단수형 명사 (C) applicant가 정답이다. 명사 (D) application(지원)은 의미상 적합하지 않다.

어휘 encourage 권장하다   submit 제출하다   exhibition 전시(회)   apply 지원[신청]하다   applicant 지원자

4 (C)
번역 쿨 리즈의 웹사이트는 공공도서관을 상대로 한 전자책 유통을 전문으로 한다.

해설 빈칸은 전치사 in의 목적어 자리이자 정관사 the 뒤의 명사 자리이므로 명사 (C) distribution이 정답이다. 명사 (B) distributor(배급업체)는 의미상 적합하지 않다.

어휘 specialize in ~을 전문으로 하다   distribute 유통[배급]하다   distribution 유통, 배급

5 (A)

번역 유머와 음악적 재능을 겸비한 아리엘리 시스터즈의 공연은 카페 배런으로 많은 관객을 끌어 모았다.

해설 빈칸은 동사 have attracted의 주어 자리로 have와 결합할 수 있는 셀 수 있는 명사의 복수형이 와야 한다. 따라서 복수형 명사 (A) performances가 정답이다.

어휘 attract 끌어 모으다 · performance 공연

6 (A)

번역 로델의 요리 인턴십 프로그램 참가자들은 식당에 있는 제라드 씨에게 보고해 첫 번째 과제를 받아야 한다.

해설 빈칸은 to부정사 to receive의 목적어 자리이자 형용사 initial의 수식을 받는 명사 자리이므로 명사 (A) assignment가 정답이다.

어휘 culinary 요리의 · receive 받다 · initial 처음의 · assignment 과제 · assign (업무를) 맡기다

7 (C)

번역 새 자동문이 설치될 수 있도록 소머스 가 입구는 하루 종일 폐쇄될 예정이다.

해설 빈칸은 뒤에 셀 수 있는 명사 day와 결합하여 '하루 종일'의 의미를 나타내는 한정사 (C) all이 정답이다. 참고로, <all+시간표현>은 '~ 내내'라는 의미의 관용 표현이다.

어휘 entrance 입구 · install 설치하다

8 (A)

번역 글래디노 아이스크림의 각 주문은 배송 중에도 냉동 상태를 유지할 수 있도록 특별 포장되어 있다.

해설 빈칸은 be동사 is의 주어인 단수명사 order를 수식하는 형용사 자리이고, '각각의 주문품'이라는 의미가 되어야 자연스러우므로 정답은 (A) Each이다. (B) Several과 (C) All은 복수명사를 수식하고, (D) Either(둘 중 하나의)는 단수명사를 수식하지만 의미상 적절하지 않다.

어휘 order 주문, 주문품 · package 포장하다 · frozen 냉동된

9 (C)

번역 페닝턴 씨는 고객들에게 판매 수익을 증대시키기 위한 유용한 제안을 제공했다.

해설 빈칸은 4형식 동사 give의 직접목적어 역할을 하는 명사 자리이다. 빈칸 앞에 관사 a가 있으므로 단수명사 (C) suggestion이 정답이다.

어휘 helpful 유용한, 도움이 되는 · sales profit 판매 수익

10 (D)

번역 직원 업무 수행 평가는 매 6개월마다 실시된다.

해설 빈칸 뒤에 있는 six months와 결합하여 '매 6개월마다'라는 의미를 나타내는 (D) every가 정답이다.

어휘 performance evaluation 업무 수행 평가

[11-14] 기사

> 튀기지 않고 속을 채운 고추를 즐기세요
>
> 저희 가족은 칠레스 렐레노스를 사랑합니다. 맛있는 치즈로 속을 채우고 기름으로 튀긴 고추를 누가 **11 참을** 수 있을까요? 하지만 다른 사람들처럼 당신도 칼로리가 높다는 이유로 자주 만들지는 않을 거예요. 이것이 바로 제가 가족이 **12 가장 좋아하게 된** 건강한 버전을 개발한 이유입니다. 통조림에 든 초록색 칠레 고추를 통으로 베이킹 접시에 놓으세요. **13 그 다음에** 고추를 토마토 그리고 저지방 치즈와 함께 겹겹이 쌓아 올리세요. 그런 다음 달걀 몇 개에 밀가루와 우유를 약간 섞어 맨 위에 끼얹으세요. **14 마지막으로 부풀어 오를 때까지 구우세요.** 저는 350도에서 약 30분 정도 요리합니다.

어휘 stuffed 속을 채운 · pepper 고추, 피망 · deep-fried 기름으로 튀긴 · filled with ~로 가득 찬 · canned 통조림으로 된 · layer 겹겹이 쌓다 · top (다른 것의) 위에 놓다 · flour 밀가루 · degree (온도) 도

11 (B)

해설 빈칸 앞 문장에서 자신의 가족이 칠레스 렐레노스를 사랑한다(My family loves chiles rellenos)고 한 뒤, 빈칸 뒤에서 맛난 치즈로 속을 채우고 기름에 튀긴 맛있게 요리된 칠레스 렐레노스(those delicious deep-fried stuffed peppers filled with yummy cheese)를 묘사하고 있다. 따라서 '칠레스 렐레노스를 참을 수 있는 사람은 없다'는 내용이 이어져야 자연스러우므로 (B) resist가 정답이다. (A) discover(발견하다), (C) import(수입하다), (D) locate(위치시키다)는 모두 의미상 적합하지 않다.

12 (D)

해설 빈칸은 명사 a healthier version을 수식하는 관계대명사절의 동사 has become의 주격 보어 자리로, 명사 a healthier version과 동격을 이루면서 바로 앞에 있는 명사 family와 복합명사를 이룰 수 있는 명사가 필요하다. '가족이 가장 좋아하는 것이 된 건강한 버전'이라는 의미가 되어야 자연스러우므로 명사 (D) favorite이 정답이다. (A) favor(호의, 친절)는 의미상 적합하지 않고, (B) favoring은 동명사/현재분사, (C) favored는 과거동사/과거분사로 품사상 적절하지 않다.

13 (A)

해설 빈칸 앞 문장에서 칠레스 렐레노스를 건강하게 만드는 방법을 설명하고 있고, 빈칸 뒤에서는 해당 조리법을 이어서 계속 설명하고 있다. 따라서 '그 다음에'라는 의미를 나타내며 이어지는 내용을 덧붙일 때 사용하는 (A) Next가 정답이다. (B) If not(그렇지 않으면), (C) In any case(아무튼), (D) Otherwise(그렇지 않으면)는 모두 의미상 적합하지 않다.

14 (C)

번역 (A) 마음에 드시면 알려주세요.
(B) 어떤 사람들은 매운 고추를 선호합니다.
(C) **마지막으로 부풀어 오를 때까지 구우세요.**
(D) 저희 어머니께 조리법을 빌렸습니다.

해설 빈칸 앞 문장에서 달걀 몇 개에 밀가루와 우유를 약간 섞어 맨 위에 끼얹으라(Then, top them with a couple of eggs mixed with a little flour and milk)고 재료를 배합하는 방법을 설명하고 있다. 따라서 빈칸에는 그 다음 순서로 재료를 익히는 방법을 설명하는 것이 글의 흐름상 자연스러우므로 (C)가 정답이다.

어휘 puffy 부푼

UNIT 03 대명사

❶ 인칭대명사

ETS 유형 연습 본책 p.153

| 1 (B) | 2 (A) | 3 (B) | 4 (B) | 5 (B) | 6 (B) |
| 7 (A) | 8 (A) | | | | |

1 (B)
번역 정비공들은 신기술을 사용하기 시작하면서 더욱 효율적이 되었다.
해설 빈칸은 접속사 as가 이끄는 부사절에서 동사 began의 주어 자리이므로 주격 인칭대명사인 (B) they가 정답이다.

2 (A)
번역 켄싱턴 씨는 최근에 다녀온 홍콩 출장에 대한 지출 결의서를 이미 제출했다.
해설 빈칸 뒤의 명사구 recent trip 앞에는 소유격을 써야 하므로 소유격 인칭대명사인 (A) his가 정답이다. 빈칸이 전치사 for 뒤에 있다고 해서 성급히 목적격인 (B) him을 고르지 않도록 주의해야 한다.

3 (B)
번역 윌리엄스 씨는 새로운 작업실 공사에 관한 상세 일정을 우리에게 제공했다.
해설 빈칸 앞의 동사 has given은 〈give+간접목적어+직접목적어〉의 구조를 취한다. 따라서 빈칸은 동사의 간접목적어 자리이므로 목적격 인칭대명사인 (B) us가 정답이다.

4 (B)
번역 직원들이 성장했지만, 이 씨는 모든 고객 회의를 계속 직접 진행한다.
해설 빈칸이 없어도 완전한 문장이 되므로 주어 Mr. Lee를 강조하는 강조 용법의 재귀대명사 (B) himself가 정답이다. 강조 용법의 재귀대명사는 생략 가능하다.

5 (B)
번역 모톨로 씨가 프리토리아에 하루 더 머물렀다면 그는 공장을 둘러볼 수 있었을 것이다.
해설 빈칸은 동사 could have toured의 주어 자리이므로 주격 인칭대명사인 (B) he가 정답이다. 소유대명사 (C) his도 주어 자리에 올 수 있지만 의미상 적합하지 않다.

6 (B)
번역 내일 휴가 정책에 대한 여러분의 질문에 답변하기 위해서 회의가 있을 예정입니다.
해설 빈칸 뒤의 명사 questions 앞에는 소유격을 써야 하고, '여러분의 질문에 답변하기 위해서'라는 의미가 되어야 자연스러우므로 소유격 인칭대명사인 (B) your가 정답이다.

7 (A)
번역 우리는 건물주로부터 임대료를 그녀에게 직접 지불해야 한다는 연락을 받았다.
해설 빈칸은 전치사 to의 목적어 자리이므로 the property owner와 대응 관계에 있는 목적격 인칭대명사 (A) her가 정답이다. 소유대명사 (B) hers와 재귀대명사 (D) herself도 목적어 자리에 올 수 있지만 의미상 적합하지 않다.

8 (A)
번역 그래픽 디자이너 직책에 지원하는 지원자들은 5월 30일까지 포트폴리오를 제출해야 한다.
해설 빈칸 뒤의 명사 portfolios 앞에는 소유격을 써야 하므로 소유격 인칭대명사인 (A) their가 정답이다.

❷ 소유대명사와 재귀대명사

ETS 유형 연습 본책 p.155

| 1 (A) | 2 (B) | 3 (A) | 4 (B) | 5 (D) | 6 (D) |
| 7 (C) | 8 (C) | | | | |

1 (A)
번역 운전자들은 흰 선 안에 주차하도록 요청 받는다.
해설 빈칸 뒤의 명사 cars 앞에는 소유격을 써야 하므로 소유격 인칭대명사인 (A) their가 정답이다.

2 (B)
번역 면접을 준비하기 위해 백 씨는 회사 약력에 대해 읽었다.
해설 빈칸은 to부정사 To prepare의 목적어 자리이자 주어인 백 씨 자신을 준비시킨다는 의미이므로 재귀대명사인 (B) himself가 정답이다.

3 (A)
번역 웡 씨는 싱가포르의 경영 세미나에 혼자 출장 갈 것이다.
해설 빈칸 앞의 전치사 on과 결합해 '혼자서'라는 의미의 on one's own을 적용하는 문제이므로 (A) his own이 정답이다. 목적격 인칭대명사 (B) him은 의미상 적합하지 않다.

133

4 (B)
번역 바튼 정비소의 직원들은 다음 달 작업 스케줄을 직접 결정했다.
해설 빈칸이 없어도 완전한 문장이 되므로 주어 Barton Maintenance employees를 강조하는 강조 용법의 재귀대명사 (B) themselves가 정답이다. 강조 용법의 재귀대명사는 생략 가능하다.

5 (D)
번역 우리는 우리 제품을 우수한 주방 가전제품 중 최고의 냉장고로 올려 놓을 것이다.
해설 빈칸은 동사 will position의 목적어 자리이자 뒤에 있는 the premier refrigerator에 대응되는 our refrigerator(우리의 냉장고)를 나타내야 하므로 소유대명사 (D) ours가 정답이다. 빈칸이 동사 will position 뒤에 있다고 해서 성급히 목적격인 (B) us를 고르지 않도록 주의해야 한다.

6 (D)
번역 슈미트 박사는 자신의 조교가 조사를 혼자서 완수할 수 있을지 확신하지 못한다.
해설 전치사 by와 결합해 '혼자서'라는 의미의 by oneself를 적용하는 문제이므로 (D) himself가 정답이다. 소유대명사 (A) his와 목적격 인칭대명사 (B) him은 의미상 적합하지 않다. by himself(혼자서)와 by him(그에 의해서)은 의미 구별에 주의해야 한다.

7 (C)
번역 고객 문의사항에 혼자서 대답하는 일은 어려울 수 있다.
해설 빈칸 앞에 전치사 on과 결합해 '혼자서'라는 의미의 on one's own을 적용하는 문제이므로 (C) your own이 정답이다. (B) yourself는 빈칸 앞에 전치사 by가 있는 경우에 적절하다.

8 (C)
번역 유 씨는 녹차가 그가 가장 좋아하는 음료라고 자주 언급하므로 차 모듬 세트는 사려 깊은 선물이 될 것이다.
해설 '단수 명사+of' 뒤에 빈칸이 있고, 문맥상 '그가 가장 좋아하는 음료'라는 의미가 되어야 자연스러우므로 소유대명사 (C) his가 정답이다. 참고로, '단수 명사+of+소유대명사'는 '소유격+명사'와 같은 의미이다.

③ 지시대명사와 부정대명사

ETS 유형 연습 본책 p.157

1 (A) 2 (B) 3 (B) 4 (B) 5 (C) 6 (C)
7 (A) 8 (B)

1 (A)
번역 이 정비사는 김 씨의 자동차 정비소에서 수년간 일해 왔다.
해설 빈칸 뒤에 단수명사인 mechanic이 있으므로 단수명사와 결합하는 지시형용사 (A) This가 정답이다. 지시형용사 (B) These 뒤에는 복수명사가 와야 한다.

2 (B)
번역 많은 직원들이 없어진 서류철을 찾기 위해 기록 보관소를 뒤지고 있다.
해설 빈칸은 동사 are searching의 주어 자리이다. 문장의 동사가 복수형인 are이므로 복수동사와 수가 일치하는 부정대명사 (B) Many가 정답이다. many는 대명사로 쓰일 때 〈many of the+복수명사+복수동사〉로 쓰이는 반면 much는 대명사로 쓰일 때 〈much of the+셀 수 없는 명사+단수동사〉로 쓰인다.

3 (B)
번역 한 씨와 스몰스 씨는 유사한 직무를 수행하는데, 두 사람 모두 승진을 바라고 있다.
해설 빈칸은 동사 hope의 주어 자리이다. 문장의 동사가 복수형인 hope이며 의미상 앞에서 언급한 두 사람(Mr. Hahn and Ms. Smalls)을 가리키고 있으므로 대명사 (B) both가 정답이다.

4 (B)
번역 히마나 박사와 웨어햄 박사는 대학생 시절부터 서로 아는 사이였다.
해설 빈칸은 동사 have known의 목적어 자리이다. 문맥상 '서로 아는 사이였다'라는 의미가 되어야 자연스러우므로 대명사 (B) each other가 정답이다. '또 다른 것'이라는 의미의 (A) another one은 의미상 적합하지 않다.

5 (C)
번역 배송 사무실에서 일하는 사람들은 새로운 우편물 발송 절차 라벨에 관한 교육을 받아야 한다.
해설 빈칸은 동사 must receive의 주어 자리이자 who가 이끄는 형용사절의 수식을 받는 명사 자리이다. '~하는 사람들'이란 의미로, who 뒤의 복수동사 work와도 수 일치가 되어야 하므로 지시대명사 (C) Those가 정답이다.

6 (C)
번역 두 휴대전화 중 하나는 800만 화소 카메라가 장착되어 있고, 다른 하나는 1,200만 화소 카메라가 장착되어 있다.
해설 빈칸은 동사 features의 주어 자리이다. Of the two mobile phones를 통해 대상이 둘임을 알 수 있는데, 대상이 둘일 때 하나는 one, 나머지 하나는 the other로 나타내므로 (C) the other가 정답이다.

7 (A)
번역 지원자 면접을 마치려면 모든 채용 담당 직원들은 하루 더 머물러야 한다.
해설 빈칸은 동사 will need의 주어 자리이자 대명사로 쓰일 때,

〈부정대명사+of the+복수명사〉의 구조로 쓰일 수 있어야 하므로 부정대명사 (A) all이 정답이다. (B) much는 대명사로 쓰일 때, 〈much of the+셀 수 없는 명사〉로 쓰인다.

8 (B)

번역 그 자리에 관심 있는 사람들은 2월 21일까지 작성한 신청서를 제출해야 한다.

해설 빈칸은 동사 should submit의 주어 자리이자 interested in the position의 수식을 받아 '그 자리에 관심이 있는 사람들'이라는 의미가 되어야 자연스러우므로 지시대명사 (B) Those가 정답이다. 참고로, Those 다음에 who are가 생략되었다.

ETS 실전 문제 본책 p.158

1 (B)   2 (B)   3 (D)   4 (D)   5 (B)   6 (B)
7 (C)   8 (A)   9 (B)   10 (B) 11 (B) 12 (D)
13 (A) 14 (C)

1 (B)

번역 다이얼라스 부티크와 갈레나 패션스 모두 그들의 웹사이트에 소셜 미디어 링크가 있다.

해설 명사 Web sites를 수식하는 자리이므로 소유격 인칭대명사 (B) their가 정답이다. (D) theirs는 소유대명사임에 유의한다.

2 (B)

번역 데밍거 뷰티 프로덕츠와 사소 화장품은 올해 수익성이 떨어졌지만, 두 회사 모두 다음 분기에는 수익이 증가하리라 예상한다.

해설 빈칸은 동사 expect의 주어 자리이다. 문장의 동사가 복수형인 expect이며 의미상 앞에서 언급한 두 회사(Daminger Beauty Products and Sasso Cosmetics)를 가리키고 있으므로 대명사 (B) both가 정답이다.

어휘 profitable 수익성 있는   revenue 수익
increase 증가하다   quarter 분기

3 (D)

번역 우리 기계에 대한 서비스 계약에 점검이 반드시 포함되도록 해 주십시오.

해설 빈칸 뒤의 명사 machinery 앞에는 소유격을 써야 하므로 소유격 인칭대명사인 (D) our가 정답이다. 전치사 for 뒤에 있다고 해서 성급히 목적격을 고르지 않도록 주의한다.

어휘 ensure 반드시 ~하게 하다   inspection 점검, 검사

4 (D)

번역 뉴먼 씨는 회계 직원 대다수가 휴가 중이므로 분기별 보고서를 직접 마무리하겠다고 말했다.

해설 빈칸이 없어도 완전한 문장이 되므로 주어 she(Ms. Newman)를 강조하는 강조 용법의 재귀대명사 (D) herself가 정답이다. 강조 용법의 재귀대명사는 생략 가능하다.

어휘 complete 마무리하다   quarterly report 분기별 보고서
accounting 회계

5 (B)

번역 메이베어 베이커리는 빵 제품에 유제품이 함유되지 않았음을 약속드립니다.

해설 빈칸은 접속사 that이 이끄는 명사절에서 주어인 명사구 bread products 앞에 있으므로 이를 수식하는 소유격 인칭대명사 (B) its가 정답이다. 빈칸이 접속사 that 뒤에 있다고 해서 성급히 주격 인칭대명사 (D) they를 고르지 않도록 주의해야 한다.

어휘 dairy 유제품   free ~이 없는

6 (B)

번역 연구 프로젝트에 직접 참여한 과학자들만 실험실에 들어가도록 허용된다.

해설 빈칸에는 주어 scientists를 수식하는 것이 와야 한다. 따라서 복수명사와 함께 쓰는 지시대명사 (B) those가 정답이다. (A) which와 (D) what도 명사를 수식할 수 있지만 '어떤 ~, 무슨 ~'이라는 의미이고, (C) this는 뒤에 단수명사가 와야 한다.

어휘 directly 직접   involved 관여한   allow 허용하다
laboratory 실험실

7 (C)

번역 마크로파 사의 사장은 회사 이윤 폭 감소의 원인을 조사하는 일을 떠맡았다.

해설 빈칸은 전치사 upon의 목적어 자리이자 주어인 사장 자신이 떠맡는다는 의미이므로 재귀대명사인 (C) himself가 정답이다.

어휘 take it upon oneself to ~하는 일을 떠맡다
investigate 조사하다   reason 원인   narrow 감소하다
profit margin 이윤 폭

8 (A)

번역 최근의 고객 의견에 따르면 우리의 갈프란 신발 라인은 가볍고 저렴하다.

해설 명사구 Galpran line of footwear 앞에는 소유격을 써야 하므로 빈칸에는 소유격 인칭대명사인 (A) our가 적합하다. 빈칸이 명사절 접속사 that 뒤에 있다고 해서 성급히 주격인 (C) we를 고르지 않도록 주의해야 한다.

어휘 recent 최근의   lightweight 가벼운   affordable 저렴한

9 (B)

번역 등산객들은 여러 언덕이 있는 등산로를 선택함으로써 체력 수준을 향상시킬 수 있다.

해설 빈칸은 명사 level을 수식하는 자리이므로 소유격 인칭대명사 (B) their가 정답이다. (C) theirs는 소유대명사임에 유의한다.

어휘 fitness 체력, 건강   trail 등산로

10 (B)

번역 샹 씨는 자신의 취향은 제쳐 두고 대다수가 선호하는 디자인을 승인했다.

해설 명사 preference 앞에는 소유격을 써야 하므로 빈칸에는 소유격 인칭대명사와 소유 관련성을 강조하여 사용하는 own이 결합된 (B) her own이 적합하다.

어휘 put aside 제쳐 두다   approve 승인하다   favor 선호하다   majority 대다수

[11-14] 이메일

수신: 전 직원
발신: 신야 후타기
날짜: 11월 17일
제목: 시스템 테스트

직원 여러분께:

다음 주에 새로운 경보 시스템을 테스트하기 위한 안전 훈련을 실시할 예정입니다. 고려할 조치가 두 가지 있습니다. 첫째, 이번 주에 작업 공간에서 가장 가까운 출구를 숙지하세요. 다음 주에 경보가 울리면 차분하고 11**질서정연**하게 건물에서 나와야 한다는 점을 기억하세요. 12**건물 내 어디에 있든 즉시 나가주세요.** 둘째, 건물 밖으로 나가면 곧장 쿠퍼 가의 인도로 가세요. 13**제가** 참석 확인을 위해 거기 있을 겁니다. 도착하시면 반드시 저와 확인해 주세요. 전체 훈련은 몇 분 밖에 14**걸리지 않을 겁니다.** 질문이나 우려 사항이 있을 경우, 저에게 연락하세요.

신야 후타기
안전 연락 담당

어휘 conduct (특정 활동을) 하다   safety drill 안전 훈련   familiarize 익숙하게 하다   workstation 작업 공간   calm 차분한   sidewalk 인도   attendance 참석   entire 전체의   concern 우려   reach out 연락을 취하다   liaison 연락자

11 (B)

해설 빈칸은 앞의 형용사 calm과 함께 명사 manner를 수식하는 형용사 자리이고, 문맥상 '차분하고 질서정연한 방식으로 건물에서 나와야 한다'는 의미가 되어야 자연스러우므로 형용사 (B) orderly가 정답이다. (A) suspicious(의심스러운), (C) previous(이전의), (D) inward(안으로 향한)는 의미상 적합하지 않다.

12 (D)

번역 (A) 경비 담당 부서에서 출입하실 때 배지를 드립니다.
(B) 버머 알람이 새로운 경보 시스템을 제공했습니다.
(C) 안전 훈련은 무작위로 시행됩니다.
(D) 건물 내 어디에 있든 즉시 나가주세요.

해설 빈칸 앞 문장에서 경보가 울리면 건물에서 나와야 한다(Please remember that next week when the alarm sounds, you should exit the building in a calm, orderly manner)는 지침을 설명하고 있으므로, 빈칸에서는 추가 지침을 언급하기 전에 앞서 설명한 건물을 나가야 한다는 점을 강조하는 것이 글의 흐름상 자연스러우므로 (D)가 정답이다.

어휘 security 경비 담당 부서   random 무작위의   immediately 즉시

13 (A)

해설 동사 will be의 주어 자리에 들어가기에 적절한 주격 인칭대명사를 골라야 한다. 빈칸 뒤에서 도착하면 자신과 확인해 달라(Be sure to check in with me once you arrive)고 요청하고 있으므로 앞 문장은 '제가 거기 있을 겁니다'라는 내용이 되어야 적절하다. 따라서 '저'를 나타내는 주격 대명사 (A) I가 정답이다.

14 (C)

해설 안전 훈련은 다음 주에 일어날 일이므로, 안전 훈련 예상 소요 시간은 미래에 대해 예측하는 내용이 되어야 한다. 따라서 '몇 분 밖에 걸리지 않을 것이다(= 고작 몇 분 걸릴 것이다)'라는 의미로 예상 및 추측을 나타낼 수 있는 (C) should take가 정답이다.

UNIT 04 형용사

1 형용사의 개념과 역할

ETS 유형 연습   본책 p.161

| 1 (A) | 2 (B) | 3 (B) | 4 (A) | 5 (C) | 6 (A) |
| 7 (C) | 8 (D) |

1 (A)

번역 특별한 기내식을 요청하시려면, 항공편 예약 시 항공권 판매원에게 말씀해 주십시오.

해설 빈칸은 부정관사 a와 명사 meal request 사이에서 명사를 수식하는 형용사 자리이므로 형용사 (A) special이 정답이다.

2 (B)

번역 그 옷가게는 품질 좋은 제복을 경쟁력 있는 가격에 팔기 때문에 성공을 거두고 있다.

해설 빈칸은 be동사 is 뒤의 보어 자리이므로 명사나 형용사가 올 수 있다. 의미상 옷가게의 상태를 나타내야 자연스러우므로 형용사인 (B) successful이 정답이다.

3 (B)

번역 진행자들은 포커스 그룹에게 건설적인 비판을 해달라고 요청하고 있다.

해설 빈칸은 to provide의 목적어인 명사 criticism을 수식하는 형용사 자리이므로 형용사 (B) constructive가 정답이다. 빈칸이 to provide 뒤에 있다고 해서 성급하게 명사 (A) construction을 고르지 않도록 주의해야 한다.

4 (A)

번역 재무 부서는 전 직원 회의에서 전략적인 성장 계획을 간략히 설명할 것이다.

해설 빈칸은 소유격 its와 명사 growth plans 사이에서 명사를 수식하는 형용사 자리이므로 형용사 (A) strategic이 정답이다.

5 (C)

번역 센터빌 도서관은 다음 달에 지역 사회를 위해서 다양한 주제에 관한 일련의 무료 수업을 주최할 예정이다.

해설 빈칸은 전치사 about의 목적어 역할을 하는 명사 subjects를 수식하는 형용사 자리이므로 형용사 (C) various가 정답이다. (A) vary와 (B) varies는 동사, (D) variously는 부사이므로 품사상 적절하지 않다.

6 (A)

번역 피에트로 파인 아이스크림은 다양한 인기 있는 맛으로 제공됩니다.

해설 빈칸은 전치사 of의 목적어 역할을 하는 명사 flavors를 수식하는 형용사 자리이므로 형용사 (A) popular가 정답이다. 명사 (C) popularity는 의미상 flavors와 복합명사를 이루지 못한다.

7 (C)

번역 경영팀에서 정한 판매 목표가 대부분의 직원들에게 현실적으로 보인다.

해설 빈칸은 동사 seems의 주어인 The sales goal을 보충 설명하는 주격 보어 자리이므로 형용사 (C) realistic이 정답이다. 명사 보어는 주어와 동일한 대상을 나타내는데, 명사 (A) realist(현실주의자)와 (B) realism(현실주의)은 주어와 동일한 대상이 아니다.

8 (D)

번역 스기야마 박사의 현재 학문 연구는 행동 심리학 분야의 협력 연구 프로젝트에 중점을 두고 있다.

해설 빈칸은 전치사 on의 목적어 역할을 하는 복합명사 research projects를 수식하는 형용사 자리이므로 형용사 (D) collaborative가 정답이다. 명사 (B) collaboration은 의미상 research projects와 복합명사를 이루지 못한다.

② 주의해야 할 형용사

ETS 유형 연습   본책 p.163

| 1 (A) | 2 (B) | 3 (B) | 4 (A) | 5 (B) | 6 (B) |
| 7 (B) | 8 (A) | | | | |

1 (A)

번역 숙련된 조립 라인 작업자들은 좀 더 세심한 경향이 있다.

해설 빈칸은 명사구 assembly-line workers를 수식하는 자리이므로 형용사 역할을 할 수 있는 과거분사 (A) Experienced가 정답이다. 현재분사 (B) Experiencing(경험하고 있는)도 형용사 역할을 할 수 있지만 의미상 적합하지 않다.

2 (B)

번역 무어 씨의 연설은 청중들에게 지속적인 인상을 남겼다.

해설 빈칸은 부정관사 a와 명사 impression 사이에서 명사를 수식하는 자리이므로 형용사 역할을 할 수 있는 현재분사 (B) lasting이 정답이다. 자동사 last(지속하다)의 과거분사 (A) lasted는 완료의 의미가 되어야 자연스러우므로 의미상 적합하지 않다.

3 (B)

번역 콘서트에 있던 모든 사람들은 빈센지 씨의 뛰어난 연주에 감명받았다.

해설 빈칸은 be동사 was의 주어인 Everyone을 보충하는 주격 보어 자리이므로 형태상으로는 형용사, 명사, 분사 모두 가능한데, 과거분사 (B) impressed가 의미상 적절하다. 형용사 (A) impressive(인상적인, 감명 깊은)는 의미상 적합하지 않다.

4 (A)

번역 웰빙 에이드 사는 고객들의 특정한 요구를 충족시키는 데 전념한다.

해설 빈칸은 be동사 is의 주어 Wellbeing Aid, Inc.를 보충 설명하는 주격 보어 자리이므로 형용사와 같은 역할을 할 수 있는 과거분사 (A) dedicated(전념하는, 헌신적인)가 정답이다. 명사 보어는 주어와 동일한 대상을 나타내는데, 명사 (B) dedication(전념, 헌신)은 주어와 동일한 대상이 아니다.

5 (B)

번역 농부들은 최근 좋은 기상 조건의 결과로 풍작을 예상하고 있다.

해설 빈칸은 복합명사 weather conditions를 수식하는 형용사 자리이므로 형용사 (B) favorable이 정답이다. 형용사 역할을 할 수 있는 현재분사 (D) favoring(형편에 맞는, 선호하는)은 의미상 적합하지 않다.

6 (B)

번역 윈스롭 전략은 일관되게 마감일을 맞추는 의욕적인 사람을 채용하려고 한다.

해설 빈칸은 명사 individual을 수식하는 자리이므로 '의욕적인'이란 뜻의 형용사인 (B) motivated가 정답이다. motivate는 '동기를 주다, 자극하다'라는 의미의 동사다.

7 (B)

번역 사무실 건물 점검은 사소한 결함은 있지만 구조적인 손상은 없음을 밝혀냈다.

해설 등위접속사 but이 동사 revealed의 목적어 flaws와 damage를 연결하고 있고, 빈칸은 한정사 no와 명사 damage 사이에서 명사를 수식하는 형용사 자리이다. '구조적인 손상'이라는 의미를 나타내는 형용사 (B) structural이 정답이다.

8 (A)

번역 새 프린터는 자주 수리해야 했던 예전 것보다 더 믿을 만하다.

해설 빈칸은 주어인 The new printer를 보충 설명하는 주격 보어 역할을 하며 부사 more의 수식을 받는 형용사 자리로, '새 프린터는 더 믿을 만하다'는 의미를 나타내는 형용사 (A) reliable이 정답이다. 나머지 (B) faithful(충실한), (C) prohibitive(과도하게 비싼), (D) methodical(체계적인)은 모두 의미상 적합하지 않다.

ETS 실전 문제   본책 p.164

1 (A)	2 (C)	3 (D)	4 (A)	5 (C)	6 (B)
7 (C)	8 (B)	9 (C)	10 (C)	11 (A)	12 (D)
13 (C)	14 (B)				

1 (A)

번역 하비 가의 가판점은 다양한 신문과 잡지를 제공한다.

해설 빈칸은 부정관사 a와 명사 selection 사이에서 명사를 수식하는 형용사 자리이므로 형용사 (A) diverse가 정답이다.

어휘 kiosk 매점, 가판대   selection 선택 가능한 것, 선정된 것
diverse 다양한   diversify 다양화하다

2 (C)

번역 컨설턴트들은 보다 효율적인 직원 채용 계획이 3개월 이내에 시행되어야 한다고 권장했다.

해설 빈칸은 비교급 부사 more와 복합명사 staffing plan 사이에서 명사를 수식하는 형용사 자리이므로 형용사 (C) efficient가 정답이다. (A) efficiency(효율성)는 staffing plan과 복합명사를 이루지 않으므로 빈칸에 들어갈 수 없다.

어휘 recommend 권장하다   staffing 직원 채용
put in place 시행하다   efficient 효율적인

3 (D)

번역 우 로지스틱스는 매우 유능한 경영진 덕분에 올해 유례없는 성장을 경험했다.

해설 빈칸은 부사 highly와 명사 management team 사이에서 명사를 수식하는 형용사 자리이므로 형용사 (D) competent가 정답이다.

어휘 highly 매우   experience 경험하다   unprecedented 유례없는   growth 성장   competency 능숙함   competent 유능한

4 (A)

번역 파텔 씨는 해이튼 인더스트리즈 사에 첫 출근하는 날이 걱정되었지만, 모든 일이 아주 순조롭게 진행되었다.

해설 빈칸은 동사 was의 주어인 Ms. Patel을 보충 설명하는 주격 보어 자리이므로 형용사 (A) anxious가 정답이다. 명사 보어는 주어와 동일한 대상을 나타내는데, 명사 (C) anxiety(불안)와 (D) anxiousness(걱정스러움)는 주어와 동일한 대상이 아니다.

어휘 extremely 아주   be anxious about ~에 대해 걱정하다

5 (C)

번역 무료 아침 식사는 매일 오전 6시부터 오전 9시 30분까지 등록된 투숙객들을 위해 매일 제공됩니다.

해설 빈칸은 전치사 for의 목적어인 명사 guests를 수식하는 형용사 자리이므로 형용사 (C) registered가 정답이다.

어휘 complimentary 무료의   serve 제공하다
register 등록하다

6 (B)

번역 자크 하트빅센의 최신 저서는 현대 건축의 역사에서 중요한 순간을 탐구한다.

해설 빈칸은 명사 moments를 수식하는 형용사 자리이다. 따라서 '중요한'이라는 뜻의 형용사 (B) significant가 정답이다.

어휘 explore 탐구하다   architecture 건축학
significantly 상당히; 의미 있게

7 (C)

번역 셀프 물품보관 업계는 현재 향상된 자동화를 위한 유망 기술들을 테스트하고 있다.

해설 빈칸은 동사 is testing의 목적어인 명사 technologies를 수식하는 형용사 자리이므로 형용사 (C) promising이 정답이다.

어휘 storage 보관   industry 산업   currently 현재
enhanced 향상된   automation 자동화
promising 유망한

8 (B)

번역 상당한 노력을 기울인 끝에, 우리는 키보드를 다시 디자인하는 데 성공했다.

해설 빈칸은 전치사 After의 목적어인 명사 effort를 수식하는 형용사 자리이므로 (B)와 (C)가 가능한데, 의미상 (B) considerable이 정답이다. 형용사 (C) considerate(사려 깊은)은 의미상 적합하지 않다.

어휘 effort 노력   succeed 성공하다   considerable 상당한

9 (C)

번역 소비자들은 자신들이 받는 원치 않는 우편물의 양을 줄이기 위한 우리의 노력에 무척 고마워하고 있다.

해설 빈칸은 have been의 주어인 Consumers를 보충 설명하는 주격 보어 자리이자 부사 very의 수식을 받는 형용사 자리이므로 형용사 (C) appreciative가 정답이다.

어휘 reduce 줄이다   amount 양   unsolicited 원치 않는
receive 받다   appreciative 고마워하는

10 (C)

번역 새로 만든 알레르기 약이 기존 알레르기 약보다 더 효과적이라는 설득력 있는 증거는 없다.

해설 빈칸은 There is/are 구문의 주어인 evidence를 수식하는 형용사 자리이므로 형용사 (C) persuasive가 정답이다.

어휘 evidence 증거 reformulate 새로 만들다 medication 약 effective 효과적인 existing 기존의 persuade 설득하다 persuasive 설득력 있는

[11-14] 광고

> 스트로베리 문이 5월 모든 매트리스에 대한 가격 인하와 함께 봄을 기념합니다!
>
> 스트로베리 문의 최첨단 매트리스로 당신의 통증과 고통을 완화하세요. 스트로베리 문의 천연 폼 매트리스는 편안한 숙면을 돕도록 제작되었으며 매일 **11 상쾌한** 기분으로 일어날 수 있도록 도와줍니다. 저희 매트리스는 허리를 **12 위한** 지지를 제공해 줄 뿐만 아니라 내구성과 편안함도 제공합니다. **13 또한**, 저희가 생산하는 모든 매트리스는 항균이 되며 저자극성입니다.
>
> **14 특별 할인을 받으시려면 5월 31일 이전에 매트리스를 구매하세요.** 이 할인 혜택에 대해 더 알아보시고 전체 제품을 둘러보시려면 www.strawberrymoon.ca를 방문해 주세요.
>
> **어휘** celebrate 기념하다 price break 가격 인하 relieve 완화하다 ache 통증 pain 고통 natural 천연의 engineer (설계하여) 제작하다 promote 촉진하다 restful 편안한 support 지지 back 허리 durability 내구성 comfort 편안함 antibacterial 항균성의 hypoallergenic 저자극성의

11 (A)

해설 feeling 이하는 부사절 접속사 while과 주어 you가 생략된 분사구문이다. 빈칸은 원래 while you feel에서 동사 feel의 주어인 you를 보충하는 주격 보어 자리로 '상쾌한 기분을 느끼며'라는 의미가 되어야 자연스러우므로 형용사 (A) refreshed가 정답이다.

12 (D)

해설 빈칸은 your back을 목적어로 취하면서 '~를 위한'을 의미하는 전치사 (D) for가 정답이다.

13 (C)

해설 빈칸 앞 문장에서 매트리스의 이점을 설명하고 있고, 빈칸 뒤에서도 매트리스가 항균이 되고 저자극성이라며 또 다른 이점을 이야기하고 있다. 따라서 '또한'이라는 의미로 유사한 정보를 추가할 때 쓰는 (C) In addition이 정답이다. (A) Nevertheless(그럼에도 불구하고), (B) Consequently(따라서), (D) To summarize(요약하자면)는 모두 의미상 적합하지 않다.

14 (B)

번역 (A) 초고강도 매트리스는 특별 주문으로만 구매 가능합니다.
(B) 특별 할인을 받으시려면 5월 31일 이전에 매트리스를 구매하세요.
(C) 저희 토론토 전시장은 6월에 월요일마다 휴무임을 참고해 주세요.
(D) 만족한 고객들이 긍정적인 후기를 남기도록 권장됩니다.

해설 빈칸 뒤 문장에서 이 할인 혜택에 대해 더 알아보라(To learn more about these savings)고 언급하고 있다. 따라서 빈칸에는 할인 행사에 대해 안내하는 내용이 나오는 것이 자연스러우므로 (B)가 정답이다.

어휘 extra-firm 초고강도의 obtain 얻다 showroom 전시장 satisfied 만족한 encourage 권장하다 post 게시하다 positive 긍정적인 review 후기

UNIT 05 부사

❶ 부사의 개념과 역할

ETS 유형 연습 본책 p.167

1 (B) **2** (A) **3** (B) **4** (B) **5** (D) **6** (C)
7 (C) **8** (D)

1 (B)

번역 당신은 그 문제에 관해 동료와 전혀 다른 의견이 있을 수 있다.

해설 빈칸은 부정관사 a와 형용사 different 사이에서 형용사 different를 수식하는 부사 자리이므로 부사 (B) completely가 정답이다.

2 (A)

번역 자외선 차단 로션을 노출된 피부에 바르고 완전히 흡수될 때까지 문질러 주세요.

해설 빈칸은 be동사 is와 과거분사 absorbed 사이에서 과거분사 absorbed를 수식하는 부사 자리이므로 부사 (A) fully가 정답이다.

3 (B)

번역 소리가 너무 크지 않도록 음량 스위치를 살짝 조정해 주세요.

해설 주어 없이 시작하는 명령문이다. 따라서 빈칸은 동사원형 adjust와 목적어 the volume knob으로 이뤄진 완전한 문장 뒤에서 동사 adjust를 수식하는 부사 자리이므로 부사 (B) slightly가 정답이다.

4 (B)

번역 시의 도로 재포장 공사는 현재 예정대로 진행되고 있다.

해설 빈칸은 be동사 is의 주어를 보충하는 전치사구 on schedule을 수식하는 부사 자리이므로 부사 (B) currently가 정답이다. 빈칸이 be동사 is 뒤에 있다고 해서 성급하게 형용사 (A) current를 고르지 않도록 주의해야 한다.

5 (D)

번역 법무부는 금요일까지 계약서를 면밀히 검토하여 피드백을 제공할 예정입니다.

해설 빈칸은 조동사 will과 동사원형 examine 사이에서 동사를 수식하는 부사 자리이고, '면밀히 검토한다'는 의미가 되어야 자연스러우므로 부사 (D) closely가 정답이다. (A) close와 (B) closer는 부사로 쓰일 경우 '(위치상) 가까이, 바싹'이라는 뜻으로 문맥상 적합하지 않다.

6 (C)

번역 오후 5시 이후에 입금된 수표는 보통 영업일 기준 2일 이내에 게시됩니다.

해설 빈칸은 be동사 are와 과거분사 posted 사이에서 동사를 수식하는 부사 자리이므로, 부사 (C) typically가 정답이다. (A) type과 (D) types는 명사/동사, (B) typical은 형용사로 품사상 빈칸에 들어갈 수 없다.

7 (C)

번역 안타깝게도, 선비 스낵의 신제품인 단백질이 풍부한 그래놀라 바는 널리 판매되지 않는다.

해설 빈칸은 be동사 are와 형용사 available 사이에서 형용사를 수식하는 부사 자리이므로 부사 (C) widely가 정답이다. (A) widening은 명사, (B) widest는 최상급 형용사, (D) wider는 비교급 형용사이므로 품사상 적합하지 않다.

8 (D)

번역 박미선 씨의 예술 작품은 고전적인 요소들을 현대적인 재료와 솜씨 있게 접목하고 있다.

해설 빈칸은 주어 Mi-Sun Park's artwork와 동사 combines 사이에서 동사를 수식하는 부사 자리이므로 부사 (D) skillfully가 정답이다.

② 빈출 부사 정리

ETS 유형 연습 본책 p.169

| 1 (A) | 2 (A) | 3 (A) | 4 (A) | 5 (C) | 6 (C) |
| 7 (C) | 8 (A) | | | | |

1 (A)

번역 하청업체들은 내일 오전 8시 직전에 보수공사를 시작할 것이라고 말한다.

해설 빈칸은 시간 표현인 before 8 A.M. tomorrow를 강조하는 부사 자리이다. '내일 오전 8시 직전에'라는 의미가 되어야 자연스러우므로 부사 (A) shortly가 정답이다. 참고로, shortly before[after]는 '~ 직전[직후]'라는 뜻이다. (B) short는 '짧은'이라는 형용사와 '짧게'라는 부사, 둘 다로 쓰인다.

2 (A)

번역 북쪽 부속 건물의 엘리베이터들은 다음 주에 정비 작업을 위해 임시로 폐쇄될 것이다.

해설 '임시로 폐쇄될 것이다'라는 의미가 되어야 자연스러우므로 부사 (A) temporarily가 정답이다. (B)는 cautiously는 '조심스럽게'라는 뜻이다.

3 (A)

번역 신차들의 판매가 이번 분기에 거의 5퍼센트 하락했다.

해설 빈칸은 숫자 표현인 five percent를 강조하는 부사 자리이다. '거의 5퍼센트'라는 의미가 되어야 자연스러우므로 부사 (A) nearly가 정답이다. (B) quite는 '꽤'라는 뜻이다.

4 (A)

번역 원래 소규모 관광호텔로 문을 연 아가피야 인은 현재 풀 서비스 리조트다.

해설 빈칸은 과거분사 opened를 수식하는 부사 자리이므로 부사 (A) Originally가 정답이다.

5 (C)

번역 말든 퍼니처의 책장은 제시간에 도착했지만 부품 중 하나가 약간 손상되어 있었다.

해설 빈칸은 be동사 was와 과거분사 damaged 사이에서 과거분사 damaged를 수식하는 부사 자리이므로 부사 (C) slightly가 정답이다.

6 (C)

번역 회의실에 의자 6개만 두고 여분은 모두 치워주세요.

해설 주어 없이 시작하는 명령문이다. 빈칸은 동사원형 leave와 목적어 six chairs 사이에서 숫자 six를 강조하는 부사 자리이다. '6개의 의자만'이라는 의미가 되어야 자연스러우므로 부사 (C) just가 정답이다.

7 (C)

번역 크리스티 드라이버 씨는 잘 알려진 치료사로, 그녀의 치료는 매우 합리적으로 가격이 책정된다.

해설 빈칸은 과거분사 priced를 수식하는 부사 자리이다. '합리적으로 가격이 책정된'이라는 의미가 적절하므로 (C) reasonably가 정답이다. (A) strongly(강하게), (B) internally(내적으로), (D) repeatedly(반복적으로)는 의미상 적합하지 않다.

8 (A)

번역 경영진은 곧 직원 사무실 의자를 교체할 계획이다.

해설 빈칸 앞은 주어(The management), 동사(plans), 목적어(to replace employee office chairs)를 모두 갖춘 완전한 문장이므로, 빈칸은 부사 자리이다. '곧 의자를 교체할 계획이다'라는 의미가 되어야 자연스러우므로 부사 (A) soon이 정답이다. (B) therefore(그러므로)와 (C) both(둘 다)는 의미상 적합하지 않고, 형용사인 (D) easy는 품사상 빈칸에 들어갈 수 없다.

ETS 실전 문제
본책 p.170

1 (D)	2 (C)	3 (B)	4 (D)	5 (D)	6 (D)
7 (C)	8 (D)	9 (D)	10 (D)	11 (A)	12 (B)
13 (D)	14 (C)				

1 (D)
번역 치열한 경쟁에도 불구하고, 타시지안 씨는 컨설팅 사업을 수익을 내면서 확장할 수 있었다.

해설 빈칸은 완전한 절 뒤에서 to부정사구 to expand his consulting business를 수식하는 부사 자리이므로 부사 (D) profitably가 정답이다.

어휘 competition 경쟁 expand 확장하다 profitable 수익성이 있는 profitably 수익성 있게

2 (C)
번역 펄 패션은 마이애미 시내에 위치한 매우 인기 있는 라이저 몰에 세 번째 매장을 열었다.

해설 빈칸은 정관사 the와 형용사 popular 사이에서 형용사 popular를 수식하는 부사 자리로, '매우 인기 있는'이라는 의미가 되어야 자연스러우므로 (C) highly가 정답이다.

어휘 tightly 단단히 evenly 고르게 solely 오로지

3 (B)
번역 모든 기계를 한꺼번에 교체하는 대신, 하트포드 공장의 기술자들은 향후 5년에 걸쳐 기계를 차차 교체하기로 결정했다.

해설 빈칸은 to부정사 to replace와 목적어 it으로 이뤄진 구 뒤에서 동사 replace를 수식하는 부사 자리로, '차차 교체하기로 결정했다'라는 의미가 되어야 자연스러우므로 (B) gradually가 정답이다.

어휘 replace 교체하다 machinery 기계 at once 한꺼번에 familiarly 친하게 previously 이전에

4 (D)
번역 비록 그 일을 완료하는 데 6시간밖에 걸리지 않았지만, 직원들은 8시간 근무에 대한 보수를 받게 된다.

해설 빈칸은 동사 took과 목적어 six hours 사이에서 숫자 six를 강조하는 부사 자리로, '겨우 6시간만 걸렸다'라는 의미가 되어야 자연스러우므로 부사 (D) only가 정답이다. 전치사 (A) during(~ 동안)과 (B) until(~까지)은 품사상 적합하지 않고 부사로도 사용되는 (C) right(정확히)은 의미상 적합하지 않다.

어휘 complete 완료하다 shift (교대) 근무

5 (D)
번역 몬스타드 건설은 우리 호텔 로비를 개조할 회사로, 적극 추천된다.

해설 빈칸은 2형식 동사 comes 뒤에서 주격 보어로 쓰인 과거분사 recommended를 수식하는 부사 자리이므로 부사 (D) highly가 정답이다. (A) high(높이)도 부사로 사용할 수 있지만 의미상 적합하지 않다.

어휘 renovate 개조하다 highly recommended 적극 추천되는

6 (D)
번역 세레나 안전 경보는 합리적인 가격의 가정용 보안 시스템을 제공합니다.

해설 빈칸은 be동사 are와 과거분사 priced 사이에서 과거분사 priced를 수식하는 부사 자리이므로 (D) reasonably가 정답이다. (A) reason은 명사/동사, (B) to reason은 to부정사, (C) reasonable은 형용사이므로 품사상 빈칸에 들어갈 수 없다.

어휘 security 보안 price 가격을 정하다 reason 이유; 판단하다 reasonable 합리적인

7 (C)
번역 지원자는 모든 지원 서류를 제출하기 전에 꼼꼼히 교정하도록 권장된다.

해설 빈칸은 to부정사 to proofread 사이에서 to부정사를 수식하는 부사 자리이므로 부사 (C) carefully가 정답이다. (A) careful은 형용사, (B) caring은 형용사/명사, (D) cares는 동사/명사이므로 품사상 적합하지 않다.

어휘 applicant 지원자 proofread 교정하다 application 지원 material 자료

8 (D)
번역 전하는 바에 따르면 확장 이전에 로마스 레스토랑은 시간당 약 50명의 고객을 응대했다고 한다.

해설 빈칸은 주어 Lomas Restaurant과 동사 served 사이에서 동사를 수식하는 부사 자리이므로 부사 (D) reportedly가 정답이다.

어휘 expansion 확장 serve 응대하다 patron 고객 reportedly 전하는 바에 따르면

9 (D)
번역 졸너 컴퍼니는 카운티 서부 지역의 건축 비용이 놀랍도록 높다는 것을 발견했다.

해설 빈칸은 to부정사구의 be동사와 형용사 high 사이에서 형용사를 수식하는 부사 자리로 '놀라울 정도로'라는 의미의 부사 (D) surprisingly가 정답이다.

10 (D)
번역 아이언 에이스의 고품질 전동 공구는 전국적으로 10,000개 이상의 소매업체에서 판매된다.

해설 빈칸은 주어(Iron Ace's high-quality power tools), 수동태 동사(are sold), 수식어구(at over 10,000 retailers)로 이뤄진 완전한 문장 뒤에서 과거분사 sold를 수식하는 부사 자리이다. 따라서 '전국적으로 팔린다'라는 의미를 나타내는 부사 (D) nationwide가 정답이다. (A) nation과 (C) nationality는 명사, (B) national은 형용사로 품사상 적절하지 않다.

어휘 high-quality 고품질의 retailer 소매업체 nationality 국적, 민족 nationwide 전국적으로

[11-14] 이메일

수신: a.crimmins@anyasgifts.com.au
발신: payments@orangebellwireless.com.au
날짜: 9월 7일
제목: 결제 처리 완료

크리민스 씨께,

귀하의 결제 금액 71.39달러를 받았습니다. 금액은 귀하의 계정에 입금되었으며, 귀하께서 취하실 **11추가적인** 조치는 없습니다. **12하지만** 다음 결제 기한을 변경하시려면 www.orangebellwireless.com.au/portal에서 계정에 로그인 하시면 가능합니다. **13또한 새롭게 개편된 휴대전화 앱을 통해 계정에 접속하실 수도 있습니다.** 고객분들께서 저희 앱의 새로운 버전이 이전 버전보다 사용하기 훨씬 더 쉽다고 말씀하십니다. 귀하께서도 **14동의하시길** 바랍니다.

충실한 고객이 되어 주셔서 감사드립니다. 귀하의 거래에 진심으로 감사드립니다.

오렌지 벨 와이어리스

어휘 payment 결제(액) process 처리하다 credit 입금하다 due date 마감일 loyal 충실한 appreciate 감사하다

11 (A)
해설 빈칸은 한정사 no와 명사 action 사이에서 명사를 수식하는 형용사 자리이고, '추가적인 조치는 없다'는 의미가 되어야 자연스러우므로 형용사 (A) further가 정답이다.

12 (B)
해설 빈칸은 문장 전체를 수식하는 부사 자리이다. 앞에서 추가로 취할 조치가 없다고 했는데, 빈칸 뒤에서는 결제 기한을 변경하려면 웹사이트 계정에 로그인 해야 한다며 추가로 조치를 취해야 한다고 말하고 있다. 따라서 '하지만'이라는 의미로 앞뒤 문장의 역접 관계를 나타내는 (B) However가 정답이다. (A) Instead(대신에), (C) In particular(특히), (D) For example(예를 들어)은 모두 의미상 적합하지 않다.

13 (D)
번역 (A) 귀하의 무선 서비스 제공업체가 되어 영광입니다.
(B) 이 정보는 귀하께 추가적인 예시를 제공할 것입니다.
(C) 귀하의 다음 결제 기한이 변경되었습니다.
(D) 또한 새롭게 개편된 휴대전화 앱을 통해 계정에 접속하실 수도 있습니다.

해설 빈칸 앞 문장에서 결제 기한을 변경하려면 웹사이트에서 계정에 로그인 하라고 안내하고 있고, 빈칸 뒤 문장에서는 새로운 버전의 앱(this new version of our app)에 대해서 언급하고 있다. 따라서 빈칸에는 웹사이트 로그인 외에 추가적인 계정 접속 방법과 새로운 버전의 앱을 동시에 언급하는 것이 문맥상 자연스러우므로 (D)가 정답이다.

어휘 privilege 영광, 특권 provider 제공업체, 공급자 reschedule 일정을 변경하다 access 접속하다, 접근하다 redesign 재설계하다

14 (C)
해설 빈칸 앞 문장에서 고객들이 앱의 새로운 버전이 이전 버전보다 사용하기 더 쉽다고 말한다(Customers tell us that they find this new version of our app much easier to use than the previous version)고 언급하고 있다. 문맥상 '귀하께서도 동의하시길 바란다'는 의미가 되어야 자연스러우므로 (C) agree가 정답이다. (A) continue(계속하다), (B) respond(응답하다), (D) join(합류하다)은 의미상 적합하지 않다.

UNIT 06 동사의 형태와 종류

1 동사의 형태

ETS 유형 연습 본책 p.173

1 (B) **2** (B) **3** (B) **4** (A) **5** (B) **6** (C)
7 (D) **8** (C)

1 (B)
번역 외출할 때는 프런트 데스크에 호텔 열쇠를 맡기세요.
해설 빈칸은 주어 없이 Please로 시작하는 명령문이므로 동사원형 (B) leave가 정답이다.

2 (B)
번역 이지수의 최근 강의는 온라인으로 시청할 수 있다.
해설 빈칸은 조동사 can 뒤의 동사원형 자리이고 뒤에 타동사 view의 목적어가 없으므로 수동태 (B) be viewed가 정답이다.

3 (B)
번역 달링스톤 호텔은 모든 손님들에게 무료 아침식사를 제공하고 있다.
해설 빈칸은 문장의 동사 자리이고 주어가 3인칭 단수 The Darlingstone Hotel이므로 단수동사인 (B) is offering이 정답이다. 준동사인 (A) offering은 동사 자리에 올 수 없다.

4 (A)
- 번역: 후 씨의 획기적인 아이디어들은 베르시어 그룹의 마케팅 직원들로부터 열렬하게 환영을 받았다.
- 해설: be동사 다음에는 현재분사나 과거분사가 올 수 있으므로 과거분사 (A) received가 정답이다.

5 (B)
- 번역: CEO는 언론과의 만남을 위한 초대를 거절했다.
- 해설: 빈칸은 명사구 an invitation을 목적어로 취하는 동사 자리이므로, 빈칸 앞의 has와 함께 현재완료 동사구를 완성하는 과거분사가 들어가야 한다. 따라서 (B) declined가 정답이다.

6 (C)
- 번역: 세탁물을 신속하게 돌려받고자 한다면, 제공된 꼬리표에 객실 번호를 써 주십시오.
- 해설: 빈칸은 주어 없이 시작하는 명령문의 동사원형 자리이므로 동사원형 (C) write가 정답이다. 문장 끝에 있는 provided(제공된)는 the tag를 수식하는 과거분사이다. 동사의 과거형과 과거분사형은 형태가 같은 것이 많으므로 주의해야 한다.

7 (D)
- 번역: 다음 주에 우리는 새로운 회계 소프트웨어 프로그램을 도입할 예정이다.
- 해설: 빈칸 뒤에 목적어 a new accounting software program이 있으므로 앞의 be동사와 결합하여 능동태를 이루는 현재분사 (D) introducing이 정답이다.

8 (C)
- 번역: 사무용품 관련 모든 주문서는 목요일 정오까지 리튼 씨에게 제출해야 한다.
- 해설: 문맥상 '모든 주문서가 제출되어야 한다'는 수동적 의미를 나타내고 있으므로 과거분사 (C) submitted가 정답이다. 현재분사 (A) submitting이 들어가면 '제출하는 중이다'라는 능동태 진행형이 되므로 어색하다.

② 자동사와 타동사

ETS 유형 연습 본책 p.175

| 1 (A) | 2 (B) | 3 (B) | 4 (B) | 5 (D) | 6 (A) |
| 7 (D) | 8 (A) | | | | |

1 (A)
- 번역: 모든 팀원은 새로운 규정을 준수해야 한다.
- 해설: 빈칸은 전치사 with와 결합하여 the new regulations를 목적어로 취할 수 있는 자동사 자리이므로 자동사 (A) comply가 정답이다. 타동사 (B) keep(지키다)은 전치사 없이 바로 목적어를 취한다.

2 (B)
- 번역: 신제품은 분명히 많은 고객을 끌어 모을 것이다.
- 해설: 빈칸은 뒤에 a lot of customers를 목적어로 바로 취할 수 있는 타동사 자리이므로 타동사 (B) attract가 정답이다. 자동사 appeal(마음에 들다, 호소하다)은 전치사 to와 결합하여 목적어를 취할 수 있다.

3 (B)
- 번역: 전 직원은 매년 12월에 연간 (직무) 평가서를 완성해야 한다.
- 해설: 빈칸은 뒤에 annual evaluations를 목적어로 바로 취할 수 있는 타동사 자리이므로 (B) complete가 정답이다. 자동사 (A) agree(동의하다)는 주로 전치사 on 또는 with와 결합하여 목적어를 취할 수 있다.

4 (B)
- 번역: 이시무라 씨는 친절하게도 초대장을 직접 전달하겠다고 했다.
- 해설: 빈칸은 뒤에 the invitation을 목적어로 바로 취할 수 있는 타동사 자리이므로 타동사 (B) deliver가 정답이다. 자동사 (A) respond(응답하다)는 전치사 to와 결합하여 목적어를 취할 수 있다.

5 (D)
- 번역: 기획팀은 보관 공간이 얼마나 필요한지 파악하기 위해 조사를 시행할 것이다.
- 해설: 빈칸 뒤의 a survey를 목적어로 취해 '조사를 시행할 것이다'라는 의미가 되어야 자연스러우므로 타동사 (D) conduct가 정답이다. (A) remain(남아 있다)은 자동사이고, (B) act(~처럼 행동하다), (C) decide(결정하다)는 의미상 적합하지 않다.

6 (A)
- 번역: 빌리카 주민 대부분은 생계를 위해 농업에 의존한다.
- 해설: 빈칸에는 agriculture를 목적어로 취하면서 자동사 rely와 결합하여 '농업에 의존한다'라는 의미를 나타내는 전치사 (A) on이 들어가야 한다.

7 (D)
- 번역: 메다텔리 푸즈는 건강에 좋은 비타민과 미네랄이 풍부한 제품 제조를 전문으로 한다.
- 해설: 빈칸은 전치사 in과 결합하여 crafting products를 목적어로 취할 수 있는 자동사 자리이므로 자동사 (D) specializes가 정답이다.

8 (A)
- 번역: 건설 근로자들은 차질 없이 마감 시한을 맞추기 위해 동료들과 협력한다.
- 해설: 빈칸은 문장의 동사 자리이고 주어가 3인칭 복수 The construction workers이므로 복수동사인 (A) collaborate가 정답이다. 자동사 collaborate는 주로 전치사 with 또는 on과 결합하여 쓰인다.

ETS 실전 문제

본책 p.176

1 (D)	2 (D)	3 (B)	4 (A)	5 (D)	6 (D)
7 (B)	8 (B)	9 (D)	10 (A)	11 (A)	12 (B)
13 (D)	14 (B)				

1 (D)

번역 재정 검토 위원회는 예산 제안서가 10페이지를 넘지 않아야 한다고 언급했다.

해설 빈칸은 조동사 may 뒤에 있으므로 동사원형 (D) exceed가 정답이다.

어휘 board 위원회 state 언급하다 budget 예산 excessive 과도한 excess 초과 exceed 초과하다

2 (D)

번역 모든 신입사원은 3일간의 오리엔테이션에 참여해야 한다.

해설 빈칸은 전치사 in과 결합하여 the three-day orientation을 목적어로 취할 수 있는 자동사 자리이므로 자동사 (D) participate가 정답이다. 타동사 (A) attend(참석하다)와 (B) take(취하다, 가지고 가다)는 전치사 없이 바로 목적어를 취한다. 자동사 (C) inquire(문의하다)는 주로 전치사 about과 결합하여 목적어를 취한다.

3 (B)

번역 지난 15년 동안 타텔라 사는 국내 완구 제조업체 상위 10위 안에 지속적으로 들었다.

해설 빈칸에는 부사 consistently의 수식을 받으면서 앞의 동사 has와 결합하여 완료를 나타낼 수 있는 과거분사가 필요하므로 (B) ranked가 정답이다.

어휘 consistently 지속적으로 leading 선두의, 일류의 manufacturer 제조업체 rank 위치하다, 순위를 차지하다

4 (A)

번역 기무라 컨설팅은 직원들의 작문 능력을 향상시킬 수 있도록 워크숍을 제공하고 있습니다.

해설 문맥상 '직원들의 작문 능력을 향상시킬 수 있도록'이라는 의미가 되어야 자연스러우므로 (A) improve가 정답이다.

어휘 improve 향상시키다 explore 탐구하다 market (시장에) 내놓다 select 선정하다

5 (D)

번역 우리 소식지를 구독하는 고객은 첫 구매 시 15퍼센트 할인 혜택을 받을 수 있습니다.

해설 빈칸은 사람 선행사 Customers를 수식하는 관계대명사절의 동사 자리이다. 전치사 to와 결합하여 our newsletter를 목적어로 취할 수 있는 자동사가 와야 하고, 문맥상 '우리 소식지를 구독하는 고객'이라는 의미가 되어야 자연스러우므로 (D) subscribe가 정답이다. (A) alert와 (C) receive는 타동사로 목적어를 직접 취하고, (B) propose는 'to+목적어'와 함께 쓸 수 있지만 의미상 적합하지 않다.

어휘 alert 경고하다 propose 프러포즈를 하다, 제안하다 receive 받다 subscribe 구독하다

6 (D)

번역 글라이드라인 테크놀로지스는 기록을 보관하고 손상된 데이터를 복구하는 것을 전문으로 한다.

해설 빈칸은 전치사 in과 결합하여 archiving records and retrieving lost data를 목적어로 취할 수 있는 자동사 자리이므로 자동사 (D) specializes가 정답이다. (A) consists는 전치사 in과 결합하여 '~에 있다'의 의미로, 전치사 of와 결합하여 '~로 구성되다'의 의미로 쓰일 수 있지만 의미상 적합하지 않다.

어휘 archive 기록을 보관하다 retrieve 복구하다 specialize 전문으로 하다

7 (B)

번역 타인사이드 레크리에이션 부서는 이달 말까지 새 프로그램에 대한 제안을 받아들일 예정이다.

해설 빈칸은 문장의 동사 자리이고 미래를 나타내는 until the end of this month가 있으므로 미래 시제인 (B) will be accepting이 정답이다.

어휘 accept 받아들이다

8 (B)

번역 케이요먼 식당은 도심에서 해안 마을에 이르기까지 아주 다양한 지역에서 볼 수 있다.

해설 빈칸은 be동사 다음에 나오므로 분사가 들어갈 수 있는데, 식당들이 '발견된다'라는 수동의 의미가 되어야 자연스러우므로 과거분사 (B) found가 정답이다. 현재분사 (A) finding은 '발견하는 중이다'라는 능동태 진행형을 나타낸다.

어휘 urban 도시의 coastal 해안의

9 (D)

번역 최상의 결과를 얻으려면 반드시 접착제가 나무 표면에 들러붙도록 20분간 건조하세요.

해설 빈칸은 뒤의 전치사 to와 결합하여 the surface of the wood를 목적어로 취할 수 있는 자동사 자리이므로 자동사 (D) adheres가 정답이다. 타동사 (A) utilizes와 (B) polishes는 전치사 없이 바로 목적어를 취한다. 자동사 (C) complies는 주로 전치사 with와 결합하여 목적어를 취한다.

어휘 glue 접착제 ensure 확실하게 하다 surface 표면 utilize 활용하다 polish 닦다 comply 따르다 adhere 들러붙다

10 (A)

번역 재무 이사와 인사부 이사는 예산 인상에 대한 질문에 아주 다르게 반응했다.

해설 빈칸은 부사 quite의 수식을 받으면서 자동사 responded

를 수식하는 부사 자리이므로 부사 (A) differently가 정답이다. respond는 자동사이므로 전치사 to와 함께 쓰여 '~에 반응하다'라는 의미를 나타내며, respond를 타동사로 착각하여 명사를 정답으로 선택하지 않도록 주의한다.

어휘 respond to ~에 반응하다 budget 예산

[11-14] 기사

멜버른 (4월 26일)—호주에서 가장 오래된 화장품 회사 중 하나인 틴리 틴트는 이번 주에 은퇴하는 클리포드 빅스비 CEO의 후임으로 스텔라 추를 임명했다. 지난 10년 동안 추 씨는 회사 내에서 다양한 지도부 직책을 맡아왔다. 가장 최근 그녀는 최고운영책임자로 근무했다. 그 **11** 직위에서 그녀는 틴리 틴트의 글로벌 입지를 빠르게 확대하는 업무를 감독했다. 틴리 틴트는 **12** 현재 20개국 이상에 유통 센터를 보유하고 있다. "이 혁신적인 회사의 리더로 **13** 선택되어 영광입니다."라고 추 씨는 보도 자료에서 말했다. "화장품 산업은 단순히 제품에 그치지 않습니다. 그것은 사람들이 자신의 개성을 표현할 수 있도록 힘을 실어주는 것입니다. 저희 직원들은 그 점을 이해하고 있습니다. **14** 그들은 틴리 틴트 성공의 공로 대부분을 인정받을 자격이 있습니다."

어휘 cosmetics 화장품 name 임명하다 replace 대체하다 retire 은퇴하다 various 다양한 position 직책 serve 근무하다 chief operating officer 최고운영책임자 oversee 감독하다 rapid 빠른 expansion 확대 presence 입지 distribution 유통 honor 영광 innovative 혁신적인 press release 보도 자료 empower 권한을 주다 express 표현하다 uniqueness 개성

11 (A)

해설 빈칸 앞 문장에서 스텔라 추가 최근 맡았던 직위(Most recently, she served as its chief operating officer)를 언급하고 있다. 따라서 빈칸이 있는 문장은 그 직위에서 맡았던 업무를 설명하는 내용이 되어야 하므로 (A) capacity가 정답이다. 나머지 (B) development(개발), (C) group(단체), (D) location(장소)은 모두 의미상 적합하지 않다.

12 (B)

해설 빈칸 앞 문장에서 스텔라 추가 틴리 틴트의 글로벌 입지를 확대했다(she oversaw the rapid expansion of Tinley Tint's global presence)고 했으므로, 그 결과 '현재 20개국 이상에 유통 센터를 보유하고 있다'는 내용이 이어져야 적절하다. 따라서 (B) now가 정답이다. (A) too(너무), (C) mostly(주로), (D) strictly(엄격하게)는 모두 의미상 적합하지 않다.

13 (D)

해설 빈칸은 가주어 It의 진짜 주어인 to부정사에서 to 뒤의 동사원형 자리이다. 뒤에 목적어가 없고 Ms. Chou가 회사의 리더로 '선택되는' 것이므로 수동태인 (D) be picked가 정답이다.

14 (B)

번역
(A) 그들이 이 상의 후보로 지명되어 매우 기쁩니다.
(B) 그들은 틴리 틴트 성공의 공로 대부분을 인정받을 자격이 있습니다.
(C) 저희 베스트셀러 립스틱은 저희가 개발한 첫 제품이었습니다.
(D) 틴리 틴트는 올해 50여 명의 직원을 채용할 예정입니다.

해설 빈칸 앞에서 틴리 틴트의 직원들은 화장품 산업이 개성을 표현할 수 있도록 힘을 실어주는 것이라는 점을 이해하고 있다고 직원들의 강점을 강조하고 있다. 따라서 빈칸에는 직원들의 공로를 치하하는 내용이 나오는 것이 문맥상 자연스러우므로 (B)가 정답이다.

어휘 delighted 기쁜 nominate (후보로) 지명하다 deserve 받을 자격이 있다 credit 공로 develop 개발하다 hire 채용하다

UNIT 07 수 일치

1 수 일치의 개념과 동사의 형태

ETS 유형 연습 본책 p.179

1 (A) 2 (B) 3 (B) 4 (B) 5 (A) 6 (C)
7 (B) 8 (B)

1 (A)

번역 도서관의 이메일 시스템은 고객들에게 새로운 운영 시간을 공지했다.

해설 빈칸은 문장의 동사 자리이고 주어가 3인칭 단수 The library's e-mail system이므로 단수동사 (A) has가 정답이다. 여기서 has는 과거분사 notified와 결합하여 완료형을 나타낸다.

2 (B)

번역 우리 연구 결과가 〈브레이크스루〉 7월호에 게재되었다.

해설 빈칸은 be동사의 복수형인 were의 주어 자리이므로 복수명사 (B) results가 정답이다.

3 (B)

번역 그 제조사는 최신 카메라 모델들의 품질 보증을 12개월까지 연장했다.

해설 빈칸은 문장의 동사 자리이고 주어가 3인칭 단수 The manufacturer이므로 단수동사 (B) has extended가 정답이다.

4 (B)

번역 2분기 수익은 우리의 기대치를 상당히 웃돌았다.

해설 빈칸은 be동사의 복수형인 were의 주어 자리이므로 복수명사 (B) earnings가 정답이다.

5 (A)
번역 행사 기획자들은 올해 예술제에 참가하는 판매 업체의 수가 증가할 것으로 기대한다.
해설 빈칸은 문장의 동사 자리이고 주어가 3인칭 복수 Event organizers이므로 복수동사 (A) anticipate이 정답이다.

6 (C)
번역 선 씨는 다가오는 이사진 회의에서 8월 수익을 부각시킬 계획이다.
해설 빈칸은 문장의 동사 자리이고 주어가 3인칭 단수 Ms. Seon이므로 단수동사 (C) plans가 정답이다.

7 (B)
번역 올해 우리의 가장 중요한 목표는 경비를 줄이고 돈을 절약하는 것이다.
해설 빈칸은 문장의 동사 자리이고 주어가 3인칭 단수 Our most important goal이므로 단수동사 (B) is가 정답이다.

8 (B)
번역 쥬비리 신발회사는 공장 실험을 통해서 자사의 운동화 디자인을 개선할 수 있었다.
해설 빈칸 뒤에 복수동사 have helped가 왔으므로 빈칸은 복수 주어가 되는 (B) tests가 정답이다.

❷ 주의해야 할 수 일치

ETS 유형 연습   본책 p.181

1 (B) **2** (A) **3** (B) **4** (B) **5** (B) **6** (A)
7 (D) **8** (C)

1 (B)
번역 테데시 슈즈는 브링클리 대학교 학생들에게 할인을 제공한다.
해설 빈칸은 문장의 동사 자리이고 주어가 3인칭 단수 Tedeschi Shoes이므로 단수동사 (B) offers가 정답이다. 대문자로 쓰여진 회사명은 복수 형태라도 단수 취급하므로 주의해야 한다.

2 (A)
번역 스마트폰 이용자들의 수가 올해 30퍼센트까지 증가할 것으로 예상된다.
해설 빈칸은 문장의 동사 자리이고 주어가 3인칭 단수 The number 이므로 단수동사 (A) is가 정답이다. 주어를 수식하는 전치사구 of smartphone users는 수 일치에 영향을 주지 않는다.

3 (B)
번역 동료들과 디자인 아이디어를 공유하면 그들로부터 피드백을 받을 수 있다.
해설 빈칸은 문장의 동사 자리이고 주어가 단수 취급하는 동명사구 Sharing design ideas with co-workers이므로 단수동사 (B) enables가 정답이다. 빈칸 앞의 복수명사 co-workers는 전치사 with와 함께 수식어구로 쓰여 수 일치에 영향을 주지 않는다.

4 (B)
번역 목요일 저녁에 열리는 재즈 콘서트의 할인 티켓은 클라인 씨 사무실에서 구입할 수 있다.
해설 빈칸은 be동사의 복수형인 are의 주어 자리이므로 복수명사 (B) tickets가 정답이다. for Thursday evening's jazz concert는 주어를 수식하는 전치사구로 수 일치에는 영향을 주지 않고, discount ticket과 같은 복합명사는 뒤에 나오는 명사가 수를 결정한다.

5 (B)
번역 그린필드 프로젝트에 연관된 모든 사람은 사택에 거주한다.
해설 빈칸은 문장의 동사 자리이고 주어가 3인칭 단수 Everyone이므로 단수동사 (B) resides가 정답이다. 빈칸 앞의 involved는 주어 Everyone을 수식하는 과거분사이다. 동사의 과거형과 과거분사형은 형태가 같은 것이 많으므로 주의해야 한다.

6 (A)
번역 조지아 버네의 최근 CD에 수록된 노래들 대부분이 10대들에게 크게 인기를 얻고 있다.
해설 Most가 주어 자리에 나올 때, 〈Most of the+복수명사〉는 복수동사로, 〈Most of the+셀 수 없는 명사〉는 단수동사로 받는다. 여기서는 복수명사 the songs가 왔으므로 (A) are가 정답이다. (D) have 역시 복수형이지만 타동사이므로 주어를 보충 설명할 때 쓰이는 형용사 popular와 어울리지 않는다.

7 (D)
번역 시의 엄격한 규정에도 불구하고 많은 차량들이 매일 밤 불법 주차되어 있다.
해설 빈칸은 문장의 동사 자리이고 주어가 한정사 A number of 뒤의 복수명사 vehicles이므로 복수동사 (D) are가 정답이다. 빈칸 뒤의 parked는 be동사와 결합해 '차량이 주차되어 있다'는 수동적 의미를 나타내는 과거분사이다.

8 (C)
번역 그 컨설턴트가 제공한 제안 사항들은 직원 생산성을 향상시킬 것으로 추정된다.
해설 빈칸은 과거분사구 provided by the consultant의 수식을 받는 주어 자리이다. 동사 are가 복수형이므로 복수명사 (C) suggestions가 정답이다.

ETS 실전 문제

본책 p.182

1 (A) 2 (A) 3 (A) 4 (B) 5 (A) 6 (A)
7 (B) 8 (A) 9 (B) 10 (D) 11 (B) 12 (A)
13 (C) 14 (D)

1 (A)

번역 그뤼빌행 열차는 월요일부터 금요일까지 아침 9시에 출발한다.

해설 빈칸은 문장의 동사 자리이고 주어가 전치사구 for Gruyville의 수식을 받는 복수명사인 Trains이므로 복수동사 (A) depart가 정답이다. 나머지 (B) is departed, (C) departs, (D) is departing은 모두 단수동사이다.

어휘 depart 출발하다

2 (A)

번역 로이스 유리 사의 무료 설치 제공은 5월 1일부터 8월 31일까지다.

해설 빈칸은 문장의 동사 자리이고 주어가 3인칭 단수 Royce Glass Company's free installation offer이므로 단수동사 (A) extends가 정답이다.

어휘 installation 설치 extend 미치다

3 (A)

번역 직무 관련 강좌 중 하나를 등록해야 하는 마감일은 2월 10일이다.

해설 빈칸은 문장의 동사 자리이고 주어가 3인칭 단수 The deadline이므로 단수동사 (A) is가 정답이다. The deadline을 수식하는 to부정사구는 수 일치에 영향을 미치지 않는다.

어휘 deadline 마감일, 마감기한 sign up for ~에 등록하다
job-related 직무와 관련된

4 (B)

번역 리셉션 장식은 J. 리스터 디자인에서 제공했다.

해설 빈칸은 동사 were supplied의 주어 자리이다. 따라서 복수명사 (B) Decorations가 정답이다. (D) Decorating을 동명사로 볼 경우, 동사 were와 수 일치되지 않고 decorate는 타동사로 뒤에 목적어가 와야 한다.

어휘 reception 리셉션; 접수처

5 (A)

번역 사무 단지는 보행자 쇼핑 구역 주변에 건설될 것이다.

해설 빈칸은 주어인 The office complex 뒤의 동사 자리이다. 빈칸 뒤에 목적어가 없는 것으로 보아 수동태가 와야 하고, 문맥상 '사무 단지는 보행자 쇼핑 구역 주변에 건설될 것이다'라는 미래의 의미를 나타내는 것이 자연스러우므로 (A) will be built가 정답이다.

어휘 outskirts 주변, 근교 pedestrian 보행자

6 (A)

번역 맥닐 프로젝트의 일정표는 1층 회의실 벽에 걸려 있다.

해설 빈칸은 동사 is hanging의 주어 자리이자 전치사구 for the MacNeill project의 수식을 받는 명사 자리이므로 단수명사 (A) schedule이 정답이다. 명사 (D) scheduler(일정 관리 프로그램)는 의미상 적합하지 않다.

어휘 hang 걸리다, 매달리다
schedule 일정(표); 일정[시간계획]을 잡다

7 (B)

번역 이번 주에 한해, 200달러 이상 주문하시면 주문품을 무료로 익일 배송해 드립니다.

해설 빈칸은 명령문 뒤에 and로 이어지는 절에서 동사 자리이고 주어가 3인칭 단수 your order이므로 단수동사 (B) qualifies가 정답이다. qualify는 자동사로 쓰일 때 주로 전치사 for와 결합하여 쓰인다.

어휘 order 주문(품); 주문하다 overnight shipping 익일 배송
qualify for ~의 자격을 얻다, ~ 대상으로 적합하다

8 (A)

번역 파일 보관함에 있는 서류들은 알파벳순으로 정리되어야 한다.

해설 빈칸은 문장의 동사 자리이고 주어가 전치사구 in the filing cabinet의 수식을 받는 3인칭 복수 The documents이므로 복수동사 (A) need가 정답이다.

어휘 filing cabinet 파일 보관함 alphabetically 알파벳순으로

9 (B)

번역 최근 통과된 세법은 그 지방의 가족 소유 업체들 대부분에게 혜택을 주었다.

해설 빈칸은 문장의 동사 자리이고 주어가 3인칭 복수 Tax laws이므로 복수동사 (B) have benefited가 정답이다. 빈칸 앞의 passed recently는 주어 Tax laws를 수식하는 과거분사구이다.

어휘 tax law 세법 pass 통과시키다 majority 대부분
family-owned 가족 소유의 province 지방
benefit 혜택을 주다

10 (D)

번역 작가 미치코 히로타가 한 연설은 에르간 사 직원들의 호평을 받았다.

해설 빈칸은 과거분사구 given by author Michiko Hirota의 수식을 받는 문장의 주어 자리이다. 동사 was가 단수형이므로 단수명사 (D) address가 정답이다.

어휘 be received well by ~의 호평을 받다
addressable 다룰 수 있는 address 연설; 주소

[11-14] 편지

데보라 수 의원
포레스트 플레이스 451번지, 1층
헉스턴, 로드아일랜드 02310

수 의원님께,

제 지역 주민들을 대표해서 시내에 더 많은 자전거 도로를 요청하기 위해 편지를 씁니다. 주거 지역 근처에 새로운 비즈니스 시설들이 생겨나면서 통근 거리가 **11 줄어들었습니다.** 홀리힐 가에 자전거 점포가 문을 열었다는 점이 자전거 사용량의 증가를 입증해 줍니다. 사실 올해 초에는 〈헉스턴 데일리〉지의 한 기사에 **12 이것이** 실리기도 했습니다.

9월 6일 의회에서 티스데일 가와 포트 대로에 자전거 도로 개발 계획을 승인한 것으로 알고 있습니다. 저는 이러한 **13 조치들**을 전적으로 지지합니다. **14 사실 더 많은 자전거 도로가 뒤따라야 한다고 생각합니다.** 자전거 도로를 추가해서 도로의 안전과 효율성을 높여 주시기 바랍니다.

감사합니다.

가브리엘 리처즈 드림

어휘 council 의회 on behalf of ~을 대표[대신]해 fellow 같은 처지의, 동료의 community member 지역 주민 bicycle lane 자전거 도로 development 개발 residential area 주거 지역 distance 거리 commute 통근하다 attest to ~을 입증하다 usage 사용(량) make note of ~을 기록하다 article 기사 approve 승인하다 fully 전적으로 efficiency 효율성 add 추가하다

11 (B)

해설 빈칸은 문장의 동사 자리이고 주어가 전치사구 of new business facilities near residential areas의 수식을 받는 3인칭 단수 The development이므로 단수동사 (B) has shortened가 정답이다. (C) shortening과 (D) to shorten은 문장의 동사 자리에 나올 수 없다.

어휘 shorten 줄이다

12 (A)

해설 빈칸은 전치사 of의 목적어 자리이자 앞 문장 (The opening of a bicycle shop on Holleyhill Avenue attests to the increase in bicycle usage) 전체를 받을 수 있는 대명사 자리이므로 (A) this가 정답이다. 참고로, 앞에 나온 내용 전체를 가리킬 때 지시대명사 this나 that을 쓴다.

13 (C)

해설 빈칸 앞 문장에서 위원회가 자전거 도로 개발 계획들을 승인했다(the council approved plans on September 6 for bicycle lane development on Teasdale Street and Port Avenue)고 언급하고 있다. 따라서 빈칸에는 '이러한 위원회의 조치들을 전적으로 지지한다'는 내용이 이어져야 자연스러우므로 (C) measures가 정답이다. 나머지 (A) companies(회사들), (B) groups(단체들), (D) factories(공장들)는 모두 의미상 부적합하다.

14 (D)

번역 (A) 사실 더 많은 자전거 안전 교육이 제공되어야 합니다.
(B) 또한 새로운 자전거 가게들이 문을 열었습니다.
(C) 다시 말씀드리면, 자전거 타기는 좋은 운동입니다.
(D) 사실 더 많은 자전거 도로가 뒤따라야 한다고 생각합니다.

해설 빈칸 앞에서 자전거 도로 개발 계획을 전적으로 지지한다(I fully support these measures)고 언급하고 있다. 따라서 빈칸에는 더 많은 자전거 도로가 만들어져야 한다는 의견을 제시하는 것이 글의 흐름상 자연스러우므로 (D)가 정답이다.

어휘 in other words 다시 말해서 follow (결과가) 뒤따르다

UNIT 08 시제

① 현재/과거/미래 시제

ETS 유형 연습   본책 p.185

| 1 (B) | 2 (A) | 3 (A) | 4 (A) | 5 (D) | 6 (C) |
| 7 (A) | 8 (A) |

1 (B)

번역 강 씨는 25년 전에 한국의 부산에서 인쇄 사업을 시작했다.

해설 빈칸은 문장의 동사 자리이고 과거를 나타내는 25 years ago가 있으므로 과거 동사 (B) started가 정답이다.

2 (A)

번역 젤라코 소프트웨어 사는 정보기술 전문가들을 빈번하게 고용한다.

해설 빈칸은 문장의 동사 자리이고 반복을 나타내는 부사 frequently(빈번하게, 자주)가 동사를 수식하고 있으므로 현재 시제 (A) hires가 정답이다. (B) hiring은 문장의 동사 자리에 올 수 없다.

3 (A)

번역 회사 창립 파티가 오는 토요일 로얄 호텔에서 열릴 예정이다.

해설 빈칸은 문장의 동사 자리이고 미래를 나타내는 this coming Saturday가 있으므로 미래 시제인 (A) will be가 정답이다.

4 (A)

번역 어젯밤 만찬에서 히로시 스즈키에게 상이 수여되었다.

해설 빈칸은 문장의 동사 자리이고 과거를 나타내는 at last night's dinner가 있으므로 과거 동사 (A) was presented가 정답이다.

5 (D)

번역 엘로리 가에 있는 사업체들은 작업반이 거리를 재포장할 수 있도록 어제 일찍 문을 닫았다.

해설 빈칸은 문장의 동사 자리이고 과거를 나타내는 early yesterday가 동사를 수식하고 있으므로 과거 동사 (D) closed가 정답이다.

6 (C)
번역 현 시스템에서는 사용자들이 비밀번호를 입력해 온라인 뱅킹 계좌에 접속하도록 허용한다.
해설 주어가 The current system으로 3인칭 단수이고 현 시스템에 대한 문장이므로 현재 시제 단수동사인 (C) allows가 정답이다.

7 (A)
번역 모든 엠버트 어플라이언스 제품들에 대한 새로운 주문 절차가 다음 달부터 시행될 것이다.
해설 빈칸은 문장의 동사 자리이고 미래를 나타내는 as of next month가 있으므로 미래 시제인 (A) will come이 정답이다.

8 (A)
번역 지난해 한스퍼드 자동차 회사 카탈로그에는 에어컨이 전 차종의 기본 사양으로 포함되었다.
해설 빈칸은 문장의 동사 자리이고 과거를 나타내는 Last year가 있으므로 과거 동사 (A) listed가 정답이다.

② 진행 시제

ETS 유형 연습　　　본책 p.187

1 (A)　2 (A)　3 (B)　4 (B)　5 (D)　6 (C)
7 (C)　8 (A)

1 (A)
번역 초과 예약 때문에 텔코 버스의 일부 승객들은 지금 다섯 시간 넘게 기다리고 있다.
해설 빈칸은 문장의 동사 자리이다. 현재를 나타내는 now가 있으므로 waiting과 결합하여 현재진행 시제를 나타내는 be동사 (A) are가 정답이다.

2 (A)
번역 포항 시민들은 다음 주 이 시간에 새 시장을 선출하기 위해 투표하고 있을 것이다.
해설 빈칸은 조동사 will 뒤의 동사원형 자리이다. 미래를 나타내는 this time next week이 있으므로 조동사 will과 결합하여 미래진행 시제를 나타내는 (A) be voting이 정답이다.

3 (B)
번역 윤 씨는 목요일에 돌아왔을 때 시차증으로 고생하고 있었다.
해설 빈칸은 문장의 동사 자리이다. 부사절 when she returned on Thursday가 과거를 나타내므로 과거진행 시제인 (B) was suffering이 정답이다. 과거진행 시제는 과거 시점에 동작이나 상태가 진행 중임을 강조하기 위해 쓴다.

4 (B)
번역 방문객들은 내일 아침 10시에 우리 생산 시설을 둘러볼 예정이다.
해설 빈칸은 문장의 동사 자리이다. 미래를 나타내는 at 10 A.M. tomorrow morning이 있으므로 touring과 결합하여 미래진행 시제를 나타내는 동사 (B) will be가 정답이다.

5 (D)
번역 PX 카피타임에서 온 서비스 기술자는 지금 고장 난 복사기를 수리하고 있다.
해설 빈칸은 문장의 동사 자리이다. at the moment(바로 지금)를 써서 지금 현재의 순간을 강조하고 있으므로 현재진행 시제인 (D) is repairing이 정답이다. 현재 시제인 (B) repairs는 주로 반복적인 동작을 나타낼 때 쓰인다.

6 (C)
번역 플런지 사는 오는 2월 투자자 회의에 새로운 대표를 파견할 예정이다.
해설 빈칸은 문장의 동사 자리로, 뒤에 목적어 a new representative가 있으므로 능동형 동사가 와야 한다. 뒤에 미래를 나타내는 next February가 있으므로 미래진행 시제인 (C) will be sending이 정답이다. 주어가 3인칭 단수 Flunge, Inc.이므로 (A) send는 수 일치되지 않는다.

7 (C)
번역 팩스톤 엔터프라이즈가 섬유 부문을 구조 조정했을 때 중간 관리자 몇 명이 해고되었다.
해설 빈칸은 접속사 When이 이끄는 부사절의 동사 자리이다. 동사의 주어가 3인칭 단수 Paxton Enterprises이고 주절의 동사가 were laid off로 과거를 나타내고 있으므로 과거진행 시제인 (C) was restructuring이 정답이다.

8 (A)
번역 모르네스 하드웨어는 다음 주 금요일에 선착순 50명의 고객들에게 무료 손전등을 제공할 예정이다.
해설 빈칸은 문장의 동사 자리이고 미래를 나타내는 next Friday가 있으므로 가까운 미래를 대신할 수 있는 현재진행 시제인 (A) is offering이 정답이다.

③ 완료시제

ETS 유형 연습　　　본책 p.189

1 (B)　2 (A)　3 (A)　4 (A)　5 (B)　6 (B)
7 (B)　8 (B)

1 (B)
번역 신임 CEO가 루파 인베스트먼츠에 합류한 이후로 근무 환경이 대단히 좋아졌다.
해설 빈칸은 문장의 동사 자리이고 과거부터 현재까지의 기간을 나타내는 부사절 since the new CEO joined Loopa Investments가 있으므로 현재완료 시제인 (B) have improved가 정답이다.

2 (A)
번역 두 회사는 한 달 전에 합병 계획에 합의했다.
해설 빈칸은 문장의 동사 자리이고 과거를 나타내는 one month ago가 있으므로 과거동사 (A) reached가 정답이다. 명확한 과거 시점을 나타내는 부사는 현재완료 시제와 함께 쓸 수 없다.

3 (A)
번역 지난 세 분기 동안 이몰라 씨의 순수익률이 약간 상승했다.
해설 빈칸은 문장의 동사 자리이고 과거부터 현재까지의 기간을 나타내는 for the last three quarters가 있으므로 과거분사 risen과 결합하여 현재완료 시제를 나타내는 동사 (A) has가 정답이다. (B) was를 쓰면 수동태가 되는데, rise는 자동사이므로 수동태가 불가능하다.

4 (A)
번역 최근 타이거 짐 헬스클럽 여러 곳이 도심부에 문을 열었다.
해설 빈칸은 문장의 동사 자리이고 과거나 현재완료 시제와 어울리는 부사 recently가 동사를 수식하고 있으므로 현재완료 시제인 (A) have opened가 정답이다.

5 (B)
번역 지난 5년 동안 과거 어느 때보다 많은 대학생들이 인턴 프로그램에 참가했다.
해설 빈칸은 문장의 동사 자리이고 과거부터 현재까지의 기간을 나타내는 in the last five years가 있으므로 현재완료 시제인 (B) have participated가 정답이다.

6 (B)
번역 오전 10시 17분 기차는 아바키 씨 팀이 역에 도착하기 전에 이미 떠났다.
해설 빈칸은 문장의 동사 자리로 부사절 before Mr. Abaki's team arrived at the station이 나타내는 과거보다 더 전에 일어난 일을 나타내고 있으므로 left와 결합하여 과거완료 시제를 나타내는 동사 (B) had가 정답이다.

7 (B)
번역 우리는 지난주에 신문 광고를 낸 이래로 10건의 문의를 받았다.
해설 빈칸은 문장의 동사 자리이고 과거부터 현재까지의 기간을 나타내는 부사절 since the advertisement ran in last week's edition of the newspaper가 있으므로 현재완료 시제인 (B) have received가 정답이다.

8 (B)
번역 발스파 씨는 퇴직할 무렵까지 회사의 시장 점유율을 상당히 높일 수 있을 것이다.
해설 빈칸은 문장의 동사 자리이고, 부사절 By the time Ms. Valspar retires는 현재 시제를 쓰고 있지만 실제로 미래를 의미하여 미래의 특정 시점까지 완료되는 것을 나타낸다. 따라서 미래완료 시제인 (B) will have managed가 정답이다.

ETS 실전 문제 (본책 p.190)

1 (B) 2 (C) 3 (B) 4 (A) 5 (D) 6 (A)
7 (C) 8 (B) 9 (A) 10 (B) 11 (B) 12 (D)
13 (C) 14 (A)

1 (B)
번역 구매 관리자인 매기 윌리엄스는 현재 매주 말에 요청 받은 비품을 주문한다.
해설 빈칸은 문장의 동사 자리로 주어가 3인칭 단수 Maggie Williams이고 부사 currently(현재)와 반복을 나타내는 at the end of each week가 있으므로 현재 시제인 (B) orders가 정답이다.
어휘 purchasing manager 구매 담당자 currently 현재 requested 요청 받은 supplies 비품, 보급품

2 (C)
번역 다음 달에, 베르제스 아트 스튜디오는 모든 수업에 25퍼센트 할인을 제공할 예정이다.
해설 빈칸은 동사 자리로, 앞에 Next month라는 미래 표현이 있으므로 미래 시제인 (C) will offer가 정답이다.

3 (B)
번역 하튼 패션 크로니클에 따르면, 많은 디자이너들이 올해의 가을 신상품에 녹색과 갈색 직물들을 사용할 것이라고 한다.
해설 빈칸은 문장의 동사 자리로 미래를 나타내는 this year가 있는데, 보기에 미래 시제가 없다. 가까운 미래는 현재진행 시제로 대신할 수 있으므로 (B) are using이 정답이다.
어휘 fabric 직물, 천 collection (의류) 신상품, 신작 발표회

4 (A)
번역 폴란스키 데이터 인터내셔널은 다음 주 리버풀에서 열리는 디지털 미디어 회의에 참석하는 모든 직원을 위해 교통편을 마련했다.
해설 빈칸은 문장의 동사 자리이고 문맥상 교통편의 마련이 완료된 상태이므로 현재완료 시제인 (A) has arranged가 정답이다.
어휘 transportation 교통(편) arrange 마련하다

5 (D)
번역 스즈키 박사는 기차가 20분 늦게 출발했는데도 불구하고 시상식에 제시간에 도착했다.
해설 빈칸은 접속사 even though가 이끄는 부사절의 동사 자리이다. 주절의 동사가 arrived로 과거를 나타내고 의미상 그 과거보다 더 전에 일어난 일을 나타내고 있으므로 과거완료 시제인 (D) had left가 정답이다.
어휘 awards ceremony 시상식 on time 제시간에 even though 비록 ~에도 불구하고

6 (A)
번역 가우드 대학교에서 졸업률은 지난 10년 동안 55퍼센트 증가했다.
해설 문장의 시제가 현재완료(has increased)이고, 문맥상 '지난 10년 동안'이라는 의미가 되어야 자연스러우므로 전치사 (A) over가 정답이다. (B) behind(~뒤에), (C) near(~가까이), (D) toward(~을 향해)는 모두 의미상 적합하지 않다.
어휘 graduation 졸업 rate 비율 decade 10년

7 (C)
번역 스트랜튼의 부동산 중개업자들은 내년에 부동산 가치가 오를 것으로 전망한다.
해설 빈칸은 접속사 that이 이끄는 명사절의 동사 자리이다. 미래를 나타내는 in the coming year가 있으므로 미래 시제인 (C) will increase가 정답이다.
어휘 real estate agent 부동산 중개업자 anticipate 전망하다 property 부동산 increasingly 점점 increase 오르다

8 (B)
번역 솔즈베리 네이처 클럽의 회계 담당자는 다음 회계분기의 예산을 검토하고 수정을 제안했다.
해설 빈칸은 문장의 동사 자리이다. 동사 두 개를 연결한 등위 접속사 and가 있으므로 빈칸의 동사도 suggested와 같은 형태여야 하므로 현재완료 시제인 (B) has examined가 정답이다. 참고로, suggested 앞에 has가 생략되어 있다.
어휘 treasurer 회계 담당자 revision 수정 budget 예산 financial quarter 회계분기 examine 검토하다

9 (A)
번역 이제 온라인에서 월별 계정 명세서를 확인할 수 있다.
해설 빈칸은 형용사 available을 수식하는 부사 자리로 현재 시제 be동사인 are와 함께 문맥상 '명세서가 이제 확인 가능하다'는 의미가 되어야 자연스러우므로 (A) now가 정답이다.
어휘 statement 명세서 available 이용 가능한 now 지금 well 잘 gently 부드럽게 brightly 밝게

10 (B)
번역 매출 급감 때문에 미켈슨 의류는 현재의 광고 캠페인을 중단했고 대폭 수정할 예정이다.
해설 빈칸은 문장의 동사 자리이다. 등위접속사 and는 두 문장을 연결하고 있는데, 주어가 동일할 경우 and 뒤에 오는 문장에서는 주어를 생략할 수 있다. 문맥상 '현재의 광고 캠페인을 중단했고 수정할 예정이다'라는 의미가 되어야 자연스러우므로 미래진행 시제 (B) will be modifying이 정답이다.
어휘 decrease 감소 suspend 중단하다 current 현재의 substantially 대폭 modify 수정하다

[11-14] 공지

전 직원 여러분:

어젯밤 우리 건물 1층에 가벼운 전기 화재가 진화되었다는 것을 알고 계실 겁니다. **11 다행히** 화재가 빠르게 진압되어 피해는 미미합니다. 하지만 오늘 주방과 테이블은 **12 이용할 수 없습니다**. 오늘 아침 배선 점검 및 교체를 위해 전기 기사들이 왔습니다. **13 작업이 끝나면 공간은 철저히 청소될 것입니다.** 신속한 조치를 취해주신 야간 보안 요원분들께 감사드립니다.

주방을 자주 사용하는지에 상관없이, 관리자는 회사 구내식당에서 무료 다과를 받을 수 있는 상품권을 배포할 수 있도록 **14 권한을 부여받았습니다.**

-주디 응, 시설 관리자

어휘 minor 가벼운, 작은 extinguish (불을) 진화하다 contain 억제하다 damage 손해 minimal 아주 적은 kitchenette 간이 주방 electrician 전기 기사 inspect 점검하다 wiring 배선 grateful 감사하는 security crew 보안 요원 regardless of ~에 상관없이 regularly 자주 distribute 배포하다 voucher 상품권 refreshment 다과 facility 시설

11 (B)
해설 빈칸 뒤에서 화재가 빠르게 진압되어 피해는 미미하다(the fire was contained quickly, so the damage is minimal)고 언급하고 있으므로, 다행스러운 상황을 표현하는 부사 (B) Fortunately가 정답이다. 나머지 (A) Repeatedly(반복적으로), (C) Normally(보통), (D) Kindly(친절하게)는 모두 의미상 적합하지 않다.

12 (D)
해설 빈칸 뒤에서 화재 복구 작업 진행(Electricians arrived this morning to inspect and replace the wiring)에 대해 언급하고 있으므로, 복구 작업 때문에 '주방과 테이블은 이용할 수 없다'는 내용이 되어야 적절하므로 (D) unavailable이 정답이다. 나머지 (A) arranged(배치된), (B) incomplete(불완전한), (C) furnished(가구가 비치된)는 모두 의미상 부적합하다.

13 (C)
번역
(A) 사무실에서 불과 한 블록 거리에 새로운 식당이 문을 열었습니다.
(B) 이 일을 위한 예산에 자금이 충분하지 않습니다.
(C) 작업이 끝나면 공간은 철저히 청소될 것입니다.
(D) 팀 오찬에 참석할 수 있는지 관리자에게 알려주세요.

해설 빈칸 앞 문장에서 배선 점검 및 교체를 위해 전기 기사들이 왔다(Electricians arrived this morning to inspect and replace the wiring)고 언급하고 있다. 따라서 빈칸에는 앞서 언급된 작업이 완료되고 난 뒤 후속 조치에 대한 내용이 나오는 것이 글의 흐름상 자연스러우므로 (C)가 정답이다.

어휘 mere 겨우 ~의 budget 예산 thoroughly 철저히 luncheon 오찬

14 (A)

해설 빈칸은 뒤에 목적어가 없으므로 수동태 동사 자리이다. 또한 문맥상 현재 관리자가 상품권 배포 권한을 부여받은 상태라는 의미가 되어야 자연스러우므로 현재완료 시제 (A) has been authorized가 정답이다. 상품권 배포 권한을 부여받은 것이 특정 과거시점보다 더 과거의 일이 아니므로 과거완료 시제 (B) had been authorized는 적절하지 않다.

UNIT 09 능동태와 수동태

① 수동태의 개념과 형태

ETS 유형 연습
본책 p.193

| 1 (A) | 2 (B) | 3 (B) | 4 (B) | 5 (D) | 6 (A) |
| 7 (D) | 8 (A) |

1 (A)

번역 그 자리에 지원하는 사람들은 이달 말까지 지원서를 제출해야 한다.

해설 빈칸은 조동사 must 뒤의 동사원형 자리이고 주어 Candidates가 목적어 their applications를 제출하는 주체이므로 능동태인 (A) submit이 정답이다.

2 (B)

번역 디자인상 후보로 지명된 엔지니어 목록이 본 이메일에 첨부되어 있다.

해설 주어 A list가 첨부되는 대상이므로 수동태를 이루는 과거분사 (B) attached가 정답이다.

3 (B)

번역 요청 정보는 제공된 공간에 신중하게 기입되어야 한다.

해설 주어 The requested information이 작성되는 대상이므로 수동태를 이루는 과거분사 (B) written이 정답이다.

4 (B)

번역 세미나에는 외식산업에 관련된 전문가들이 참석할 것이다.

해설 수동태 문장에서 빈칸 뒤의 professionals가 동사 attend의 주체가 되므로 '~에 의해'라는 뜻으로 행위자를 나타내는 전치사 (B) by가 정답이다.

5 (D)

번역 항공사 파업으로 자벨라 씨는 로마 여행 계획을 미뤄야 했다.

해설 빈칸은 문장의 동사 자리이고 주어 Mr. Jarvela가 목적어 his plans를 연기하는 주체이므로 능동태인 (D) had to postpone이 정답이다. 준동사인 (A) postponing과 (B) to postpone은 동사 자리에 올 수 없다.

6 (A)

번역 우리 회사의 품질 관리부는 소매업자들에게 배송되기 전에 모든 제품을 검사한다.

해설 접속사 before가 이끄는 부사절에서 주어 they(= all products)가 배송되는 대상이므로 수동태를 이루는 과거분사 (A) shipped가 정답이다.

7 (D)

번역 시의 열차 시스템에 대한 보고서는 지난 화요일 일반인들에게 공개되었다.

해설 주어 The report on the city's train system이 발표되는 대상이므로 수동태인 (D) was released가 정답이다.

8 (A)

번역 아일랜드 호퍼의 웹페이지에 업데이트된 취업기회 목록이 게시되어 있다.

해설 주어 An updated list of job opportunities가 게시되는 대상이므로 수동태인 (A) is posted가 정답이다.

② 능동태와 수동태 구별하기

ETS 유형 연습
본책 p.195

| 1 (B) | 2 (A) | 3 (B) | 4 (B) | 5 (B) | 6 (A) |
| 7 (B) | 8 (D) |

1 (B)

번역 사내 지침서는 급여 및 상여금, 초과 근무의 주제를 다루고 있다.

해설 빈칸은 문장의 동사 자리인데, 뒤에 목적어 the topics가 나오므로 능동태 (B) covers가 정답이다.

2 (A)

번역 소형 보트를 위한 최고의 트레일러는 토우-웰 제조사에 의해 제조된다.

해설 빈칸은 문장의 동사 자리로, 뒤에 목적어가 없이 전치사가 나오므로 수동태 (A) is made가 정답이다.

3 (B)

번역 더 나은 마케팅 전략들이 항상 개발될 수 있다.

해설 빈칸은 조동사 can 뒤의 동사원형 자리이고 뒤에 목적어가 없으므로 수동태 (B) be developed가 정답이다.

4 (B)

번역 디자이너들과 사진작가들 모두 가을 카탈로그에 만족한다.

해설 빈칸은 the fall catalog를 목적어로 취하면서 수동태 동사 are satisfied와 결합하여 '가을 카탈로그에 만족한다'라는 의미를 나타내는 전치사 (B) with가 정답이다. be satisfied with는 '~에 만족하다'라는 뜻이다.

5 (B)

번역 링 씨는 초청 연사들과 쇼 진행자에게 수정된 일정표를 나눠주고 있다.

해설 빈칸 앞에 be동사 is가 있고 뒤에 목적어 a revised schedule이 있으므로 진행형 능동태를 이루는 현재분사 (B) distributing이 정답이다.

6 (A)

번역 팀원 대다수가 다가오는 워크숍에 관심을 갖고 있다.

해설 빈칸은 the upcoming workshop을 목적어로 취하면서 수동태 동사 are interested와 결합하여 '다가오는 워크숍에 관심이 있다'는 의미를 나타내는 전치사 (A) in이 정답이다. be interested in은 '~에 관심이 있다'라는 뜻이다.

7 (B)

번역 모든 시계의 뒷면에는 모델 번호와 일련 번호가 둘 다 새겨져 있다.

해설 빈칸은 문장의 동사 자리이고 주어 Both the model number and the serial number가 새겨지는 대상이므로 수동태 (B) are engraved가 정답이다.

8 (D)

번역 자물쇠에 자주 발생하는 문제들은 간단한 수리나 조절로 해결할 수 있다.

해설 빈칸은 문장의 동사 자리이고 주어 Many problems가 해결되는 대상이므로 수동태 동사 (D) can be solved가 정답이다.

ETS 실전 문제   본책 p.196

1 (D)	2 (D)	3 (B)	4 (A)	5 (B)	6 (B)
7 (C)	8 (A)	9 (D)	10 (B)	11 (C)	12 (D)
13 (B)	14 (A)				

1 (D)

번역 알세이저 출신의 변호사 데이브 민센트는 시의회에 복무하도록 선출되었다.

해설 주어 Dave Minsent, a lawyer from Alsager는 선출하는 주체가 아니라 선출되는 대상이므로 '알세이저 출신의 변호사 데이브 민센트는 선출되었다'라는 수동의 의미가 적절하다. 따라서 과거분사 (D) elected가 정답이다. 빈칸 뒤에 목적어가 없는 구조로도 수동태 문장임을 판단할 수 있다.

어휘 serve 복무하다 council 의회 election 선거 electoral 선거의 elect 선출하다

2 (D)

번역 현재 실바우 디비전은 시 바로 외곽에 있는 새로운 현대적 시설에서 모든 종류의 철강 제품을 생산하고 있다.

해설 빈칸은 a full line of steel products를 목적어로 취하면서 '모든 종류의 철강 제품을 생산하고 있다'는 능동적 의미를 나타내는 현재분사 (D) manufacturing이 정답이다.

어휘 facility 시설, 설비 manufacture 생산하다

3 (B)

번역 모든 승객은 버스가 이동하는 동안 자리에 앉아 있어야 한다.

해설 빈칸은 문장의 동사 자리로, 뒤에 목적어가 없으므로 수동태 (B) are required가 정답이다.

어휘 passenger 승객 be required to ~해야 한다

4 (A)

번역 재 권의 사진집은 산 경관을 가로지르는 빛의 미묘한 변화를 드러낸다.

해설 빈칸은 문장의 동사 자리이고 주어 Jae Kwon's collection이 3인칭 단수명사이자 목적어 the subtle changes of light를 드러내는 주체이므로 능동태 단수동사 (A) exposes가 정답이다.

어휘 collection 모음집, 소장품 photograph 사진 subtle 미묘한 landscape 경치 expose 드러내다

5 (B)

번역 최근 개조한 실험실은 최첨단 연구 장비와 보안 카메라를 갖추고 있다.

해설 빈칸은 state-of-the-art research equipment and security cameras를 목적어로 취하면서 수동태 동사 is equipped와 결합하여 '최첨단 연구 장비와 보안 카메라를 갖추고 있다'라는 의미를 나타내는 전치사 (B) with가 정답이다. be equipped with는 '~를 갖추다'라는 뜻이다.

어휘 newly 최근 laboratory 실험실, 연구실 state-of-the-art 최첨단의 equipment 장비 security 보안

6 (B)

번역 트루 포토 프린터용 기술 설명서들은 A-랭귀지 사의 계약자들에 의해 스페인어로 번역되었다.

해설 빈칸은 문장의 동사 자리이고 주어 The technical manuals가 번역이 되는 대상이므로 수동태 (B) were translated가 정답이다.

어휘 technical manual 기술 설명서 contractor 계약자 translate 번역하다

7 (C)
번역 분실된 창고 열쇠를 찾는 사람은 누구든지 샤 씨에게 반환해야 한다.

해설 빈칸은 대명사 Anyone을 수식하는 관계대명사절의 동사 자리이다. who가 대신하는 주어인 Anyone이 단수이고 뒤에 목적어가 있으므로 능동태인 단수동사 (C) finds가 정답이다.

어휘 missing 분실된 warehouse 창고

8 (A)
번역 연봉 인상을 결정하는 데 사용되는 다양한 척도를 공적 기준이라고 한다.

해설 빈칸은 문장의 동사 자리이고 뒤에 타동사 refer의 목적어가 없으므로 수동태 (A) are referred가 정답이다.

어휘 measure 척도 determine 결정하다 annual 연간의 salary increase 급여 인상 merit 공적 criteria 기준 refer to as ~라고 부르다

9 (D)
번역 회사 지역 봉사 클럽의 겨울 안건은 이따가 오늘 오후에 배포될 것이다.

해설 빈칸은 문장의 동사 자리로, 주어 The winter agenda of the company's community service club이 유포되는 대상이고 미래를 나타내는 later this afternoon이 있으므로 미래 시제 수동태 (D) will be circulated가 정답이다.

어휘 agenda 안건 community 지역 circulate 배포하다

10 (B)
번역 밀러 철물점의 웹사이트는 휴대폰에서 볼 수 있도록 간소화되어 있다.

해설 be동사 뒤에 알맞은 형태를 고르는 문제이다. 문맥상 '웹사이트가 간소화되다'라는 의미가 적절하므로 수동태의 과거분사 (B) simplified가 정답이다. (A) simplification은 보어로서 be동사 뒤에 쓰일 수 있지만 주어(Web site)와 동격을 이루지 않으므로 오답이다.

어휘 hardware store 철물점 simplification 간소화

[11-14] 가이드라인

〈오팔우드 트리뷴〉은 독자 여러분의 편지를 환영합니다. 공간에 제약이 있어 저희가 받는 11**모든** 제출물을 게재할 수는 없습니다. 저희는 지역 관심사에 대해 새로운 시각을 제공하는 편지에 우선권을 부여하는데 특히, 이 문제가 최근 기사에서 12**언급된** 경우 우선권이 부여됩니다. 저희는 또한 200단어를 넘지 않는 편지를 선호합니다. 13**그보다 긴 제출물은 편집될 수 있습니다.**

편지가 출판을 위해 14**선정되면** 편집자가 통지할 수 있도록 이름과 연락처 정보를 반드시 넣으세요.

어휘 limited 제약이 있는 submission 제출(물) priority 우선권 perspective 시각 interest 관심 particularly 특히 recent 최근의 exceed 넘다 editor 편집자 notify 통지하다 publication 출판(물)

11 (C)
해설 빈칸 앞 문장에서 공간이 제한되어 있다(Because space is limited)고 이유를 대고 있다. 따라서 빈칸에는 모든 제출물을 게재할 수 없다는 내용이 이어져야 자연스러우므로 (C) all이 정답이다. 나머지 (A) any(어느), (B) total(전체의), (D) original(원래의)은 모두 의미상 적합하지 않다.

12 (D)
해설 빈칸은 접속사 if가 이끄는 부사절에서 동사 자리로 뒤에 목적어가 없으므로 수동태 (D) was mentioned가 정답이다. (C) being mentioned는 동사 자리에 올 수 없다.

13 (B)
번역 (A) 따라서 저희는 익명의 편지는 출판하지 않습니다.
(B) 그보다 긴 제출물은 편집될 수 있습니다.
(C) 저희 출판물에서는 그런 말을 사용하는 것이 허용되지 않습니다.
(D) 이보다 더 자주 저희에게 편지하지 마세요.

해설 빈칸 앞 문장에서 200단어를 넘지 않는 편지를 선호한다(We also prefer letters that do not exceed 200 words)고 언급하고 있다. 따라서 빈칸에는 200자를 초과하는 원고에 대한 대응을 나타내는 것이 글의 흐름상 자연스러우므로 (B)가 정답이다.

어휘 therefore 따라서 anonymous 익명의 edit 편집하다 frequently 자주

14 (A)
해설 빈칸 앞에서 편집자가 통지할 수 있도록 이름과 연락처 정보를 요구(Please be sure to include your name and contact information so the editors can notify you)하고 있다. 따라서 '출판을 위해 선정된다면'이라는 의미가 되어야 자연스러우므로 (A) selected(선정된)가 정답이다. 나머지 (B) completed(완성된), (C) opened(열린), (D) continued(계속되는)는 모두 의미상 적합하지 않다.

UNIT 10 to부정사와 동명사

1 to부정사의 형태와 역할

ETS 유형 연습   본책 p.199

| 1 (B) | 2 (B) | 3 (B) | 4 (A) | 5 (A) | 6 (D) |
| 7 (D) | 8 (A) | | | | |

1 (B)
번역 관리팀은 예산의 제약 때문에 그 프로젝트를 취소하기로 결정했다.

해설 빈칸은 동사 decided의 목적어 자리로 the project를 목적어로 취하면서 명사 역할을 할 수 있는 to부정사 (B) to cancel이 정답이다. decide는 to부정사를 목적어로 취한다.

2 (B)
번역 컴퓨터 프로그래머로서 당신의 업무 중 하나는 우리 웹 사이트를 업데이트하는 것이다.

해설 빈칸은 be동사 is의 주어인 One of your tasks와 동일한 대상을 나타내는 주격 보어 자리로 our Web site를 목적어로 취하면서 명사 역할을 할 수 있는 to부정사 (B) to update가 정답이다.

3 (B)
번역 도슨 씨는 완료해야 할 업무가 너무 많아서 하루 휴가를 낼 수가 없다.

해설 빈칸은 명사구 so many assignments를 수식하는 수식어 자리로 동사원형 complete와 결합하여 형용사 역할을 할 수 있는 to부정사의 (B) to가 정답이다.

4 (A)
번역 훌륭한 가구를 만들기 위해, 테일러 씨는 상점에서 구할 수 없는 특별한 목재를 사용한다.

해설 빈칸은 fine furniture를 목적어로 취하면서 '~하기 위하여'라는 목적의 의미를 나타낼 수 있는 to부정사 (A) To build가 정답이다.

5 (A)
번역 보석 상자에 진열된 반지는 어떤 손가락에도 맞도록 치수를 바꿀 수 있다.

해설 빈칸 앞이 완전한 절이므로, 빈칸 이하는 수식어구가 된다. 동사원형 fit과 결합하여 부사 역할을 할 수 있는 (A) to가 정답이다. 참고로, '~하기 위해'라는 의미의 부사 역할을 하는 to부정사는 〈in order+to부정사〉나 〈so as+to부정사〉로 바꿔 쓸 수 있다.

6 (D)
번역 라라도어 병원 관계자들은 병원 자원봉사자들에게 감사하는 뜻에서 다과를 제공할 것이다.

해설 빈칸은 to부정사를 이루는 To 뒤의 동사원형 자리로 동사원형 (D) thank가 정답이다. to부정사의 to와 전치사 to는 형태가 같으므로 빈칸 앞의 to를 전치사로 오인하여 동명사를 고르지 않도록 주의해야 한다.

7 (D)
번역 이 기계는 제대로 기능하려면 정기적으로 서비스를 받아야 한다.

해설 빈칸은 In order to 뒤의 동사원형 자리로 동사원형 (D) function이 정답이다. 〈in order to+동사원형(~하기 위해)〉은 부사 역할을 한다.

8 (A)
번역 로봇은 여러 가지 일을 동시에 수행하는 것이 가능하다.

해설 빈칸은 be동사 is의 주어 자리로 문장의 진짜 주어인 for a robot to carry out several tasks at the same time을 대신하는 가주어 (A) It이 정답이다.

② 자주 출제되는 to부정사 표현

ETS 유형 연습
본책 p.201

| 1 (A) | 2 (B) | 3 (A) | 4 (A) | 5 (B) | 6 (B) |
| 7 (C) | 8 (C) |

1 (A)
번역 애드리나 씨는 재무 보고서를 마치는 마감일을 연장하기를 바란다.

해설 앞에 to부정사를 목적어로 취하는 동사 hope가 있으므로 빈칸은 to부정사를 이루는 동사원형 (A) extend가 정답이다. to부정사의 to와 전치사 to는 형태가 같으므로 빈칸 앞의 to를 전치사로 오인하여 동명사를 고르지 않도록 주의해야 한다.

2 (B)
번역 선생님들은 신입생을 맞이하기 위해 월요일에 일찍 출근할 것으로 예상된다.

해설 빈칸은 be동사 are의 주어인 Teachers를 보충하는 주격 보어 자리이자 '선생님들은 일찍 출근할 것으로 예상된다'는 수동의 의미를 나타내고 있으므로 과거분사 (B) expected가 정답이다. expect는 능동태에서 주로 〈expect+목적어+목적격 보어(to부정사)〉의 구조로 쓰이며, 수동태로 바꾸면 〈be expected to부정사〉의 구조가 된다.

3 (A)
번역 던컨 엔터프라이즈는 올해 마닐라에 첫 점포를 열 계획이다.

해설 빈칸은 동사 plans의 목적어 자리로 its first store를 목적어로 취하면서 명사와 같은 역할을 할 수 있는 to부정사 (A) to open이 정답이다. plan은 to부정사를 목적어로 취한다.

4 (A)
번역 우리는 관심사에 대한 구독자들의 편지를 독자들에게 발표할 수 있게 되어 기쁩니다.

해설 빈칸은 과거분사 pleased를 수식하는 자리로 subscribers' letters를 목적어로 취하면서 부사 역할을 할 수 있는 to부정사 (A) to publish가 정답이다. 〈be pleased to부정사〉는 '~하게 되어 기쁘다'의 의미이다.

5 (B)
번역 저희 TPG 파이낸셜 플래닝은 귀사에 사업상 도움을 드릴 기회를 갖게 되어 기쁩니다.

해설 빈칸은 명사 the opportunity를 수식하는 자리로 you를 목적어로 취하면서 형용사 역할을 할 수 있는 to부정사 (B) to assist가 정답이다.

6 (B)
번역 내셔널 은행 임원진은 컴퓨터 시스템 장애의 재발을 막는 데 필요한 조치를 취했다.
해설 빈칸은 명사구 the necessary steps를 수식하는 자리로 another computer system failure를 목적어로 취하면서 형용사 역할을 할 수 있는 to부정사 (B) to prevent가 정답이다.

7 (C)
번역 시 합창단은 신축 도서관 건물 개관식에서 공연할 예정이다.
해설 빈칸 앞에 is scheduled가 있고 문맥상 '공연할 예정이다'라는 의미가 되어야 자연스러우므로 (C) to perform이 정답이다. 〈be scheduled to부정사〉는 '~할 예정이다'의 의미이다.

8 (C)
번역 리 앤 장 사 이사회는 컴퓨터 네트워크를 업그레이드할 때라고 결론 내렸다.
해설 빈칸은 명사 time을 수식하는 자리로 the computer network를 목적어로 취하면서 형용사 역할을 할 수 있는 to부정사 (C) to upgrade가 정답이다.

③ 동명사의 개념과 명사와의 차이점

ETS 유형 연습   본책 p.203

| 1 (A) | 2 (B) | 3 (A) | 4 (A) | 5 (D) | 6 (B) |
| 7 (D) | 8 (D) |

1 (A)
번역 연체료를 지불하지 않으려면 기일까지 도서를 반납해야 한다.
해설 빈칸은 to부정사 To avoid의 목적어 자리로 a late fee를 목적어로 취하면서 명사 역할을 할 수 있는 동명사 (A) paying이 정답이다. avoid는 동명사를 목적어로 취한다.

2 (B)
번역 청중에게 자신을 소개하는 것이 프레젠테이션의 첫 번째 단계이다.
해설 빈칸은 문장의 주어 자리로 yourself를 목적어로 취하면서 명사 역할을 할 수 있는 동명사 (B) Introducing이 정답이다.

3 (A)
번역 공항에 도착하는 대로 호텔 마로이스행 무료 셔틀 버스를 타세요.

해설 동명사 arriving을 목적어로 취하면서 '~하자마자'의 의미를 나타내는 전치사 (A) On이 정답이다.

4 (A)
번역 영양사들은 매일 균형 잡히고 건강에 좋은 아침 식사를 하라고 권한다.
해설 빈칸은 동사 recommend의 목적어 자리로 a well-balanced and healthy breakfast를 목적어로 취하면서 명사 역할을 할 수 있는 동명사 (A) eating이 정답이다. recommend는 동명사를 목적어로 취한다.

5 (D)
번역 직원들은 보관실에서 기밀 문서를 꺼내기 전에 기록부에 서명해야 한다.
해설 before 뒤에 주어가 없으므로, 여기서 before는 전치사로 쓰이고 있음을 알 수 있다. 전치사 뒤에는 명사와 동명사가 올 수 있지만 뒤에 목적어 any confidential papers가 나오기 때문에 동명사 (D) removing이 정답이다.

6 (B)
번역 매가 일렉트로닉스 사는 지난해 1백만 달러가 넘는 돈을 신형 휴대전화를 개발하는 데 썼다.
해설 빈칸은 생략된 전치사 in의 목적어 자리로 new mobile phones를 목적어로 취하면서 명사 역할을 할 수 있는 동명사 (B) developing이 정답이다. spend는 〈spend+시간[돈]+(in) -ing(~하는 데 시간[돈]을 쓰다)〉의 구조로 주로 쓰인다.

7 (D)
번역 고위 경영진은 회사 컴퓨터의 개인적인 사용을 금지하는 조치 시행을 고려해 왔다.
해설 빈칸은 동사 has considered의 목적어 자리로 a ban을 목적어로 취하면서 명사 역할을 할 수 있는 동명사 (D) instituting이 정답이다. consider는 동명사를 목적어로 취한다.

8 (D)
번역 플레이오 건설은 우리 회사가 모든 프로젝트에서 목표를 성취하도록 돕는 데 중대한 역할을 한다.
해설 빈칸에는 뒤에 온 동명사 helping을 목적어로 취할 수 있는 말이 들어가야 한다. '~하는 데 (중요한) 역할을 하다'는 play a (critical) role in -ing로 표현하므로, (D) in이 정답이다.

ETS 실전 문제   본책 p.204

1 (C)	2 (B)	3 (A)	4 (C)	5 (B)	6 (A)
7 (A)	8 (B)	9 (C)	10 (A)	11 (C)	12 (C)
13 (D)	14 (B)

1 (C)
번역 비즈니스 컨설턴트는 협상이 시작되기 전에 합병안을 세밀하게 검토하라고 제안한다.
해설 빈칸은 동사 suggests의 목적어 자리로 the merger plan을 목적어로 취하면서 명사 역할을 할 수 있는 동명사 (C) reviewing이 정답이다. suggest는 동명사를 목적어로 취한다.
어휘 merger 합병 negotiation 협상

2 (B)
번역 오디오 북을 추가로 구입하는 것은 도서관 장서들을 현대화하려는 도서관장 계획의 일환이다.
해설 빈칸은 be동사 is의 주어 자리로 additional audio books를 목적어로 취하면서 명사 역할을 할 수 있는 동명사 (B) Purchasing이 정답이다.
어휘 head librarian 도서관장 modernize 현대화하다 collection 소장품

3 (A)
번역 히베이루 에이전시는 고객과의 모든 의사소통을 명확하고 간결하게 하도록 노력한다.
해설 빈칸은 동사 strive의 목적어 자리로 all communication with our clients를 목적어로 취하면서 명사 역할을 할 수 있는 to부정사 (A) to make가 정답이다. strive는 to부정사를 목적어로 취한다.
어휘 strive to ~하기 위해 노력하다 to the point 간결한

4 (C)
번역 퓨쳐 스타일즈 사의 모든 직원들은 새로운 디자이너들을 만나기를 기대하고 있다.
해설 빈칸은 전치사 to의 목적어 자리로 their new designers를 목적어로 취하면서 명사 역할을 할 수 있는 동명사 (C) meeting이 정답이다. to부정사의 to와 전치사 to는 형태가 같아 주의해야 하는데, 여기서 look forward와 함께 쓰이는 to는 전치사이다.

5 (B)
번역 우리의 목표는 매출 성장을 증대하기 위해 공급망 효율성을 구축하는 것이다.
해설 빈칸 앞에 완전한 절이 있고, 뒤에는 동사원형이 있으므로 '매출 성장을 증대하기 위해서'라는 의미를 완성하는 (B) in order to가 정답이다. (A) while은 접속사, (C) also는 부사, (D) by the time은 부사 또는 접속사로 구조상 빈칸에 들어갈 수 없다.
어휘 supply chain 공급망 efficiency 효율성 revenue 수익

6 (A)
번역 출판사의 목표는 내년도까지 일일 판매 부수 8만 부를 넘기는 것이다.
해설 빈칸은 be동사 is의 주어인 The publisher's goal과 동일한 대상을 나타내는 주격 보어 자리로 the daily circulation figure를 목적어로 취하면서 명사 역할을 할 수 있는 to부정사 (A) to surpass가 정답이다. 동명사 (D) surpassing도 보어 역할을 할 수 있지만 goal과 같이 미래 지향적 주어의 보어로는 동명사가 아닌 to부정사를 쓴다는 것을 알아두자.
어휘 publisher 출판사 circulation figure 판매 부수 surpass 능가하다

7 (A)
번역 정 씨는 마케팅 조사 결과를 검토하는 기회를 가진 후 사장에게 보고할 것이다.
해설 빈칸은 명사 chance를 수식하는 자리로 them을 목적어로 취하면서 형용사 역할을 할 수 있는 to부정사 (A) to review가 정답이다.
어휘 result 결과 review 검토하다

8 (B)
번역 신용카드를 이용해 이번 컴퓨터 워크숍 비용을 지불하려면 린다 와그너에게 555-4236번으로 연락하세요.
해설 빈칸은 전치사 by의 목적어 자리로 your credit card를 목적어로 취하면서 명사 역할을 할 수 있는 동명사 (B) using이 정답이다. 전치사 by는 동명사와 결합하여 주로 '~함으로써'의 의미를 나타낸다.
어휘 pay for ~의 비용을 지불하다

9 (C)
번역 기업들은 자격을 갖춘 직원들을 계속 보유하려면 전문성을 개발할 기회를 제공하는 것이 중요하다.
해설 빈칸은 가주어 It의 진짜 주어 자리로 professional development opportunities를 목적어로 취하면서 명사 역할을 할 수 있는 to부정사 (C) to offer가 정답이다. 동명사 (A) offering도 명사 역할을 할 수 있지만 가주어 it으로 바꿔 쓰지 않는다.
어휘 professional development 전문성 개발 in order to ~하기 위해 retain (계속) 보유하다 qualified 자격이 있는 staff (집합적) 직원, 사원

10 (A)
번역 머콕스 화장품은 시장을 확대하여 고객 수 증가 면에서 1위를 지키기를 바란다.
해설 빈칸은 동사 hopes의 목적어 자리로 its number one ranking을 목적어로 취하면서 명사 역할을 할 수 있는 to부정사 (A) to defend가 정답이다. hope는 to부정사를 목적어로 취한다.
어휘 ranking 순위 consumer 소비자 growth 증가, 성장 expand 확장하다 defend 지키다, 방어하다

[11-14] 기사

> **제한된 공간에서 텃밭 가꾸기**
>
> 많은 채소 애호가들이 가정에서 직접 먹을거리를 재배하는 것을 즐긴다. **11그러나 키우고 싶은 모든 것을 위한 공간을 찾는 것은 힘든 일일 수 있다.** 공간을 절약하기 위해 다른 식물을 함께 키울 수 있다. **12예를 들어** 부시 콩은 빠르게 자라는 식물이라서 느리게 자라는 식물인 토마토 사이에 심을 수 있다. **13추가로 심은** 식물은 토마토가 커가는 동안 잡초의 성장을 막는 데 도움이 될 것이다. 콩이 다 자라면 채소는 수확하고 식물은 제거할 수 있다. 이렇게 하면 토마토가 **14계속** 자라날 공간이 생기고 토양에는 귀중한 영양분이 남게 된다. 결국, 텃밭의 수확량이 증가하고 식물의 건강이 크게 개선될 것이다.
>
> **어휘** plant 식물; 심다   grower ~하게 자라는 식물   prevent 막다, 방지하다   weed 잡초   mature 성숙하다   harvest 수확하다   valuable 귀중한   nutrient 영양분   ultimately 결국, 궁극적으로   yield 수확량   significantly 크게

11 (C)

번역
(A) 토마토 식물은 가정 텃밭에서 흔하게 보인다.
(B) 텃밭 가꾸기는 시간이 많이 걸릴 수 있다.
(C) 그러나 키우고 싶은 모든 것을 위한 공간을 찾는 것은 힘든 일일 수 있다.
(D) 무엇을 키울지 결정하는 것은 과정의 필수적인 부분이다.

해설 빈칸 앞에서 직접 먹을거리를 재배하는 것을 즐기는 사람이 많다고 했는데, 빈칸 뒤 문장에서 공간을 절약할 수 있는 재배 방법(To save space, you can grow different plants together)을 제시하고 있다. 따라서 빈칸에는 가정에서 식물을 재배하는 데 필요한 공간의 제약에 대해 언급하는 것이 글의 흐름상 자연스러우므로 (C)가 정답이다.

어휘 commonly 흔히   time-consuming 시간이 걸리는   struggle 힘든 일   essential 필수적인   process 과정

12 (C)

해설 빈칸의 앞 문장에서 서로 다른 식물을 함께 키울 수 있다고 언급한 후, 빈칸 뒤에서는 부시 콩과 토마토를 함께 심는 것을 예로 들고 있다. 따라서 '예를 들어'라는 의미로 예시를 제시할 때 쓰는 접속부사인 (C) for example이 정답이다. (A) however(하지만), (B) as a result(그 결과), (D) on the other hand(다른 한편으로는)는 문맥상 적절하지 않다.

13 (D)

해설 빈칸 앞 문장에서 서로 다른 식물을 함께 키우는 예로 토마토와 부시 콩(Bush beans, for example, are fast growers and can be planted between tomatoes, a slower-growing plant)을 언급하고 있다. 따라서 빈칸에는 추가로 심은 식물을 언급하는 것이 자연스러우므로 '추가의'라는 의미의 (D) extra가 정답이다. (A) natural(자연의), (B) colorful(형형색색의), (C) rare(드문)는 모두 의미상 적합하지 않다.

14 (B)

해설 주어(This), 동사(will create), 목적어(room)가 있는 완전한 절이 있으므로, for 이하는 명사 room을 꾸며주는 수식어 자리이다. 빈칸 앞에 to부정사의 의미상 주어인 for the tomatoes가 왔으므로 '토마토가 계속 자라날 수 있는 공간'이라는 의미를 완성하는 to부정사가 오는 것이 적절하다. 따라서 (B) to continue가 정답이다.

UNIT 11   분사

① 분사의 형태와 역할

ETS 유형 연습   본책 p.207

1 (B)   **2** (A)   **3** (B)   **4** (A)   **5** (B)   **6** (D)
7 (B)   **8** (D)

1 (B)

번역 국가의 감소하는 수출은 경제 전문가들 사이에서 큰 우려를 야기했다.

해설 빈칸은 소유격 The country's 뒤에서 명사 exports를 수식하는 자리로 형용사 역할을 할 수 있는 현재분사 (B) decreasing이 정답이다.

2 (A)

번역 시의 건축 법규는 따르기에 무척 복잡해졌다.

해설 빈칸은 주어 The city's building codes를 보충하는 주격 보어 자리로, '복잡해졌다'라는 수동적 의미를 나타내면서 형용사 역할을 할 수 있는 과거분사 (A) complicated가 정답이다. 참고로 complicated는 '복잡한'이라는 의미의 형용사로 관용적으로 쓰인다.

3 (B)

번역 법률 소송에 연루된 사람은 누구나 변호사와 상담할 것을 권한다.

해설 빈칸은 주어 Any person을 수식하는 자리로 '관련된 사람'이라는 수동적 의미를 나타내면서 형용사 역할을 할 수 있는 과거분사 (B) involved가 정답이다. 현재분사 (A) involving은 능동적 의미를 나타낸다. 동사의 과거형과 과거분사형은 형태가 같은 것이 많으므로 주의해야 한다.

4 (A)

번역 이 광고가 게재되기 전에 구입한 표에 대해서는 할인이 유효하지 않습니다.

해설 빈칸은 전치사 on의 목적어 tickets를 수식하는 자리로 '구매된 표'라는 수동적 의미를 나타내면서 형용사 역할을 할 수 있는 과거분사 (A) purchased가 정답이다.

5 (B)
번역 경미한 교량 보수로 인해 5월 12일부터 5월 25일까지 열차의 운행 빈도가 줄어들 예정입니다.

해설 빈칸은 전치사 with의 목적어 역할을 하는 명사 frequency를 수식하는 형용사 자리이므로 형용사 역할을 하는 과거분사 (B) reduced가 정답이다. (A) reduce와 (C) reduces는 동사로 품사상 빈칸에 들어갈 수 없고, 명사인 (D) reduction은 frequency와 복합명사를 이루지 않는다.

6 (D)
번역 귀하의 개인 디지털 파일은 저희 온라인 서버에 안전하게 저장되어 있을 것입니다.

해설 빈칸은 주어 Your personal digital files를 보충 설명하는 주격 보어 자리로 '저장된'이라는 수동적 의미를 나타내면서 형용사 역할을 할 수 있는 과거분사 (D) stored가 정답이다.

7 (B)
번역 무역 박람회의 모든 공급업체를 나열한 안내책자가 다음 주에 발송될 예정이다.

해설 빈칸은 주어 The brochure를 수식하는 수식어 자리로 all the vendors를 목적어로 취해 '모든 공급업체를 나열한 안내책자'라는 의미가 되어야 하므로 현재분사 (B) listing이 정답이다. (A) list와 (C) lists는 명사/동사이므로 품사상 빈칸에 들어갈 수 없고, (D) listed는 과거분사로 뒤에 목적어가 올 수 없다.

8 (D)
번역 바르가스 씨는 신입사원을 위한 환영 카드에 잊지 않고 손으로 쓴 메모를 포함시킨다.

해설 빈칸은 동명사 including의 목적어인 명사 notes를 수식하는 자리로 형용사 역할을 할 수 있는 과거분사 (D) handwritten이 정답이다.

② 현재분사 vs. 과거분사

ETS 유형 연습   본책 p.209

| 1 (A) | 2 (B) | 3 (B) | 4 (B) | 5 (B) | 6 (D) |
| 7 (C) | 8 (A) |

1 (A)
번역 분실되거나 파손된 수하물을 신고하시려면, 넥스트레어 수하물 서비스 부스를 방문하세요.

해설 빈칸은 to부정사의 목적어인 baggage를 수식하는 자리로 '파손된 수하물'이라는 수동적 의미를 나타내면서 형용사 역할을 할 수 있는 과거분사 (A) damaged가 정답이다. 참고로, damaged는 '파손된'이라는 의미의 형용사로 관용적으로 쓰인다.

2 (B)
번역 정부는 소유주들이 세입자들에게 재활용 서비스를 제공하도록 요구하는 규정을 공표했다.

해설 빈칸은 동사 has published의 목적어 regulations를 수식하는 자리로 owners를 목적어로 취하면서 능동의 의미로 형용사 역할을 할 수 있는 현재분사 (B) requiring이 정답이다.

3 (B)
번역 3월에 시 오케스트라는 재능 있는 신입 멤버인 마리아 크루즈가 출연하는 흥미진진한 오페라를 선보일 예정이다.

해설 빈칸은 부정관사 an 뒤에서 명사 opera를 수식하는 자리이다. 감정을 유발하는 주체인 opera가 '흥미롭게 하는'이라는 능동적 의미를 나타내므로 현재분사 (B) exciting이 정답이다. 감정을 유발하는 주체인 사물은 현재분사와, 감정을 느끼는 대상인 사람은 과거분사와 결합하여 주로 쓰인다.

4 (B)
번역 그 판매사원은 고객들의 부정적인 의견에 실망했다.

해설 빈칸은 주어 The sales representative를 보충하는 주격 보어 자리이다. 감정을 느끼는 대상인 The sales representative가 '실망했다'는 수동적 의미를 나타내므로 과거분사 (B) disappointed가 정답이다.

5 (B)
번역 이토 씨는 국제 거래를 관리한 경력이 있기 때문에 해외 지사를 담당할 것이다.

해설 빈칸은 전치사 Because of의 목적어 his experience를 수식하는 자리로 international accounts를 목적어로 취하면서 형용사 역할을 할 수 있는 현재분사 (B) supervising이 정답이다. 분사가 명사를 뒤에서 수식하는 경우 분사 뒤에 목적어가 있으면 현재분사를, 목적어가 없으면 과거분사를 주로 쓴다.

6 (D)
번역 경제학 고급 학위는 리플러 사의 수석 애널리스트 직책에 필수적이다.

해설 빈칸은 부정관사 An과 명사 degree 사이에서 명사를 수식하는 자리이고, '고급 학위'라는 의미가 되어야 적절하므로 (D) advanced가 정답이다. 명사 (A) advancement(진보)와 (C) advances(발전)는 degree와 복합명사를 이루지 않으므로 빈칸에 들어갈 수 없고, (B) advancing(나이가 들어도)은 의미가 적합하지 않다. 참고로, advanced는 형용사로 쓰임이 굳어진 분사이다.

7 (C)
번역 불필요한 수수료를 줄이기 위해 관광부에서 제시한 계획은 큰 호응을 얻었다.

해설 빈칸은 명사 The plan을 수식하는 자리로 '제시된 계획'이라는 수동적 의미를 나타내면서 형용사 역할을 할 수 있는 과거분사 (C) presented가 정답이다.

8 (A)

번역 다가오는 계약 협상에 대한 모든 추천 사항은 다음 주까지 리 씨와 공유될 것 같습니다.

해설 빈칸은 정관사 the와 명사구 contract negotiations 사이에서 명사를 수식하는 자리로, '다가오는 계약 협상'이라는 의미가 되어야 적절하므로 (A) upcoming이 정답이다. (B) estimated(추측의), (C) permanent(영구적인), (D) accurate(정확한)는 모두 의미상 적합하지 않다.

③ 분사구문

ETS 유형 연습 본책 p.211

1 (B)	2 (B)	3 (A)	4 (B)	5 (A)	6 (A)
7 (C)	8 (C)				

1 (B)

번역 그 호텔은 시 관광 명소 중 하나에 인접해 있어서 많은 관광객들을 유치하고 있다.

해설 분사구문의 생략된 주어 the hotel이 '위치되어 있다'는 수동적 의미를 나타내고 있으므로 과거분사 (B) Located가 정답이다. 빈칸 앞에는 '~ 때문에'라는 의미의 부사절 접속사가 생략되어 있다.

2 (B)

번역 켈빈 씨는 계약서 초안을 살펴보다가 잘못된 부분을 몇 군데 발견했다.

해설 분사구문의 생략된 주어 Mr. Kelvin이 동사 review의 주체로서 능동적 의미를 나타내고 있으므로 현재분사 (B) Reviewing이 정답이다. 빈칸 앞에는 '~하는 동안'이라는 의미의 부사절 접속사가 생략되어 있다. 동사원형 (A)가 들어가면 콤마 앞이 명령문이 되는데, 이 경우 뒷문장과 이어지기 위해 접속사가 필요하다.

3 (A)

번역 모든 전기 장치의 플러그를 뽑은 후 그 시설 관리자는 퇴근했다.

해설 분사구문의 생략된 주어 the facility manager가 동사 unplug의 주체로서 능동적 의미를 나타내고 있으므로 현재분사 (A) Unplugging이 정답이다. 빈칸 앞에는 '~ 후에'라는 의미의 부사절 접속사가 생략되어 있다.

4 (B)

번역 그 전시회장은 30년 전에 건설되었기 때문에 보수 공사가 필요하다.

해설 분사구문의 생략된 주어인 the exhibition hall이 '건설되었다'는 수동적 의미를 나타내고 있으므로 과거분사 (B) Constructed가 정답이다. 빈칸 앞에는 '~ 때문에'라는 의미의 부사절 접속사가 생략되어 있다.

5 (A)

번역 주요 업계 보고서를 인용하면서 임원진은 트럭 타이어 생산을 늘리기로 결정했다.

해설 콤마 앞부분은 접속사와 주어 없이 뒷문장과 이어지고 있으므로 분사구문이다. 빈칸 뒤에 목적어가 있으므로 현재분사 (A) Citing이 정답이다. 빈칸 앞에는 '~하면서'라는 의미의 부사절 접속사가 생략되어 있다.

6 (A)

번역 건강과 영양을 다루는 그 잡지는 쉬운 말로 쓰여서 읽기 쉽다.

해설 분사구문의 형태는 뒤의 목적어 유무를 통해 결정할 수 있다. 빈칸 뒤에 목적어 없이 전치사구가 나오므로 과거분사 (A) Written이 정답이다. 빈칸 앞에는 '~ 때문에'라는 의미의 부사절 접속사가 생략되어 있다.

7 (C)

번역 JK 일렉트로닉스 사는 아시아 시장까지 확장해 국제 시장에서의 시장 점유율을 높였다.

해설 빈칸 이하는 연속 동작을 나타내는 분사구문이다. 분사구문의 생략된 주어 JK Electronics, Inc.가 '시장 점유율을 높인다'는 능동적 의미를 나타내고 있으므로 현재분사 (C) increasing이 정답이다.

8 (C)

번역 ZJA 회의에 등록할 때는 회원 번호를 제공해야 한다.

해설 분사구문에서 주어만 생략된 경우다. 생략된 주어 you가 동사 register의 주체로서 능동적 의미를 나타내고 있으므로 현재분사 (C) registering이 정답이다. 참고로, register는 주로 전치사 for와 함께 쓰인다.

ETS 실전 문제 본책 p.212

1 (C)	2 (D)	3 (B)	4 (D)	5 (B)	6 (B)
7 (B)	8 (B)	9 (D)	10 (C)	11 (A)	12 (B)
13 (D)	14 (A)				

1 (C)

번역 피치파워 소프트웨어의 신입사원들은 채용 시 매우 빠듯한 2주간의 연수 코스에 참가해야 한다.

해설 빈칸은 동사 attend의 목적어 two-week training course를 수식하는 자리이다. '매우 빠듯한 2주간의 연수 코스'라는 능동적 의미를 나타내는 현재분사 (C) demanding이 정답이다.

어휘 employee 사원 hire 채용하다 demand 요구하다 demanding 빠듯한, 요구 사항이 많은

2 (D)

번역 신입 인턴들은 투어 중 공장 운영의 효율성에 감명을 받았다.

해설 빈칸은 be동사 were의 주어 the new interns를 보충 설명하는 주격 보어 자리이다. 감정을 느끼는 대상인 the new interns가 '감명받았다'는 수동적 의미가 되어야 하므로 (D) impressed가 정답이다. 나머지는 모두 과거분사로 주격 보어 역할을 할 수 있지만 의미상 적합하지 않다. 참고로, impressed는 형용사로 쓰임이 굳어진 과거분사이다.

어휘 efficiency 효율성   operation 운영
conduct (특정 활동을) 하다   discover 발견하다
promote 홍보하다   impressed 감명받은

3 (B)

번역 광고팀은 늦게 시작했음에도 불구하고 놀라울 정도로 만회하여 일정보다 일주일 앞당겨 프로젝트를 끝냈다.

해설 빈칸은 부정관사 an 뒤에서 형용사처럼 명사 recovery를 수식하는 자리이다. 감정을 유발하는 주체인 recovery가 '놀라게 하는'이라는 능동적 의미를 나타내므로 현재분사 (B) amazing이 정답이다. 감정을 유발하는 주체인 사물은 현재분사와, 감정을 느끼는 대상인 사람은 과거분사와 결합하여 주로 쓰인다.

어휘 recovery 회복   ahead of schedule 일정보다 앞서

4 (D)

번역 최근의 졸업생들은 하넘 사가 좋은 승진 기회를 제공하기 때문에 그 회사에 지원한다.

해설 빈칸은 동사 offers의 목적어 opportunities를 수식하는 자리로, '좋은, 뛰어난'이라는 의미의 형용사 (D) outstanding이 정답이다. 참고로 outstanding은 '미결제된'이라는 의미로도 쓰인다.

어휘 apply for ~에 지원하다   advancement 승진, 발전

5 (B)

번역 오토 테크 컴퓨터는 유지 보수 패키지와 함께 구입하면 3년간 품질 보증이 된다.

해설 접속사 When 뒤에 주어가 없으므로 분사구문임을 알 수 있다. 분사구문의 생략된 주어 the Auto Tech Computer가 '구매되는' 대상이므로 과거분사 (B) purchased가 정답이다. 동사 (A) was purchasing, (C) is purchased, (D) purchases는 모두 앞에 주어가 있어야 한다.

어휘 in combination with ~와 결합하여
maintenance 유지 보수   warranty 품질 보증

6 (B)

번역 지난밤 로레인에서는 폭풍우가 몰아치는 날씨로 정전이 발생해 일부 주민은 전기 없이 지내야 했다.

해설 빈칸 이하는 연속 동작을 나타내는 분사구문이다. 빈칸 뒤에 목적어 some residents가 있으므로 현재분사 (B) leaving이 정답이다. 동사 (A) will leave, (C) have left, (D) leaves는 빈칸 앞에 접속사가 필요하다.

어휘 stormy 폭풍우가 몰아치는   power outage 정전
resident 주민, 거주자   electricity 전기

7 (B)

번역 이메일로 기자의 질문을 받은 직원은 답장을 작성할 때 형식과 내용을 모두 고려해야 한다.

해설 접속사 when 뒤에 주어가 없으므로 분사구문임을 알 수 있다. 빈칸 뒤에 목적어가 있으므로 능동 의미를 나타내는 현재분사 (B) formulating이 정답이다.

어휘 reporter 기자   form 형식   content 내용   response 답장   formulate 만들어 내다, 표현[진술]하다

8 (B)

번역 베이징과 리스본에 있는 팀들은 긴밀히 협조해야 하므로, 이메일은 이 프로젝트를 위해 선호되는 의사소통 수단이다.

해설 빈칸은 정관사 the 뒤에서 명사 method를 수식하는 자리로 '선호되는 수단'이라는 수동적 의미를 나타내면서 형용사와 같은 역할을 할 수 있는 과거분사 (B) preferred가 정답이다.

어휘 closely 긴밀하게   method 방법, 방식
preferred 선호되는, 바람직한

9 (D)

번역 새 아야메 꽃집 자리로 제안된 장소 근처에 꽃 시장이 있어서 다른 장소를 물색하고 있다.

해설 빈칸은 정관사 the와 명사 site 사이에서 명사를 수식하는 형용사 자리이다. '제안된 장소'라는 수동의 의미를 나타내며 형용사 역할을 할 수 있는 과거분사 (D) proposed가 정답이다.

어휘 exist 있다, 존재하다   seek 물색하다   obliged 고마운
voluntary 자발적인   deliberate 의도적인   proposed 제안된

10 (C)

번역 큐랩 사에서 보람 있게 9년을 보낸 로젠 씨는 전무이사 직에서 사임하고 새로운 벤처사업을 추진할 예정이다.

해설 빈칸은 전치사 After의 목적어인 years를 수사 nine 뒤에서 수식하는 형용사 자리이다. '보람 있는 9년'이라는 의미를 나타내며 형용사 역할을 할 수 있는 현재분사 (C) rewarding이 정답이다.

어휘 resign 사임하다   executive director 전무이사
pursue 추진하다   reward 보상하다   rewarding 보람 있는

[11-14] 기사

펀 판다, 리치몬드에 오다

리치몬드 (8월 24일)—버지니아 주에서 내년 초에 첫 펀 판다 레스토랑을 볼 수 있을 것으로 기대된다. 싱가포르에 **11 본사를 둔** 이 아시아 패스트푸드 체인점은 10년 전 북미로 확장하기 시작하여 빠르게 인기를 얻었다. **12 현재는** 미국 전역에 53개 지점을 보유하고 있다. 하지만 리치몬드 지역에는 펀 판다 레스토랑이 없으며, 리치몬드에서 **13 가장 가까운** 곳은 275킬로미터 떨어진 노스캐롤라이나 주 롤리에 있다.

새로운 펀 판다는 이전에 홈타운 다이너가 있던 쿠퍼 대로의 건물에 위치할 예정이다. **14 개점 날짜는 아직 발표되지 않았다.**

어휘 expand 확장하다 popularity 인기 location 지점
boulevard 대로 formerly 이전에 house 수용하다

11 (A)

해설 콤마 뒤로 완전한 문장이 나오므로, 빈칸은 in Singapore와 결합해 수식어구가 되어야 한다. 따라서 수식어구를 이끌 수 있는 to부정사나 분사가 정답의 후보인데, 빈칸 뒤에 목적어가 없으므로 수동의 의미를 나타내는 과거분사 (A) Based가 정답이다. 나머지 (B) Basing, (C) To base, (D) Having based는 모두 목적어가 필요하다.

12 (B)

해설 빈칸 앞 문장에서 펀 판다가 10년 전 북미로 확장하기 시작해 빠르게 인기를 얻었다(the Asian fast-food chain started expanding to North America ten years ago and quickly grew in popularity)고 했으므로, 뒤에는 그 결과로 '현재 미국 전역에 53개 지점이 있다'는 내용이 이어져야 자연스러우므로 (B) now가 정답이다. 나머지 (A) mainly(주로), (C) fully(완전히), (D) instead(대신에)는 모두 의미상 적합하지 않다.

13 (D)

해설 빈칸 앞에서 펀 판다가 리치몬드 지역에 없다(there are no Fun Panda restaurants in the Richmond area)고 언급하고 있고, 빈칸 뒤로는 리치몬드와의 거리가 언급되고 있다. 따라서 빈칸은 '리치몬드에서 가장 가까운 곳'이라는 의미가 되어야 자연스러우므로 (D) closest가 정답이다.

14 (A)

번역 (A) 개점일은 아직 발표되지 않았다.
(B) 미국에서 최근 아시아 음식의 인기가 높아졌다.
(C) 쿠퍼 대로는 여러 호텔 체인의 본거지이다.
(D) 리치몬드는 선택할 수 있는 다양한 레스토랑으로 유명하다.

해설 빈칸 앞 문장에서 레스토랑의 새 지점이 문을 열게 될 위치에 대해 언급하고 있다. 따라서 빈칸에는 개점과 관련된 추가 정보가 나오는 것이 글의 흐름상 자연스러우므로 개점일을 언급한 (A)가 정답이다.

UNIT 12 전치사와 접속사

① 전치사의 개념과 역할

ETS 유형 연습 본책 p.215

1 (B) 2 (A) 3 (B) 4 (B) 5 (D) 6 (D)
7 (A) 8 (A)

1 (B)

번역 그 동영상은 중소기업 재무 관리를 위한 모범 사례를 설명한다.

해설 문맥상 중소기업의 재무를 관리하기 위한 '목적이나 용도'를 나타내는 전치사 (B) for가 정답이다.

2 (A)

번역 귀하의 신용카드 유효기간을 알려 주시기 바랍니다.

해설 your credit card를 목적어로 취하면서 the expiration date를 수식하는 형용사 역할을 할 수 있는 전치사 (A) of가 정답이다.

3 (B)

번역 고객들은 정상 영업 시간 동안 전화로 담당자와 상담할 수 있다.

해설 빈칸 뒤 normal business hours를 목적어로 취하면서 '정상 영업 시간 동안'이라는 의미를 나타내는 전치사 (B) during이 정답이다.

4 (B)

번역 모든 여행객은 적절한 여행 서류들을 구비할 책임이 있다.

해설 빈칸은 전치사 for의 목적어 자리로 proper travel documents를 목적어로 취하는 동명사 (B) obtaining이 정답이다.

5 (D)

번역 주요 시장 세 곳은 우리의 주 생산 공장으로부터 반경 500마일 이내에 있다.

해설 a five-hundred-mile radius를 목적어로 취하면서 '~ 이내에'를 의미하는 전치사 (D) within이 정답이다.

6 (D)

번역 우리는 전액 환불 서면 요청서와 함께 파손된 상품을 동봉했다.

해설 빈칸은 a written request를 목적어로 취하는 전치사 자리로 '서면 요청서와 함께'라는 의미를 나타내는 소지의 전치사 (D) with가 정답이다.

7 (A)

번역 높은 등록 인원 수 때문에, 학교 행정 담당자들은 더 많은 수업을 추가할 계획이다.

해설 빈칸은 high registration numbers를 목적어로 취하면서 '높은 등록 인원 수 때문에'라는 의미를 나타내는 전치사 (A) Because of가 정답이다. (B) Otherwise(그렇지 않으면)와 (C) Therefore(그러므로)는 부사, (D) Not only(~뿐만 아니라)는 〈not only A but also B〉의 구조로 사용되는 상관접속사로 품사상 적합하지 않다.

8 (A)

번역 야마구치 씨는 기차가 지연되어 역에서 두 시간 넘게 기다려야만 했다.

해설 빈칸은 the station을 목적어로 취하면서 to부정사를 수식하는 전치사 자리로 '역에서'라는 의미를 나타내는 장소의 전치사 (A) at이 정답이다. wait는 뒤에 기다리는 대상이 올 때

for를 쓰므로 의미 파악 없이 (B) for를 고르지 않도록 유의해야 한다.

② 전치사의 종류와 의미

ETS 유형 연습　　　　　　　　본책 p.217

| 1 (A) | 2 (B) | 3 (A) | 4 (A) | 5 (C) | 6 (B) |
| 7 (A) | 8 (B) | | | | |

1　(A)
번역　새로 장만한 브라이트스타 사진기에 대해 보다 자세한 정보를 원하시면 저희 웹사이트를 방문해 주세요.
해설　빈칸은 your new Brightstar camera를 목적어로 취하는 전치사 자리로, '사진기에 대한'이라는 의미를 만드는 전치사 (A) about이 정답이다.

2　(B)
번역　지역 재활용 행사를 위한 계획은 7월 12일에 시작될 것으로 예상된다.
해설　빈칸은 날짜 명사구 July 12를 목적어로 취하는 전치사 자리로 '7월 12일에'라는 의미를 나타내는 시점 전치사 (B) on이 정답이다.

3　(A)
번역　차량 판매 보고서는 매주 월요일 오전 8시까지 제출되어야 한다.
해설　빈칸 뒤 시점 표현 8:00 A.M.을 목적어로 취하는 전치사 자리로 '오전 8시까지'라는 의미를 나타내는 전치사 (A) by가 정답이다.

4　(A)
번역　JHB 은행은 적절한 서류 없이는 대출 신청을 처리할 수 없다.
해설　빈칸은 the proper documentation을 목적어로 취하는 전치사 자리로 '적절한 서류 없이'라는 의미를 이루는 (A) without이 정답이다.

5　(C)
번역　단체 행사에 대한 자세한 정보는 월요일부터 금요일까지 오전 9시부터 오후 5시 사이에 사무실로 전화 주십시오.
해설　빈칸은 9:00 A.M. and 5:00 P.M.을 목적어로 취하여 '오전 9시부터 오후 5시 사이에'라는 의미를 나타내는 전치사 (C) between이 정답이다.

6　(B)
번역　브롬즈 셔츠 컴퍼니 직원들의 최선의 노력에도 불구하고 일부 고객들은 주문품을 제때 받지 못했다.
해설　빈칸은 명사구 the best efforts를 목적어로 취하는 전치사 자리로 '최선의 노력에도 불구하고'라는 의미를 나타내는 전치사 (B) Despite가 정답이다.

7　(A)
번역　작업 환경은 동료들 간의 협업을 촉진하도록 설계되었다.
해설　빈칸은 coworkers를 목적어로 취하면서 '~ 사이에서'를 의미하는 전치사 (A) among이 정답이다.

8　(B)
번역　시 보건부는 일년 내내 의료 종사자를 대상으로 몇 가지 무료 강습을 운영한다.
해설　빈칸은 the year를 목적어로 취하는 전치사 자리로 '일년 내내'라는 의미를 나타내는 기간의 전치사 (B) throughout이 정답이다.

③ 등위접속사와 상관접속사

ETS 유형 연습　　　　　　　　본책 p.219

| 1 (B) | 2 (A) | 3 (B) | 4 (B) | 5 (D) | 6 (A) |
| 7 (C) | 8 (B) | | | | |

1　(B)
번역　암바니 씨는 프랑스어는 하지 못하지만 구자라트어와 표준 중국어는 유창하다.
해설　빈칸은 앞뒤에 있는 대등한 절과 절을 연결하는 등위접속사 자리로 문맥상 앞뒤가 대조적 의미를 나타내고 있으므로 등위접속사 (B) but이 정답이다.

2　(A)
번역　야카모토 씨는 오노 씨와 시몬 씨 둘 다를 승진 대상으로 추천했다.
해설　빈칸 뒤의 and와 함께 짝을 이루어 'A와 B 둘 다'의 의미를 나타내는 (A) both가 정답이다.

3　(B)
번역　오슬로에서 베르겐으로 가기 위해 우 씨는 비행기를 타거나 산맥을 통과하는 기차를 탈 수 있다.
해설　빈칸 앞의 either와 함께 짝을 이루어 'A나 B 둘 중 하나'의 의미를 나타내는 (B) or가 정답이다.

4　(B)
번역　탱 씨와 쑤리 씨 모두 환경 정책에 관한 기자회견에 참석하지 않았다.
해설　빈칸 앞의 Neither와 함께 짝을 이루어 'A도 B도 아닌'의 의미를 나타내는 (B) nor가 정답이다.

5 (D)
번역 최 씨는 훌륭한 대중 연설가일 뿐만 아니라 재능 있는 작가이기도 하다.
해설 빈칸 앞의 not only와 함께 짝을 이루어 'A뿐만 아니라 B도'의 의미를 나타내는 (D) but이 정답이다. 빈칸 뒤의 부사 also는 생략할 수 있다.

6 (A)
번역 경력 개발 세미나에는 시간제 직원과 정규직 직원 모두 참석할 수 있다.
해설 빈칸 앞의 both와 함께 짝을 이루어 'A와 B 둘 다'의 의미를 나타내는 (A) and가 정답이다.

7 (C)
번역 직원들은 교육 과정에 참가하거나 온라인 개별 학습을 이수하는 것 중에서 선택할 수 있다.
해설 빈칸은 전치사 of의 목적어인 attending a training class와 completing an online tutorial을 연결하는 등위접속사 자리로 문맥상 앞뒤가 선택 대상을 나타내고 있으므로 '또는'을 뜻하는 (C) or가 정답이다.

8 (B)
번역 마주리 가구는 우리와 계약을 갱신했지만, 레노라 조명은 그렇지 않았다.
해설 빈칸은 문장과 문장을 이어주는 접속사 자리이다. 문맥상 앞뒤가 대조적 의미를 나타내고 있으므로 등위접속사 (B) but이 정답이다.

ETS 실전 문제
본책 p.220

1 (A) 2 (C) 3 (D) 4 (A) 5 (A) 6 (A)
7 (B) 8 (A) 9 (C) 10 (B) 11 (B) 12 (D)
13 (A) 14 (A)

1 (A)
번역 심 씨는 1월부터 영업팀을 이끌어 왔다.
해설 빈칸은 January를 목적어로 취하는 전치사 자리로 '1월부터'라는 뜻을 나타내는 전치사 (A) since가 정답이다. (B) already는 부사, (C) last는 형용사/부사/명사/동사, (D) recently는 부사로 품사상 적합하지 않다.

2 (C)
번역 모든 에어프레시 에어컨은 구입일로부터 1년 이내에 고장나면 무료로 수리되거나 교체된다.
해설 빈칸은 one year of the purchase date를 목적어로 취하는 전치사 자리로 '구입일로부터 1년 이내에'라는 의미를 이루는 (C) within이 정답이다.
어휘 repair 수리하다 replace 교체하다 free of charge 무료로 malfunction 고장나다 purchase 구매

3 (D)
번역 정 씨는 테슬러 씨나 사토 씨 중 한 사람이 다음 달에 열릴 회의에 참석해야 한다고 제안했다.
해설 빈칸 뒤의 or와 함께 짝을 이루어 'A나 B 둘 중 하나'의 의미를 나타내는 (D) either가 정답이다.
어휘 conference 회의, 회담

4 (A)
번역 메이올 은행의 보안팀은 승인되지 않은 접속으로부터 고객의 개인정보를 보호합니다.
해설 동사 protects는 전치사 from과 함께 쓰여 '~로부터 …를 보호하다'라는 의미로 쓰이는데, 문맥상 '승인되지 않은 접속으로부터 개인 정보를 보호한다'는 의미가 되어야 하므로 (A) from이 정답이다.
어휘 security 보안 unauthorized 승인되지 않은 access 접속, 접근

5 (A)
번역 귀하의 업체가 세금 환급을 받을 자격이 되는지 알아볼 수 있는 최고의 방법은 클레이 카운티 웹사이트를 통하는 것입니다.
해설 빈칸은 명사구 the Clay County Web site를 목적어로 취하면서 '클레이 웹사이트를 통해'라는 의미를 완성하는 수단의 전치사 (A) through가 정답이다. (B) beside(~ 옆에), (C) among((여럿) 중에서), (D) upon(~ 위에)은 의미상 적절하지 않다.
어휘 be entitled to ~할 자격이 있다 tax rebate 세금 환급

6 (A)
번역 새로운 기계의 작동을 위한 설명은 월요일 교육 세션 동안 모든 직원에게 제공될 것이다.
해설 빈칸은 Monday's training session을 목적어로 취하면서 '~ 동안'을 의미하는 기간 전치사 (A) during이 정답이다.
어휘 instruction 설명 operate 작동하다 machinery 기계류

7 (B)
번역 오늘 루이스 리지 광업 주주들은 카시아스 메탈에 구리 사업부를 매각하는 안을 승인하거나 기각할 것이다.
해설 빈칸은 이 문장의 동사 approve와 reject를 연결하는 등위접속사 자리로 문맥상 앞뒤가 선택 대상을 나타내고 있으므로 '또는'을 뜻하는 (B) or가 정답이다.
어휘 shareholder 주주 approve 승인하다 reject 기각하다 copper 구리

8 (A)
번역 요나손 도서관은 필요한 건물 정비로 2월 4일 월요일 정오까지 문을 열지 않습니다.

해설 빈칸은 necessary building maintenance를 목적어로 취하면서 '필요한 건물 정비 때문에'라는 뜻을 나타내는 전치사 (A) due to가 정답이다. (B) instead of(~ 대신에)는 의미상 어울리지 않고, 접속사 (C) even though(비록 ~ 이지만), (D) now that(~이므로)은 품사상 적합하지 않다.

어휘 necessary 필요한   maintenance 정비

9 (C)

번역 금요일 오후 4시 이후에 제출된 전자 결제는 빨라도 화요일 오전에나 처리될 것입니다.

해설 빈칸은 Tuesday morning을 목적어로 취하는 전치사 자리로, 빈칸 앞의 not과 함께 not A until B의 구조로 'B가 되어서야 A하다'라는 의미를 완성하는 (C) until이 정답이다. (D) while은 절을 연결하는 접속사이므로 품사상 적합하지 않다.

어휘 electronic 전자의   payment 결제   submit 제출하다   process 처리하다   at the earliest 빨라도

10 (B)

번역 저자는 머리말과 맺음말을 쓰는 것 외에도 유명 소설가에게 자신의 책을 위한 서문을 작성해 달라고 요청했다.

해설 빈칸은 동명사구 writing an introduction and an epilogue를 목적어로 취하는 전치사 자리로, '머리말과 맺음말을 쓰는 것 외에도'라는 의미를 완성하는 전치사 (B) Besides가 정답이다. (C) In contrast to(~와 대조적으로)는 의미상 어울리지 않고, 접속부사인 (A) For example과 접속사인 (D) If는 품사상 적합하지 않다.

어휘 introduction 머리말, 소개   epilogue 맺음말   author 작가   novelist 소설가   preface 서문

[11-14] 회람

수신: 전 직원
발신: 파트리시오 멘도사, 총지배인
날짜: 9월 17일
제목: 고객 참여

고객 만족도 연구에 따르면 슈퍼마켓 직원이 **11 고객과** 대화를 나눌 때 고객은 쇼핑 경험에서 더 큰 즐거움을 찾는다고 합니다. **12 따라서 직원들이 고객과 대화하는 데 더 많은 시간을 보내도록 권장합니다.** 주제에는 특히 날씨, 음악, 스포츠, 지역 행사가 포함될 수 있습니다. 우리는 마을에서 가장 도움이 되는 슈퍼마켓이라는 평판을 얻고자 하며, 이 **13 목표를** 달성하도록 여러분이 도움을 주시리라 기대합니다. 그리고 여러분의 참여를 얼마나 소중히 여기는지 증명하기 위해 다음 달부터 이달의 친절한 직원에게 100달러 상품권으로 **14 사례하고자 합니다.**

어휘 engagement 참여   satisfaction 만족   engage in ~에 참여하다   among others 특히   reputation 평판   count on 기대하다   value 소중히 여기다   participation 참여   friendly 친절한   gift certificate 상품권

11 (B)

해설 빈칸은 customers를 대신하는 대명사 them을 목적어로 취하는 전치사 자리로, '그들과 함께 대화를 나눈다'라는 의미를 나타내는 (B) with가 정답이다.

12 (D)

번역 (A) 그러나 우리는 이 연구 결과에 동의하지 않습니다.
(B) 우리 정책의 전체 목록은 웹사이트에서 확인할 수 있습니다.
(C) 고객 여론 조사는 항상 진지하게 고려되어야 합니다.
(D) 따라서 직원들이 고객과 대화하는 데 더 많은 시간을 보내도록 권장합니다.

해설 빈칸 앞 문장에서 직원이 고객과 대화를 나눌 때 고객이 쇼핑을 더 즐거워한다는 연구 결과에 대해 언급하고 있다. 따라서 빈칸에는 직원들에게 고객과의 대화를 권장하는 내용이 나오는 것이 글의 흐름상 자연스러우므로 (D)가 정답이다.

어휘 disagree 동의하지 않다   result 결과   opinion poll 여론 조사   seriously 진지하게   encourage 권장하다

13 (A)

해설 빈칸 앞에서 마을에서 가장 도움이 되는 슈퍼마켓이라는 평판을 얻고자 한다(We seek to develop a reputation as the most helpful supermarket in town)는 목표에 대해 언급하고 있다. 따라서 빈칸에는 '이 목표를 달성하도록 도와달라'는 의미가 되어야 적절하므로 (A) goal이 정답이다. 나머지 (B) level(수준), (C) number(숫자), (D) destination(목적지)은 모두 의미상 부적절하다.

14 (A)

해설 빈칸은 주어 we의 동사 자리로, 빈칸 뒤에 목적어 our friendliest employee of the month가 있고 미래를 나타내는 표현 beginning next month와 함께 쓰였으므로 미래 시제 능동태 (A) will be rewarding이 정답이다.

어휘 reward 사례하다

UNIT 13 부사절 접속사

1 시간·조건의 부사절 접속사

ETS 유형 연습   본책 p.223

1 (A)   2 (B)   3 (B)   4 (A)   5 (C)   6 (A)
7 (B)   8 (B)

1 (A)

번역 처방전을 수령하는 고객은 릴로 약국 카운터에 도착할 때 개인 신분증을 제시해야 합니다.

해설 빈칸 뒤에 〈주어(they)+동사(arrive)〉가 있으므로 접속사 (A) when이 정답이다. (B) during은 전치사이다.

2 (B)

번역 새로운 시간 관리 소프트웨어가 설치된 이후 직원들은 생산성이 향상되었다.

해설 빈칸은 앞뒤로 완전한 절이 나오므로 부사절 접속사 자리로 '설치된 이래로'의 의미를 나타내는 시간의 부사절 접속사 (B) since가 정답이다. 참고로 부사절 접속사 since는 주절의 시제가 현재완료, 부사절의 시제가 과거일 때, '~ 이래로'의 의미를 나타내고 그 외의 시제가 나올 경우 '~ 때문에'의 의미를 나타낸다.

3 (B)

번역 신분증이 2개 있을 경우 고객들은 수표를 발행할 수 있다.

해설 빈칸은 앞뒤로 완전한 절이 나오므로 부사절 접속사 자리이다. '가지고 있다면'이라는 의미를 나타내는 조건의 부사절 접속사 (B) if가 정답이다.

4 (A)

번역 셀렉트 소프트웨어에 등록하면 고객 식별 번호를 받게 됩니다.

해설 빈칸은 뒤에 있는 완전한 절을 이끌면서 콤마 뒤의 완전한 문장 전체를 수식하는 부사절 접속사 자리로 '일단 등록하면'의 의미를 나타내는 조건의 부사절 접속사 (A) Once가 정답이다. 부사 (B) Next는 절을 이끌지 못한다.

5 (C)

번역 모든 지원서들이 접수된 후에 위원회는 면접 대상자 명단을 확정할 것이다.

해설 빈칸은 뒤에 있는 완전한 절을 이끌면서 콤마 뒤의 완전한 문장 전체를 수식하는 부사절 접속사 자리로 '접수된 후에'라는 의미를 나타내는 시간의 부사절 접속사 (C) After가 정답이다. 전치사 (A) About, (B) Except, (D) With는 품사상 적합하지 않다.

6 (A)

번역 헬스장 회원권은 취소가 요청되지 않는 한 고객의 가입 기념일에 자동으로 갱신됩니다.

해설 빈칸은 앞뒤로 완전한 절이 나오므로 부사절 접속사 자리이다. '취소가 요청되지 않는 한'이라는 의미가 되어야 문맥상 적절하므로 조건 접속사 (A) unless(~하지 않는 한)가 정답이다. (B) although(비록 ~일지라도)는 의미상 적합하지 않고, 형용사인 (C) few와 (D) just는 품사상 적합하지 않다.

7 (B)

번역 울트라패스트 오일의 고객은 차량이 정비되는 것을 기다리는 동안 라운지에서 휴식을 취할 수 있다.

해설 빈칸 앞에 완전한 절이 있으므로 waiting for their vehicles to be serviced는 분사구문으로 볼 수 있다. 문맥상 '기다리는 동안'이라는 의미가 되어야 적절하므로 분사구문을 이끄는 부사절 접속사 (B) while이 정답이다. 참고로, (D) as도 '~하는 동안'이라는 의미를 나타낼 수 있지만 분사구문 앞에서 쓰이지 않으므로 정답이 될 수 없다.

8 (B)

번역 저희는 일단 관련 서류를 받는 즉시 발레호 씨의 대출 신청을 처리할 것입니다.

해설 빈칸은 앞뒤로 완전한 절이 나오므로 부사절 접속사 자리로 '받자마자'의 의미를 나타내는 조건의 부사절 접속사 (B) once가 정답이다. 부사 (A) just(막)와 (D) still(여전히), 전치사 (C) upon(~위에, ~하자마자)은 품사상 적합하지 않다.

2 이유·양보·기타의 부사절 접속사

ETS 유형 연습   본책 p.225

1 (A) 2 (A) 3 (A) 4 (A) 5 (C) 6 (C)
7 (D) 8 (C)

1 (A)

번역 호제 씨는 원거리 통근에 지쳐서 시내로 이사했다.

해설 빈칸은 앞뒤로 완전한 절이 나오므로 부사절 접속사 자리이다. '지쳤기 때문에'라는 의미를 나타내는 이유의 부사절 접속사 (A) because가 정답이다.

2 (A)

번역 티아넨 씨 팀은 부지런히 보고서를 작성하고 있음에도 불구하고 아직 보고서는 끝나지 않았다.

해설 빈칸은 뒤에 있는 완전한 절을 이끌면서 콤마 뒤의 완전한 문장 전체를 수식하는 부사절 접속사 자리로 '부지런히 보고서를 작성하고 있음에도 불구하고'의 의미를 나타내는 양보의 부사절 접속사 (A) Even though가 정답이다.

3 (A)

번역 그 제품은 너무 비싸서 쇼핑객들 대부분이 그것을 구입하기를 주저한다.

해설 빈칸은 be동사 is의 주격 보어인 형용사 expensive를 수식하는 부사 자리로 접속사 that과 결합하여 '너무 ~해서 …하다'라는 의미를 나타내는 부사 (A) so가 정답이다. 참고로 '너무 ~해서 …하다'는 〈so+형용사/부사+that+완전한 절〉이나 〈such a(n)+(형용사)+명사+that+완전한 절〉의 형태로 쓰인다.

4 (A)

번역 아야 코두라는 전국 투어 중에도 엄격한 연습 일정을 유지했다.

해설 빈칸은 뒤에 있는 명사구 her national tour를 목적어로 취하는 전치사 자리로 '전국 투어 동안'이라는 의미를 나타내는 기간의 전치사 (A) during이 정답이다. 부사절 접속사 (B) while 뒤에는 완전한 절이 나온다.

5 (C)

번역 조 씨는 동료들이 그녀와 함께 할 수 없었는데도 불구하고 부산의 새 연구소를 방문하기로 결정했다.

해설 빈칸은 앞뒤로 완전한 절이 나오므로 부사절 접속사 자리이고, '동료들이 함께 할 수 없었는데도 불구하고'라는 의미가 되어야 자연스러우므로 (C) even though가 정답이다. (A) rather than(~보다는)과 (D) wherever(~하는 곳 어디든)은 의미상 적합하지 않고 (B) regardless of(~에 상관없이)는 전치사이므로 품사상 답이 될 수 없다.

6 (C)
번역 토요일에 있을 콘서트의 취소는 예상치 못한 음향 시스템의 문제 때문이었다.
해설 빈칸은 명사구 unexpected problems를 목적어로 취하면서 앞의 be동사 was의 주어인 The cancellation을 보충 설명하는 주격 보어 자리로 '예상치 못한 문제 때문에'라는 의미를 나타내는 이유의 전치사 (C) due to가 정답이다. 부사절 접속사 (A) because, (B) as if, (D) unless 뒤에는 완전한 절이 나온다.

7 (D)
번역 션 맥크리는 보고서 초안을 입력하는 반면에 마리오 다미코는 사실들을 확인하는 업무를 맡았다.
해설 빈칸은 앞뒤로 완전한 절이 나오므로 부사절 접속사 자리이다. '입력하는 반면에'라는 의미를 나타내는 대조의 부사절 접속사 (D) while이 정답이다. 부사 (A) also(또한)와 (C) moreover(게다가, 더욱이)는 품사상 적합하지 않다.

8 (C)
번역 버커트 파이낸셜의 본사는 작업팀이 로비의 카펫을 교체할 수 있도록 월요일에 한 시간 늦게 문을 열 것이다.
해설 빈칸은 앞뒤로 완전한 절이 나오는 부사절 접속사 자리이므로 부사절 접속사 (C) so that이 정답이다. 전치사 (A) according to와 분사구문 (B) based on, to부정사 (D) to allow는 품사상 부적합하다.

ETS 실전 문제
본책 p.226

1 (A) 2 (B) 3 (C) 4 (A) 5 (B) 6 (C)
7 (B) 8 (C) 9 (A) 10 (A) 11 (A) 12 (D)
13 (D) 14 (C)

1 (A)
번역 재무 담당 최고책임자가 업무 차 자리를 비웠기 때문에 예산 회의는 월요일로 일정이 변경되었다.
해설 빈칸은 뒤에 있는 완전한 절을 이끌면서 콤마 뒤의 완전한 문장 전체를 수식하는 부사절 접속사 자리로 '자리를 비웠기 때문에'의 의미를 나타내는 이유의 부사절 접속사 (A) Since가 정답이다. 대명사 (B) Either(어느 하나의)는 품사상 적합하지 않다.
어휘 chief financial officer 재무 담당 최고책임자(CFO) budget 예산 reschedule 일정을 변경하다

2 (B)
번역 코시모 식료품점은 구매한 식품을 최대한 활용할 수 있도록 고객에게 실용적인 요리 비법을 제공한다.
해설 빈칸은 부사절 접속사 자리로 '활용할 수 있도록'이라는 의미를 나타내는 목적의 부사절 접속사 (B) so that이 정답이다. so that 대신 in order that으로 바꿔 쓸 수 있다. (A) in addition(게다가), (C) just as(꼭 ~처럼), (D) in case(~의 경우에는)는 의미상 적합하지 않다.
어휘 practical 실용적인 make the most of ~을 최대한 활용하다 purchase 구매하다

3 (C)
번역 바랑기아 마케팅 서비스는 고작 4년 동안 영업해 왔음에도 불구하고 기업 광고의 선두주자가 되었다.
해설 빈칸은 앞뒤로 완전한 절이 나오므로 부사절 접속사 자리이다. '영업해 왔음에도 불구하고'라는 의미를 나타내는 양보의 부사절 접속사 (C) even though가 정답이다. 전치사 (A) owing to와 부사 (D) instead는 품사상 적합하지 않고 시간의 부사절 접속사 (B) before는 의미상 적합하지 않다.
어휘 advertising 광고 in business 영업하는 owing to ~ 덕분에 instead 대신에

4 (A)
번역 음악이 건물 내의 다른 입주자들에게 방해만 되지 않는다면, 세입자는 악기를 연주할 수 있다.
해설 빈칸은 부사절 접속사 자리로 '방해하지 않는다면'이라는 의미를 나타내는 조건의 부사절 접속사 (A) provided that이 정답이다. 이때 that은 생략할 수 있다. 전치사 (B) such as(~와 같은), (C) in case of(~ 경우에), (D) owing to(~ 때문에)는 모두 품사상 적합하지 않다.
어휘 tenant 세입자, 임차인 musical instrument 악기 disturb (작업·수면 등을) 방해하다 resident 거주자, 주민 provided that 만일 ~이라면, ~라는 조건으로

5 (B)
번역 28번 고속도로는 공사가 완전히 끝날 때까지 폐쇄된다.
해설 빈칸은 앞뒤로 완전한 절이 나오므로 부사절 접속사 자리이다. 문맥상 '공사가 완전히 끝날 때까지'라는 의미를 나타내는 시간의 부사절 접속사 (B) until이 정답이다. (A) during(~동안), (C) along(~을 따라), (D) past(~을 지나서)는 전치사이므로 품사상 적합하지 않다.

6 (C)
번역 칼스톤 시의 대중교통 시스템을 확장하기 위한 몇 가지 아이디어가 제시되었지만, 예산 범위 내에 있는 것은 하나도 없다.
해설 빈칸은 뒤에 있는 완전한 절을 이끌면서 콤마 뒤의 완전한 문장 전체를 수식하는 부사절 접속사 자리로 '제시되었지만'이라는 의미를 나타내는 양보의 부사절 접속사 (C) Although가 정답이다.
어휘 expand 확장하다 public transportation 대중교통 budget 예산

7 (B)
번역 인사과에서 휴가 정책을 수정한 것은 많은 직원이 과거 정책이 혼란스럽다고 생각했기 때문이다.

해설 빈칸은 앞뒤로 완전한 절이 나오므로 부사절 접속사 자리이다. '혼란스럽다고 생각했기 때문에'라는 의미를 나타내는 이유의 부사절 접속사 (B) because가 정답이다. 부사 (D) thus(따라서)는 품사상 적합하지 않다.

어휘 revise 수정하다   policy 정책   employee 직원   confusing 혼란스러운

8 (C)
번역 정화 활동이 끝났으므로 작업장에서 대형 쓰레기통을 치울 것이다.

해설 빈칸은 뒤에 있는 완전한 절을 이끌면서 콤마 뒤의 완전한 문장 전체를 수식하는 부사절 접속사 자리로 '끝났으므로'라는 의미를 나타내는 이유의 부사절 접속사 (C) Now that이 정답이다.

어휘 trash 쓰레기   remove 치우다   in particular 특히   now that ~이므로   for instance 예를 들어

9 (A)
번역 베가 씨의 환급 요청은 그녀의 상관이 서류에 서명하자마자 처리될 것이다.

해설 빈칸은 앞뒤로 완전한 절이 나오는 부사절 접속사 자리로 '서명하자마자'라는 의미를 나타내는 부사절 접속사 (A) once가 정답이다. (B) alike는 형용사/부사, (C) such as는 전치사, (D) sooner는 부사이므로 품사상 적합하지 않다.

어휘 reimbursement 환급   process 처리하다   supervisor 상관   form (서류·문서의) 양식

10 (C)
번역 산티니 씨가 10분 안에 공항에 도착하지 않으면 나중 비행기를 타야 할 것이다.

해설 빈칸은 뒤에 있는 완전한 절을 이끌면서 콤마 뒤의 완전한 문장 전체를 수식하는 부사절 접속사 자리로 '도착하지 않는다면'의 의미를 나타내는 조건의 부사절 접속사 (C) Unless가 정답이다. 부사 (A) Regardless(그럼에도 불구하고)와 (D) Rather(꽤, 오히려)는 품사상 적합하지 않다.

어휘 take a later flight 나중 비행기를 타다

[11-14] 공지
클리어데일 아파트 입주민들께 알려 드립니다:

보일러 연간 정비 및 청소가 10월 18일에 실시될 예정임을 안내드립니다. **11** 이 프로젝트는 오전 10시부터 대략 오후 1시까지 계속될 예정입니다. 이 시간 동안 건물 전체의 수도 공급이 중단됩니다. **12** 따라서 세탁실은 폐쇄됩니다.

이번 일이 **13** 야기할 수 있는 불편함에 대해 사과드립니다. 이 중요한 작업을 완성하는 **14** 데 협조해 주셔서 미리 감사드립니다.

루이스 베렐라, 건물 관리자

어휘 tenant 입주민, 세입자   annual 연간의   maintenance 정비   take place 일어나다   supply 공급   entire 전체의   laundry 세탁   apologize for ~에 대해 사과하다   inconvenience 불편   cooperation 협조

11 (A)
번역 (A) 이 프로젝트는 오전 10시부터 대략 오후 1시까지 계속될 예정입니다.
(B) 잔디 위 쓰레기를 줍기 위해 자원봉사자 몇 사람을 구하고 있습니다.
(C) 모든 연체 임대료는 이 날짜까지 제출해야 합니다.
(D) 새 기계는 더욱 강력하고 신뢰할 수 있을 것입니다.

해설 빈칸 앞에서 보일러 연간 정비 및 청소 실시 날짜(the annual maintenance and cleaning of the boiler has been scheduled to take place on October 18)를 알리고 있다. 따라서 글의 흐름상 빈칸에는 이 작업의 소요 시간에 관한 내용이 와야 자연스러우므로 (A)가 정답이다.

어휘 approximately 대략   overdue 연체된   submit 제출하다   reliable 신뢰할 수 있는

12 (C)
해설 빈칸은 문장 전체를 수식하는 부사 자리이다. 문맥상 '따라서 세탁실은 폐쇄된다'라고 하는 것이 자연스러우므로 (C) Consequently가 정답이다. 나머지 (A) Nevertheless(그럼에도 불구하고), (B) Elsewhere(다른 곳에), (D) Alternatively(대신에)는 모두 의미상 적합하지 않다.

13 (D)
해설 빈칸은 앞의 사물 명사 any inconvenience를 수식하는 관계대명사절의 동사 자리로 '이것이 야기할 수 있는'이라는 의미를 나타내는 것이 자연스러우므로 (D) may cause가 정답이다. any inconvenience 뒤에는 목적격 관계대명사 which[that]가 생략되어 있다.

14 (C)
해설 빈칸은 앞뒤로 완전한 절이 나오므로 부사절 접속사 자리이다. '이 중요한 작업을 완성할 때'라는 의미를 나타내는 시간의 부사절 접속사 (C) as가 정답이다. (A) so와 (D) that은 의미상, 부사 (B) also는 품사상 적합하지 않다.

UNIT 14 관계대명사

❶ 관계대명사의 개념과 종류

ETS 유형 연습   본책 p.229

1 (B)   2 (A)   3 (A)   4 (B)   5 (A)   6 (C)
7 (D)   8 (D)

1 (B)
번역 인터뷰를 한 많은 사람들은 더 큰 자동차가 필요 없다고 생각했다.
해설 빈칸은 뒤에 있는 동사 were interviewed의 주어 역할을 하면서 앞의 사람 명사 Many people을 수식하는 관계대명사 자리로 주격 관계대명사 (B) who가 정답이다.

2 (A)
번역 약 2,000명의 사람들이 지난달에 열린 취업 박람회에 참석했다.
해설 빈칸은 뒤에 있는 동사 was held의 주어 역할을 하면서 앞의 사물 명사 the job fair를 수식하는 관계대명사 자리로 주격 관계대명사 (A) which가 정답이다.

3 (A)
번역 이 부츠는 내구성이 강하고 세탁하기 쉬운 합성피혁으로 제작되었다.
해설 빈칸은 뒤에 있는 동사 is의 주어 역할을 하면서 앞의 사물 명사 synthetic leather를 수식하는 관계대명사 자리로 주격 관계대명사 (A) that이 정답이다. 참고로 that은 주격과 목적격 관계대명사 둘 다로 쓰이며 또한 사물 명사와 사람 명사를 모두 수식할 수 있다.

4 (B)
번역 여권을 검사하는 세관 직원은 방문 비자를 발급할 권한도 갖고 있다.
해설 빈칸은 뒤에 있는 동사 inspects의 주어 역할을 하면서 앞의 사람 명사 The customs agent를 수식하는 관계대명사 자리로 주격 관계대명사 (B) who가 정답이다.

5 (A)
번역 레스턴 씨와 판쏭 씨는 지난주에 고객들을 방문했던 사장들 중 두 사람이다.
해설 빈칸은 뒤에 있는 동사 visited의 주어 역할을 하면서 앞의 사람 명사 the senior partners를 수식하는 관계대명사 자리로 주격 관계대명사 (A) who가 정답이다.

6 (C)
번역 필름스 나우는 구독자 추천에 대한 보상을 제공하는 새로운 인터넷 스트리밍 서비스이다.
해설 빈칸은 뒤에 있는 동사 offers의 주어 역할을 하면서 앞의 사물 명사 a new Internet-streaming service를 수식하는 관계대명사 자리로 주격 관계대명사 (C) that이 정답이다.

7 (D)
번역 토요일에 있을 창고 정리 세일로 곧 입고될 다음 시즌 상품을 보관할 공간을 마련할 것이다.
해설 빈칸은 뒤에 있는 동사 will arrive의 주어 역할을 하면서 앞의 사물 명사 next season's products를 수식하는 관계대명사 자리로 주격 관계대명사 (D) which가 정답이다.

8 (D)
번역 무역 박람회에 참석하는 직원들은 잠재 고객에게 나눠줄 명함을 항상 준비하고 있어야 한다.
해설 빈칸은 앞의 사람 명사 Employees를 수식하는 관계대명사 절의 동사 자리로, 선행사 Employees가 복수이므로 복수동사 (D) attend가 정답이다.

2 목적격 관계대명사와 소유격 관계대명사

ETS 유형 연습   본책 p.231

1 (B)   2 (B)   3 (A)   4 (B)   5 (D)   6 (C)
7 (D)   8 (C)

1 (B)
번역 오가와 씨가 수행해야 하는 업무는 그녀의 고용 계약서에 간략히 서술되어 있다.
해설 빈칸은 뒤에 있는 동사 must carry out의 목적어 역할을 하면서 앞의 사물 명사 The tasks를 수식하는 관계대명사 자리로 목적격 관계대명사 (B) that이 정답이다. 참고로 목적격 관계대명사는 생략할 수 있다.

2 (B)
번역 배송 중 주문품이 파손된 모든 고객에게 환불을 해줄 것이다.
해설 빈칸은 뒤에 있는 동사 are damaged의 주어인 orders를 수식하면서 앞의 사람 명사 all customers를 수식하는 관계대명사 자리로 소유격 관계대명사 (B) whose가 정답이다. 여기서 all customers와 orders는 '모든 고객들의 주문'이라는 소유 관계를 나타낸다.

3 (A)
번역 귀하께서 어제 주문하신 책은 내일 오전에 배송될 것입니다.
해설 빈칸은 앞의 The book을 수식하는 관계대명사절의 주어 자리로 주격 인칭대명사 (A) you가 정답이다. The book 뒤에는 목적격 관계대명사 which[that]가 생략되어 있다.

4 (B)
번역 이 이메일에 첨부된 파일은 면밀히 검토되어야 한다.
해설 빈칸은 뒤에 있는 동사 must be examined의 주어 The file을 수식하는 수식어 자리로 '첨부된 파일'이라는 수동적 의미를 나타내는 과거분사 (B) attached가 정답이다. 이때, 빈칸 앞에는 주격 관계대명사 which[that]와 동사 is가 생략되어 있다고 볼 수 있다.

5 (D)
번역 그 교수가 추천한 지원자가 곧 면접을 보러 올 것이다.
해설 빈칸은 뒤에 있는 동사 recommended의 목적어 역할을 하면서 선행사 The applicant를 수식하는 관계대명사 자리로 목적격 관계대명사 (D) that이 정답이다.

6 (C)

번역 아직 제목이 확정되지 않은 아키라 쓰카다의 소설은 내년에 출간될 것이다.

해설 빈칸은 뒤에 있는 동사 hasn't been finalized의 주어인 title을 수식하면서 앞의 사물 명사 Akira Tsukada's novel을 수식하는 관계대명사 자리로 소유격 관계대명사 (C) whose가 정답이다. 여기서 Akira Tsukada's novel과 title은 '아키라 쓰카다 소설의 제목'이라는 소유 관계를 나타낸다.

7 (D)

번역 폴라 코는 규정 준수를 보장하기 위해 크린사이드 호텔 주변 지역을 점검하는 계약을 맺었다.

해설 빈칸은 앞에 있는 명사 the area를 수식하는 수식어 자리로 '크린사이드 호텔을 둘러싸고 있는 지역'이라는 능동적 의미를 나타내면서 형용사 역할을 할 수 있는 현재분사 (D) surrounding이 정답이다. 이때, 빈칸 앞에는 주격 관계대명사 which[that]와 동사 is가 생략되어 있다고 볼 수 있다.

8 (C)

번역 계약서에 포함된 품질 관리 절차들은 기술부장의 검토를 받아야 한다.

해설 빈칸은 주어인 The quality-control procedures를 수식하는 자리로 '포함된 품질 관리 절차'라는 수동적 의미를 나타내면서 형용사 역할을 할 수 있는 과거분사 (C) included가 정답이다. 이때, 빈칸 앞에는 주격 관계대명사 which[that]와 동사 are가 생략되어 있다고 볼 수 있다.

ETS 실전 문제　　　　　　본책 p.232

1 (C)	2 (B)	3 (A)	4 (B)	5 (C)	6 (A)
7 (A)	8 (C)	9 (C)	10 (A)	11 (B)	12 (B)
13 (A)	14 (D)				

1 (C)

번역 퍼버 시스템즈의 총괄 비서직에 지원한 후보자들 중 많은 사람이 충분한 자격을 갖추고 있었다.

해설 빈칸은 뒤에 있는 동사 applied for의 주어 역할을 하면서 앞의 사람 명사 the candidates를 수식하는 관계대명사 자리로 주격 관계대명사 (C) who가 정답이다.

어휘 candidate 후보자, 지원자　administrative assistant 총괄 비서　highly qualified 충분한 자격을 갖춘

2 (B)

번역 런버그 최초의 교원 사택으로 쓰였던 메인 가의 헴튼 하우스가 사적으로 지정되었다.

해설 빈칸은 뒤에 있는 동사 served의 주어 역할을 하면서 앞의 사물 명사 Hemton House를 수식하는 관계대명사 자리로 주격 관계대명사 (B) which가 정답이다. 일반적으로 주격 관계대명사 바로 뒤에는 동사가 나온다.

어휘 schoolhouse 교원 사택　designate 지정하다　historical landmark 사적

3 (A)

번역 산업 장비를 조작하는 공장 직원은 1년에 한 번 안전 교육에 참여해야 한다.

해설 빈칸은 뒤에 있는 be동사 is의 주어인 job을 수식하는 동시에 앞의 사람 명사 Factory personnel을 수식하는 관계대명사 자리로 소유격 관계대명사 (A) whose가 정답이다. 여기서 Factory personnel과 job은 '공장 직원의 일'이라는 소유관계를 나타낸다.

어휘 personnel (조직의) 직원　operate (기계를) 조작하다　industrial machinery 산업 장비　attend 참석하다　safety 안전　once a year 1년에 한 번

4 (B)

번역 마케팅 부장에 의해 검토된 모든 사업 계획서 중에서 마틴 씨의 안이 가장 인상적이다.

해설 빈칸은 전치사 Of의 목적어 all the business plans를 수식하는 수식어 자리이다. '검토된 모든 사업 계획서'라는 수동적 의미를 나타내면서 형용사 역할을 할 수 있는 과거분사 (B) reviewed가 정답이다. 이때, 분사 앞에는 주격 관계대명사 which[that]와 동사 were가 생략되어 있다고 볼 수 있다.

어휘 impressive 인상적인　review 검토하다, 비평하다

5 (C)

번역 바타미 금융그룹은 경제 연구와 분석을 토대로 한 전문가 컨설팅 서비스를 제공한다.

해설 빈칸은 뒤에 있는 동사 are based의 주어 역할을 하는 동시에 앞의 사물 명사 expert consulting services를 수식하는 관계대명사 자리로 주격 관계대명사 (C) that이 정답이다.

어휘 expert 전문가　research 연구　analysis 분석

6 (A)

번역 스카이타운 항공사는 승객들에게 그들이 겪은 지연에 대해 사과했다.

해설 빈칸은 앞의 사물 명사 the delays를 수식하는 관계대명사 절의 주어 자리로 주격 인칭대명사 (A) they가 정답이다. 명사(the delays) 뒤에 (대)명사와 동사가 연달아 나오므로 빈칸 앞에 목적격 관계대명사가 생략됐음을 알 수 있다.

어휘 apologize 사과하다

7 (A)

번역 기조연설자는 J. M. 림이었는데, 림의 풍력에 관한 연구는 대체 에너지 산업이 틀을 갖추는 데 일조했다.

해설 빈칸은 뒤에 있는 동사 has helped의 주어인 research on wind power를 수식하는 동시에 앞의 사람 명사 J. M. Lim을 수식하는 관계대명사 자리로 소유격 관계대명사 (A)

170

whose가 정답이다. 여기서 J. M. Lim과 research on wind power는 'J. M. 림의 풍력에 관한 연구'라는 소유 관계를 나타낸다.

어휘 keynote speaker 기조연설자 alternative 대체의

8 (C)

번역 ZG 치과는 지난주 피츠버그에서 열린 전국 치과 엑스포에서 마케팅 자료를 배부한 모든 직원들에게 감사드립니다.

해설 빈칸은 앞의 사람 명사 all staff members를 수식하는 관계대명사절의 동사 자리이다. who가 이끄는 절에 과거를 나타내는 at last week's National Dentistry Expo가 있으므로 과거동사 (C) distributed가 정답이다. 일반적으로 주격 관계대명사 바로 뒤에는 동사가 나온다.

어휘 dentistry 치과학 distribute 배포하다

9 (C)

번역 화니타는 우리가 데리고 있는 직원 중 가장 믿음직해서, 그녀가 이 계약을 처리하도록 믿고 맡길 수 있다.

해설 빈칸은 뒤에 있는 동사 have의 목적어 역할을 하면서 앞의 사람 명사 the most reliable employee를 수식하는 관계대명사 자리로 목적격 관계대명사 (C) that이 정답이다. 선행사가 최상급의 수식을 받고 있으면, who와 which보다 that이 주로 쓰인다.

어휘 depend on ~에 의지하다 handle 처리하다, 다루다

10 (A)

번역 공원 부지를 기부한 단체는 그곳에 피크닉 쉼터를 건립할 기금 또한 제공할 것이다.

해설 빈칸은 뒤에 있는 동사 donated의 주어 역할을 하면서 앞의 사물 명사 The organization을 수식하는 관계대명사 자리로 주격 관계대명사 (A) that이 정답이다. (B) likewise(마찬가지로)는 부사, (C) whereas(반면에)는 부사절 접속사, (D) has는 동사이므로 품사상 빈칸에 들어갈 수 없다.

어휘 organization 단체 donate 기부하다 fund 기금 shelter 쉼터

[11-14] 광고

리빙 룸 컨셉트

새 가구가 필요하신가요? 거실 공간을 새롭게 단장하고 싶으신가요? 리빙 룸 컨셉트는 최고의 편안함과 고급스러움을 제공합니다. 저희의 의자, 2인용 안락의자, 소파는 최고의 휴식 경험을 제공합니다. 저희의 러그, 미술품과, **11 램프를** 확인해 보세요. 이 부대용품들은 따뜻함과 스타일을 더해줍니다. 사내 인테리어 디자이너 마이클 네이선에게 무료 상담을 요청하시면, **12 그가 공간에 어울리는 가구와 원단을 선택하는 것을 도와드릴 것입니다. 13 그가 시작하는 데 필요한 것은 고객님 방의 치수뿐입니다.**

저희 매장을 방문하셔서 이 광고를 **14 언급하시고** 구매 금액의 10퍼센트를 할인받으세요! 저희는 웰링턴에 크레센트 대로 37번지와 고스포트 가 145번지 두 곳의 매장이 있습니다.

어휘 freshen up 단장하다 comfort 편안함 loveseat 2인용 안락의자 ultimate 최고의 relaxation 휴식 warmth 따뜻함 consultation 상담 in-house (조직) 내부의 fabric 원단 suit 어울리다

11 (B)

해설 빈칸 뒤 문장에서 부대용품들(These accessories will add warmth and style)을 언급하고 있다. 따라서 빈칸에는 러그, 미술품과 함께 부대용품에 속할 수 있는 제품이 들어가야 하므로 (B) lamps가 정답이다. 나머지 (A) beds(침대), (C) appliances(가전제품), (D) countertops(조리대)는 모두 부대용품에 속하지 않는다.

12 (B)

해설 빈칸은 뒤에 있는 동사 will help의 주어 역할을 하면서 앞의 사람 명사 interior designer를 수식하는 관계대명사 자리로 주격 관계대명사 (B) who가 정답이다.

13 (A)

번역 (A) 그가 시작하는 데 필요한 것은 고객님 방의 치수뿐입니다.
(B) 점포 전체 세일이 곧 끝나니 서두르세요!
(C) 배송비는 저희 창고와의 거리에 따라 다릅니다.
(D) 네이선 씨는 효율적인 팀워크를 장려합니다.

해설 빈칸 앞 문장에서 사내 인테리어 디자이너 마이클 네이선에게 상담하면 공간에 어울리는 제품 선택을 도와줄 것이라고 언급하고 있다. 따라서 빈칸에는 그에게 실내 장식 상담을 받는 것과 관련된 구체적인 내용이 뒤따르는 것이 글의 흐름상 자연스러우므로 (A)가 정답이다.

어휘 dimension 치수 storewide 점포 전체의 delivery charge 배송비 vary 다르다 depending on ~에 따라 distance 거리 warehouse 창고 efficient 효율적인

14 (D)

해설 빈칸 뒤에서 구매 금액의 10퍼센트를 할인받으라(to get 10 percent off your purchase)고 했으므로, 문맥상 '이 광고를 언급하고 할인을 받으라'는 내용이 되어야 자연스럽다. 따라서 (D) mention이 정답이다. 나머지 (A) publish(출판하다), (B) avoid(피하다), (C) expect(기대하다)는 모두 의미상 적합하지 않다.

UNIT 15 명사절 접속사

❶ 명사절 접속사 that, whether, if

ETS 유형 연습 본책 p.235

1 (A) 2 (A) 3 (B) 4 (A) 5 (C) 6 (C)
7 (A) 8 (C)

1 (A)
번역 그 위원회의 의견은 우리가 탁아 시설을 지어야 한다는 것이다.
해설 빈칸은 앞의 be동사 is의 보어 역할을 하는 명사절 접속사 자리로 '~라는 것'이라는 의미를 나타내는 명사절 접속사 (A) that이 정답이다.

2 (A)
번역 글래드삭 직원들은 올해 상여금을 받을지 여부를 알지 못한다.
해설 빈칸은 뒤에 있는 완전한 절을 이끌면서 앞의 동사 do not know의 목적어 역할을 하는 명사절 접속사 자리로 '~인지 아닌지'의 의미를 나타내는 명사절 접속사 (A) if가 정답이다. 등위접속사 (B) and는 대등한 구조를 연결한다.

3 (B)
번역 귀하가 서명할 계약서 한 부가 이 편지와 같이 들어 있다는 것에 유념해 주십시오.
해설 빈칸은 동사 note의 목적어 역할을 하는 명사절 접속사 자리로 '~라는 것'의 의미를 나타내는 (B) that이 정답이다.

4 (A)
번역 함 플라스틱 사는 현재 제주시에 새로운 지사를 개설할지 여부를 결정하고 있다.
해설 빈칸은 뒤에 있는 to부정사 구문을 이끌면서 앞의 동사 is deciding의 목적어 역할을 하는 명사절 접속사 자리로 '~인지 아닌지'의 의미를 나타내는 명사절 접속사 (A) whether가 정답이다. 명사절 접속사 whether는 〈whether+완전한 절〉 또는 〈whether+to부정사〉의 형태로 쓰일 수 있다. (B) if도 '~인지 아닌지'라는 의미의 명사절 접속사로 쓰이지만, to부정사가 뒤에 나올 수는 없다.

5 (C)
번역 그 경쟁사가 트롤만 사를 상대로 소송을 제기할지 여부는 두고 보아야 한다.
해설 빈칸은 뒤의 동사 remains의 주어 역할을 하는 명사절 접속사 자리로 '~인지 아닌지'의 의미를 나타내는 명사절 접속사 (C) Whether가 정답이다.

6 (C)
번역 영업 사원들은 자신들의 분기 매출 목표치를 달성해야 한다는 것을 알고 있다.
해설 빈칸은 뒤에 있는 완전한 절을 이끌면서 앞의 동사 know의 목적어 역할을 할 수 있는 명사절 접속사 자리로 '~라는 것'의 의미를 나타내는 명사절 접속사 (C) that이 정답이다. (B) what도 '~라는 것'의 의미를 나타내지만, 뒤에 불완전한 절이 나온다. 전치사 (A) about과 대명사 (D) it은 품사상 적합하지 않다.

7 (A)
번역 톰슨 씨가 그 프로젝트를 이끌 최선의 사람인지 아닌지를 결정하기가 어렵다.
해설 빈칸은 뒤에 있는 완전한 절을 이끌면서 앞의 to determine의 목적어 역할을 할 수 있는 명사절 접속사 자리로 '~인지 아닌지'의 의미를 나타내는 명사절 접속사 (A) whether가 정답이다. (B) what 뒤에는 불완전한 절이 나온다. 부사절 접속사 (C) so that(~하기 위해)은 목적어 역할을 할 수 없고 전치사 (D) for는 품사상 적합하지 않다.

8 (C)
번역 지원자를 고용할지 여부에 대한 회사의 결정은 추천서 검토 결과에 달려 있을 것이다.
해설 빈칸은 a candidate를 목적어로 취하면서 명사절 접속사 whether와 결합하여 전치사 on의 목적어 역할을 할 수 있는 to부정사 (C) to hire가 정답이다. 명사절 접속사 whether는 〈whether+완전한 절〉 또는 〈whether+to부정사〉의 형태로 쓰일 수 있다.

❷ 의문사 형태의 명사절 접속사

ETS 유형 연습
본책 p.237

1 (A) 2 (A) 3 (B) 4 (B) 5 (B) 6 (C)
7 (D) 8 (D)

1 (A)
번역 인사부장은 누가 서울 사무실로 전근될지 결정하지 못했다.
해설 빈칸은 뒤에 있는 동사 will be transferred의 주어가 없는 불완전한 절을 이끌면서 앞의 동사 has not decided의 목적어 역할을 하는 명사절 접속사 자리로 '누가'의 의미를 나타내는 (A) who가 정답이다. (B) when 뒤에는 완전한 절이 나온다.

2 (A)
번역 대부분의 회의 참석자들은 지금 발표자가 하는 말을 이해하지 못한다.
해설 빈칸은 뒤에 있는 동사 is saying의 목적어가 없는 불완전한 절을 이끌면서 앞의 동사 do not understand의 목적어 역할을 하는 명사절 접속사 자리로 '~하는 것, 무엇'의 의미를 나타내는 (A) what이 정답이다. 명사절 접속사 (B) that도 '~하는 것'의 의미를 나타내지만 뒤에 완전한 절이 이어져야 한다.

3 (B)
번역 무료 바이러스 보호 소프트웨어는 아직 그 소프트웨어가 없는 사람은 누구든지 이용할 수 있다.
해설 빈칸은 뒤에 있는 동사 does not have의 주어가 없는 불완전한 절을 이끌면서 앞의 전치사 to의 목적어 역할을 하는 명사절 접속사 자리로 '~한 사람은 누구든지'의 의미를 나타내는 (B) whoever가 정답이다. 참고로 whoever는 anyone who(주격 관계대명사)로 분리해 쓸 수 있다.

4 (B)

번역 능 출판사에서 고객들은 표현하고 싶은 것은 무엇이든지 쓰도록 독려 받는다.

해설 빈칸은 뒤에 있는 to express의 목적어가 없는 불완전한 절을 이끌면서 앞의 to write의 목적어 역할을 하는 명사절 접속사 자리로 '~한 것은[을] 무엇이든지'의 의미를 나타내는 (B) whatever가 정답이다.

5 (B)

번역 내일 (교육)시간에는 참가자들에게 해외 수송 컨테이너를 준비하는 방법에 대해 교육할 것이다.

해설 빈칸은 뒤에 있는 to부정사 구문을 이끌면서 앞의 전치사 on의 목적어 역할을 하는 명사절 접속사 자리로, '~하는 방법'이라는 의미를 나타내는 (B) how가 정답이다. how는 〈how+완전한 절〉 또는 〈how+to부정사〉의 형태로 쓰인다. (A) what도 〈what+to부정사〉의 형태로 쓰이지만 what 뒤에는 목적어가 없는 불완전한 to부정사 구문이 나온다.

6 (C)

번역 직원 명부에는 이용자들에게 다양한 부서 관련 질문에 누가 대답할 수 있는지를 말해 주는 부분이 있다.

해설 빈칸은 뒤에 있는 동사 can answer의 주어가 없는 불완전한 절을 이끌면서 앞의 동사 tells의 직접목적어 역할을 할 수 있는 명사절 접속사 자리로 '누가'라는 의미를 나타내는 (C) who가 정답이다. 명사절 접속사 (A) if와 (B) how 뒤에는 완전한 절이 나온다.

7 (D)

번역 프리모 출판사는 아직 신제품 소프트웨어의 최신 기능을 언제 소개할지 결정하지 못했다.

해설 빈칸은 뒤에 있는 완전한 절을 이끌면서 앞의 동사 has not decided의 목적어 역할을 할 수 있는 명사절 접속사 자리로 '언제'라는 의미를 나타내는 (D) when이 정답이다. (A) which, (B) who, (C) what 뒤에는 불완전한 절이 나온다.

8 (D)

번역 식당 설문조사에 응답하는 사람은 모두 랭글리 카페의 10달러짜리 상품권을 받을 것이다.

해설 빈칸은 동사 will receive의 주어 자리로, 뒤에 있는 responding to the restaurant survey의 수식을 받아 '식당 설문조사에 응답하는 모든 사람'이라는 의미를 나타내는 대명사 (D) Everyone이 정답이다. (A) Whoever와 (B) Whose 뒤에는 절이 나와야 하고, 대명사 (C) Someone(누군가)은 의미상 적합하지 않다.

ETS 실전 문제
본책 p.238

1 (D)	2 (B)	3 (C)	4 (D)	5 (B)	6 (A)
7 (A)	8 (B)	9 (C)	10 (C)	11 (B)	12 (C)
13 (B)	14 (B)				

1 (D)

번역 이번 연구는 논톡 카운티에 새 우물을 뚫는 것이 지하수 수위에 상당한 영향을 미칠지 여부를 판단할 것이다.

해설 빈칸은 뒤에 있는 완전한 절을 이끌면서 앞의 동사 will determine의 목적어 역할을 하는 명사절 접속사 자리로 '~인지 아닌지'의 의미를 나타내는 명사절 접속사 (D) whether가 정답이다. 명사절 접속사 whether는 〈whether+완전한 절〉 또는 〈whether+to부정사〉의 형태로 쓰일 수 있다.

어휘 determine 판단하다 drill 뚫다 significant 상당한 impact 영향 groundwater 지하수

2 (B)

번역 만능 조리기구 사용 설명서에 따르면 이 기구는 곡물과 채소 모두에 사용할 수 있다.

해설 빈칸은 뒤에 있는 완전한 절을 이끌면서 앞의 동사 indicates의 목적어 역할을 할 수 있는 명사절 접속사 자리로 '~라는 것'의 의미를 나타내는 명사절 접속사 (B) that이 정답이다. (A) but과 (D) so는 대등한 구조를 연결한다. 부사절 접속사 (C) while도 완전한 두 개의 절을 연결한다.

어휘 instruction manual 사용 설명서 food processor 만능 조리기구 indicate 나타내다 grain 곡물

3 (C)

번역 이사진은 핵심 기술을 어떻게 관리할지에 대해 논의하고 있다.

해설 빈칸은 뒤에 있는 완전한 절을 이끌면서 앞의 동사 is discussing의 목적어 역할을 할 수 있는 명사절 접속사 자리로 '어떻게'의 의미를 나타내는 (C) how가 정답이다. (A) who, (B) which, (D) what 뒤에는 불완전한 절이 나온다.

어휘 maintain 관리하다 core technology 핵심 기술

4 (D)

번역 제품 개발팀은 신제품이 언제 출시될지 알려 주지 못하고 있다.

해설 빈칸은 뒤에 있는 완전한 절을 이끌면서 앞의 동사 cannot say의 목적어 역할을 할 수 있는 명사절 접속사 자리로 '언제'라는 의미를 나타내는 (D) when이 정답이다. (A) which, (B) who, (C) what 뒤에는 불완전한 절이 나온다.

어휘 release 출시하다, 공개하다

5 (B)

번역 〈농업협회보〉에 실린 한 보고서에 따르면, 소비자들은 농산물이 어디에서 재배되는지에 대해 점점 더 많은 관심을 쏟고 있다.

해설 빈칸은 뒤에 있는 완전한 절을 이끌면서 앞의 전치사 about의 목적어 역할을 할 수 있는 명사절 접속사 자리로 '어디에서'라는 의미를 나타내는 (B) where가 정답이다. (C) what 뒤에는 불완전한 절이 나오고 명사절 접속사 (D) that은 전치사 뒤에 나올 수 없다.

어휘 agricultural 농업의 increasingly 점점 더 be concerned about ~에 관심을 쏟다, 걱정하다 produce 농산물

6 (A)

번역 〈젠킨스 비즈니스 리뷰〉지는 다양한 직업의 사람들 수천 명에게 자신들의 직업에 수반되는 것이 무엇인지 물었다.

해설 빈칸은 뒤에 있는 동사 entail의 목적어가 없는 불완전한 절을 이끌면서 앞의 to describe의 목적어 역할을 할 수 있는 명사절 접속사 자리로 '~한 것, 무엇'의 의미를 나타내는 (A) what이 정답이다. (B) how와 (C) when 뒤에는 완전한 절이 나오고, (D) which 뒤에는 불완전한 절이 올 수 있지만 의미상 적합하지 않다.

어휘 thousands of 수천의, 많은   a wide range of 다양한, 광범위한   profession 직업, 직종   entail 수반하다

7 (A)

번역 영업팀이 발표 일정을 변경해야 하는지 여부를 금요일까지 고위 경영진에게 알려 주세요.

해설 빈칸은 뒤에 있는 완전한 절을 이끌면서 know의 목적어 역할을 하는 명사절 접속사 자리로 '~인지 아닌지'라는 의미를 나타내는 (A) whether가 정답이다. (B) either는 상관접속사로 〈either A or B〉의 구조를 이루고, (C) rather는 부사, (D) yet은 부사/등위접속사로 품사상 적합하지 않다

어휘 senior 고위의

8 (B)

번역 투자자들은 마란딕 모터스의 새로운 전기차 판매가 증가할지에 대해 반신반의했다.

해설 빈칸은 뒤에 있는 완전한 절을 이끌면서 전치사 about의 목적어 역할을 하는 명사절 접속사 자리로 '~인지 아닌지'의 의미를 나타내는 명사절 접속사 (B) whether가 정답이다. (A) unless, (C) even if, (D) in case는 모두 부사절 접속사로 목적어 역할을 하는 절을 이끌 수 없다.

어휘 express 표현하다   uncertainty 반신반의

9 (C)

번역 딤킨네 아이스크림 가게의 개점 행사에 가장 먼저 오는 사람은 누구든지 무료 티셔츠를 받을 것이다.

해설 빈칸은 뒤에 있는 동사 arrives의 주어가 없는 불완전한 절을 이끌면서 뒤의 동사 will receive의 주어 역할을 할 수 있는 명사절 접속사 자리로 '~한 사람은 누구든지'의 의미를 나타내는 (C) Whoever가 정답이다. (A) Who와 (B) What 뒤에는 불완전한 절이 올 수 있지만 의미상 적합하지 않고, (D) That 뒤에는 완전한 절이 나온다.

어휘 grand opening 개업

10 (C)

번역 회사 임원들은 하노이 공장에서 비용 절감을 위해 쓸 수 있는 모든 선택사항을 조사하라고 응우옌 씨에게 요청했다.

해설 빈칸은 have requested의 목적어 역할을 하는 that절에서 주어 Ms. Nguyen의 동사 자리이다. requested처럼 요청을 나타내는 that절에서는 동사원형을 사용해야 하므로 동사원형 (C) investigate가 정답이다. 주어와 동사 사이에 should가 생략되어 있다.

어휘 officer 임원   reduce 절감하다   investigate 조사하다

[11-14] 보도자료

> **긴급 보도자료** 11월 18일
>
> 트레퍼드 시—시 폐기물 관리국(CWMA)은 재활용을 목적으로 전자제품 폐기물을 수거하기 위해 지역 재활용 처리 시설인 GDA 폐기물 솔루션즈와 손을 잡았다.
>
> 이 **11협력 관계**로 주민들은 휴대전화와 노트북 같은 오래된 기기를 퍼 가에 있는 주민센터에 수용으로 내버릴 수 있게 됐다. **12물건은 주민센터의 정규 운영 시간에 접수 가능하다.** 주민들은 센터가 문을 닫은 후에는 센터 밖에 물건을 두지 말아야 한다. "회수 프로그램은 우리의 새로운 '청정 도시' 캠페인의 일환입니다." CWMA 국장 로이드 잉그램 씨가 말했다. "이제 **13어떻게** 이 캠페인을 활성화할지는 주민들이 결정할 때입니다." 그 목적을 달성하기 위해 다음 주 목요일 오후 7시 시청 B 회의실에서 활성화 방안에 대한 지역주민 의견을 수렴하기 위한 공청회가 **14열릴 예정이다.**
>
> 더 많은 정보는 www.cwma-ewaste.org에서 볼 수 있다.

어휘 authority 당국   team up with ~와 협력하다   recycling facility 재활용 처리 시설   collect 수거하다   resident 주민   drop off 수거용으로 특정 장소에 버리다   leave 놓아두다   promote 활성화하다, 촉진하다   to that end 그 목적을 달성하기 위해   public meeting 공청회   seek 구하다, 찾다   input 의견, 조언

11 (B)

해설 빈칸 바로 앞 문장에서 재활용 목적으로 전자 쓰레기를 수거하기 위해 지역 재활용 처리 시설과 손을 잡았다(The City Waste Management Authority(CWMA) has teamed up with GDA Waste Solutions, a local recycling facility, to collect electronic waste for recycling)고 언급하고 있다. 따라서 이러한 '협력 관계'로 가능해진 일을 이어서 설명하는 것이 자연스러우므로 (B) partnership이 정답이다. 나머지 (A) modification(수정, 변경), (C) separation(분리), (D) law(법)는 모두 의미상 적합하지 않다.

12 (C)

번역 (A) 이 기기들은 이번에는 재활용품으로 분류되지 않는다.
(B) 서면 견적서에는 총 수리 비용이 포함될 것이다.
(C) 물건은 주민센터의 정규 운영 시간에 접수 가능하다.
(D) 이 회사의 신제품은 더 에너지 효율적이다.

해설 빈칸 뒤에서 센터가 문을 닫은 후에는 센터 밖에 물건을 두지 말아야 한다(Residents are asked not to leave items outside the center after it has closed)고 언급하고 있다. 따라서 빈칸에는 접수 가능한 센터의 정규 운영 시간에 관한 내용이 오는 것이 글의 흐름상 자연스러우므로 (C)가 정답이다.

어휘 consider 간주하다   recyclable 재활용이 가능한   estimate 견적(서)   repair 수리   accept 받아들이다   energy-efficient 에너지 효율적인

13 (B)
해설 빈칸 뒤에 있는 to부정사 구문을 이끌면서 앞의 to decide의 목적어 역할을 할 수 있는 명사절 접속사 자리로 '~하는 방법'을 나타내는 (B) how가 정답이다. how는 ⟨how+완전한 절⟩ 또는 ⟨how+to부정사⟩의 형태로 쓰인다.

14 (B)
해설 빈칸은 문장의 동사 자리로 미래를 나타내는 next Thursday가 동사를 수식하고 있으므로 미래 시제 (B) will be held가 정답이다.

UNIT 16 비교구문

1 비교급과 원급

ETS 유형 연습
본책 p.241

| 1 (A) | 2 (B) | 3 (A) | 4 (A) | 5 (A) | 6 (B) |
| 7 (C) | 8 (B) | | | | |

1 (A)
번역 새로운 바이러스 방지 소프트웨어는 과거 버전보다 훨씬 성능이 좋다.
해설 빈칸 앞의 비교급 형용사 more powerful과 결합하여 '~보다 더 강력한'의 의미를 나타내는 (A) than이 정답이다.

2 (B)
번역 레드 배지 사는 현재 경쟁업체인 테일로 시큐리티만큼 유명하다.
해설 빈칸은 형용사 famous를 수식하는 부사 자리로 뒤에 있는 ⟨형용사+as⟩와 결합하여 '~만큼 유명한'의 의미를 나타내는 (B) as가 정답이다.

3 (A)
번역 플라스틱은 오늘날 예전보다 훨씬 더 용도가 다양한 건축 자재이다.
해설 빈칸은 뒤의 비교급 형용사 more versatile을 수식하는 부사 자리로 비교급 강조 부사 (A) much가 정답이다. (B) very는 원급 형용사를 수식하는 부사이다. 참고로 비교급 강조 부사로는 much, even, still, far, a lot 등이 있다.

4 (A)
번역 의료비 상환은 가능한 한 빨리 지급될 것입니다.
해설 빈칸은 동사 will be paid를 수식하는 부사 자리로 빈칸 앞의 as, 뒤의 as possible과 결합하여 '가능하면 빨리'의 의미를 나타내는 원급 부사 (A) quickly가 정답이다. ⟨as+원급+as possible⟩의 관용적 표현을 기억한다.

5 (A)
번역 그 편집직에는 학력만큼이나 업무 경력이 중요하다.
해설 빈칸은 형용사 important를 수식하는 부사 자리로 뒤에 있는 ⟨형용사+as⟩와 결합하여 '~만큼 중요한'의 의미를 나타내는 (A) as가 정답이다.

6 (B)
번역 내일 교육은 입사한 지 1년 미만인 직원들을 대상으로 마련된 것이다.
해설 빈칸은 뒤의 숫자 표현 one year를 수식하는 부사 자리로 '1년보다 더 적은'이라는 의미를 나타내는 (B) less than이 정답이다. 나머지 (A) rather than(~보다는), (C) no longer(더 이상 ~않은), (D) by far(훨씬, 단연)는 모두 의미상 적합하지 않다.

7 (C)
번역 설문에 참여한 소비자들은 제품의 새로운 포장에 대해 예상보다 훨씬 더 호의적으로 반응했다.
해설 빈칸은 부사 even의 수식을 받으면서 앞의 동사 responded를 수식하는 부사 자리로 뒤의 than과 결합하여 '~보다 훨씬 더 호의적으로'라는 의미를 나타내는 비교급 부사 (C) more favorably가 정답이다.

8 (B)
번역 찬 씨는 직원들에게 늦어도 오후 5시까지 근무 시간 기록표를 제출해 달라고 요청했다.
해설 빈칸은 앞의 no, 뒤의 than과 결합하여 '~보다 더 늦지 않게, 늦어도 ~까지는'의 의미를 나타내는 비교급 부사 (B) later가 정답이다.

2 최상급

ETS 유형 연습
본책 p.243

| 1 (B) | 2 (A) | 3 (B) | 4 (B) | 5 (D) | 6 (A) |
| 7 (C) | 8 (B) | | | | |

1 (B)
번역 AC 오토즈 사의 NX 2016 모델은 세계에서 가장 빠른 자동차 중 하나다.
해설 빈칸은 전치사 of의 목적어인 cars를 수식하는 형용사 자리로 앞의 정관사 the, 뒤의 in the world와 결합하여 '세상에서 가장 빠른'이라는 의미를 나타내는 최상급 형용사 (B) fastest가 정답이다. 최상급은 ⟨one of the+최상급 형용사+복수명사⟩의 형태로 자주 쓰인다.

2 (A)
번역 어제 축제는 팰리스 극장이 여태껏 주최한 것 중 가장 활기 넘치는 공연 몇몇을 보여 줬다.

해설 빈칸은 전치사 of의 목적어인 performances를 수식하는 형용사 자리로 앞에 정관사 the와 결합하여 '가장 활기찬'의 의미를 나타내는 최상급 형용사 (A) most lively가 정답이다.

3 (B)

번역 부장이 면접한 지원자들 중에서 포위트 씨가 가장 적합한 자격을 갖췄다.

해설 빈칸 앞에 정관사 the가 있는데 빈칸 뒤에 명사가 없다. 따라서 여기서 the는 최상급 앞에 붙는 것임을 알 수 있으므로 최상급을 이루는 (B) most가 정답이다.

4 (B)

번역 발표된 세 개의 프레젠테이션 중에서 샨티 그룹의 것이 가장 인상적이었다.

해설 빈칸은 be동사 was의 주어인 the one을 보충 설명하는 주격 보어 자리로 콤마 앞의 Of the three presentations, 바로 앞의 정관사 the와 결합하여 '셋 중 가장 인상적인'이라는 의미를 나타내는 최상급 형용사 (B) most impressive가 정답이다.

5 (D)

번역 소린스 레이크뷰 그릴은 우리가 지금까지 스웬센 시에서 가 본 곳 중에서 가장 큰 식당이다.

해설 빈칸은 명사 restaurant을 수식하는 형용사 자리로 앞의 정관사 the, 뒤의 형용사절 that we've ever been to in the city of Swensen과 결합하여 '가본 적이 있는 가장 큰'의 의미를 나타내는 최상급 형용사 (D) largest가 정답이다.

6 (A)

번역 써니덱 리조트는 몇몇 업체들로부터 받은 제안서를 검토하고 있으며, 가장 적당한 입찰가를 선택할 것이다.

해설 빈칸은 명사 bid를 수식하는 형용사 자리로, 빈칸 앞의 정관사 the와 결합하여 '제안서들 중 가장 가격이 적당한'이라는 의미를 나타내는 최상급 형용사 (A) most affordable이 정답이다.

7 (C)

번역 애플바움 시장은 도시가 10년 만에 가장 탄탄한 고용 시장을 누리고 있다고 발표했다.

해설 빈칸은 명사구 job market을 수식하는 형용사 자리로 앞의 정관사 the, 뒤의 전치사구 in a decade와 결합하여 '10년 만에 가장 탄탄한 고용 시장'이라는 의미를 나타내는 최상급 형용사 (C) strongest가 정답이다.

8 (B)

번역 에드워즈 앤 선즈 플러밍은 올해의 설문에서 고객 만족 부분에 대해 가장 높은 평가를 받았다.

해설 빈칸은 명사 ratings를 수식하는 형용사 자리로 빈칸 앞의 정관사 the, 뒤에 있는 in this year's survey와 결합하여 '~ 설문에서 가장 높은'의 의미를 나타내는 최상급 형용사 (B) highest가 정답이다.

ETS 실전 문제   본책 p.244

1 (B)	2 (B)	3 (B)	4 (D)	5 (C)	6 (B)
7 (A)	8 (C)	9 (C)	10 (D)	11 (A)	12 (B)
13 (A)	14 (B)				

1 (B)

번역 기술 지원 사무소에 이메일을 보내면 대체로 전화보다 더 빨리 응답 받는다.

해설 빈칸은 부정관사 a와 명사 response 사이에서 명사를 수식하는 형용사 자리로 빈칸 뒤의 than과 결합하여 '~보다 더 빠른 응답'의 의미를 나타내는 비교급 형용사 (B) quicker가 정답이다.

어휘 assistance 지원   generally 대체로   response 응답

2 (B)

번역 종합건설업자는 마운틴 오피스 공원이 늦어도 다음 달까지는 입주 준비가 되리라 예상한다.

해설 빈칸은 앞의 no, 뒤의 than과 결합하여 '늦어도 ~까지, ~보다 더 늦지 않게'의 의미를 나타내는 비교급 부사 (B) later가 정답이다.

어휘 general contractor 종합건설업자   expect 예상하다   occupancy 입주   no later than 늦어도 ~까지   lately 최근에

3 (B)

번역 봄 의류 판매 계획에 관해서 가능한 한 빨리 슈리드하르 씨에게 연락하십시오.

해설 빈칸은 동사 contact를 수식하는 부사 자리로 빈칸 앞의 as, 뒤의 as possible과 결합하여 '가능하면 빨리'의 의미를 나타내는 원급 부사 (B) soon이 정답이다.

어휘 as soon as possible 가능한 한 빨리

4 (D)

번역 추가 인력은 예정되지 않았지만 재고 검토는 예상보다 빨리 마무리됐다.

해설 빈칸은 동사 was completed를 수식하는 부사 자리로 빈칸 뒤에 있는 than과 결합하여 '~보다 더 빨리'라는 의미를 나타내는 비교급 부사 (D) more rapidly가 정답이다.

어휘 additional 추가의   inventory 재고   complete 마무리하다   than expected 예상보다

5 (C)

번역 일단 최신 업데이트가 설치되면 전화 플랫폼이 더 이상 이 애플리케이션을 지원하지 않게 된다.

해설 빈칸은 동사 support를 수식하는 부사 자리로 빈칸 뒤에 있는 longer와 결합하여 '더 이상 ~아닌'이라는 의미를 나타내는 (C) no가 정답이다.

어휘 once 일단 ~하면   most recent 최신의
install 설치하다   support 지원하다

6 (B)

번역 설계된 다리에 관한 건축가들의 모형은 도면만 있을 때보다 훨씬 더 이해하기 쉽다.

해설 빈칸은 뒤의 비교급 형용사 easier를 수식하는 부사 자리로 비교급 강조 부사 (B) much가 정답이다. 나머지 (A) very, (C) so, (D) too는 모두 원급 형용사를 수식하는 부사이다. 참고로 비교급 강조 부사로는 much, even, still, far, a lot 등이 있다.

7 (A)

번역 CCAR 미술감독 후보자 세 사람 중 쇼 씨가 가장 경력이 많다.

해설 빈칸은 뒤의 명사 the three candidates를 목적어로 취하면서 콤마 뒤의 최상급 the most experience를 한정할 수 있도록 the three candidates와 결합하여 '세 후보 중'이라는 의미를 나타내는 전치사 (A) Of가 정답이다. 부사와 접속사로 사용되는 (C) Yet과 (D) So는 품사상 적합하지 않다.

어휘 candidate 후보자   experience 경력

8 (C)

번역 건축가를 찾을 때 로페즈 씨보다 더 정확한 디자이너를 찾기를 바랄 수는 없다.

해설 빈칸은 명사 designer를 수식하는 형용사 자리로 뒤에 있는 than과 결합하여 '~보다 더 정확한'이라는 의미를 나타내는 비교급 형용사 (C) more accurate이 정답이다.

어휘 architect 건축가   accurately 정확하게
accurate 정확한

9 (C)

번역 라모스 씨는 능 파이낸셜 대신 에타 뱅킹에서 직책을 맡기로 결정했다.

해설 문맥상 '능 파이낸셜 대신'이라는 의미가 되어야 자연스러우므로 빈칸은 '~대신 차라리, ~보다 오히려'라는 의미의 비교급 관용 표현인 (C) rather than이 정답이다. (A) subsequently와 (B) moreover는 부사로 빈칸에 들어갈 수 없고, (D) in regard to는 '~에 관하여'라는 의미로 적절하지 않다.

어휘 position 직책   subsequently 이후에
moreover 게다가

10 (D)

번역 새로 출시된 니비도 휴대전화는 그 회사의 다른 모델들보다 거의 2배 만큼 비싸다.

해설 빈칸은 원급 비교인 as expensive as를 수식하는 배수사 자리로 '2배만큼 비싼'의 의미를 나타내는 배수사 (D) twice가 정답이다. 유사한 의미의 double은 〈as+원급+as〉 앞에 쓰이지 않는다.

어휘 released 출시된, 공개된   almost 거의

[11-14] 광고

파티, 회의 및 기타 사교 모임을 계획 중이시라면 인바이팅 디자인스를 이용하십시오. **11 저희는 모든 손님을 품위 있게 초대하는 일을 도와 드립니다.** 저희는 미리 만들어진 초대장을 폭넓게 구비해 놓고 있기 때문에 다른 카드 회사들보다 이용하시기에 **12 더 쉽습니다.** 아주 바쁜 기획자분들은 수십 가지 각기 다른 행사에 완벽하게 적합한 이들 초대장 **13 견본** 중에서 고르실 수 있습니다. 혹시 **14 특별한** 디자인이 필요하시다면 오직 당신만을 위한 맞춤 패키지를 만들어 드릴 수도 있습니다. 어떤 것이 필요하시든 오늘 전화 주셔서 초대 받는 분이 외면할 수 없는 인바이팅 디자인스 초대장을 주문하십시오!

어휘 extensive 폭넓은, 광범위한   premade 미리 만들어진
invitation 초대장   planner 기획자   in a rush 아주 바쁜
be suited to ~에 적합하다   occasion 행사, 경우
customized 맞춤 제작된   ignore 무시하다

11 (A)

번역 (A) 저희는 모든 손님을 품위 있게 초대하는 일을 도와 드립니다.
(B) 파티는 사람들에게 저희 서비스를 홍보할 적기입니다.
(C) 저희 초대장은 모두 당신을 위해 특별히 제작됩니다.
(D) 저희는 각종 행사 준비에 필요한 모든 용품을 제공합니다.

해설 빈칸 뒷 문장에서 이 업체가 초대장을 제작하는 카드 회사임을 알 수 있다. 따라서 빈칸 뒤에서 인바이팅 디자인스에서 제공하는 서비스에 대해 상세히 설명하기 전에 이곳에서 하는 일을 언급하는 것이 글의 흐름상 자연스러우므로 (A)가 정답이다. 모든 카드가 특별 제작되는 것은 아니며, 모든 행사용품을 취급하는 것도 아니므로 (C)와 (D)는 적합하지 않다.

12 (B)

해설 빈칸은 be동사 are의 주어인 We를 보충 설명하는 주격 보어 자리로 빈칸 뒤의 to use than과 결합하여 '~보다 사용하기 더 쉬운'이라는 의미를 나타내는 비교급 형용사 (B) easier가 정답이다.

13 (A)

해설 빈칸은 동사구 choose from의 목적어로 앞의 명사 invitation과 결합하여 '초대장 견본 중에서 고를 수 있다'라는 의미를 나타내는 것이 자연스러우므로 (A) templates가 정답이다. 나머지 (B) fonts(폰트), (C) designers(디자이너), (D) enhancements(향상, 강화)는 모두 의미상 적합하지 않다.

14 (B)

해설 빈칸 뒤에 있는 문장에서 맞춤 패키지를 만들어 줄 수 있다(we can create a customized package just for you)고 언급하고 있다. 따라서 앞에는 '특화된 디자인이 필요하면'이라는 의미를 나타내는 것이 자연스러우므로 (B) specialized가 정답이다. 나머지 (A) typical(전형적인), (C) reusable(재사용할 수 있는), (D) sensitive(세심한)는 모두 의미상 적합하지 않다.

UNIT 17 　어휘 1: 명사/형용사

▶ 기출 어휘 – 명사 1

ETS 유형 연습　　　　　　　　　본책 p.247

| 1 (A) | 2 (B) | 3 (B) | 4 (A) | 5 (B) | 6 (D) |
| 7 (A) | 8 (C) |

1　(A)
번역　디트리치 덴티스트리는 환자들에게 예정된 예약을 취소하려면 24시간 전에 통지해 달라고 요청한다.
해설　빈칸은 to cancel의 목적어 자리로 '예정된 예약을 취소하기 위하여'라는 의미가 되어야 자연스러우므로 (A) appointment가 정답이다.

2　(B)
번역　프로젝트의 실제 비용에 대한 우려로 경기장 확장 계획이 지연되었다.
해설　빈칸은 동사 have delayed의 주어 자리로 뒤의 about the actual cost of the project와 결합하여 '실제 비용에 대한 우려'라는 의미가 되어야 적절하므로 (B) Concerns가 정답이다.

3　(B)
번역　권 회계와 선우 청소 서비스는 계약이 만료되기 전에 현재 계약을 재협상할 예정이다.
해설　빈칸에는 their current와 결합하여 동사 will renegotiate의 목적어가 될 말이 필요하다. before 이하가 '만료되다'를 나타내므로 이와 어울릴 수 있는 (B) contract가 정답이다.

4　(A)
번역　하울랜드 제조사가 발송하는 모든 물품은 있을지 모르는 결함을 위해 세심하게 검사 받는다.
해설　빈칸은 전치사 for의 목적어 자리로 앞의 possible과 결합하여 '있을지 모르는 결함'이라는 의미가 되어야 적절하므로 (A) defects가 정답이다.

5　(B)
번역　드완 합병 프로젝트를 위해 지속적으로 기여해준 사우스필드 지사 팀의 노고에 감사합시다.
해설　빈칸은 뒤의 to the Dewan merger project와 결합하여 '합병 프로젝트에 대한 지속적인 기여'라는 의미가 되어야 자연스러우므로 (B) contributions가 정답이다. 참고로 contribution은 주로 전치사 to와 함께 쓰인다.

6　(D)
번역　은도리 산업은 시의회로부터 제안된 건설 프로젝트에 필요한 모든 승인을 받았다.
해설　빈칸은 동사 received의 목적어 자리로 all the necessary와 결합하여 '필요한 모든 승인'이라는 의미가 되어야 자연스러우므로 (D) approvals가 정답이다.

7　(A)
번역　미나벳 카운티 산림청은 필요할 때 휴양 단지를 조기 폐쇄할 수 있는 권한을 갖고 있다.
해설　빈칸은 뒤의 to close recreational areas early와 결합하여 '휴양 단지를 조기 폐쇄할 수 있는 권한'이라는 의미가 되어야 자연스러우므로 (A) authority가 정답이다.

8　(C)
번역　마즈덴 제조사는 더 많은 인력 자원에 대한 현재의 수요를 해결하기 위해 임시 직원을 고용하고 있다.
해설　빈칸은 to address의 목적어 자리로, 뒤의 for greater personnel resources와 결합하여 '더 많은 인력 자원에 대한 수요'라는 의미가 되어야 자연스러우므로 (C) demand가 정답이다.

▶ 기출 어휘 – 명사 2

ETS 유형 연습　　　　　　　　　본책 p.249

| 1 (B) | 2 (B) | 3 (B) | 4 (A) | 5 (B) | 6 (B) |
| 7 (C) | 8 (B) |

1　(B)
번역　보조 통계학자의 직무 내용에는 자료 수집, 코딩, 통계 분석이 포함되어 있다.
해설　빈칸에는 job과 결합하여 동사 includes의 주어가 될 말이 필요하다. includes의 목적어로 나열된 여러 예시가 '직무 내용'을 나타내므로 (B) description이 정답이다.

2　(B)
번역　주모리토 타일 회사는 단계별 설치 지침을 제공하는 무료 DVD를 제공한다.
해설　빈칸은 관계대명사 that이 이끄는 절에서 동사 provides의 목적어 자리로, step-by-step의 수식을 받으며 installation과 복합명사 구조를 이루어 '단계별 설치 지침'이라는 의미가 되어야 자연스러우므로 (B) instructions가 정답이다.

3　(B)
번역　연구에 따르면 생명공학 산업은 다른 관련 분야보다 빠르게 성장하고 있다.
해설　빈칸은 that절에서 동사 is growing의 주어 자리로 the biotechnology와 복합명사 구조를 이루어 '생명공학 산업'의 의미가 되어야 자연스러우므로 (B) industry가 정답이다.

4 (A)
번역 어제 3분기 재무제표에서 바르가스 인더스트리즈 사는 주가의 15퍼센트 증가를 보고했다.

해설 빈칸은 뒤의 in value와 결합하여 '가치에서 15퍼센트 증가'의 의미가 되어야 자연스러우므로 (A) gain이 정답이다.

5 (B)
번역 파벨라 테스팅 랩의 회사 사무실 지도와 길 안내는 아래 링크를 클릭하세요.

해설 빈칸은 뒤의 전치사구 to Pavella Testing Lab's corporate office와 결합하여 '파벨라 테스팅 랩 회사 사무실로의 길 안내'라는 의미가 되어야 자연스러우므로 (B) directions가 정답이다. directions는 주로 전치사 to와 함께 쓰인다.

6 (B)
번역 노헤이븐 어소시에이츠 사는 고객에게 3년간의 전문적인 시장 전망을 제공한다.

해설 빈칸은 전치사 with의 목적어 자리로 expert의 수식을 받으며 market과 복합명사의 구조를 이루어 '전문적인 시장 전망'이라는 의미가 되어야 자연스러우므로 (B) forecasts가 정답이다.

7 (C)
번역 주민센터 개보수 계획에 반대하는 주민들은 월요일 밤 회의에서 우려 사항에 대해 의견을 제시할 수 있다.

해설 빈칸은 have의 목적어 자리로 뒤의 to the plan과 결합하여 '계획에 대한 반대'의 의미가 되어야 자연스러우므로 (C) objections가 정답이다.

8 (B)
번역 테크린드 사는 권한이 없는 사용자가 기밀 정보에 접근하는 것을 방지하기 위해 엄격한 보안 조치를 시행한다.

해설 빈칸은 동사 implements의 목적어 자리로 strict의 수식을 받으면서 명사 security와 복합명사 구조를 이루어 '엄격한 보안 조치'라는 의미가 되어야 자연스러우므로 (B) measures가 정답이다.

▶ **기출 어휘 – 명사 3**

ETS 유형 연습
본책 p.251

| 1 (B) | 2 (A) | 3 (A) | 4 (B) | 5 (D) | 6 (C) |
| 7 (A) | 8 (C) | | | | |

1 (B)
번역 스태퍼드 케이블은 여러 가지 결제 옵션을 제공하므로 고객들은 가장 편리한 납부 방법을 선택할 수 있다.

해설 빈칸은 동사 offers의 목적어 자리로 several의 수식을 받으며 payment와 복합명사 구조를 이루어 '여러 가지 결제 옵션'이라는 의미가 되어야 자연스러우므로 (B) options가 정답이다.

2 (A)
번역 디바드 사는 유망한 신인 음악가의 홍보를 전담하는 작은 홍보회사다.

해설 빈칸은 뒤에 온 of promising new musicians와 결합하여 '유망한 신인 음악가의 홍보'라는 의미가 되어야 자연스러우므로 (A) promotion이 정답이다.

3 (A)
번역 대회 규칙을 준수하지 않는 출품작은 자동으로 실격될 것이다.

해설 빈칸은 관계대명사 that절이 수식하는 주어 자리로, that are out of compliance with contest rules와 결합하여 '대회 규칙을 준수하지 않는 출품작'이라는 의미가 되어야 자연스러우므로 (A) Submissions가 정답이다.

4 (B)
번역 회의 비용과 이동 경비는 디렉스코에서 지불하지만, 식사 비용은 참가자의 책임입니다.

해설 빈칸은 be동사 are의 주어인 dining expenses를 설명하는 주격 보어 자리이다. '식사 비용은 참가자의 책임'이라는 의미가 되어야 자연스러우므로 (B) responsibility가 정답이다.

5 (D)
번역 우수한 고객 서비스에 대한 명성 덕분에 메이즈 미용실은 이 지역 동종 업계에서 가장 인기있는 사업체이다.

해설 빈칸은 뒤의 for outstanding customer service와 결합하여 '우수한 고객 서비스에 대한 명성'이라는 의미가 되어야 자연스러우므로 (D) reputation이 정답이다.

6 (C)
번역 레골로스 사는 고객 정보 보호의 중요성을 인식하고 있기 때문에 자료 보호를 최우선 순위로 삼았다.

해설 빈칸은 동사 has made의 목적어인 data privacy를 설명하는 목적격 보어 자리이다. '자료 보호를 최우선 순위로 삼다'는 의미가 되어야 자연스러우므로 (C) priority가 정답이다.

7 (A)
번역 예상되는 수요로 인하여 에메랄드 폰드 인은 최소 한 달 전에 예약할 것을 권장합니다.

해설 빈칸은 동사 recommends의 목적어 역할을 하는 동명사 making의 목적어 자리로, making과 함께 '예약을 할 것'이라는 의미가 되어야 자연스러우므로 (A) reservations가 정답이다.

8 (C)
번역 항공사 안전 규정은 승무원뿐만 아니라 승객들도 준수해야 한다.

해설 빈칸에는 Airline safety와 결합하여 동사 must be followed의 주어가 될 말이 필요하다. '항공사 안전 규정은 준수되어야 한다'라는 의미가 되어야 적절하므로 (C) regulations가 정답이다.

▶ 기출 어휘 - 형용사 1

ETS 유형 연습
본책 p.253

| 1 (B) | 2 (B) | 3 (B) | 4 (A) | 5 (B) | 6 (A) |
| 7 (C) | 8 (A) | | | | |

1 (B)
번역 그 엔터테인먼트 복합단지는 주말이면 개인적인 행사를 위해 이용할 수 있다.
해설 빈칸은 be동사 is의 주어인 The entertainment complex를 보충 설명하는 주격 보어 자리이다. 뒤의 for private functions와 결합하여 '개인적인 행사를 위해 이용 가능한'이라는 의미가 되어야 자연스러우므로 (B) available이 정답이다.

2 (B)
번역 귀하가 선택한 물품들은 7일에서 10일 후에 도착할 예정이며, 뒤이어 매 6주마다 추가로 배송됩니다.
해설 빈칸은 전치사 by의 목적어인 deliveries를 수식하는 형용사 자리이다. 뒤의 every six weeks와 결합하여 '매 6주마다 추가적인 배송'이라는 의미가 되어야 자연스러우므로 (B) additional이 정답이다.

3 (B)
번역 톰킨스빌 도로 안내서는 상세한 전국 지도와 지역 지도를 바탕으로 편찬되었다.
해설 빈칸은 뒤에 온 national and local maps를 수식하는 형용사 자리이다. '상세한 전국 지도와 지역 지도'라는 의미가 되어야 자연스러우므로 (B) detailed가 정답이다.

4 (A)
번역 에디스 코직스 사는 기간제 직원들도 유급 휴가를 받을 자격이 있다는 것을 보장한다.
해설 빈칸은 temporary employees를 보충 설명하는 주격 보어 자리이다. 뒤의 for paid holidays와 결합하여 '유급 휴가를 받을 자격이 있는'의 의미가 되어야 자연스러우므로 (A) eligible이 정답이다. 형용사 eligible은 주로 전치사 for와 함께 쓰인다.

5 (B)
번역 실험실 직원은 이 설명서의 지침을 적힌 대로 정확히 따르는 것이 중요하다.
해설 빈칸은 be동사 is의 진짜 주어인 that laboratory employees follow the instructions in this manual exactly as written을 보충 설명하는 주격 보어 자리로 that 이하와 결합하여 '지침을 따르는 것이 중요하다'는 의미가 되어야 자연스러우므로 (B) critical이 정답이다.

6 (A)
번역 〈글로벌 플라이웨이즈〉는 올란 항공 승객들에게 서비스로 제공되는 무료 잡지다.
해설 빈칸은 magazine을 수식하는 형용사 자리이다. '무료 잡지'라는 의미가 되어야 자연스러우므로 (A) complimentary가 정답이다.

7 (C)
번역 콴 씨는 독창성에 대한 명성에 걸맞게 신공항 터미널 설계를 위한 가장 창의적인 제안서를 제출했다.
해설 빈칸은 최상급을 나타내는 the most와 명사 proposal 사이에서 명사를 수식하는 형용사 자리로, '가장 창의적인 제안서'라는 의미가 되어야 자연스러우므로 (C) creative가 정답이다.

8 (A)
번역 중세의 성이 조약돌 길을 내려다보고 있는 매혹적인 도시 류블라냐는 사랑받는 관광지이다.
해설 정관사 the와 명사 town 사이에서 명사를 수식하는 형용사 자리로 관광지를 홍보하는 문맥상 '매혹적인 도시'라는 의미가 되어야 적절하므로 (A) captivating이 정답이다.

▶ 기출 어휘 - 형용사 2

ETS 유형 연습
본책 p.255

| 1 (B) | 2 (A) | 3 (A) | 4 (B) | 5 (D) | 6 (B) |
| 7 (C) | 8 (A) | | | | |

1 (B)
번역 건축자재 비용을 상당히 절감한 것이 민브로 건설의 수익 증대에 기여했다.
해설 빈칸은 문장의 주어 savings를 수식하는 형용사 자리로 '상당한 절감'이라는 의미가 되어야 자연스러우므로 (B) Significant가 정답이다.

2 (A)
번역 덜레스 테크에서 15년간 일한 덕택에 듀바르 씨는 회사 정책을 철저하게 이해하고 있다.
해설 빈칸은 동사 has의 목적어인 understanding을 수식하는 형용사 자리이다. 뒤의 of company policies와 결합하여 '회사 정책의 철저한 이해'라는 의미가 되어야 자연스러우므로 (A) thorough가 정답이다.

3 (A)

번역 치과 보조직 지원자들은 뉴욕 주에서 유효한 자격증을 소지해야 합니다.

해설 빈칸은 주격 관계대명사 that이 이끄는 절에서 a license를 보충 설명하는 주격 보어 자리이다. '유효한 자격증'이란 의미가 되어야 자연스러우므로 (A) valid가 정답이다.

4 (B)

번역 분석가들은 웨스턴빌 파이낸셜이 오랫동안 지속적인 수익성을 올린 기록이 있기 때문에 안정적인 회사로 규정한다.

해설 빈칸은 전치사 as의 목적어인 company를 수식하는 형용사 자리이다. '안정적인 회사'라는 의미가 되어야 자연스러우므로 (B) stable이 정답이다.

5 (D)

번역 회사 방침에 따르면, 직원들은 개인적인 목적으로 직장 내 이메일 계정을 사용해서는 안 된다.

해설 빈칸은 전치사 for의 목적어인 purposes를 수식하는 형용사 자리로, '개인적인 목적으로'라는 의미를 나타내야 하므로 (D) personal이 정답이다. 나머지 (A) entire(전체의), (B) active(활동적인), (C) cautious(신중한)는 모두 의미상 적합하지 않다.

6 (B)

번역 베닝필드 농가는 워크허스트 시내에 유일하게 남아 있는 18세기 건물이다.

해설 빈칸은 the only와 명사구 eighteenth-century building 사이에 들어가 '유일하게 남아 있는 18세기 건물'이라는 의미가 되어야 적절하므로 (B) remaining이 정답이다. (A) gradual(점진적인), (C) mutual(상호적인), (D) delayed(지연된)는 모두 의미상 적합하지 않다.

7 (C)

번역 관객들과 평론가들로부터 널리 찬사를 받은 〈19개 무지개〉는 올해 가장 흥미로운 영화 중 하나로 간주된다.

해설 빈칸은 최상급 부사 most와 명사 films 사이에서 films를 수식하는 형용사 자리이다. '가장 흥미로운 영화'라는 의미가 되어야 자연스러우므로 (C) exciting이 정답이다.

8 (A)

번역 많은 고용 담당자들은 자격을 갖춘 후보자를 찾는 데 도움이 될 수 있도록 소셜 네트워킹 사이트를 이용한다.

해설 빈칸은 명사 candidates를 수식하는 형용사 자리로, '자격을 갖춘 후보자'라는 의미가 되어야 자연스러우므로 (A) qualified가 정답이다.

ETS 실전 문제
본책 p.256

1 (A)	2 (C)	3 (A)	4 (B)	5 (D)	6 (D)
7 (B)	8 (C)	9 (A)	10 (D)	11 (D)	12 (D)
13 (D)	14 (C)	15 (A)	16 (B)		

1 (A)

번역 스코틀랜드 소설가 엘시 백스터는 매우 상상력이 풍부한 등장인물들로 찬사를 받아왔다.

해설 빈칸은 전치사 for의 목적어 역할을 하는 자리로, 앞의 her highly imaginative와 결합하여 '그녀의 매우 상상력이 풍부한 등장인물들'이라는 의미가 되어야 자연스러우므로 (A) characters가 정답이다.

어휘 Scottish 스코틀랜드의 novelist 소설가 praise 칭찬하다 imaginative 상상력이 풍부한 packager 포장업자 exercise 운동 possibility 가능성

2 (C)

번역 해리스 레스토랑의 손님들은 모든 저녁 식사에 곁들일 수 있는 수프나 샐러드를 선택할 수 있다.

해설 빈칸은 동사 have의 목적어 역할을 하는 명사 자리로, 빈칸 뒤 전치사구 of soup or salad의 수식을 받아 '수프나 샐러드를 선택할 수 있다'는 의미가 되어야 적절하므로 (C) choice가 정답이다.

어휘 accompany 곁들이다 wish 소망 taste 맛 choice 선택 piece 조각

3 (A)

번역 사우스 베이 해양 박물관은 이 지역의 조선 역사에 관한 전시회를 선보이고 있다.

해설 빈칸은 동사 is featuring의 목적어 역할을 하는 명사 자리로, 문맥상 '박물관은 전시를 선보이고 있다'는 의미가 되어야 적절하므로 (A) exhibit이 정답이다.

어휘 maritime 해양의 feature 특별히 포함하다 shipbuilding 조선 exhibit 전시 advertisement 광고 expression 표현 indication 표시

4 (B)

번역 고마르 셰프의 요리 아카데미의 등록 기간이 시작되면 이메일로 알림을 받게 되실 것입니다.

해설 빈칸은 전치사 for의 목적어 역할을 하는 명사 자리로, 문맥상 '요리 아카데미의 등록을 위한 기간'이라는 의미가 되어야 자연스러우므로 명사 (B) enrollment가 정답이다.

어휘 notify 알리다 period 기간 culinary 요리의 enrollment 등록 appearance 외관 convenience 편리 replacement 교체

5 (D)

번역 경영진은 베를린에 지사를 개설하여 회사의 국제적 존재감을 높일 계획이다.

해설 빈칸은 to increase의 목적어 자리로 '회사의 국제적 존재감을 높일 계획'이라는 의미가 되어야 적절하므로 (D) presence가 정답이다.

어휘 branch 지사 expedition 탐험 evaluation 평가 collection 수집 presence 존재감

6 (D)

번역 윈스턴 배관 회사는 75년 이상 운영되어 왔다.

해설 빈칸은 전치사 in의 목적어 역할을 하는 명사 자리로 in과 결합하여 be동사 has been의 보어 역할을 하며 '운영되어 왔다'는 의미가 되어야 자연스러우므로 (D) operation이 정답이다.

어휘 plumbing 배관 statement 성명, 진술

7 (B)

번역 창고 내부 작업에는 대용량 파란색 페인트가 최소 30통은 필요할 것이다.

해설 빈칸은 전치사 of의 목적어 역할을 하는 자리로 앞의 the interior of the와 결합하여 '창고의 내부'라는 의미가 되어야 자연스러우므로 (B) warehouse가 정답이다. (A) combination(조합), (C) tent(텐트), (D) party(파티)는 모두 의미상 적합하지 않다.

어휘 at least 최소한 interior 내부

8 (C)

번역 엔지니어들이 그 문제에 대해 두 시간 동안 논의했지만 해결책에 합의하지 못했다.

해설 빈칸은 전치사 on의 목적어 역할을 하는 명사 자리로, '문제에 대해 논의했지만 해결책에 합의하지 못했다'는 의미가 적절하므로 (C) solution이 정답이다.

어휘 trouble 문제 solution 해결책 progress 진전

9 (A)

번역 넬틴 코퍼레이션은 모든 고객 데이터를 무단 접근에서 보호하기 위해 적절한 보안 조치를 취한다.

해설 빈칸은 security measures를 수식하는 형용사 자리이다. '적절한 보안 조치'라는 의미가 되어야 자연스러우므로 (A) appropriate이 정답이다.

어휘 measure 조치 safeguard 보호하다 unauthorized 무단의 access 접근 appropriate 적절한 dependent 의존적인 receptive 잘 수용하는 concerned 걱정하는

10 (D)

번역 업계 잡지 기자들은 여전히 에어리타의 신기술과 그것이 어떻게 시장에 막대한 영향을 끼칠 수 있는지를 대체로 인식하지 못하고 있다.

해설 빈칸은 동사 remain의 주어인 Trade magazine writers를 보충 설명하는 주격 보어 자리이다. '인식하지 못하고 있다'라는 의미가 되어야 자연스러우므로 (D) unaware가 정답이다. 참고로 형용사 unaware는 주로 전치사 of와 함께 쓰인다.

어휘 trade magazine 업계 잡지 writer 기자, 필자 remain (여전히) ~한 상태로 있다 largely 대체로 drastically 막대하게, 급격하게 affect 영향을 끼치다 severe 심각한 indicative ~을 나타내는 subtle 미묘한

11 (D)

번역 이 설문지에 제공하신 정보는 엄격히 기밀이며 다른 어떤 판매업체와도 공유되지 않습니다.

해설 빈칸은 be동사 is의 주어인 The information을 보충 설명하는 주격 보어 자리이다. 뒤의 and will not be shared with any other vendors와 결합하여 '정보는 기밀로 다른 판매업체와 공유되지 않는다'는 의미가 되어야 자연스러우므로 (D) confidential이 정답이다.

어휘 questionnaire 설문지 strictly 엄밀히, 정확히 share 공유하다, 함께 쓰다 vendor 판매업체, 판매인 potential 잠재적인, 가능성 있는 concentrated 집중한, 응집된 dedicated 헌신적인, 몰두하는

12 (D)

번역 전체 조직이 올너 씨의 은퇴식에 초대되어서 그룹의 규모가 클 것이다.

해설 빈칸 뒤의 명사 organization을 수식해 '전체 조직이 초대되었다'는 의미가 되어야 자연스러우므로 (D) entire가 정답이다. (A) attentive(배려하는), (B) solid(단단한), (C) final(최종의)은 모두 의미상 적합하지 않다.

어휘 organization 조직 retirement 은퇴 entire 전체의

13 (D)

번역 목요일에 대표이사는 레미니 금융 서비스와의 합병 계획에 관한 기자회견을 열었다.

해설 빈칸은 plans를 목적어로 취하면서 a press conference를 수식하는 전치사 자리로, '계획에 관한'이라는 의미를 만드는 (D) concerning이 정답이다.

어휘 press conference 기자회견 merge 합병 except ~을 제외하고 versus ~에 비해 concerning ~에 관한

14 (C)

번역 JQT 코퍼레이션의 사업 목표는 신뢰할 수 있는 시장조사 없이는 달성할 수 없다.

해설 빈칸은 market research를 수식하는 형용사 자리이다. '신뢰할 수 있는 시장조사'라는 의미가 되어야 자연스러우므로 (C) reliable이 정답이다.

어휘 fulfill 달성하다 contented 만족하는 convinced 확신하는 reliable 신뢰할 수 있는 right 옳은

15 (A)
번역 내일 세미나는 오전 9시 정각에 시작되므로 참석자들은 시간을 지키도록 노력해야 한다.

해설 '시간을 지키도록 노력해야 한다'라는 의미를 나타내는 (A) punctual이 정답이다.

어휘 sharp 정각에 attendee 참석자 punctual 시간을 지키는 advanced 고급의, 앞선 instant 즉시의 sudden 갑작스러운

16 (B)
번역 헤데스 살롱의 스타일리스트들은 헤어, 뷰티, 고객 만족에 대해 진실된 열정을 보여준다.

해설 빈칸은 부정관사 a와 명사 passion 사이에서 명사를 수식하는 형용사 자리로, passion과 결합하여 '진실된 열정'이라는 의미가 되어야 자연스러우므로 (B) genuine이 정답이다.

어휘 passion 열정 satisfaction 만족 trimmed 손질된 genuine 진실한 straight 곧은 hospitable 친절한

UNIT 18 어휘 2: 동사/부사

▶ 기출 어휘 - 동사 1

ETS 유형 연습 본책 p.259

| 1 (B) | 2 (B) | 3 (A) | 4 (B) | 5 (C) | 6 (C) |
| 7 (B) | 8 (B) |

1 (B)
번역 시장은 오늘 연설에서 도로 개선사업의 문제를 다룰 것이다.

해설 빈칸 뒤의 목적어 the issue와 결합하여 '문제를 다루다'라는 의미가 되어야 자연스러우므로 (B) address가 정답이다. (A) educate(교육하다)는 의미상 적합하지 않다.

2 (B)
번역 다음 달 런던에서 개최되는 영업 전시회에 참가하고 싶은 직원들은 자신의 부장들에게 알려야 한다.

해설 빈칸 뒤의 목적어 the sales exposition과 결합하여 '영업 전시회에 참가하다'라는 의미가 되어야 자연스러우므로 타동사 (B) attend가 정답이다. (A) participate(참가하다)는 자동사로 전치사 in과 결합하여 목적어를 취할 수 있다.

3 (A)
번역 두 회사의 임원들은 곧 제안된 합병의 조건에 대해 확정할 준비가 될지도 모른다.

해설 빈칸 뒤의 목적어 the terms와 결합하여 '조건들을 확정하다'라는 의미가 되어야 자연스러우므로 타동사 (A) confirm이 정답이다. (B) collaborate(협력하다)는 자동사로 전치사 with 또는 on 없이 바로 목적어를 취할 수 없다.

4 (B)
번역 우리 계약업체에서 제작한 초기 모델은 우리가 그 업체에 제공한 명세 사항을 준수하지 못했다.

해설 빈칸 뒤의 전치사구 with the specifications와 결합하여 '명세 사항을 준수하다'라는 의미가 되어야 자연스러우므로 자동사 (B) comply가 정답이다. (A) approach(접근하다)는 타동사로 전치사 없이 바로 목적어를 취한다.

5 (C)
번역 파웰 사는 올해 지역 고등학생들에게 15개 이상의 교육 장학금을 수여했다.

해설 빈칸 뒤의 목적어 more than fifteen educational scholarships와 결합하여 '15개 이상의 교육 장학금을 수여했다'라는 의미가 되어야 자연스러우므로 (C) awarded가 정답이다.

6 (C)
번역 어떻게 린더우드 공장의 가구 생산 속도를 높일지가 다음 관리자 회의의 주제다.

해설 빈칸 뒤의 목적어 production과 결합하여 '생산 속도를 높이다'라는 의미를 나타내는 타동사 (C) accelerate가 정답이다. 자동사 (A) appeal(호소하다)과 (D) subscribe(구독하다)는 주로 전치사 to와 함께 쓴다.

7 (B)
번역 시내에 있는 식당들은 건강 및 안전 기준 준수 여부를 검증 받기 위해 검사관에 의해 자주 평가 받는다.

해설 빈칸은 주어 Eating establishments를 보충 설명하는 주격 보어 자리이다. frequently와 결합하여 '자주 평가 받는'이라는 의미가 되어야 자연스러우므로 (B) assessed가 정답이다.

8 (B)
번역 델워 코스메틱스는 다음 주 기자 회견에서 브리그먼 사와의 제휴를 발표할 예정이다.

해설 빈칸은 뒤의 its partnership을 목적어로 취하는 동사 자리로 '제휴를 발표할 예정이다'라는 의미가 되어야 자연스러우므로 (B) announce가 정답이다. (A) consist(이루어져 있다)는 자동사로 목적어를 취할 수 없고, 나머지는 의미상 적합하지 않다.

▶ 기출 어휘 - 동사 2

ETS 유형 연습 본책 p.261

| 1 (B) | 2 (A) | 3 (B) | 4 (B) | 5 (D) | 6 (D) |
| 7 (B) | 8 (D) |

1 (B)
번역 크로이돈 교통은 소포를 항상 제시간에 배송하겠습니다.
해설 빈칸 뒤의 목적어 your parcel과 결합하여 '당신의 소포를 배달하다'라는 의미가 되어야 자연스러우므로 타동사 (B) deliver가 정답이다. (A) exceed(초과하다)는 의미상 적합하지 않다.

2 (A)
번역 국제적 제휴 관계를 형성하는 것은 회사가 시장을 확장하는 효과적인 방법이다.
해설 빈칸 뒤의 목적어 its market과 결합하여 '시장을 확장하다'라는 의미가 되어야 자연스러우므로 (A) expand가 정답이다. (B) include(포함하다)는 의미상 적합하지 않다.

3 (B)
번역 리워스의 커피 자회사는 지너스 빈스라는 이름으로 운영될 것이다.
해설 빈칸 뒤의 under the name of Genus Beans와 결합하여 '지너스 빈스라는 이름으로 운영되다'라는 의미가 되어야 자연스러우므로 (B) operate가 정답이다.

4 (B)
번역 아걸 사의 최고 경영자는 이번 주 늦게 언론에 성명서를 발표하리라 예상된다.
해설 빈칸 뒤의 목적어 a statement와 결합하여 '성명을 발표하다'라는 의미가 되어야 자연스러우므로 (B) issue가 정답이다. (A) speak는 '말하다'의 의미일 때, 주로 자동사로 쓰인다.

5 (D)
번역 헬로글라스는 향후 5년 동안 태양광 패널의 생산을 늘릴 계획이다.
해설 빈칸은 동사 plans의 목적어 역할을 하는 to부정사의 to 뒤 동사원형 자리이다. 빈칸 뒤의 목적어 its production과 결합하여 '생산을 늘릴 계획이다'라는 의미가 되어야 자연스러우므로 (D) increase가 정답이다.

6 (D)
번역 모든 프로그래머가 취업 면접을 잘 수행했지만, 수잔 트래포드는 나머지보다 돋보였다.
해설 빈칸 뒤의 수식어구 well in their job interviews와 결합하여 '취업 면접을 잘 수행했다'라는 의미를 나타내는 (D) performed가 정답이다. (A) treat(취급하다), (B) reveal(드러내다), (C) handle(취급하다)은 바로 뒤에 목적어가 온다.

7 (B)
번역 여름 인턴 멘토 활동에 관심 있는 사람은 인사과 샤밀라 쿠마르에게 통보해야 한다.
해설 빈칸 뒤의 목적어 Sharmila Kumar와 결합하여 '샤밀라 쿠마르에게 통보하다'라는 의미가 되어야 자연스러우므로 (B) notify가 정답이다. (C) respond(응답하다)는 자동사로 전치사 to와 결합하여 목적어를 취할 수 있다.

8 (D)
번역 고위 경영진은 직원들에게 직장 만족도를 높이기 위한 아이디어를 인사과에 제출하도록 독려한다.
해설 빈칸 뒤의 목적어 employees와 결합하여 '직원들을 독려하다'라는 의미가 되어야 자연스러우므로 (D) encourages가 정답이다. (A) respond(응답하다)는 전치사 to 없이 바로 목적어를 취할 수 없다.

▶ **기출 어휘 - 동사 3**

ETS 유형 연습 본책 p.263

1 (B) **2** (B) **3** (A) **4** (A) **5** (B) **6** (C)
7 (D) **8** (C)

1 (B)
번역 메란 투자는 신규 본사를 매입하는 계약을 체결했다.
해설 빈칸 뒤의 목적어 an agreement와 결합하여 '계약서에 서명했다'라는 의미가 되어야 자연스러우므로 (B) signed가 정답이다.

2 (B)
번역 우리는 모든 방문객들에게 건물에 들어오기 전에 사진이 부착된 신분증을 제시하도록 요구한다.
해설 빈칸 뒤의 목적어 photo identification과 결합하여 '사진이 부착된 신분증을 제시하다'라는 의미가 되어야 자연스러우므로 (B) present가 정답이다. (A) notify(통지하다)는 주로 통지를 받는 대상이 목적어 자리에 나온다.

3 (A)
번역 팀장들은 워크숍 참석자들이 서로 의견을 되풀이하지 않도록 노력해야 한다.
해설 빈칸 뒤의 목적어 workshop attendees와 from repeating과 결합하여 '워크숍 참석자들이 되풀이하는 것을 막다'라는 의미가 되어야 자연스러우므로 (A) prevent가 정답이다. prevent는 〈prevent+목적어+from+-ing〉의 구조를 취한다.

4 (A)
번역 호텔 피트니스 센터에 가려면 메인 로비 뒤쪽에 있는 계단을 이용하세요.
해설 빈칸 뒤의 목적어 the hotel fitness center와 결합하여 '호텔 피트니스 센터에 가다'라는 의미가 되어야 자연스러우므로 (A) reach가 정답이다.

5 (B)
번역 워크숍 참가자들은 발표자들을 위해 지정된 앞줄 좌석들을 제외하고는 강당에서 아무 좌석이나 선택할 수 있습니다.

해설 주격 관계대명사 which(those=seats)가 이끄는 절의 빈칸은 수동태를 이루는 과거분사가 들어갈 자리이다. 의미상 주어가 되는 선행사 those(=seats)와 어울리는 것은 '(자리 등을) 따로 잡아두다'라는 뜻의 reserve이므로 (B) reserved가 정답이다.

6 (C)
번역 출장비를 환급 받으려면, 직원들은 출장에서 돌아온 후 30일 이내에 경비 보고서를 제출해야 한다.

해설 빈칸은 within 30 days of와 from their trip과 결합하여 '여행에서 돌아온 후 30일 이내에'라는 의미가 되어야 자연스러우므로 (C) returning이 정답이다.

7 (D)
번역 컴퓨터 기술자들은 영업 사원들에게 고객 데이터베이스 접근에 관한 상세한 설명을 제공한다.

해설 빈칸 뒤의 목적어 sales representatives와 결합하여 '영업 사원들에게 제공한다'라는 의미가 되어야 자연스러우므로 (D) provide가 정답이다. (A) offer(제공하다)는 전치사 with 없이 detailed instructions를 직접목적어로 취할 수 있다.

8 (C)
번역 모든 육상 선수들은 점프하거나 전력 질주하기 전에 몸을 풀라고 권고된다.

해설 빈칸은 앞의 be동사 are와 뒤의 to부정사 to warm up과 결합하여 '몸을 풀라고 권고된다'라는 의미가 되어야 자연스러우므로 (C) urged가 정답이다.

▶ 기출 어휘 - 부사 1

ETS 유형 연습   본책 p.265

| 1 (A) | 2 (B) | 3 (B) | 4 (A) | 5 (C) | 6 (D) |
| 7 (C) | 8 (C) |

1 (A)
번역 변경된 작업 계획은 즉시 시작될 예정이며 최소 3개월 동안 유효할 것이다.

해설 빈칸은 to begin을 수식하는 부사 자리로 '즉시 시작할 것이다'라는 의미가 되어야 자연스러우므로 (A) immediately가 정답이다.

2 (B)
번역 새 사무 장비 요청은 처리에 보통 한 달 걸린다.

해설 빈칸은 문장의 동사 take를 수식하는 부사 자리로 one month to process와 결합하여 '처리에 보통 한 달 걸린다'라는 의미가 되어야 자연스러우므로 (B) generally가 정답이다.

3 (B)
번역 부서장에게 정식으로 소개되기 전, 로렌 씨는 일주일 동안 클로스 파이버스에서 근무했다.

해설 빈칸은 introduced를 수식하는 부사 자리로, '부서장에게 정식으로 소개되기 전'이라는 의미가 되어야 자연스러우므로 (B) formally가 정답이다.

4 (A)
번역 티호미르 토이즈 직원들은 회사 상품의 품질을 확보하기 위해 부지런히 일한다.

해설 빈칸은 동사 work를 수식하는 부사 자리로 '부지런히 일한다'라는 의미가 되어야 자연스러우므로 (A) diligently가 정답이다.

5 (C)
번역 빠른 처리를 위해 양식의 모든 부분들이 완전히 작성되게 하세요.

해설 빈칸은 동사 are filled out을 수식하는 부사 자리로 '완전히 작성되다'라는 의미가 되어야 자연스러우므로 (C) completely가 정답이다.

6 (D)
번역 현금 인출을 자주 하는 고객들은 우리의 신규 온라인 뱅킹 서비스에 관심이 있을지도 모른다.

해설 빈칸은 주격 관계대명사 who가 이끄는 형용사절에서 동사 make를 수식하는 부사 자리이다. '자주 현금 인출을 하는'이라는 의미가 되어야 자연스러우므로 (D) frequently가 정답이다.

7 (C)
번역 잉캠 카메라의 플래시는 자동으로 작동하므로 사진 찍는 사람이 플래시를 켤 필요가 없다.

해설 빈칸은 문장의 동사 activates를 수식하는 부사 자리로 '자동으로 작동하다'의 의미가 되어야 자연스러우므로 (C) automatically가 정답이다.

8 (C)
번역 사이토 박사의 연구 프로젝트는 점점 시간이 많이 걸리고 재정 부담이 커져서 중단되었다.

해설 빈칸은 형용사 time-consuming을 수식하는 부사 자리로 '점점 시간이 많이 걸리는'의 의미가 되어야 자연스러우므로 (C) increasingly가 정답이다.

기출 어휘 - 부사 2

ETS 유형 연습 본책 p.267

| 1 (B) | 2 (B) | 3 (B) | 4 (A) | 5 (A) | 6 (A) |
| 7 (C) | 8 (B) |

1 (B)
번역 타이러덱스 조립 라인 근로자들은 그들의 일을 신속하지만 정확하게 해낼 것으로 기대된다.
해설 빈칸은 앞의 to do를 수식하는 부사 자리이다. 뒤의 but accurately와 결합하여 '신속하지만 정확하게'의 의미가 되어야 자연스러우므로 (B) rapidly가 정답이다.

2 (B)
번역 만타르 사의 최근 결성된 고객 자문 부서가 현재 재무 전문가를 채용 중이다.
해설 빈칸은 명사를 수식하는 과거분사 formed를 수식하는 부사 자리이다. '최근에 결성된'이라는 의미가 되어야 자연스러우므로 (B) recently가 정답이다.

3 (B)
번역 〈실비나 상법〉의 최신 디지털 판에는 전에 이용할 수 없었던 온라인 리뷰 섹션이 있다.
해설 빈칸은 형용사 available을 수식하는 부사 자리로 not과 결합하여 '전에 이용할 수 없었던'이라는 의미가 되어야 자연스러우므로 (B) previously가 정답이다.

4 (A)
번역 회사 연회에서 사진을 찍을 자원봉사자, 특히 행사 촬영 경험이 있는 사람들이 필요하다.
해설 빈칸 뒤의 절 those who have experience in event photography를 수식하는 부사 자리로 '특히 행사 촬영 경험이 있는 사람들'의 의미가 되어야 자연스러우므로 (A) specifically가 정답이다.

5 (A)
번역 지난 시즌 해변 호텔들의 총 객실 이용률은 일기 예보관들이 경고한 장마 때문에 예측대로 낮았다.
해설 빈칸은 주격 보어인 형용사 low를 수식하는 부사 자리로, '예측대로 낮았다'는 의미가 되어야 적절하므로 (A) predictably가 정답이다.

6 (A)
번역 모든 비스멧 용품 매장의 장비 부서에서 매출이 꾸준히 증가했다.
해설 빈칸은 동사 have risen을 수식하는 부사 자리로 '꾸준히 증가했다'는 의미가 되어야 자연스러우므로 (A) steadily가 정답이다.

7 (C)
번역 뜻하지 않은 초과 인출을 방지하기 위해 주기적으로 예금 계좌 잔액을 확인하는 것이 필수적이다.
해설 빈칸은 앞의 to monitor를 수식하는 부사 자리로 '주기적으로 확인하는 것'이라는 의미가 되어야 자연스러우므로 (C) periodically가 정답이다.

8 (B)
번역 드포 씨는 조경사들에게 퇴근하고 작업을 나중에 끝내도 된다고 말했다.
해설 빈칸은 동사 finish를 수식하는 부사 자리로 '작업을 나중에 끝낸다'는 의미가 되어야 자연스러우므로 (B) later가 정답이다.

ETS 실전 문제 본책 p.268

1 (D)	2 (C)	3 (B)	4 (C)	5 (C)	6 (A)
7 (B)	8 (B)	9 (D)	10 (D)	11 (C)	12 (A)
13 (A)	14 (D)	15 (A)	16 (D)

1 (D)
번역 코 미술관의 전시회는 보통 6만에서 10만 명의 방문객을 유치한다.
해설 빈칸 뒤의 목적어 between 60,000 and 100,000 visitors와 결합하여 '6만에서 10만 명의 방문객을 유치한다'라는 의미가 되어야 자연스러우므로 (D) attract가 정답이다.
어휘 exhibition 전시회 typically 보통

2 (C)
번역 전통적인 폴란드 음식을 제공하는 비에타스 카페는 이전에 키스포트 비스트로가 사용하던 사우스 스트리트 위치에 문을 열었다.
해설 빈칸은 명사구 the South Street location을 뒤에서 수식하는 과거분사 자리로 by Keesport Bistro와 결합하여 '키스포트 비스트로에 의해 사용되던'이라는 의미가 되어야 자연스러우므로 (C) occupied가 정답이다.
어휘 serve 제공하다 traditional 전통의 Polish 폴란드의 fare 음식 formerly 이전에 finalize 마무리짓다 postpone 연기하다 occupy (건물 등을) 사용하다, 차지하다 accompany 동반하다

3 (B)
번역 스캐그힐 수산은 작업장 안전 지침을 초과 달성하여 지역 당국에게 칭찬을 받았다.
해설 빈칸은 have been의 주어 Skaghill Fisheries를 보충 설명하는 주격 보어 자리로 뒤의 by local authorities와 결합하여 '지역 당국에게 칭찬 받은'이라는 의미가 되어야 자연스러우므로 과거분사 (B) commended가 정답이다.

어휘 fishery 수산 회사 authority 당국 exceed 초과하다 propose 제안하다 commend 칭찬하다 perceive 인지하다 assert 주장하다

4 (C)
번역 러들로 고양이 병원의 수의사들은 고양이들에게 전문적인 치료를 제공하는 데 헌신하고 있다.

해설 빈칸은 전치사 to의 목적어 역할을 하는 동명사 자리이고, expert care를 목적어로 취해 '전문적인 치료를 제공하는 것'이라는 의미가 되어야 자연스러우므로 (C) providing이 정답이다.

어휘 veterinarian 수의사 dedicated 헌신적인 expert 전문적인 feline 고양이과 동물 commit 저지르다 entrust 맡기다

5 (C)
번역 임원들은 서비스의 개선이 컴퓨터 시스템을 더 빨리 작동하도록 만드는 소프트웨어 업그레이드 덕분이라고 여긴다.

해설 attribute A to B(A를 B의 덕분으로 여기다) 구문에서 '소프트웨어 업그레이드 덕분에 서비스가 개선되었다'라는 해석이 자연스러우므로 (C) improvement가 정답이다.

어휘 official 임원, 공무원 run 작동하다 exchange 교환; 교환하다 relief 경감, 안심 lift 승강기; 들어 올리다

6 (A)
번역 설문조사 결과는 직원들이 일반적으로 그들의 연금 제도에 만족하고 있다는 것을 보여준다.

해설 빈칸은 뒤의 that절 that employees are generally satisfied with their pension plan을 목적어로 취해 '직원들이 연금 제도에 만족한다는 것을 보여준다'는 의미가 되어야 자연스러우므로 (A) suggest가 정답이다.

어휘 result 결과 generally 일반적으로 satisfied 만족하는 pension 연금 plan 제도, 계획 suggest 시사하다, 암시하다 discover 발견하다 believe 믿다 require 요구하다

7 (B)
번역 시 관계자들은 새로 개관한 미술관이 관광을 활성화해주기를 바라고 있다.

해설 빈칸 뒤의 목적어 tourism과 결합하여 '관광을 활성화해줄 것이다'라는 의미를 나타내는 (B) stimulate가 정답이다.

어휘 official 관계자, 공무원 defend 방어하다 stimulate 활성화하다, 자극하다 prefer 선호하다 negotiate 협상하다

8 (B)
번역 셰이디 오크 강연 시리즈는 여러 지역 단체에서 후원을 받는다.

해설 빈칸은 앞의 be동사 is와 결합하여 수동태를 이루는 과거분사 자리로, '여러 단체에 의해 후원을 받는다'는 의미가 되어야 하므로 (B) sponsored가 정답이다.

어휘 organization 단체 trade 거래하다 sponsor 후원하다 explore 탐구하다 achieve 달성하다

9 (D)
번역 우리의 숙련된 직원들은 우리 부서의 성장을 가속화하는 데 필요한 기술을 보유하고 있다.

해설 빈칸은 주어 Our experienced employees의 동사 자리로 the skills를 목적어로 취해 '직원들은 기술을 보유하고 있다'는 의미가 되어야 적절하므로 (D) possess가 정답이다.

어휘 accelerate 가속화하다 division 부서 enlarge 확대하다 benefit 혜택을 입다 contain ~이 들어 있다 possess 보유하다, (자질 등을) 지니다

10 (D)
번역 올해에만 V1X 자동차 산업대상은 연비가 좋은 자동차를 생산하는 제조업체에게만 수여될 것이다.

해설 빈칸은 뒤의 전치사구 to manufacturers를 수식하는 부사 자리로 '오로지 제조업체에게'라는 의미가 되어야 자연스러우므로 (D) exclusively가 정답이다.

어휘 manufacturer 제조업체 energy-efficient 연비가 좋은 vehicle 자동차 exceptionally 유난히 routinely 일상적으로 exclusively 오로지

11 (C)
번역 여러 해 동안, 글렌뷰 연구소는 고객들에게 비용 효율이 높은 우수한 서비스를 한결같이 제공해 왔다.

해설 빈칸은 조동사와 과거분사 사이의 부사 자리로 '한결같이 제공해 왔다'는 의미가 되어야 자연스러우므로 (C) consistently가 정답이다.

어휘 quality 양질의, 우수한; 품질 cost-effective 비용 효율이 높은 broadly 널리 formerly 전에 consistently 한결같이, 지속적으로 repetitiously 되풀이하여

12 (A)
번역 일요일 세션 중 시간을 절약하기 위해 원탁 토론은 회의 일정에서 의도적으로 생략되었다.

해설 빈칸은 be동사와 과거분사 사이의 부사 자리로 '의도적으로 생략되었다'는 의미가 되어야 자연스러우므로 (A) intentionally가 정답이다.

어휘 omit 생략하다 intentionally 의도적으로 arguably 아마 틀림없이 commonly 흔히 vitally 필수적으로

13 (A)
번역 지난 12월 수립된 스피디 프린트의 새로운 배출 감소 전략은 다음 달에 마침내 시행될 예정이다.

해설 빈칸은 조동사 will과 동사 be implemented 사이의 부사 자리로 '마침내 시행될 예정이다'라는 의미가 되어야 자연스러우므로 (A) finally가 정답이다.

어휘 emission (가스 등의) 배출 reduction 감소 strategy 전략 implement 시행하다 finally 마침내 recently

최근에　lastly 마지막으로　exactly 정확히

14 (D)

번역 그레이필드 인더스트리의 직원들은 승진 결정이 내려지기 전에 매년 평가받는다.

해설 빈칸은 동사 are reviewed를 수식하는 부사 자리로, 뒤에 평가 시기에 대해 언급하는 내용과 자연스럽게 연결될 수 있도록 '매년 평가받는다'라는 의미를 나타내는 (D) annually가 정답이다.

어휘 review 평가하다　promotion 승진　decision 결정 certainly 확실히　subsequently 그 후에　densely 빽빽하게

15 (A)

번역 메타 전자는 호가에 맞는 제안을 기다리고 있기 때문에 오래된 건물을 팔지 않았다.

해설 빈칸은 전치사 for의 목적어 자리이자 관계대명사 that절의 수식을 받는 명사 자리이다. that meets the asking price와 결합하여 '호가에 맞는 제안'이라는 의미가 되어야 자연스러우므로 (A) offer가 정답이다.

어휘 asking price 호가, 부르는 값　offer 제안　expense 비용　addition 추가　incident 사건

16 (D)

번역 그 숙소는 여러 식당과 상점이 도보 거리 이내에 있어 위치가 편리하다.

해설 빈칸은 be동사 is와 과거분사 located 사이에서 과거분사 located를 수식하는 부사 자리이다. '편리하게 위치한'이라는 의미가 적절하므로 부사 (D) conveniently가 정답이다. (A) widely(널리), (B) quickly(빨리), (C) gradually(점차적으로)는 의미상 적합하지 않다.

어휘 distance 거리

PART 7 READING COMPREHENSION

UNIT 19 편지 / 이메일

ETS 기출 예제 본책 p.274

이메일

오스본 씨께

아프로디테 스포츠용품(ASG)은 최근 저희 파일에 있는 고객님의 주소로 여름 카탈로그 한 부를 발송했습니다. 안타깝게도 해당 물품은 "배송 불가"로 표시되어 반송되었습니다.

저희는 고객님께 카탈로그를 보내 드리고 싶습니다. 고객님의 지난 구매 내역을 볼 때 고객님은 신상 테니스 장비에 관심이 있으실 것 같습니다. **고객님의 현재 우편물 발송 주소를 알려 주시면 유용한 쿠폰과 함께 카탈로그를 다시 보내 드리겠습니다.**

저희는 우편 주문 서비스도 개선했습니다. 이제 온라인 주문 추적 서비스를 제공하고 50달러 이상의 주문에 대해 더 이상 배송비를 청구하지 않습니다.

고객님의 답변을 기다리고 있겠습니다.

트랭 민 팜

Q 이메일의 목적은 무엇인가?
(A) 환불 받는 방법을 설명하려고
(B) 기프트 카드를 제공하려고
(C) 연락처 정보를 얻으려고
(D) 주문에 대한 세부 사항을 제공하려고

ETS 유형 연습 본책 p.275

1 (B)　**2** (B)

[1] 이메일

수신: 밍 라이 〈mlai@azurewingimports.com.hk〉
발신: 마르코 세린자 〈mcerinza@cerinzajewellery.com.ph〉
제목: 정보
첨부: ⓞ 세린자1; 세린자2

라이 씨께:

주문한 보석을 받았습니다. 하지만 **제가 주문한 시계 10개가 배송물에 포함되어 있지 않았습니다.** 시계가 송장에는 기재되어 있지만 첫 번째 상자에 들어 있던 포장 목록에는 없습니다. 두 문서의 스캔본을 첨부했습니다. 시계의 배송 상태를 알려주세요.

마르코 세린자

Q 이메일의 목적은 무엇인가?
(A) 실수에 대해 사과하려고
(B) 누락된 품목에 대해 문의하려고

해설 **주제/목적**
두 번째 문장에서 주문한 시계가 배송물에서 빠져 있다(the ten watches I ordered were not in any of the packages)고 보고하고 있으므로 (B)가 정답이다.

[2] 편지

고메즈 씨께:

다음 달부터 영업부의 2개 국어 구사 고객 서비스직에 공석이 생기리라 예상합니다. 지난해에 찾은 2개 국어 구사자 사무직 가용 인력 중에서 귀하의 지원서가 보관되어 있었습니다. 아직 관심이 있으신지, 또 올해 상근으로 일할 수 있으신지 알고 싶습니다. 만약 그러하시다면 5월 15일 금요일까지 604-555-0009로 저에게 연락하시면 상세 내용을 알려 드리겠습니다.

파멜라 핀치

Q 직위에 필요한 자격 요건은 무엇인가?
(A) 영업 경력
(B) 2개 국어 유창

해설 **세부 사항**
첫 문장에서 영업부의 2개 국어 구사 고객 서비스직에 공석이 생길 것(We anticipate an opening for a bilingual customer service associate in our sales department starting next month)이라고 했다. 이를 통해 2개 국어에 유창한 것이 자격 요건이라는 것을 알 수 있으므로 (B)가 정답이다.

Paraphrasing 지문의 bilingual → 보기의 Fluency in two languages

ETS 실전 문제 본책 p.276

1 (B)	2 (C)	3 (A)	4 (D)	5 (A)	6 (D)
7 (A)	8 (D)	9 (A)	10 (A)	11 (A)	12 (B)
13 (D)	14 (A)	15 (B)	16 (A)	17 (C)	

[1-2] 이메일

수신: ayang@winklightmail.net
발신: hughes@knowltoninn.com
날짜: 10월 20일
제목: 귀하의 체류

양 씨께,

놀턴 인에 머무르기로 결정해 주셔서 감사합니다. **2** 저희는 새로운 첨단 비즈니스 센터와 최근 리모델링된 식당 프레쉬 퍼스펙티브즈를 포함한 호텔의 멋진 시설들에 자부심을 가지고 있습니다.

1 소중한 고객으로서, 고객님의 의견은 저희에게 중요합니다. 잠시 시간을 내 www.knowltoninn.com/guest_comments에서 간단한 설문조사를 작성해 주세요. 11월 1일까지 작성해 주시면, 고객님이 다음 번에 프레시 퍼스펙티브즈를 방문하실 때 쓸 수 있는 25퍼센트 할인 쿠폰을 우편으로 보내 드리겠습니다.

다시 한 번 놀턴 인을 선택해 주셔서 감사합니다. 체류가 즐거우셨기를 바랍니다.

해리스 휴즈, 매니저
놀턴 인

어휘 facility 시설 state-of-the-art 첨단의 newly 최근에 valued 소중한 opinion 의견 important 중요한 fill out 작성하다 survey 설문조사 voucher 쿠폰

1 휴즈 씨가 이메일을 보낸 이유는 무엇인가?
(A) 예약을 확인하려고
(B) 고객에게 의견을 요청하려고
(C) 고객 불만에 응대하려고
(D) 지불을 요청하려고

해설 **주제/목적**
두 번째 단락의 첫 문장에서 고객의 의견이 중요하다(As a valued customer, your opinions are important to us)며 설문을 작성해 달라고 요청(Please take a moment to fill out a brief survey at www.knowltoninn.com/guest_comments)하고 있으므로 (B)가 정답이다.

어휘 reservation 예약 complaint 불만

Paraphrasing 지문의 a brief survey
→ 보기의 feedback

2 놀턴 인에 대해 암시되는 것은 무엇인가?
(A) 시의 역사적 지역에 위치한다.
(B) 곧 웹사이트 디자인을 고칠 것이다.
(C) 최근에 변화를 겪었다.
(D) 합리적인 가격 책정으로 유명하다.

해설 **추론**
첫 번째 단락의 두 번째 문장에서 새로운 첨단 비즈니스 센터와 최근 리모델링된 식당 등에 자부심을 가지고 있다(We are proud of the wonderful facilities at our inn, including our new state-of-the-art business center and our newly remodeled restaurant, Fresh Perspectives)고 했다. 이를 통해 최근 시설에 변화가 있었다는 것을 알 수 있으므로 (C)가 정답이다.

어휘 recently 최근에 undergo 겪다
noted for ~로 유명한 reasonable 합리적인

[3-4] 편지

5월 26일

켄 이즈무
웨스트레이크 행군 밴드
웰스 포인트 대로 5443번지
킹스랜드, 미주리 64160

이즈무 씨께,

축하합니다! **3** 귀하의 행군 밴드가 킹스랜드 여름 퍼레이드에서 연주하도록 선정되었습니다. 퍼레이드는 6월 20일 토요일 오후 2시

에 시작됩니다. 연주자들에게 늦어도 오후 1시 30분까지 컨벤션 센터에 도착하라고 이야기해 주세요. 4공연자들은 컨벤션 센터 남문 근처에 모여서 출발해 서쪽 메인 가를 향하다 시청을 지나 조플린 다리 쪽으로 향할 예정입니다. 축제 행사는 페리우드 공원에서 끝나는데 이곳에서 컨벤션 센터로 돌아가는 셔틀버스를 이용할 수 있습니다.

거기서 뵙겠습니다!

메리앤 존스
행사 코디네이터

어휘 perform 연주[공연]하다   no later than 늦어도 ~까지
head 향하다   past ~을 지나서

3 이즈무 씨는 누구이겠는가?
(A) 밴드 리더   (B) 버스 기사
(C) 컨벤션 센터 직원   (D) 퍼레이드 주최자

해설 추론
Ken Izumu라는 이름은 편지의 첫 부분에서 나오므로 편지를 받는 사람이다. 두 번째 문장에서 이즈무 씨의 행군 밴드가 퍼레이드에서 연주하도록 선정되었다(Your marching band has been selected to perform in the Kingsland summer parade)고 했다. 이를 통해 이즈무 씨는 밴드 리더임을 알 수 있으므로 (A)가 정답이다.

어휘 organizer 주최자

4 퍼레이드는 어디에서 시작되는가?
(A) 시청   (B) 조플린 다리 밑
(C) 페리우드 공원   (D) 컨벤션 센터

해설 세부 사항
중반부에서 공연자들은 컨벤션 센터 남문 근처에 모여서 출발한다(Performers will gather near the south gate of the convention center to start)고 했다. 따라서 퍼레이드는 컨벤션 센터에서 시작된다는 것을 알 수 있으므로 (D)가 정답이다.

[5-7] 이메일

수신: 장진희 〈jchang@bottlepress.co.uk〉
발신: 르마르 제이콥슨 〈ljacobson@balogcentre.jm〉
날짜: 9월 2일
제목: 제안
첨부: @ 센터 정보

장 선생님께,

7저는 자메이카 킹스턴에 있는 발로그 비즈니스 리더십 센터의 책임자입니다. 저는 저희 센터에서 매달 진행하는 초빙 연사 시리즈의 기획 또한 맡고 있습니다. 5최근 연구에 대해 저희 센터에서 발표를 하시는 데 관심이 있으신지 여쭤보려고 글을 씁니다. 올해 11월과 내년 3월, 4월에 가능한 날짜가 있습니다. 저희 측에서 기꺼이 항공료를 부담하며 강연료를 제공해 드리겠습니다. 또한 6저희 센터 내 게스트 하우스가 지난 6월에 완공되어 2박을 위한 숙소를 무료로 제공할 수 있습니다.

저희 센터와 발표 방침에 대한 정보를 첨부했습니다. 회신을 기다리겠습니다.

르마르 제이콥슨

어휘 deliver (강연 등을) 하다   latest 최근의   cover (비용을) 대다   airfare 항공료   on-site 현장의   accommodation 숙소

5 이메일의 목적은?
(A) 사과문을 발표하려고
(B) 추천을 요청하려고
(C) 초청을 하려고
(D) 예약을 확인하려고

해설 주제/목적
초반부에서 최근 연구에 대해 센터에서 발표를 하는 데 관심이 있는지 묻기 위해 글을 쓴다(I am writing to ask whether you might be interested in delivering a presentation at the centre about your latest research)고 했다. 이를 통해 제이콥슨 씨가 장 씨에게 센터에서 초빙 강사로서 발표해 줄 수 있는지 제안하려고 이메일을 보냈다는 것을 알 수 있으므로 정답은 (C)이다.

어휘 referral (인재 등의) 추천, 소개
extend an invitation 초청하다

6 이메일에 따르면, 6월에 있었던 일은?
(A) 항공 요금이 변경되었다.
(B) 행사가 취소되었다.
(C) 객실 요금이 인상되었다.
(D) 건물 건설이 완료되었다.

해설 세부 사항
첫 번째 단락 마지막 문장에서 게스트 하우스가 6월에 완공되었다(our on-site guest house was completed last June)고 했으므로 정답은 (D)이다.

어휘 rate 요금

Paraphrasing 지문의 guest house was completed
→ 보기의 Construction on a building ended

7 [1], [2], [3], [4]로 표시된 곳 중에서 다음 문장이 들어가기에 가장 적합한 위치는?
"저는 저희 센터에서 매달 진행하는 초빙 연사 시리즈의 기획 또한 맡고 있습니다."
(A) [1]   (B) [2]
(C) [3]   (D) [4]

해설 문장 삽입
[1] 앞 문장에서 제이콥슨 씨가 자신은 자메이카 킹스턴에 있는 발로그 비즈니스 리더십 센터의 책임자(I am the director of the Balog Centre for Business Leadership in Kingston, Jamaica)라고 자신을 소개하면서 직함을 밝히고 있다. 자신이 맡고 있는 업무 내용에 대한 추가 정보는 문맥상 그 뒤에 들어가는 것이 자연스러우므로 (A)가 정답이다.

[8-10] 이메일

수신: jayliu@onyxmail.com
발신: customerservice@hilindasupplies.com
9 날짜: 12월 22일
제목: 배송 알림

리우 씨께,

힐린다 용품에서 주문해 주셔서 감사합니다. 9 어제 귀하의 자동차 부품 온라인 주문을 받았습니다. 8 저희가 선호하는 배송 회사인 피트슨 포스트에서 1월 3일까지 제품을 배송할 예정입니다.

주문을 추적하시려면 www.pittsonpost.com을 방문하셔서 주문 번호 34513을 입력하십시오. 추적 정보는 2시간마다 사이트에서 업데이트됩니다. 10 배송물이 제때 도착하지 않는 경우 피트슨 포스트의 웹사이트 www.pittsonpost.com에서 챗봇 기능을 사용하여 문제를 신고해 주십시오.

고객 서비스
힐린다 용품

어휘 part 부품   track 추적하다   enter 입력하다
function 기능   report 신고하다, 보고하다

8 힐린다 용품에 대해 암시된 것은?
(A) 두 시간 이내에 주문을 처리한다.
(B) 이전에 리우 씨의 주문을 이행한 적이 있다.
(C) 피트슨 포스트의 시설 근처에 위치해 있다.
(D) 피트슨 포스트와 자주 거래하고 있다.

해설 **추론**
첫 단락 세 번째 문장에서 피트슨 포스트는 힐린다 용품에서 선호하는 배송 회사(Pittson Post, our preferred shipping company)라고 한 것으로 보아 힐린다 용품은 피트슨 포스트에 자주 배송을 맡긴다는 것을 짐작할 수 있으므로 정답은 (D)이다.

어휘 process 처리하다   fill 이행하다   facility 시설
regularly 자주, 정기적으로

9 리우 씨는 언제 주문을 했는가?
(A) 12월 21일   (B) 12월 22일
(C) 1월 3일   (D) 1월 4일

해설 **세부 사항**
이메일의 작성 날짜가 12월 22일(Date: December 22)이고 첫 단락 두 번째 문장에서 작성일 전날인 어제 리우 씨의 주문을 받았다(We received your auto parts online order yesterday)고 했으므로 정답은 (A)이다.

10 배송품이 제때 도착하지 않을 경우 리우 씨는 무엇을 하라고 요청받는가?
(A) 배송 서비스 업체에 연락하기
(B) 직접 매장 방문하기
(C) 힐린다 용품 부서에 전화하기
(D) 피트슨 포스트에서 보낸 이메일에 회신하기

해설 **세부 사항**
두 번째 단락 마지막 문장에서 배송물이 제때 도착하지 않는 경우 피트슨 포스트의 웹사이트에서 문제를 신고해 달라(If your package does not arrive on time, please use the chatbot function on Pittson Post's Web site, www.pittsonpost.com, to report the problem)고 했으므로 정답은 (A)이다.

어휘 in person 직접

Paraphrasing 지문의 use the chatbot function on Pittson Post's Web site → 보기의 Contact

[11-13] 이메일

수신: 페리스 호마이디 〈f.homaidi@harpco.com〉
발신: 마리 달만스 〈m.daalmans@mgmttax.com〉
날짜: 11월 10일
제목: 후속 연락

호마이디 씨께,

이번 주말 컨퍼런스에서 편안히 귀가하셨기를 바랍니다. 11 11월 18일 수요일 오후 2시 30분에 열리는 저희 회사의 무료 "연말 임금 대장 준비" 웨비나에 대해 상기시켜드리고자 후속 연락 드립니다. 저희 전문가들이 급여 규정 준수를 위한 연말 양식 처리법을 설명할 예정입니다. 연중 내내 회사의 재정을 적법하게 관리하는 방법에 관한 조언도 공유해 드립니다.

또한, 13 귀하께서 저희의 상업용 세금 준비 서비스에 대해 알아보는 데 관심이 있을 것 같다고 말씀하셨습니다. 12 저희는 귀사와 같은 소규모 기업이 이 절차를 잘 처리할 수 있도록 돕는 일에 자부심을 갖고 있습니다. 저희가 제공하는 것에 대해 더 자세히 말씀드리고 싶습니다. 13 이번 주 목요일 오후, 금요일 오전 또는 다음 주 초 중 통화가 가능할까요?

귀하의 회신을 기다리겠습니다.

마리 달만스
MGMT 세금 컨설팅 그룹

어휘 journey (장거리) 이동, 여행   reminder 상기시키는 글   complimentary 무료의   payroll 임금 대장, 급여
form 양식   compliance (규정) 준수   in order 적법한
commercial 상업용의   tax 세금   preparation 준비
take pride in ~에 자부심이 있다   navigate 처리하다
process 절차

11 달만스 씨는 호마이디 씨에게 무엇을 상기시키는가?
(A) 무료 온라인 프레젠테이션
(B) 구직 면접 요청
(C) 이전에 일정을 잡은 회의
(D) 서명해야 할 서류 꾸러미

해설 **세부 사항**
첫 단락의 두 번째 문장에서 달만스 씨는 호마이디 씨에게 자신의 회사에서 제공하는 무료 "연말 임금 대장 준비" 웨비나에 대해 상기시켜주고자 후속 연락한다(I wanted to follow up with a reminder about my firm's complimentary "Preparing for Year-End Payroll" webinar taking place on Wednesday, November 18, at 2:30 P.M.)고 했으므로 정답은 (A)이다.

191

어휘 virtual 가상의　previously 이전에　packet 꾸러미

12 호마이디 씨에 대해 명시된 것은?
(A) 전문 세무 대리인이다.
(B) 소규모 업체를 운영한다.
(C) 자주 출장을 다닌다.
(D) 최근 컨퍼런스에서 연사였다.

해설　**Not / True**
두 번째 단락의 두 번째 문장에서 호마이디 씨의 업체를 소규모 기업(We take pride in helping small businesses like yours navigate the process)이라고 언급하고 있으므로 (B)가 정답이다.

어휘　tax preparer 세무 대리인　frequently 자주

13 [1], [2], [3], [4]로 표시된 곳 중에서 다음 문장이 들어가기에 가장 적합한 위치는?
"저희가 제공하는 것에 대해 더 자세히 말씀드리고 싶습니다."
(A) [1]　　　　　　(B) [2]
(C) [3]　　　　　　**(D) [4]**

해설　**문장 삽입**
두 번째 단락 첫 문장에서 호마이디 씨가 회사의 상업용 세금 준비 서비스에 관심을 보였음(you mentioned that you might be interested in learning about our commercial tax-preparation services)을 상기시키고 있고, [4]번 뒤 문장에서는 호마이디 씨에게 통화가 가능한 시간대를 묻고(Are you available for a call ~ ?) 있다. 따라서 회사의 서비스 내용에 대해 더 상세히 안내하고 싶다는 제안은 그 사이에 들어가는 것이 자연스러우므로 (D)가 정답이다.

[14-17] 편지

4월 3일
크리스틴 천
뉴포트 로 304번지
샐리어스빌, 켄터키 41465

천 씨께,

저희 브라이트스타 2200 스트리밍 장치를 구매해 주셔서 감사합니다. 저희 지원 기술자와 대화하신 내용에 따른 후속 조치를 위해 편지를 씁니다. **14**장치를 설치하는 데 어려움이 있으신 점 죄송합니다. 지원팀에서 문제의 원인을 파악하고 다음의 지침을 제공했습니다.

먼저, 브라이트스타 2200과 텔레비전의 전원을 끄고 플러그를 뽑아 주세요. **15**이 봉투 안에 새 HDMI 선이 들어 있습니다. 이것을 사용해서 브라이트스타 2200을 텔레비전에 연결해 주세요.

다음으로, 브라이트스타 2200의 전원을 켜고 시작될 때까지 기다려 주세요. **16**시작 과정이 완료될 때까지 텔레비전을 끈 상태로 유지해 주세요. 작은 불빛이 깜빡임을 멈추면 장치가 재부팅되었다는 것을 알 수 있습니다. 이 작업은 몇 초 정도 걸립니다.

16텔레비전의 전원을 켜 주세요. 이제 텔레비전과 브라이트스타 2200이 연결되어 있을 겁니다. 텔레비전이 브라이트스타 2200을 인식하면 설정 메뉴로 들어가서 인터넷 연결을 설정해 주세요.

추가 도움이 필요하시면 606-555-0130으로 전화해 주세요. **17**추가적인 문제에 대해 신속하게 해결해 드릴 것을 약속드립니다.

카렌 응, 고객 서비스 담당자
브라이트스타 스트리밍

어휘　purchase 구매하다　streaming 스트리밍, 실시간 재생　device 장치　follow up 후속 조치를 하다　support 지원　set up 설치[설정]하다　determine 파악하다　cause 원인　instructions 지침　unplug 플러그를 뽑다　cable 전선　process 과정　complete 완료하다　reboot 재부팅하다　blink 깜박이다　link 연결하다　recognize 인식하다　address 해결하다　further 추가적인　promptly 신속하게

14 편지의 목적은 무엇인가?
(A) 새로운 유형의 제품을 소개하려고
(B) 제품을 반품하는 방법을 설명하려고
(C) 잠재적인 문제에 대해 경고하려고
(D) 문제를 해결하는 방법을 설명하려고

해설　**주제 / 목적**
첫 단락에서 장치 설치에 어려움을 겪고 있는 점에 대해 사과(We are sorry that you are having trouble setting up the device)하며 지원팀에서 문제 원인을 파악하여 지침을 제공했다(The support team has determined the cause of the problem and provided the following instructions)고 했다. 따라서 문제를 해결하는 방법을 설명하려고 편지를 썼다는 것을 알 수 있으므로 정답은 (D)이다.

어휘　introduce 소개하다　explain 설명하다　return 반품하다　warn 경고하다　potential 잠재적인　fix 해결하다, 고치다

Paraphrasing　지문의 provided the following instructions → 보기의 explain

15 편지와 함께 온 것은 무엇인가?
(A) 새로운 전원 코드
(B) 새로운 HDMI 선
(C) 새로운 스트리밍 장치
(D) 새로운 텔레비전 리모컨

해설　**세부 사항**
두 번째 단락 두 번째 문장에서 봉투 안에 새 HDMI 선이 들어 있다(In this envelope is a new HDMI cable)고 했으므로 정답은 (B)이다.

어휘　remote control 리모컨

16 지침에 따르면, 천 씨는 언제 텔레비전을 켜야 하는가?
(A) 브라이트스타 2200을 켜자마자
(B) 인터넷 연결을 설정한 후
(C) 브라이트스타 2200을 텔레비전에 연결하기 전에
(D) 브라이트스타 2200의 작은 불빛이 깜박이는 것을 멈춘 후

해설　**세부 사항**
지문 중반에서 TV를 끈 상태로 유지하다가 작은 불빛이 깜박임을 멈추면 장치가 재부팅된 것(Leave your

television turned off until the start-up process is completed. You will know the device has rebooted when the small light stops blinking)이고 그 뒤 TV의 전원을 켜라(Turn on your television)고 설명하고 있다. 따라서 정답은 (D)이다.

17 다섯 번째 단락 1행의 "address"와 의미상 가장 가까운 단어는?
(A) 인사하다
(B) 겨냥하다
(C) 처리하다
(D) 이야기하다

해설 **동의어**
address는 문맥상 '해결하다, 다루다'라는 의미로 쓰인 것이므로 (C)가 정답이다.

UNIT 20 회람 / 공지 / 광고 / 기사

ETS 기출 예제
본책 p.282

공지

맨테로 시 주민 센터
하계 요리 강좌

맨테로 시 주민 센터에서는 이번 여름에 다음과 같이 요리 강좌를 열 것입니다:

강좌	날짜	시간	비용
수프와 애피타이저	7월 9일	오후 4시 - 오후 6시	20달러
가금류와 육류 요리	7월 11일	오후 1시 - 오후 3시	30달러
간단한 파스타 요리	7월 13일	오전 9시 - 오전 11시	25달러

강좌는 맨테로 시 스프링데일 대로 3535번지에 위치한 맨테로 시 주민 센터에서 열립니다. 등록은 7월 1일에 시작됩니다. 자리를 예약하시려면 **D행정실을 방문해 주십시오.** 다른 방법으로는, **C로자 모랄레즈 씨에게 928-555-0198번으로 귀하의 정보를 팩스로 보내시거나 A rmorales@manterocc.net으로 이메일을 보내실 수 있습니다.** 성함, 수강하고자 하는 강좌명과 전화번호를 꼭 기재해 주십시오.

Q 독자들에게 응답 방법으로 제시하지 않은 것은 무엇인가?
(A) 이메일
(B) 전화
(C) 팩스
(D) 직접 방문

ETS 유형 연습
본책 p.283

1 (B)　2 (A)

[1] **광고**

젠텔 프리미엄 후크
모든 스포츠용품 매장에서 구매 가능합니다

- 최고급 금속
- 첨단 기술
- 다용도와 신뢰도
- 다양한 크기와 스타일

배스 후크, 서클 후크, 더블 후크, 플라이 후크, 지그 후크 등등!
"젠텔 프리미엄 후크는 세계 최고입니다!" – 〈베터 태클 매거진〉
"낚시 장비 성능 부문 최고 등급" – 〈스포츠 타이머 가제트〉

Q 광고되고 있는 것은 무엇인가?
(A) 캠핑 장비 가게
(B) 낚시 장비의 한 종류

해설 **주제/목적**
광고 전체에 걸쳐 hook(낚시 바늘)가 언급되고 있고, 마지막 문장에서 〈스포츠 타이머 가제트〉 잡지로부터 낚시 장비 성능 부문 최고 등급 평가를 받았다(Top ratings in our fishing-gear performance category)고 했으므로 낚시 장비 브랜드를 광고하고 있다는 것을 알 수 있다. 따라서 (B)가 정답이다.

Paraphrasing 지문의 fishing-gear → 보기의 fishing equipment

[2] **회람**

발신: 하은미, 최고경영자
수신: 전 직원
제목: 1월 10일 회의
날짜: 1월 13일

에너지 비용 절감 계획의 일환으로 대부분 직원들의 정규 근무 시간을 변경할 예정입니다. 대체로 연료비가 늦은 오후에 높기 때문에 오전에 더 많이 근무하는 것이 우리에게 유리할 것입니다. 따라서, 2월 24일 월요일부터 근무 시간은 공식적으로 오전 9시가 아니라 오전 8시에 시작할 것이며, 오후 5시가 아니라 오후 4시에 끝날 것입니다. 기존 일정은 2월 21일 금요일이 마지막이 될 것입니다.

Q 직원들은 무엇을 하도록 요청 받는가?
(A) 정규 근무 스케줄을 조정할 것
(B) 에너지 효율이 좋은 전구로 교체할 것

해설 **세부 사항**
첫 번째 문장에서 에너지 비용 절감 계획의 일환으로 직원들의 정규 근무 시간을 변경할 예정(We will be changing the regular work hours for most employees as part of our initiative to reduce energy costs)이라고 하였으며, 이어지는 글에서 변경된 근무 시간을 구체적으로 언급하고 있으므로 (A)가 정답이다.

Paraphrasing 지문의 changing the regular work hours → 보기의 Adjust their typical work schedules

ETS 실전 문제

본책 p.284

1 (D) 2 (C) 3 (D) 4 (D) 5 (C) 6 (A)
7 (D) 8 (C) 9 (A) 10 (D) 11 (D) 12 (A)
13 (C) 14 (B) 15 (D) 16 (C) 17 (A)

[1-2] 광고

디나스
www.deenas.com

40년이 넘는 기간 동안 **1** 디나스는 의상과 화려한 장식품부터 대여 테이블 및 의자에 이르기까지 명절 모임, 생일 축하 행사 또는 기타 사교 행사에 필요한 모든 품목을 구매할 수 있는 이 지역의 단골 가게였습니다.

대규모 행사의 경우, 지금 10% 할인가에 저희의 특별 제품을 확인하세요.

클래식 종이 입장권 100, 300, 500롤

- 다양한 글꼴, 색상, 크기, 스타일로 구매가 가능합니다.
- **2** 입장권 소지자가 고객님의 브랜드를 기억할 수 있도록 회사 또는 후원사 로고를 추가하세요—이 특별 주문은 신속히 처리해 드립니다!

어휘 go-to destination 단골 가게(식당, 호텔 등) gathering 모임 celebration 축하 행사 occasion 행사 costume 의상 decoration 장식품 featured 특색으로 한 admission 입장 sponsor 후원사 turnaround 작업을 완료해서 회송하는 데 걸리는 시간

1 디나스는 어떤 업체인가?
(A) 행사 기획 대행사
(B) 유니폼 제조업체
(C) 음식 공급 회사
(D) 파티용품점

해설 추론
첫 단락에서 각종 행사에 필요한 모든 품목을 구매할 수 있는 이 지역의 단골 가게(Deena's has been the area's go-to destination for every item you might need for a holiday gathering, a birthday celebration, or any other social occasion ~)라고 소개하고 있으므로 디나스는 파티용품을 판매하는 가게라는 것을 알 수 있다. 따라서 정답은 (D)이다.

어휘 agency 대행사 manufacturer 제조업체 catering 음식 공급 supply 용품

Paraphrasing 지문의 a holiday gathering, a birthday celebration, or any other social occasion → 보기의 party

2 광고에서 특별 제품에 대해 명시하는 것은?
(A) 곧 품절될 것이다.
(B) 무료 배송이 가능하다.
(C) 주문 제작할 수 있다.
(D) 최근에 새로 디자인되었다.

해설 Not / True
마지막 문장에서 특별 주문에 회사 또는 후원사 로고를 추가할 수 있다(Add your company or sponsor logo so that ticket holders remember your brand)고 언급하고 있으므로 (C)가 정답이다.

어휘 out of stock 품절인 eligible ~할 수 있는, 자격이 있는 customize 주문 제작하다

Paraphrasing 지문의 Add your company or sponsor logo → 보기의 customized

[3-5] 회람

3 수신: 전 직원
발신: 스튜어트 웬트워스, 운영 부사장
날짜: **4** 1월 26일 월요일
제목: 겨울 폭풍

3,4 눈보라가 임박한 관계로, 젤만 건축은 내일 문을 닫습니다. 카운티 교통부는 긴급하지 않은 모든 차량은 도로에 나오지 말도록 요청했습니다.

4 직원들은 정규 업무 시간에 집에서 업무를 수행하고, 이메일로 부서장과 계속 연락을 취해야 합니다. 관리자들은 모든 월말 마감일이 그대로 유효하다는 점에 유의하십시오.

눈보라는 수요일 오전 일찍 그치리라 예상됩니다. **5** 제설 작업반에게 주차장을 치울 충분한 시간을 주기 위해, 직원들은 수요일 오전 10시 30분 이후에 도착하십시오. 평소에 하는 수요일 오전 직원회의는 당일 더 늦은 시간으로 옮길 예정입니다.

협조해 주셔서 감사합니다.

어휘 impending 임박한 nonemergency 긴급하지 않은 vehicle 차량 be expected to ~해야 한다, ~하리라 예상되다 assignment 업무, 과제 in effect 유효한 snowplow 제설기, 제설차 no earlier than ~ 이후에

3 회람의 목적은 무엇인가?
(A) 새로운 규정을 설명하려고
(B) 직원에게 새로운 마감일을 상기시키려고
(C) 직원에게 연장근무를 요청하려고
(D) 직원에게 사무실 폐쇄를 통지하려고

해설 주제 / 목적
To: All staff를 통해 모든 직원들에게 보내는 회람임을 알 수 있고, 첫 번째 단락에서 젤만 건축이 내일 문을 닫을 것(Because of the impending snowstorm, Zelman Architects will be closed tomorrow)이라고 했으므로 (D)가 정답이다.

어휘 extended 연장된 notify 통지하다

4 관리자들은 1월 27일 화요일에 무엇을 해야 하는가?
(A) 오후에 직원회의 참석
(B) 평소보다 늦게 출근
(C) 수정된 일정에 대해 웬트워스 씨에게 연락
(D) 직원과 이메일 소통 유지

해설 **추론**

공지의 날짜가 1월 26일(January 26)이며 이날을 기준으로 하루 뒤에 업체는 문을 닫는다고 했다. 두 번째 단락에서 직원들은 정규 업무 시간에 집에서 업무를 수행하고, 이메일로 부서장과 계속 연락을 취해야 한다(Employees are expected to work on assignments at home during regular business hours and to stay in touch with their department managers by e-mail)고 했다. 이를 통해 1월 27일 화요일에 부서장들은 직원들과 이메일로 연락을 취해야 한다는 것을 알 수 있으므로 (D)가 정답이다.

어휘 revised 수정된

Paraphrasing 지문의 stay in touch with their department managers by e-mail → 보기의 Maintain e-mail communication with staff

5 젤만 건축에 대해 암시된 것은 무엇인가?
(A) 교통부와 계약을 맺고 있다.
(B) 여러 곳에 사무소가 있다.
(C) 차로 통근하는 사람을 많이 고용하고 있다.
(D) 특별한 회사 행사를 연기해야 했다.

해설 **추론**

세 번째 단락에서 제설 작업반이 주차장을 치울 시간을 주기 위해 젤만 건축의 직원들은 수요일 오전 10시 30분 이후에 출근해 달라(To give the snowplow crews enough time to clear the parking areas, employees are asked to arrive no earlier than 10:30 A.M. on Wednesday)고 했다. 이를 통해 차로 통근하는 직원이 많다는 것을 알 수 있으므로 (C)가 정답이다.

어휘 commute 통근하다

[6-7] 구인 광고

> 7록 리먼은 성장하는 사업을 위해 파트타임으로 일하며 그래픽을 개발할 창의적인 인재를 모집합니다. 6지원자는 광고, 메뉴, 식탁용 매트, 간판을 디자인한 경험이 있어야 합니다. 이력서, 작업 샘플, 그리고 기술 및 경험 요약 또는 웹사이트 링크를 질 시먼스에게 j.seamans@lochleman.co.uk로 이메일을 보내주세요.

어휘 creative 창의적인 individual 개인 develop 개발하다 applicant 지원자 advertisement 광고 place mat 식탁용 매트 CV 이력서 summary 요약

6 록 리먼은 어느 업계에서 운영되고 있는 것 같은가?
(A) 음식 서비스   (B) 인테리어 디자인
(C) 컴퓨터 프로그래밍   (D) 식당 건설

해설 **추론**

두 번째 문장에서 지원자는 광고, 메뉴, 식탁용 매트, 간판을 디자인한 경험이 있어야 한다(Applicants must have experience designing advertisements, menus, place mats, and signs)고 했다. 메뉴와 식탁용 매트를 디자인하는 업무가 있는 것으로 보아 록 리먼은 음식 관련 업계에 있다는 것을 짐작할 수 있으므로 정답은 (A)이다.

어휘 operate 운영하다

7 이 일자리에 적합한 후보자는 누구일 것 같은가?
(A) 은행 임원   (B) 비즈니스 분석가
(C) 조경 디자이너   (D) 그래픽 디자이너

해설 **추론**

첫 문장에서 그래픽을 개발할 창의적인 인재를 모집한다(Loch Leman seeks a creative individual to work part-time developing graphics for our growing business)고 했으므로 정답은 (D)이다.

어휘 candidate 후보자 executive 임원 analyst 분석가 landscape 조경

Paraphrasing 지문의 a creative individual to work part-time developing graphics → 보기의 A graphic designer

[8-10] 공지

> 8마이어 아몬드 가루를 구매해 주셔서 감사합니다!
>
> 맛있게 빻은 아몬드로 만든 마이어 아몬드 제품을 구입하신 것을 축하드립니다. 9마이어 아몬드 가루는 아몬드 껍질을 그대로 사용해 만든 경쟁사들의 거친 아몬드 가루 제품과는 다릅니다. 저희 아몬드는 물에 짧은 시간 동안 끓여 질긴 껍질을 제거한 다음, 잘게 빻고 체에 걸러 베이킹에 이상적인 밝은 색의 맛있는 가루로 만들어집니다. 저희 아몬드 가루는 또한 항산화제, 단백질, 섬유질이 풍부해 건강에 좋습니다. 10마이어 가문은 대를 이어 수십 년간 고품질 아몬드 제품을 만들기 위해 헌신해 왔습니다. 이 특별한 제품이 마음에 드시기를 바랍니다. 문의사항이나 의견이 있으시면 www.meyeralmond.com을 방문하세요.

어휘 flour (곡물의) 가루 grind (곡식 등을) 갈다, 빻다 competitor 경쟁사 coarse 거친 almond meal 표백한 아몬드의 굵은 가루 intact 그대로인 briefly 잠시 sift 체로 거르다 antioxidant 항산화제 fiber 섬유질 generation 세대 committed 헌신적인 decade 10년

8 공지는 어디에서 찾을 수 있을 것 같은가?
(A) 공장의 문   (B) 배송 차량
(C) 포장물의 측면   (D) 사무실 게시판

해설 **추론**

제목에서 마이어 아몬드 가루를 구매해 주셔서 감사하다(Thank you for your purchase of Meyer Almond Flour!)고 하는 것을 보아 공지는 마이어 아몬드 가루 제품의 포장물에 있다는 것을 짐작할 수 있으므로 정답은 (C)이다.

어휘 vehicle 차량 bulletin board 게시판

9 마이어 아몬드 제품에 대해 명시된 것은?
(A) 아몬드 껍질이 들어 있지 않다.
(B) 질감이 무겁고 거칠다.
(C) 긴 요리 시간이 필요하다.
(D) 환불 보증이 제공된다.

해설 **Not / True**
두 번째 문장에서 마이어 아몬드 가루는 아몬드 껍질을 그대로 사용해 만든 경쟁사들의 거친 아몬드 가루 제품과는 다르다(Meyer Almond Flour is different from our competitors' coarse almond-meal products that are made with almond skins intact)고 한 뒤 껍질을 제거하는 방법을 설명했으므로 정답은 (A)이다.

어휘 contain ~이 들어 있다 texture 질감
money-back 환불 guarantee 보증, 보장

10 마이어 아몬드 회사에 대해 암시된 것은?
(A) 제품을 수제로 만든다.
(B) 제품에 방부제를 첨가한다.
(C) 수년간 운영되어 왔다.
(D) 최근에 더 큰 시설로 이전했다.

해설 **추론**
후반부에서 마이어 가문은 대를 이어 수십 년간 고품질 아몬드 제품을 만들기 위해 헌신해 왔다(Generations of the Meyer family have been committed to creating high-quality almond products for decades)고 했으므로 정답은 (C)이다.

어휘 preservative 방부제 operate 운영되다
relocate 이전하다 facility 시설

Paraphrasing 지문의 for decades → 보기의 for many years

[11-13] 회람

수신: 전 직원
발신: 닐 할데란, CEO, 할데란 파이낸셜 사
날짜: 1월 25일
제목: 구직

많이들 아시겠지만, **11,12**당사는 최근 할데란 파이낸셜 사의 신임 부사장을 찾는 것을 면밀히 진행했습니다. 치에코 사카이 씨가 그 자리에 임명되었다는 것을 알리게 되어 기쁩니다.

사카이 씨는 지난 5년간 BRI 투자 그룹의 전무로 재직했습니다. 그 전에는 2년간 웰튼 보험 주식회사에서 영업직 일반사원으로 근무한 후 간부직에 올랐고 3년 동안 같은 회사에서 영업직 간부로 근무했습니다. 그녀는 노스몬트 대학교에서 경영학 이학사와 경영학 석사 학위를 받았습니다.

13할데란 파이낸셜로 오신 사카이 씨를 환영하기 위해 2월 4일 금요일 오후 5시에서 7시 사이에 브로드 가에 있는 라운드 하우스 레스토랑에서 환영회를 열 예정입니다. 모든 직원의 참석을 환영합니다. 사카이 씨는 오늘 새로운 직책을 맡았습니다.

어휘 recently 최근에 thorough 면밀한, 꼼꼼한 appoint 임명하다 attain 얻다, 이루다 bachelor of science 이학사 degree 학위 master 석사 business administration 경영학 assume 맡다

11 회람을 보낸 이유는 무엇인가?
(A) 마케팅 계획을 설명하려고
(B) 구인 공고를 하려고
(C) 직원 오리엔테이션을 준비하려고
(D) 새 직원을 소개하려고

해설 **주제/목적**
첫 번째 단락에서 할데란 파이낸셜 사의 신임 부사장을 찾는 것을 면밀히 진행했다(we have recently conducted a thorough search for a new vice president of Halderan Financial, Inc.)면서 치에코 사카이 씨가 그 자리에 임명되었다(We are pleased to announce that Ms. Chieko Sakai has been appointed to the position)고 했다. 이후 사카이 씨에 대한 소개가 이어지고 있으므로 (D)가 정답이다.

12 사카이 씨의 현재 직함은 무엇인가?
(A) 부사장   (B) 전무
(C) 영업직 간부   (D) 영업직 일반사원

해설 **세부 사항**
첫 번째 단락에서 치에코 사카이 씨가 신임 부사장으로 임명되었다(we have recently conducted a thorough search for a new vice president of Halderan Financial, Inc. We are pleased to announce that Ms. Chieko Sakai has been appointed to the position)고 했다. 따라서 치에코 사카이 씨는 현재 할데란 파이낸셜 사의 부사장이라는 것을 알 수 있으므로 (A)가 정답이다.

13 2월 4일에 무슨 일이 있겠는가?
(A) 취업 면접을 실시한다.   (B) 대학 강좌가 시작된다.
(C) 모임을 갖는다.   (D) 기업이 매각된다.

해설 **세부 사항**
마지막 단락에서 사카이 씨의 환영회를 2월 4일에 열 예정(To welcome Ms. Sakai to Halderan Financial, we will be holding a reception at the Round House Restaurant on Broad Street between 5 and 7 P.M. on Friday, February 4)이라고 했으므로 (C)가 정답이다.

Paraphrasing 지문의 we will be holding a reception → 보기의 A gathering will be held.

[14-17] 기사

공원 관리부, 계획안 공개 평가 요청

미드론 (7월 12일)—우리 지역 공원 관리부에서 이번 주에 미드론 공원의 서쪽 구역 재설계를 위한 계획 초안을 발표했다. **14** 서쪽 구역의 개선 필요성은 공원 동쪽 구역에 있는 미드론 문화 센터의 최근 확장에 따른 것이다. **17** 문화 센터 주변에는 석재 보도와 피크닉 테이블이 있는 야외 모임 공간이 조성되었다. 또한 이곳에는 이제 야외 극장도 있다. **14**공원의 개발 구역과 자연 구역 사이의 균형을

유지하기 위해 공원 관리부는 서쪽을 대부분 녹지로 유지하기를 원한다.

이달 초 열린 일련의 공개 회의에서 공원 관리부의 직원들은 공원 서쪽을 개선하기 위한 가능한 방안들을 제시했다. 경치 좋은 습지 위에 산책로를 건설하자는 계획은 회의 참석자들로부터 호응을 얻었다. **15몇몇 미드론 주민들은 지역 구성원들이 기념 행사를 위해 예약할 수 있는 옥외 별관을 지을 것을 제안했다.** 하지만 이 아이디어는 공원 관리부에 의해 채택되지 않았다. 소프트볼이나 축구장을 개발하자는 제안들도 마찬가지로 고려되지 않았다.

공원 관리부는 계획들을 추려 현재 웹사이트에서 지역 주민들에게 온라인 피드백을 요청하고 있다. **16주민들은 공원 관리부가 당일 저녁에 열릴 사업 회의 전에 검토할 수 있도록 8월 17일 정오까지 계획을 검토하고 의견을 제출하도록 요청된다.**

어휘 release 발표하다 draft 초안 expansion 확장 gathering 모임 perimeter 주변 balance 균형 representative 직원, 대표 potential 가능성이 있는 enhance 개선하다 scenic 경치가 좋은 wetland 습지 favorable 호의적인 attendee 참석자 pavilion 별관 reserve 예약하다 celebratory 기념하는 likewise 마찬가지로 discount 고려에 넣지 않다 narrow down 줄이다, 좁히다 solicit 요청하다

14 공원 관리부는 왜 미드론 공원의 한 구역에 대한 제안들을 고려 중인가?
(A) 지역 스포츠 팀의 요구를 충족시키려고
(B) 녹지 보존을 도우려고
(C) 문화 센터의 인기를 높이려고
(D) 시의 구역 설정 규정을 준수하려고

해설 세부 사항

첫 단락의 두 번째 문장에서 미드론 문화 센터의 확장에 따른 서쪽 구역의 개선 필요성(The need to improve the west section follows the recent expansion of the Midlawn Culture Center in the east section of the park)을 언급했고 같은 단락 마지막 문장에서 공원 관리부는 개발 구역과 자연 구역 사이의 균형 유지를 위해 서쪽을 대부분 녹지로 유지하기를 원한다(the parks department wants to keep the west side mostly green)고 했으므로 정답은 (B)이다.

어휘 preserve 보존하다 popularity 인기 municipal 시의 zoning 구역제 regulation 규정

Paraphrasing 지문의 keep the west side mostly green → 보기의 preserve green space

15 공원 서쪽 구역 개선에 대해 일부 지역 구성원들이 제안한 것은?
(A) 방문객 교육을 위한 자연 센터
(B) 자전거 도로
(C) 확장된 주차 공간
(D) 야외 행사 개최를 위한 구조물

해설 세부 사항

두 번째 단락 세 번째 문장에서 일부 미드론 주민들이 기념 행사를 위해 예약할 수 있는 옥외 별관을 지을 것을 제안했다 (Several Midlawn residents suggested building an open-air pavilion that community members could reserve for celebratory events)고 했으므로 (D)가 정답이다.

어휘 path 길 enlarged 확장된 structure 구조물

Paraphrasing 지문의 open-air pavilion → 보기의 structure for holding outdoor events

16 8월 17일에 무엇이 일어날 예정인가?
(A) 공원 관리자들이 기자 회견에 참석할 것이다.
(B) 보수 공사 작업이 시작될 것이다.
(C) 제안에 대한 피드백이 논의될 것이다.
(D) 설문 조사 결과가 온라인으로 발표될 것이다.

해설 세부 사항

마지막 문장에서 주민들은 공원 관리부가 당일 저녁에 열릴 사업 회의 전에 검토할 수 있도록 8월 17일 정오까지 계획을 검토하고 의견을 제출하도록 요청된다(Residents are asked to review the plans and submit comments no later than noon on August 17 so that the parks department can review them before its business meeting later that evening)고 했으므로 정답은 (C)이다.

어휘 official 관리자 renovation 보수

17 [1], [2], [3], [4]로 표시된 곳 중에서 다음 문장이 들어가기에 가장 적합한 위치는?
"또한 이곳에는 이제 야외 극장도 있다."
(A) [1]   (B) [2]
(C) [3]   (D) [4]

해설 문장 삽입

[1]번 앞 문장에서 문화 센터 주변에 조성된 공간들에 대해 나열(Outdoor gathering spaces with stone walkways and picnic tables were created around the perimeter of the culture center)하고 있으므로, 이곳에 조성된 공간을 추가로 언급하고 있는 문장이 그 뒤에 들어가는 것이 흐름상 자연스러우므로 (A)가 정답이다.

어휘 open-air 야외의

UNIT 21 기타 양식

ETS 기출 예제
본책 p.290

문자 메시지

폴라 말론 [오전 8시 53분]
부탁 좀 들어 주실래요? 제가 9시에 체육관에서 체육 수업이 있는데 늦을 거 같아요. 제가 탄 기차에 기계적 결함이 있어서 예정보다 15분 늦게 출발했거든요.

마틴 빌렉 [오전 8시 54분]
이런. 어떻게 도와 드릴까요?

폴라 말론 [오전 8시 55분]
수업을 취소하거나 학생들에게 제가 9시 15분쯤에 도착할 거라고 알려 주시겠어요?

마틴 빌렉 [오전 8시 57분]
학생들 대부분이 벌써 와 있어서 취소하기는 좀 그러네요. 수키도 오늘 근무라서 일찍 나와 있어요. 제가 수키에게 수업을 바꿔 달라고 부탁하면 말론 씨가 10시 수업을 할 수 있을 거예요.

폴라 말론 [오전 8시 58분]
그럼 정말 좋죠. 고마워요.

Q 오전 8시 58분에 말론 씨가 "그럼 정말 좋죠"라고 쓴 의도는?
(A) 빌렉 씨의 아이디어가 마음에 든다.
(B) 아침 운동을 좋아한다.
(C) 새 직장에 대해 흥분된다.
(D) 비번이라서 기분이 좋다.

ETS 유형 연습 본책 p.291

1 (B) **2** (B)

[1] 간판

보스코 앤 선즈
고품질 지붕 및 외벽 마감
증축 및 수리
업체와 주택을 대상으로 서비스를 제공합니다.
www.boskoandsons.com
완전 보험 적용 • 무료 견적 • 라이선스 KE404

Q 보스코 앤 선즈는 어떤 종류의 업체인가?
(A) 소규모 기업 컨설팅 회사 (B) 건설 회사

해설 추론
지문 전반에 걸쳐 지붕과 외벽 마감(Quality roofing and siding), 증축 및 수리(Additions and repairs) 등의 건설 관련 서비스를 제공한다고 언급하고 있으므로 (B)가 정답이다.

[2] 양식

아멜리아 이모네의 케이크
가정식 케이크, 타르트 등등!

구매해 주셔서 감사합니다. 저희는 고객의 의견을 소중히 생각합니다. 잠시 시간을 내서 동봉된 설문지를 작성하신 후 저희가 제공해 드린, 주소가 명기된 반송용 봉투에 넣어 보내 주시기 바랍니다. 답례로 고객님께 다음 구매 시 20퍼센트 가격 할인을 받을 수 있는 쿠폰을 보내 드리겠습니다.

5를 '훌륭하다', 1을 '형편없다'라고 판단하여 다음 항목들을 1~5등급으로 평가해 주십시오.

맛	1	2	3	4	⑤
식감	1	2	3	4	⑤
장식(해당되는 경우)	①	2	3	4	5
전체 모양	①	2	3	4	5

Q 고객들은 무슨 요청을 받고 있는가?
(A) 케이크 수령
(B) 서식을 우편으로 발송

해설 세부 사항
세 번째 문장에서 잠시 시간을 내서 설문지를 작성한 후 주소가 명기된 반송용 봉투에 넣어 보내 달라(Please take the time to fill out the enclosed survey and return it in the addressed, postage-paid envelope we have provided)고 하므로 (B)가 정답이다.

ETS 실전 문제 본책 p.292

1 (D) **2** (C) **3** (C) **4** (A) **5** (B) **6** (C)
7 (C) **8** (D) **9** (A) **10** (B) **11** (C) **12** (C)
13 (A) **14** (C) **15** (B) **16** (D)

[1-2] 영수증

콩그라니 커피
매장 #10380, 워터포드 키 7번지, 피피티아 웰링턴
04-555-0128

영수증 번호: 9374
날짜: 6월 10일

품목	수량	총계($)
치아바타 롤	2	9.98
²아이스 라즈베리 모카	1	3.45
찻잎 상자	1	12.95
기프트 카드	1	20.00
할인:	²보상 음료	-3.45
합계:		42.93

보상 번호: 1028-493-02
¹결제 형태: 신용카드 XXXXXXXXXXXX0192
카드 소지자 이름: 에밀리아 오캄포

어휘 receipt 영수증 reward 보상 beverage 음료

1 영수증에 명시된 것은?
(A) 치아바타 롤 1개는 9.98달러이다.
(B) 기프트 카드 2장이 구매되었다.
(C) 콩그라니 커피는 6월 10일에 문을 닫았다.
(D) 결제는 신용카드로 이루어졌다.

해설 Not / True
후반부의 결제 형태(Payment type: Credit Card XXXXXXXXXXXX0192)를 통해 신용카드를 이용해 결제했다는 것을 확인할 수 있으므로 정답은 (D)이다.

2 어떤 보상이 제공되었는가?
(A) 차 한 상자 (B) 무료 기프트 카드
(C) 무료 음료 (D) 향후 구매 시 할인

해설 **세부 사항**
중반부의 Iced raspberry mocha 3.45($)와 Discounts: Reward beverage -3.45를 통해 3.45달러짜리 아이스 라즈베리 모카를 보상으로 무료 제공받았다는 것을 알 수 있으므로 정답은 (C)이다.

어휘 complimentary 무료의

> **Paraphrasing** 지문의 Reward beverage
> → 보기의 complimentary drink

[3-4] 양식

```
http://www.rosnayassoc.com/facilities/workorder
```

로즈네 앤 어소시에이츠
시설부
내부 작업 주문 요청서

날짜:	2월 5일
요청한 사람:	나렌드라 시타라만
제목:	인사부장
이메일/전화:	sitharamann@rosnayassoc.com / 785-555-0131

설명:
³2월 17일 월요일, 유키 후지모토와 아서 탕이 회계부에 합류합니다. ⁴그들의 사무실인 510호와 514호에 표준 품목 컴퓨터와 전화가 설치되어야 합니다. 514호에는 탁상용 프린터와 스캐너도 비치해야 합니다. 구매품과 인건비는 5876-02 계정으로 청구하세요.

요청 완료일: 2월 13일

[제출]

어휘 description 설명 install 설치하다 latter 후자의 furnish 비치하다 purchase 구매(품) labor 일, 노동

3 로즈네 앤 어소시에이츠는 최근에 무엇을 했겠는가?
(A) 회계법인과 합병했다.
(B) 컴퓨터 시스템을 업그레이드했다.
(C) 직원을 추가로 채용했다.
(D) 구매 절차를 바꿨다.

해설 **추론**
양식이 쓰여진 시기는 2월 5일(February 5)이며 설명 첫 번째 문장에서 2월 17일에 유키 후지모토와 아서 탕이 회계부에 합류한다(On Monday, February 17, Yuki Fujimoto and Arthur Tang will be joining our accounting department)고 했으므로 최근에 직원을 채용했다는 것을 알 수 있다. 따라서 (C)가 정답이다.

어휘 merge 합병하다

4 무엇을 위한 주문인가?
(A) 장비 설치 (B) 가구 조립
(C) 프린터 수리 (D) 사무실 청소

해설 **세부 사항**
설명 두 번째 문장에서 510호와 514호에 컴퓨터와 전화를 설치해야 한다(Standard-issue computers and telephones should be installed in their offices, 510 and 514)고 했고, 이어지는 문장에서 514호에는 탁상용 프린터와 스캐너도 비치해야 한다(The latter office should also be furnished with a desk printer and scanner)고 했으므로 (A)가 정답이다.

> **Paraphrasing** 지문의 computers and telephones should be installed / should also be furnished with a desk printer and scanner → 보기의 Equipment setup

[5-6] 문자 메시지

에이미 모로 [오후 2시 17분]
안녕하세요, 케빈. 저는 사무용품 매장에 있어요. 지금 명찰이 할인 중이에요. 우리는 늘 이게 필요한 것 같더라고요. 하계 인턴사원들용으로 몇 개 살까요? 곧 그들을 위한 용품을 준비할 거죠?

케빈 조 [오후 2시 18분]
네, 맞아요. 그리고 그걸 사는 게 좋겠어요. 사실, ⁵인턴 7명이 2주 후에 사무실에서 교육을 시작할 거예요.

에이미 모로 [오후 2시 19분]
알겠어요. 다른 용품들도 할인되는 것 같아요. ⁶봉투, 폴더나 노트패드 같은 다른 게 필요한가요?

케빈 조 [오후 2시 20분]
확인해 볼게요.

에이미 모로 [오후 2시 20분]
네.

케빈 조 [오후 2시 22분]
괜찮아요.

에이미 모로 [오후 2시 23분]
알겠어요. 30분 뒤에 사무실에 도착할 것 같아요.

어휘 name badge 명찰 currently 지금, 현재 grab 구하다, 마련하다 intern 인턴(사원) prepare 준비하다 material 용품, 재료 envelope 봉투

5 메시지 작성자들에 따르면, 2주 후에 무슨 일이 일어날 것인가?
(A) 몇몇 쿠폰이 만료된다. (B) 인턴 몇 명이 온다.
(C) 판매 행사가 종료된다. (D) 휴가 기간이 시작된다.

해설 **세부 사항**
2시 18분에 조 씨가 인턴 7명이 2주 후에 사무실에서 교육받기 시작할 것(The seven interns will be in the office in two weeks to start training)이라고 했으므로 정답은 (B)이다.

어휘 conclude 끝나다 period 기간

> **Paraphrasing** 지문의 will be in the office → 보기의 will arrive

6 오후 2시 22분에 조 씨가 "괜찮아요"라고 쓴 의도는?
(A) 프로젝트 마감일에 대해 걱정하지 않는다.
(B) 업무팀에 직원이 충분히 있다.
(C) 다른 사무용품은 필요하지 않다.
(D) 나중에 매장을 방문할 계획이다.

해설 **의도 파악**
2시 19분에 모로 씨가 봉투, 폴더나 노트패드 같은 다른 게 필요한지(Do you need anything else, like envelopes, folders, or notepads?) 물은 데 대해 조씨는 괜찮다고 대답했다. 이는 더 이상 필요한 용품이 없다는 의도로 한 말이므로 (C)가 정답이다.

어휘 concerned 걱정하는 deadline 마감일

Paraphrasing 지문의 anything else, like envelopes, folders, or notepads → 보기의 any other office supplies

---

[7-9] 송장

발신: 콜든 사
콜든 사
익스텐션 로 5번지
모빌, 앨라배마 36606
전화: 251-555-0152

수신:
랜더스 레스토랑
웨스트 찰스 가 71번지
채플 힐, 노스캐롤라이나 27515

품번	명세	수량	단가	소계
121-B	샐러드 접시 (12/상자)	4	25.59달러	
8 782-A	조각 수프 스푼 (12/팩)	4	5.78달러	23.12달러
78-K	수프 그릇 (48/상자)	1	58.19달러	58.19달러
59-C	천 냅킨 (12/팩)	8	13.29달러	106.32달러
193-W	5쿼트 스테인리스 스틸 소테 팬과 뚜껑	3	46.31달러	138.93달러

총 비용 326.56달러
배송 17.92달러
지불할 요금 344.48달러

메모: **7,8 주문하신 조각 스푼은 저희 소매점 중 한 곳에서 별도로 직송됩니다.** 주문하신 샐러드 접시는 현재 재고가 없어 2-3주 동안은 구할 수 없습니다. **9 이 품목은 배송 이후에 청구될 예정이며 배송비는 50퍼센트 할인됩니다.** 불편을 끼쳐 드려 죄송합니다.

어휘 engrave 조각하다 separately 별도로 retail 소매의 currently 현재 out of stock 재고가 없는 reduce 할인하다 apologize for ~에 대해 사과하다 inconvenience 불편

7 콜든 사는 무엇이겠는가?
(A) 지역 급식 서비스   (B) 주간 선박회사
(C) 주방용품 체인점   (D) 고급 식당

해설 **추론**
하단 메모에서 조각 스푼이 소매점 중 한 곳에서 직송된다(The engraved spoons you ordered will be shipped separately, directly from one of our retail locations)는 점에서 발신자인 콜든 사는 주방용품 체인점이라는 것을 알 수 있으므로 (C)가 정답이다.

어휘 interstate 주와 주 사이의 exclusive 고급의

8 품목 782-A에 대해 언급된 것은 무엇인가?
(A) 카탈로그에 라벨이 잘못 붙어 있었다.
(B) 파손된 채 도착했다.
(C) 요청된 색상은 구할 수 없다.
(D) 소매점에서 발송된다.

해설 **Not/True**
중반부의 782-A Engraved soup spoons (12/pack)를 통해 782-A는 수프 스푼임을 알 수 있고, 하단 메모에서 조각 스푼은 소매점 중 한 곳에서 직송된다(The engraved spoons you ordered will be shipped separately, directly from one of our retail locations)고 했다. 이를 통해 스푼은 소매점에서 발송된다는 것을 알 수 있으므로 (D)가 정답이다.

Paraphrasing 지문의 will be shipped separately, directly from one of our retail locations → 보기의 is being sent from a retail store

9 물품 발송에 대해 명시된 것은 무엇인가?
(A) 한 품목은 할인 배송될 것이다.
(B) 한 품목은 기상 악화로 배송할 수 없었다.
(C) 일부 품목들은 익일 배송될 것이다.
(D) 일부 물품들은 엉뚱한 주소로 배송되었다.

해설 **Not/True**
하단의 메모에서 샐러드 접시의 배송비가 50퍼센트 할인된다(You will not be charged for that item until it is shipped, and the shipping charge for that item will be reduced by 50 percent)고 했으므로 (A)가 정답이다.

Paraphrasing 지문의 the shipping charge for that item will be reduced → 보기의 One item will be shipped at a discount.

[10-12] 웹페이지

https://www.eastbayuniversity.ac.uk/garden-ideas

증가하는 관심사

10 일년 중 가정 정원을 계획하기 시작할 시기가 다시 돌아왔습니다. 이스트 베이 대학교의 식물학자들이 이번 시즌에 물을 절약하려는 사람들에게 도움이 될 만한 몇 가지 사실을 공유했습니다.

• 토마토는 뿌리가 빠르게 성장하여 표면에 물이 적을 때 땅속 깊은 곳에서 수분을 끌어올 수 있습니다.

- 멜론도 토마토처럼 뿌리가 깊게 자라며 시즌 초기에 충분한 물을 공급받으면 지면이 건조할 때 살아남을 수 있습니다.
- **11**콩은 건조한 환경에 잘 적응합니다. 일부 품종은 사막 지역에서 유래했으며 다른 환경에서 재배될 때 적은 양의 물만 필요합니다.
- **12**무, 아스파라거스, 근대, 가지, 겨잣잎, 고추는 물 보존에 도움이 될 수 있는 식물들 중 일부입니다. 이것들은 짧은 기간 동안만 물을 주면 되기 때문입니다.

과학자들은 또한 각 식물이 적절한 양의 물을 받을 수 있도록 물이 비슷하게 필요한 채소들을 함께 심기를 권합니다.

어휘 botanist 식물학자 conserve 절약하다 root 뿌리 draw 끌어당기다 moisture 수분 surface 표면 adapt 적응하다 conditions 환경, 조건 originate 유래하다 desert 사막 environment 환경 radish 무 Swiss chard 근대 eggplant 가지 mustard green 겨잣잎 pepper 고추 aid 돕다 conservation 보존

10 웹페이지에서 논의하는 것은 무엇인가?
 (A) 대학교의 새로운 연구 프로젝트
 (B) 가정 정원을 가꾸는 사람들을 위한 유용한 정보
 (C) 지역 농부의 프로필
 (D) 대학교의 식물학 프로그램의 역사

해설 주제/목적
첫 단락에서 가정 정원에 대한 계획 수립과 관련하여 물을 절약하는 데 도움이 될 정보에 대해 언급(It is once again the time of year to begin planning a home garden. ~ some facts that may be helpful to those who are looking to conserve water this season)하고 있다. 따라서 정답은 (B)이다.

어휘 research 연구 botany 식물학

Paraphrasing 지문의 some facts that may be helpful
→ 보기의 Useful information

11 어떤 식물군이 사막에서 자라온 것으로 언급되는가?
 (A) 토마토 (B) 멜론
 (C) 콩 (D) 무

해설 세부 사항
네 번째 단락에서 콩은 건조한 환경에 잘 적응하고 일부 품종은 사막 지역에서 유래했다(Beans are well adapted to dry conditions. Some varieties originated in desert areas)고 했으므로 정답은 (C)이다.

Paraphrasing 지문의 originated in desert areas
→ 질문의 having grown in the desert

12 [1], [2], [3], [4]로 표시된 곳 중에서 다음 문장이 들어가기에 가장 적합한 위치는?
"이것들은 짧은 기간 동안만 물을 주면 되기 때문입니다."
 (A) [1] (B) [2]
 (C) [3] (D) [4]

해설 문장 삽입
다섯 번째 단락에서 무, 아스파라거스, 근대, 가지, 겨잣잎, 고추는 물 보존에 도움이 될 수 있는 식물들 중 일부(Radishes, asparagus, Swiss chard, eggplant, mustard greens, and peppers are among those plants that can aid in the conservation of water)라고 했다. 문맥상 이 식물들을 they로 대신해 물 보존에 도움이 되는 이유를 제시하는 문장이 그 뒤에 들어가는 것이 흐름상 자연스러우므로 (C)가 정답이다.

어휘 brief 짧은 length of time 기간

[13-16] 온라인 채팅

레일라 은디디 [오전 10시 18분] 오스카와 야엘, 안녕하세요. **13**다음 달 관광 컨퍼런스에 가실 계획인가요?

오스카 본마티 [오전 10시 22분] 네, 전 갈 거예요. 당신은요?

야엘 라소 [오전 10시 22분] 네, 기대돼요.

레일라 은디디 [오전 10시 25분] 저는 방금 등록했어요. 아마 기차를 탈 것 같아요.

오스카 본마티 [오전 10시 27분] 저도요. **14**같은 기차를 예약할까요?

레일라 은디디 [오전 10시 28분] 좋은 계획 같아요. 야엘은요?

야엘 라소 [오전 10시 29분] 보통은 기차를 탈 텐데 스프링필드에 있는 여동생네 집에서 운전해서 갈 예정이에요.

레일라 은디디 [오전 10시 31분] **15**컨퍼런스 전에 여동생을 방문할 기회가 돼서 좋겠어요. 오스카랑 제가 안부 전한다고 해주세요.

오스카 본마티 [오전 10시 33분] 네, 꼭이요. 그나저나 우리 각자 다른 세션에 참석하고 나중에 필기한 걸 주고받을까 생각해 봤어요. 어떻게 생각하세요?

야엘 라소 [오전 10시 34분] 좋은 생각이네요.

오스카 본마티 [오전 10시 35분] 그리고 **16**호텔 예약할 때 사용할 컨퍼런스 할인 코드가 있지 않나요? 지금 제가 못 찾고 있어요.

레일라 은디디 [오전 10시 36분] 있어요. **16**그게 언급된 이메일을 지금 바로 전달해 줄게요.

오스카 본마티 [오전 10시 37분] 고마워요!

어휘 tourism 관광 register 등록하다 trade 주고받다 forward (편지, 이메일 등을) 전달하다

13 은디디 씨는 왜 본마티 씨와 라소 씨에게 연락했는가?
 (A) 출장 계획을 조율하려고
 (B) 회의 일정을 잡으려고
 (C) 컨퍼런스 계획에 도움을 요청하려고
 (D) 컨퍼런스 세션의 필기 내용을 요청하려고

해설 주제/목적
10시 18분에 은디디 씨가 본마티 씨와 라소 씨에게 컨퍼런스에 갈 계획인지(Are you planning to go to the tourism conference next month?) 묻고 있는 것으로 보아 컨퍼런스 출장을 준비하기 위해 동료들에게 연락했다는 것을 알 수 있다. 따라서 정답은 (A)이다.

어휘 coordinate 조율하다, 조정하다

14 오전 10시 28분에 은디디 씨가 "좋은 계획 같아요"라고 쓴 의도는?
(A) 컨퍼런스 신청서를 작성할 것이다.
(B) 동료들을 간절히 보고 싶어 한다.
(C) **본마티 씨와 같은 기차를 타고 싶어 한다.**
(D) 라소 씨가 가족 방문을 할 수 있어서 기쁘다.

해설 의도 파악
10시 27분에 본마티 씨가 은디디 씨에게 같은 기차를 예약할지(Should we try to book the same one?) 제안하자 은디디 씨는 좋은 계획 같다고 호응하고 있다. 이는 본마티 씨와 같은 기차를 타기를 원한다는 뜻으로 한 말이므로 (C)가 정답이다.

어휘 complete 작성하다   registration form 신청서
colleague 동료

15 은디디 씨와 본마티 씨에 대해 암시된 것은?
(A) 스프링필드에 산다.
(B) **라소 씨의 여동생을 알고 있다.**
(C) 라소 씨에게 직접 보고한다.
(D) 해외 여행을 즐긴다.

해설 추론
10시 31분에 은디디 씨가 라소 씨에게 여동생을 방문하게 되어 좋겠다며 본마티 씨와 자신의 안부를 전해달라(That's nice that you'll have a chance to visit her before the conference. Please tell her that Oscar and I say hello)고 한 것으로 보아 두 사람은 라소 씨의 여동생을 알고 있다는 것을 짐작할 수 있다. 따라서 (B)가 정답이다.

어휘 directly 직접, 바로

16 은디디 씨는 다음에 무엇을 할 것 같은가?
(A) 기차표를 구매
(B) 호텔 예약
(C) 컨퍼런스 행사장으로 운전
(D) **본마티 씨에게 정보 전송**

해설 세부 사항
10시 35분에 본마티 씨가 컨퍼런스 할인 코드가 있지 않냐(isn't there a conference discount code to use when booking the hotel?)고 묻자 10시 36분에 은디디 씨가 해당 정보가 언급된 이메일을 바로 전달해 주겠다(I'll forward you the e-mail that mentions it right away)고 했으므로 정답은 (D)이다.

어휘 reservation 예약   venue 장소

UNIT 22 복수 지문

ETS 기출 예제   본책 p.298

공지 + 편지

예술가들이여, 모여라!
아마추어 혹은 전문 그래픽 작가이십니까? 렐링 교통(RT) 센터는 창사 이래 첫 로고 콘테스트를 개최하고 있습니다. 8월 2일부터 22일까지 렐링 터미널에 위치한 렐링 교통 본부에서 버스 또는 열차 여행과 관련된 로고들을 접수합니다. 예선을 통과한 30점을 유니온 스트리트 역 내부 벽면에 전시할 예정입니다. 9월 1일부터 30일까지 일반 대중들은 가장 마음에 드는 로고에 투표할 수 있습니다. 총 4개의 상을 수여할 예정입니다.

1위: *옐로 패스*. 5일간 렐링 교통의 지역 열차 또는 버스를 무제한 탑승할 수 있는 자유승차권
2위: *블루 패스*. 3일간 렐링 교통의 지역 열차를 무제한 탑승할 수 있는 자유승차권
3위: *그린 패스*. 목적지를 불문하고 렐링 교통의 급행열차 1회 왕복 탑승권
4위: *레드 패스*. 목적지를 불문하고 렐링 교통의 급행버스 1회 왕복 탑승권

이반코바 씨께:

렐링 교통 센터의 로고 콘테스트 당선을 축하드립니다. 동봉한 것은 귀하께 드리는 부상입니다. 이 패스는 정해진 개시일이 없음을 양지하시기 바랍니다. 언제든 원하시는 날짜부터 5일간 유효합니다.

렐링 교통 센터를 대표하여 콘테스트를 빛내 주셔서 감사하다는 말씀을 전합니다.

리타 라즈왈
렐링 교통 센터, 지역사회 연계 프로그램 담당자

Q   이반코바 씨는 무엇을 받았는가?
(A) **옐로 패스**   (B) 블루 패스
(C) 그린 패스   (D) 레드 패스

ETS 유형 연습   본책 p.299

1 (A)   **2** (B)

[1-2] 웹페이지 + 댓글

https://www.cuisinetoday.com/testkitchen

| 홈 | 레스토랑 | 테스트 키친 | 정보 |

퀴진 투데이의 최고 버터 브랜드

매달 퀴진 투데이에서는 최고로 뽑힌 음식을 소개합니다. 이번 달에는 버터에 대해 이야기합니다. **1우리가 선정한 최고의 제품들을 살펴보시고 정보 탭으로 이동하셔서 이 브랜드들을 어디에서 구입할 수 있는지 확인해 보세요.**

그린필드 팜즈: 이 버터는 크리미한 식감과 독특한 풍미를 지녀 베이킹에 가장 적합한 제품입니다.

2밸리 크리머리: 이 버터는 맛있고 풍부한 맛이 나며 빵에 펴 바르기에 좋습니다. **2거의 흰색에 가깝고 샘플링한 버터 중 가장 색이 연합니다.**

가장 마음에 드는 버터는 무엇인가요? 온라인에 댓글을 남겨주세요.

댓글 작성자: 와타루 사노

저는 전문 케이크 디자이너이며, 프리미엄 팜즈 브랜드의 버터를 한동안 사용해 왔습니다. 그래서 목록에 있는 버터들을 사용해보

고 싶은 호기심이 생겼습니다. **2흰색 케이크를 만들어야 해서 가장 밝은 색의 버터를 먼저 사용해 보았는데** 결과가 매우 만족스러웠습니다. 그런 다음 다른 버터들도 사용해 보았고 목록에 있는 모든 브랜드의 결과에 만족했습니다. 그린필드 팜즈 버터에 대한 평가에 동의한다는 말도 덧붙여야겠네요.

1 독자들은 정보 탭에서 무엇을 찾을 수 있는가?
(A) 목록에 있는 브랜드의 판매처
(B) 다양한 브랜드의 버터 가격

해설 세부 사항
웹페이지의 첫 번째 단락 마지막 문장에서 우리가 선정한 최고의 제품들을 살펴보고 정보 탭으로 이동하여 이 브랜드들을 어디에서 구입할 수 있는지 확인해 보라(Take a look at our top choices, and go to the Information tab to see where these brands are available)고 했으므로 정답은 (A)이다.

2 사노 씨가 가장 먼저 사용해 본 웹페이지 목록의 버터 브랜드는 무엇인가?
(A) 그린필드 팜즈   (B) 밸리 크리머리

해설 연계
웹페이지의 세 번째 단락에서 밸리 크리머리가 샘플링한 버터 중 가장 색이 연하다(It is nearly white and has the palest color of all those we sampled)는 것을 알 수 있고, 댓글의 중반부에서 사노 씨가 가장 밝은 색의 버터를 먼저 사용해 보았다(I needed to make a white cake, so I used the lightest-colored butter first)고 했으므로 정답은 (B)이다.

ETS 실전 문제   본책 p.300

1 (A)	2 (D)	3 (C)	4 (B)	5 (C)
6 (A)	7 (C)	8 (B)	9 (C)	10 (D)
11 (D)	12 (B)	13 (A)	14 (A)	15 (B)
16 (A)	17 (B)	18 (D)	19 (A)	20 (D)

[1-5] 편지 + 블로그 게시물

아트랜드 인 하트랜드
퀸 가 4525번지
캔자스시티, 미주리 64111
미국

8월 8일

마커스 하마다
힐튼 브라가 로 357번지
리우데자네이루 - 리우데자네이루주, 22640-102
브라질

하마다 씨께:

저희 회사에 대해 문의해 주신 편지에 감사드립니다. **1현재 채용을 하고 있지 않다고 말씀드리게 되어 죄송합니다.** 하지만 **2,3유머 카**

드 사업부를 위해 보내주신 이미지는 매우 훌륭하다고 생각합니다. 향후 연하장을 그릴 정규직 삽화가가 필요하게 되면 반드시 연락드리겠습니다.

귀하의 커리어 노력에 행운이 함께하길 바랍니다.

말리나 로즈
아트랜드 인 하트랜드

어휘 inquire 문의하다   division 부서   greeting card 연하장   certainly 분명히   endeavor 노력, 시도

마커스 하마다의 장대한 예술
욜란다 노리스 글

9월 19일–독자 여러분도 아시다시피, 저는 지난 주말 브라질에 도착했습니다. 가장 먼저 리우데자네이루의 거리 예술 축제에 참석해서 많은 뛰어난 현지 예술가들의 작품을 접했습니다. 축제는 또한 스페인, 멕시코, 미국, 영국, 이스라엘 출신의 놀라운 예술가들도 소개하고 있었습니다. 하지만 가장 인상적이었던 것은 대중에게 처음 작품을 선보이던 마커스 하마다라는 젊은 현지 예술가의 작품이었습니다.

4하마다 씨의 작품은 분명히 많은 관객들을 매료시키고 있습니다. 그의 크고 화려한 아크릴화와 유화에 경탄하는 미술품 중개상뿐만 아니라 그의 현대적이고 밝은 파스텔화를 감상하는 가족들도 그의 부스를 방문하고 있습니다. **3그의 재미있는 펜화 일러스트를 유심히 살펴보는 젊은이들도 있었는데, 우스꽝스러운 연하장에서 볼 수 있는 그런 종류였습니다.** 이 유쾌한 작품들은 티셔츠, 머그컵, 그리고 기타 저렴한 기념품 유형의 제품들에도 옮겨져 있었습니다.

5한 작가의 작품으로 이렇게 다양하게 구성된 컬렉션은 본 적이 없습니다. 앞으로 하마다 씨의 커리어가 어떻게 펼쳐질지 기대됩니다.

어휘 magnificent 장대한   encounter 접하다   exceptional 뛰어난   showcase 소개하다, 전시하다   incredible 놀라운, 믿을 수 없는   present 보여 주다   appeal to ~을 매료시키다, ~의 흥미를 끌다   booth 부스   dealer 중개인   marvel 경탄하다   acrylic 아크릴로 그린   eye 감상하다   peruse (자세히) 살피다   amusing 재미있는   delightful 유쾌한   transfer 옮기다   affordable (가격이) 적당한   diverse 다양한

1 편지의 목적은 무엇인가?
(A) 회사에 공석이 없음을 설명
(B) 채용 공고의 정보 수정
(C) 회사의 제품 홍보
(D) 예술가에게 작품 전시 요청

해설 주제/목적
편지의 두 번째 문장에서 현재 채용을 하고 있지 않다고 말씀드리게 되어 죄송하다(I am sorry to inform you that we are not hiring now)고 했으므로 (A)가 정답이다.

어휘 job opening 취직자리   job posting 채용 공고

Paraphrasing 지문의 are not hiring → 보기의 has no job openings

2 아트랜드 인 하트랜드는 어떤 종류의 업체인 것 같은가?
(A) 박물관 (B) 미술관
(C) 디자인 학교 **(D) 연하장 제조업체**

해설 추론
편지의 세 번째 문장에서 유머 카드 사업부를 위해 보내준 이미지를 언급(we feel that the images you sent for our humorous card division are quite good)하며 향후 연하장을 그릴 정규직 삽화가가 필요하게 되면 연락하겠다(Should we need a full-time greeting card illustrator in the future, we will certainly reach out)고 했다. 사내에 유머 카드 사업부와 연하장 삽화가 일자리가 있으므로 아트랜드 인 하트랜드는 연하장 제조업체라는 것을 짐작할 수 있다. 따라서 정답은 (D)이다.

3 하마다 씨는 로즈 씨에게 보낸 샘플을 만드는 데 무엇을 사용했을 것 같은가?
(A) 파스텔 (B) 유화 물감
(C) 펜과 잉크 (D) 아크릴 물감

해설 연계
편지의 세 번째 문장에서 유머 카드 사업부를 위해 보내준 이미지가 훌륭하다(we feel that the images you sent for our humorous card division are quite good)고 한 점을 통해 하마다 씨는 로즈 씨에게 유머 카드 이미지를 보냈다는 것을 알 수 있고, 블로그 게시물의 두 번째 단락 세 번째 문장에서 우스꽝스러운 연하장에서 볼 수 있을 만한 재미있는 펜화 일러스트(his amusing pen-and-ink illustrations, the kind seen on funny greeting cards)를 언급했으므로 하마다 씨가 보낸 샘플이 펜과 잉크를 사용한 일러스트라는 것을 알 수 있다. 따라서 정답은 (C)이다.

4 블로그 게시물의 두 번째 단락 1행의 "appeals to"와 의미상 가장 가까운 단어는?
(A) 보호하다 **(B) 마음을 끌다, 매혹하다**
(C) 요청하다 (D) 주장하다

해설 동의어
문맥상 '매료시키다'라는 의미로 쓰인 것이므로 '마음을 끌다, 매혹하다'라는 의미의 (B) attracts가 정답이다.

5 노리스 씨가 하마다 씨에 대해 가장 인상 깊게 생각한 점은 무엇인가?
(A) 밝은 색상의 사용
(B) 자신의 예술을 마케팅하는 능력
(C) 다양한 예술 창작품들
(D) 젊은 관객들 사이에서의 인기

해설 세부 사항
블로그 게시물의 마지막 단락 첫 문장에서 한 작가의 작품으로 이렇게 다양하게 구성된 컬렉션은 본 적이 없다(I have never seen such a diverse collection of works from one artist)며 놀라움을 표현하고 있으므로 정답은 (C)이다.

어휘 market (상품을) 마케팅하다, 광고하다   creation 창작품   popularity 인기

Paraphrasing 지문의 a diverse collection of works from one artist → 보기의 wide variety of artistic creations

[6-10] 이메일 + 온라인 양식

수신: 강소희 〈skang@worldmail.com〉
발신: 앤드루 벨 〈abelle@invernessbank.co.uk〉
날짜: 12월 13일
제목: 인버네스 은행이 더 좋아지도록 도와주세요

강 씨께,

저희 기록에 따르면 **9**고객님께서는 12월 6일에 인버네스 은행의 글래스고 지점을 방문하셨습니다. **6, 7, 9**www.invernessbank.co.uk/survey에서 설문조사에 참여하셔서 저희 서비스가 어땠는지 알려주세요. **9**고객 ID 번호 5851을 사용하세요. 또한 **7**info@invernessbank.co.uk로 이메일을 보내서 저희 팀원 중 한 명에게 의견을 공유하실 수도 있습니다. 고객님께서 제공하시는 모든 정보는 향후 직원 회의에서 검토될 것입니다.

시간을 내주셔서 미리 감사드립니다.

앤드루 벨

어휘 improve 개선하다   branch 지점   comment 의견   review 검토하다   in advance 미리

9인버네스 은행 고객 만족 설문조사 - 고객 ID 5851
다음 문항에 대한 고객님의 응답을 1점(전혀 동의하지 않음)부터 4점(매우 동의함)까지의 척도로 표시해 주세요. 각 응답에 대한 설명을 추가해 주시면 감사하겠습니다.

1. 인버네스 직원은 개인적으로 상냥하고 친절한 태도를 보였다.
의견: **8**나를 맞이해 준 은행원인 줄리아는 예의 바르고 제 문제를 해결하도록 열심히 도와주었습니다. 하지만 직장에서 첫 근무일이라서 그런지 조금 벅차 보였습니다. 결국 그녀는 지점장에게 제 문제를 해결하는 데 도움을 달라고 요청했습니다.

2. 인버네스 직원은 나의 요구 사항을 잘 듣고 그것을 처리하기 위한 적절한 조치를 취했다. ① ② ● ④
의견: **9**저는 인버네스 모바일 앱을 이용해 제 은행 계좌에 보안 단계를 한 가지 더 추가하는 데 도움이 필요했습니다. 지점장인 짐은 불편을 끼친 점에 대해 사과했으며 제 계좌를 안전하게 보호하는 방법을 보여주었습니다. 그는 또한 문제를 겪게 될 경우 그에게 직접 전화하거나 이메일을 보내도 된다고 했습니다.

3. 다른 사람들에게 인버네스 은행을 추천할 것 같다.
의견: 짐이 도와준 이후, 저는 이제 앱을 사용하여 집에서 은행 업무를 봅니다. 게다가 **10**지점을 방문해야 할 경우에도 귀사는 대부분의 다른 은행과 달리 지점이 많고 운영 시간이 깁니다.

어휘 satisfaction 만족   indicate 표시하다   scale 척도   disagree 동의하지 않다   kindly 부디, 제발   representative 직원   engaging 상냥한   friendly 친절한

demeanor 태도 bank teller 은행원 polite 예의 바른 eager 열심인 address 해결하다 overwhelmed 벅찬 appropriate 적절한 layer 단계 security 보안 apologize(= apologise) 사과하다 secure 안전하게 보호하다 refer 추천하다 extended 길어진, 연장된

6 벨 씨는 강 씨에게 무엇을 요청하는가?
(A) 피드백 제공
(B) 오류 수정
(C) 최근 거래 확인
(D) 새로운 은행 지점 방문

해설 **세부 사항**
이메일의 두 번째 문장에서 벨 씨가 강 씨에게 설문조사에 참여해 서비스에 대해 평가해 달라(Please let us know how we did by taking our survey)고 요청하고 있으므로 정답은 (A)이다.

어휘 correct 수정하다 error 오류 confirm 확인하다 transaction 거래

Paraphrasing 지문의 let us know how we did
→ 보기의 Provide some feedback

7 이메일에 따르면, 벨 씨는 누구인 것 같은가?
(A) 인사 전문가
(B) 웹사이트 디자이너
(C) 고객 서비스 관리자
(D) 인버네스 은행 변호사

해설 **추론**
이메일의 두 번째 문장에서 벨 씨는 고객에게 서비스에 대한 피드백을 요청(Please let us know how we did by taking our survey)하고 있고, 네 번째 문장에서 자신의 팀원에게 의견을 공유해도 된다(You may also share your comments with one of my team members)고 했다. 이를 통해 벨 씨는 인버네스 은행의 고객 서비스를 담당하는 직원임을 알 수 있으므로 정답은 (C)이다.

어휘 specialist 전문가

8 한 은행원에 대해 암시된 것은?
(A) 인버네스 은행의 모바일 앱 제작을 도왔다.
(B) 새로운 근무 환경에 적응하고 있다.
(C) 대부분의 주말에 근무한다.
(D) 최근에 자신의 계좌를 개설했다.

해설 **추론**
온라인 양식 첫 번째 항목에서 은행원 줄리아가 열심히 도와주었지만 첫 근무일이라서 조금 벅차 보였다(The bank teller who welcomed me, Julia, was polite and eager to help ~. However, as it was her first day on the job, she seemed a bit overwhelmed)고 했다. 이를 통해 은행원 줄리아가 인버네스 은행 업무에 적응하는 중임을 알 수 있으므로 정답은 (B)이다.

어휘 adjust 적응하다 environment 환경

Paraphrasing 지문의 her first day on the job
→ 보기의 adjusting to a new work environment

9 강 씨는 왜 12월 6일에 글래스고 지점을 방문했는가?
(A) 새 은행 계좌를 개설하려고
(B) 고객 서비스에 대해 불만을 제기하려고
(C) 계좌의 보안을 강화하려고
(D) 연례 회의에 참석하려고

해설 **연계**
이메일의 첫 문장에서 강 씨가 12월 6일 글래스고 지점을 방문(you visited Inverness Bank's Glasgow branch on 6 December)하여 고객 ID 번호 5851을 사용해 설문조사에 참여해달라는 요청(Please let us know how we did by taking our survey ~. Use customer ID number 5851)을 받았다는 것을 알 수 있다. 또한, 온라인 양식의 고객 ID가 5851(Inverness Bank Customer Satisfaction Survey—Customer ID 5851)이므로 작성자는 강 씨라는 점을 알 수 있고, 두 번째 항목에서 강 씨는 은행 계좌에 보안 단계를 한 가지 더 추가(I needed help adding another layer of security to my bank account using the Inverness mobile app)하려고 은행을 방문했다고 했다. 따라서 (C)가 정답이다.

어휘 complain 불평하다 strengthen 강화하다 annual 연례의

10 온라인 양식에 따르면, 강 씨가 인버네스 은행을 추천할 수도 있는 이유는 무엇인가?
(A) 이자율
(B) 개인 대출
(C) 평판
(D) 편리함

해설 **추론**
온라인 양식의 마지막 문장에서 강 씨는 지점이 많고 운영 시간이 길다(if I need to visit a branch, your bank has many locations with extended hours, unlike most other banks)는 편리함을 인버네스 은행의 강점으로 꼽고 있으므로 정답은 (D)이다.

어휘 loan 대출 reputation 평판

Paraphrasing 지문의 many locations with extended hours → 보기의 convenience

[11-15] 이메일 + 광고 + 후기

수신: 트리나 첸
발신: 해럴드 렌바
날짜: 11월 1일
제목: 신규 진열 품목

안녕하세요, 트리나.

아래 제품들을 창고에서 찾아 매장의 지정된 통로에 진열해 주세요. 내일 중으로 이 작업을 완료 부탁드립니다.

통로	분류	품목 번호	제조사; 설명
13 2	사포	A222	아이들리; 다양한 석질
3	가위	**11** RJ283	피피즈; 원예용 가위
4	톱	D727	코클리; 가로톱
5	나사	H01017	잰콘; 강철 십자머리 나사

205

감사합니다.
해럴드

어휘 shelve 선반에 얹다　designated 지정된　aisle 통로
task 작업, 일　sandpaper 사포　grit 석질, 자갈　shears
큰 가위　crosscut saw 가로톱　screw 나사
Phillips-head 십자 홈 나사못 대가리　steel 강철

렌바 철물점
1일 할인 행사: 11월 3일

병 생수 특별 판매
아카디 스파: 상자당 3.99달러
15블루웰 퓨어: 상자당 5.99달러
탑스 스프링트리: 상자당 7.99달러
월 마운틴: 상자당 8.99달러

그 외 할인 품목:
12모든 낚시 장비 및 페인트 10퍼센트 할인

어휘 hardware store 철물점

매장 후기: 렌바 철물점
앤 에이버리 글

(11월 10일)—저는 렌바 철물점을 매우 좋아해요! 이곳은 가족이 운영하는 작은 가게로, 철물점에 있을 거라고 기대하지 않을 물건들을 포함해 상상할 수 있는 거의 모든 품목을 취급합니다. 하지만 **14보통 있을 거라고 예상되는 곳에 물건이 없는 것 같아 제가 사러 온 물건이 어디에 있는지 가게 점원에게 종종 물어봐야 합니다.**

예를 들어, **13**지난 월요일에 하논의 모형용 접착제 한 병을 사러 갔습니다. 제품이 있을 거라고 생각했던 예술 공예품 코너가 아니라 페인트 코너의 사포 옆에 있었습니다. 그리고 제가 필요했던 잰콘 강철 십자머리 나사는 철물 제품이 아닌 음료와 함께 있었습니다.

제가 렌바에서 정기적으로 쇼핑을 하는 또 다른 이유는 매일 있는 특가 제품 때문입니다. 그래서 제가 방문한 날에도 가게는 병 생수 1일 할인 행사를 했습니다. **15**블루웰 생수 한 상자를 평소 내던 가격의 반값보다 싸게 구입했습니다!

그러니까 **14**매장 배치가 다소 혼란스럽기는 하지만 보통 제가 찾고 있는 건 뭐든지 있기 때문에 적어도 일주일에 한 번은 그곳에 갑니다.

어휘 family-owned 가족이 운영하는　establishment 시설　imagine 상상하다　ordinarily 보통　glue 접착제 arts and crafts 미술 공예　beverage 음료　regularly 정기적으로, 자주　bargain 특가품　layout 배치　puzzling 혼란스러운　generally 보통

---

11 이메일에 따르면, 품목 RJ283은 무엇인가?
(A) 잰콘이 제조한 나사 　(B) 코클리가 제조한 톱
(C) 사포 종류　(D) **원예용 도구**

해설 세부 사항
이메일의 표에서 RJ283이 원예용 가위(RJ283 - Fifi's; gardening shears)라는 것을 확인할 수 있으므로 정답은 (D)이다.

12 렌바 철물점의 할인 행사에 대해 광고에 언급된 것은?
(A) 일주일 동안 계속된다.
(B) 낚시 장비가 포함되어 있다.
(C) 매년 11월에 열린다.
(D) 철물 전 제품이 10퍼센트 할인된다.

해설 세부 사항
광고의 하단에 모든 낚시 장비 및 페인트가 10퍼센트 할인(10 percent off all fishing equipment and paint)이라는 점을 통해 할인 품목에 낚시 장비가 포함되어 있다는 것을 알 수 있으므로 (B)가 정답이다.

어휘 last 지속되다　take place 열리다, 개최되다
feature ~을 특징으로 하다

13 에이버리 씨가 접착제를 발견했을 것 같은 곳은?
(A) 2번 통로　(B) 3번 통로
(C) 4번 통로　(D) 5번 통로

해설 연계
후기의 두 번째 단락 첫 문장에서 에이버리 씨가 접착제를 사러 갔는데(last Monday, I went in to buy a bottle of Hannon's model glue), 제품이 예술 공예품 코너가 아닌 페인트 코너의 사포 옆에 있었다(Rather than in the arts and crafts section where I thought it would be, it was in the paint department, next to the sandpaper)고 했고, 이메일의 표 상단 Aisle—2, Sandpaper를 통해 사포는 2번 통로에 있다는 것을 알 수 있으므로 정답은 (A)이다.

14 에이버리 씨가 후기에서 렌바 철물점에 대해 명시한 것은?
(A) 구성이 다소 혼란스럽다.
(B) 고객을 잘 대우하지 않는다.
(C) 재고가 충분하지 않다.
(D) 큰 규모가 부담스러울 수 있다.

해설 Not / True
에이버리 씨는 후기의 첫 단락에서 물건이 예상되는 곳에 없어서 종종 가게 점원의 도움을 청한다(I often have to ask the shop assistant where the product is that I came in for since it never seems to be where I would ordinarily expect it)고 했고, 마지막 문장에서 매장 배치가 다소 혼란스럽다(the store's layout is somewhat puzzling to me)고 했으므로 (A)가 정답이다.

어휘 organization 구성　confusing 혼란스러운
treat 대우하다　stock (재고를 갖추고) 있다
overwhelming 압도적인

Paraphrasing 지문의 layout is somewhat puzzling
→ 보기의 organization is a bit confusing

15 에이버리 씨가 구입한 생수의 할인가는?
(A) 3.99달러　**(B) 5.99달러**
(C) 7.99달러　(D) 8.99달러

해설 연계

후기의 세 번째 단락 마지막 문장에서 에이버리 씨가 블루웰 생수를 구입했다(I bought a case of Bluewell bottled water at less than half the price I usually pay!)고 했고, 광고에서 블루웰 퓨어는 상자당 5.99달러(Bluewell Pure: $5.99 per case)라는 것을 확인할 수 있으므로 (B)가 정답이다.

[16-20] 이메일 + 송장 + 이메일

발신: 토드 굿윈 〈t.goodwin@ossieofficesupply.com〉
수신: OOS 운영팀 〈management@ossieofficesupply.com〉
날짜: 7월 2일
제목: 팀 회의 안건
첨부: ❶ 쿠르미노프 기사

팀원 여러분, 안녕하세요.

오늘 운영 회의 안건입니다. 오후 1시에 뵈어요!
1. 신입사원 교육 일정. **16** 이번 주 카렌 박이 채용돼 7월 8일부터 교육을 시작합니다. 회의 전에 일정을 확인하고 교육 근무를 할 준비를 해서 오세요.
2. 2분기 판매 결과. 훌리오 고메즈가 매장 내 판매에 대해 논평합니다. 저는 온라인 판매를 논의합니다.
3. 온라인 판매. 온라인 판매 신장에 관한 첨부된 기사를 읽고 아이디어를 토의할 준비를 해서 회의에 오세요. **18** 온라인 판매를 늘려야 하므로 저는 무료 배송이나 반품, 원 플러스 원 특가, 또는 재구매 고객을 위한 10퍼센트 충성고객 할인 제공을 고려해야 한다고 생각합니다.
4. 새 배송업체 물색 진행 상황. 지난달 6월 14일 저는 고객 설문조사 결과를 발표했는데, 조사에 따르면 고객들은 소포 추적이 되기를 바랍니다. 고객들은 배송비 인하도 원합니다. **17** 줄리 린트가 고려할 만한 배송업체 몇 군데에 관해 발표합니다.

토드 굿윈
오시 사무용품 본부장

어휘 agenda 안건 buy-one-get-one-free 원 플러스 원 return customer 재구매 고객 progress 진행 track 추적하다 shipping rate 배송비

발신: 오시 사무용품 〈invoice@ossieofficesupply.com〉
수신: 시마 샤 〈s.shah@gopromail.com〉
날짜: 8월 18일
제목: 청구서 #08912

오시 사무용품에서 구매해 주셔서 감사합니다! 아래 청구서를 보세요.

품목	수량	단가	총 가격
검정 볼펜(8팩)	10	2.99달러	29.90달러
빨강 볼펜(8팩)	2	2.99달러	5.98달러
백색 인쇄용지(500매)	20	4.29달러	85.80달러
		소계	121.68달러
		18 할인: (10% 할인)	12.17달러
		세금: 5%	6.08달러
		배송: (특송)	10.00달러
		지불 금액:	125.59달러

온라인 주문은 배송 전까지 수정 또는 취소할 수 있습니다. 변경이 필요하면 (413) 555-0130으로 전화 주세요. **19** 배송 진행 상황은 짚 쉽 웹사이트에서 추적 번호 0008971을 사용해 추적할 수 있습니다(zipship.com/trackmypackage).

어휘 revise 수정하다

발신: 시마 샤 〈s.shah@gopromail.com〉
수신: OOS 고객 서비스 〈customerservice@ossieofficesupply.com〉
20 날짜: 8월 22일
제목: 없어진 주문품

안녕하세요.

청구서 #08912와 관련하여 씁니다. **20** 오늘 도착 예정이었지만 이제 업무종료 시간인데 아직 도착하지 않았습니다. 전에는 귀사에서 주문품을 제시간에 받는 데 문제가 한 번도 없었습니다. **19** 주문품 도착 시간을 알 수 있는 방법을 알려 주세요. 금요일 전에 받지 못하면 주문을 취소하고 매장으로 가야 합니다.

감사합니다.

시마 샤
고 프로 이그제큐티브즈, 사무장

어휘 due to ~하기로 예정된

16 굿윈 씨가 운영팀 팀원들에게 요청한 일은 무엇인가?
(A) 신입사원 교육 돕기
(B) 팀별 판매 결과 제출
(C) 기사 편집
(D) 반품 정책 검토

해설 세부 사항

첫 번째 이메일의 운영 회의 안건 1에서 이메일의 발신자 굿윈 씨가 수신자인 운영팀에게 신입 직원의 교육 근무를 준비해 달라(Karen Park was hired this week and will begin training on July 8. Please look at your schedules before the meeting and come prepared to take a training shift)고 요청하고 있다는 것을 알 수 있으므로 (A)가 정답이다.

17 배송업체에 관해 발표할 사람은 누구인가?
(A) 박 씨   (B) 린트 씨
(C) 굿윈 씨   (D) 고메즈 씨

해설 세부 사항

첫 번째 이메일의 운영 회의 안건 4에서 린트 씨가 배송업체에 관해 발표를 할 것(Julie Lindt will present on a few shipping companies for us to consider)이라고 했으므로 (B)가 정답이다.

18 굿윈 씨의 제안 중 그룹이 무엇에 찬성했겠는가?
(A) 무료 배송   (B) 무료 반품
(C) 원 플러스 원 특가 (D) 충성고객 할인

해설 연계
첫 번째 이메일의 운영 회의 안건 3에서 굿윈 씨는 재구매 고객에게 무료 배송이나 반품, 원 플러스 원 특가, 10퍼센트의 충성고객 할인 제공을 제안(We need to boost online sales, so I think we should consider offering free shipping or returns, a buy-one-get-one-free special, or a 10 percent loyalty discount for return customers)했다는 것을 알 수 있다. 그리고 송장의 Discount: (10% off)를 통해 고객이 10퍼센트 할인을 받았다는 것을 확인할 수 있으므로 (D)가 정답이다.

19 고객 지원 담당자는 샤 씨에게 무엇을 하라고 요청하겠는가?
(A) 짚 쉽 웹사이트 방문
(B) 주문 취소
(C) 오시 사무용품 매장 방문
(D) 고객 서비스 번호로 전화하기

해설 연계
두 번째 이메일 네 번째 문장에서 메일 발신인 샤 씨는 수신인 고객 서비스 부서에 주문 도착 시간을 어떻게 알 수 있는지(Please let me know how I can find out when our order will arrive) 묻고 있고, 송장 하단에서 짚 쉽 웹사이트에서 배송 진행 상황을 추적할 수 있다(The progress of your shipment can be tracked on Zip Ship's Website using tracking number 0008971)고 했다. 이를 통해 고객 지원 담당자는 샤 씨에게 짚 쉽 웹사이트 방문을 요청할 것임을 알 수 있으므로 (A)가 정답이다.

20 샤 씨의 배송품은 언제 도착하기로 되어 있었는가?
(A) 6월 14일   (B) 7월 2일
(C) 8월 18일   (D) 8월 22일

해설 추론
두 번째 이메일의 두 번째 문장에서 오늘 도착 예정인 주문품이 아직 도착하지 않았다(It was due to arrive today, but it is now the close of business, and it has not yet arrived)고 했고 이메일은 8월 22일(August 22)에 쓰였으므로 (D)가 정답이다.

YBM

ETS 토익
단기공략
650⁺
실전 모의고사

LISTENING TEST

In the Listening test, you will be asked to demonstrate how well you understand spoken English. The entire Listening test will last approximately 45 minutes. There are four parts, and directions are given for each part. You must mark your answers on the separate answer sheet. Do not write your answers in your test book.

PART 1

Directions: For each question in this part, you will hear four statements about a picture in your test book. When you hear the statements, you must select the one statement that best describes what you see in the picture. Then find the number of the question on your answer sheet and mark your answer. The statements will not be printed in your test book and will be spoken only one time.

Statement (C), "They're sitting at a table," is the best description of the picture, so you should select answer (C) and mark it on your answer sheet.

1.

2.

3.

4.

5.

6.

PART 2

Directions: You will hear a question or statement and three responses spoken in English. They will not be printed in your test book and will be spoken only one time. Select the best response to the question or statement and mark the letter (A), (B), or (C) on your answer sheet.

7. Mark your answer on your answer sheet.
8. Mark your answer on your answer sheet.
9. Mark your answer on your answer sheet.
10. Mark your answer on your answer sheet.
11. Mark your answer on your answer sheet.
12. Mark your answer on your answer sheet.
13. Mark your answer on your answer sheet.
14. Mark your answer on your answer sheet.
15. Mark your answer on your answer sheet.
16. Mark your answer on your answer sheet.
17. Mark your answer on your answer sheet.
18. Mark your answer on your answer sheet.
19. Mark your answer on your answer sheet.
20. Mark your answer on your answer sheet.
21. Mark your answer on your answer sheet.
22. Mark your answer on your answer sheet.
23. Mark your answer on your answer sheet.
24. Mark your answer on your answer sheet.
25. Mark your answer on your answer sheet.
26. Mark your answer on your answer sheet.
27. Mark your answer on your answer sheet.
28. Mark your answer on your answer sheet.
29. Mark your answer on your answer sheet.
30. Mark your answer on your answer sheet.
31. Mark your answer on your answer sheet.

PART 3

Directions: You will hear some conversations between two or more people. You will be asked to answer three questions about what the speakers say in each conversation. Select the best response to each question and mark the letter (A), (B), (C), or (D) on your answer sheet. The conversations will not be printed in your test book and will be spoken only one time.

32. What kind of event are the speakers discussing?
    (A) A dance performance
    (B) A retirement party
    (C) A community festival
    (D) A music competition

33. What kind of business do the speakers most likely work for?
    (A) A bank
    (B) An amusement park
    (C) A bakery
    (D) A shipping company

34. What problem does the woman tell the man about?
    (A) An equipment delivery was delayed.
    (B) A vehicle is not working.
    (C) An order form is missing.
    (D) An employee has not arrived.

35. What is the man working on?
    (A) A vacation policy
    (B) An upcoming workshop
    (C) A training manual
    (D) An employee retreat

36. What does the man mention about the internship program?
    (A) It was a great success.
    (B) It needs more mentors.
    (C) It has a small budget.
    (D) It is no longer running.

37. What does the woman suggest?
    (A) Adjusting a deadline
    (B) Hiring temporary employees
    (C) Creating some guidelines
    (D) Gathering staff feedback

38. Who most likely are the speakers?
    (A) Restaurant servers
    (B) Tour guides
    (C) Security guards
    (D) Taxi drivers

39. According to the woman, what has caused a delay?
    (A) An absent employee
    (B) A computer error
    (C) A severe storm
    (D) A traffic jam

40. What does the man plan to do next?
    (A) Head to an office
    (B) Upload a schedule
    (C) Share some news
    (D) Purchase some beverages

41. Who most likely is the woman?
    (A) An athlete
    (B) A marketing specialist
    (C) A journalist
    (D) A shoe designer

42. Why are the speakers meeting?
    (A) To test a product line
    (B) To negotiate a contract
    (C) To practice a presentation
    (D) To review some feedback

43. What does the woman mention about the men's company's products?
    (A) She has a lot of them.
    (B) She usually buys them online.
    (C) They have a lightweight design.
    (D) They are popular worldwide.

GO ON TO THE NEXT PAGE

44. Who most likely are the speakers?

    (A) Repair technicians
    (B) Real estate agents
    (C) Hotel clerks
    (D) Administrative assistants

45. What kind of business is Primrose Inc.?

    (A) A plumbing company
    (B) A graphic design firm
    (C) A camping supply company
    (D) An electronics manufacturer

46. What does the woman offer to do?

    (A) Revise a pamphlet
    (B) Speak to a manager
    (C) Report a complaint
    (D) Work additional hours

47. What are the speakers applying for?

    (A) A license renewal
    (B) A building permit
    (C) A business loan
    (D) A research grant

48. What does the man mean when he says, "I saved it in the shared folder"?

    (A) Some work procedures have changed.
    (B) Another storage drive was full.
    (C) Some information is not confidential.
    (D) A file has not been lost.

49. What devices do the speakers hope to include?

    (A) Smart speakers
    (B) Emergency generators
    (C) Security cameras
    (D) Portable heaters

50. Where most likely do the speakers work?

    (A) At a waste management firm
    (B) At a government office
    (C) At an art supply store
    (D) At a fashion design company

51. What does the woman want to do?

    (A) Conduct a survey
    (B) Offer a disposal service
    (C) Launch a loyalty program
    (D) Promote some employees

52. What does the man say he will do tomorrow?

    (A) Contact a consultant
    (B) Move some shelves
    (C) Design a poster
    (D) Get some cost estimates

53. Who most likely is the woman?

    (A) A professor
    (B) An actor
    (C) An author
    (D) A librarian

54. What problem does the woman tell the man about?

    (A) An event is too short.
    (B) Some expenses have increased.
    (C) She will be arriving late.
    (D) Tickets have not been selling well.

55. What will the man probably do next?

    (A) Send an invitation
    (B) Set up a seating area
    (C) Reserve a room
    (D) Consult a business owner

56. In what industry do the speakers most likely work?

(A) Transportation
(B) Agriculture
(C) Health care
(D) Finance

57. Why does the man interrupt the conversation?

(A) To remind the women about a project
(B) To deliver some urgent packages
(C) To volunteer to do a task
(D) To explain a problem with a timeline

58. What will happen next?

(A) The man will read some online reviews.
(B) The man will submit some documents.
(C) The women will contact some businesses.
(D) The women will review test results.

---

59. How did the woman find out about the business?

(A) By speaking to a coworker
(B) By receiving a promotional e-mail
(C) By being handed a flyer
(D) By getting a relative's recommendation

60. What does the man mean when he says, "I completed a project there last week"?

(A) He is free to start right away.
(B) A travel distance is not too far.
(C) The woman can view a property.
(D) He is familiar with regulations.

61. What does the man say he will need?

(A) Some measurements
(B) An initial deposit
(C) A product sample
(D) Some photographs

62. What does the man say he will do next week?

(A) Move to a new home
(B) Launch a business
(C) Return some furniture
(D) Host some guests

63. Look at the graphic. Which product does the man want to order?

(A) #401
(B) #426
(C) #459
(D) #477

64. What does the woman tell the man about?

(A) A bulk discount on items
(B) A free delivery option
(C) An extended warranty
(D) An offer for a free gift

GO ON TO THE NEXT PAGE

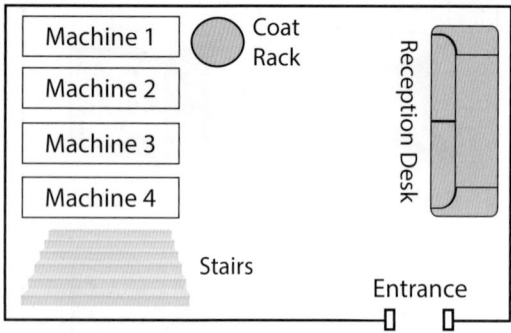

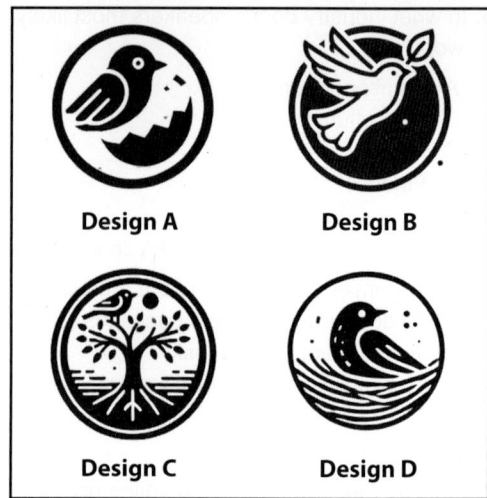

65. Why did the man visit Ames Logistics?

(A) To give a demonstration
(B) To plan an anniversary party
(C) To inspect a facility
(D) To take part in an interview

66. Look at the graphic. Which vending machine should the man not use?

(A) Machine 1
(B) Machine 2
(C) Machine 3
(D) Machine 4

67. What will the man most likely do next?

(A) Show a photo ID
(B) Write his license number
(C) Provide his signature
(D) View a building map

68. What are the speakers preparing for?

(A) A sports competition
(B) A fund-raising event
(C) A nature hike
(D) A community picnic

69. Look at the graphic. Which design does the woman select?

(A) Design A
(B) Design B
(C) Design C
(D) Design D

70. What does the man ask the woman to bring?

(A) Some decorations
(B) Some storage boxes
(C) Some business cards
(D) Some banking details

PART 4

Directions: You will hear some talks given by a single speaker. You will be asked to answer three questions about what the speaker says in each talk. Select the best response to each question and mark the letter (A), (B), (C), or (D) on your answer sheet. The talks will not be printed in your test book and will be spoken only one time.

71. What most likely is the advertisement about?

    (A) A pharmacy
    (B) A health clinic
    (C) A gym
    (D) A beauty salon

72. What recent change at the business is mentioned?

    (A) The interior has been remodeled.
    (B) The number of branches has increased.
    (C) The business is under new management.
    (D) The staff has completed special training.

73. According to the speaker, why should listeners visit a Web site?

    (A) To leave a review
    (B) To download a coupon
    (C) To check a price list
    (D) To view some photographs

74. Who most likely is the speaker addressing?

    (A) Journalists
    (B) Accountants
    (C) Factory workers
    (D) Medical technicians

75. What will be the topic of Ms. Drake's talk?

    (A) Efficiency improvements
    (B) Professional networking
    (C) Stress management
    (D) Personal finance

76. What does the speaker suggest listeners do?

    (A) Read a book
    (B) Take many notes
    (C) Set a goal
    (D) Join a debate

77. Where most likely does the speaker work?

    (A) At a moving company
    (B) At a car dealership
    (C) At an architecture firm
    (D) At a real estate agency

78. What does the speaker say is necessary?

    (A) An application fee
    (B) An insurance policy
    (C) A mailing address
    (D) A letter of reference

79. What does the speaker mean when he says, "She has been here for a long time"?

    (A) Another customer must be served first.
    (B) A colleague can handle some inquiries.
    (C) Some paperwork has already been prepared.
    (D) A project had a significant delay.

80. What is the announcement mainly about?

    (A) A reminder to audience members about theater etiquette
    (B) Rules regarding food and beverages in a theater
    (C) Items that are available for purchase at a theater
    (D) A correction that has been made to a theater schedule

81. What is mentioned about the June 5 performance?

    (A) Some performers will sign posters.
    (B) Discounts are available to groups.
    (C) Its tickets have already sold out.
    (D) The start time has been changed.

82. What can listeners receive if they sign up for a membership today?

    (A) A parking pass
    (B) A performance ticket
    (C) A section upgrade
    (D) A complimentary bag

GO ON TO THE NEXT PAGE

83. What is the purpose of the call?
    (A) To register for an industry conference
    (B) To invite the listener to give a talk
    (C) To offer transportation to the listener
    (D) To remind the listener to reserve a ticket

84. What did the speaker do at the Sherwood Center last year?
    (A) He attended a wedding.
    (B) He applied for a job.
    (C) He hosted a family reunion.
    (D) He took part in a trade show.

85. What is the speaker looking forward to doing?
    (A) Giving a presentation
    (B) Learning about a winner
    (C) Meeting an industry leader
    (D) Attending an engineering course

86. Who most likely is the speaker?
    (A) An architect
    (B) A fashion designer
    (C) A lawyer
    (D) A restaurant chef

87. What type of item does the speaker mention?
    (A) Appliances
    (B) Flooring
    (C) Furniture
    (D) Lights

88. Why does the speaker say, "those figures include installation"?
    (A) To express a concern
    (B) To decline some assistance
    (C) To avoid a misunderstanding
    (D) To make an offer

89. Who is the speaker?
    (A) An event planner
    (B) A newspaper reporter
    (C) A safety inspector
    (D) A city employee

90. What is the speaker discussing?
    (A) The renewal of a business contract
    (B) The addition of some sports facilities
    (C) The creation of a bicycle trail
    (D) The celebration of an achievement

91. According to the speaker, why is a project being carried out?
    (A) To attract more tourists
    (B) To prevent air pollution
    (C) To promote outdoor activities
    (D) To reduce operating costs

92. How is the speaker helping the listener?
    (A) By organizing an office
    (B) By editing a presentation
    (C) By booking a flight
    (D) By renting a car

93. What does the speaker imply when he says, "they're roughly the same price"?
    (A) A coupon code did not work.
    (B) Some figures must be incorrect.
    (C) The listener can choose freely.
    (D) The listener should research further.

94. Why does the speaker say he might not answer his phone?
    (A) He has a low phone battery.
    (B) He will be in a meeting.
    (C) He needs the information in writing.
    (D) He plans to leave work early.

Foster Bank	
Teller Services	Counter 1
Foreign Currency Exchange	Counter 2
Loan Applications	Counter 3
Business Accounts	Counter 4

Music Lineup	
6:30 P.M.	Echoes of Time
7:00 P.M.	The Collective
7:30 P.M.	The Rio Trio
8:00 P.M.	Edge-Makers

95. According to the speaker, what has happened recently?

(A) New employees have been hired.
(B) Banking regulations have changed.
(C) The number of customers has increased.
(D) A building has been made larger.

96. Look at the graphic. Which counter is currently closed?

(A) Counter 1
(B) Counter 2
(C) Counter 3
(D) Counter 4

97. How does the speaker say that listeners can save time?

(A) By picking up a brochure
(B) By signing up for a newsletter
(C) By scheduling an appointment
(D) By calling a helpline

98. What type of music is the speaker discussing?

(A) Jazz
(B) Folk
(C) Classical
(D) Rock and roll

99. Look at the graphic. When does the recommended performance start?

(A) At 6:30 P.M.
(B) At 7:00 P.M.
(C) At 7:30 P.M.
(D) At 8:00 P.M.

100. Who is Dominic Briggs?

(A) A radio host
(B) A studio owner
(C) A singer
(D) A teacher

This is the end of the Listening test. Turn to Part 5 in your test book.

GO ON TO THE NEXT PAGE

READING TEST

In the Reading test, you will read a variety of texts and answer several different types of reading comprehension questions. The entire Reading test will last 75 minutes. There are three parts, and directions are given for each part. You are encouraged to answer as many questions as possible within the time allowed.

You must mark your answers on the separate answer sheet. Do not write your answers in your test book.

PART 5

Directions: A word or phrase is missing in each of the sentences below. Four answer choices are given below each sentence. Select the best answer to complete the sentence. Then mark the letter (A), (B), (C), or (D) on your answer sheet.

101. If ------- products do not meet customers' expectations, they can be returned.

    (A) we
    (B) ours
    (C) our
    (D) ourselves

102. The factory requires a ------- supply of raw materials to meet its production demands.

    (A) steady
    (B) rough
    (C) rigid
    (D) durable

103. The Association of Organic Farmers ------- a new set of guidelines for growers next month.

    (A) has released
    (B) will release
    (C) released
    (D) releasing

104. Thanks to a bulk discount, Tyson Manufacturing bought the wire at ------- low rates.

    (A) actively
    (B) finally
    (C) gradually
    (D) surprisingly

105. Compliance with new industry standards will require a policy -------.

    (A) revises
    (B) revision
    (C) revised
    (D) revisional

106. Owing to upgraded equipment, Kendell Manufacturing is ------- 20 percent more appliances than before.

    (A) solving
    (B) producing
    (C) fostering
    (D) affecting

107. Ms. Han notes that technical issues during our video conferences are ------- common.

    (A) regrettably
    (B) regret
    (C) regretted
    (D) regrettable

108. Damato Finance's research consultants prepared a report ------- a broad range of investment options.

    (A) as
    (B) to
    (C) by
    (D) on

109. All documents relating to the contract should be reviewed by a senior -------.
   (A) executive
   (B) execute
   (C) executing
   (D) execution

110. Section 3 of the staff handbook explains that most accidents are ------- through careful planning.
   (A) prevent
   (B) preventing
   (C) preventable
   (D) prevention

111. Carolina Outdoors bicycles are ------- to be the most durable option for any riding in off-road conditions.
   (A) encountered
   (B) affected
   (C) insisted
   (D) considered

112. Mr. Rasmussen is the food critic ------- was the first to praise the bistro's unique flavors.
   (A) whose
   (B) whenever
   (C) who
   (D) what

113. Although teamwork is important, managers assess employees' performance -------.
   (A) individual
   (B) individuals
   (C) individually
   (D) individuality

114. Due to the thin walls, speaking with a microphone may cause disturbances in ------- rooms.
   (A) accessible
   (B) adjacent
   (C) spacious
   (D) formal

115. The construction of the new public library was delayed by ------- nine months.
   (A) between
   (B) major
   (C) late
   (D) over

116. Rowley Solutions is recruiting software engineers ------- the development of an investment smartphone application.
   (A) about
   (B) for
   (C) like
   (D) since

117. Vance Inc.'s board members debated whether the ------- partnership offer should be reconsidered in the next quarter.
   (A) withdraw
   (B) withdrawal
   (C) withdraws
   (D) withdrawn

118. Regarding the contract, the terms will continue for one year unless both parties agree -------.
   (A) namely
   (B) otherwise
   (C) indeed
   (D) almost

119. Thus far, Eastfall Logistics ------- agreements with more than twenty major retail chains across the country.
   (A) to secure
   (B) has secured
   (C) was securing
   (D) secure

120. Mr. Allen would ------- need several years of further education to meet the requirements of the job.
   (A) either
   (B) only
   (C) still
   (D) much

GO ON TO THE NEXT PAGE

121. The laboratory technicians require intense ------- while mixing the chemicals needed for the experiment.
    (A) concentrate
    (B) concentrates
    (C) concentration
    (D) concentrated

122. To ------- the job duties, Emerson Clothing's employees must be familiar with all policies.
    (A) incur
    (B) remit
    (C) fulfill
    (D) obtain

123. The committee members ------- recalled the details of Ms. Turner's presentation at the last meeting.
    (A) vaguely
    (B) vague
    (C) vaguest
    (D) vagueness

124. ------- the bank transfer request is received by 1 P.M., it will be processed the same day.
    (A) Rather than
    (B) As long as
    (C) Due to
    (D) In light of

125. Mr. Jackson questioned whether the business could ------- all of the proposed upgrades.
    (A) affordable
    (B) afford
    (C) afforded
    (D) affording

126. The consultant for Kirkland Studios suggested the scenic mountain range as a promising ------- for the film shoot.
    (A) location
    (B) function
    (C) population
    (D) phase

127. Because the actual materials' prices did not align with ------- in the original quote, the project's final cost was much higher.
    (A) outside
    (B) those
    (C) including
    (D) toward

128. Personal e-mails are ------- in the office during working hours in an effort to maintain productivity.
    (A) prohibited
    (B) demolished
    (C) broken
    (D) chosen

129. To attract exceptional ------- to the sales role, Mr. Presley is offering an attractive bonus.
    (A) reasons
    (B) candidates
    (C) practices
    (D) results

130. Ms. Huang is busy with bookkeeping tasks year-round but ------- during the tax season.
    (A) fortunately
    (B) tightly
    (C) especially
    (D) permanently

PART 6

Directions: Read the texts that follow. A word, phrase, or sentence is missing in parts of each text. Four answer choices for each question are given below the text. Select the best answer to complete the text. Then mark the letter (A), (B), (C), or (D) on your answer sheet.

Questions 131-134 refer to the following notice.

Dear Rivendell Clinic Staff:

The annual Southwest Medical Convention will be held on June 21, and the clinic will pay the related costs for any staff members who wish to take part in it. ------- can listen to lectures, participate in workshops, and watch panel discussions. There is a registration form for the event, which should ------- by May 10. So, please let Amber Flynn know if you are interested as soon as possible. -------. Going to the convention is a great way to build ------- connections with other medical professionals as well as learn more about the medical field.

131. (A) Passengers
(B) Messengers
(C) Attendees
(D) Guides

132. (A) have submitted
(B) have been submitted
(C) be submitted
(D) be submitting

133. (A) Applications will only be accepted until the end of May.
(B) The sessions throughout the day were informative and engaging.
(C) All presenters will have rooms booked at the same hotel.
(D) She will make the necessary arrangements on your behalf.

134. (A) strongest
(B) strong
(C) strength
(D) strongly

GO ON TO THE NEXT PAGE

Questions 135-138 refer to the following memo.

To: Forster Advertising Staff
From: Valentina Blakely
Date: October 16
Subject: Congratulations!

I ------- (135.) spoke to a representative of the National Advertising Council who informed me that our company has made the list of nominees for the Innovative Advertising Award. The judges were impressed with the creative transitions in our Nuzum Footwear advertisement. It was wonderful to hear ------- (136.) praise for our work. ------- (137.) . I will let you know as soon as I find out the result. This nomination is an honor, and it is great publicity for our business. ------- (138.) , it demonstrates the talent of our team.

135. (A) soon
(B) rarely
(C) just
(D) yet

136. (A) my
(B) it
(C) their
(D) your

137. (A) It can be seen both on television and online.
(B) Be sure to fill out the nomination form completely.
(C) Sales increased noticeably after the advertisement ran.
(D) The winner will be announced on November 5.

138. (A) Nonetheless
(B) To illustrate
(C) Above all
(D) In contrast

Questions 139-142 refer to the following press release.

FOR IMMEDIATE RELEASE

CONTACT: Ines Fiorentini, (203) 555-9748

(May 5)—The Lakewood History Museum announces the grand opening of its newest exhibit, "Legacies of the Ancient World." Visitors are encouraged ------- (139.) this collection of items from ancient Egypt that highlight the development of its writing and culture. The centerpiece is a recently ------- (140.) scroll that describes a local ceremony. ------- (141.), there are several tools for early writing, such as reed pens and ink containers. The exhibit is open from Tuesday to Sunday from 10:00 A.M. to 5:30 P.M. The museum offers a variety of ways to enjoy the exhibit. ------- (142.). We hope everyone will enjoy this wonderful event!

139. (A) exploring
 (B) to explore
 (C) the exploration of
 (D) they explored

140. (A) discovering
 (B) discovery
 (C) discovered
 (D) discover

141. (A) Until then
 (B) Consequently
 (C) In advance
 (D) Furthermore

142. (A) Some visitors requested more thorough explanations.
 (B) They were found at an archeological dig site.
 (C) Maps of the museum may be outdated.
 (D) These include group tours and audio guides.

Questions 143-146 refer to the following memo.

To: All Ermin Sales Employees
From: Vineet Nayar, Office Manager
Date: November 29
Subject: Change regarding travel

As it has become increasingly difficult to ------- staff members' business-related travel receipts and reimbursements, Ermin Sales will adopt a new policy. From January 1, the administrative office will book all flights and hotels for staff members. -------. These can be used for smaller expenses arising during business trips, such as meals and local transportation. We know that some of you enjoy making your own travel arrangements, but this is no longer ------- enough. Please rest assured that ------- regarding the change can be brought up and discussed at the next staff meeting.

143. (A) sort out
(B) measure
(C) pay with
(D) possess

144. (A) For example, first class is much more expensive.
(B) Many of our new clients are based overseas.
(C) We will also be issuing company credit cards.
(D) This software requires a very secure password.

145. (A) substantial
(B) actual
(C) restricted
(D) efficient

146. (A) comments
(B) to comment
(C) comment
(D) commented

PART 7

Directions: In this part you will read a selection of texts, such as magazine and newspaper articles, e-mails, and instant messages. Each text or set of texts is followed by several questions. Select the best answer for each question and mark the letter (A), (B), (C), or (D) on your answer sheet.

Questions 147-148 refer to the following receipt.

SUNNYVALE HOTEL
Room Service

- Call the front desk to order (dial 0)
- Available 6 A.M. to 11 P.M. daily
- Dishes can be adapted for those with food allergies

ORDER	PRICE
Salmon cream pasta	$18.00
Garden salad	$9.00
Cola	$3.50
Subtotal	$30.50
Tax	$2.44
TOTAL	$32.94

October 17, 7:29 P.M.
Charged to credit card: XXXX-XXXX-XXXX-7495
Name and room number: Craig Alvarado, 322
Delivered by: Peggy Stanfield

147. What is indicated about the food service?

(A) Its recipes can be altered.
(B) It is available around the clock.
(C) Its prices are lower for groups.
(D) It can be charged to the room.

148. Who most likely is Mr. Alvarado?

(A) A front desk receptionist
(B) A guest at Sunnyvale Hotel
(C) A delivery person
(D) An on-site hotel chef

GO ON TO THE NEXT PAGE

Questions 149-150 refer to the following e-mail.

To:	Brandi Pollard <brandi@agmaxrentals.com>
From:	Felix Dawson <fdawson@cambriamail.com>
Date:	May 11
Subject:	Willowgreen Farm

Hi Brandi,

Thank you for confirming that you have received the deposit for my rental of a liquid fertilizer sprayer for my farm. I know that I asked for it to be delivered on May 16 and picked up the following day. However, would it be possible to have the two-day rental begin on May 13 instead? Very high winds are expected beginning May 15, so I would like to spray on May 13 and 14. Please let me know if this is possible.

Thank you,

Felix Dawson

149. What is the purpose of the e-mail?
 (A) To negotiate a lower fee for machinery
 (B) To ask where to send a deposit
 (C) To request a change in a rental period
 (D) To make a complaint about a transaction

150. According to the e-mail, by when does Mr. Dawson want to complete a task?
 (A) May 13
 (B) May 14
 (C) May 15
 (D) May 16

Questions 151-152 refer to the following notification.

Hi, Mr. Janik. Your Breeze Electronics order #083119 containing 3 items has been dispatched and is now with our courier. The estimated arrival time at the address indicated on the order form is 2:00 P.M.–3:00 P.M., and your courier is Derren B. Please note that we cannot leave items outside the property or with a neighbor. If you will not be home to accept the item, please select a new time and date through your customer account page. Thank you for choosing Breeze Electronics!

151. Why was Mr. Janik sent a notification?
 (A) An item is currently out of stock.
 (B) A package is out for delivery.
 (C) A refund has been approved.
 (D) An order is awaiting payment.

152. What is mentioned in the notification about Breeze Electronics?
 (A) It is open daily until 3:00 P.M.
 (B) It charges a fee for returns.
 (C) It upgraded its account page.
 (D) It does not give items to third parties.

Questions 153-154 refer to the following online chat discussion.

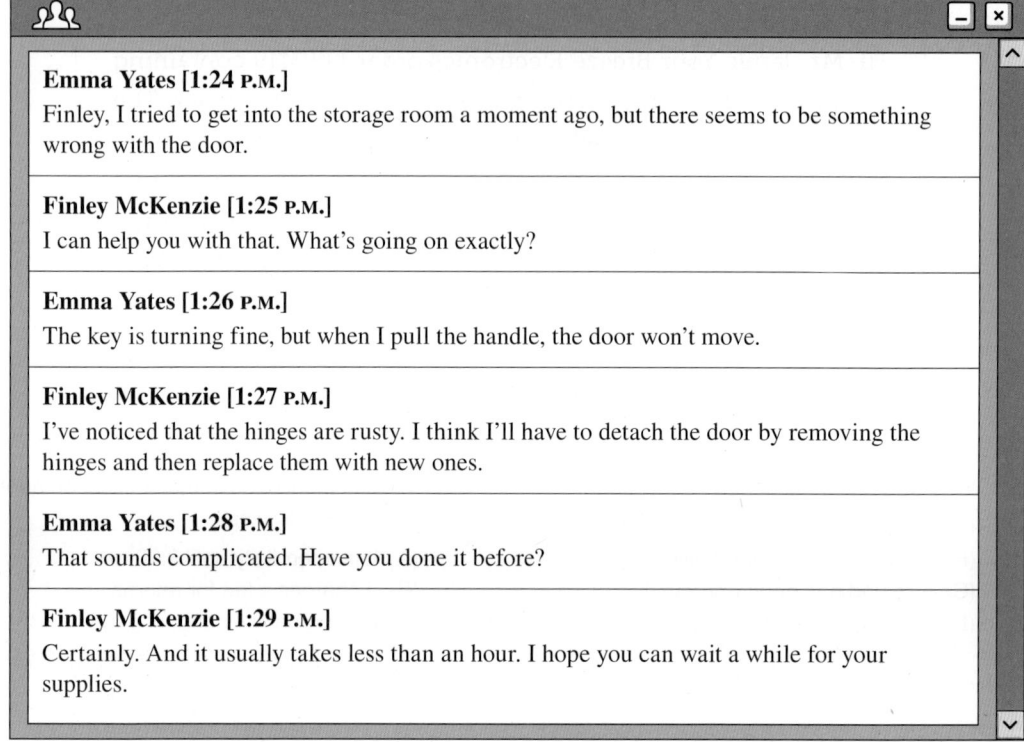

Emma Yates [1:24 P.M.]
Finley, I tried to get into the storage room a moment ago, but there seems to be something wrong with the door.

Finley McKenzie [1:25 P.M.]
I can help you with that. What's going on exactly?

Emma Yates [1:26 P.M.]
The key is turning fine, but when I pull the handle, the door won't move.

Finley McKenzie [1:27 P.M.]
I've noticed that the hinges are rusty. I think I'll have to detach the door by removing the hinges and then replace them with new ones.

Emma Yates [1:28 P.M.]
That sounds complicated. Have you done it before?

Finley McKenzie [1:29 P.M.]
Certainly. And it usually takes less than an hour. I hope you can wait a while for your supplies.

153. Why did Ms. Yates contact Mr. McKenzie?
 (A) She cannot lift some containers in a storage area.
 (B) She needs to place an order for supplies.
 (C) She is having difficulty accessing a space.
 (D) She does not have her key for a locked door.

154. At 1:29 P.M., what does Mr. McKenzie most likely mean when he writes, "Certainly"?
 (A) He has experience performing a task.
 (B) Some tools can be borrowed by Ms. Yates.
 (C) He knows where to buy some components.
 (D) A repair has already been completed.

Questions 155-157 refer to the following notice.

NOTICE: PARKERSBURG AUTUMN TRIATHLON UPDATE

As autumn approaches, we are once again asking staff members to support the Parkersburg Autumn Triathlon. The event will be held on October 3, and the swimming portion will take place here at the Waves Swim Center. A record number of athletes are expected because the triathlon had to be called off last autumn due to severe weather. More lifeguards than usual will be needed. These will be paid positions funded by the event's sponsor, Hawkin Apparel, so you will need to share information about your bank account for the payment processing.

Sherry Valdez is our site's point of contact for this event. If you are interested in participating, please speak to her directly or send her an e-mail at valdezsherry@wavessc.com. A representative from Hawkin Apparel will lead a brief meeting on September 1 at 10 A.M. He will answer any questions you may have and give you a form to complete regarding payment. Please bring a government-issued ID.

155. For whom is the notice intended?
 (A) Event coordinators
 (B) Hawkin Apparel representatives
 (C) Triathlon athletes
 (D) Swim center employees

156. What does the notice indicate about the event?
 (A) Its admission is free.
 (B) Its date may change.
 (C) It was canceled last year.
 (D) It is for people of all ages.

157. What will meeting participants do on September 1 ?
 (A) Pose for an ID photo
 (B) Receive their first payment
 (C) Provide banking details
 (D) Give a tour of a swimming area

Questions 158-160 refer to the following e-mail.

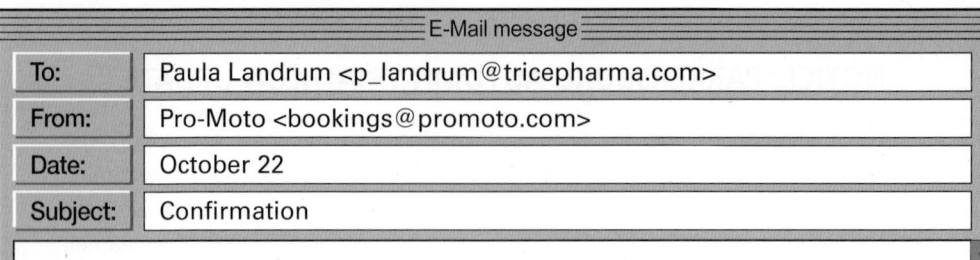

Dear Ms. Landrum,

Thank you for reserving a vehicle from Pro-Moto during your visit to Atlanta. On October 28, you can pick up the four-door hybrid car at our counter in Terminal 3, and your confirmation code is R48797. Please present this code to expedite the process. You must also bring your driver's license and a credit card or debit card. As you plan to use your own insurance, you must provide proof of the policy at the time of pick-up. There will be a brief form for you to fill out, and then you'll be set.

We look forward to serving you.

The Pro-Moto Team

158. What is suggested about Ms. Landrum in the e-mail?

(A) She requested a reservation change.
(B) She recently got a new job.
(C) She has used Pro-Moto before.
(D) She plans to drive in Atlanta.

159. What does Ms. Landrum NOT need to bring on October 28?

(A) Proof of address
(B) Proof of insurance
(C) A form of payment
(D) A confirmation code

160. The word "set" in paragraph 1, line 7, is closest in meaning to

(A) ready
(B) fixed
(C) strict
(D) decided

Questions 161-163 refer to the following notice.

NOTICE TO HOLDENBY RESIDENTS

Thanks to the receipt of a government grant, the town of Holdenby will launch a tree-planting initiative next month. — [1] —. Maple and oak trees will be planted all along Caxton Street and Ashley Street. — [2] —. This is an investment in the future, which will enhance the appearance of major roads as well as provide vital wildlife habitats.

Residents can also pick up free saplings from City Hall to plant on their own property. Those who do so are reminded to check the locations of underground utility lines, particularly gas and electric, before doing any digging. — [3] —. A map detailing utility line locations can be downloaded from the city's Web site. Painted lines near Caxton Street and Ashley Street will also indicate utility lines, as these references will be needed for city workers. Regarding any remaining funds from the grant, officials are assessing several development plans for Terrace Park. — [4] —.

161. Why was the notice written?
 (A) To provide details of a community program
 (B) To explain the benefits of regular tree trimming
 (C) To gather information about tree preferences
 (D) To invite residents to apply for a grant

162. According to the notice, how can residents find out the location of utility lines?
 (A) By visiting City Hall in person
 (B) By calling gas and electric companies
 (C) By asking city workers to paint lines
 (D) By downloading a map online

163. In which of the positions marked [1], [2], [3], and [4] does the following sentence best belong?

 "We will make an announcement once one has been approved."

 (A) [1]
 (B) [2]
 (C) [3]
 (D) [4]

Questions 164-167 refer to the following letter.

Timothy Cordero
2121 Ellis Avenue
Toledo, OH 43604

August 18

Anton Hinson
Jarrell Industrial
190 Zeller Road
Toledo, OH 43727

Dear Mr. Hinson:

I would like to express my interest in the commercial plumbing position at Jarrell Industrial. Please find enclosed my résumé along with copies of my licenses and certifications. I learned of this job opportunity from Wesley Lowery, who is a former employee of yours. Mr. Lowery and I completed the plumbing certification program together at the Elliston Institute.

For the past five years, I have worked full-time for Delgado Plumbing, carrying out large-scale plumbing projects at retail spaces, office complexes, hotels, and more. The owner of the company, Simon Delgado, is retiring, so he is closing the business soon. I have provided Mr. Delgado's contact details should you wish to contact him for a reference. He can confirm that I meet the qualifications you are looking for.

Throughout my career, I have always worked hard, kept informed of local building codes and regulations, and carried out my projects with efficiency and attention to detail. In fact, in a six-month project for Northside Hospital, I rerouted the pipe system to make it more streamlined, saving the client thousands on materials and building trust in the company.

I would be happy to discuss my experience in more detail anytime.

Best,

Timothy Cordero
Timothy Cordero
Enclosure

164. Who most likely is Mr. Lowery?

(A) An institute founder
(B) A certified plumber
(C) A class instructor
(D) A job recruiter

165. What does Mr. Cordero mention about his current employer?

(A) He will shut down his business.
(B) He is difficult to contact as a reference.
(C) He gave Mr. Cordero an award.
(D) He met Mr. Cordero six months ago.

166. The word "meet" in paragraph 2, line 4, is closest in meaning to

(A) locate
(B) allow
(C) encounter
(D) satisfy

167. What accomplishment does Mr. Cordero mention?

(A) He drastically cut costs on a project.
(B) He completed some hospital work early.
(C) He brought in a major client for the company.
(D) He managed a team of workers.

Questions 168-171 refer to the following article.

Worker Health

A recent study conducted in the town of Branford has highlighted significant health and fitness challenges among office workers. — [1] —. Questionnaire responses revealed that despite the recommendation to achieve at least 8,000 steps per day, 75 percent of workers did not even reach 4,000 daily steps. As physical inactivity has been linked to a number of health issues, companies are looking into possible solutions. — [2] —.

One approach is to introduce standing desks, which can help increase daily physical activity. If stools are provided, employees can alternate between sitting and standing throughout the day, which promotes good circulation. The small movements associated with standing can boost energy levels and help keep employees focused.

Another effective strategy is offering flexible work-from-home options. By reducing their commuting times, employees have more free time to incorporate physical activities, such as daily walks, into their routines. — [3] —. This option also contributes to a healthy work-life balance.

Providing on-site exercise facilities at the workplace is another solution. — [4] —. With an easily accessible gym, employees can work out during breaks or before/after work due to the convenient location of the equipment. When staff members use a fitness area together, it can foster a culture of health and well-being within the workplace, as well as build good relationships among employees. Having opportunities to exercise at the workplace was one of the top-rated requests from questionnaire respondents.

By taking action to support employees' health, companies can help bridge the gap between recommended and actual levels of physical activity.

168. What is one reason the article was written?

(A) To urge workers to complete a survey
(B) To explain the most effective exercises
(C) To present some research findings
(D) To report on the area's healthcare facilities

169. What is suggested about the majority of office workers in Branford?

(A) They have reduced their workout time by seventy-five percent.
(B) They fail to meet recommended exercise targets.
(C) They have a high rate of illness due to stress.
(D) They work more hours compared to people in other cities.

170. What is NOT mentioned in the article as a way to improve employee fitness?

(A) Supplying exercise equipment at work
(B) Allowing employees to work remotely
(C) Attending group fitness classes as a team
(D) Using desks at which people can stand

171. In which of the positions marked [1], [2], [3], and [4] does the following sentence best belong?

"Of course, this may not be possible for operations with limited space."

(A) [1]
(B) [2]
(C) [3]
(D) [4]

Questions 172-175 refer to the following text-message chain.

Arlene Brunelle [10:11 A.M.] Hira and Lucien, this morning, I spoke to Rossana Shuman, the site manager of Ettlewood Hall. She informed me that their outdoor fountain has yet to be repaired, and she wondered whether we want to postpone our project.

Hira Nandi [10:12 A.M.] We can't. Everything else is ready for shooting a scene there on Saturday. I thought they were having it fixed. Didn't Ms. Shuman guarantee that on Tuesday?

Lucien Doyle [10:13 A.M.] Yes. When I was there in person, I pointed out the problem. Ms. Shuman assured me that someone would come to resolve the issue that afternoon.

Arlene Brunelle [10:15 A.M.] We can't delay the filming schedule. I guess we'll have to add in the water digitally later, like we did with the Cartwright project last year. But the services from the visual effects studio were quite expensive, if I remember correctly.

Hira Nandi [10:16 A.M.] If we check their invoice, we could get a better idea.

Lucien Doyle [10:17 A.M.] I'm sure I have it.

Hira Nandi [10:18 A.M.] Thanks, Lucien.

Arlene Brunelle [10:19 A.M.] I'll let Ms. Shuman know that we will go ahead as we first planned.

172. In what industry do the writers most likely work?

    (A) Construction
    (B) Fashion
    (C) Media
    (D) Healthcare

173. When was a repair promised?

    (A) On Monday
    (B) On Tuesday
    (C) On Thursday
    (D) On Saturday

174. At 10:17 A.M., what does Mr. Doyle most likely mean when he writes, "I'm sure I have it"?

    (A) He will provide directions to Ettlewood Hall.
    (B) He forgot to send an important invoice.
    (C) He can supply some cost information.
    (D) He thinks they do not need to purchase anything.

175. What will Ms. Brunelle probably do next?

    (A) Send an updated bill to Ms. Shuman
    (B) Inform staff members of a postponement
    (C) Research some of the site options
    (D) Give confirmation of the original schedule

Questions 176-180 refer to the following brochure and e-mail.

CHARACK SOLUTIONS
contact@characksolutions.com / 878-555-4357

Turn any room into a space that you love!

We can help to transform your residence or commercial premises. Interior design is more than just choosing between wallpaper and paint or carpets and hardwood floors. Of course we'll help you with that, but we'll also work to create a cohesive design that is a true reflection of who you are. We'll suggest the right furniture, as well as curtains or blinds, to tie everything together.

The initial advisory session is provided at no charge.

Our team has a diverse range of styles to suit customers of all tastes.

Nicole Boone – Modern Style: sleek lines, functional furniture, and following the latest trends

Jay Kocher – Minimalist Style: light colors and natural materials with a "less is more" approach

Alia Marwah – Traditional Style: classic elegance, antique furniture, and ornate accessories

Tara Hess – Industrial Style: rough and edgy, with exposed brick, open layout, and lots of metal

View portfolios of our designers' work at characksolutions.com/gallery.

From:	<victoria@synergy-mgmt.net>
To:	<contact@characksolutions.com>
Date:	September 29
Subject:	Inquiry

Dear Charack Solutions,

My property management firm is relocating soon. The new unit needs to be completely redecorated. We want customers to have a positive response to the space when they first walk in. Currently, we have several beautiful pieces of furniture that are over one hundred years old. We'd like to incorporate them into the new design, as we're once again going for some kind of timeless look. We don't have a clear vision yet but would like to book a meeting with one of your designers.

Sincerely,

Victoria Barrett

176. What is NOT mentioned as being handled by Charack Solutions?

(A) Light fixtures
(B) Flooring
(C) Window coverings
(D) Walls

177. What is indicated about Charack Solutions?

(A) It is under new management.
(B) It does not work on residential properties.
(C) It was founded by Ms. Boone.
(D) It offers free consultations.

178. Why did Ms. Barrett send the e-mail?

(A) She is seeking a service at a lower price.
(B) She had a different designer cancel on her.
(C) She wants to make a good impression on clients.
(D) She hopes to get customers from Charack Solutions.

179. What is suggested about Ms. Barret's new office?

(A) Ms. Hess would most likely decorate it.
(B) Ms. Marwah's designs would best suit it.
(C) Its location is near Charack Solutions.
(D) It does not have much space for furniture.

180. In the e-mail, the word "clear" in paragraph 1, line 5, is closest in meaning to

(A) distinct
(B) transparent
(C) pure
(D) alert

Questions 181-185 refer to the following article and e-mail.

BURLINGTON (March 19)—The construction of BX Center, Burlington's new multi-sport stadium, was officially finished yesterday, one week ahead of schedule. The building is a much-needed facility for sports and community events, and it will be used primarily for football and soccer games, along with the Avery Complex, which is already in use. The building houses a small souvenir shop as well as Super Snacks, a snack bar that will be open two hours before the start time of any game.

Mitchell Taylor, coach of the town's semi-professional soccer team, has been looking forward to having another sports facility in town. "Due to scheduling conflicts at the Avery Complex, we often had to practice at Rosemont Stadium, a 40-minute drive for our players. This will be so much more convenient."

To view a schedule of events, visit www.bxcenter.com.

E-Mail message

To: Eric Kinney <ekinney@sardismail.com>
From: Isaac Vogel <vogeli@bxsupersnacks.com>
Date: April 4
Subject: First day at Super Snacks

Hi Eric,

Welcome to the Super Snacks team! We're pleased to have you on board.

Your first day of work will be April 9 during the soccer game against the Johnstown Rangers. Please arrive at 1:30 P.M., as we need to open the snack bar at 2:00 P.M. Your shift will last for 4 hours on your first day. You do not need to prepare anything in advance, as the assistant manager, Olivia Nelson, will train you on-site and tell you what to do.

All employees wear a red polo shirt with our logo along with a red cap. I will get these ready for you to change into when you arrive. Please wear black trousers and any closed-toe footwear. If you have any questions before your first day, please let me know.

Sincerely,

Isaac Vogel
Manager, Super Snacks

181. Why was the article written?

(A) To announce the completion of a sports venue
(B) To report on the delay in a city's building project
(C) To explain how to purchase tickets for sports events
(D) To introduce the new coach of a local team

182. What is mentioned about Mr. Taylor's players?

(A) They always used to practice at the Avery Complex.
(B) They will host a tournament in the BX Center.
(C) They sometimes had to travel far for practice.
(D) They are expected to win a tournament.

183. What does Mr. Vogel say he will prepare for Mr. Kinney?

(A) A feedback form
(B) A monthly schedule
(C) An employee parking pass
(D) A staff uniform

184. What time does the game start on April 9?

(A) At 1:30 P.M.
(B) At 2:00 P.M.
(C) At 3:30 P.M.
(D) At 4:00 P.M.

185. What will Mr. Kinney do on April 9?

(A) Get instructions from Ms. Nelson
(B) Read some equipment manuals
(C) Sign an employment contract
(D) Make deliveries to the Johnstown Rangers

Questions 186-190 refer to the following e-mail, business card, and review.

To:	Ali Pacheco <a.pacheco@straitoninc.com>
From:	Precision Automotive <admin@precisionauto.com>
Date:	March 28
Subject:	Vehicle inspection

Dear Ms. Pacheco,

Your vehicle is scheduled to undergo a routine inspection at Precision Automotive on April 3 at 7:30 P.M. Please reply if you need to reschedule.

As you are a new customer, please bring a photo ID along with proof of ownership of the vehicle. We request that you complete some forms upon arrival. Please also ensure that your car is free of personal items. The inspection will take approximately one hour. If we identify a problem that requires further work, we will text you for written confirmation before carrying out repairs.

Thank you for your patronage.

Sincerely,

Tegan Murrell
Scheduling Coordinator, Precision Automotive

Precision Automotive
821 Fieldcrest Road S
Westbury, NY 11590
contact@precisionauto.com

Auto Repairs, Maintenance, Assessment

Our experienced team is here to help you!

Business Hours: 8:00 A.M. to 9:00 P.M. Mondays, 8:00 A.M. to 6:00 P.M. Tuesdays to Saturdays

Call 516-555-7059 to make an appointment, or simply drop off your vehicle without prior arrangement.

> https://www.precisionauto.com/reviews

I took my vehicle to Precision Automotive for the first time, and I was very satisfied with the overall experience. The appointment was for a routine inspection, but the mechanic, Adam, noticed that the brake pads were quite worn. He made the repairs promptly and for a reasonable price. The team at Precision Automotive was incredibly thorough when working on my vehicle.

The company offers an easy booking process. I also liked the modern and clean reception area. The only downside of the business is the location. Customers dropping off a vehicle may have difficulty because there are no bus stops nearby. However, this did not apply to me, as the business is within walking distance of my new apartment.

I wholeheartedly recommend Precision Automotive, and I plan to use it for all of my future vehicle repair needs.

—Ali Pacheco, April 7

---

186. What is Ms. Pacheco asked to do before the inspection?

(A) Provide proof of her car insurance
(B) Remove her personal belongings
(C) E-mail copies of some paperwork
(D) Create a new customer account

187. What day did Ms. Pacheco receive a service?

(A) Monday
(B) Wednesday
(C) Thursday
(D) Saturday

188. According to the business card, what is true about Precision Automotive?

(A) It has recently expanded its services.
(B) It does not require appointments.
(C) It is open every day of the week.
(D) It collects a deposit upon booking.

189. What is suggested about Adam?

(A) He dropped off Ms. Pacheco's vehicle for her.
(B) He gets to work by public transportation.
(C) He specializes in rare vehicle models.
(D) He sent a text message to Ms. Pacheco.

190. What does the review indicate about Ms. Pacheco?

(A) She works near the Precision Automotive building.
(B) She noticed that her brakes were making strange noises.
(C) She read good reviews about Precision Automotive.
(D) She recently moved into her current residence.

GO ON TO THE NEXT PAGE

Questions 191-195 refer to the following Web page and e-mails.

---

www.rentabusdc.com/about

Have a great time out with your private group with help from Rent-A-Bus, whether it's for a few hours, days, or even weeks! You can choose any pick-up or drop-off point in the Washington, D.C. area, or beyond (additional charges may apply), and our staff can help to make your tour memorable.

All of our buses are equipped with Wi-Fi, onboard entertainment systems, and restroom facilities. Our largest buses also have leather seats and charging ports. We can accommodate a wide range of group sizes with the following buses: mini bus (max. 30 passengers), mid-sized bus (max. 45 passengers), full-sized bus (max. 65 passengers), and double-decker bus (max. 90 passengers).

You can also decide how much or how little involvement you require from our team:

Standard Package: Vehicle and driver only
Silver Package: Standard Package plus a knowledgeable tour guide
Gold Package: Silver Package plus a customized sightseeing schedule
Platinum Package: Gold Package plus all meals

For inquiries and bookings, please contact Alan Dobson at a.dobson@rentabusdc.com. We look forward to making your next journey safe, comfortable, and memorable.

To:	Mae Houck <mae_houck@ds-distributors.com>
From:	Alan Dobson <a.dobson@rentabusdc.com>
Date:	April 25
Subject:	Rent-A-Bus

Dear Ms. Houck,

Thank you for your interest in booking a bus for your upcoming team-building activity. We do have availability on the date you mentioned in your voice mail message. The Rhapsody Hotel is not out of our regular service range, so there would be no additional charge regarding pick-up and drop-off. I understand that you had a mid-sized bus in mind, but, unfortunately, that won't be large enough for your group.

As you said you would like our highest-tier package, we can begin planning the meals we will provide as soon as you send us information about any dietary restrictions. We look forward to planning a great tour for you and your guests.

Warmest regards,

Alan Dobson

To:	Alan Dobson <a.dobson@rentabusdc.com>
From:	Mae Houck <mae_houck@ds-distributors.com>
Date:	April 27
Subject:	RE: Rent-A-Bus

Dear Mr. Dobson,

Thank you for following up. Our planning committee remains interested in having you plan the tour's itinerary. However, due to group members' requests for a lot of different cuisine options, we plan to have them do mealtimes on their own, so we would not need that service from you. I'm also wondering if it is possible to have you collect our group at the Rhapsody Hotel as the first stop but leave us at the Darton Center as our final stop. Please let me know a good time when we can discuss the details further.

Thank you,

Mae Houck

191. What does the Web page indicate about Rent-A-Bus?
    (A) Customers can hire their own driver.
    (B) All of its buses include charging ports.
    (C) Its buses can be rented overnight.
    (D) It will add Wi-Fi to its buses soon.

192. Why did Mr. Dobson write the first e-mail?
    (A) To respond to an inquiry
    (B) To suggest changes to an agreement
    (C) To report a double-booking
    (D) To confirm receipt of a payment

193. What is suggested about Ms. Houck's group?
    (A) It has a larger budget than it did last year.
    (B) It has more than forty-five people in it.
    (C) Its members are visiting from overseas.
    (D) Its members prefer sitting in leather seats.

194. Which package will most likely be booked by Ms. Houck?
    (A) The Standard Package
    (B) The Silver Package
    (C) The Gold Package
    (D) The Platinum Package

195. What does Ms. Houck request?
    (A) A list of restaurant suggestions
    (B) Information about peak travel times
    (C) Different pick-up and drop-off sites
    (D) Special equipment on the bus

Questions 196-200 refer to the following invoice and e-mails.

FLEX GYM

Membership Number: 04938
Issue Date: March 3
Due Date: April 10

Carl Lang
3209 Brannon Street
Irvine, CA 92614

Description	Billing Code	Amount
February Membership Fee	201	$125.00
Personal Training 4-session Package	477	$180.00
Zumba Dance Class	525	$18.00
Health and Wellness Consultation	800	$35.00
	TOTAL	**$358.00**

We appreciate your business, and we would particularly like to thank those who attended our Grand Reopening Event on February 1. We look forward to helping you achieve your fitness goals! Feel free to contact us at contact@flexgym.net.

E-Mail

To:	Flex Gym <contact@flexgym.net>
From:	Carl Lang <langc@lathaminc.com>
Date:	March 4
Subject:	Inquiries

Dear Flex Gym,

I have been enjoying visiting Flex Gym since I joined on February 1, and I can already see improvements in my health and fitness level. I hope to spend even more time at the facility, so my personal trainer recommended renting my own locker there. Could you please let me know how I can do this?

I am also wondering about the invoice I received. On it, there is a charge for a dance class that I took on February 6. However, I was told that I could try one class for free to see whether or not I liked it. It was the first class of that kind that I attended, so I believe this charge is incorrect, even though I've paid it. Could you please look into this matter?

Thank you,

Carl Lang

To:	Carl Lang <langc@lathaminc.com>
From:	Yolanda Moreno <yolanda@flexgym.net>
Date:	March 5
Subject:	RE: Inquiries

Dear Mr. Lang,

Thank you for contacting us with your inquiries. Unfortunately, at the moment, all of our lockers are rented. However, I have added your name to the waiting list, and we will contact you by e-mail as soon as one is available.

With regard to your invoice, I sincerely apologize for the incorrect charge. A credit in the amount of the overpayment will be provided in the next billing cycle, the invoice for which will be sent one month after this current one. By way of apology, we would like to give you a free Flex Gym water bottle. I'll leave it at the front desk with Allison, so just ask for it the next time you visit.

Thank you for your understanding,

Yolanda Moreno
Client Services, Flex Gym

196. What is suggested in the invoice about Flex Gym?

(A) It is open seven days a week.
(B) It has more than one location.
(C) It offers different membership levels.
(D) It had a temporary closure.

197. In the first e-mail, what does Mr. Lang say he wants to do?

(A) Upgrade his membership status
(B) Sign up for more classes
(C) Change his personal trainer
(D) Rent a storage area

198. What fee does Mr. Lang dispute?

(A) $18.00
(B) $35.00
(C) $125.00
(D) $180.00

199. When will Mr. Lang's next invoice be issued?

(A) On March 6
(B) On April 3
(C) On April 10
(D) On May 10

200. Who most likely is Allison?

(A) A receptionist
(B) A business owner
(C) A maintenance worker
(D) An accountant

Stop! This is the end of the test. If you finish before time is called, you may go back to Parts 5, 6, and 7 and check your work.

Answer Key

650+

1 (B)	2 (A)	3 (B)	4 (D)	5 (C)	6 (C)	7 (A)	8 (C)	9 (B)	10 (B)
11 (C)	12 (A)	13 (C)	14 (C)	15 (A)	16 (C)	17 (B)	18 (C)	19 (C)	20 (C)
21 (B)	22 (A)	23 (A)	24 (B)	25 (A)	26 (A)	27 (A)	28 (C)	29 (B)	30 (C)
31 (B)	32 (A)	33 (C)	34 (B)	35 (A)	36 (D)	37 (B)	38 (B)	39 (D)	40 (D)
41 (A)	42 (B)	43 (A)	44 (A)	45 (B)	46 (D)	47 (C)	48 (D)	49 (B)	50 (C)
51 (B)	52 (B)	53 (C)	54 (A)	55 (D)	56 (B)	57 (D)	58 (C)	59 (A)	60 (D)
61 (A)	62 (A)	63 (C)	64 (D)	65 (A)	66 (D)	67 (C)	68 (B)	69 (C)	70 (A)
71 (D)	72 (B)	73 (D)	74 (A)	75 (C)	76 (C)	77 (D)	78 (A)	79 (B)	80 (C)
81 (B)	82 (D)	83 (C)	84 (A)	85 (B)	86 (A)	87 (B)	88 (C)	89 (D)	90 (B)
91 (C)	92 (D)	93 (C)	94 (B)	95 (D)	96 (B)	97 (A)	98 (B)	99 (B)	100 (D)
101 (C)	102 (A)	103 (B)	104 (D)	105 (B)	106 (B)	107 (A)	108 (D)	109 (A)	110 (C)
111 (D)	112 (C)	113 (C)	114 (B)	115 (D)	116 (B)	117 (D)	118 (B)	119 (B)	120 (C)
121 (C)	122 (C)	123 (A)	124 (B)	125 (B)	126 (A)	127 (B)	128 (A)	129 (B)	130 (C)
131 (C)	132 (C)	133 (D)	134 (B)	135 (C)	136 (C)	137 (D)	138 (C)	139 (B)	140 (C)
141 (D)	142 (D)	143 (A)	144 (C)	145 (D)	146 (A)	147 (A)	148 (B)	149 (C)	150 (B)
151 (B)	152 (D)	153 (C)	154 (A)	155 (D)	156 (C)	157 (C)	158 (D)	159 (A)	160 (A)
161 (A)	162 (D)	163 (D)	164 (B)	165 (A)	166 (D)	167 (A)	168 (C)	169 (B)	170 (C)
171 (D)	172 (C)	173 (B)	174 (C)	175 (D)	176 (A)	177 (D)	178 (C)	179 (B)	180 (A)
181 (A)	182 (C)	183 (D)	184 (D)	185 (A)	186 (B)	187 (A)	188 (B)	189 (D)	190 (D)
191 (C)	192 (A)	193 (B)	194 (C)	195 (C)	196 (D)	197 (D)	198 (A)	199 (B)	200 (A)

ANSWER SHEET

실전 모의고사

수험번호

응시일자 : 20   년   월   일

성명: 한글 / 한자 / 영자

LISTENING (Part I ~ IV)

READING (Part V ~ VII)

ANSWER SHEET

실전 모의고사